Dictionary

Dutch – English
English – Dutch

Woordenboek

Nederlands – Engels
Engels – Nederlands

Berlitz Publishing / APA Publications GmbH & Co.
Verlag KG, Singapore Branch, Singapore

Contacting the Editors
Every effort has been made to provide accurate information in this publication, but changes are inevitable. The publisher cannot be responsible for any resulting loss, inconvenience or injury. We would appreciate it if readers would call our attention to any errors or outdated information by contacting Berlitz Publishing, 193 Morris Ave., Springfield, NJ 07081, USA. Fax: 1-908-206-1103, e-mail: comments@berlitzbooks.com

Cover photo: ©ID Image Direkt CD-ROM GmbH, Germany

Contents

Inhoud

Preface

In selecting the vocabulary and phrases for this dictionary, the editors have had the traveller's needs foremost in mind. This book will prove a useful companion to casual tourists and business travellers who appreciate the reassurance a small and practical dictionary can provide. It offers them—as well as beginners and students—all the basic vocabulary they will encounter and have to use, providing key words and expressions to allow them to cope in everyday situations.

Like our successful phrase books and travel guides, these dictionaries—created with the help of a computer data bank—are designed to slip into your pocket or purse, and thus have a role as handy companions at all times.

Besides just about everything you normally find in dictionaries, there are these Berlitz bonuses:

- simplified pronunciation after each foreign-word entry, making it easy to read and enunciate words whose spelling may look forbidding

- a unique, practical glossary to simplify reading a foreign restaurant menu and to take the mystery out of complicated dishes and indecipherable names on bills of fare

- useful information on how to tell the time and how to count, on conjugating irregular verbs, commonly used abbreviations and converting to the metric system, in addition to basic phrases.

While no dictionary of this size can pretend to completeness, we are confident this dictionary will help you get most out of your trip abroad.

Berlitz Publishing

Voorwoord

Bij het selecteren van de woordbegrippen voor dit woordenboek stond de redactie in de allereerste plaats de behoeften van de reiziger voor ogen. Dit boekje zal van grote waarde blijken te zijn voor de vele reizigers, toeristen en zakenmensen die zich graag verzekerd weten van een klein en praktisch woordenboek. Het biedt hen – evenals beginners en gevorderden – de benodigde woordenschat, alsook sleutelwoorden en uitdrukkingen voor dagelijks gebruik.

Zoals onze succesvolle taal- en reisgidsen, zijn deze woordenboekjes – tot stand gekomen met behulp van een computer data bank – speciaal ontworpen om in jaszak of handtas gestoken te worden.

Behalve wat u normaliter in woordenboeken vindt, biedt Berlitz nog de volgende extra's:

• een transcriptie van elk grondwoord in het internationale fonetische alfabet (IPA), hetgeen het uitspreken van woorden waarvan de spelling moeilijk lijkt vergemakkelijkt

• een unieke, praktische woordenlijst van culinaire begrippen om het lezen van een menu in een buitenlands restaurant te vereenvoudigen en de mysteries te ontrafelen van bijzondere gerechten

• nuttige informatie over tijdsaanduiding, getallen, de vervoeging van onregelmatige werkwoorden, veel gebruikte afkortingen en een lijst van veel voorkomende uitdrukkingen.

Hoewel geen enkel woordenboek van dit formaat kan pretenderen volledig te zijn, verwachten wij toch dat de gebruiker van dit boek zich goed uitgerust zal voelen om buitenlandse reizen met vertrouwen te ondernemen.

Dutch-English

Nederlands-Engels

Introduction

This dictionary has been designed to cater for your practical needs. Unnecessary linguistic information has been avoided. The entries are listed in alphabetical order regardless of whether the entry word is a single word, hyphened or two or more separate words.

When an entry is followed by sub-entries such as expressions and locutions, these, too, have been listed in alphabetical order.

Each main-entry word is followed by a phonetic transcription (see Guide to pronunciation). Following the transcription is the part of speech of the entry word whenever applicable. When an entry word may be used in more than one part of speech, the translations are grouped together after the respective part of speech.

Considering the complexity of the rules for constructing the plural of Dutch nouns, we have supplied the plural form whenever in current use. Each time an entry word is repeated in plurals or in sub-entries, a tilde (~) is used to represent the full entry word.

In plurals of long words, only the part that changes is written out fully, whereas the unchanged part is represented by a hyphen.

Entry: beker (pl ~s)   Plural: bekers
       kind (pl ~eren)   kinderen
       leslokaal (pl -kalen)   leslokalen

An asterisk (*) in front of a verb indicates that the verb is irregular. For details, refer to the list of irregular verbs.

Abbreviations

adj	adjective	*num*	numeral
adv	adverb	*p*	past tense
Am	American	*pl*	plural
art	article	*plAm*	plural (American)
c	common gender	*pp*	past participle
conj	conjunction	*pr*	present tense
f	feminine	*pref*	prefix
m	masculine	*prep*	preposition
n	noun	*pron*	pronoun
nAm	noun (American)	*v*	verb
nt	neuter	*vAm*	verb (American)

Guide to Pronunciation

Each main entry in this part of the dictionary is followed by a phonetic transcription which shows you how to pronounce the words. This transcription should be read as if it were English. It is based on Standard British pronunciation, though we have tried to take account of General American pronunciation also. Below, only those letters and symbols are explained which we consider likely to be ambiguous or not immediately understood.

The syllables are separated by hyphens, and stressed syllables are printed in *italics*.

Of course, the sounds of any two languages are never exactly the same, but if you follow our indications carefully, you should be able to pronounce the foreign words in such a way that you'll be understood. To make your task easier, our transcriptions occasionally slightly simplify the sound system of the language while still reflecting the essential sound differences.

Consonants

g	a **g**-sound where the tongue doesn't quite close the air passage between itself and the roof of the mouth, so that the escaping air produces audible friction; often fairly hard, so that it resembles **kh**
kh	like g, but based on a **k**-sound; therefore hard and voiceless, like **ch** in Scottish lo**ch**
ñ	as in Spanish se**ñ**or, or like **ni** in o**ni**on
s	always hard, as in **s**o
zh	a soft, voiced **sh**, like **s** in plea**s**ure

1) In everyday speech, the **n** in the ending of verbs and plurals of nouns is usually dropped.
2) We use the transcription **v** for two different sounds (written **v** and **w** in Dutch) because the difference between them is often inaudible to foreigners.

Vowels and Diphthongs

aa	long **a**, as in c**a**r, without any **r**-sound
ah	a short version of **aa**; between **a** in c**a**t and **u** in c**u**t
ai	like **air**, without any **r**-sound
eh	like **e** in g**e**t
er	as in oth**er**, without any **r**-sound
ew	a "rounded **ee**-sound"; say the vowel sound **ee** (as in s**ee**), and while saying it, round your lips as for **oo** (as in s**oo**n), without moving your tongue; when your lips are in the **oo** position, but your tongue is in the **ee** position, you should be pronouncing the correct sound
I	like **i** in b**i**t
igh	as in s**igh**
o	always as in h**o**t (British pronunciation)
ou	as in l**ou**d
ur	as in f**ur**, but with rounded lips and no **r**-sound

1) A bar over a vowel symbol (e.g. $\overline{oo}$) shows that this sound is long.
2) Raised letters (e.g. **aa**^{ee}, **t**^{y}, ^{y}**eh**) should be pronounced only fleetingly.
3) Dutch vowels (i.e. not diphthongs) are pure. Therefore, you should try to read a transcription like $\overline{oa}$ without moving tongue or lips while pronouncing the sound.
4) Some Dutch words borrowed from French contain nasal vowels, which we transcribe with a vowel symbol plus **ng** (e.g. **ahng**). This **ng** should *not* be pronounced, and serves solely to indicate nasal quality of the preceding vowel. A nasal vowel is pronounced simultaneously through the mouth and the nose.

aal (aal) *c* (pl alen) eel

aambeien (*aam*-bay-ern) *pl* haemorrhoids *pl*, piles *pl*

aan (aan) *prep* to; on

aanbetaling (*aam*-ber-taa-lıng) *c* (pl ~en) down payment

***aanbevelen** (*aam*-ber-vay-lern) *v* recommend

aanbeveling (*aam*-ber-vay-lıng) *c* (pl ~en) recommendation

aanbevelingsbrief (*aam*-ber-vay-lıngs-breef) *c* (pl -brieven) letter of recommendation

***aanbidden** (*aam*-bı-dern) *v* worship

***aanbieden** (*aam*-bee-dern) *v* offer; present

aanbieding (*aam*-bee-dıng) *c* (pl ~en) offer

aanblik (*aam*-blık) *c* sight; appearance

aanbod (*aam*-bot) *nt* offer; supply; *Am* bid

aanbranden (*aam*-brahn-dern) *v* *burn

aandacht (*aan*-dahkht) *c* attention; notice, consideration; ~ **besteden aan** attend to

aandeel (*aan*-dayl) *nt* (pl -delen) share

aandenken (*aan*-dehng-kern) *nt* (pl ~s) remembrance; keepsake

aandoening (*aan*-dōō-nıng) *c* (pl ~en) affection

aandoenlijk (aan-*dōōn*-lerk) *adj* touching

***aandrijven** (*aan*-dray-vern) *v* propel

***aandringen** (*aan*-drı-ngern) *v* insist

aanduiden (*aan*-dur^ew^-dern) *v* indicate

***aangaan** (*aang*-gaan) *v* concern

aangaande (aang-*gaan*-der) *prep* as regards

aangeboren (aang-ger-*bōa*-rern) *adj* natural

aangelegenheid (aang-ger-*lay*-gern-hayt) *c* (pl -heden) matter, concern; affair, business

aangenaam (*aang*-ger-naam) *adj* agreeable, pleasing, pleasant

aangesloten (*aang*-ger-*slōa*-tern) *adj* affiliated

***aangeven** (*aang*-gay-vern) *v* indicate; declare; *give, hand, pass

aangezien (aang-ger-*zeen*) *conj* as, since; because

aangifte (*aang*-gıf-ter) *c* (pl ~n) declaration

aangrenzend (aang-*grehn*-zernt) *adj* neighbo(u)ring

aanhalen (*aan*-haa-lern) *v* tighten; quote

aanhalingstekens (*aan*-haa-lıngs-tay-kerns) *pl* quotation marks

aanhangen (*aan*-hahng-ern) *v* cling to

aanhangwagen (*aan*-hahng-vaa-gern) *c* (pl ~s) trailer

aanhankelijk (aan-*hahng*-ker-lerk) *adj* affectionate

***aanhebben** (*aan*-heh-bern) *v* *wear

aanhechten (*aan*-hehkh-tern) *v* attach

aanhoren (*aan*-hōa-rern) *v* listen

***aanhouden** (*aan*-hou-dern) *v* insist; **aanhoudend** constant

aanhouding (*aan*-hou-dıng) *c* (pl ~en) arrest

***aankijken** (*aang*-kay-kern) *v* look at

aanklacht (*aang*-klahkht) *c* (pl ~en) charge

aanklagen (*aang*-klaa-gern) *v* accuse, charge

aankleden (*aang*-klay-dern) *v* dress; *get dressed

***aankomen** (*aang*-kōa-mern) *v* arrive

aankomst (*aang*-komst) *c* arrival

aankomsttijd (*aang*-koms-tayt) *c* (pl ~en) time of arrival

aankondigen (*aang*-kon-der-gern) *v*
announce

aankondiging (*aang*-kon-der-ging) *c*
(pl ~en) notice, announcement

aankoop (*aang*-kōap) *c* (pl -kopen)
purchase

aankruisen (*aang*-krur^{ew}-sern) *v* mark

aanleg (*aan*-lehkh) *c* talent

aanleggen (*aan*-leh-gern) *v* dock

aanleiding (*aan*-lay-ding) *c* (pl ~en)
cause, occasion

aanlengen (*aan*-leh-ngern) *v* dilute

aanmelden (*aan*-mehl-dern): **zich ~**
report

aanmerkelijk (aa-*mehr*-ker-lerk) *adj*
considerable

aanmerken (*aa*-mehr-kern) *v*
comment

aanmoedigen (*aa*-mōō-der-gern) *v*
encourage

*aannemen (*aa*-nāy-mern) *v* accept;
assume, suppose; adopt;
aangenomen dat supposing that

aannemer (*aa*-nāy-merr) *c* (pl ~s)
contractor

aanpak (*aam*-pahk) *c* method,
approach

aanpassen (*aam*-pah-sern) *v* adapt;
suit; adjust

aanplakbiljet (*aam*-plahk-bil-^yeht) *nt*
(pl ~ten) placard

*aanprijzen (*aam*-pray-zern) *v*
recommend

*aanraden (*aan*-raa-dern) *v* advise,
recommend

aanraken (*aan*-raa-kern) *v* touch

aanraking (*aan*-raa-king) *c* (pl ~en)
touch; contact

aanranden (*aan*-rahn-dern) *v* assault

aanrichten (*aan*-rikh-tern) *v* cause

aanrijding (*aan*-ray-ding) *c* (pl ~en)
collision

aanschaffen (*aan*-skhah-fern) *v* *buy

*aansluiten (*aan*-slur^{ew}-tern) *v*
connect

aansluiting (*aan*-slur^{ew}-ting) *c* (pl ~en)
connection

aansporen (*aan*-spōa-rern) *v* incite;
urge

aanspraak (*aan*-spraak) *c* (pl -spraken)
claim

aansprakelijk (aan-*spraa*-ker-lerk) *adj*
liable; responsible

aansprakelijkheid (aan-*spraa*-ker-
lerk-hayt) *c* liability; responsibility

*aanspreken (*aan*-sprāy-kern) *v*
address; appeal

aanstekelijk (aan-*stāy*-ker-lerk) *adj*
contagious

*aansteken (*aan*-stāy-kern) *v* *light;
infect

aansteker (*aan*-stāy-kerr) *c* (pl ~s)
lighter, cigarette lighter

aanstellen (*aan*-steh-lern) *v* appoint

aanstoot (*aan*-stōat) *c* offense *Am*,
offence

aanstootgevend (aan-stōat-*khāy*-
vernt) *adj* offensive

aanstrepen (*aan*-strāy-pern) *v* tick off

aantal (*aan*-tahl) *nt* (pl ~len) number;
quantity

aantekenen (*aan*-tāy-ker-nern) *v*
record; register

aantekening (*aan*-tāy-ker-ning) *c* (pl
~en) note

aantonen (*aan*-tōa-nern) *v* prove;
demonstrate, *show

aantrekkelijk (aan-*treh*-ker-lerk) *adj*
attractive

*aantrekken (*aan*-treh-kern) *v* attract;
tempt; *put on; tighten

aantrekking (*aan*-treh-king) *c*
attraction

aantrekkingskracht (*aan*-treh-kings-
krahkht) *c* (pl ~en) appeal

aanvaarden (aan-*vaar*-dern) *v* accept

aanval (*aan*-vahl) *c* (pl ~len) attack; fit

*aanvallen (*aan*-vah-lern) *v* attack;

assault

aanvang (*aan*-vahng) *c* beginning

*aanvangen (*aan*-vah-ngern) *v* *begin

aanvankelijk (aan-*vahng*-ker-lerk) *adv* originally, at first

aanvaring (*aan*-vaa-rɪng) *c* (pl ~en) collision

aanvoer (*aan*-vōōr) *c* supply

aanvoerder (*aan*-vōōr-derr) *c* (pl ~s) leader

aanvraag (*aan*-vraakh) *c* (pl -vragen) application

aanwezig (aan-*vāy*-zerkh) *adj* present

aanwezigheid (aan-*vāy*-zerkh-hayt) *c* presence

*aanwijzen (*aan*-vay-zern) *v* point out; designate

aanwijzing (*aan*-vay-zɪng) *c* (pl ~en) indication; hint; ~en geven *v* hint

aanzetten (*aan*-zeh-tern) *v* turn on

aanzien (*aan*-zeen) *nt* aspect; esteem; ten ~ van regarding

aanzienlijk (aan-*zeen*-lerk) *adj* considerable, substantial

aap (aap) *c* (pl apen) monkey

aard (aart) *c* nature

aardappel (*aar*-dah-perl) *c* (pl ~s, ~en) potato

aardappelpuree (*aar*-dah-perl pew-rāy) *c* mashed potatoes

aardbei (*aart*-bay) *c* (pl ~en) strawberry

aardbeving (*aart*-bāy-vɪng) *c* (pl ~en) earthquake

aardbol (*aart*-bol) *c* globe

aarde (*aar*-der) *c* earth; soil

aardewerk (*aar*-der-vehrk) *nt* crockery, pottery, ceramics *pl*

aardig (*aar*-derkh) *adj* pleasant; nice, kind

aardrijkskunde (*aar*-drayks-kern-der) *c* geography

aartsbisschop (*aarts*-bɪ-skhop) *c* (pl ~pen) archbishop

aarzelen (*aar*-zer-lern) *v* hesitate

aas (aass) *nt* bait

abces (ahp-*sehss*) *nt* (pl ~sen) abscess

abdij (ahb-*day*) *c* (pl ~en) abbey

abonnee (ah-bo-*nāy*) *c* (pl ~s) subscriber

abonnement (ah-bo-ner-*mehnt*) *nt* (pl ~en) subscription

abonnementskaart (ah-bo-ner-*mehnts*-kaart) *c* (pl ~en) season ticket

abortus (ah-*bor*-terss) *c* (pl ~sen) abortion

abrikoos (ah-bree-*kōāss*) *c* (pl -kozen) apricot

absoluut (ahp-sōā-*lewt*) *adj* sheer; *adv* absolutely

abstract (ahp-*strahkt*) *adj* abstract

absurd (ahp-*serrt*) *adj* absurd

abuis (aa-*bu̇ewss*) *nt* (pl abuizen) mistake

academie (aa-kaa-*dāy*-mee) *c* (pl ~s) academy

accent (ahk-*sehnt*) *nt* (pl ~en) accent

accepteren (ahk-sehp-*tāy*-rern) *v* accept

accessoires (ahk-seh-*svaa*-rerss) *pl* accessories *pl*

accijns (ahk-*sayns*) *c* (pl -cijnzen) Customs duty

accommodatie (ah-ko-mōā-*daa*-tsee) *c* accommodation

accu (*ah*-kew) *c* (pl ~'s) battery

acht (ahkht) *num* eight

achteloos (*ahkh*-ter-lōāss) *adj* careless

achten (*ahkh*-tern) *v* esteem; count

achter (*ahkh*-terr) *prep* behind; after

achteraan (ahkh-ter-*raan*) *adv* behind

achterbuurt (*ahkh*-terr-bēwrt) *c* (pl ~en) slum

achterdochtig (ahkh-terr-*dokh*-terkh) *adj* suspicious

achtergrond (*ahkh*-terr-gront) *c* (pl ~en) background

achterkant (*ahkh*-terr-kahnt) *c* (pl

~en) rear

*achterlaten (*ahkh*-terr-laa-tern) *v*
*leave behind

achterlicht (*ahkh*-terr-lıkht) *nt* (pl
~en) taillight, rear light

achternaam (*ahkh*-terr-naam) *c* (pl
-namen) family name, surname

achterstallig (ahkh-terr-*stah*-lerkh)
adj overdue

achteruit (ahkh-ter-*rur^(ew)t*) *adv*
backwards

*achteruitrijden (ahkh-ter-*rur^(ew)t*-ray-
dern) *v* reverse

achterwerk (*ahkh*-terr-vehrk) *nt* (pl
~en) bottom, behind

achting (*ahkh*-tıng) *c* respect, esteem

achtste (*ahkht*-ster) *num* eighth

achttien (*ahkh*-teen) *num* eighteen

achttiende (*ahkh*-teen-der) *num*
eighteenth

acne (*ahk*-nāy) *c* acne

acquisitie (ah-kvee-*zee*-tsee) *c* (pl ~s)
acquisition

acteur (ahk-*tūrr*) *m* (pl ~s) actor

actie (*ahk*-see) *c* (pl ~s) action

actief (ahk-*teef*) *adj* active

activiteit (ahk-tee-vee-*tayt*) *c* (pl ~en)
activity

actrice (ahk-*tree*-ser) *f* (pl ~s) actress

actueel (ahk-tēw-*vāyl*) *adj* topical,
current

acuut (ah-*kēwt*) *adj* acute

adel (*aa*-derl) *c* nobility

adellijk (*aa*-der-lerk) *adj* noble

adem (*aa*-derm) *c* breath

ademen (*aa*-der-mern) *v* breathe

ademhaling (*aa*-derm-haa-lıng) *c*
breathing, respiration

adequaat (ah-dāy-*kvaat*) *adj* adequate

ader (*aa*-derr) *c* (pl ~s, ~en) vein

administratie (aht-mee-nee-*straa*-
tsee) *c* (pl ~s) administration

administratief (aht-mee-nee-straa-
teef) *adj* administrative

adopteren (ah-dop-*tāy*-rern) *v* adopt

adres (aa-*drehss*) *nt* (pl ~sen) address

adresseren (aa-dreh-*sāy*-rern) *v*
address

advertentie (aht-ferr-*tehn*-see) *c* (pl ~s)
advertisement

advies (aht-*feess*) *nt* (pl adviezen)
advice

adviseren (aht-fee-*zāy*-rern) *v* advise

advocaat (aht-fōā-*kaat*) *m* (f -cate, pl
-caten) lawyer; barrister; solicitor;
attorney

af (ahf) *adv* off; finished; ~ **en toe**
occasionally

afbeelding (*ahf*-bāyl-dıng) *c* (pl ~en)
picture

afbetalen (*ahf*-ber-taa-lern) *v* *pay on
account; pay off

afbetaling (*ahf*-ber-taa-lıng) *c* (pl ~en)
instalment

*afblijven (*ahf*-blay-vern) *v* *keep off

afbraak (*ahf*-braak) *c* demolition

*afbreken (*ahf*-brāy-kern) *v* chip

afdaling (*ahf*-daa-lıng) *c* (pl ~en)
descent

afdanken (*ahf*-dahng-kern) *v* discard

afdeling (*ahf*-dāy-lıng) *c* (pl ~en)
division, department; section

*afdingen (*ahf*-dı-ngern) *v* bargain

afdrogen (*ahf*-drōā-gern) *v* dry

afdruk (*ahf*-drerk) *c* (pl ~ken) print

*afdwingen (*ahf*-dvı-ngern) *v* extort

affaire (ah-*fai*-rer) *c* (pl ~s) deal; affair

affiche (ah-*fee*-sher) *nt* (pl ~s) poster

afgeladen (*ahf*-kher-laa-dern) *adj*
packed, replete

afgelegen (*ahf*-kher-lāy-gern) *adj*
remote, far-off, out of the way

afgelopen (*ahf*-kher-lōā-pern) *adj* past

afgerond (*ahf*-kher-ront) *adj* rounded

afgevaardigde (*ahf*-kher-vaar-derg-
der) *c* (pl ~n) deputy

afgezien van (*ahf*-kher-zeen-vahn)
apart from

afgod (*ahf*-khot) *c* (pl ~en) idol

afgrijzen (*ahf*-khray-zern) *nt* horror

afgrond (*ahf*-khront) *c* (pl ~en) precipice, abyss

afgunst (*ahf*-khernst) *c* envy

afgunstig (ahf-*khern*-sterkh) *adj* envious

afhalen (*ahf*-haa-lern) *v* collect, fetch

afhandelen (*ahf*-hahn-der-lern) *v* settle

***afhangen van** (*ahf*-hah-ngern) depend on

afhankelijk (ahf-*hahng*-ker-lerk) *adj* dependant, depending

afhellend (*ahf*-heh-lernt) *adj* sloping

afkeer (*ahf*-kāyr) *c* dislike; antipathy

afkerig (ahf-*kāy*-rerkh) *adj* averse

afkeuren (*ahf*-kūr-rern) *v* disapprove; reject

afknippen (*ahf*-knı-pern) *v* *cut off

afkondigen (*ahf*-kon-der-gern) *v* proclaim

afkorting (*ahf*-kor-tıng) *c* (pl ~en) abbreviation

afleiden (*ahf*-lay-dern) *v* deduce, infer

afleiding (*ahf*-lay-dıng) *c* diversion

afleren (*ahf*-lāy-rern) *v* unlearn

afleveren (*ahf*-lāy-ver-rern) *v* deliver

***aflopen** (*ahf*-lōa-pern) *v* end; expire

aflossen (*ahf*-lo-sern) *v* relieve; *pay off

afluisteren (*ahf*-lur^ew^-ster-rern) *v* eavesdrop

afmaken (*ahf*-maa-kern) *v* finish

afmeting (*ahf*-māy-tıng) *c* (pl ~en) size

***afnemen** (*ahf*-nāy-mern) *v* decrease; *take away

afpersing (*ahf*-pehr-sıng) *c* (pl ~en) extortion

***afraden** (*ahf*-raa-dern) *v* dissuade from

afremmen (*ahf*-reh-mern) *v* slow down

Afrika (aa-free-kaa) Africa

Afrikaan (aa-free-*kaan*) *m* (f ~se, pl -kanen) African

Afrikaans (aa-free-*kaans*) *adj* African

afschaffen (*ahf*-skhah-fern) *v* abolish

afscheid (*ahf*-skhayt) *nt* parting

afschrift (*ahf*-skhrıft) *nt* (pl ~en) copy

afschuw (*ahf*-skhēw^oo^) *c* horror, disgust

afschuwelijk (ahf-*skhēw*-ver-lerk) *adj* horrible, awful, disgusting; hideous

***afsluiten** (*ahf*-slur^ew^-tern) *v* *cut off

***afsnijden** (*ahf*-snay-dern) *v* *cut off; chip

afspraak (*ahf*-spraak) *c* (pl -spraken) appointment; engagement; ~je date

afstammeling (*ahf*-stah-mer-lıng) *c* (pl ~en) descendant

afstamming (*ahf*-stah-mıng) *c* origin

afstand (*ahf*-stahnt) *c* (pl ~en) distance; space, way

afstandsmeter (*ahf*-stahnts-māy-terr) *c* (pl ~s) range finder

afstellen (*ahf*-steh-lern) *v* adjust

afstemmen (*ahf*-steh-mern) *v* tune in

afstotelijk (ahf-*stōa*-ter-lerk) *adj* repellent

aftekenen (*ahf*-tāy-ker-nern) *v* endorse

***aftrekken** (*ahf*-treh-kern) *v* deduct; subtract

aftrap (*ahf*-trahp) *c* kickoff

afvaardiging (ah-*faar*-der-gıng) *c* (pl ~en) delegation

afval (*ah*-fahl) *nt* garbage, litter, rubbish, refuse

afvegen (ah-*fāy*-gern) *v* wipe

afvoer (*ah*-fōor) *c* drain

***afvragen: zich ~** (ah-*fraa*-gern) wonder

afwachten (*ahf*-vahkh-tern) *v* await

afwasmachine (*ahf*-vahs-mah-shee-ner) *c* (pl ~s) dishwasher

afwassen (*ahf*-vah-sern) *v* wash up

afwateren (*ahf*-vaa-ter-rern) *v* drain

afwenden (*ahf*-vehn-dern) *v* avert

afwezig (ahf-*vāy*-zerkh) *adj* absent
afwezigheid (ahf-*vāy*-zerkh-hayt) *c* absence
***afwijken** (*ahf*-vay-kern) *v* deviate
afwijking (*ahf*-vay-kıng) *c* (pl ~en) deviation
***afwijzen** (*ahf*-vay-zern) *v* reject
afwisselen (*ahf*-vı-ser-lern) *v* vary; **afwisselend** alternate
afwisseling (*ahf*-vı-ser-lıng) *c* variation; **voor de ~** for a change
***afzeggen** (*ahf*-seh-gern) *v* cancel
afzender (*ahf*-sehn-derr) *m* (f -zendster, pl ~s) sender
afzetting (*ahf*-seh-tıng) *c* (pl ~en) deposit
afzonderlijk (ahf-*son*-derr-lerk) *adj* individual; separate; *adv* apart
afzwakken (*ahf*-zvah-kern) *v* understate
agenda (aa-*gehn*-daa) *c* (pl ~'s) diary; agenda
agent (aa-*gehnt*) *m* (f ~e, pl ~en) policeman; distributor, agent
agentschap (aa-*gehnt*-skhahp) *nt* (pl ~pen) agency
agressief (ah-greh-*seef*) *adj* aggressive
AIDS (eets) *nt* AIDS
airbag (*ehr*-behk) *c* (pl ~s) air bag *c*
airco (*ehr*-ko) *c*, **airconditioning** *c* air conditioning *c*
akelig (*aa*-ker-lerkh) *adj* nasty
akker (*ah*-kerr) *c* (pl ~s) field
akkoord (ah-*kōart*) *nt* (pl ~en) agreement
akte (*ahk*-ter) *c* (pl ~n, ~s) act, certificate
aktentas (*ahk*-tern-tahss) *c* (pl ~sen) briefcase, attaché case
al (ahl) *adj* all; *adv* already
alarm (aa-*lahrm*) *nt* alarm
alarmeren (aa-lahr-*māy*-rern) *v* alarm
album (*ahl*-berm) *nt* (pl ~s) album

alcohol (*ahl*-kōa-hol) *c* alcohol, *colloquial* booze
alcoholisch (ahl-kōa-*hōa*-leess) *adj* alcoholic
alcoholist (ahl-kōa-ho-*lıst*) *c* (pl ~en) alcoholic
aldoor (*ahl*-dōar) *adv* all the time
alfabet (*ahl*-faa-beht) *nt* alphabet
algebra (*ahl*-ger-braa) *c* algebra
algemeen (ahl-ger-*māyn*) *adj* general; universal, public; **in het ~** in general
Algerije (ahl-ger-*ray*-er) Algeria
Algerijn (ahl-ger-*rayn*) *m* (f ~se, pl ~en) Algerian
Algerijns (ahl-ger-*rayns*) *adj* Algerian
alhoewel (ahl-hōō-*vehl*) *conj* though
alikruik (aa-lee-krur^(ew)k) *c* (pl ~en) winkle
alinea (aa-*lee*-nāy-aa) *c* (pl ~'s) paragraph
alledaags (ah-ler-*daakhs*) *adj* ordinary; everyday
alleen (ah-*lāyn*) *adv* only, just; alone; by itself
allemaal (ah-ler-*maal*) *num* all
allergie (ah-lehr-*gee*) *c* (pl ~ën) allergy
allergisch (ah-*lehr*-geess) *adj* allergic
allerlei (*ah*-lerr-lay) *adj* various; all sorts of
alles (*ah*-lerss) *pron* everything
almachtig (ahl-*mahkh*-terkh) *adj* omnipotent
almanak (*ahl*-maa-nahk) *c* (pl ~ken) almanac
als (ahls) *conj* if; when; as, like
alsof (ahl-*zof*) *conj* as if; ***doen ~** pretend
alstublieft (ahl-stēw-*bleeft*) here you are; please
alt (ahlt) *c* (pl ~en) alto
altaar (*ahl*-taar) *nt* (pl altaren) altar
alternatief (ahl-terr-naa-*teef*) *nt* (pl -tieven) alternative
altijd (*ahl*-tayt) *adv* always, ever

amandel (aa-*mahn*-derl) *c* (pl ~en, ~s)
almond; **amandelen** tonsils *pl*

amandelontsteking (aa-*mahn*-derl-
ont-stāȳ-kıng) *c* (pl ~en) tonsilitis

ambacht (*ahm*-bahkht) *nt* (pl ~en)
trade

ambassade (ahm-bah-*saa*-der) *c* (pl
~s) embassy

ambassadeur (ahm-bah-saa-*dūrr*) *m*
(f -drice, pl ~s) ambassador

ambitie (ahm-*bee*-tsee) *c* ambition

ambitieus (ahm-bee-*tsʸūrss*) *adj*
ambitious

ambt (ahmt) *nt* (pl ~en) office

ambtenaar (*ahm*-ter-naar) *c* (pl
-naren) civil servant

ambulance (ahm-bēw-*lahn*-ser) *c* (pl
~s) ambulance

Amerika (aa-*māȳ*-ree-kaa) America

Amerikaan (aa-māȳ-ree-*kaan*) *m* (f
~se, pl -kanen) American

Amerikaans (aa-māȳ-ree-*kaans*) *adj*
American

amethist (ah-mer-*tist*) *c* (pl ~en)
amethyst

amicaal (aa-mee-*kaal*) *adj* friendly

ammonia (ah-*mōā*-nee-ʸaa) *c*
ammonia

amnestie (ahm-nehss-*tee*) *c* amnesty

amper (*ahm*-perr) *adj* hardly

amulet (aa-mēw-*leht*) *c* (pl ~ten) lucky
charm, charm

amusant (aa-mēw-*zahnt*) *adj* amusing;
entertaining

amusement (aa-mēw-zer-*mehnt*) *nt*
amusement; entertainment

amuseren (aa-mēw-z*āȳ*-rern) *v* amuse

analfabeet (ahn-ahl-faa-*bāȳt*) *m* (f
-bete, pl -beten) illiterate

analist (ah-naa-*lıst*) *c* (pl ~en) analyst

analyse (ah-naa-lee-zer) *c* (pl ~n, ~s)
analysis

analyseren (ah-naa-lee-z*āȳ*-rern) *v*
analyse

analyticus (ah-naa-*lee*-tee-kerss) *c* (pl
-ci) analyst, psychoanalyst

ananas (*ah*-nah-nahss) *c* (pl ~sen)
pineapple

anarchie (ah-nahr-*khee*) *c* anarchy

anatomie (ah-naa-tōā-*mee*) *c* anatomy

ander (*ahn*-derr) *adj* other; different;
een ~ another; **onder andere** among
other things

anders (*ahn*-derrs) *adv* else; otherwise

andersom (ahn-derr-*som*) *adv* the
other way round

angst (ahngst) *c* (pl ~en) fright, fear;
terror

angstig (*ahng*-sterkh) *adj* afraid

angstwekkend (ahngst-*veh*-kernt) *adj*
terrifying

animo (aa-nee-*mōā*) *c* zest

anker (*ahng*-kerr) *nt* (pl ~s) anchor

annexeren (ah-nehk-*sāȳ*-rern) *v* annex

annuleren (ah-nēw-*lāȳ*-rern) *v* cancel

annulering (ah-nēw-*lāȳ*-rıng) *c* (pl
~en) cancellation

anoniem (ah-nōā-*neem*) *adj*
anonymous

ansichtkaart (*ahn*-zıkht-kaart) *c* (pl
~en) postcard, picture postcard

ansjovis (ahn-*shōā*-vıss) *c* (pl ~sen)
anchovy

antenne (ahn-*teh*-ner) *c* (pl ~s) aerial

antibioticum (ahn-tee-bee-ʸ*ōā*-tee-
kerm) *nt* (pl -ca) antibiotic

antiek (ahn-*teek*) *adj* antique

antipathie (ahn-tee-paa-*tee*) *c* dislike,
antipathy

antiquair (ahn-tee-*kair*) *c* (pl ~s)
antique dealer

antiquiteit (ahn-tee-kvee-*tayt*) *c* (pl
~en) antique

antivries (ahn-tee-*vreess*) *c* antifreeze

antwoord (*ahnt*-vōārt) *nt* (pl ~en)
reply, answer; **als ~** in reply

antwoorden (ahnt-vōar-dern) *v* reply,
answer

apart (aa-*pahrt*) *adv* apart, separately

aperitief (aa-p $\overline{ay}$ -ree-*teef*) *nt/c* (pl -tieven) aperitif

apotheek (aa-p $\overline{oa}$ -*t $\overline{ay}$ k*) *c* (pl -theken) pharmacy, chemist's; drugstore *nAm*

apotheker (aa-p $\overline{oa}$ -*t $\overline{ay}$* -kerr) *m* (f ~es, pl ~s) chemist, pharmacist

apparaat (ah-paa-*raat*) *nt* (pl -raten) appliance; machine; apparatus

appartement (ah-pahr-ter-*mehnt*) *nt* (pl ~en) apartment *nAm*

appel (*ah*-perl) *c* (pl ~s) apple

applaudisseren (ah-plou-dee-*s $\overline{ay}$* -rern) *v* clap, applaud

applaus (ah-*plouss*) *nt* applause

april (ah-*prɪl*) April

aquarel (aa-kvaa-*rehl*) *c* (pl ~len) watercolo(u)r

ar (ahr) *c* (pl ~ren) sleigh

Arabier (aa-raa-*beer*) *m* (f Arabische, pl ~en) Arab

Arabisch (aa-*raa*-beess) *adj* Arab

arbeid (*ahr*-bayt) *c* labo(u)r, work

arbeidbesparend (*ahr*-bayt-ber-spaa-rernt) *adj* labo(u)r-saving

arbeider (*ahr*-bay-derr) *m* (f -ster, pl ~s) labo(u)rer, workman, worker

arbeidsbureau (*ahr*-bayts-b $\overline{ew}$ -r $\overline{oa}$) *nt* (pl ~s) job center *Am*, job centre

archeologie (ahr-kh $\overline{ay}$ - $\overline{oa}$ -l $\overline{oa}$ -gee) *c* archaeology

archeoloog (ahr-kh $\overline{ay}$ - $\overline{oa}$ -*l $\overline{oa}$ akh*) *c* (pl -logen) archaeologist

archief (ahr-*kheef*) *nt* (pl -chieven) archives *pl*

architect (ahr-shee-*tehkt*) *c* (pl ~en) architect

architectuur (ahr-shee-tehk-*t $\overline{ew}$ r*) *c* architecture

arena (aa-*r $\overline{ay}$* -naa) *c* (pl ~'s) bullring, arena

arend (*aa*-rernt) *c* (pl ~en) eagle

Argentijn (ahr-gern-*tayn*) *m* (f ~se, pl ~en) Argentinian

Argentijns (ahr-gern-*tayns*) *adj* Argentinian

Argentinië (ahr-gern-*tee*-nee- ^{y} er) Argentina

argument (ahr-g $\overline{ew}$ -*mehnt*) *nt* (pl ~en) argument

argumenteren (ahr-g $\overline{ew}$ -mehn-*t $\overline{ay}$* -rern) *v* argue

argwaan (*ahrkh*-vaan) *c* suspicion

argwanend (ahrkh-*vaa*-nernt) *adj* suspicious

arm[1] (ahrm) *adj* poor

arm[2] (ahrm) *c* (pl ~en) arm

armband (*ahrm*-bahnt) *c* (pl ~en) bracelet; bangle

armoede (ahr-*m $\overline{oo}$* -der) *c* poverty

armoedig (ahr-*m $\overline{oo}$* -derkh) *adj* poor

aroma (aa-*r $\overline{oa}$* -maa) *nt* aroma

arrestatie (ah-rehss-*taa*-tsee) *c* (pl ~s) arrest

arresteren (ah-rehss-*t $\overline{ay}$* -rern) *v* arrest

arrogant (ah-r $\overline{oa}$ -*gahnt*) *adj* presumptuous

artikel (ahr-*tee*-kerl) *nt* (pl ~en, ~s) article; item

artisjok (ahr-tee-*shok*) *c* (pl ~ken) artichoke

artistiek (ahr-tɪss-*teek*) *adj* artistic

arts (ahrts) *c* (pl ~en) doctor

as[1] (ahss) *c* (pl ~sen) axle

as[2] (ahss) *c* ash

asbak (*ahss*-bahk) *c* (pl ~ken) ashtray

asbest (*ahss*-behst) *nt* asbestos

asfalt (*ahss*-fahlt) *nt* asphalt

asiel (aa-*zeel*) *nt* asylum

aspect (ahss-*pehkt*) *nt* (pl ~en) aspect

asperge (ahss-*pehr*-zher) *c* (pl ~s) asparagus

aspirine (ahss-pee-*ree*-ner) *c* aspirin

assistent (ah-see-*stehnt*) *c* (pl ~en) assistant

associëren (ah-s $\overline{oa}$ -*sh $\overline{ay}$* -rern) *v* associate

assortiment (ah-sor-tee-*mehnt*) *nt* (pl

~en) assortment

assurantie (ah-sēw-*rahn*-see) *c* (pl -ties, -tiën) insurance

astma (*ahss*-maa) *nt* asthma

astronaut (ahss-trōā-*nout*) *m* (f ~e, pl ~en) astronaut

atheïst (aa-tāy-ɪst) *m* (f ~e, pl ~en) atheist

Atlantische Oceaan (aht-*lahn*-tee-ser ōā-say-*aan*) Atlantic

atleet (aht-*lāyt*) *c* (pl -leten) athlete

atletiek (aht-lāy-*teek*) *c* athletics *pl*

atmosfeer (aht-moss-*fāyr*) *c* atmosphere

atomisch (aa-*tōā*-meess) *adj* atomic

atoom (aa-*tōām*) *nt* (pl atomen) atom; **atoom-** atomic

attent (ah-*tehnt*) *adj* considerate

attest (ah-*tehst*) *nt* (pl ~en) certificate

attractie (ah-*trahk*-see) *c* (pl ~s) attraction

aubergine (ōā-behr-*zhee*-ner) *c* (pl ~s) eggplant

augustus (ou-*gerss*-terss) August

aula (*ou*-laa) *c* (pl ~'s) auditorium

Australië (ou-*straa*-lee-Yer) Australia

Australiër (ou-*straa*-lee-Yerr) *m* (f Australische, pl ~s) Australian

Australisch (ou-*straa*-leess) *adj* Australian

auteur (ōā-*tūrr*) *c* (pl ~s) author

authentiek (ōā-tehn-*teek*) *adj* authentic

auto (*ōā*-tōā) *c* (pl ~'s) car; motorcar, automobile

automaat (ōā-tōā-*maat*) *c* (pl -maten) slot machine

automatisch (ōā-tōā-*maa*-teess) *adj* automatic

automatisering (ōā-tōā-maa-tee-*zāy*-rɪng) *c* automation

automobielclub (ōā-tōā-mōā-*beel*-klerp) *c* (pl ~s) automobile club

automobilisme (ōā-tōā-mōā-bee-*lɪss*-mer) *nt* motoring

automobilist (ōā-tōā-mōā-bee-*lɪst*) *m* (f ~e, pl ~en) motorist

autonoom (ōā-tōā-*nōām*) *adj* autonomous

autoped (*ōā*-tōā-peht) *c* (pl ~s) scooter

autopsie (ōā-top-see) *c* autopsy

***autorijden** (*ōā*-tōā-ray-dern) *v* motor

autorit (*ōā*-tōā-rɪt) *c* (pl ~ten) drive

autoritair (ōā-tōā-ree-*tair*) *adj* authoritarian

autoriteiten (ōā-tōā-ree-*tay*-tern) *pl* authorities *pl*

autoverhuur (*ōā*-tōā-verr-*hēwr*) *c* car hire; car rental *Am*

autoweg (*ōā*-tōā-vehk) *c* (pl ~en) motoway, highway *nAm*

avond *c* (pl ~en) night, evening

avondeten (*aa*-vernt-*āy*-tern) *nt* dinner; supper

avondkleding (*aa*-vernt-klāy-dɪng) *c* evening dress

avondschemering (*aa*-vernt-skhāy-mer-rɪng) *c* dusk

avontuur (aa-von-*tēwr*) *nt* (pl -turen) adventure

Aziaat (aa-zee-Yaat) *c* (f Aziatische, pl Aziaten) Asian

Aziatisch (aa-zee-Yaa-teess) *adj* Asian

Azië (*aa*-zee-Yer) Asia

azijn (aa-*zayn*) *c* vinegar

B

baai (baaᵉᵉ) c (pl ∼en) bay
baan (baan) c (pl banen) job; orbit
baard (baart) c (pl ∼en) beard
baarmoeder (baar-mōō-derr) c womb
baars (baars) c (pl baarzen) bass, perch
baas (baass) m (f bazin, pl bazen) boss; master
baat (baat) c benefit; profit
babbelen (bah-ber-lern) v chat
babbelkous (bah-berl-kouss) c (pl ∼en) chatterbox
babbeltje (bah-berl-tᵞer) nt (pl ∼s) chat
baby (bāy-bee) c (pl ∼'s) baby
bacil (bah-sɩl) c (pl ∼len) germ
bacterie (bahk-tāy-ree) c (pl -riën) bacterium
bad (baht) nt (pl ∼en) bath; **een ∼ *nemen** bathe
baden (baa-dern) v bathe
badhanddoek (baht-hahn-dōōk) c (pl ∼en) bath towel
badjas (baht-ᵞahss) c (pl ∼sen) bathrobe
badkamer (baht-kaa-merr) c (pl ∼s) bathroom
badmeester (baht-māyss-terr) m (pl ∼s) pool attemdant
badmuts (baht-merts) c (pl ∼en) bathing cap
badpak (baht-pahk) nt (pl ∼ken) bathing suit
badplaats (baht-plaats) c (pl ∼en) seaside resort
badstof (baht-stof) c towel(l)ing
badzout (baht-sout) nt bath salts
bagage (bah-gaa-zher) c baggage; luggage
bagagedepot (bah-gaa-zher-dāy-pōa) nt (pl ∼s) left luggage office; baggage deposit office Am
bagagenet (bah-gaa-zher-neht) nt (pl ∼ten) luggage rack

bagageoverschot (bah-gaa-zher-ōa-verr-skhot) nt overweight
bagagerek (bah-gaa-zher-rehk) nt (pl ∼ken) luggage rack
bagageruimte (bah-gaa-zher-rurᵉʷm-ter) c (pl ∼n, ∼s) boot, nAm trunk
bagagewagen (bah-gaa-zher-vaa-gern) c (pl ∼s) luggage van
bakboord (bahk-bōart) nt port
baken (baa-kern) nt (pl ∼s) landmark
bakermat (baa-kerr-maht) c cradle
bakkebaarden (bah-ker-baar-dern) pl whiskers pl, sideburns pl
*bakken (bah-kern) v bake; fry
bakker (bah-kerr) m (f -ster, pl ∼s) baker
bakkerij (bah-ker-ray) c (pl ∼en) bakery
baksteen (bahk-stāyn) c (pl -stenen) brick
bal¹ (bahl) c (pl ∼len) ball
bal² (bahl) nt (pl ∼s) ball
balans (bah-lahns) c (pl ∼en) balance
baldadig (bahl-daa-derkh) adj rowdy
balie (baa-lee) c (pl ∼s) counter
balk (bahlk) c (pl ∼en) beam
balkon (bahl-kon) nt (pl ∼s) balcony; circle
ballet (bah-leht) nt (pl ∼ten) ballet
balling (bah-lɩng) c (pl ∼en) exile
ballingschap (bah-lɩng-skhahp) c exile
ballon (bah-lon) c (pl ∼s) balloon
ballpoint (bol-poᵞnt) c (pl ∼s) ballpoint pen; Biro®
bamboe (bahm-bōō) nt bamboo
banaan (baa-naan) c (pl bananen) banana
band (bahnt) c (pl ∼en) tape; band; tyre, tire; **lekke ∼** flat tyre, puncture
bandenpech (bahn-der-pehkh) c blowout, puncture

bandenspanning (*bahn*-der-spah-nıng) *c* tyre pressure

bandiet (bahn-*deet*) *m* (pl ~en) bandit

bandrecorder (*bahnt*-rer-kor-derr) *c* (pl ~s) tape recorder, recorder

bang (bahng) *adj* frightened, afraid; ~ ***zijn** *v* be afraid

bank (bahngk) *c* (pl ~en) bank; bench

bankbiljet (*bahngk*-bıl-ʸeht) *nt* (pl ~ten) banknote

banket (bahng-*keht*) *nt* (pl ~ten) banquet

banketbakker (bahng-*keht*-bah-kerr) *m* (f -ster, pl ~s) confectioner

banketbakkerij (bahng-keht-bah-ker-*ray*) *c* (pl ~en) pastry shop

bankrekening (*bahngk*-rāy-ker-nıng) *c* (pl ~en) bank account

bankroet (bahngk-*rōōt*) *adj* bankrupt

bar (bahr) *c* (pl ~s) bar; saloon

barbecue (*bahr*-ber-kʸew̅̅̅) *c* (pl ~s) barbecue

barbecuen (*bahr*-ber-kʸew̅̅̅-ern) *v* barbecue

baret (baa-*reht*) *c* (pl ~ten) beret

bariton (*baa*-ree-ton) *m* (pl ~s) baritone

barjuffrouw (*bahr*-ʸer-frou) *f* (pl ~en) barmaid

barman (*bahr*-mahn) *m* (pl ~nen) bartender, barman

barmhartig (bahr-*mahr*-terkh) *adj* merciful

barnsteen (*bahrn*-stāyn) *nt* amber

barok (baa-*rok*) *adj* baroque

barometer (*bah*-rōa-māy-terr) *c* (pl ~s) barometer

barrière (bah-ree-ʸ*ai*-rer) *c* (pl ~s) barrier

barst (bahrst) *c* (pl ~en) crack

*barsten (*bahrs*-tern) *v* crack, *burst, *split; *get cracked

bas (bahss) *c* (pl ~sen) bass

baseren (baa-*zāy*-rern) *v* base

basiliek (baa-zee-*leek*) *c* (pl ~en) basilica

basis (*baa*-zerss) *c* (pl bases) basis; base

basiscrème (*baa*-zerss-kraim) *c* (pl ~s) foundation cream

basiskennis (*baa*-zerss-keh-nerss) *c* basics

bast (bahst) *c* (pl ~en) bark

bastaard (*bahss*-taart) *c* (pl ~en, ~s) bastard

baten (*baa*-tern) *v* *be of use

batterij (bah-ter-*ray*) *c* (pl ~en) battery

beambte (ber-*ahm*-ter) *c* (pl ~n) clerk

beamen (be-*aa*-mern) *v* affirm

beantwoorden (ber-*ahnt*-vōar-dern) *v* answer

bebloed (be-*blōōt*) *adj* bloody

bebost (ber-*bost*) *adj* wooded; ~ **gebied** woodland

bebouwen (ber-*bou*-ern) *v* cultivate

bed (beht) *nt* (pl ~den) bed

bedaard (ber-*daart*) *adj* quiet

bedachtzaam (ber-*dahkht*-saam) *adj* cautious

bedanken (ber-*dahng*-kern) *v* thank

bedaren (ber-*daa*-rern) *v* calm down

beddegoed (*beh*-der-gōōt) *nt* bedding

bedeesd (ber-*dāyst*) *adj* timid

bedekken (ber-*deh*-kern) *v* cover

bedelaar (*bāy*-der-laar) *m* (f -ster, -ares, pl ~s) beggar

bedelen (*bāy*-der-lern) *v* beg

*bedelven (ber-*dehl*-vern) *v* bury

*bedenken (ber-*dehng*-kern) *v* *think of

*bederven (ber-*dehr*-vern) *v* *spoil; mess up

bedevaart (*bāy*-der-vaart) *c* (pl ~en) pilgrimage

bediende (ber-*deen*-der) *c* (pl ~n, ~s) domestic, servant; valet; (servant) boy

bedienen (ber-*dee*-nern) *v* serve; wait on; attend on

bediening (ber-*dee*-nıng) *c* service

bedieningsgeld (ber-*dee*-nɪngs-khehlt) *nt* service charge

bedoelen (ber-*doo*-lern) *v* *mean; intend

bedoeling (ber-*doo*-lɪng) *c* (pl ~en) purpose, intention

bedrag (ber-*drahkh*) *nt* (pl ~en) amount

***bedragen** (ber-*draa*-gern) *v* amount to

bedreigen (ber-*dray*-gern) *v* threaten

bedreiging (ber-*dray*-gɪng) *c* (pl ~en) threat

***bedriegen** (ber-*dree*-gern) *v* deceive; cheat

bedrijf (ber-*drayf*) *nt* (pl bedrijven) business, concern; plant; act

bedrijvig (ber-*dray*-verkh) *adj* active; industrious

bedroefd (ber-*drooft*) *adj* sad, sorry

bedroefdheid (ber-*drooft*-hayt) *c* sadness; grief

bedrog (ber-*drokh*) *nt* deceit; fraud

beëindigen (ber-*ayn*-der-gern) *v* end, finish

beek (bāyk) *c* (pl beken) brook, stream

beeld (bāylt) *nt* (pl ~en) picture, image

beeldhouwer (*bāylt*-hou-err) *m* (pl ~s) sculptor

beeldhouwwerk (*bāylt*-hou-vehrk) *nt* (pl ~en) sculpture

beeldscherm (*bāylt*-skhehrm) *nt* (pl ~en) screen

been¹ (bāyn) *nt* (pl benen) leg

been² (bāyn) *nt* (pl beenderen, benen) bone

beer (bāyr) *c* (pl beren) bear

beest (bāyst) *nt* (pl ~en) beast

beestachtig (*bāyst*-ahkh-terkh) *adj* brutal

beet (bāyt) *c* (pl beten) bite

beetje (*bāy*-tʸer) *nt* (pl ~s) bit, ounce

***beetnemen** (*bāyt*-nāy-mern) *v* kid

befaamd (ber-*faamt*) *adj* noted

begaafd (ber-*gaaft*) *adj* gifted, talented

***begaan** (ber-*gaan*) *v* commit

begeerlijk (ber-*gāyr*-lerk) *adj* desirable

begeerte (ber-*gāyr*-ter) *c* (pl ~n) desire

begeleiden (ber-ger-*lay*-dern) *v* accompany; conduct

begeren (ber-*gāy*-rern) *v* desire

***begeven** (ber-*gāy*-vern): **zich ~ onder** *v* mingle

begin (ber-*gɪn*) *nt* start, beginning; **begin-** initial

beginneling (ber-gɪ-ner-lɪng) *m* (f ~e, pl ~en) learner, beginner

***beginnen** (ber-gɪ-nern) *v* start, commence, *begin, initiate

beginner (ber-gɪ-nerr) *c* (pl ~s) learner

beginsel (ber-gɪn-serl) *nt* (pl ~en, ~s) principle

begraafplaats (ber-*graaf*-plaats) *c* (pl ~en) cemetery

begrafenis (ber-*graa*-fer-nɪss) *c* (pl ~sen) burial; funeral

***begraven** (ber-*graa*-vern) *v* bury

***begrijpen** (ber-*gray*-pern) *v* *understand; *see, *take; **begrijpend** sympathetic

begrip (ber-*grɪp*) *nt* (pl ~pen) notion, concept; idea, conception; understanding

begroeid (ber-*groo*ᵉᵉt) *adj* overgrown

begroeten (ber-*groo*-tern) *v* say hello to

begroting (ber-*groa*-tɪng) *c* (pl ~en) budget

begunstigde (ber-*gern*-sterkh-der) *c* (pl ~n) payee

begunstigen (ber-*gern*-ster-gern) *v* favo(u)r

beha (*bāy*-haa) *c* (pl ~'s) bra

behalen (ber-*haa*-lern) *v* obtain

behalve (ber-*hahl*-ver) *prep* but, except; beyond, besides

behandelen (ber-*hahn*-der-lern) *v*

treat, handle

behandeling (ber-*hahn*-der-lıng) *c* (pl ~en) treatment

behang (ber-*hahng*) *nt* wallpaper

beheer (ber-*hāȳr*) *nt* management; administration

beheersen (ber-*hāȳr*-sern) *v* master

beheksen (ber-*hehk*-sern) *v* bewitch

*behelpen (ber-*hehl*-pern): **zich ~ met** *make do with

behendig (ber-*hehn*-derkh) *adj* skil(l)ful

beheren (ber-*hāȳ*-rern) *v* manage

behoedzaam (ber-*hōōt*-saam) *adj* wary

behoefte (ber-*hōōf*-ter) *c* (pl ~n) need, want

behoeven (ber-*hōō*-vern) *v* need; **ten behoeve van** on behalf of

behoorlijk (ber-*hōār*-lerk) *adj* proper

behoren (ber-*hōā*-rern) *v* belong to; *ought

behoudend (ber-*hou*-dernt) *adj* conservative

beide (*bay*-der) *adj* both; **een van ~** either; **geen van ~** neither

beige (*bai*-zher) *adj* beige

beïnvloeden (ber-ın-vlōō-dern) *v* influence; affect

beitel (*bay*-terl) *c* (pl ~s) chisel

bejaard (ber-ʸaart) *adj* aged; elderly

bek (behk) *c* (pl ~ken) mouth; beak

bekend (ber-*kehnt*) *adj* well-known

bekende (ber-*kehn*-der) *c* (pl ~n) acquaintance

bekendmaken (ber-*kehnt*-maa-kern) *v* announce

bekendmaking (ber-*kehnt*-maa-kıng) *c* (pl ~en) announcement

bekennen (ber-*keh*-nern) *v* admit, confess

bekentenis (ber-*kehn*-ter-nıss) *c* (pl ~sen) confession

beker (*bāȳ*-kerr) *c* (pl ~s) mug;

tumbler; cup

bekeren (ber-*kāȳ*-rern) *v* convert

*bekijken (ber-*kay*-kern) *v* regard, view

bekken (*beh*-kern) *nt* (pl ~s) basin; pelvis

beklagen (ber-*klaa*-gern) *v* pity

bekleden (ber-*klāȳ*-dern) *v* upholster

beklemmen (ber-*kleh*-mern) *v* oppress

*beklimmen (ber-*klı*-mern) *v* ascend

beklimming (ber-*klı*-mıng) *c* (pl ~en) ascent

beknopt (ber-*knopt*) *adj* concise; brief

bekommeren (ber-*ko*-mer-rern): **zich ~ om** care about

bekoring (ber-*kōā*-rıng) *c* (pl ~en) attraction, charm

bekritiseren (ber-kree-tee-*zāȳ*-rern) *v* criticize

bekrompen (ber-*krom*-pern) *adj* narrow-minded

bekronen (ber-*krōā*-nern) *v* crown

bekwaam (ber-*kvaam*) *adj* able, capable; skil(l)ful

bekwaamheid (ber-*kvaam*-hayt) *c* (pl -heden) ability, faculty, capacity

bel (behl) *c* (pl ~len) bell; bubble

belachelijk (ber-*lah*-kher-lerk) *adj* ridiculous, ludicrous

belang (ber-*lahng*) *nt* (pl ~en) interest; importance; **van ~ *zijn** matter

belangrijk (ber-*lahng*-rayk) *adj* important; capital

belangstellend (ber-lahng-*steh*-lernt) *adj* interested

belangstelling (ber-lahng-*steh*-lıng) *c* interest

belasten (ber-*lahss*-tern) *v* charge; tax; **belast met** in charge of

belasting (ber-*lahss*-tıng) *c* (pl ~en) charge; tax; taxation

belastingvrij (ber-lahss-tıng-*vray*) *adj* duty-free; tax-free

beledigen (ber-*lāȳ*-der-gern) *v* insult;

offend; **beledigend** offensive

belediging (ber-*lay*-der-gɪng) c (pl ~en) insult; offense Am, offence

beleefd (ber-*layft*) adj polite; civil

belegering (ber-*lay*-ger-rɪng) c (pl ~en) siege

beleggen (ber-*leh*-gern) v invest

belegging (ber-*leh*-gɪng) c (pl ~en) investment

beleid (ber-*layt*) nt policy

belemmeren (ber-*leh*-mer-rern) v impede

belemmering (ber-*leh*-mer-rɪng) c (pl ~en) impediment

beletsel (ber-*leht*-serl) nt (pl ~s, ~en) impediment

beletten (ber-*leh*-tern) v prevent

beleven (ber-*lay*-vern) v experience

Belg (behlkh) m (f Belgische, pl ~en) Belgian

België (*behl*-gee-ᵞer) Belgium

Belgisch (*behl*-geess) adj Belgian

belichting (ber-*lɪkh*-tɪng) c exposure

belichtingsmeter (ber-*lɪkh*-tɪngs-*may*-terr) c (pl ~s) exposure meter

*belijden (ber-*lay*-dern) v confess

bellen (*beh*-lern) v *ring

belofte (ber-*lof*-ter) c (pl ~n) promise

belonen (ber-*lōa*-nern) v reward

beloning (ber-*lōa*-nɪng) c (pl ~en) reward; prize

beloven (ber-*lōa*-vern) v promise

bemachtigen (ber-*mahkh*-ter-gern) v secure

bemanning (ber-*mah*-nɪng) c (pl ~en) crew

bemerken (ber-*mehr*-kern) v notice; perceive

bemiddelaar (ber-*mɪ*-der-laar) m (f ~ster, pl ~s) mediator

bemiddeld (ber-*mɪ*-derlt) adj well-to-do

bemiddelen (ber-*mɪ*-der-lern) v mediate

bemind (ber-*mɪnt*) adj beloved

bemoeien (ber-*mōōᵉᵉ*-ern): **zich ~ met** interfere with

benadrukken (ber-*naa*-drer-kern) v emphasize, stress

benaming (ber-*naa*-mɪng) c (pl ~en) denomination

benauwd (ber-*nout*) adj stuffy

bende (*behn*-der) c (pl ~n, ~s) gang

beneden (ber-*nay*-dern) prep under, below; adv underneath, beneath; below; downstairs; **naar ~** downwards, down; downstairs

benieuwd (ber-*neeᵒᵒt*) adj curious

benijden (ber-*nay*-dern) v envy

benoemen (ber-*nōō*-mern) v nominate, appoint

benoeming (ber-*nōō*-mɪng) c (pl ~en) nomination, appointment

benutten (ber-*ner*-tern) v utilize

benzine (behn-*zee*-ner) c petrol; fuel; gasoline nAm, gas nAm; **loodvrije ~** unleaded petrol

benzinepomp (behn-*zee*-ner-pomp) c (pl ~en) petrol pump; fuel pump Am; gas pump Am

benzinestation (behn-*zee*-ner-staa-shon) nt (pl ~s) service station, petrol station; gas station Am

benzinetank (behn-*zee*-ner-tehngk) c (pl ~s) petrol tank

beoefenen (ber-*ōō*-fer-nern) v practise

beogen (ber-*ōa*-gern) v aim at

beoordelen (ber-*ōar*-day-lern) v judge

beoordeling (ber-*ōar*-day-lɪng) c (pl ~en) judgment

bepaald (ber-*paalt*) adj definite; certain

bepalen (ber-*paa*-lern) v define, determine; stipulate

bepaling (ber-*paa*-lɪng) c (pl ~en) stipulation; definition

beperken (ber-*pehr*-kern) v limit

beperking (ber-*pehr*-kɪng) c (pl ~en)
restriction

beproeven (ber-*prōō*-vern) v attempt

beraad (ber-*raat*) nt deliberation

beraadslagen (ber-*raat*-slaa-gern) v
deliberate

beramen (ber-*raa*-mern) v devise

bereid (ber-*rayt*) adj prepared, willing

bereiden (ber-*ray*-dern) v cook

bereidwillig (ber-rayt-vɪ-lerkh) adj co-
operative

bereik (ber-*rayk*) nt reach; range

bereikbaar (ber-*rayk*-baar) adj
attainable

bereiken (ber-*ray*-kern) v reach;
achieve, accomplish, attain

berekenen (ber-*rāy*-ker-nern) v
calculate; charge

berekening (ber-*rāy*-ker-nɪng) c (pl
~en) calculation

berg (behrkh) c (pl ~en) mountain;
mount

bergachtig (*behrkh*-ahkh-terkh) adj
mountainous

bergketen (*behrkh*-kāy-tern) c (pl ~s)
mountain range

bergpas (*behrkh*-pahss) c (pl ~sen)
mountain pass

bergplaats (*behrkh*-plaats) c (pl ~en)
depository

bergrug (*behrkh*-rerg) c (pl ~gen) ridge

bergsport (*behrkh*-sport) c
mountaineering

bericht (ber-*rɪkht*) nt (pl ~en) message;
notice

berispen (ber-*rɪss*-pern) v reprimand,
scold

berk (behrk) c (pl ~en) birch

berm (behrm) c (pl ~en) wayside

beroemd (ber-*rōōmt*) adj famous

beroemdheid (ber-*rōōmt*-hayt) c (pl
~heden) VIP

beroep (ber-*rōōp*) nt (pl ~en)
profession; appeal; **in ~ gaan** v appeal;

beroeps- professional

beroerd (ber-*rōōrt*) adj miserable

beroerte (ber-*rōōr*-ter) c (pl ~n, ~s)
stroke

berouw (ber-*rou*) nt repentance

beroven (ber-*rōa*-vern) v rob

beroving (ber-*rōa*-vɪng) c (pl ~en)
robbery

berucht (ber-*rerkht*) adj notorious

bes (behss) c (pl ~sen) berry; currant;
zwarte ~ blackcurrant

beschaafd (ber-*skhaaft*) adj civilized;
cultured

beschaamd (ber-*skhaamt*) adj
ashamed

beschadigen (ber-*skhaa*-der-gern) v
damage

beschaving (ber-*skhaa*-vɪng) c (pl
~en) civilization; culture

bescheiden (ber-*skhay*-dern) adj
modest

bescheidenheid (ber-*skhay*-dern-
hayt) c modesty

beschermen (ber-*skhehr*-mern) v
protect

bescherming (ber-*skhehr*-mɪng) c
protection

beschikbaar (ber-*skhɪk*-baar) adj
available

beschikken over (ber-*skhɪ*-kern)
dispose of

beschikking (ber-*skhɪ*-king) c disposal

beschimmeld (ber-*skhɪ*-merlt) adj
mouldy

beschouwen (ber-*skhou*-ern) v
consider; regard; reckon

*beschrijven (ber-*skhray*-vern) v
describe

beschrijving (ber-*skhray*-vɪng) c (pl
~en) description

beschuldigen (ber-*skherl*-der-gern) v
accuse; blame

beschutten (ber-*skher*-tern) v shelter

beschutting (ber-*skher*-tɪng) c cover,

shelter
beseffen (ber-*seh*-fern) v realize
beslag (ber-*slahk*) nt batter; ~ **leggen op** confiscate
beslissen (ber-*slı*-sern) v decide
beslissing (ber-*slı*-sıng) c (pl ~en) decision
beslist (ber-*slıst*) adv without fail; certainly
besluit (ber-*slur^{ew}t*) nt (pl ~en) decision
***besluiten** (ber-*slur^{ew}-tern*) v decide
besmettelijk (ber-*smeh*-ter-lerk) adj contagious, infectious
besmetten (ber-*smeh*-tern) v infect
besneeuwd (ber-*snāy^{oo}t*) adj snowy
bespelen (ber-*spāy*-lern) v play
bespottelijk (ber-*spo*-ter-lerk) adj ridiculous, ludicrous
bespotten (ber-*spo*-tern) v ridicule; mock
***bespreken** (ber-*sprāy*-kern) v discuss; reserve
bespreking (ber-*sprāy*-kıng) c (pl ~en) booking; review; discussion
best (behst) adj best
bestaan (ber-*staan*) nt existence
***bestaan** (ber-*staan*) v exist; ~ **uit** consist of
bestanddeel (ber-*stahn*-dāyl) nt (pl -delen) ingredient; element
besteden (ber-*stāy*-dern) v *spend
bestek (ber-*stehk*) nt (pl ~ken) cutlery
bestelauto (ber-*stehl*-ōa-tōa) c (pl ~'s) van; delivery van, pick-up van
bestelformulier (ber-*stehl*-for-mēw-leer) nt (pl ~en) order form
bestellen (ber-*steh*-lern) v order
bestelling (ber-*steh*-lıng) c (pl ~en) order
bestemmen (ber-*steh*-mern) v destine
bestemming (ber-*steh*-mıng) c (pl ~en) destination
bestendig (ber-*stehn*-derkh) adj permanent

***bestijgen** (ber-*stay*-gern) v mount
bestraten (ber-*straa*-tern) v pave
***bestrijden** (ber-*stray*-dern) v combat
besturen (ber-*stēw*-rern) v *drive
bestuur (ber-*stēwr*) nt (pl besturen) direction; board; rule
bestuurlijk (ber-*stēwr*-lerk) adj administrative
bestuursrecht (ber-*stēwrs*-rehkht) nt administrative law
betalen (ber-*taa*-lern) v *pay
betaling (ber-*taa*-lıng) c (pl ~en) payment
betasten (ber-*tahss*-tern) v *feel
betekenen (ber-*tāy*-ker-nern) v *mean
betekenis (ber-*tāy*-ker-nıss) c (pl ~sen) meaning; sense
beter (*bāy*-terr) adj better; superior
beteugelen (ber-*tūr*-ger-lern) v curb
betogen (ber-*tōā*-gern) v demonstrate
betoging (ber-*tōā*-gıng) c (pl ~en) demonstration
beton (ber-*ton*) nt concrete
betoveren (ber-*tōā*-ver-rern) v bewitch; **betoverend** enchanting, glamorous
betovering (ber-*tōā*-ver-rıng) c (pl ~en) spell
betrappen (ber-*trah*-pern) v *catch
***betreden** (ber-*trāy*-dern) v enter
***betreffen** (ber-*treh*-fern) v concern; affect, touch; **wat betreft** as regards
betreffende (ber-*treh*-fern-der) prep as regards, regarding, about, concerning
betrekkelijk (ber-*treh*-ker-lerk) adj relative
***betrekken** (ber-*treh*-kern) v implicate, *get involved; obtain
betrekking (ber-*treh*-kıng) c (pl ~en) post, position, job; reference; **met ~ tot** regarding, with reference to
betreuren (ber-*trur*-rern) v regret
betrokken (ber-*tro*-kern) adj cloudy,

overcast; concerned, involved; interested

betrouwbaar (ber-*trou*-baar) *adj* trustworthy, reliable

betuigen (ber-*tur^{ew}*-gern) *v* express

betwijfelen (ber-*tvay*-fer-lern) *v* doubt, query

betwisten (ber-*tvıss*-tern) *v* dispute

beu (bur) *adj* tired of, fed up with

beuk (burk) *c* (pl ~en) beech

beul (burl) *m* (pl ~en) executioner

beurs (burrs) *c* (pl beurzen) purse; stock exchange; fair; grant

beurt (burrt) *c* (pl ~en) turn

bevaarbaar (ber-*vaar*-baar) *adj* navigable

*bevallen (ber-*vah*-lern) *v* please

bevallig (ber-*vah*-lerkh) *adj* graceful

bevalling (ber-*vah*-lıng) *c* (pl ~en) delivery, childbirth

*bevaren (ber-*vaa*-rern) *v* sail

bevatten (ber-*vah*-tern) *v* contain; include

bevel (ber-*vehl*) *nt* (pl ~en) command, order

*bevelen (ber-*vāy*-lern) *v* command, order, bid

bevelhebber (ber-*vehl*-heh-berr) *m* (pl ~s) commander

beven (*bāy*-vern) *v* tremble

bever (*bāy*-verr) *c* (pl ~s) beaver

bevestigen (ber-*vehss*-ter-gern) *v* acknowledge, confirm, affirm; fasten; **officieel ~** attest; **bevestigend** affirmative

bevestiging (ber-*vehss*-ter-gıng) *c* (pl ~en) confirmation

*bevinden (ber-*vın*-dern): **zich ~** *be

bevlieging (ber-*vlee*-gıng) *c* (pl ~en) whim

bevochtigen (ber-*vokh*-ter-gern) *v* damp, moisten

bevoegd (ber-*vōōkht*) *adj* qualified

bevoegdheid (ber-*vōōkht*-hayt) *c* (pl ~heden) qualification

bevolking (ber-*vol*-kıng) *c* population

bevoorrechten (ber-*vōa*-raykh-tern) *v* favo(u)r

bevorderen (ber-*vor*-der-rern) *v* promote

bevredigen (ber-*vrāy*-der-gern) *v* satisfy

bevredigend (ber-*vrāy*-der-gernt) *adj* satisfactory

bevrediging (ber-*vrāy*-der-gıng) *c* (pl ~en) satisfaction

*bevriezen (ber-*vree*-zern) *v* *freeze

bevrijden (ber-*vray*-dern) *c* liberate; **~ van** rid of

bevrijding (ber-*vray*-dıng) *c* liberation

bevuild (ber-*vur^{ew}lt*) *adj* soiled

bewaken (ber-*vaa*-kern) *v* guard

bewaker (ber-*vaa*-kerr) *m* (f bewaakster, pl ~s) guard; warden

bewapenen (ber-*vaa*-per-nern) *v* arm

bewaren (ber-*vaa*-rern) *v* *hold; preserve; *keep

bewaring (ber-*vaa*-rıng) *c* preservation

beweeglijk (ber-*vāykh*-lerk) *adj* mobile

beweegreden (ber-*vāykh*-rāy-dern) *c* (pl ~en) cause

*bewegen (ber-*vāy*-gern) *v* move; stir

beweging (ber-*vāy*-gıng) *c* (pl ~en) movement; motion

beweren (ber-*vāy*-rern) *v* claim

bewerken (ber-*vehr*-kern) *v* edit

bewijs (ber-*vayss*) *nt* (pl bewijzen) proof, evidence; token; voucher

*bewijzen (ber-*vay*-zern) *v* prove

bewind (ber-*vınt*) *nt* rule, government

bewolking (ber-*vol*-kıng) *c* clouds

bewolkt (ber-*volkt*) *adj* cloudy

bewonderen (ber-*von*-der-rern) *v* admire

bewondering (ber-*von*-der-rıng) *c* admiration

bewonen (ber-*voa*-nern) *v* inhabit

bewoner (ber-*voa*-nerr) *m* (f bewoonster, pl ~s) inhabitant; occupant

bewoonbaar (ber-*voan*-baar) *adj* habitable, inhabitable

bewust (ber-*verst*) *adj* conscious, aware

bewusteloos (ber-*verss*-ter-loass) *adj* unconscious

bewustzijn (ber-*verst*-sayn) *nt* consciousness

bezem (*bay*-zerm) *c* (pl ~s) broom

bezeren (ber-*zay*-rern) *v* *hurt

bezet (ber-*zeht*) *adj* engaged, occupied

bezeten (ber-*zay*-tern) *adj* possessed

bezetten (ber-*zeh*-tern) *v* occupy

bezetting (ber-*zeh*-ting) *c* (pl ~en) occupation

bezielen (ber-*zee*-lern) *v* inspire

bezienswaardigheid (ber-zeen-*svaar*-derkh-hayt) *c* (pl -heden) sight

bezig (*bay*-zerkh) *adj* engaged, busy

***bezighouden** (*bay*-zerkh-hou-dern): **zich ~ met** attend to

bezinksel (ber-*zingk*-serl) *nt* (pl ~s) deposit

bezit (ber-*zit*) *nt* property; possession

***bezitten** (ber-*zi*-tern) *v* possess, own

bezitter (ber-*zi*-terr) *m* (f -ster, pl ~s) owner

bezittingen (ber-*zi*-ting-ern) *pl* belongings *pl*

bezoek (ber-*zook*) *nt* (pl ~en) call, visit

***bezoeken** (ber-*zoo*-kern) *v* visit; call on

bezoeker (ber-*zoo*-kerr) *m* (f -ster, pl ~s) visitor

bezoekuren (ber-*zook*-ew-rern) *pl* visiting hours

bezonnen (ber-*zo*-nern) *adj* sober

bezorgd (ber-*zorkht*) *adj* anxious, concerned

bezorgdheid (ber-*zorkht*-hayt) *c* worry, anxiety

bezorgen (ber-*zor*-gern) *v* deliver; supply

bezorging (ber-*zor*-ging) *c* delivery

bezwaar (ber-*zvaar*) *nt* (pl bezwaren) objection; ~ *hebben tegen object to; mind

***bezwijken** (ber-*zvay*-kern) *v* collapse; succumb

bibberen (*bi*-ber-rern) *v* shiver

bibliotheek (bee-blee-*voa*-tayk) *c* (pl -theken) library

***bidden** (*bi*-dern) *v* pray

biecht (beekht) *c* (pl ~en) confession

biechten (*beekh*-tern) *v* confess

***bieden** (*bee*-dern) *v* offer; bid

biefstuk (*beef*-sterk) *c* (pl ~ken) steak

bier (beer) *nt* (pl ~en) beer; ale

bies (beess) *c* (pl biezen) rush

bieslook (*beess*-loak) *nt* chives *pl*

biet (beet) *c* (pl ~en) beet

big (bikh) *c* (pl ~gen) piglet

bij¹ (bay) *prep* near, at, with, by; to

bij² (bay) *c* (pl ~en) bee

bijbel (*bay*-berl) *c* (pl ~s) bible

bijbetekenis (*bay*-ber-tay-ker-niss) *c* (pl ~sen) connotation

bijdrage (*bay*-draa-ger) *c* (pl ~n) contribution

bijeen (bay-*ayn*) *adv* together

***bijeenbrengen** (bay-*ayn*-breh-ngern) *v* assemble

***bijeenkomen** (bay-*ayng*-koa-mern) *v* gather

bijeenkomst (bay-*ayng*-komst) *c* (pl ~en) meeting; rally; assembly, congress

bijenkorf (*bay*-er-korf) *c* (pl -korven) beehive

bijgebouw (*bay*-ger-bou) *nt* (pl ~en) annex

bijgeloof (*bay*-ger-loaf) *nt* superstition

bijgevolg (bay-ger-*volkh*) *adv* consequently

*bijhouden (*bay*-hou-dern) *v* *keep up with

bijknippen (*bay*-knı-pern) *v* trim

bijkomend (*bay*-kōa-mernt) *adj* additional

bijkomstig (bay-*kom*-sterkh) *adj* additional; subordinate

bijl (bayl) *c* (pl ⁓en) axe

bijlage (*bay*-laa-ger) *c* (pl ⁓n) appendix, annex; enclosure

bijna (*bay*-naa) *adv* nearly, almost

bijnaam (*bay*-naam) *c* (pl -namen) nickname

bijouterie (bee-zhōō-ter-*ree*) *c* jewelry *Am*, jewellery

*bijsluiten (*bay*-slur^{ew}-tern) *v* enclose

*bijstaan (*bay*-staan) *v* assist, aid

bijstand (*bay*-stahnt) *c* assistance; social security, *nAm* welfare

*bijten (*bay*-tern) *v* *bite

bijvoegen (*bay*-vōō-gern) *v* attach

bijvoeglijk naamwoord (bay-*vōōkh*-lerk *naam*-vōart) adjective

bijvoorbeeld (ber-*vōar*-bāylt) *adv* for instance, for example

bijwonen (*bay*-vōa-nern) *v* assist at, attend

bijwoord (*bay*-vōart) *nt* (pl ⁓en) adverb

bijziend (bay-*zeent*) *adj* short-sighted

bijzonder (bee-*zon*-derr) *adj* special, particular; peculiar; **in het ⁓** in particular, specially

bijzonderheid (bee-*zon*-derr-hayt) *c* (pl -heden) detail

bil (bıl) *c* (pl ⁓len) buttock

biljart (bıl-*y'ahrt*) *nt* billiards *pl*

billijk (*bı*-lerk) *adj* right, fair, reasonable

*binden (*bın*-dern) *v* *bind; tie

binnen (*bı*-nern) *prep* within, inside; *adv* inside, indoors; in; indoor; **naar ⁓** inwards; **van ⁓** within, inside

binnenband (*bı*-ner-bahnt) *c* (pl ⁓en) inner tube

*binnengaan (*bı*-ner-gaan) *v* enter, *go in

binnenkant (*bı*-ner-kahnt) *c* interior, inside

*binnenkomen (*bı*-nern-kōa-mern) *v* enter

binnenkomst (*bı*-ner-komst) *c* entrance

binnenkort (bı-ner-*kort*) *adv* shortly

binnenlands (*bı*-ner-lahnts) *adj* domestic

binnenst (*bı*-nerst) *adj* inside; **binnenste buiten** *adv* inside out

*binnenvallen (*bı*-ner-vah-lern) *v* invade; barge in

biologie (bee-^yōa-lōa-*gee*) *c* biology

bioscoop (bee-^yoss-*kōap*) *c* (pl -scopen) cinema; pictures; movie theater *Am*, movies *Am*

biscuit (bıss-*kvee*) *nt* (pl ⁓s) cookie *nAm*

bisschop (*bıss*-khop) *m* (pl ⁓pen) bishop

bitter (*bı*-terr) *adj* bitter

blaar (blaar) *c* (pl blaren) blister

blaas (blaass) *c* (pl blazen) bladder; blister

blaasontsteking (*blaass*-ont-stāy-kıng) *c* (pl ⁓en) cystitis

blad[1] (blaht) *nt* (pl ⁓eren, blaren) leaf

blad[2] (blaht) *nt* (pl ⁓en) sheet; magazine

bladgoud (*blaht*-khout) *nt* gold leaf

bladzijde (*blaht*-say-der) *c* (pl ⁓n) page

blaffen (*blah*-fern) *v* bark; bay

blanco (*blahng*-kōa) *adj* blank

blank (blahngk) *adj* white

blankvoorn (*blahngk*-fōa-rern) *c* (pl ⁓s) roach

blauw (blou) *adj* blue

*blazen (*blaa*-zern) *v* *blow

blazer (*blāy*-zerr) *c* (pl ⁓s) blazer

bleek (blāyk) *adj* pale

bleken (*blay*-kern) *v* bleach

blessure (bleh-*sew*-rer) *c* (pl ~s) injury

blij (blay) *adj* glad; happy, joyful

blijkbaar (*blayk*-baar) *adv* apparently

*****blijken** (*blay*-kern) *v* prove; appear

blijspel (*blay*-spehl) *nt* (pl ~en) comedy

*****blijven** (*blay*-vern) *v* stay, remain; *keep; **blijvend** lasting; permanent

blik (blɪk) *nt* (pl ~ken) tin, can; *c* look; glimpse, glance; **een ~ *werpen** glance

blikopener (*blɪk*-ōa-per-nerr) *c* (pl ~s) tin opener, can opener

bliksem (*blɪk*-serm) *c* lightning

blind[1] (blɪnt) *nt* (pl ~en) shutter

blind[2] (blɪnt) *adj* blind

blindedarm (blɪn-der-*dahrm*) *c* (pl ~en) appendix

blindedarmontsteking (blɪn-der-*dahrm*-ont-stāy-king) *c* (pl ~en) appendicitis

*****blinken** (*blɪng*-kern) *v* *shine; **blinkend** bright

blocnote (*blok*-nōat) *c* (pl ~s) writing pad

bloed (blōōt) *nt* blood

bloedarmoede (*blōōt*-ahr-mōō-der) *c* anaemia

bloeddruk (*blōō*-drerk) *c* blood pressure

bloeden (*blōō*-dern) *v* *bleed

bloederig (*blōō*-de-rerkh) *adj* bloody

bloeding (*blōō*-dɪng) *c* (pl ~en) h(a)emorrhage

bloedsomloop (*blōōt*-som-lōap) *c* circulation

bloedvat (*blōōt*-faht) *nt* (pl ~en) blood vessel

bloedvergiftiging (*blōōt*-ferr-gɪf-ter-gɪng) *c* blood poisoning

bloem[1] (blōōm) *c* flour

bloem[2] (blōōm) *c* (pl ~en) flower

bloemblad (*blōōm*-blaht) *nt* (pl ~en) petal

bloembol (*blōōm*-bol) *c* (pl ~len) bulb

bloemenwinkel (*blōō*-mer-vɪng-kerl) *c* (pl ~s) flower shop

bloemist (blōō-*mɪst*) *m* (f ~e, pl ~en) florist

bloemkool (*blōōm*-kōal) *c* (pl -kolen) cauliflower

bloemperk (*blōōm*-pehrk) *nt* (pl ~en) flowerbed

bloesem (*blōō*-serm) *c* (pl ~s) blossom *nt*

blok (blok) *nt* (pl ~ken) block; **blokje** *nt* cube

blokkeren (blo-*kāy*-rern) *v* block

blond (blont) *adj* fair, blond, blonde

blondine (blon-*dee*-ner) *c* (pl ~s) blond, blonde

bloot (blōat) *adj* bare; naked

blootleggen (*blōat*-leh-gern) *v* uncover

blootstellen (*blōat*-steh-lern) *v* expose

blootstelling (*blōat*-steh-lɪng) *c* (pl ~en) exposure

blouse (*blōō*-zer) *c* (pl ~s) blouse

blozen (*blōa*-zern) *v* blush

blussen (*bler*-sern) *v* extinguish

bocht (bokht) *c* (pl ~en) turning, bend; curve, turn

bod (bot) *nt* bid

bode (*bōa*-der) *m* (pl ~n, ~s) messenger

bodem (*bōa*-derm) *c* (pl ~s) bottom; ground; soil

boef (bōōf) *m* (pl boeven) villain

boei (bōō-ee) *c* (pl ~en) buoy

boeien (*bōō*-ee-ern) *v* fascinate

boek (bōōk) *nt* (pl ~en) book

boeken (*bōō*-kern) *v* book

boekenstalletje (*bōō*-ker-stah-ler-t'er) *nt* (pl ~s) bookstand

boeket (bōō-*keht*) *nt* (pl ~ten) bouquet

boekhandel (*bōōk*-hahn-derl) *c* (pl ~s) bookstore

boekhandelaar (*bōōk*-hahn-der-laar) *m* (pl -laren) bookseller

boekwinkel (*boōk*-vɪng-kerl) *c* (pl ⁓s) bookstore

boel (boōl) *c* lot

boer (boōr) *m* (pl ⁓en) farmer; peasant; knave

boerderij (boōr-der-*ray*) *c* (pl ⁓en) farm; farmhouse

boerin (boō-*rɪn*) *f* (pl ⁓nen) farmer's wife

boete (*boō*-ter) *c* (pl ⁓n, ⁓s) penalty, fine

boetiek (boō-*teek*) *c* boutique *c*

boetseren (boōt-*say*-rern) *v* model

bof (bof) *c* mumps

bok (bok) *c* (pl ⁓ken) goat, buck

boksen (*bok*-sern) *v* box

bokswedstrijd (*boks*-veht-strayt) *c* (pl ⁓en) boxing match

bol (bol) *c* (pl ⁓len) bulb; sphere

Boliviaan (boā-lee-vee-*ʸaan*) *m* (f ⁓se, pl -vianen) Bolivian

Boliviaans (boā-lee-vee-*ʸaans*) *adj* Bolivian

Bolivië (boā-*lee*-vee-ʸer) Bolivia

bom (bom) *c* (pl ⁓men) bomb

bombarderen (bom-bahr-*day*-rern) *v* bomb

bon (bon) *c* (pl ⁓nen) coupon; ticket; voucher

bonbon (bom-*bon*) *c* (pl ⁓s) chocolate

bond (bont) *c* (pl ⁓en) league, federation

bondgenoot (*bont*-kher-noāt) *m* (pl -noten) associate

bondgenootschap (*bont*-kher-noāt-skhahp) *nt* (pl ⁓pen) alliance

bons (bons) *c* (pl bonzen) bump

bont (bont) *adj* colo(u)rful, loud

bontjas (*bont*-tʸahss) *c* (pl ⁓en) fur coat

bontwerker (*bont*-tvehr-kerr) *m* (pl ⁓s) furrier

bonzen (*bon*-zern) *v* bump

boodschap (*boāt*-skhahp) *c* (pl ⁓pen) errand; message

boodschappentas (*boāt*-skhah-per-tahss) *c* (pl ⁓sen) shopping bag

boog (boākh) *c* (pl bogen) arch; bow

boogvormig (*boākh*-for-merkh) *adj* arched

boom (boām) *c* (pl bomen) tree

boomgaard (*boām*-gaart) *c* (pl ⁓en) orchard

boomkwekerij (boām-kvaȳ-ker-*ray*) *c* (pl ⁓en) nursery

boon (boān) *c* (pl bonen) bean

boor (boār) *c* (pl boren) drill

boord (boārt) *nt/c* (pl ⁓en) collar; **aan boord** aboard; **van boord *gaan** disembark

boordenknoopje (*boār*-der-knoā-pʸer) *nt* (pl ⁓s) collar-stud

boos (boāss) *adj* cross

boosaardig (boā-*zaar*-derkh) *adj* malicious, vicious

boosheid (*boāss*-hayt) *c* anger, temper

boot (boāt) *c* (pl boten) boat, ship

bootje (*boā*-tʸer) *nt* (pl ⁓s) dinghy

boottocht (*boā*-tokht) *c* (pl ⁓en) cruise

bord (bort) *nt* (pl ⁓en) dish, plate; board

bordeel (bor-*dayl*) *nt* (pl -delen) brothel

borduren (bor-*dew*-rern) *v* embroider

borduurwerk (bor-*dewr*-vehrk) *nt* (pl ⁓en) embroidery

boren (*boā*-rern) *v* drill, bore

borgsom (*borkh*-som) *c* (pl ⁓men) bail

borrel (*boa*-rerl) *c* (pl ⁓s) drink

borrelhapje (*bo*-rerl-hahp-ʸer) *nt* (pl ⁓s) appetizer

borst (borst) *c* (pl ⁓en) chest; breast, bosom

borstel (*bor*-sterl) *c* (pl ⁓s) brush

borstelen (*bor*-ster-lern) *v* brush

borstkas (*borst*-kahss) *c* (pl ⁓sen) chest

bos (boss) *nt* (pl ⁓sen) forest, wood; *c* bunch

bosje (*bo*-sher) *nt* (pl ⁓s) grove

boswachter (*boss*-vahkh-terr) *m* (pl

~s) forester

bot¹ (bot) *adj* dull, blunt

bot² (bot) *nt* (pl ~ten) bone

boter (bōa-terr) *c* butter

boterham (bōa-terr-hahm) *c* (pl ~men) sandwich

botsen (bot-sern) *v* bump; collide, crash

botsing (bot-sɪng) *c* (pl ~en) collision, crash

bougie (bōō-zhee) *c* (pl ~s) sparking plug

bout (bout) *c* (pl ~en) bolt

boutique (bōō-teek) *c* (pl ~s) boutique

bouw (bou) *c* construction

bouwen (bou-ern) *v* *build; construct

bouwkunde (bou-kern-der) *c* architecture

bouwvallig (bou-vah-lerkh) *adj* dilapidated

boven (bōa-vern) *prep* above, over; *adv* above; upstairs; **naar ~** upwards; up; upstairs

bovendek (bōa-vern-dehk) *nt* main deck

bovendien (bōa-vern-deen) *adv* furthermore, moreover, besides

bovenkant (bōa-verng-kahnt) *c* (pl ~en) top side, top

bovenop (bōa-vern-op) *prep* on top of

bovenst (bōa-verst) *adj* upper, top

braaf (braaf) *adj* good

braak (braak) *adj* waste

braam (braam) *c* (pl bramen) blackberry

*braden (braa-dern) *v* fry; roast

braken (braa-kern) *v* vomit

brand (brahnt) *c* (pl ~en) fire

brandalarm (brahnt-aa-lahrm) *nt* fire alarm

brandblusapparaat (brahnt-blerss-ahpaa-raat) *nt* (pl -raten) fire extinguisher

branden (brahn-dern) *v* *burn

brandkast (brahnt-kahst) *c* (pl ~en) safe

brandmerk (brahnt-mehrk) *nt* (pl ~en) brand

brandpunt (brahnt-pernt) *nt* (pl ~en) focus

brandstof (brahnt-stof) *c* (pl ~fen) fuel

brandtrap (brahn-trahp) *c* (pl ~pen) fire escape

brandvrij (brahnt-fray) *adj* fireproof

brandweer (brahn-tvayr) *c* fire brigade

brandweerman (brahn-tvayr-mahn) *c* firefighter

brandwond (brahn-tvont) *c* (pl ~en) burn

Braziliaan (braa-zee-lee-ʸaan) *m* (f ~se, pl -lianen) Brazilian

Braziliaans (braa-zee-lee-ʸaans) *adj* Brazilian

Brazilië (braa-zee-lee-ʸer) Brazil

breed (brāyt) *adj* broad, wide

breedte (brāy-ter) *c* (pl ~n, ~s) breadth, width

breedtegraad (brāy-ter-graat) *c* (pl -graden) latitude

breekbaar (brāyk-baar) *adj* fragile

breekijzer (brāy-kay-zerr) *nt* (pl ~s) crowbar

breien (bray-ern) *v* *knit

*breken (brāy-kern) *v* *break; *burst, crack; fracture

*brengen (breh-ngern) *v* *bring; *take

bres (brehss) *c* (pl ~sen) gap, breach

bretels (brer-tehls) *pl* braces *pl*; suspenders *plAm*

breuk (brurk) *c* (pl ~en) break; fracture; hernia

brief (breef) *c* (pl brieven) letter; **aangetekende ~** registered letter

briefkaart (breef-kaart) *c* (pl ~en) card, postcard

briefopener (breef-ōa-per-nerr) *c* (pl ~s) paper knife

briefpapier (breef-paa-peer) *nt*

notepaper

briefwisseling (*breef*-vi-ser-lıng) *c* correspondence

bries (breess) *c* breeze

brievenbus (*bree*-ver-berss) *c* (pl ~sen) letterbox, pillarbox; mailbox *nAm*

bril (brıl) *c* (pl ~len) spectacles, glasses

briljant (brıl-*^yahnt*) *adj* brilliant

Brit (brıt) *m* (f ~se, pl ~ten) Briton

Brits (brıts) *adj* British

broche (bro-sher) *c* (pl ~s) brooch

brochure (bro-*shéw*-rer) *c* (pl ~s) brochure

broeder (*brōō*-derr) *m* (pl ~s) brother

broederschap (*brōō*-derr-skhahp) *c* fraternity

broeikas (*brōō^{ee}*-kahss) *c* (pl ~sen) greenhouse

broek (brōōk) *c* (pl ~en) trousers *pl*, slacks *pl*; pants *plAm*; **korte ~** shorts *pl*

broekpak (*brōōk*-pahk) *nt* (pl ~ken) pant suit

broer (brōōr) *m* (pl ~s) brother

brok (brok) *nt* (pl ~ken) morsel; lump

bromfiets (*brom*-feets) *c* (pl ~en) moped

brommen (*bro*-mern) *v* buzz

brommer (*bro*-merr) *c* (pl ~s) motorbike *nAm*

bron (bron) *c* (pl ~nen) well; fountain, source, spring; **geneeskrachtige ~** spa

bronchitis (brong-*khee*-terss) *c* bronchitis

brons (brons) *nt* bronze

bronzen (*bron*-zern) *adj* bronze

brood (brōāt) *nt* (pl broden) bread; loaf

broodje (*brōā*-t^yer) *nt* (pl ~s) roll, bun

broos (brōāss) *adj* fragile

brouwen (*brou*-ern) *v* brew

brouwerij (brou-er-*ray*) *c* (pl ~en) brewery

brug (brerkh) *c* (pl ~gen) bridge

bruid (brur^wt) *f* (pl ~en) bride

bruidegom (*brur^{ew}*-der-gom) *m* (pl ~s) bridegroom, groom

bruikbaar (*brur^{ew}k*-baar) *adj* usable; useful

bruiloft (*brur^{ew}*-loft) *c* (pl ~en) wedding

bruin (brur^{ew}n) *adj* brown

brullen (*brer*-lern) *v* roar

brunette (brēw-*neh*-ter) *f* (pl ~s) brunette

brutaal (brēw-*taal*) *adj* bold, impertinent, insolent, *colloquial* cheeky

bruto (*brōō*-tōa) *adj* gross

budget (ber-*jeht*) *nt* (pl ~ten, ~s) budget

buffet (bēw-*feht*) *nt* (pl ~ten) buffet

bui (bur^{ew}) *c* (pl ~en) shower

buidel (*bur^{ew}*-derl) *c* (pl ~s) pouch

buigbaar (*bur^{ew}kh*-baar) *adj* flexible

***buigen** (*bur^{ew}*-gern) *v* *bend; bow

buigzaam (*bur^{ew}kh*-saam) *adj* supple

buik (bur^{ew}k) *c* (pl ~en) belly

buikpijn (*bur^{ew}k*-payn) *c* stomach ache

buis (bur^{ew}ss) *c* (pl buizen) tube; telly

buiten (*bur^{ew}*-tern) *prep* outside, out of; *adv* out; outside, outdoors; **naar ~** outwards

buitengewoon (*bur^{ew}*-ter-ger-*vōan*) *adj* extraordinary, exceptional

buitenhuis (*bur^{ew}*-ter-hur^{ew}ss) *nt* (pl -huizen) cottage

buitenkant (*bur^{ew}*-ter-kahnt) *c* (pl ~en) outside, exterior

buitenland (*bur^{ew}*-tern-lahnt) foreign country; **in het ~** abroad; **naar het ~** abroad

buitenlander (*bur^{ew}*-ter-lahn-derr) *m* (f -se, pl ~s) alien, foreigner

buitenlands (*bur^{ew}*-ter-lahnts) *adj* alien, foreign

buitensporig (bur^{ew}-ter-*spōā*-rerkh) *adj* excessive

buitenwijk (*bur^{ew}*-ter-vayk) *c* (pl ~en) suburb; outskirts *pl*

bukken: (*ber*-kern) **zich ~** *bend down

Bulgaar (berl-*gaar*) *m* (f ~se, pl -garen) Bulgarian

Bulgaars (berl-*gaars*) *adj* Bulgarian

Bulgarije (berl-gaa-*ray*-er) Bulgaria

bulletin (ber-ler-*tañg*) *c* (pl ~s) bulletin

bult (berlt) *c* (pl ~en) lump

bumper (berm-perr) *c* (pl ~s) bumper

bundel (*bern*-derl) *c* (pl ~s) bundle

bundelen (*bern*-der-lern) *v* bundle

burcht (berrkht) *c* (pl ~en) stronghold

bureau (bew-*roā*) *nt* (pl ~s) agency, office; bureau, desk; **~ voor gevonden voorwerpen** lost property office

bureaucratie (bew-roā-kraa-*tsee*) *c* bureaucracy

burgemeester (berr-ger-*māyss*-terr) *m* (pl ~s) mayor

burger (*berr*-gerr) *m* (f ~es, pl ~s) citizen; civilian; **burger-** civilian, civic

burgerlijk (*berr*-gerr-lerk) *adj* bourgeois, middle-class; square; **~ recht** civil law

bus (berss) *c* (pl ~sen) coach, bus; tin, canister

buste (*bēw*-ster) *c* (pl ~s, ~n) bust

bustehouder (*bēw*-ster-hou-derr) *c* (pl ~s) bra

buur (bēwr) *m* (pl buren) neighbo(u)r

buurman (*bēwr*-mahn) *m* (f buurvrouw, pl buurlui) neighbo(u)r

buurt (bēwrt) *c* (pl ~en) neighbo(u)rhood, vicinity

C

cabaret (kaa-baa-*reht*) *nt* (pl ~s) cabaret

cabine (kaa-*bee*-ner) *c* (pl ~s) cabin

cadeau (kaa-*doā*) *nt* (pl ~s) gift, present

café (kaa-*fāy*) *nt* (pl ~s) café; public house, pub

cafeïnevrij (*kah*-fāyy-ıne-vray) *adj* decaf(feinated)

cafetaria (kah-fer-taa-ree-*Ya*a) *c* (pl ~'s) cafeteria

caissière (kah-*shai*-rer) *f* (pl ~s) cashier

cake (kāyk) *c* (pl ~s) cake

calcium (*kahl*-see-*Y*erm) *nt* calcium

calorie (kah-*loā*-ree) *c* (pl ~ën) calorie

calvinisme (kahl-vee-*nıss*-mer) *nt* Calvinism

camee (kaa-*māy*) *c* (pl ~ën) cameo

campagne (kahm-*pah*-ñer) *c* (pl ~s) campaign

camping (*kehm*-pıng) *c* (pl ~s) camping site, camping

Canada (*kaa*-naa-daa) Canada

Canadees (kaa-naa-*dāyss*) *adj* Canadian

capabel (kaa-*paa*-berl) *adj* able

capaciteit (kah-paa-see-*tayt*) *c* (pl ~en) capacity

cape (kāyp) *c* (pl ~s) cape

capitulatie (kah-pee-tēw-*laa*-tsee) *c* (pl ~s) capitulation

capsule (kahp-*sēw*-ler) *c* (pl ~s) capsule

caravan (*keh*-rer-vern) *c* (pl ~s) caravan

carbonpapier (kahr-*bon*-paa-peer) *nt* carbon paper

carburateur (kahr-bēw-raa-*tūrr*) *c* (pl ~s) carburettor

carillon (kaa-rıl-*Yon*) *nt* (pl ~s) chimes *pl*

carnaval (*kahr*-naa-vahl) *nt* carnival

carrière (kah-ree-*ᵞai*-rer) *c* (pl ~s)
career

carrosserie (kah-ro-ser-*ree*) *c* (pl ~ën)
motor body *Am*

casino (kaa-*zee*-nōa) *nt* (pl ~'s) casino

catacombe (kah-tah-*kom*-ber) *c* (pl
~n) catacomb

catalogus (kah-*taa*-lōa-gerss) *c* (pl
-gussen, -gi) catalogue

catarre (kaa-*tahr*) *c* catarrh

catastrofe (kaa-taa-*straw*-fer) *c* (pl ~s)
catastrophe, disaster

categorie (kaa-ter-gōa-*ree*) *c* (pl ~ën)
category

cavia (*kaa*-vee-ᵞaa) *c* (pl ~'s) guinea pig

CD (ser-*dāy*) *c* (pl ~'s) CD

CD-ROM (sāy-dāy-*rom*) *c* (pl ~s) CD-
ROM

CD-speler (ser-*dāy*-spāy-lerr) *c* (pl ~s)
CD player

cel (sehl) *c* (pl ~len) cell

celibaat (sāy-lee-*baat*) *nt* celibacy

cellofaan (seh-loa-*faan*) *nt* cellophane

celsius (*sehl*-see-ᵞerss) centigrade

cement (ser-*mehnt*) *nt* cement

censuur (sehn-*zēwr*) *c* censorship

centimeter (*sehn*-tee-māy-terr) *c* (pl
~s) centimeter *Am*, centimetre; tape
measure

centraal (sehn-*traal*) *adj* central; ~
station central station; **centrale
verwarming** central heating

centraliseren (sehn-traa-lee-*zāy*-
rern) *v* centralize

centrifuge (sehn-tree-*fēw*-zher) *c* (pl
~s) dryer

centrum (*sehn*-trerm) *nt* (pl centra)
center *Am*, centre

ceramiek (sāy-raa-*meek*) *c* ceramics *pl*

ceremonie (sāy-rer-*mōa*-nee) *c* (pl
-niën, -nies) ceremony

certificaat (sehr-tee-fee-*kaat*) *nt* (pl
-caten) certificate

chalet (shaa-*leht*) *nt* (pl ~s) chalet

champagne (shahm-*pah*-ñer) *c* (pl ~s)
champagne

champignon (shahm-pee-*ñon*) *c* (pl
~s) mushroom

chantage (shahn-*taa*-zher) *c*
blackmail

chanteren (shahn-*tāy*-rern) *v*
blackmail

chaos (*khaa*-oss) *c* chaos

chaotisch (khaa-*ōa*-teess) *adj* chaotic

charlatan (*shahr*-laa-tahn) *m* (pl ~s)
quack

charmant (shahr-*mahnt*) *adj* charming

charme (*shahr*-mer) *c* (pl ~s) charm

chartervlucht (*chahr*-terr-vlerkht) *c*
(pl ~en) charter flight

chassis (shah-*see*) *nt* (pl ~) chassis

chauffeur (shōa-*fūrr*) *m* (f chauffeuse,
pl ~s) driver, chauffeur

chef (shehf) *m* (f cheffin, pl ~s) boss,
manager, chief

chef-kok (shehf-*kok*) *m* (f -kokkin, pl
~s) chef

chemie (khāy-*mee*) *c* chemistry

chemisch (*khāy*-meess) *adj* chemical

cheque (shehk) *c* (pl ~s) cheque; check
nAm

chequeboekje (*shehk*-bōa-k*ᵞ*er) *nt* (pl
~s) chequebook; checkbook *nAm*

chic (sheek) *adj* smart; posh

Chileen (shee-*lāyn*) *m* (f ~se, pl -lenen)
Chilean

Chileens (shee-*lāyns*) *adj* Chilean

Chili (*shee*-lee) Chile

China (*shee*-naa) China

Chinees (shee-*nāyss*) *adj* Chinese

chirurg (shee-*rerrkh*) *m* (pl ~en)
surgeon

chloor (khlōar) *nt* chlorine

chocola (shōa-kōa-*laa*) *c* chocolate

chocolademelk (shōa-kōa-*laa*-der-
mehlk) *c* chocolate; **warme ~** cocoa

christelijk (*krıss*-ter-lerk) *adj*
Christian

christen (*kriss*-tern) *m* (f christin, pl ~en) Christian

Christus (*kriss*-terss) Christ

chronisch (*khrōa*-neess) *adj* chronic

chronologisch (khrōa-nōa-*lōa*-geess) *adj* chronological

chroom (khrōam) *nt* chromium

cijfer (*say*-ferr) *nt* (pl ~s) number, figure; digit; mark

cilinder (see-*lin*-derr) *c* (pl ~s) cylinder

cilinderkop (see-*lin*-derr-kop) *c* (pl ~pen) cylinder head

circa (*sir*-kaa) *adv* approximately

circulatie (sir-kew-*laa*-tsee) *c* circulation

circus (*sir*-kerss) *nt* (pl ~sen) circus

cirkel (*sir*-kerl) *c* (pl ~s) circle

citaat (see-*taat*) *nt* (pl citaten) quotation

citeren (see-*tāy*-rern) *v* quote

citroen (see-*trōon*) *c* (pl ~en) lemon

civiel (see-*veel*) *adj* civil

clausule (klou-*sēw*-ler) *c* (pl ~s) clause

claxon (*klahk*-son) *c* (pl ~s) horn, hooter

claxonneren (klahk-so-*nāy*-rern) *v* hoot; toot *vAm*, honk *vAm*

clementie (klāy-*mehn*-tsee) *c* mercy

cliënt (klee-*ʸehnt*) *m* (f ~e, pl ~en) customer, client

closetpapier (klōa-*zeht*-pah-peer) *nt* toilet paper

club (klerp) *c* (pl ~s) club, society

cocaïne (kōa-kaa-*ee*-ner) *c* cocaine

cocktail (kok-*tāyl*) *c* (pl ~s) cocktail *c*

code (*kōa*-der) *c* (pl ~s) code

coffeïne (ko-fāy-*ee*-ner) *c* caffeine

coffeïnevrij (ko-fāy-*ee*-ner-vray) *adj* decaffeinated

cognac (ko-*ñahk*) *c* cognac

coiffure (kvah-*fēw*-rer) *c* (pl ~s) hairdo

colbert (kol-*bair*) *c* (pl ~s) jacket

collaboreren (ko-laa-bōa-*rāy*-rern) *v* collaborate, cooperate

collectant (ko-lehk-*tahnt*) *m* (f ~e, pl ~en) collector

collecteren (ko-lehk-*tāy*-rern) *v* collect

collectie (ko-*lehk*-see) *c* (pl ~s) collection

collectief (ko-lehk-*teef*) *adj* collective

collega (ko-*lāy*-gaa) *c* (pl ~'s) colleague

college (ko-*lāy*-zher) *nt* (pl ~s) lecture

Colombiaans (kōa-lom-bee-*ʸaans*) *adj* Colombian

coma (*kōa*-maa) *nt* coma

combinatie (kom-bee-*naa*-tsee) *c* (pl ~s) combination

combineren (kom-bee-*nāy*-rern) *v* combine

comfortabel (kom-for-*taa*-berl) *adj* comfortable

comité (ko-mee-*tāy*) *nt* (pl ~s) committee

commentaar (ko-mehn-*taar*) *nt* (pl -taren) comment

commercieel (ko-mehr-*shāyl*) *adj* commercial

commissie (ko-*mi*-see) *c* (pl ~s) committee; commission

commode (ko-*mōa*-der) *c* (pl ~s) chest of drawers; bureau *nAm*

commune (ko-*mēw*-ner) *c* (pl ~s) commune

communicatie (ko-mēw-nee-*kaa*-tsee) *c* communication

communiqué (ko-mēw-nee-*kāy*) *nt* (pl ~s) communiqué

communisme (ko-mēw-*niss*-mer) *nt* communism

compact (kom-*pahkt*) *adj* compact

compact disk (*kom*-pahkt disk) *c* compact disc; ~ **speler** CD-player

compagnon (kom-pah-*ñon*) *c* (pl ~s) partner

compensatie (kom-pehn-z*aa*-tsee) *c* (pl ~s) compensation

compenseren (kom-pehn-*zay*-rern) *v* compensate

compleet (kom-*playt*) *adj* complete

compliment (kom-plee-*mehnt*) *nt* (pl ~en) compliment

componist (kom-poā-*nıst*) *m* (f ~e, pl ~en) composer

compositie (kom-poā-*zee*-tsee) *c* (pl ~s) composition

compromis (kom-proā-*mee*) *nt* (pl ~sen) compromise

computer (kom-*pyoo*-terr) *nt* computer

computerspel (kom-*pyoo*-terr-spehl) *nt* video game

concentratie (kon-sehn-*traa*-tsee) *c* (pl ~s) concentration

concentreren (kon-sehn-*tray*-rern) *v* concentrate

conceptie (kon-*sehp*-see) *c* conception

concert (kon-*sehrt*) *nt* (pl ~en) concert

concertzaal (kon-*sehrt*-saal) *c* (pl -zalen) concert hall

concessie (kon-*seh*-see) *c* (pl ~s) concession

conciërge (kon-*shehr*-zheh) *c* (pl ~s) janitor; caretaker, concierge

conclusie (kong-*klew*-zee) *c* (pl ~s) conclusion

concreet (kong-*krayt*) *adj* concrete

concurrent (kong-kew-*rehnt*) *m* (f ~e, pl ~en) competitor; rival

concurrentie (kong-kew-*rehn*-tsee) *c* competition; rivalry

conditie (kon-*dee*-tsee) *c* (pl ~s) condition

conditioner (kon-*dish*-er-nerr) *nt* conditioner

condoom (kon-*doom*) *nt* condom

conducteur (kon-derk-*turr*) *m* (f -trice, pl ~s) ticket collector

confectie- (kon-*fehk*-see) *adj* ready-made

conferencier (kon-fer-rahng-*shay*) *c* (pl ~s) entertainer

conferentie (kon-fer-*rehn*-see) *c* (pl ~s) conference

conflict (kon-*flıkt*) *nt* (pl ~en) conflict

congregatie (kong-grāy-*gaa*-tsee) *c* (pl ~s) congregation

congres (kong-*grehss*) *nt* (pl ~sen) congress

consequentie (kon-ser-*kvehn*-see) *c* (pl ~s) consequence

conservatief (kon-zerr-vaa-*teef*) *adj* conservative

conservatorium (kon-zerr-vaa-*toā*-ree-^yerm) *nt* (pl ~s) music academy

conserven (kon-*sehr*-vern) *pl* tinned food

consideratie (kon-see-der-*raa*-tsee) *c* consideration

constant (kon-*stahnt*) *adj* even

constateren (koan-staa-*tay*-rern) *v* note, ascertain; diagnose

constipatie (kon-stee-*paa*-tsee) *c* constipation

constructie (kon-*strerk*-see) *c* (pl ~s) construction

construeren (kon-strĕw^{oo}-*ay*-rern) *v* construct

consulaat (kon-zēw-*laat*) *nt* (pl -laten) consulate

consult (kon-*zerlt*) *nt* (pl ~en) consultation

consultatiebureau (kon-zerl-*taa*-tsee-bēw-roā) *nt* (pl ~s) health center *Am*, health centre

consument (kon-zew-*mehnt*) *m* (f ~e, pl ~en) consumer

consumeren (kon-zew-*mehren*) *v* consume

contact (kon-*tahkt*) *nt* (pl ~en) contact; touch

contactlenzen (kon-*tahkt*-lehn-zern) *pl* contact lenses

container (kon-*tay*-nerr) *c* (pl ~s)

dustbin, container

contanten (kon-*tahn*-tern) *pl* cash

continent (kon-tee-*nehnt*) *nt* (pl ~en) continent

continentaal (kon-tee-nehn-*taal*) *adj* continental

contra (*kon*-traa) *prep* versus

contract (kon-*trahkt*) *nt* (pl ~en) agreement, contract

contrast (kon-*trahst*) *nt* (pl ~en) contrast

controle (kon-*traw*-ler) *c* (pl ~s) control; supervision, inspection

controleren (kon-tröa-*lay*-rern) *v* control, check

controlestrook (kon-*traw*-ler-strōak) *c* (-stroken) counterfoil, stub

controversieel (kon-tröa-vehr-*zhäyl*) *adj* controversial

conversatie (kon-verr-*zaa*-tsee) *c* (pl ~s) conversation

coöperatie (köa-ōa-per-*raa*-tsee) *c* (pl ~s) co-operative

coöperatief (köa-ōa-per-raa-*teef*) *adj* co-operative

coördinatie (köa-or-dee-*naa*-tsee) *c* coordination

coördineren (köa-or-dee-*näy*-rern) *v* coordinate

corpulent (kor-pēw-*lehnt*) *adj* corpulent, stout, fat

correct (ko-*rehkt*) *adj* correct

correctie (ko-*rehk*-see) *c* (pl ~s) correction

correspondent (ko-rehss-pon-*dehnt*) *m* (f ~e, pl ~en) correspondent

correspondentie (ko-rehss-pon-*dehn*-see) *c* correspondence

corresponderen (ko-rehss-pon-*däy*-rern) *v* correspond

corrigeren (ko-ree-*zhäy*-rern) *v* correct

corrupt (ko-*rerpt*) *adj* corrupt

coupé (kōō-*pay*) *c* (pl ~s) compartment

couplet (kōō-*pleht*) *nt* (pl ~ten) stanza, verse

coupon (kōō-*pon*) *c* (pl ~s) coupon

creatief (kräy-aa-*teef*) *adj* creative

crèche (krehsh) *c* (pl ~s) nursery

crediteren (kräy-dee-*täy*-rern) *v* credit

creëren (kräy-*äy*-rern) *v* create

crème (kraim) *c* (pl ~s) cream; **vochtinbrengende ~** moisturizing cream

criminaliteit (kree-mee-naa-lee-*tayt*) *c* criminality

crimineel (kree-mee-*näyl*) *adj* criminal

crisis (*kree*-serss) *c* (pl -ses) crisis

criticus (*kree*-tee-kerss) *m* (pl -ci) critic

Cuba (*kēw*-baa) Cuba; **Cubaan** (kēw-*baan*) *m* (f ~se, pl -banen) Cuban; **Cubaans** (kēw-*baans*) *adj* Cuban

cultuur (kerl-*tēwr*) *c* (pl -turen) culture

cursus (*kerr*-zerss) *c* (pl ~sen) course

cyclus (*see*-klerss) *c* (pl ~sen) cycle

cynisch (*see*-neess) *adj* cynical

D

daad (daat) *c* (pl daden) deed, act

daar (daar) *adv* there

daarheen (*daar*-häyn) *adv* there

daarom (*daa*-rom) *conj* therefore

dadel (*daa*-derl) *c* (pl ~s) date

dadelijk (*daa*-der-lerk) *adv* at once, immediately; presently

dag (dahkh) *c* (pl ~en) day; **per ~** per

day; **dag!** hello!; goodbye!

dagblad (*dahkh*-blaht) *nt* (pl ~en) daily

dagboek (*dahkh*-book) *nt* (pl ~en) diary

dagelijks (*daa*-ger-lerks) *adj* daily

dageraad (*daa*-ger-raat) *c* daybreak, dawn

daglicht (*dahkh*-lıkht) *nt* daylight

dak (dahk) *nt* (pl ~en) roof

dakpan (*dahk*-pahn) *c* (pl ~nen) tile

dal (dahl) *nt* (pl ~en) valley

dalen (*daa*-lern) *v* descend

dam (dahm) *c* (pl ~men) dam; dike

dame (*daa*-mer) *f* (pl ~s) lady

damestoilet (*daa*-merss-tvah-leht) *nt* (pl ~ten) powder room, ladies' room

damp (dahmp) *c* (pl ~en) vapo(u)r

damspel (*dahm*-spehl) *nt* draughts; checkers *plAm*

dan (dahn) *adv* then; *conj* than; **nu en ~** occasionally

dankbaar (*dahngk*-baar) *adj* grateful, thankful

dankbaarheid (*dahngk*-baar-hayt) *c* gratitude

danken (*dahng*-kern) *v* thank; **dank u** thank you; **te ~ *hebben aan** owe

dans (dahns) *c* (pl ~en) dance

dansen (*dahn*-sern) *v* dance

danszaal (*dahn*-saal) *c* (pl -zalen) ballroom

dapper (*dah*-perr) *adj* brave, courageous

dapperheid (*dah*-perr-hayt) *c* courage

darm (dahrm) *c* (pl ~en) gut, intestine; **darmen** bowels *pl*

das (dahss) *c* (pl ~sen) necktie, tie; scarf

dashboard (*dehsh*-bort) *c* (pl ~s) dashboard

dat (daht) *pron* which; *conj* that

dateren (daa-*tay*-rern) *v* date

datum (*daa*-term) *c* (pl data) date

dauw (dou) *c* dew

de (der) *art* the *art*

debat (der-*baht*) *nt* (pl ~ten) discussion, debate

debatteren (day-bah-*tay*-rern) *v* argue

debet (*day*-beht) *nt* debit

december (day-*sehm*-berr) December

deeg (daykh) *nt* dough

deel (dayl) *nt* (pl delen) part; share; volume

*deelnemen (*dayl*-nay-mern) *v* participate

deelnemer (*dayl*-nay-merr) *m* (f -ster, pl ~s) participant

deels (dayls) *adv* partly

Deen (dayn) *m* (f ~se, pl Denen) Dane

Deens (dayns) *adj* Danish

defect[1] (der-*fehkt*) *adj* defective, faulty

defect[2] (der-*fehkt*) *nt* (pl ~en) fault

defensie (day-*fehn*-zee) *c* defense *Am*, defence

definiëren (day-fi-ni-*ay*-rern) *v* define

definitie (day-fee-*nee*-tsee) *c* (pl ~s) definition

degelijk (*day*-ger-lerk) *adj* thorough; sound

dek (dehk) *nt* deck

deken (*day*-kern) *c* (pl ~s) blanket

dekhut (*dehk*-hert) *c* (pl ~ten) deck cabin

deksel (*dehk*-serl) *nt* (pl ~s) lid; cover, top

delegatie (day-ler-*gaa*-tsee) *c* (pl ~s) delegation

delen (*day*-lern) *v* divide; share

delfstof (*dehlf*-stof) *c* (pl ~fen) mineral

delicatessen (day-lee-kaa-*teh*-sern) *pl* delicatessen

delicatessenwinkel (day-lee-kaa-*teh*-ser-vıng-kerl) *c* (pl ~s) delicatessen

delikaat (day-lee-*kaat*) *adj* delicate

deling (*day*-lıng) *c* (pl ~en) division

delinquent (day-lıng-*kvehnt*) *m* (pl ~en) criminal

*delven (*dehl*-vern) *v* *dig

democratie (day-*mōa*-kraa-*tsee*) *c* (pl

~ën) democracy

democratisch (dāy-mōa-*kraa*-teess) *adj* democratic

demonstratie (dāy-mon-*straa*-tsee) *c* (pl ~s) demonstration

demonstreren (dāy-mon-*strāy*-rern) *v* demonstrate

den (dehn) *c* (pl ~nen) fir tree

Denemarken (*dāy*-ner-mahr-kern) Denmark

denkbeeld (*dehngk*-bāyld) *nt* (pl ~en) idea

denkbeeldig (dehngk-*bāyl*-derkh) *adj* imaginary

***denken** (*dehng*-kern) *v* *think; guess, reckon; ~ **aan** *think of

denker (*dehng*-kerr) *m* (pl ~s) thinker

dennenboom (*deh*-ner-bōam) *c* (pl -bomen) fir tree

deodorant (dāy-ᵞōa-dōa-*rahnt*) *c* deodorant

departement (dāy-pahr-ter-*mehnt*) *nt* (pl ~en) department

deponeren (dāy-pōa-*nāy*-rern) *v* bank; deposit

depressie (dāy-*preh*-see) *c* (pl ~s) depression

deprimeren (dāy-pree-*māy*-rern) *v* depress

derde (*dehr*-der) *num* third

dergelijk (*dehr*-ger-lerk) *adj* such; similar

dermate (*dehr*-maa-ter) *adv* so

dertien (*dehr*-teen) *num* thirteen

dertiende (*dehr*-teen-der) *num* thirteenth

dertig (*dehr*-terkh) *num* thirty

dertigste (*dehr*-terkh-ster) *num* thirtieth

deserteren (dāy-zehr-*tāy*-rern) *v* desert

deskundig (dehss-*kern*-derkh) *adj* expert

deskundige (dehss-*kern*-der-ger) *c* (pl

~n) expert

dessert (deh-*sair*) *nt* (pl ~s) dessert

detail (dāy-*tigh*) *nt* (pl ~s) detail

detailhandel (dāy-*tigh*-hahn-derl) *c* retail trade

detaillist (dāy-tah-ᵞ*ɪst*) *c* (pl ~en) retailer

detective (dāy-*tehk*-tɪf) *m* (pl ~s) detective

detectiveroman (dāy-*tehk*-tɪf-rōa-mahn) *c* (pl ~s) detective story

deugd (dūrkht) *c* (pl ~en) virtue

deugniet (*dūrkh*-neet) *m* (pl ~en) rascal

deuk (dūrk) *c* (pl ~en) dent

deur (dūrr) *c* (pl ~en) door

deurbel (*dūrr*-behl) *c* (pl ~len) doorbell

deurwaarder (*dūrr*-vaar-derr) *c* (pl ~s) bailiff

devaluatie (dāy-vaa-lēw-*vaa*-tsee) *c* (pl ~s) devaluation

devalueren (dāy-vaa-lēw-*vāy*-rern) *v* devalue

devies (der-*veess*) *nt* (pl deviezen) motto

deze (*dāy*-zer) *pron* this; these

dia (*dee*-ᵞaa) *c* (pl ~'s) slide

diabetes (dee-ᵞaa-*bāy*-terss) *c* diabetes

diabeticus (dee-ᵞaa-*bāy*-tee-kerss) *m* (f -ca, pl -ci) diabetic

diagnose (dee-ᵞahkh-*nōā*-zer) *c* (pl ~n, ~s) diagnosis; **een ~ stellen** diagnose

diagonaal[1] (dee-'aa-gōā-*naal*) *adj* diagonal

diagonaal[2] (dee-'aa-gōā-*naal*) *c* (pl -nalen) diagonal

diagram (dee-ᵞaa-*grahm*) *nt* (pl ~men) diagram

dialect (dee-ᵞaa-*lehkt*) *nt* (pl ~en) dialect

diamant (dee-ᵞaa-*mahnt*) *c* (pl ~en) diamond

diarree (dee-*Y*ah-*rāy*) c diarrh(o)ea

dicht (dıkht) adj dense; thick; closed, shut

dichtbevolkt (dıkht-ber-*volkt*) adj populous

dichtbij (dıkht-*bay*) adj near

dichtdraaien (*dıkh*-draa^{ee}-ern) v turn off

dichter (*dıkh*-terr) m (f ~es, pl ~s) poet

dichtkunst (*dıkht*-kernst) c poetry

***dichtslaan** (*dıkht*-slaan) v slam

dictaat (dık-*taat*) nt (pl-taten) dictation

dictafoon (dık-taa-*fōan*) c (pl ~s) dictaphone

dictator (dık-taa-tor) c (pl ~s) dictator

dictee (dık-*tāy*) nt (pl ~s) dictation

dicteren (dık-*tāy*-rern) v dictate

die (dee) pron that; those; who

dieet (dee-*Yāyt*) nt diet

dief (deef) m (f dievegge, pl dieven) robber, thief

diefstal (*deef*-stahl) c (pl~len) robbery, theft

dienblad (*deen*-blaht) nt (pl ~en) tray

dienen (*dee*-nern) v serve

dienst (deenst) c (pl ~en) service; **in ~ *nemen** engage

dienstmeid (*deenst*-mayt) f (pl ~en) housemaid

dienstplichtige (deenst-*plıkh*-ter-ger) c (pl ~n) conscript

dienstregeling (*deenst*-rāy-ger-lıng) c (pl ~en) schedule, timetable

diep (deep) adj deep; low

diepte (*deep*-ter) c (pl ~n, ~s) depth

diepvrieskast (*deep*-freess-kahst) c (pl ~en) deep-freeze, freezer

diepzinnig (deep-sı-nerkh) adj profound

dier (deer) nt (pl ~en) animal

dierbaar (*deer*-baar) adj dear; precious

dierenarts (*dee*-rern-ahrts) c (pl ~en) veterinary surgeon

dierenriem (*dee*-rer-reem) c zodiac

dierentuin (dee-rer-tur^{ew}n) c (pl ~en) zoological gardens; zoo

diesel (*dee*-serl) c diesel

difterie (dıf-ter-*ree*) c diphtheria

digitaal (die-gie-*taal*) adj digital

dij (day) c (pl ~en) thigh

dijk (dayk) c (pl ~en) dike; dam

dik (dık) adj corpulent; thick; fat, stout, big

dikte (*dık*-ter) c (pl ~n, ~s) thickness; fatness

dikwijls (*dık*-verls) adv frequently, often

dineren (dee-*nāy*-rern) v dine

ding (dıng) nt (pl ~en) thing

dinsdag (*dıns*-dahkh) c Tuesday

diploma (dee-*plōa*-maa) nt (pl ~'s) certificate, diploma; **een ~ behalen** graduate

diplomaat (dee-plōa-*maat*) c (pl -maten) diplomat

direct (dee-*rehkt*) adj direct; adv straight away

directeur (dee-rerk-*tūrr*) m (f -trice, pl ~en, ~s) executive, manager, director; headmaster, principal

directie (dee-*rehk*-see) c (pl ~s) management

dirigent (dee-ree-*gehnt*) c (pl ~en) conductor

dirigeren (dee-ree-*gāy*-rern) v conduct

discipline (dee-see-*plee*-ner) c (pl ~s) discipline

disconto (dıss-*kon*-tōa) nt (pl ~'s) bank rate

discreet (dıss-*krāyt*) adj modest

discussie (dıss-*ker*-see) c (pl ~s) discussion, argument

discussiëren (dıss-ker-*shāy*-rern) v discuss; argue

distel (*dıss*-terl) c (pl ~s) thistle

district (dıss-*trıkt*) nt (pl ~en) district

dit (dıt) pron this

divan (*dee*-vahn) *c* (pl ~s) couch

docent (dōa-*sehnt*) *m* (f ~e, pl ~en) teacher

doch (dokh) *conj* but

dochter (*dokh*-terr) *f* (pl ~s) daughter

doctor (*dok*-tor) *c* (pl ~en, ~s) doctor

document (dōa-kēw-*mehnt*) *nt* (pl ~en) document

dodelijk (*dōa*-der-lerk) *adj* mortal, fatal

doden (*dōa*-dern) *v* kill

doei (dōōy) *colloquial* bye-bye

doek (dōōk) *c* (pl ~en) cloth; *nt* curtain

doel (dōōl) *nt* (pl ~en) objective, aim, purpose; object, goal, design, target

doelman (*dōōl*-mahn) *m* (pl ~nen) goalkeeper

doelmatig (dōōl-*maa*-terkh) *adj* efficient

doelpunt (*dōōl*-pernt) *nt* (pl ~en) goal

doeltreffend (dōōl-*treh*-fernt) *adj* effective

***doen** (dōōn) *v* *do; cause to

dof (dof) *adj* mat, dim

dok (dok) *nt* (pl ~ken) dock

dokter (*dok*-terr) *c* (pl ~s) doctor, physician

dollar (*do*-lahr) *c* (pl ~s) dollar, *colloquial* buck

dom¹ (dom) *adj* dumb, stupid

dom² (dom) *c* cathedral

dominee (dōa-mee-*nāy*) *m* (pl ~s) clergyman, parson, rector

dompelaar (*dom*-per-laar) *c* (pl ~s) immersion heater

donateur (dōa-naa-*tūrr*) *m* (pl ~s) donor

donder (*don*-derr) *c* thunder

donderdag (*don*-derr-dahkh) *c* Thursday

donderen (*don*-der-rern) *v* thunder

donker (*dong*-kerr) *adj* dark, dim

donor (*dōa*-nor) *m* (pl ~s) donor

dons (dons) *nt* down; **donzen dekbed** eiderdown

dood (dōat) *adj* dead; *c* death

doodstraf (*dōat*-strahf) *c* death penalty

doof (dōaf) *adj* deaf

dooi (dōaⁱ) *c* thaw

dooien (*dōaⁱ*-ern) *v* thaw

dooier (*dōaⁱ*-err) *c* (pl ~s) yolk

doolhof (*dōal*-hof) *nt* (pl -hoven) maze; labyrinth

doop (dōap) *c* baptism, christening

doopsel (*dōap*-serl) *nt* baptism

door (dōar) *prep* through; by

doorboren (dōar-*bōa*-rern) *v* pierce

***doorbrengen** (*dōar*-breh-ngern) *v* *spend

doordat (dōar-*daht*) *conj* because

***doordringen** (*dōar*-drı-ngern) *v* penetrate

***doorgaan** (*dōar*-gaan) *v* continue, *go on; carry on; *go ahead; ~ **met** *keep on

doorgang (*dōar*-gahng) *c* (pl ~en) passage

doorlichten (*dōar*-lıkh-tern) *v* X-ray

doorlopend (dōar-*lōa*-pernt) *adj* continuous

doormaken (*dōar*-maa-kern) *v* *go through

doorn (dōarn) *c* (pl ~en, ~s) thorn

doorreis (*dōar*-rayss) *c* passage

doorslag (*dōar*-slahkh) *c* (pl ~en) carbon copy

doorsturen (*dōar*-stēw-rern) *v* forward

doorweken (dōar-*vāy*-kern) *v* soak

doorzichtig (dōar-*zıkh*-terkh) *adj* transparent, sheer

***doorzoeken** (dōar-*zōō*-kern) *v* search

doos (dōass) *c* (pl dozen) box

dop (dop) *c* (pl ~pen) shell

dopen (*dōa*-pern) *v* baptize, christen

dorp (dorp) *nt* (pl ~en) village

dorst (dorst) *c* thirst

dorstig (*dors*-terkh) *adj* thirsty

dosis (*dōa*-zerss) *c* (pl doses) dose

dossier (do-*shay*) *nt* (pl ~s) file

douane (dōō-*vaa*-ner) *c* Customs *pl*

douanebeambte (dōō-*vaa*-ner-ber-ahm-ter) *c* (pl ~n) Customs officer

douche (dōōsh) *c* (pl ~s) shower

doven (*dōa*-vern) *v* extinguish

dozijn (dōa-*zayn*) *nt* (pl ~en) dozen

draad (draat) *c* (pl draden) thread; wire; **draadloos** wireless

draagbaar (*draakh*-baar) *adj* portable

draaglijk (*draakh*-lerk) *adj* tolerable

draai (draa^ee) *c* (pl ~en) turn; twist

draaideur (*draa^ee*-dūrr) *c* (pl ~en) revolving door

draaien (*draa^ee*-ern) *v* turn; twist; *spin

draaimolen (*draa^ee*-mōa-lern) *c* (pl ~s) merry-go-round

draak (draak) *c* (pl draken) dragon

*****dragen** (*draa*-gern) *v* carry, *bear; *wear

drager (*draa*-gerr) *m* (f draagster, pl ~s) bearer

drama (*draa*-maa) *nt* (pl ~'s) drama

dramatisch (draa-*maa*-teess) *adj* dramatic

drang (drahng) *c* urge

drank (drahngk) *c* (pl ~en) drink, beverage; **sterke ~** spirits, liquor

dreigement (dray-ger-*mernt*) *nt* (pl ~en) threat

dreigen (*dray*-gern) *v* threaten

drek (drehk) *c* muck

drempel (*drehm*-perl) *c* (pl ~s) threshold

dresseren (dreh-*say*-rern) *v* train

dreun (drūrn) *c* smash

dreunen (*drūr*-nern) *v* smash

drie (dree) *num* three

driehoek (*dree*-hōōk) *c* (pl ~en) triangle

driehoekig (dree-*hōō*-kerkh) *adj* triangular

driekwart (*dree*-kvahrt) *adj*

threequarter

driemaandelijks (*dree*-maan-der-lerks) *adj* quarterly

drift (drıft) *c* passion

driftig (*drıf*-terkh) *adj* quick-tempered; hot-tempered

drijfkracht (*drayf*-krahkht) *c* driving force

*****drijven** (*dray*-vern) *v* float

*****dringen** (*drı*-ngern) *v* push; **dringend** pressing, urgent

drinkbaar (*drıngk*-baar) *adj* for drinking

*****drinken** (*drıng*-kern) *v* *drink

drinkwater (*drıngk*-vaa-terr) *nt* drinking water

droefheid (*drōōf*-hayt) *c* sorrow

droevig (*drōō*-verkh) *adj* sad

drogen (*drōa*-gern) *v* dry

drogisterij (drōa-gıss-ter-*ray*) *c* (pl ~en) pharmacy, chemist's; drugstore *nAm*

dromen (*drōa*-mern) *v* *dream

dronken (*drong*-kern) *adj* drunk; intoxicated

droog (drōakh) *adj* dry

droogleggen (*drōakh*-leh-gern) *v* drain

droogte (*drōakh*-ter) *c* drought

droom (drōam) *c* (pl dromen) dream

droombeeld (*drōam*-baylt) *nt* (pl ~en) illusion

drop (drop) *c* liquorice

druif (drur^ew f) *c* (pl ~ven) grape

druk (drerk) *adj* busy; crowded; *c* pressure

drukken (*drer*-kern) *v* press; print

drukknop (*drer*-knop) *c* (pl ~pen) push button

drukte (*drerk*-ter) *c* bustle; fuss; excitement

drukwerk (*drerk*-vehrk) *nt* printed matter

druppel (*drer*-perl) *c* (pl ~s) drop

dubbel (*der*-berl) *adj* double

dubbelzinnig (der-berl-*zɪ*-nerkh) *adj* ambiguous

duidelijk (*dur*ᵉʷ-der-lerk) *adj* distinct, plain, clear; apparent, evident; obvious

duif (durᵉʷf) *c* (pl duiven) pigeon

duikboot (*dur*ᵉʷk-bōāt) *c* (pl -boten) submarine

duikbril (*dur*ᵉʷk-brɪl) *c* (pl ⁓len) goggles *pl*

*****duiken** (*dur*ᵉʷ-kern) *v* dive

duim (durᵉʷm) *c* (pl ⁓en) thumb; inch (2.54 cm)

duin (durᵉʷn) *nt* (pl ⁓en) dune

duister (*dur*ᵉʷ-sterr) *adj* obscure, dark; *nt* gloom

duisternis (*dur*ᵉʷ-sterr-nɪss) *c* dark

Duits (durᵉʷts) *adj* German

Duitser (*dur*ᵉʷt-serr) *m* (f Duitse, pl ⁓s) German

Duitsland (*dur*ᵉʷts-lahnt) Germany

duivel (*dur*ᵉʷ-verl) *m* (pl ⁓s) devil

duizelig (*dur*ᵉʷ-zer-lerkh) *adj* giddy, dizzy

duizeligheid (*dur*ᵉʷ-zer-lerkh-hayt) *c* giddiness, dizziness

duizend (*dur*ᵉʷ-zernt) *num* thousand

dulden (*derl*-dern) *v* *bear

dun (dern) *adj* thin; sheer

dupe (*dēw*-per) *c* (pl ⁓s) victim

duren (*dēw*-rern) *v* last

durf (derrf) *c* nerve

durven (*derr*-vern) *v* dare

dus (derss) *conj* so

dutje (*der*-tʸer) *nt* (pl ⁓s) nap

duur (dēwr) *adj* dear, expensive; *c* duration

duurzaam (*dēwr*-zaam) *adj* lasting, permanent

duw (dēwᵒᵒ) *c* (pl ⁓en) push

duwen (*dēw*ᵒᵒ-ern) *v* push

dwaas¹ (dvaass) *adj* foolish, crazy, silly

dwaas² (dvaass) *c* (pl dwazen) fool

dwalen (*dvaa*-lern) *v* err

dwarsbomen (dvahrs-*bōā*-mern) *v* spite

dwerg (dvehrkh) *m* (pl ⁓en) dwarf, midget; leprechaun

*****dwingen** (*dvɪ*-ngern) *v* force; compel

dynamo (dee-*naa*-mōā) *c* (pl ⁓'s) dynamo

E

eb (ehp) *c* low tide

ebbehout (*eh*-ber-hout) *nt* ebony

echo (*eh*-khōā) *c* (pl ⁓'s) echo

echt (ehkht) *adj* genuine, true, authentic, real; *adv* really; *c* matrimony

echter (*ehkh*-terr) *conj* however, yet

echtgenoot (*ehkht*-kher-nōāt) *m* (pl -noten) husband

echtgenote (*ehkht*-kher-nōā-ter) *f* (pl ⁓n) wife

echtpaar (*ehkht*-paar) *nt* (pl -paren) married couple

echtscheiding (*ehkht*-skhay-dɪng) *c* (pl ⁓en) divorce

economie (*āy*-kōā-nōā-*mee*) *c* economy

economisch (*āy*-kōā-*nōā*-meess) *adj* economic

econoom (*āy*-kōā-*nōām*) *m* (pl -nomen) economist

eczeem (ehk-*sāym*) *nt* eczema

edel (*āy*-derl) *adj* noble

edelmoedigheid (*āy*-derl-*mōō*-derkh-hayt) c generosity

edelsteen (a̅y̅-derl-sta̅yn) c (pl -stenen) gem, stone

editie (a̅y̅-*dee*-tsee) c (pl ~s) edition

eed (a̅y̅t) c (pl eden) oath, vow

eekhoorn (a̅y̅k-ho̅a̅rn) c (pl ~s) squirrel

een¹ (ern) art a art

een² (a̅y̅n) num one

eenakter (a̅y̅n-ahk-terr) c (pl ~s) oneact play

eend (a̅y̅nt) c (pl ~en) duck

eender (a̅y̅n-derr) adj alike

eenheid (a̅y̅n-hayt) c (pl -heden) unit; unity

eenmaal (a̅y̅n-maal) adv once

eenmalig (a̅y̅n-maa-lerkh) adv for once

eenrichtingsverkeer (a̅y̅n-*rɪkh*-tɪngs-ferr-ka̅y̅r) nt one-way traffic

eens (a̅y̅ns) adv once; some time, some day; **het ~ *zijn** agree

eentonig (a̅y̅n-to̅a̅-nerkh) adj monotonous

eenvoudig (a̅y̅n-*vou*-derkh) adj plain, simple; adv simply

eenzaam (a̅y̅n-zaam) adj lonely

eenzijdig (a̅y̅n-*zay*-derkh) adj one-sided

eer (a̅y̅r) c honour; glory

eerbied (a̅y̅r-beet) c respect

eerbiedig (a̅y̅r-*bee*-derkh) adj respectful

eerbiedwaardig (a̅y̅r-beet-*vaar*-derkh) adj venerable

eerder (a̅y̅r-derr) adv before; rather

eergevoel (a̅y̅r-ger-vo̅o̅l) nt sense of honour

eergisteren (a̅y̅r-gɪss-ter-rern) adv the day before yesterday

eerlijk (a̅y̅r-lerk) adj honest; fair; straight; sincere

eerlijkheid (a̅y̅r-lerk-hayt) c honesty

eerst (a̅y̅rst) adj first; primary; initial; adv at first

eersteklas (a̅y̅r-ster-klahss) adj first-class

eersterangs (a̅y̅r-ster-rahngs) adj first-rate

eerstvolgend (a̅y̅rst-*fol*-gernt) adj following

eervol (a̅y̅r-vol) adj honourable

eerzaam (a̅y̅r-zaam) adj respectable; honourable

eetbaar (a̅y̅t-baar) adj edible

eetkamer (a̅y̅t-kaa-merr) c (pl ~s) dining room

eetlepel (a̅y̅t-la̅y̅-perl) c (pl ~s) tablespoon

eetlust (a̅y̅t-lerst) c appetite

eetservies (a̅y̅t-sehr-veess) nt (pl -viezen) dinner service

eetzaal (a̅y̅t-saal) c (pl -zalen) dining room

eeuw (a̅y̅°°) c (pl ~en) century

eeuwig (a̅y̅°°-erkh) adj eternal; adv eeuwig, voor goed; altijd

eeuwigheid (a̅y̅°°-erkh-hayt) c eternity

effect (eh-*fehkt*) nt (pl ~en) effect; **effecten** stocks and shares

effectenbeurs (eh-*fehk*-term-bŭrrs) c (pl -beurzen) stock market, stock exchange

effectief (eh-fehk-*teef*) adj effective

effen (eh-fern) adj level; smooth, even

efficiënt (eh-fee-*shehnt*) adj efficient

egaal (a̅y̅-*gaal*) adj level

egaliseren (a̅y̅-gaa-lee-*za̅y̅*-rern) v level

egel (a̅y̅-gerl) c (pl ~s) hedgehog

egocentrisch (a̅y̅-go̅a̅-*sehn*-treess) adj self-centered Am, self-centred

egoïsme (a̅y̅-go̅a̅-*vɪss*-mer) nt selfishness

egoïstisch (a̅y̅-go̅a̅-*vɪss*-teess) adj selfish, ego(t)istic

Egypte (a̅y̅-*gɪp*-ter) Egypt

Egyptenaar (a̅y̅-*gɪp*-ter-naar) m (f

-nares, pl -naren) Egyptian

Egyptisch (ay-*gıp*-teess) *adj* Egyptian

ei (ay) *nt* (pl ~eren) egg

eierdooier (ay-err-dōa^{ee}-err) *c* (pl ~s) egg yolk

eierdopje (ay-err-dop-^yer) *nt* (pl ~s) eggcup

eigen (ay-gern) *adj* own

eigenaar (ay-ger-naar) *m* (f -nares, -pl ~s, -naren) owner, proprietor

eigenaardig (ay-ger-*naar*-derkh) *adj* singular, peculiar

eigenaardigheid (ay-ger-*naar*-derkh-hayt) *c* (pl -heden) peculiarity

eigendom (ay-gern-dom) *nt* (pl ~men) property; possessions

eigengemaakt (ay-gern-ger-maakt) *adj* home-made

eigenlijk (ay-gern-lerk) *adj* actual; *adv* as a matter of fact, really

eigenschap (ay-gern-skhahp) *c* (pl ~pen) property, quality

eigentijds (ay-gern-*tayts*) *adj* contemporary

eigenwijs (ay-gern-*vayss*) *adj* pig-headed, stubborn

eik (ayk) *c* (pl ~en) oak

eikel (ay-kerl) *c* (pl ~s) acorn

eiland (ay-lahnt) *nt* (pl ~en) island

einde (ayn-der) *nt* end, finish; ending, issue

eindelijk (ayn-der-lerk) *adv* at last

eindigen (ayn-der-gern) *v* finish

eindpunt (aynt-pernt) *nt* (pl ~en) terminal

eindstreep (aynt-strāyp) *c* (pl -strepen) finish

eis (ayss) *c* (pl ~en) demand, claim

eisen (ay-sern) *v* demand

eiwit (ay-vıt) *nt* (pl ~ten) protein

ekster (ehk-sterr) *c* (pl ~s) magpie

eksteroog (ehk-sterr-ōakh) *nt* (pl -ogen) corn

eland (āy-lahnt) *c* (pl ~en) moose

elastiek (āy-lahss-*teek*) *nt* (pl ~en) rubber band, elastic

elastisch (āy-*lahss*-teess) *adj* elastic

elders (ehl-derrs) *adv* elsewhere

elegant (āy-ler-*gahnt*) *adj* elegant

elegantie (āy-ler-*gahnt*-see) *c* elegance

elektricien (āy-lehk-tree-*shahng*) *m* (pl ~s) electrician

elektriciteit (āy-lehk-tree-see-*tayt*) *c* electricity

elektriciteitscentrale (āy-lehk-tree-see-*tayt*-sehn-traa-ler) *c* power station

elektrisch (āy-*lehk*-treess) *adj* electric

elektronisch (āy-lehk-*trōa*-neess) *adj* electronic; ~ **spel** electronic game

element (āy-ler-*mehnt*) *nt* (pl ~en) element

elementair (āy-ler-mehn-*tair*) *adj* primary

elf[1] (ehlf) *num* eleven

elf[2] (ehlf) *c* (pl ~en) elf

elfde (ehlf-der) *num* eleventh

elftal (ehlf-tahl) *nt* (pl ~len) soccer team

elimineren (āy-lee-mee-*nāy*-rern) *v* eliminate

elk (ehlk) *adj* each, every

elkaar (ehl-*kaar*) *pron* each other

elleboog (eh-ler-*bōakh*) *c* (pl -bogen) elbow

ellende (eh-*lehn*-der) *c* misery

ellendig (eh-*lehn*-derkh) *adj* miserable

email (āy-*migh*) *nt* enamel

e-mail (ee-māyl) *c* (pl ~s) e-mail

e-mailen (ee-māy-lern) *v* e-mail

emailleren (āy-migh-āy-rern) *v* glaze

emancipatie (āy-mahn-see-*paa*-tsee) *c* emancipation

embargo (ehm-*bahr*-gōa) *nt* embargo

embleem (ehm-*blāym*) *nt* (pl -blemen) emblem

emigrant (āy-mee-*grahnt*) *m* (f ~e, ~en) emigrant

emigratie (āy-mee-*graa*-tsee) *c*

emigration

emigreren ($\overline{ay}$-mee-*gr$\overline{ay}$*-rern) *v*
emigrate

eminent ($\overline{ay}$-mee-*nehnt*) *adj*
outstanding

emmer (*eh*-merr) *c* (pl ~s) bucket, pail

emotie ($\overline{ay}$-*m$\overline{oa}$*-tsee) *c* (pl ~s) emotion

employé (ahm-plvah-*$^y\overline{ay}$*) *m* (f -yee, pl
~s) employee

en (ehn) *conj* and

encyclopedie (ehn-see-kl$\overline{oa}$-pay-*dee*)
c (pl ~ën) encyclop(a)edia

endeldarm (*ehn*-derl-dahrm) *c* (pl~en)
rectum

energie ($\overline{ay}$-nehr-*zhee*) *c* energy;
power

energiek ($\overline{ay}$-nehr-*zheek*) *adj* energetic

eng (ehng) *adj* narrow; creepy

engel (*eh*-ngerl) *c* (pl ~en) angel

Engeland (*eh*-nger-lahnt) England;
Britain

Engels (*eh*-ngerls) *adj* English; British

Engelse (*eh*-ngerl-ser) *f* (pl Engelsen)
Englishwoman

Engelsman (*eh*-ngerls-mahn) *m* (pl
Engelsen) Englishman; Briton

enig ($\overline{ay}$-nerkh) *adj* sole, only; *pron* any;
enige *pron* some

enigszins ($\overline{ay}$-nerkh-sıns) *adv*
somewhat

enkel[1] (*ehng*-kerl) *adj* single; **enkele**
pron some

enkel[2] (*ehng*-kerl) *c* (pl ~s) ankle

enkeling (*ehng*-ker-lıng) *c* (pl ~en)
individual

enkelvoud (*ehng*-kerl-vout) *nt*
singular

enorm ($\overline{ay}$-*norm*) *adj* tremendous,
enormous, huge

enquête (ahng-*kai*-ter) *c* (pl ~s)
enquiry

enthousiasme (ahn-t$\overline{oo}$-*zhahss*-mer)
nt enthusiasm

enthousiast (ahn-t$\overline{oo}$-*zhahst*) *adj*

enthusiastic; keen

entree (ahn-*tr$\overline{ay}$*) *c* entry; entrance fee

envelop (ahng-ver-*lop*) *c* (pl ~pen)
envelope

enzovoort (*ehn*-z$\overline{oa}$-v$\overline{oa}$rt) and so on,
etcetera

epidemie ($\overline{ay}$-pee-der-*mee*) *c* (pl ~ën)
epidemic

epilepsie ($\overline{ay}$-pee-lehp-*see*) *c* epilepsy

epiloog ($\overline{ay}$-pee-*l$\overline{oa}$kh*) *c* (pl -logen)
epilogue

episch ($\overline{ay}$-peess) *adj* epic

episode ($\overline{ay}$-pee-*z$\overline{oa}$*-der) *c* (pl ~n, ~s)
episode

epos ($\overline{ay}$-poss) *nt* (pl epen, ~sen) epic

equipe ($\overline{ay}$-*keep*) *c* (pl ~s) team

equivalent ($\overline{ay}$-kvee-vaa-*lehnt*) *adj*
equivalent

er (ehr) *adv* there; *pron* of them

erbarmelijk (ehr-*bahr*-mer-lerk) *adj*
lamentable

eredienst ($\overline{ay}$-rer-deenst) *c* (pl ~en)
worship

eren ($\overline{ay}$-rern) *v* honour

erf (ehrf) *nt* (pl erven) yard

erfelijk (*ehr*-fer-lerk) *adj* hereditary

erfenis (*ehr*-fer-nıss) *c* (pl ~sen)
inheritance; legacy

erfgenaam (*ehrf*-ger-naam) *m* (pl
-namen) heir

erfgename (*ehrf*ger-naamer) *f* (pl
-namen) heiress

erg (ehrkh) *adj* bad; *adv* very; **erger**
worse; **ergst** worst

ergens (*ehr*-gerns) *adv* somewhere

ergeren (*ehr*-ger-rern) *v* annoy

ergernis (*ehr*-gerr-nıss) *c* annoyance

erkennen (ehr-*keh*-nern) *v* recognize;
acknowledge

erkenning (ehr-*keh*-nıng) *c* (pl ~en)
recognition

erkentelijk (ehr-*kehn*-ter-lerk) *adj*
grateful

ernst (ehrnst) *c* seriousness; gravity

ernstig (*ehrn*-sterkh) *adj* serious; grave, bad, severe

erts (ehrts) *nt* (pl ~en) ore

***ervaren** (ehr-*vaa*-rern) *v* experience

ervaring (ehr-*vaa*-rıng) *c* (pl ~en) experience

erven (*ehr*-vern) *v* inherit

erwt (ehrt) *c* (pl ~en) pea

escorte (ehss-*kor*-ter) *nt* (pl ~s) escort

escorteren (ehss-kor-*tay*-rern) *v* escort

esdoorn (*ehss*-doarn) *c* (pl ~s) maple

essay (eh-*say*) *nt* (pl ~s) essay

essentie (eh-*sehn*-see) *c* essence

essentieel (eh-sehn-*shayl*) *adj* vital, essential

etage (ay-*taa*-zher) *c* (pl ~s) floor, stor(e)y; apartment *nAm*

etalage (ay-taa-*laa*-zher) *c* (pl ~s) shopwindow

etappe (ay-*tah*-per) *c* (pl ~n, ~s) stage; lap

eten (*ay*-tern) *nt* food

***eten** (*ay*-tern) *v* *eat

ether (*ay*-terr) *c* ether

Ethiopië (ay-tee-*yoa*-pee-*y*er) Ethiopia

Ethiopiër (ay-tee-*yoa*-pee-*y*err) *m* (f -ische, pl ~s) Ethiopian

Ethiopisch (ay-tee-*yoa*-peess) *adj* Ethiopian

etiket (ay-tee-*keht*) *nt* (pl ~ten) label, tag

etiketteren (ay-tee-keh-*tay*-rern) *v* label

etmaal (*eht*-maal) *nt* (pl -malen) twenty-four hours

ettelijk (*eh*-ter-lerk) *adj* several

etter (*eh*-terr) *c* pus

etui (ay-*tvee*) *nt* (pl ~s) case

euro (*ur*-roa) *c* euro

Europa (ur-*roa*-paa) Europe

Europeaan (ur-roa-pay-*aan*) *m* (f -ese, pl -anen) European

Europees (ur-roa-*payss*) *adj* European

Europese Unie (eur-oo-*peeser y*-nie) European Union

evacueren (ay-vaa-kew-*vay*-rern) *v* evacuate

evangelie (ay-vahng-*gay*-lee) *nt* (pl -liën, ~s) gospel

even (*ay*-vern) *adj* even; *adv* equally, as

evenaar (*ay*-ver-naar) *c* equator

evenals (*ay*-ver-nahls) *conj* as well as

evenaren (*ay*-ver-*naa*-rern) *v* equal

eveneens (ay-ver-*nayns*) *adv* as well, likewise, also

evenredig (ay-ver-*ray*-derkh) *adj* proportional

eventueel (ay-vern-*tew*-*vayl*) *adj* possible, eventual

evenveel (*ay*-ver-*vayl*) *adv* as much

evenwel (*ay*-ver-*vehl*) *adv* however

evenwicht (*ay*-ver-vıkht) *nt* balance

evenwijdig (*ay*-ver-*vay*-derkh) *adj* parallel

evenzeer (*ay*-ver-*zayr*) *adv* as much

evenzo (ay-ver-*zoa*) *adv* likewise

evolutie (ay-voa-*lew*-tsee) *c* (pl ~s) evolution

exact (ehk-*sahkt*) *adj* precise

examen (ehk-*saa*-mern) *nt* (pl ~s) examination

excentriek (ehk-sehn-*treek*) *adj* eccentric

exces (ehk-*sehss*) *nt* (pl ~sen) excess

exclusief (ehks-klew-*zeef*) *adj* exclusive

excursie (ehks-*kerr*-zee) *c* (pl ~s) day trip, excursion

excuseren (ehks-kew-*zay*-rern) *v* excuse

excuus (ehks-*kewss*) *nt* (pl excuses) apology, excuse

exemplaar (ehk-serm-*plaar*) *nt* (pl -plaren) specimen; copy

exotisch (ehk-*soa*-teess) *adj* exotic

expeditie (ehks-per-*dee*-tsee) *c* (pl ~s) expedition

experiment (ehks-pay-ree-*mehnt*) *nt* (pl ~en) experiment
experimenteren (ehks-pay-ree-mehn-*tay*-rern) *v* experiment
expert (ehks-*pair*) *c* (pl ~s) expert
expliciet (ehks-plee-*seet*) *adj* explicit
exploderen (ehks-ploa-*day*-rern) *v* explode, *blow up
exploiteren (ehks-plvah-*tay*-rern) *v* exploit
explosie (ehks-*ploa*-zee) *c* (pl ~s) blast, explosion
explosief (ehks-ploa-*zeef*) *adj* explosive

export (*ehk*-sport) *c* exports *pl*, export
exporteren (ehk-spor-*tay*-rern) *v* export
expositie (ehk-spoa-*zee*-tsee) *c* (pl ~s) exhibition
expresse- (ehk-*spreh*-ser) express; special delivery
extase (ehk-*staa*-zer) *c* ecstasy
extra (*ehk*-straa) *adj* additional, extra; spare
extravagant (ehk-straa-vaa-*gahnt*) *adj* extravagant
extreem (ehk-*straym*) *adj* extreme
ezel (*ay*-zerl) *c* (pl ~s) donkey

F

faam (faam) *c* fame
fabel (*faa*-berl) *c* (pl ~s, ~en) fable
fabriceren (faa-bree-*say*-rern) *v* manufacture
fabriek (faa-*breek*) *c* (pl ~en) factory; mill, works *pl*
fabrikant (faa-bree-*kahnt*) *m* (f ~e, pl ~en) manufacturer
factor (*fahk*-tor) *c* (pl ~en) factor
factureren (fahk-tew-*ray*-rern) *v* bill
factuur (fahk-*tewr*) *c* (pl-turen) invoice
facultatief (faa-kerl-taa-*teef*) *adj* optional
faculteit (faa-kerl-*tayt*) *c* (pl ~en) faculty
failliet (fah-*ʸeet*) *adj* bankrupt
fakkel (*fah*-kerl) *c* (pl ~s) torch
falen (*faa*-lern) *v* fail
familiaar (fah-mee-lee-*ʸaar*) *adj* familiar
familie (faa-*mee*-lee) *c* (pl ~s) family
familielid (faa-*mee*-lee-lɪt) *nt* (pl -leden) relative
fanatiek (faa-naa-*teek*) *adj* fanatical

fanfarekorps (fahm-*faa*-rer-korps) *nt* (pl ~en) brass band
fantasie (fahn-taa-*zee*) *c* (pl ~ën) fantasy, fancy
fantastisch (fahn-*tahss*-teess) *adj* fantastic
farmacologie (fahr-maa-koa-loa-*gee*) *c* pharmacology
fascinerend (fah-see-*nay*-rernt) *adj* glamorous
fascisme (fah-sɪss-mer) *nt* fascism
fascist (fah-sɪst) *m* (pl ~en) fascist
fascistisch (fah-sɪss-teess) *adj* fascist
fase (*faa*-zer) *c* (pl ~s, ~n) stage, phase
fataal (faa-*taal*) *adj* fatal
fatsoen (faht-*soon*) *nt* decency
fatsoenlijk (faht-*soon*-lerk) *adj* decent
fauteuil (foa-*tur*ᵉʷ) *c* (pl ~s) armchair
favoriet (faa-voa-*reet*) *c* (pl ~en) favo(u)rite
fax (faks) *c* fax; **een ~ versturen** send a fax
fazant (faa-*zahnt*) *c* pheasant
februari (fay-brew-*vaa*-ree) February

federaal (fāy-der-*raal*) *adj* federal

federatie (fāy-der-*raa*-tsee) *c* (pl ~s) federation

fee (fāy) *f* (pl ~ën) fairy

feest (fāyst) *nt* (pl ~en) feast; party

feestdag (*fāyss*-dahkh) *c* (pl ~en) holiday

feestelijk (*fāy*-ster-lerk) *adj* festive

feestje (*fāy*-sher) *nt* (pl ~s) party

feilloos (*fay*-lōass) *adj* faultless, infallible

feit (fayt) *nt* (pl ~en) fact; **in feite** in fact

feitelijk (*fay*-ter-lerk) *adj* factual; *adv* as a matter of fact, actually, in effect

fel (fehl) *adj* fierce

felicitatie (fāy-lee-see-*taa*-tsee) *c* (pl ~s) congratulation

feliciteren (fāy-lee-see-*tāy*-rern) *v* congratulate; compliment

feodaal (fāy-*rō*oa-*daal*) *adj* feudal

festival (*fehss*-tee-vahl) *nt* (pl ~s) festival

feuilleton (fur^ew-er-*ton*) *nt* (pl ~s) serial

fiasco (fee-*y*ahss-kōa) *nt* (pl ~'s) failure; disaster

fiche (*fee*-sher) *c* (pl ~s) chip

fictie (*fik*-see) *c* (pl ~s) fiction

fiets (feets) *c* (pl ~en) cycle, bicycle

fietser (*fee*-tserr) *m* (f -ster, pl ~s) cyclist

figuur (fee-*gēwr*) *c* (pl -guren) figure; diagram

fijn (fayn) *adj* enjoyable; fine; delicate

fijnhakken (*fayn*-hah-kern) *v* mince

***fijnmalen** (*fayn*-maa-lern) *v* *grind

fijnproever (*faym*-prōo-verr) *m* (pl ~s) gourmet

fijnstampen (*fayn*-stahm-pern) *v* mash

filiaal (fee-lee-*y*aal) *nt* (-ialen) branch

Filippijnen (fee-lɪ-*pay*-nern) *pl* Philippines *pl*

Filippijns (fee-lɪ-*payns*) *adj* Philippine

film (film) *c* (pl ~s) film; movie

filmcamera (*film*-kaa-mer-raa) *c* (pl ~'s) camera

filmen (*fil*-mern) *v* film

filmjournaal (*film*-zhōor-naal) *nt* newsreel

filosofie (fee-lōa-zōa-*fee*) *c* (pl ~ën) philosophy

filosoof (fee-lōa-*zōaf*) *m* (f -sofe, pl -sofen) philosopher

filter (*fil*-terr) *nt* (pl ~s) filter

Fin (fɪn) *m* (f ~se, pl ~nen) Finn

financieel (fee-nahn-*shāyl*) *adj* financial

financiën (fee-*nahn*-see-*y*ern) *pl* finances *pl*

financieren (fee-nahn-*see*-rern) *v* finance

Finland (*fin*-lahnt) Finland

Fins (fɪns) *adj* Finnish

firma (*fir*-maa) *c* (pl ~'s) company, firm

fitting (*fɪ*-tɪng) *c* (pl ~en) socket

flacon (flaa-*kon*) *c* (pl ~s) flask

flamingo (flaa-*mɪng*-gōa) *c* (pl ~'s) flamingo

flanel (flaa-*nehl*) *nt* flannel

flat (fleht) *c* (pl ~s) flat; apartment *nAm*

flatgebouw (*fleht*-kher-bou) *nt* (pl ~en) block of flats; apartment house *Am*

flauw (flou) *adj* faint

***flauwvallen** (*flou*-vah-lern) *v* faint

fles (flehss) *c* (pl ~sen) bottle

flesopener (*fleh*-zōa-per-nerr) *c* (pl ~s) bottle opener

flessehals (*fleh*-ser-hahls) *c* bottleneck

flets (flehts) *adj* dull

flink (flɪngk) *adj* considerable; brave, plucky

flits (flɪts) *c* (pl ~en) flash

flitslampje (*flɪts*-lahm-p^yer) *nt* (pl ~s) flash bulb

fluisteren (*flur*^ewss-ter-rern) *v* whisper

fluit (flur^ewt) *c* (pl ~en) flute

***fluiten** (*flur*^ew-tern) *v* whistle

fluitje (*flur*^ew-t^yer) *nt* (pl ~s) whistle

fluitketel (*flur^(ew)t*-kaȳ-terl) *c* (pl ∽s) ketel

fluweel (flēw-vāyl) *nt* velvet

foefje (*fōo*-f^yer) *nt* (pl ∽s) trick

foei! (fōo^(ee)) shame!

fokken (*fo*-kern) *v* *breed; raise

folklore (fol-*klōa*-rer) *c* folklore

fonds (fons) *nt* (pl ∽en) fund

fonetisch (fōa-*nāy*-teess) *adj* phonetic

fonkelend (*fong*-ker-lernt) *adj* sparkling

fontein (fon-*tayn*) *c* (pl ∽en) fountain

fooi (fōa^(ee)) *c* (pl ∽en) tip; gratuity

foppen (*fo*-pern) *v* fool

forceren (for-*sāy*-rern) *v* strain; force

forel (fōa-*rehl*) *c* (pl ∽len) trout

forens (fōa-*rehns*) *c* (pl ∽en, forenzen) commuter

formaat (for-*maat*) *nt* (pl -maten) size

formaliteit (for-maa-lee-*tayt*) *c* (pl ∽en) formality

formeel (for-*māyl*) *adj* formal

formule (for-*mēw*-ler) *c* (pl ∽s) formula

formulier (for-mēw-*leer*) *nt* (pl ∽en) form

fornuis (for-*nur^(ew)ss*) *nt* (pl -nuizen) cooker, stove

fors (fors) *adj* robust

fortuin (for-*tur^(ew)n*) *nt* (pl ∽en) fortune

foto (*fōa*-tōa) *c* (pl ∽'s) photograph, photo

fotocopie (fōa-tōa-kōa-*pee*) *c* (pl ∽ën) photocopy

fotograaf (fōa-tōa-*graaf*) *m* (f -grafe, pl -grafen) photographer

fotograferen (fōa-tōa-graa-*fāy*-rern) *v* photograph

fotografie (fōa-tōa-graa-*fee*) *c* photography

fototoestel (*fōa*-tōa-tōo-stehl) *nt* (pl ∽len) camera

fotowinkel (*fōa*-tōa-vɪng-kerl) *c* (pl ∽s) camera shop

fouilleren (fōo-^y*āy*-rern) *v* search

fout¹ (fout) *adj* mistaken, wrong

fout² (fout) *c* (pl ∽en) error, mistake, fault

foutloos (*fout*-lōass) *adj* faultless

foyer (fvah-^y*āy*) *c* (pl ∽s) foyer; lobby

fractie (*frahk*-see) *c* (pl ∽s) fraction

fragment (frahkh-*mehnt*) *nt* (pl ∽en) fragment; extract

framboos (frahm-*bōass*) *c* (pl -bozen) raspberry

franje (*frah*-ñer) *c* (pl ∽s) fringe

frankeren (frahng-*kāy*-rern) *v* stamp

frankering (frahng-*kāy*-rɪng) *c* (pl ∽en) postage

franko (*frahng*-kōa) *adj* postage paid, post-paid

Frankrijk (*frahng*-krayk) France

Frans (frahns) *adj* French

Fransman (*frahns*-mahn) *m* (f Franse, pl Fransen) Frenchman

frappant (frah-*pahnt*) *adj* striking

fraude (*frou*-der) *c* (pl ∽s) fraud

frequent (frer-*kvehnt*) *adj* frequent

frequentie (frer-*kvehn*-tsee) *c* (pl ∽s) frequency

friet (freet) *pl* chips; French fries

fris (frɪss) *adj* fresh

frisdrank (*frɪss*-drahngk) *c* soft drink, soda *nAm*

frites (freet) *pl* chips; French fries

fruit (frur^(ew)t) *nt* fruit

fuif (fur^(ew)f) *c* (pl fuiven) party

functie (*ferngk*-see) *c* (pl ∽s) function; position

functioneren (ferngk-shōa-*nāy*-rern) *v* work

fundamenteel (fern-daa-mehn-*tāyl*) *adj* fundamental, basic

fuseren (fēw-*zāy*-rern) *v* merge

fusie (*fēw*-zee) *c* (pl ∽s) merger

fysica (*fee*-zee-kaa) *c* physics

fysiek (fee-*zeek*) *adj* physical

fysiologie (fee-zee-^y*ōa*-lōa-*gee*) *c* physiology

G

*gaan (gaan) *v* *go; ***~ door** pass
through

gaarne (*gaar*-ner) *adv* gladly

*gadeslaan (*gaa*-der-slaan) *v* watch

gal (gahl) *c* gall, bile

galblaas (*gahl*-blaass) *c* (pl -blazen)
gall bladder

galerij (gah-ler-*ray*) *c* (pl ~en) arcade;
gallery

galg (gahlkh) *c* (pl ~en) gallows *pl*

galop (gaa-*lop*) *c* gallop

galsteen (*gahl*-stayn) *c* (pl -stenen)
gallstone

gammel (*gah*-merl) *adj* ramshackle,
shaky

gang (gahng) *c* (pl ~en) corridor; pace;
course

gangbaar (*gahng*-baar) *adj* current

gangpad (*gahng*-paht) *nt* (pl ~en) aisle

gans (gahns) *c* (pl ganzen) goose

gapen (*gaa*-pern) *v* yawn

garage (gaa-*raa*-zher) *c* (pl ~s) garage

garanderen (gaa-rahn-*day*-rern) *v*
guarantee

garantie (gaa-*rahn*-tsee) *c* (pl ~s)
guarantee

garderobe (gahr-der-*raw*-ber) *c* (pl ~s)
wardrobe, cloakroom; checkroom
nAm

garen (*gaa*-rern) *nt* (pl ~s) thread, yarn

garnaal (gahr-*naal*) *c* (pl -nalen) prawn,
shrimp

gas (gahss) *nt* (pl ~sen) gas

gasfabriek (*gahss*-faa-breek) *c* (pl ~en)
gasworks

gasfornuis (*gahss*-for-nur^{ew}ss) *nt* (pl
-nuizen) gas cooker

gaskachel (*gahss*-kah-kherl) *c* (pl ~s)
gas stove

gaspedaal (*gahss*-per-daal) *nt* (pl
-dalen) accelerator

gasstel (*gah*-stehl) *nt* (pl ~len) gas
cooker

gast (gahst) *c* (pl ~en) guest

gastheer (*gahst*-hayr) *m* (pl -heren)
host

gastvrij (gahst-*fray*) *adj* hospitable

gastvrijheid (gahst-*fray*-hayt) *c*
hospitality

gastvrouw (*gahst*-frou) *f* (pl ~en)
hostess

gat (gaht) *nt* (pl ~en) hole, gap

gauw (gou) *adv* soon

gave (*gaa*-ver) *c* (pl ~n) gift, faculty

gazon (gaa-*zon*) *nt* (pl ~s) lawn

geacht (ger-*ahkht*) *adj* esteemed;
geachte heer Dear Sir

geadresseerde (ger-ah-dreh-*sayr*-
der) *c* (pl ~n) addressee

geaffecteerd (ger-ah-fehk-*tayrt*) *adj*
affected

gearmd (ger-*ahrmt*) *adv* arm-in-arm

gebaar (ger-*baar*) *nt* (pl gebaren) sign

gebak (ger-*bahk*) *nt* cake, pastry

gebaren (ger-*baa*-rern) *v* gesticulate

gebed (ger-*beht*) *nt* (pl ~en) prayer

gebergte *nt* mountain range

gebeuren (ger-*bur*-rern) *v* occur;
happen

gebeurtenis (ger-*burr*-ter-nıss) *c* (pl
~sen) event; happening, occurrence

gebied (ger-*beet*) *nt* (pl ~en) region;
zone, area, field, territory

geblokt (ger-*blokt*) *adj* chequered

gebogen (ger-*bōa*-gern) *adj* curved

geboorte (ger-*bōar*-ter) *c* (pl ~n) birth

geboorteland (ger-*bōar*-ter-lahnt) *nt*
native country

geboorteplaats (ger-*bōar*-ter-plaats) *c*
place of birth

geboren (ger-*bōa*-rern) *adj* born

gebouw (ger-*bou*) *nt* (pl ~en)
construction, building

gebrek (ger-*brehk*) *nt* (pl ~en)

deficiency, fault; want, lack, shortage

gebrekkig (ger-*breh*-kerkh) *adj* defective, faulty

gebruik (ger-*brur*^{ew}k) *nt* (pl ~en) use, usage; custom

gebruikelijk (ger-*brur*^{ew}-ker-lerk) *adj* customary; common, usual

gebruiken (ger-*brur*^{ew}-kern) *v* use; employ; apply

gebruiker (ger-*brur*^{ew}-kerr) *m* (f -ster, pl ~s) user

gebruiksaanwijzing (ger-*brur*^{ew}k-saan-vay-zıng) *c* (pl ~en) directions for use

gebruiksvoorwerp (ger-*brur*^{ew}ks-fōar-vehrp) *nt* (pl ~en) utensil

gebruind (ger-*brur*^{ew}nt) *adj* tanned

gebrul (ger-*brerl*) *nt* roar

gecompliceerd (ger-kom-plee-*sāyrt*) *adj* complicated

gedachte (ger-*dahkh*-ter) *c* (pl ~n) thought; idea

gedachtenstreepje (ger-*dahkh*-ter-strāyp-^{y}er) *nt* (pl ~s) dash

gedeelte (ger-*dāyl*-ter) *nt* (pl ~n, ~s) part

gedeeltelijk (ger-*dāyl*-ter-lerk) *adj* partial; *adv* partly

gedelegeerde (ger-dāy-ler-*gāyr*-der) *c* (pl ~n) delegate

gedenkteken (ger-*dehngk*-tāy-kern) *nt* (pl ~s) memorial; monument

gedenkwaardig (ger-dehngk-*vaar*-derkh) *adj* memorable

gedetailleerd (ger-dāy-tah-^{y}*āyrt*) *adj* detailed

gedetineerde (ger-dāy-tee-*nāyr*-der) *c* (pl ~n) prisoner

gedicht (ger-*dıkht*) *nt* (pl ~en) poem

geding (ger-*dıng*) *nt* (pl ~en) lawsuit

gediplomeerd (ger-dee-plōa-*māyrt*) *adj* qualified

gedrag (ger-*drahkh*) *nt* conduct, behavio(u)r

*****gedragen** (ger-*draa*-gern): **zich** ~ act, behave

geduld (ger-*derlt*) *nt* patience

geduldig (ger-*derl*-derkh) *adj* patient

gedurende (ger-*dēw*-rern-der) *prep* during; for

gedurfd (ger-*derrft*) *adj* daring

geel (gāyl) *adj* yellow

geelkoper (gāyl-kōa-perr) *nt* brass

geelzucht (gāyl-zerkht) *c* jaundice

geëmailleerd (ger-āy-mah-^{y}*āyrt*) *adj* enamelled

geen (gāyn) *adj* no; none

geenszins (gāyn-sıns) *adv* by no means

geest (gāyst) *c* (pl ~en) spirit, mind; soul; ghost

geestelijk (gāy-ster-lerk) *adj* spiritual, mental

geestelijke (gāy-ster-ler-ker) *c* (pl ~n) clergyman

geestig (gāy-sterkh) *adj* witty, humorous

geeuwen (gāy^{oo}-ern) *v* yawn

gefluister (ger-*flur*^{ew}-sterr) *nt* whisper

gegadigde (ger-gaa-derkh-der) *c* (pl ~n) candidate

gegeneerd (ger-zher-*nāyrt*) *adj* embarrassed

gegeven (ger-*gāy*-vern) *nt* (pl ~s) data *pl*

gegrond (ger-*gront*) *adj* well-founded

gehandicapt (ger-*hehn*-dee-kehpt) *adj* disabled

gehecht aan (ger-*hekht* aan) *adj* attached to

geheel (ger-*hāyl*) *adj* entire, whole, total; *adv* completely; *nt* whole

geheelonthouder (ger-*hāyl*-ont-hou-derr) *m* (pl ~s) teetotaller

geheim[1] (ger-*haym*) *adj* secret

geheim[2] (ger-*haym*) *nt* (pl ~en) secret

geheimzinnig (ger-haym-zı-nerkh) *adj* mysterious

geheugen (ger-*hūr*-gern) *nt* memory

gehoor (ger-*hōar*) *nt* hearing

gehoorzaam (ger-*hōar*-zaam) *adj* obedient

gehoorzaamheid (ger-*hōar*-zaam-hayt) *c* obedience

gehoorzamen (ger-*hōar*-zaa-mern) *v* obey

gehorig (ger-*hōa*-rerkh) *adj* noisy

gehucht (ger-*herrkht*) *nt* (pl ~en) hamlet

geïnteresseerd (ger-ın-trer-*sāyrt*) *adj* interested

geïsoleerd (ger-ee-zōa-*lāyrt*) *adj* isolated; insulated

geit (gayt) *c* (pl ~en) goat

geiteleer (*gay*-ter-lāyr) *nt* kid

gek[1] (gehk) *adj* crazy, mad

gek[2] (gehk) *c* (pl ~ken) fool

geklets (ger-*klehts*) *nt* chat; rubbish

gekleurd (ger-*klūrt*) *adj* colo(u)red

gekraak (ger-*kraak*) *nt* crack

gekruid (ger-*krur^ew^t*) *adj* spiced

gelaatstrek (ger-*laats*-trehk) *c* (pl ~ken) feature

gelach (ger-*lahkh*) *nt* laughter

geld (gehlt) *nt* money; **buitenlands ~** foreign currency; **contant ~** cash

geldautomaat (*gehlt*-oo-too-maat) *c* cash dispenser, ATM, cash point

geldbelegging (*gehlt*-ber-leh-gıng) *c* (pl ~en) investment

*gelden (*gehl*-dern) *v* apply

geldig (*gehl*-derkh) *adj* valid

geldstuk (*gehlt*-sterk) *nt* (pl ~ken) coin

geleden (ger-*lāy*-dern) ago; **kort ~** recently

geleerde (ger-*lāyr*-der) *c* (pl ~n) scholar, scientist

gelegen (ger-*lay*-gern) *adj* situated

gelegenheid (ger-*lāy*-gern-hayt) *c* (pl -heden) occasion, chance, opportunity; facilities

gelei (zher-*lay*) *c* (pl ~en) jelly

geleidehond (ger-*lay*-der-hont) *c* (pl ~en) guide dog

geleidelijk (ger-*lay*-der-lerk) *adj* gradual

gelijk (ger-*layk*) *adj* equal, like, alike; level, even; **~ *hebben** *be right; **~ maken** equalize

gelijkenis (ger-*lay*-ker-nıss) *c* (pl ~sen) resemblance, similarity

gelijkgezind (ger-layk-kher-*zınt*) *adj* like-minded

gelijkheid (ger-*layk*-hayt) *c* equality

gelijkstroom (ger-*layk*-strōam) *c* direct current

gelijktijdig (ger-layk-*tay*-derkh) *adj* simultaneous

gelijkwaardig (ger-layk-*vaar*-derkh) *adj* equivalent

gelofte (ger-*lof*-ter) *c* (pl ~n) vow

geloof (ger-*lōaf*) *nt* belief; faith

geloofwaardig (ger-lōaf-*vaar*-derkh) *adj* credible

geloven (ger-*lōa*-vern) *v* believe

geluid (ger-*lur^ew^t*) *nt* (pl ~en) sound; noise

geluiddicht (ger-lur^ew^-*dıkht*) *adj* soundproof

geluk (ger-*lerk*) *nt* happiness; luck, fortune

gelukkig (ger-*ler*-kerkh) *adj* happy; fortunate

gelukwens (ger-*lerk*-vehns) *c* (pl ~en) congratulation

gelukwensen (ger-*lerk*-vehn-sern) *v* congratulate, compliment

gemak (ger-*mahk*) *nt* leisure; ease; comfort; convenience

gemakkelijk (ger-*mah*-ker-lerk) *adj* easy; convenient

gematigd (ger-*maa*-terkht) *adj* moderate

gember (*gehm*-berr) *c* ginger

gemeen (ger-*māyn*) *adj* foul, mean

gemeenschap (ger-*māyn*-skhahp) *c*

(pl ~pen) community; intercourse

gemeenschappelijk (ger-mayn-skhah-per-lerk) adj common

gemeente (ger-mayn-ter) c (pl ~n, ~s) congregation

gemeentebestuur (ger-mayn-ter-ber-stewr) nt municipality

gemeentelijk (ger-mayn-ter-lerk) adj municipal

gemêleerd (ger-meh-layrt) adj mixed

gemengd (ger-mehngt) adj mixed; miscellaneous

gemiddeld (ger-mɪ-derlt) adj average, medium; adv on the average

gemiddelde (ger-mɪ-derl-der) nt (pl ~n) average, mean

gemis (ger-mɪss) nt want, lack

genade (ger-naa-der) c mercy; grace

geneeskunde (ger-nayss-kern-der) c medicine

geneeskundig (ger-nayss-kern-derkh) adj medical

geneesmiddel (ger-nayss-mɪ-derl) nt (pl ~en) medicine; remedy, drug

genegen (ger-nay-gern) adj inclined

genegenheid (ger-nay-gern-hayt) c affection

geneigd (ger-naykht) adj inclined

generaal (gay-ner-raal) m (pl ~s) general

generatie (gay-ner-raa-tsee) c (pl ~s) generation

generator (gay-ner-raa-tor) c (pl ~en, ~s) generator

***genezen** (ger-nay-zern) v heal; cure; recover

genezing (ger-nay-zɪng) c (pl ~en) cure; recovery

genie (zher-nee) nt (pl ~ën) genius

***genieten van** (ger-nee-tern) enjoy

genoeg (ger-nookh) adv enough; sufficient

genoegen (ger-noo-gern) nt (pl ~s) pleasure

genootschap (ger-noat-skhahp) nt (pl ~pen) society; association

genot (ger-not) nt joy; delight; enjoyment

geologie (gay-ʸoa-loa-gee) c geology

gepast (ger-pahst) adj suitable, proper

gepensioneerd (ger-pehn-shoa-nayrt) adj retired

geprikkeld (ger-prɪ-kerlt) adj excited

geraamte (ger-raam-ter) nt (pl ~n, ~s) skeleton

geraas (ger-raass) nt roar

gerecht (ger-rehkht) nt (pl ~en) dish; law court

gerechtigheid (ger-rehkh-terkh-hayt) c justice

gereed (ger-rayt) adj ready

gereedschap (ger-rayt-skhahp) nt (pl ~pen) tool; utensil, implement

gereedschapskist (ger-rayt-skhahps-kɪst) c (pl ~en) tool kit

geregeld (ger-ray-gerlt) adj regular

gereserveerd (ger-ray-zehr-vayrt) adj reserved

gerief (ger-reef) nt comfort

geriefelijk (ger-ree-fer-lerk) adj comfortable, easy; convenient

gering (ger-rɪng) adj minor; slight, small; **geringst** least

geroddel (ger-ro-derl) nt gossip

gerst (gehrst) c barley

gerucht (ger-rerkht) nt (pl ~en) rumour

geruit (ger-rurᵉᵘt) adj chequered

gerust (ger-rerst) adj confident

geruststellen (ger-rerst-steh-lern) v reassure

gescheiden (ger-skhay-dern) adj separate

geschenk (ger-skhehngk) nt (pl ~en) gift, present

geschiedenis (ger-skhee-der-nɪss) c history

geschiedkundig (ger-skheet-kern-derkh) adj historical

geschiedkundige (ger-skheet-*kern*-der-ger) *c* (pl ~n) historian

geschikt (ger-*skhıkt*) *adj* convenient, suitable, proper, appropriate, fit; ~ ***zijn** qualify

geschil (ger-*skhıl*) *nt* (pl ~len) dispute

geslacht (ger-*slahkht*) *nt* (pl ~en) sex; gender

geslachtelijk (ger-*slahkh*-ter-lerk) *adj* genital

geslachtsziekte (ger-*slahkht*-seek-ter) *c* (pl ~n, ~s) venereal disease

gesloten (ger-*slōa*-tern) *adj* closed, shut

gesp (gehsp) *c* (pl ~en) buckle

gespannen (ger-*spah*-nern) *adj* tense

gespierd (ger-*speert*) *adj* muscular

gespikkeld (ger-*spı*-kerlt) *adj* spotted

gesprek (ger-*sprehk*) *nt* (pl ~ken) discussion, conversation, talk; **interlokaal** ~ long-distance call; **lokaal** ~ local call

gestalte (ger-*stahl*-ter) *c* (pl ~n, ~s) figure

gesticht (ger-*stıkht*) *nt* (pl ~en) asylum

gestorven (ger-*stor*-vern) *adj* dead

gestreept (ger-*strāypt*) *adj* striped

getal (ger-*tahl*) *nt* (pl ~len) number

getij (ger-*tay*) *nt* (pl ~en) tide

getrouw (ger-*trou*) *adj* true

getuige (ger-*turᵉᵂ*-ger) *c* (pl ~n) witness

getuigen (ger-*turᵉᵂ*-gern) *v* testify; attest

getuigschrift (ger-*turᵉᵂ*kh-skhrıft) *nt* (pl ~en) certificate

geur (gŭrr) *c* (pl ~en) smell, odo(u)r; scent

gevaar (ger-*vaar*) *nt* (pl -varen) danger; risk, peril

gevaarlijk (ger-*vaar*-lerk) *adj* dangerous; perilous

geval (ger-*vahl*) *nt* (pl ~len) case; instance; event; **in elk** ~ at any rate, anyway; **in** ~ **van** in case of

gevangene (ger-*vah*-nger-ner) *c* (pl ~n) prisoner

gevangenis (ger-*vah*-nger-nıss) *c* (pl ~sen) prison; jail

gevangenschap (ger-*vah*-ngern-skhahp) *c* imprisonment

gevarieerd (ger-vaa-ree-ᵛ*āyrt*) *adj* varied

gevatheid (ger-*vaht*-hayt) *c* wit

gevecht (ger-*vehkht*) *nt* (pl ~en) combat, battle, fight

gevel (*gāy*-verl) *c* (pl ~s) façade

geveltop (*gāy*-verl-top) *c* (pl ~pen) gable

*geven (*gāy*-vern) *v* *give; ~ **om** mind

gevoel (ger-*vōōl*) *nt* feeling; sensation

gevoelig (ger-*vōō*-lerkh) *adj* sensitive

gevoelloos (ger-*vōō*-lōass) *adj* numb

gevogelte (ger-*vōa*-gerl-ter) *nt* fowl; poultry

gevolg (ger-*volkh*) *nt* (pl ~en) result, consequence; issue, effect; **ten gevolge van** owing to

gevolgtrekking (ger-*volkh*-treh-kıng) *c* (pl ~en) conclusion

gevorderd (ger-*vor*-derrt) *adj* advanced

gevuld (ger-*verlt*) *adj* stuffed

gewaad (ger-*vaat*) *nt* (pl gewaden) robe

gewaagd (ger-*vaakht*) *adj* risky

gewaarwording (ger-*vaar*-vor-dıng) *c* (pl ~en) perception; sensation

gewapend (ger-*vaa*-pernt) *adj* armed

geweer (ger-*vāyr*) *nt* (pl geweren) rifle, gun

geweld (ger-*vehlt*) *nt* violence; force

gewelddaad (ger-*vehl*-daat) *c* (pl -daden) outrage

gewelddadig (ger-vehl-*daa*-derkh) *adj* violent

geweldig (ger-vehl-*derkh*) *adj* terrific; huge

gewelf (ger-*vehlf*) nt (pl gewelven) arch, vault

gewend (ger-*vehnt*) adj accustomed

gewest (ger-*vehst*) nt (pl ~en) province

geweten (ger-*vay*-tern) nt conscience

gewicht (ger-*vikht*) nt (pl ~en) weight

gewichtig (ger-*vikh*-terkh) adj important; big

gewillig (ger-*vi*-lerkh) adj co-operative

gewond (ger-*vont*) adj injured

gewoon (ger-*voan*) adj normal, ordinary; common, regular, plain, simple; customary, habitual; accustomed; ~ **zijn** *be used to; would

gewoonlijk (ger-*voan*-lerk) adj customary; adv as a rule, usually

gewoonte (ger-*voan*-ter) c (pl ~n, ~s) habit; custom

gewoonweg (ger-*voan*-vehkh) adv simply

gewricht (ger-*vrikht*) nt (pl ~en) joint

gezag (ger-*zahkh*) nt authority

gezagvoerder (ger-*zahkh*-foor-derr) m (pl ~s) captain

gezamenlijk (ger-*zaa*-mer-lerk) adj joint; adv jointly

gezang (ger-*zahng*) nt (pl ~en) hymn

gezant (ger-*zahnt*) m (f ~e, pl ~en) envoy

gezellig (ger-*zeh*-lerkh) adj cosy

gezelschap (ger-*zehl*-skhahp) nt (pl ~pen) company; society

gezet (ger-*zeht*) adj corpulent; stout

gezicht (ger-*zikht*) nt (pl ~en) face; sight

gezichtscrème (ger-*zikhts*-kraim) c (pl ~s) face cream

gezichtsmassage (ger-*zikhts*-mah-saa-zher) c (pl ~s) face massage

gezichtspoeder (ger-*zikhts*-poo-derr) nt/c (pl ~s) face-powder

gezien (ger-*zeen*) prep considering

gezin (ger-*zin*) nt (pl ~nen) family

gezond (ger-*zont*) adj healthy; well; wholesome

gezondheid (ger-*zont*-hayt) c health

gezondheidsattest (ger-*zont*-hayts-ah-tehst) nt (pl ~en) health certificate

gezwel (ger-*zvehl*) nt (pl ~len) tumo(u)r, growth

gids (gits) c (pl ~en) guide; guidebook

giechelen (*gee*-kher-lern) v giggle

gier (geer) c (pl ~en) vulture

gierig (*gee*-rerkh) adj stingy

***gieten** (*gee*-tern) v pour

gietijzer (*gee*-tay-zerr) nt cast iron

gift (gift) c (pl ~en) donation

giftig (*gif*-terkh) adj poisonous

gijzelaar (*gay*-zer-laar) m (f ~ster, pl ~s) hostage

gil (gil) c (pl ~len) scream, yell, shriek

gillen (*gi*-lern) v scream, yell, shriek

ginds (gins) adv over there

gips (gips) nt plaster

gissen (*gi*-sern) v guess

gissing (*gi*-sing) c (pl ~en) guess

gist (gist) c yeast

gisten (*giss*-tern) v ferment

gisteren (*giss*-ter-rern) adv yesterday

gitaar (gee-*taar*) c (pl -taren) guitar

glad (glaht) adj slippery; smooth

glans (glahns) c gloss

glanzen (*glahn*-zern) v *shine; **glanzend** glossy

glas (glahss) nt (pl glazen) glass; **gebrandschilderd** ~ stained glass

glazen (*glaa*-zern) adj glass

gletsjer (*gleht*-sherr) c (pl ~s) glacier

gleuf (glurf) c (pl gleuven) slot

glibberig (*gli*-ber-rerkh) adj slippery

glijbaan (*glay*-baan) c (pl -banen) slide

***glijden** (*glay*-dern) v glide, *slide

glimlach (*glim*-lahkh) c smile

glimlachen (*glim*-lah-khern) v smile

glimp (glimp) c glimpse

globaal (gloa-*baal*) adj broad

gloed (gloot) c glow

gloeien (*gloo*ee-ern) v glow

gloeilamp (*gloo͞oee*-lahmp) *c* (pl ~en) light bulb

glooien (*gloa͞ee*-ern) *v* slope

glooiing (*gloa͞ee*-ing) *c* (pl ~en) ramp

glorie (*gloa͞a*-ree) *c* glory

gluren (*glew*-rern) *v* peep

god (got) *m* (pl ~en) god

goddelijk (*go*-der-lerk) *adj* divine

godin (*goa͞a*-dın) *f* (pl ~nen) goddess

godsdienst (*gots*-deenst) *c* (pl ~en) religion

godsdienstig (gots-*deen*-sterkh) *adj* religious

goed (goo͞ot) *adj* good; right, correct; kind; *adv* well; **goed!** all right!

goederen (*goo͞o*-der-rern) *pl* goods *pl*

goederentrein (*goo͞o*-der-rern-trayn) *c* (pl ~en) goods train; freight train *nAm*

goedgelovig (goo͞ot-kher-*loa͞a*-verkh) *adj* credulous

goedgeluimd (goo͞ot-kher-*lurᵍᵂ* mt) *adj* good-tempered

goedgestemd (goo͞ot-kher-*stehmt*) *adj* good-tempered; in a good mood

goedhartig (goo͞ot-*hahr*-terkh) *adj* good-natured

goedkeuren (*goo͞ot*-kūr-rern) *v* approve

goedkeuring (*goo͞ot*-kur-rng) *c* (pl ~en) approval

goedkoop (goo͞ot-*koa͞ap*) *adj* cheap; inexpensive

gok (gok) *c* chance

golf¹ (golf) *c* (pl golven) wave; gulf

golf² (golf) *nt* golf

golfbaan (*golf*-baan) *c* (pl -banen) golf links; golf course

golfclub (*golf*-klerp) *c* (pl ~s) golfclub

golflengte (*golf*-lehng-ter) *c* (pl ~n, ~s) wavelength

golvend (*gol*-vernt) *adj* wavy

gom (gom) *c/nt* (pl ~men) eraser; gum

gondel (*gon*-derl) *c* (pl ~s) gondola

goochelaar (*goa͞a*-kher-laar) *m* (f~ster, pl ~s) magician

goochelen (*goa͞a*-kher-lern) *v* *do magic; juggle

gooi (goa͞aee) *c* (pl ~en) throw

gooien (*goa͞aee*-ern) *v* *throw; *cast; toss

goot (goa͞at) *c* (pl goten) gutter

gootsteen (*goa͞at*-staȳn) *c* (pl -stenen) sink

gordijn (gor-*dayn*) *nt* (pl ~en) curtain, *nAm* drape

gorgelen (*gor*-ger-lern) *v* gargle

goud (gout) *nt* gold

gouden (*gou*-dern) *adj* golden

goudmijn (*gout*-mayn) *c* (pl ~en) goldmine

goudsmid (*gout*-smıt) *m* (pl -smeden) goldsmith

gouvernante (goo͞o-verr-*nahn*-ter) *f* (pl ~s) governess

gouverneur (goo͞o-verr-*nūr̄r*) *m* (pl ~s) governor

graad (graat) *c* (pl graden) degree; grade

graaf (graaf) *m* (pl graven) count; earl

graafschap (*graaf*-skhahp) *nt* (pl ~pen) county

graag (graakh) *adv* gladly, willingly

graan (graan) *nt* (pl granen) corn, grain

graat (graat) *c* (pl graten) bone, fishbone

gracht (grahkht) *c* (pl ~en) canal; moat

graf (grahf) *nt* (pl graven) grave; tomb

grafiek (graa-*feek*) *c* (pl ~en) graph, diagram; chart

grafisch (*graa*-feess) *adj* graphic

grafsteen (*grahf*-staȳn) *c* (pl -stenen) tombstone, gravestone

gram (grahm) *nt* (pl ~men) gram

grammatica (grah-*maa*-tee-kaa) *c* grammar

grammaticaal (grah-maa-tee-*kaal*) *adj* grammatical

grammofoonplaat (grah-moa͞a-*foa͞an*-plaat) *c* (pl -platen) disc, record

graniet (graa-*neet*) *nt* granite

grap (grahp) c (pl ~pen) joke
grappig (grah-perkh) adj funny,
humorous
gras (grahss) nt grass
grasspriet (grahss-spreet) c (pl ~en)
blade of grass
grasveld (grahss-fehlt) nt (pl ~en) lawn
gratie (graa-tsee) c grace; pardon
gratis (graa-terss) adv free of charge,
free, gratis
grauw (grou) adj grey
*graven (graa-vern) v *dig
graveren (graa-vay-rern) v engrave
graveur (graa-vūrr) c (pl ~s) engraver
gravin (graa-vın) f (pl ~nen) countess
gravure (graa-vēw-rer) c (pl ~s, ~n)
engraving
grazen (graa-zern) v graze
greep (grayp) c (pl grepen) grip; grasp,
clutch, grab
grendel (grehn-derl) c (pl ~s) bolt
grens (grehns) c (pl grenzen) frontier,
border; boundary, bound
grenzeloos (grehn-zer-lōass) adj
unlimited
grenzen (grehn-zern) v border (on),
adjoin; verge
greppel (greh-perl) c (pl ~s) ditch
Griek (greek) m (f ~se, pl ~en) Greek
Griekenland (gree-kern-lahnt)
Greece
Grieks (greeks) adj Greek
griep (greep) c flu, influenza
griet (greet) c (pl ~en) brill; vulgar
chick, bird
griezelig (gree-zer-lerkh) adj scary,
creepy
grijns (grayns) c grin
grijnzen (grayn-zern) v grin
*grijpen (gray-pern) v *catch, grip,
grasp, seize
grijs (grayss) adj grey
gril (grıl) c (pl ~len) whim, fancy
grimmig (grı-merkh) adj grim

grind (grınt) nt gravel
grinniken (grı-ner-kern) v chuckle
groef (grōōf) c (pl groeven) groove
groei (grōō⁽ᵉᵉ⁾) c growth
groeien (grōō⁽ᵉᵉ⁾-ern) v *grow
groen (grōōn) adj green
groente c (pl ~n, ~s) vegetable,
vegetables
groenteboer (grōōn-ter-bōōr) m (pl
~en) greengrocer; vegetable merchant
groep (grōōp) c (pl ~en) group; bunch,
set, party
groet (grōōt) c (pl ~en) greeting; **met
vriendelijke ~** kind regards
groeten (grōō-tern) v greet; salute; say
hello to
groeve (grōō-ver) c (pl ~n) pit
grof (grof) adj gross, coarse; rude
grommen (gro-mern) v growl
grond (gront) c ground; earth, soil;
begane ~ ground floor
grondbeginselen (gront-ber-gın-ser-
lern) c basics
grondig (gron-derkh) adj thorough
grondslag (gront-slahkh) c (pl ~en)
basis, base
grondstof (gront-stof) c (pl ~fen) raw
material
grondwet (gront-veht) c (pl ~ten)
constitution
groot (grōōt) adj big; great, large, tall;
major; **grootst** major, main; **groter**
major; superior
*grootbrengen (grōōt-breh-ngern) v
*bring up, raise; rear
Groot-Brittannië (grōōt-brı-tah-
nee-ʸer) Great Britain
groothandel (grōōt-hahn-derl) c
wholesale
grootmoeder (grōōt-mōō-derr) f (pl
~s) grandmother
grootouders (grōōt-ou-derrs) pl
grandparents pl
groots (grōōts) adj grand, superb,

magnificent

grootte (*grōā*-ter) *c* (pl ~n, ~s) size

grootvader (*grōāt*-faa-derr) *m* (pl ~s) grandfather

gros (gross) *nt* (pl ~sen) gross

grossier (gro-*seer*) *m* (pl ~s) wholesale dealer

grot (grot) *c* (pl ~ten) cave; grotto

gruis (grur^ew^ss) *nt* grit

gruwelijk (*grēw*-ver-lerk) *adj* horrible

GSM (gāy-ehs-*ehm*) *c* mobile phone

gul (gerl) *adj* generous

gulheid (*gerl*-hayt) *c* generosity

gulp (gerlp) *c* (pl ~en) fly

gulzig (*gerl*-zerkh) *adj* greedy

gunnen (*ger*-nern) *v* grant

gunst (gernst) *c* (pl ~en) favo(u)r

gunstig (*gern*-sterkh) *adj* favo(u)rable

guur (gēwr) *adj* bleak

gymnast (gɪm-*nahst*) *c* (pl ~en) gymnast

gymnastiek (gɪm-nahss-*teek*) *c* gymnastics *pl*

gymnastiekbroek (gɪm-nahss-*teek*-brōōk) *c* (pl ~en) trunks *pl*

gymnastiekzaal (gɪm-nahss-*teek*-saal) *c* (pl -zalen) gymnasium

gymschoenen (*gɪm*-skhōō-nern) *pl* gym shoes, plimsolls *pl*; sneakers *plAm*

gynaecoloog (gee-nāy-kōā-*lōākh*) *m* (f -loge, pl -logen) gynaecologist

H

haai (haa^ee^) *c* (pl ~en) shark

haak (haak) *c* (pl haken) hook; **tussen twee haakjes** by the way

haalbaar (*haal*-baar) *adj* attainable, realizable, feasible

haan (haan) *m* (pl hanen) cock

haar[1] (haar) *nt* (pl haren) hair

haar[2] (haar) *pron* her, its

haarborstel (*haar*-bor-sterl) *c* (pl ~s) hairbrush

haarcrème (*haar*-kraim) *c* (pl ~s) hair cream

haard (haart) *c* (pl ~en) hearth, fireplace

haardroger (*haar*-drōā-gerr) *c* (pl ~s) hairdryer

haargel (*haar*-zhel) *c* hair gel

haarlak (*haar*-lahk) *c* (pl ~ken) hair spray

haarnetje (*haar*-neh-t^y^er) *nt* (pl ~s) hair net

haarspeld (*haar*-spehlt) *c* (pl ~en)

hairpin, hairgrip; bobby pin *Am*

haarstukje (*haar*-ster-k^y^er) *nt* (pl ~s) hair piece

haarversteviger (*haar*-verr-stāy-ver-gerr) *c* setting lotion

haas (haass) *c* (pl hazen) hare

haast[1] (haast) *adv* nearly, almost

haast[2] (haast) *c* haste, hurry

haasten (*haass*-tern): **zich ~** hasten, rush, hurry

haastig (*haass*-terkh) *adj* hasty; *adv* in a hurry

haat (haat) *c* hatred, hate

hachelijk (*hah*-kher-lerk) *adj* precarious, critical

hagedis (haa-ger-dɪs) *c* (pl ~sen) lizard

hagel (*haa*-gerl) *c* hail

hak (hahk) *c* (pl ~ken) heel

haken (*haa*-kern) *v* crochet

hakken (*hah*-kern) *v* chop

hal (hahl) *c* (pl ~len) lobby, hall

halen (*haa*-lern) *v* *get, fetch; *make;

*catch; ***laten** ~ *send for

half (hahlf) *adj* half; semi-; *adv* half

hallo! (hah-*lōa*) hello!

hals (hahls) *c* (pl halzen) throat; neck

halsband (*hahls*-bahnt) *c* (pl ~en) collar

halsketting (*hahls*-keh-tɪng) *c* (pl ~en) necklace

halt! (hahlt) stop!

halte (*hahl*-ter) *c* (pl ~n, ~s) stop

halveren (hahl-*vāy*-rern) *v* halve

halverwege (*hahl*-verr-vāy-ger) *adv* halfway

ham (hahm) *c* (pl ~men) ham

hamburger (*hahm*-berr-gerr) *c* (pl ~s) hamburger, beefburger

hamer (*haa*-merr) *c* (pl ~s) hammer; **houten** ~ mallet

hand (hahnt) *c* (pl ~en) hand; **hand**-manual; **met de** ~ **gemaakt** handmade

handbagage (*hahnt*-bah-gaa-zher) *c* hand luggage; hand baggage *Am*

handboeien (*hahnt*-bōō^ee^-ern) *pl* handcuffs *pl*

handboek (*hahnt*-bōōk) *nt* (pl ~en) handbook, manual

handcrème (*hahnt*-kraim) *c* (pl ~s) hand cream

handdoek (*hahn*-dōōk) *c* (pl ~en) towel

handdruk (*hahn*-drerk) *c* handshake

handel (*hahn*-derl) *c* commerce, trade; business; ~ ***drijven** trade; **handels**-commercial

handelaar (*hahn*-der-laar) *m* (f ~ster, pl ~s, -laren) tradesman, merchant; dealer, trader

handelen (*hahn*-der-lern) *v* act

handeling (*hahn*-der-lɪng) *c* (pl ~en) action; deed, plot

handelsmerk (*hahn*-derls-mehrk) *nt* (pl ~en) trademark

handelsrecht (*hahn*-derls-rehkht) *nt* commercial law

handelswaar (*hahn*-derls-vaar) *c* merchandise

handenarbeid (*hahn*-der-nahr-bayt) *c* handicraft

handhaven (*hahnt*-haa-vern) *v* maintain

handig (*hahn*-derkh) *adj* handy

handicap (*hehn*-dɪ-kehp) *c* handicap

handpalm (*hahnt*-pahlm) *c* (pl ~en) palm

handrem (*hahnt*-rehm) *c* (pl ~men) handbrake

handschoen (*hahnt*-skhōōn) *c* (pl ~en) glove

handschrift (*hahnt*-skhrɪft) *nt* (pl ~en) handwriting

handtas (*hahn*-tahss) *c* (pl ~sen) handbag, bag

handtekening (*hahnt*-tāy-ker-nɪng) *v* (pl ~en) signature

handvat (*hahnt*-faht) *nt* (pl ~ten) handle

handvol (*hahnt*-fol) *c* handful

handwerk (*hahnt*-vehrk) *nt* handwork, handicraft; needlework

hangbrug (*hahng*-brerkh) *c* (pl ~gen) suspension bridge

*hangen (*hah*-ngern) *v* *hang

hangmat (*hahng*-maht) *c* (pl ~ten) hammock

hangslot (*hahng*-slot) *nt* (pl ~en) padlock

hanteerbaar (hahn-*tāy*r-baar) *adj* manageable

hanteren (hahn-*tāy*-rern) *v* handle

hap (hahp) *c* (pl ~pen) bite

hard (hahrt) *adj* hard; loud

harddraverij (hahr-draa-ver-*ray*) *c* (pl ~en) horserace

hardnekkig (hahrt-*neh*-kerkh) *adj* obstinate, dogged, stubborn

hardop (hahrt-*op*) *adv* aloud

harig (*haa*-rerkh) *adj* hairy

haring (*haa*-rıng) *c* (pl ~en) herring

hark (hahrk) *c* (pl ~en) rake

harmonie (hahr-*mōa*-*nee*) *c* harmony

harnas (*hahr*-nahss) *nt* (pl ~sen) armour

harp (hahrp) *c* (pl ~en) harp

hars (hahrs) *nt/c* resin

hart (hahrt) *nt* (pl ~en) heart

hartaanval (*hahr*-taan-vahl) *c* (pl ~len) heart attack

hartelijk (*hahr*-ter-lerk) *adj* hearty, cordial; sympathetic

harteloos (*hahr*-ter-lōass) *adj* heartless

hartklopping (*hahrt*-klo-pıng) *c* (pl ~en) palpitation

hartstocht (*hahrts*-tokht) *c* passion

hartstochtelijk (hahrts-*tokh*-ter-lerk) *adj* passionate

hatelijk (*haa*-ter-lerk) *adj* spiteful

haten (*haa*-tern) *v* hate

haven (*haa*-vern) *c* (pl ~s) port, harbour

havenarbeider (*haa*-vern-ahr-bay-derr) *m* (pl ~s) docker

haver (*haa*-verr) *c* oats *pl*

havik (*haa*-vık) *c* (pl ~en) hawk

hazelnoot (*haa*-zerl-nōat) *c* (pl -noten) hazelnut

hazewind (haa-zer-*vınt*) *c* (pl ~en) greyhound

*****hebben** (*heh*-bern) *v* *have

Hebreeuws (hāy-*brāy*^{oo}ss) *nt* Hebrew

hebzucht (*hehp*-serkht) *c* greed

hebzuchtig (hehp-*serkh*-terkh) *adj* greedy

hechten (*hehkh*-tern) *v* attach; sew up; ~ **aan** attach to

hechtenis (*hehkh*-ter-nıss) *c* custody

hechting (*hehkh*-tıng) *c* (pl ~en) stitch

hechtpleister (*hehkht*-play-sterr) *c* (pl ~s) adhesive tape

heden (*hāy*-dern) *nt* present

hedendaags (*hāy*-dern-daakhs) *adj* contemporary

heel (hāyl) *adj* entire, whole; unbroken; *adv* quite

heelal (hāy-*lahl*) *nt* universe, space

heelhuids (*hāyl*-hur^{ew}ts) *adj* unhurt

*****heengaan** (*hāyng*-gaan) *v* depart

heer (hāyr) *m* (pl heren) gentleman; lord

heerlijk (*hāyr*-lerk) *adj* lovely, wonderful; delightful, delicious

heerschappij (hāyr-skhah-*pay*) *c* (pl ~en) rule; dominion

heersen (*hāyr*-sern) *v* rule

heerser (*hāyr*-serr) *m* (f~es, pl~s) ruler

hees (hāyss) *adj* hoarse

heet (hāyt) *adj* hot; warm

hefboom (*hehf*-bōam) *c* (pl -bomen) lever

*****heffen** (*heh*-fern) *v* raise

heftig (*hehf*-terkh) *adj* violent

heg (hehkh) *c* (pl ~gen) hedge

heide (*hay*-der) *c* (pl ~n) heath; moor; heather

heiden (*hay*-dern) *c* (pl ~en) heathen, pagan

heidens (*hay*-derns) *adj* heathen, pagan

heiig (*hay*-erkh) *adj* hazy

heilbot (*hayl*-bot) *c* (pl ~ten) halibut

heilig (*hay*-lerkh) *adj* holy, sacred

heiligdom (*hay*-lerkh-dom) *nt* (pl ~men) shrine

heilige (*hay*-ler-ger) *c* (pl ~n) saint

heiligschennis (*hay*-lerkh-skheh-nerss) *c* sacrilege

heimwee (*haym*-vāy) *nt* homesickness

hek (hehk) *nt* (pl ~ken) fence; gate; railing

hekel (*hāy*-kerl) *c* dislike; **een ~ *hebben aan** hate, dislike

heks (hehks) *f* (pl ~en) witch

hel (hehl) *c* hell

helaas (hāy-*laass*) *adv* unfortunately

held (hehlt) *m* (pl ~en) hero

helder (*hehl*-derr) *adj* clear; serene;

bright

helderziend (hehl-derr-*zeent*) *adj*
psychic

heleboel (hāy-ler-*bool*) *c* plenty

helemaal (*hāy*-ler-maal) *adv* entirely,
altogether, completely, wholly; quite;
at all

helft (hehlft) *c* (pl ~en) half

helicopter (hāy-lı-kop-terr) *c* (pl ~s)
helicopter

hellen (*heh*-lern) *v* slant; **hellend**
slanting

helling (*heh*-lıng) *c* (pl ~en) slope;
hillside; gradient, incline

helm (hehlm) *c* (pl ~en) helmet

helpen (*hehl*-pern) *v* help; assist, aid

helper (*hehl*-perr) *c* (pl ~s) helper

hem (hehm) *pron* him

hemd (hehmt) *nt* (pl ~en) shirt; vest;
undershirt

hemel (*hāy*-merl) *c* (pl ~s, ~en) sky;
heaven

hen¹ (hehn) *pron* them

hen² (hehn) *f* (pl ~nen) hen

hendel (*hehn*-derl) *c* (pl ~s) lever

hengel (*heh*-ngerl) *c* (pl ~s) fishing rod

hengelen (*heh*-nger-lern) *v* angle, fish

hennep (*heh*-nerp) *c* hemp

herberg (*hehr*-behrkh) *c* (pl ~en)
hostel, tavern, inn

herbergen (*hehr*-behr-gern) *v* lodge

herdenking (hehr-*dehng*-kıng) *c* (pl
~en) commemoration

herder (*hehr*-derr) *m* (f ~in, pl ~s)
shepherd

herenhuis (*hāy*-rern-hur^(ew)ss) *nt* (pl
-huizen) mansion, manor house

herenigen (heh-*rāy*-ner-gern) *v*
reunite

herentoilet (*hāy*-rern-tvah-leht) *nt* (pl
~ten) men's room

herfst (hehrfst) *c* autumn; fall *nAm*

herhalen (hehr-*haa*-lern) *v* repeat

herhaling (hehr-*haa*-lıng) *c* (pl ~en)

repetition

herinneren (heh-*rı*-ner-rern) *v*
remind; **zich ~** remember, recollect,
recall

herinnering (heh-*rı*-ner-rıng) *c* (pl
~en) memory; remembrance

herkennen (hehr-*keh*-nern) *v*
recognize

herkomst (*hehr*-komst) *c* origin

hernia (*hehr*-nee-ᵛaa) *c* slipped disc

herrie (*heh*-ree) *c* noise; fuss

herroepen (heh-*roo*-pern) *v* recall

hersenen (*hehr*-ser-nern) *pl* brain

hersenschudding (*hehr*-sern-skher-
dıng) *c* (pl ~en) concussion

herstel (hehr-*stehl*) *nt* repair; recovery;
revival

herstellen (hehr-*steh*-lern) *v* repair,
mend; **zich ~** recover

hert (hehrt) *nt* (pl ~en) deer

hertog (*hehr*-tokh) *m* (pl ~en) duke

hertogin (hehr-*tōa*-gın) *f* (pl ~nen)
duchess

hervatten (hehr-*vah*-tern) *v* resume,
recommence

herzien (hehr-*zeen*) *v* revise

herziening (hehr-*zee*-nıng) *c* (pl ~en)
revision

het (heht, ert) *art* the; *pron* it

heten (*hāy*-tern) *v* *be called

heteroseksueel (hāy-ter-rōa-sehk-
sēw-*vāyl*) *adj* heterosexual

hetzij ... hetzij (heht-*say*) either ... or

heup (hūrp) *c* (pl ~en) hip

heuvel (*hūr*-verl) *c* (pl ~s) hill; mound

heuvelachtig (*hūr*-ver-lahkh-terkh)
adj hilly

heuveltop (*hūr*-verl-top) *c* (pl ~pen)
hilltop

hevig (*hāy*-verkh) *adj* severe, violent;
intense

hiel (heel) *c* (pl ~en) heel

hier (heer) *adv* here

hiërarchie (hee-ᵛer-rahr-*khee*) *c* (

hij (hay) *pron* he

hijgen (*hay*-gern) *v* pant

*hijsen (*hay*-sern) *v* hoist

hijskraan (*hayss*-kraan) *c* (pl -kranen) crane

hik (hık) *c* hiccup

hinderen (*hın*-der-rern) *v* hinder, inhibit; bother

hinderlaag (*hın*-derr-laakh) *c* (pl -lagen) ambush

hinderlijk (*hın*-derr-lerk) *adj* annoying

hindernis (*hın*-derr-nıss) *c* (pl ~sen) obstacle

hinken (*hıng*-kern) *v* limp

hint (hınt) *c* (pl ~s) hint

historisch (hee-*stōā*-reess) *adj* historic

hit (hıt) *c* hit

hitte (*hı*-ter) *c* heat

hobbelig (*ho*-ber-lerkh) *adj* bumpy

hobbelpaard (*ho*-berl-paart) *nt* (pl ~en) hobbyhorse

hobby (*ho*-bee) *c* (pl ~'s) hobby

hoe (hōō) *adv* how; ~ ... **hoe** the ... the; ~ **dan ook** anyhow, any way; at any rate

hoed (hōōt) *c* (pl ~en) hat

hoede (*hōō*-der) *c* custody

hoeden (*hōō*-dern): **zich ~** beware

hoef (hōōf) *c* (pl hoeven) hoof

hoefijzer (*hōōf*-ay-zerr) *nt* (pl ~s) horseshoe

hoek (hōōk) *c* (pl ~en) corner; angle

hoer (hōōr) *c* (pl ~en) whore

hoes (hōōss) *c* (pl hoezen) sleeve

hoest (hōōst) *c* cough

hoesten (*hōōss*-tern) *v* cough

hoeveel (hōō-*vāyl*) *pron* how much; how many

hoeveelheid (*hōō*-*vāyl*-hayt) *c* (pl -heden) quantity; amount

hoeven (*hōō*-vern) *v* need

hoewel (hōō-*vehl*) *conj* although, though

hof (hof) *nt* (pl hoven) court

hoffelijk (*ho*-fer-lerk) *adj* courteous

hokje (*ho*-kʸer) *nt* (pl ~s) booth

hol¹ (hol) *nt* (pl ~en) den; cavern

hol² (hol) *adj* hollow

Holland (*ho*-lahnt) Holland

Hollander (*ho*-lahn-derr) *m* (pl ~s) Dutchman

Hollands (*ho*-lahnts) *adj* Dutch

Hollandse (*ho*-lahnt-ser) *f* (pl ~n) Dutch woman

holte (*hol*-ter) *c* (pl ~s, ~n) cavity

homoseksueel (hōā-mōā-sehk-*sēw*-vāyl) *adj* homosexual, *colloquial* gay

hond (hont) *c* (pl ~en) dog

hondehok (*hon*-der-hok) *nt* (pl ~ken) kennel

honderd (*hon*-derrt) *num* hundred

hondsdolheid (honts-*dol*-hayt) *c* rabies

Hongaar (hong-*gaar*) *m* (f ~se, pl -garen) Hungarian

Hongaars (hong-*gaars*) *adj* Hungarian

Hongarije (hong-gaa-*ray*-er) Hungary

honger (*ho*-ngerr) *c* hunger

hongerig (*ho*-nger-rerkh) *adj* hungry

honing (*hōā*-nıng) *c* honey

honkbal (*hongk*-bahl) *nt* baseball

honorarium (hōā-nōā-*raa*-ree-ʸerm) *nt* (pl -ria) fee

hoofd (hōāft) *nt* (pl ~en) head; **het ~ *bieden aan** face; **hoofd-** primary, main, chief; cardinal; capital; **over het ~ *zien** overlook; **uit het ~** by heart; **uit het ~ leren** memorize

hoofdkantoor (*hōāft*-kahn-tōār) *nt* (pl ~oren) headquarters *pl*

hoofdkussen (*hōāft*-ker-sern) *nt* (pl ~s) pillow

hoofdkwartier (*hōāft*-kvahr-teer) *nt* (pl ~en) headquarters *pl*

hoofdleiding (*hōāft*-lay-dıng) *c* (pl ~en) mains *pl*

hoofdletter (*hōāft*-leh-terr) *c* (pl ~s) capital letter

hoofdlijn (*hōāft*-layn) *c* (pl ~en) main line

hoofdpijn (*hōāft*-payn) *c* headache

hoofdstad (*hōāft*-staht) *c* (pl -steden) capital

hoofdstraat (*hōāft*-straat) *c* (pl -straten) main street, thoroughfare

hoofdweg (*hōāft*-vehkh) *c* (pl ~en) main road, thoroughfare; highway

hoofdzakelijk (*hōāft*-saa-ker-lerk) *adv* mainly

hoog (hōākh) *adj* high; tall; **hoger** upper; superior; **hoogst** foremost, extreme

hoogachtend (hōākh-*ahr*-ternt) *adj* yours sincerely

hooghartig (hōākh-*hahr*-terkh) *adj* haughty

hoogleraar (hōākh-*lāy*-raar) *m* (pl -leraren, ~s) professor

hoogmoedig (hōākh-*mōō*-derkh) *adj* proud

hoogseizoen (hōākh-say-*zōōn*) *nt* high season, peak season

hoogstens (*hōākh*-sterns) *adv* at most

hoogte (*hōākh*-ter) *c* (pl ~n, ~s) height; altitude

hoogtepunt (*hōākh*-ter-pernt) *nt* (pl ~en) height

hooguit (hōākh-ur^(ew)t) *adv* at most

hoogvlakte (*hōākh*-flahk-ter) *c* (pl ~n, ~s) uplands *pl*; plateau

hooi (hōā^(ee)) *nt* hay

hooikoorts (*hōā^(ee)*-kōārts) *c* hay fever

hoon (hōān) *c* scorn

hoop¹ (hōāp) *c* (pl hopen) heap, lot

hoop² (hōāp) *c* hope

hoopvol (*hōāp*-fol) *adj* hopeful

hoorbaar (*hōār*-baar) *adj* audible

hoorn (*hōā*-rern) *c* (pl ~en, ~s) horn

hoorzitting (*hōā*-r-zɪ-tɪng) *c* (pl ~en) hearing

hop (hop) *c* hop

hopeloos (*hōā*-per-lōāss) *adj* hopeless

hopen (*hōā*-pern) *v* hope

horen (*hōā*-rern) *v* *hear

horizon (*hōā*-ree-zon) *c* horizon

horizontaal (hōā-ree-zon-*taal*) *adj* horizontal

horloge (hor-*lōā*-zher) *nt* (pl ~s) watch

horlogebandje (hor-*lōā*-zher-bahn-t^(y)er) *nt* (pl ~s) watchstrap

horlogemaker (hor-*lōā*-zher-maa-kerr) *m* (pl ~s) watchmaker

hors d'œuvre (awr-*dūr*-vrer) *c* (pl ~s) hors d'œuvre

hospes (*hoss*-perss) *m* (pl ~sen) landlord

hospita (*hoss*-pee-taa) *f* (pl ~'s) landlady

hospitaal (*hoss*-pee-taal) *nt* (pl -talen) hospital

hotel (hōā-*tehl*) *nt* (pl ~s) hotel

***houden** (hou-dern) *v* *hold; *keep; ~ van love; like, care for, *be fond of; **niet ~ van** dislike

houding (hou-dɪng) *c* (pl ~en) position; attitude

hout (hout) *nt* wood

houtblok (*hout*-blok) *nt* (pl ~ken) log

houten (*hou*-tern) *adj* wooden

houtskool (*houts*-kōāl) *c* charcoal

***houtsnijden** (*hout*-snay-dern) *v* carve

houtsnijwerk (*hout*-snay-vehrk) *nt* wood carving

houtzagerij (hout-saa-ger-*ray*) *c* (pl ~en) sawmill

houvast (hou-*vahst*) *nt* grip

huichelaar (hur^(ew)-kher-laar) *m* (f ~ster, pl ~s) hypocrite

huichelachtig (hur^(ew)-kherl-ahkh-terkh) *adj* hypocritical

huichelarij (hur^(ew)-kher-laa-*ray*) *c* hypocrisy

huichelen (hur^(ew)-kher-lern) *v* simulate

huid (hur^(ew)t) *c* (pl ~en) skin; hide

huidcrème (hur^(ew)t-kraim) *c* (pl ~s) skin

cream
huidig (*hur^{ew}*-derkh) *adj* current
huiduitslag (*hur^{ew}t*-ur^{ew}t-slahkh) *c* rash
huilen (*hur^{ew}*-lern) *v* cry, *weep
huis (hur^{ew}ss) *nt* (pl huizen) house; home; **naar ~** home
huisarts (*hur^{ew}ss*-ahrts) *c* (pl ~en) general practitioner
huisbaas (*hur^{ew}ss*-baass) *m* (pl -bazen) landlord
huisdier (*hur^{ew}ss*-deer) *nt* (pl ~en) pet; domestic animal
huiselijk (*hur^{ew}*-ser-lerk) *adj* domestic
huishouden (*hur^{ew}ss*-hou-dern) *nt* (pl ~s) household; housework, housekeeping
huishoudster (*hur^{ew}ss*-hout-sterr) *f* (pl ~s) housekeeper
huiskamer (*hur^{ew}ss*-kaa-merr) *c* (pl ~s) living room
huissleutel (*hur^{ew}*-slūr-terl) *c* (pl ~s) latchkey
huisvrouw (*hur^{ew}ss*-frou) *f* (pl ~en) housewife
huiswerk (*hur^{ew}ss*-vehrk) *nt* homework
huizenblok (*hur^{ew}*-zern-blok) *nt* (pl ~ken) house block *nAm*
hulde (*herl*-der) *c* tribute, homage
huldigen (*herl*-der-gern) *v* honour
hulp (herlp) *c* help; assistance, aid; **eerste ~** first aid; **eerste hulppost**
first aid post
hulpvaardig (herlp-*faar*-derkh) *adj* helpful
humeur (hew-*mūrr*) *nt* (pl ~en) mood
humor (*hēw*-mor) *c* humo(u)r
humoristisch (hēw-mōā-*rɪss*-teess) *adj* humorous
hun (hern) *pron* their
huppelen (*her*-per-lern) *v* hop, skip
huren (*hēw*-rern) *v* hire, rent; lease
hut (hert) *c* (pl ~ten) hut; cabin
huur (hēwr) *c* (pl huren) rent; **te ~** for hire
huurcontract (*hēwr*-kon-trahkt) *nt* (pl ~en) lease
huurder (*hēwr*-derr) *m* (f -ster, pl ~s) tenant
huurkoop (*hēwr*-kōāp) *c* hire purchase, *nAm* instal(l)ment plan
huwelijk (*hēw*-ver-lerk) *nt* (pl ~en) wedding, marriage
huwelijksreis (*hēw*-ver-lerks-rayss) *c* (pl -reizen) honeymoon
huwen (*hēw^{oo}*-ern) *v* marry
hygiëne (hee-gee-*'ay*-ner) *c* hygiene
hygiënisch (hee-gee-*'ay*-neess) *adj* hygienic
hypocriet (hee-pōā-*kreet*) *adj* hypocritical
hypotheek (hee-pōā-*tāyk*) *c* (pl -theken) mortgage
hysterisch (hee-*stāy*-reess) *adj* hysterical

I

ideaal[1] (ee-*dāy*-'aal) *adj* ideal
ideaal[2] (ee-dāy-*'aal*) *nt* (pl idealen) ideal
idee (ee-*dāy*) *nt/c* (pl ~ën, ~s) idea
identiek (ee-dehn-*teek*) *adj* identical
identificatie (ee-dehn-tee-fi-*kaa*-tsee) *c* identification
identificeren (ee-dehn-tee-fee-*sāy*-rern) *v* identify
identiteit (ee-dehn-ti-*tayt*) *c* identity

identiteitskaart (ee-dehn-tee-*tayts*-kaart) *c* (pl ~en) identity card, ID card

idiomatisch (ee-dee-*y͞oa-maa*-teess) *adj* idiomatic

idioom (ee-dee-*y͞oam*) *nt* (pl idiomen) idiom

idioot[1] (ee-dee-*ʾoat*) *adj* idiotic

idioot[2] (ee-dee-*ʾoat*) *c* (pl idioten) idiot

idool (ee-*doal*) *nt* (pl idolen) idol

ieder (*ee*-derr) *pron* each, every; everyone

iedereen (ee-der-*rayn*) *pron* everyone, everybody; anyone

iemand (*ee*-mahnt) *pron* someone, somebody

iep (eep) *c* (pl ~en) elm

Ier (eer) *m* (pl ~en) Irishman

Ierland (*eer*-lahnt) Ireland

Iers (eers) *adj* Irish

Ierse (*eer*-ser) *f* (pl ~n) Irishwoman

iets (eets) *pron* something; some

ijdel (*ay*-derl) *adj* vain; idle

ijs (ayss) *nt* ice; ice cream

ijsbaan (*ayss*-baan) *c* (pl -banen) skating rink

ijsje (*ay*-sher) *nt* (pl ~s) ice cream

ijskast (*ayss*-kahst) *c* (pl ~en) fridge, refrigerator

ijskoud (*ayss*-kout) *adj* freezing

IJsland (*ayss*-lahnt) Iceland

IJslander (*ayss*-lahn-derr) *c* (pl ~s) Icelander

IJslands (*ayss*-lahnts) *adj* Icelandic

ijswater (*ayss*-vaa-terr) *nt* iced water

ijver (*ay*-verr) *c* zeal; diligence

ijverig (*ay*-ver-rerkh) *adj* zealous; diligent

ijzer (*ay*-zerr) *nt* iron

ijzerdraad (*ay*-zerr-draat) *nt* wire

ijzeren (*ay*-zer-rern) *adj* iron

ijzerwaren (*ay*-zerr-vaa-rern) *pl* hardware

ik (ık) *pron* I; self

ikoon (ee-*k͞oan*) *c* (pl ikonen) icon

illegaal (ee-ler-*gaal*) *adj* illegal

illusie (ı-*lew*-zee) *c* (pl ~s) illusion

illustratie (ı-lew-*straa*-tsee) *c* (pl ~s) illustration

illustreren (ı-lew-*stray*-rern) *v* illustrate

imitatie (ee-mee-*taa*-tsee) *c* (pl ~s) imitation

imiteren (ee-mee-*tay*-rern) *v* imitate

immigrant (ı-mee-*grahnt*) *m* (f ~e, pl ~en) immigrant

immigratie (ı-mee-*graa*-tsee) *c* immigration

immigreren (ı-mee-*gray*-rern) *v* immigrate

immuniteit (ı-mew-nee-*tayt*) *c* immunity

impliceren (ım-plee-*say*-rern) *v* imply, involve

imponeren (ım-p͞oa-*nay*-rern) *v* impress

impopulair (ım-p͞oa-pew-*lair*) *adj* unpopular

import (*ım*-port) *c* import

importeren (ım-por-*tay*-rern) *v* import

importeur (ım-por-*turr*) *c* (pl ~s) importer

impotent (ım-p͞oa-*tehnt*) *adj* impotent

impotentie (ım-p͞oa-*tehn*-see) *c* impotence

improviseren (ım-pr͞oa-vee-*say*-rern) *v* improvise

impuls (ım-*perls*) *c* (pl ~en) impulse

impulsief (ım-perl-*zeef*) *adj* impulsive

in (ın) *prep* in; into, inside; at; *adv* trendy

inademen (*ın*-aa-der-mern) *v* inhale

inbegrepen (*ın*-ber-*gray*-pern) *adj* included; **alles** ~ all in

inboorling (*ım*-b͞oar-lıng) *m* (f ~e, pl ~en) native

***inbreken** (*ım*-bray-kern) *v* burgle

inbreker (*ım*-bray-kerr) *c* (pl ~s) burglar

incasseren (ıng-kah-*say*-rern) *v* cash

incident (ın-see-*dehnt*) *nt* (pl ⁓en)
incident

inclusief (ıng-klew-*zeef*) *adv* inclusive

incompleet (ıng-kom-*playt*) *adj*
incomplete

indelen (*ın*-day-lern) *v* classify

*****indenken** (*ın*-dehng-kern): **zich ⁓**
imagine

inderdaad (ın-derr-*daat*) *adv* indeed

index (*ın*-dehks) *c* (pl ⁓en) index

India (*ın*-dee-ʸah) India

Indiaan (ın-dee-ʸ*aan*) *m* (f ⁓se, pl
Indianen) Indian

Indiaans (ın-dee-ʸ*aans*) *adj* Indian

indien (ın-*deen*) *conj* in case, if

Indiër (*ın*-dee-ʸerr) *m* (f Indische, pl ⁓s)
Indian

indigestie (ın-dee-*gehss*-tee) *c*
indigestion

indirect (*ın*-dee-rehkt) *adj* indirect

Indisch (*ın*-deess) *adj* Indian

individu (ın-dee-vee-*dew*) *nt* (pl ⁓en,
⁓'s) individual

individueel (ın-dee-vee-dew-*vayl*) *adj*
individual

Indonesië (ın-dōa-*nay*-zee-ʸer)
Indonesia

Indonesiër (ın-dōa-*nay*-zee-ʸerr) *m* (f
Indonesische, pl ⁓s) Indonesian

Indonesisch (ın-dōa-*nay*-zeess) *adj*
Indonesian

indringer (*ın*-drı-ngerr) *m* (f -ster, pl
⁓s) trespasser

indruk (*ın*-drerk) *c* (pl ⁓ken)
impression; **⁓ maken op** impress

indrukken (*ın*-drer-kern) *v* press

indrukwekkend (ın-drerk-*veh*-kernt)
adj impressive, imposing

industrie (ın-derss-*tree*) *c* (pl ⁓ën)
industry

industrieel (ın-derss-tree-ʸ*ayl*) *adj*
industrial

industriegebied (ın-derss-*tree*-ger-
beet) *nt* (pl ⁓en) industrial area

ineens (ı-*nayns*) *adv* suddenly; at once

inenten (*ın*-ehn-tern) *v* vaccinate,
inoculate

inenting (*ın*-ehn-tıng) *c* (pl ⁓en)
vaccination, inoculation

infanterie (*ın*-fahn-ter-ree) *c* infantry

infectie (ın-*fehk*-see) *c* (pl ⁓s) infection

inferieur (ın-*fay*-ree-ʸ*urr*) *adj* inferior

inflatie (ın-*flaa*-tsee) *c* inflation

informatie (ın-for-*maa*-tsee) *c* (pl ⁓s)
information; enquiry; **⁓ *inwinnen** *v*
inquire

informatiebureau (ın-for-*maa*-tsee-
bew-rōa) *nt* (pl ⁓s) inquiry office

informeel (ın-for-*mayl*) *adj* informal

informeren (ın-for-*may*-rern) *v*
enquire; inform

infrarood (*ın*-fraa-rōat) *adj* infra-red

*****ingaan** (*ıng*-gaan) *v* enter; *take effect

ingang (*ıng*-gahng) *c* (pl ⁓en) entrance,
way in; entry; **met ⁓ van** as from

ingenieur (ın-zhern-ʸ*urr*) *c* (pl ⁓s)
engineer

ingenomen (*ıng*-ger-nōa-mern) *adj*
pleased

ingevolge (ıng-ger-*vol*-ger) *prep* in
accordance with

ingewanden (*ıng*-ger-vahn-dern) *pl*
bowels *pl*, intestines, insides

ingewikkeld (ıng-ger-vı-kerlt) *adj*
complicated; complex

ingrediënt (ıng-gray-dee-ʸ*ehnt*) *nt* (pl
⁓en) ingredient

*****ingrijpen** (*ıng*-gray-pern) *v* intervene

inhalen (*ın*-haa-lern) *v* *overtake; pass
vAm; **⁓ verboden** no overtaking; no
passing *Am*

inham (*ın*-hahm) *c* (pl ⁓men) creek,
inlet

inheems (ın-*hayms*) *adj* native

inhoud (*ın*-hout) *c* contents *pl*

*****inhouden** (*ın*-hou-dern) *v* contain;
imply; restrain

inhoudsopgave (*ın*-houts-op-khaa-ver) *c* (pl ∿n) table of contents

initiatief (ee-nee-shaa-*teef*) *nt* (pl -tieven) initiative

injectie (in-*y*ehk-see) *c* (pl ∿s) shot, injection

inkomen (ing-*kōā*-mern) *nt* (pl ∿s) revenue, income, living

inkomsten (ing-kom-stern) *pl* earnings *pl*

inkomstenbelasting (ing-kom-ster-ber-lahss-ting) *c* income tax

inkt (ingkt) *c* ink

inleiden (*in*-lay-dern) *v* introduce; **inleidend** preliminary

inleiding (*in*-lay-ding) *c* (pl ∿en) introduction

inlichten (*in*-likh-tern) *v* inform

inlichting (*in*-likh-ting) *c* (pl ∿en) information

inlichtingenkantoor (*in*-likh-ti-nger-kahn-*tōār*) *nt* (pl -toren) information bureau

inloggen (*in*-lo-gern) *v* log in

inmaken (*in*-maa-kern) *v* preserve

inmenging (*in*-mehng-ing) *c* (pl ∿en) interference

inmiddels (in-*mi*-derls) *adv* in the meantime

***innemen** (*i*-*nāy*-mern) *v* *take up; occupy; capture

inneming (*i*-*nāy*-ming) *c* capture

innen (*i*-nern) *v* cash

inpakken (*im*-pah-kern) *v* wrap; pack up, pack

inrichten (*in*-rikh-tern) *v* furnish; decorate

inrichting (*in*-rikh-ting) *c* (pl ∿en) institution

inschakelen (*in*-skhaa-ker-lern) *v* switch on; plug in

***inschenken** (*in*-skhehng-kern) *v* pour

inschepen (*in*-skh*āy*-pern) *v* embark

inscheping (*in*-skh*āy*-ping) *c* embarkation

***inschrijven** (*in*-skhray-vern) *v* enter, book; **zich ~** register, check in

inschrijvingsformulier (*in*-skhray-vings-for-m*ēw*-leer) *nt* (pl ∿en) registration form

inscriptie (in-*skrip*-see) *c* (pl ∿s) inscription

insekt (in-*sehkt*) *nt* (pl ∿en) insect; bug *nAm*

insekticide (in-sehk-tee-*see*-der) *c* (pl ∿n) insecticide

inslikken (*in*-sli-kern) *v* swallow

***insluiten** (*in*-slur*ew*-tern) *v* *shut in; encircle; include; enclose

inspanning (*in*-spah-ning) *c* (pl ∿en) strain, effort

inspecteren (in-spehk-*tāy*-rern) *v* inspect

inspecteur (in-spehk-*tūrr*) *m* (f -trice, pl ∿s) inspector

inspectie (in-*spehk*-see) *c* (pl ∿s) inspection

***inspuiten** (*in*-spur*ew*-tern) *v* inject

installatie (in-stah-*laa*-tsee) *c* (pl ∿s) installation, facilities

installeren (in-stah-*lāy*-rern) *v* install

instappen (*in*-stah-pern) *v* *get on; embark

instellen (*in*-steh-lern) *v* institute

instelling (*in*-steh-ling) *c* (pl ∿en) institution, institute

instemmen (*in*-steh-mern) *v* consent; **~ met** approve of

instemming (*in*-steh-ming) *c* approval, consent

instinct (in-*stingkt*) *nt* (pl ∿en) instinct

instituut (in-stee-*tēwt*) *nt* (pl -tuten) institute

instorten (*in*-stor-tern) *v* collapse

instructie (in-*strerk*-see) *c* (pl ∿s) direction

instrument (in-strew-*mehnt*) *nt* (pl ∿en) instrument

intact (in-*tahkt*) *adj* intact

integendeel (ın-*tay*-gern-dāyl) on the
contrary

integreren (ın-ter-*grāy*-rern) *v*
integrate

intellect (ın-ter-*lehkt*) *nt* intellect

intellectueel (ın-ter-lehk-tēw-*vāyl*) *adj*
intellectual

intelligent (ın-ter-lee-*gehnt*) *adj*
clever, intelligent

intelligentie (ın-ter-lee-*gehn*-see) *c*
intelligence

intens (ın-*tehns*) *adj* intense

interessant (ın-ter-rer-*sahnt*) *adj*
interesting

interesse (ın-ter-*reh*-ser) *c* interest

interesseren (ın-ter-reh-*sāy*-rern) *v*
interest

intermezzo (ın-terr-*mehd*-zōā) *nt* (pl
~'s) interlude

intern (ın-*tehrn*) *adj* internal; resident

internaat (ın-terr-*naat*) *nt* (pl -naten)
boarding school

internationaal (ın-terr-naht-shōā-
naal) *adj* international

Internet (*ın*-terr-net) *nt* Internet

interview (*ın*-terr-vyēw°°) *nt* interview

intiem (ın-*teem*) *adj* intimate

introduceren (ın-trōā-dēw-*sāy*-rern) *v*
introduce

intussen (ın-*ter*-sern) *adv* meanwhile

inval (*ın*-vahl) *c* (pl ~len) brain wave,
idea; raid, invasion

*invallen (*ın*-vah-lern) *v* invade

invalide[1] (ın-vaa-*lee*-der) *adj* disabled,
invalid

invalide[2] (ın-vaa-*lee*-der) *c* (pl ~n)
invalid

invasie (ın-*vaa*-zee) *c* (pl ~s) invasion

inventaris (ın-vehn-*taa*-rerss) *c* (pl
~sen) inventory

investeerder (ın-vehss-*tāyr*-derr) *m*
(pl ~s) investor

investeren (ın-vehss-*tāy*-rern) *v* invest

investering (ın-vehss-*tāy*-rıng) *c* (pl

~en) investment

inviteren (ın-vee-*tāy*-rern) *v* invite

invloed (*ın*-vlōōt) *c* (pl ~en) influence

invloedrijk (*ın*-vlōōt-rayk) *adj*
influential

invoegen (*ın*-vōō-gern) *v* insert

invoer (*ın*-vōōr) *c* import

invoeren (*ın*-vōō-rern) *v* introduce;
import

invoerrecht (*ın*-vōō-rehkht) *nt* (pl ~en)
duty, import duty

invullen (*ın*-ver-lern) *v* fill in; fill out
Am

inwendig (ın-*vehn*-derkh) *adj* inner;
internal

inwilligen (*ın*-vı-ler-gern) *v* grant

inwijden (*ın*-vay-dern) *v* initiate

inwoner (*ın*-vōā-nerr) *m* (f inwoonster,
pl ~s) inhabitant; resident

inzet (*ın*-zeht) *c* (pl ~ten) bet

inzetten (*ın*-zeh-tern) *v* launch

inzicht (*ın*-zıkht) *nt* (pl ~en) insight

*inzien (*ın*-zeen) *v* *see

Iraaks (ee-*raaks*) *adj* Iraqi

Iraans (ee-*raans*) *adj* Iranian

Irak (ee-*raak*) Iraq

Irakees (ee-raa-*kāyss*) *m* (pl -kezen)
Iraqi

Iran (ee-*raan*) Iran

Iraniër (ee-raa-nee-*y*err) *m* (pl ~s)
Iranian

ironie (ee-rōā-*nee*) *c* irony

ironisch (ee-*rōā*-neess) *adj* ironical

irriteren (ı-ree-*tāy*-rern) *v* annoy,
irritate

isolatie (ee-zōā-*laa*-tsee) *c* insulation;
isolation

isolator (ee-zōā-*laa*-tor) *c* (pl ~en, ~s)
insulator

isolement (ee-zōā-ler-*mehnt*) *nt*
isolation

isoleren (ee-zōā-*lāy*-rern) *v* insulate;
isolate

Israël (*ıss*-raa-ehl) Israel

Israëliër (ıss-raa-$\overline{ay}$-lee-^{y}err) *m* (pl ~s) Israeli

Israëlisch (ıss-raa-$\overline{ay}$-leess) *adj* Israeli

Italiaan (ee-taa-lee-^{y}aan) *c* (f ~se, pl -lianen) Italian

Italiaans (ee-taa-lee-^{y}aans) *adj* Italian

Italië (ee-*taa*-lee-^{y}er) Italy

ivoor (ee-$\overline{voo}$ar) *nt* ivory

J

ja (^{y}aa) yes

jaar (^{y}aar) *nt* (pl jaren) year

jaarboek (^{y}aar-b$\overline{oo}$k) *nt* (pl ~en) annual

jaargetijde (^{y}aar-ger-tay-der) *nt* (pl ~n) season

jaarlijks (^{y}aar-lerks) *adj* annual, yearly; *adv* per annum

jacht¹ (^{y}ahkht) *c* hunt; chase

jacht² (^{y}ahkht) *nt* (pl ~en) yacht

jachthuis (^{y}ahkht-hur^{ew}ss) *nt* (pl -huizen) lodge

jade (^{y}aa-der) *nt/c* jade

jagen (^{y}aa-gern) *v* hunt

jager (^{y}aa-gerr) *c* (pl ~s) hunter

jaloers (^{y}aa-l$\overline{oo}$rs) *adj* envious, jealous

jaloezie (^{y}aa-l$\overline{oo}$-zee) *c* (pl ~ën) jealousy, envy; blind

jam (zhehm) *c* jam, jelly

jammer! (^{y}ah-merr) what a pity!

janboel (^{y}ahn-b$\overline{oo}$l) *c* mess, shambles

janken (^{y}ahn-kern) *v* yelp; whine, whimper

januari (^{y}ah-n$\overline{ew}$-*vaa*-ree) January

Japan (^{y}aa-*pahn*) Japan

Japanner (^{y}aa-*pah*-nerr) *m* (pl ~s) Japanese

Japans (^{y}aa-*pahns*) *adj* Japanese

japon (^{y}aa-*pon*) *c* (pl ~nen) dress; gown

jargon (^{y}ahr-*gon*) *nt* slang

jarretelgordel (zhah-rer-*tehl*-gor-derl) *c* (pl ~s) garter belt *Am*

jas (^{y}ahss) *c* (pl ~sen) coat

jasje (^{y}ah-sher) *nt* (pl ~s) jacket

je (^{y}er) *pron* you; yourself; yourselves

jegens ($^y\overline{ay}$-gerns) *prep* towards

jeugd ($^y\overline{urk}$ht) *c* youth; childhood

jeugdherberg ($^y\overline{urk}$ht-hehr-behrkh) *c* (pl ~en) youth hostel

jeugdig ($^y\overline{urk}$h-derkh) *adj* juvenile

jeuk ($^y\overline{urk}$) *c* itch

jeuken ($^y\overline{ur}$-kern) *v* itch

jicht (^{y}ıkht) *c* gout

jij (^{y}ay) *pron* you

joch (^{y}okh) *nt* boy, lad

jodium ($^y\overline{oa}$-dee-^{y}erm) *nt* iodine

jong (^{y}ong) *adj* young; **jonger** junior; younger

jongen (^{y}o-ngern) *m* (pl ~s) boy; lad

jongleren (^{y}ong-*lay*-rern) *v* juggle

jood ($^y\overline{oa}$t) *m* (f jodin, pl joden) Jew

joods ($^y\overline{oa}$ts) *adj* Jewish

Jordaans (^{y}or-*daans*) *adj* Jordanian

Jordanië (^{y}or-*daa*-nee-^{y}er) Jordan

Jordaniër (^{y}or-*daa*-nee-^{y}err) *m* (pl ~s) Jordanian

jou (^{y}ou) *pron* you; **van ~** yours

journaal (zh$\overline{oo}$r-*naal*) *nt* news

journalist (zh$\overline{oo}$r-naa-*lıst*) *m* (f ~e, pl ~en) journalist

journalistiek (zh$\overline{oo}$r-naa-lıss-*teek*) *c* journalism

jouw (^{y}ou) *pron* your

jubileum ($^y\overline{ew}$-bee-*lay*-'erm) *nt* (pl ~s, -lea) jubilee

juffrouw (^{y}er-frou) *f* (pl ~en) miss

juichen (^{y}ur^{ew}-khern) *v* cheer

juist (^{y}ur^{ew}st) *adj* right, correct, just; proper, appropriate

juistheid (*'ur^{ew}st*-hayt) *c* correctness
juk (*'erk*) *nt* (pl ~ken) yoke
jukbeen (*'erk*-bayn) *nt* (pl ~deren, -benen) cheekbone
juli (*'ew*-lee) July
jullie (*'er*-lee) *pron* you; your; **van ~** yours
juni (*'ew*-nee) June
juridisch (Vew-*ree*-deess) *adj* legal

jurist (Vew-*rıst*) *m* (f ~e, pl ~en) lawyer
jurk (Verrk) *c* (pl ~en) frock, robe, dress
jury (*zhew*-ree) *c* (pl ~'s) jury
jus (zhew) *c* gravy
juweel (Vew-*vayl*) *nt* (pl -welen) jewel; gem; **juwelen** jewelry *Am*, jewellery
juwelier (Vew-ver-*leer*) *c* (pl ~s) jeweller

K

kaak (kaak) *c* (pl kaken) jaw
kaal (kaal) *adj* bald; naked, bare
kaap (kaap) *c* (pl kapen) cape
kaars (kaars) *c* (pl ~en) candle
kaart (kaart) *c* (pl ~en) map; card; **groene ~** green card
kaartenautomaat (*kaar*-tern-oa-toa-maat) *c* (pl -maten) ticket machine
kaartje (*kaar*-t^yer) *nt* (pl ~s) ticket
kaartjesautomaat (*kaar*-t^yers-oa-toa-maat) *c* (pl -maten) ticket machine
kaas (kaass) *c* (pl kazen) cheese
kabaal (kaa-*baal*) *nt* racket
kabel (*kaa*-berl) *c* (pl ~s) cable
kabeljauw (kah-berl-^you) *c* (pl ~en) cod
kabinet (kaa-bee-*neht*) *nt* (pl ~ten) cabinet
kachel (*kah*-kherl) *c* (pl ~s) heater; stove
kade (*kaa*-der) *c* (pl ~n) quay; embankment; dock, wharf
kader (*kaa*-derr) *nt* (pl ~s) cadre
kajuit (kaa-^yur^{ew}t) *c* (pl ~en) cabin
kak (kahk) *adj* posh
kaki (*kaa*-kee) *nt* khaki
kalender (kaa-*lehn*-derr) *c* (pl ~s) calendar
kalf (kahlf) *nt* (pl kalveren) calf

kalfsleer (*kahlfs*-layr) *nt* calf skin
kalfsvlees (*kahlfs*-flayss) *nt* veal
kalk (kahlk) *c* lime
kalkoen (kahl-*koon*) *m* (pl ~en) turkey
kalm (kahlm) *adj* calm; quiet, serene
kalmeren (kahl-*may*-rern) *v* calm down
kam (kahm) *c* (pl ~men) comb
kameel (kaa-*mayl*) *m* (pl kamelen) camel
kamer (*kaa*-merr) *c* (pl ~s) room; chamber
kameraad (kah-mer-*raat*) *m* (pl -raden) comrade
kamerbewoner (*kaa*-merr-ber-voa-nerr) *m* (pl ~s) lodger
kamerjas (*kaa*-merr-^yahss) *c* (pl ~sen) dressing gown
kamerlid (*kaa*-merr-lıt) *nt* (pl -leden) Member of Parliament
kamertemperatuur (*kaa*-merr-tehm-per-raa-tewr) *c* room temperature
kammen (*kah*-mern) *v* comb
kamp (kahmp) *nt* (pl ~en) camp
kampeerder (kahm-*payr*-derr) *m* (f -ster, pl ~s) camper
kampeerterrein (kahm-*payr*-teh-rayn) *nt* (pl ~en) camping site
kampeerwagen (kahm-*payr*-vaa-

gern) *c* (pl ~s) trailer *nAm*

kamperen (kahm-*pay*-rern) *v* camp

kampioen (kahm-pee-*yoon*) *m* (f ~e, pl ~en) champion

kan (kahn) *c* (pl ~nen) jug

kanaal (kaa-*naal*) *nt* (pl kanalen) canal; channel; **het Kanaal** English Channel

kanarie (kaa-*naa*-ree) *c* (pl ~s) canary

kandidaat (kahn-dee-*daat*) *m* (f -date, pl -daten) candidate

kaneel (kaa-*nayl*) *c* cinnamon

kangoeroe (*kahng*-ger-roo) *c* (pl ~s) kangaroo

kanker (*kahng*-kerr) *c* cancer

kano (*kaa*-noa) *c* (pl ~'s) canoe

kanon (kaa-*non*) *nt* (pl ~nen) gun

kans (kahns) *c* (pl ~en) chance; opportunity

kansel (*kahn*-serl) *c* (pl ~s) pulpit

kant¹ (kahnt) *c* (pl ~en) side; way; edge; **aan de andere ~ van** across

kant² (kahnt) *nt* lace

kantine (kahn-*tee*-ner) *c* (pl ~s) canteen

kantlijn (*kahnt*-layn) *c* (pl ~en) margin

kantoor (kahn-*toar*) *nt* (pl -toren) office

kantoorbediende (kahn-*toar*-ber-deen-der) *c* (pl ~n, ~s) clerk

kantoorboekhandel (kahn-*toar*-book-hahn-derl) *c* (pl ~s) stationer's

kantooruren (kahn-*toar*-*ew*-rern) *pl* business hours, office hours

kap (kahp) *c* (pl ~pen) hood

kapel (kaa-*pehl*) *c* (pl ~len) chapel

kapelaan (kah-per-*laan*) *m* (pl ~s) chaplain

kapen (*kaa*-pern) *v* hijack

kaper (*kaa*-perr) *c* (pl ~s) hijacker

kapitaal (kah-pee-*taal*) *nt* capital

kapitalisme (kah-pee-taa-*lɪss*-mer) *nt* capitalism

kapitein (kah-pee-*tayn*) *m* (pl ~s) captain

kapot (kaa-*pot*) *adj* broken

kapper (*kah*-perr) *m* (pl ~s) barber; hairdresser

kapsel (*kahp*-serl) *nt* (pl ~s) hairdo

kapstok (*kahp*-stok) *c* (pl ~ken) hat rack

kar (kahr) *c* (pl ~ren) cart

karaat (kaa-*raat*) *nt* carat

karakter (kaa-*rahk*-terr) *nt* (pl ~s) character

karakteristiek (kaa-rahk-ter-rɪss-*teek*) *adj* characteristic

karaktertrek (kaa-*rahk*-terr-trehk) *c* (pl ~ken) characteristic

karamel (kaa-raa-*mehl*) *c* (pl ~s, ~len) caramel

karbonade (kahr-boa-*naa*-der) *c* (pl ~s) cutlet, chop

kardinaal (kahr-dee-*naal*) *m* (pl -nalen) cardinal; *adj* cardinal

karper (*kahr*-perr) *c* (pl ~s) carp

karton (kahr-*ton*) *nt* cardboard

kartonnen (kahr-*to*-nern) *adj* cardboard; **~ doos** carton

karwei (kahr-*vay*) *nt* (pl ~en) job

kas (kahss) *c* (pl ~sen) greenhouse

kasjmier (*kahsh*-meer) *nt* cashmere

kassa (*kah*-saa) *c* (pl ~'s) pay desk; box office

kassier (kah-*seer*) *m* (pl ~s) cashier

kast (kahst) *c* (pl ~en) cupboard, closet

kastanje (kahss-*tah*-ñer) *c* (pl ~s) chestnut

kasteel (kahss-*tayl*) *nt* (pl -telen) castle

kat (kaht) *c* (pl ~ten) cat

kater (*kaa*-terr) *m* (pl ~s) tomcat; hangover

kathedraal (kaa-tay-*draal*) *c* (pl -dralen) cathedral

katholiek (kaa-toa-*leek*) *adj* catholic

katoen (kaa-*toon*) *nt/c* cotton

katoenen (kaa-*too*-nern) *adj* cotton

katoenfluweel (kaa-*toon*-flew-vayl) *nt* velveteen

katrol (kaa-*trol*) *c* (pl ∼len) pulley

kattekwaad (*kah*-ter-kvaat) *nt* mischief

kauwen (*kou*-ern) *v* chew

kauwgom (*kou*-gom) *c/nt* chewing gum

kaviaar (kaa-vee-*ʸaar*) *c* caviar

kazerne (kaa-*zehr*-ner) *c* (pl ∼s, ∼n) barracks *pl*

keel (kāyl) *c* (pl kelen) throat

keelontsteking (*kāyl*-ont-stāy-kıng) *c* (pl ∼en) laryngitis

keelpijn (*kāyl*-payn) *c* sore throat

keer (kāyr) *c* (pl keren) time

keerpunt (*kāyr*-pernt) *nt* (pl ∼en) turning point

keerzijde (*kāyr*-zay-der) *c* (pl ∼n) reverse

kegelbaan (*kāy*-gerl-baan) *c* (pl -banen) bowling alley

kegelspel (*kāy*-gerl-spehl) *nt* bowling

keizer (*kay*-zerr) *m* (pl ∼s) emperor

keizerin (kay-zer-*rın*) *f* (pl ∼nen) empress

keizerlijk (*kay*-zer-lerk) *adj* imperial

keizerrijk (*kay*-zer-rayk) *nt* (pl ∼en) empire

kelder (*kehl*-derr) *c* (pl ∼s) cellar; basement

kelner (*kehl*-nerl) *c* (pl ∼s) waiter

kenmerk (*kehn*-mehrk) *nt* (pl ∼en) characteristic, feature

kenmerken (*kehn*-mehr-kern) *v* characterize, mark; **kenmerkend** characteristic, typical

kennel (*keh*-nerl) *c* (pl ∼s) kennel

kennen (*keh*-nern) *v* *know

kenner (*keh*-nerr) *m* (pl ∼s) connoisseur

kennis[1] (*keh*-nerss) *c* knowledge

kennis[2] (*keh*-nerss) *c* (pl ∼sen) acquaintance

kenteken (*kehn*-tāy-kern) *nt* (pl ∼s) registration number; licence number

Am

Kenya (*kāy*-nee-ʸaa) Kenya

kerel (*kāy*-rerl) *m* (pl ∼s) fellow

keren (*kāy*-rern) *v* turn

kerk (kehrk) *c* (pl ∼en) church; chapel

kerkhof (*kehrk*-hof) *nt* (pl -hoven) cemetery, graveyard, churchyard

kerktoren (*kehrk*-tōa-rern) *c* (pl ∼s) steeple

kermis (*kehr*-merss) *c* (pl ∼sen) fair

kern (kehrn) *c* (pl ∼en) nucleus; heart, core; essence; **kern-** nuclear

kernenergie (*kehrn*-āy-nehr-zhee) *c* nuclear energy

kerrie (*keh*-ree) *c* curry

kers (kehrs) *c* (pl ∼en) cherry

Kerstmis (*kehrs*-merss) Xmas, Christmas

kerven (*kehr*-vern) *v* carve

ketel (*kāy*-terl) *c* (pl ∼s) kettle

keten (*kāy*-tern) *c* (pl ∼s, ∼en) chain

ketting (*keh*-tıng) *c* (pl ∼en) chain

keuken (*kūr*-kern) *c* (pl ∼s) kitchen

keurig (*kūr*-rerkh) *adj* neat

keus (kūrss) *c* (keuzen) pick, choice

keuze (*kūr*-zer) *c* (pl ∼n) selection, choice

kever (*kāy*-verr) *c* (pl ∼s) beetle; bug

kiekje (*keek*-ʸer) *nt* (pl ∼s) snapshot

kiel (keel) *c* (pl ∼en) keel

kiem (keem) *c* (pl ∼en) germ

kies (keess) *c* (pl kiezen) molar

kiesdistrict (*keess*-dıss-trıkt) *nt* (pl ∼en) constituency

kieskeurig (keess-*kūr*-rerkh) *adj* particular

kiesrecht (*keess*-rehkht) *nt* franchise, suffrage

kietelen (*kee*-ter-lern) *v* tickle

kieuw (kee°°) *c* (pl ∼en) gill

kievit (*kee*-veet) *c* (pl ∼en) pewit

kiezel (*kee*-zerl) *c* (pl ∼s) pebble; gravel

*kiezen (*kee*-zern) *v* *choose; pick; elect; dial

kiezer (*kee*-zer) *m* (f ~es, pl ~s) voter

***kijken** (*kay*-kern) *v* look; ~ **naar** look at; watch

kijker (*kay*-kerr) *c* (pl ~s) spectator

kijkje (*kayk*-ᵞer) *nt* (pl ~s) look

kikker (*kı*-kerr) *c* (pl ~s) frog

kil (kıl) *adj* chilly

kilo (*kee*-lōā) *nt* (pl ~'s) kilogram

kilometer (*kee*-lōā-māy-terr) *c* (pl ~s) kilometer *Am*, kilometre

kilometertal (*kee*-lōā-māy-terr-tahl) *nt* distance in kilometres (kilometers *Am*)

kim (kım) *c* horizon

kin (kın) *c* (pl ~nen) chin

kind (kınt) *nt* (pl ~eren) child; kid

kinderjuffrouw (*kın*-derr-ᵞer-frou) *f* (pl ~en) nurse

kinderkamer (*kın*-derr-kaa-merr) *c* (pl ~s) nursery

kinderverlamming (*kın*-derr-verr-lah-mıng) *c* polio

kinderwagen (*kın*-derr-vaa-gern) *c* (pl ~s) pram; baby carriage *Am*

kiosk (kee-ᵞosk) *c* (pl ~en) kiosk

kip (kıp) *f* (pl ~pen) hen; chicken

kippevel (*kı*-per-vehl) *nt* goose flesh

kist (kıst) *c* (pl ~en) chest

klaar (klaar) *adj* ready

klaarblijkelijk (klaar-*blay*-ker-lerk) *adv* apparently

klaarmaken (*klaar*-maa-kern) *v* prepare; cook

klacht (klahkht) *c* (pl ~en) complaint

klachtenboek (*klahkh*-tern-bōōk) *nt* (pl ~en) complaints book

klagen (*klaa*-gern) *v* complain

klank (klahngk) *c* (pl ~en) sound; tone

klant (klahnt) *c* (pl ~en) customer; client

klap (klahp) *c* (pl ~pen) blow; smack, slap

klappen (*klah*-pern) *v* clap, applaud

klaproos (*klahp*-rōāss) *c* (pl -rozen) poppy

klas (klahss) *c* (pl ~sen) class; form

klasgenoot (*klahss*-kher-nōāt) *m* (pl -noten) classmate

klasse (*klah*-ser) *c* (pl ~n) class

klassiek (klah-*seek*) *adj* classical

klauw (klou) *c* (pl ~en) claw

klaver (*klaa*-verr) *c* (pl ~s) clover; shamrock

kleden (*klāy*-dern): **zich ~** dress

kleding (*klāy*-dıng) *c* clothes *pl*; clothing

kleedhokje (*klāyt*-hok-ᵞer) *nt* (pl ~s) cabin

kleedje (*klāy*-tᵞer) *nt* (pl ~s) rug

kleedkamer (*klāyt*-kaa-merr) *c* (pl ~s) dressing room

kleerhanger (*klāyr*-hah-ngerr) *c* (pl ~s) hanger, coat hanger

kleerkast (*klāyr*-kahst) *c* (pl ~en) closet *nAm*

kleermaker (*klāyr*-maa-kerr) *m* (pl ~s) tailor

klei (klay) *c* clay

klein (klayn) *adj* little, small; minor, petty, short; **kleiner** minor; **kleinst** least

kleindochter (*klayn*-dokh-terr) *f* (pl ~s) granddaughter

kleingeld (*klayn*-gehlt) *nt* change, petty cash

kleinhandel (*klayn*-hahn-derl) *c* retail trade

kleinhandelaar (*klayn*-hahn-der-laar) *m* (pl -laren, ~s) retailer

kleinkind (*klayn*-kınt) *nt* (pl ~eren) grandchild

kleinood (*klay*-nōāt) *nt* (pl -noden) gem

kleinzoon (*klayn*-zōān) *m* (pl -zonen) grandson

klem (klehm) *c* (pl ~men) clamp

klemschroef (*klehm*-skhrōōf) *c* (pl -schroeven) clamp

kleren (*klāy*-rern) *pl* clothes *pl*
klerenhaak (*klāy*-rern-haak) *c* (pl -haken) peg
klerenkast (*klāy*-rer-kahst) *c* (pl ~en) wardrobe
klerk (klehrk) *m* (pl ~en) clerk
kletsen (*kleht*-sern) *v* chat; talk rubbish
kleur (klūrr) *c* (pl ~en) colo(u)r; suit (cards)
kleuren (*klūr*-re) *v* colo(u)r
kleurenblind (*klūr*-rerm-blint) *adj* colo(u)r-blind
kleurenfilm (*klūr*-rer-film) *c* (pl ~s) colo(u)r film
kleurrijk (*klūr*-rayk) *adj* colo(u)rful
kleuter (*klūr*-terr) *m* (pl ~s) tot
kleuterschool (*klūr*-terr-skhōal) *c* (pl -scholen) kindergarten
kleven (*klāy*-vern) *v* *stick
kleverig (*klāy*-ver-rerkh) *adj* sticky
klier (kleer) *c* (pl ~en) gland; bully
klikken (*klı*-kern) *v* click
klimaat (klee-*maat*) *nt* (pl -maten) climate
***klimmen** (*klı*-mern) *v* climb
klimop (klı-*mop*) *c* ivy
kliniek (klee-*neek*) *c* (pl ~en) clinic
***klinken** (*klıng*-kern) *v* sound
klinker (*klıng*-kerr) *c* (pl ~s) vowel
klip (klıp) *c* (pl ~pen) cliff
klok (klok) *c* (pl ~ken) clock; bell
klokhuis (*klok*-hur^(ew)ss) *nt* (pl -huizen) core
klomp (klomp) *c* (pl ~en) wooden shoe, clog
klont (klont) *c* (pl ~en) lump
klonterig (*klon*-ter-rerkh) *adj* lumpy
kloof (klōaf) *c* (pl kloven) cleft; chasm
klooster (*klōa*-sterr) *nt* (pl ~s) monastery; convent; cloister
klop (klop) *c* (pl ~pen) knock, tap
kloppen (*klo*-pern) *v* knock, tap; whip
kluis (klur^(ew)ss) *c* (pl kluizen) safe, vault; ~je *nt* locker

knaap (knaap) *m* (pl knapen) boy
knalpot (*knahl*-pot) *c* (pl ~ten) silencer; muffler *nAm*
knap (knahp) *adj* smart, clever; pretty, handsome, good-looking
knapperig (*knah*-per-rerkh) *adj* crisp
knapzak (*knahp*-sahk) *c* (pl ~ken) knapsack
kneuzen (*knūr*-zern) *v* bruise
kneuzing (*knūr*-zıng) *c* (pl ~en) bruise
knie (knee) *c* (pl ~ën) knee
knielen (*knee*-lern) *v* *kneel
knieschijf (*knee*-skhayf) *c* (pl -schijven) kneecap
***knijpen** (*knay*-pern) *v* pinch, squeeze
knik (knık) *c* nod
knikken (*knı*-kern) *v* nod
knikker (*knı*-kerr) *c* (pl ~s) marble
knippen (*knı*-pern) *v* *cut
knoflook (*knof*-lōak) *nt/c* garlic
knokkel (*kno*-kerl) *c* (pl ~s) knuckle
knoop (knōap) *c* (pl knopen) button; knot
knooppunt (*knōa*-pernt) *nt* (pl ~en) junction
knoopsgat (*knōaps*-khaht) *nt* (pl ~en) buttonhole
knop (knop) *c* (pl ~pen) bud; knob
knopen (*knōa*-pern) *v* button; tie, knot
knots (knots) *c* (pl ~en) club
knuffelen (*kner*-fer-lern) *v* cuddle
knuppel (*kner*-perl) *c* (pl ~s) club
knus (knerss) *adj* cosy
koe (kōō) *f* (pl koeien) cow
koek (kōōk) *c* (pl ~en) cake
koekepan (*kōō*-ker-pahn) *c* (pl ~nen) frying pan
koekje (*kōōk*-^(y)er) *nt* (pl ~s) biscuit; cookie
koekoek (*kōō*-kōōk) *c* (pl ~en) cuckoo
koel (kōōl) *adj* cool
koelkast (*kōōl*-kahst) *c* (pl ~en) fridge, refrigerator
koeltas (*kōōl*-tahss) *c* (pl ~sen) ice bag

koepel ($k\overline{oo}$-perl) *c* (pl ~s) dome

koers ($k\overline{oo}$rs) *c* (pl ~en) exchange rate; course

koets ($k\overline{oo}$ts) *c* (pl ~en) carriage, coach

koffer (*ko*-ferr) *c* (pl ~s) case, suitcase, bag; trunk

kofferruimte (*ko*-fer-rur^(ew)m-ter) *c* trunk *nAm*

koffie (*ko*-fee) *c* coffee

kogel ($k\overline{oa}$-gerl) *c* (pl ~s) bullet

kok (kok) *m* (f kokkin, pl ~s) cook

koken ($k\overline{oa}$-kern) *v* cook; boil

kokosnoot ($k\overline{oa}$-koss-n$\overline{oa}$t) *c* (pl -noten) coconut

kolen ($k\overline{oa}$-lern) *pl* coal

kolom ($k\overline{oa}$-*lom*) *c* (pl ~men) column

kolonel ($k\overline{oa}$-l$\overline{oa}$-*nehl*) *m* (pl ~s) colonel

kolonie ($k\overline{oa}$-l$\overline{oa}$-nee) *c* (pl ~s, -niën) colony

kolonne ($k\overline{oa}$-*lo*-ner) *c* (pl ~s) column

kom (kom) *c* (pl ~men) basin

komedie ($k\overline{oa}$-*may*-dee) *c* (pl ~s) comedy

***komen** ($k\overline{oa}$-mern) *v* *come

komfort (koam-*foar*) *nt* comfort

komiek (koa-*meek*) *m* (pl ~en) comedian

komisch ($k\overline{oa}$-meess) *adj* comic

komkommer (kom-*ko*-merr) *c* (pl ~s) cucumber

komma (*ko*-maa) *c* (pl ~'s) comma

kompas (kom-*pahss*) *nt* (pl ~sen) compass

komplot (kom-*plot*) *nt* (pl ~ten) plot, intrigue

komst (komst) *c* coming; arrival

konijn ($k\overline{oa}$-*nayn*) *nt* (pl ~en) rabbit

koning ($k\overline{oa}$-nıng) *m* (pl ~en) king

koningin ($k\overline{oa}$-nı-*ngın*) *f* (pl ~nen) queen

koninklijk ($k\overline{oa}$-nıng-klerk) *adj* royal

koninkrijk ($k\overline{oa}$-nıng-krayk) *nt* (pl ~en) kingdom

kooi (koa^(ee)) *c* (pl ~en) cage; bunk

kookboek ($k\overline{oa}$k-b$\overline{oa}$k) *nt* (pl ~en) cookery book; cookbook *nAm*

kookgelegenheid ($k\overline{oa}$k- ger-*lay*-gern-hayt) *c* cooking facilities

kool ($k\overline{oa}$l) *c* (pl kolen) cabbage

koop ($k\overline{oa}$p) *c* purchase; **te ~** for sale

koophandel ($k\overline{oa}$p-hahn-derl) *c* trade

koopje ($k\overline{oa}$p-^(y)er) *nt* (pl ~s) bargain

koopman ($k\overline{oa}$p-mahn) *c* (pl kooplieden) dealer, merchant

koopprijs ($k\overline{oa}$-prayss) *c* (pl -prijzen) purchase price

koopwaar ($k\overline{oa}$p-vaar) *c* merchandise

koor ($k\overline{oa}$r) *nt* (pl koren) choir

koord ($k\overline{oa}$rt) *nt* (pl ~en) cord

koorts ($k\overline{oa}$rts) *c* fever

koortsig ($k\overline{oa}$rt-serkh) *adj* feverish

kop (kop) *c* (pl ~pen) head; headline

***kopen** ($k\overline{oa}$-pern) *v* *buy; purchase

koper[1] ($k\overline{oa}$-perr) *nt* brass; copper

koper[2] ($k\overline{oa}$-perr) *m* (f koopster, pl ~s) buyer, purchaser

kopie ($k\overline{oa}$-*pee*) *c* (pl ~ën) copy

kopiëren ($k\overline{oa}$-pee-^(y)*ay*-rern) *v* copy

kopje (*kop*-^(y)er) *nt* (pl ~s) cup

koplamp (*kop*-lahmp) *c* (pl ~en) headlight, headlamp

koppeling (*ko*-per-lıng) *c* clutch

koppelteken (*ko*-perl-*tay*-kern) *nt* (pl ~s) hyphen

koppig (*ko*-perkh) *adj* obstinate, headstrong

koraal ($k\overline{oa}$-*raal*) *c* (pl -ralen) coral

koren ($k\overline{oa}$-rern) *nt* corn, grain

korenveld ($k\overline{oa}$-rer-vehlt) *nt* (pl ~en) cornfield

korhoen (kor-h$\overline{oo}$n) *nt* (pl ~ders) grouse

korrel (*ko*-rerl) *c* (pl ~s) corn, grain

korset (kor-*seht*) *nt* (pl ~ten) corset

korst (korst) *c* (pl ~en) crust

kort (kort) *adj* brief, short

korting (*kor*-tıng) *c* (pl ~en) discount,

reduction, rebate

kortsluiting (*kort*-slur^{ew}-tıng) *c* short circuit

kortstondig (kort-*ston*-derkh) *adj* momentary

kosmetica (koss-*may*-tee-kaa) *pl* cosmetics *pl*

kost (kost) *c* food, fare; livelihood; **~en inwoning** room and board, board and lodging, bed and board

kostbaar (*kost*-baar) *adj* precious, valuable, expensive

kostbaarheden (*kost*-baar-hay-dern) *pl* valuables *pl*

kosteloos (*koss*-ter-loass) *adj* free of charge

kosten (*koss*-tern) *v* *cost; *pl* cost, expenditure

kostganger (*kost*-khah-ngerr) *m* (f -gangster, pl ~s) boarder

kostuum (koss-tewm) *nt* (pl ~s) suit

kotelet (koa-ter-*leht*) *c* (pl ~ten) chop

kou (kou) *c* cold; **~ vatten** catch a cold

koud (kout) *adj* cold

kous (kouss) *c* (pl ~en) stocking

kraag (kraakh) *c* (pl kragen) collar

kraai (kraa^{ee}) *c* (pl ~en) crow

kraakbeen (*kraak*-bayn) *nt* cartilage

kraal (kraal) *c* (pl kralen) bead

kraam (kraam) *c* (pl kramen) stand, stall; booth

kraan (kraan) *c* (pl kranen) tap; faucet *nAm*

krab (krahp) *c* (pl ~ben) crab

krabben (*krah*-bern) *v* scratch

kracht (krahkht) *c* (pl ~en) force, strength; energy, power

krachtig (*krahkh*-terkh) *adj* strong

kraken (*kraa*-kern) *v* creak, crack

kralensnoer (*kraa*-ler-snoor) *nt* (pl ~en) beads *pl*

kramp (krahmp) *c* (pl ~en) cramp; convulsion

krankzinnig (krahngk-*sı*-nerkh) *adj*

insane; lunatic, crazy, mad

krankzinnige (krahngk-*sı*-ner-ger) *c* (pl ~n) lunatic

krankzinnigheid (krahngk-*sı*-nerkh-hayt) *c* lunacy

krant (krahnt) *c* (pl ~en) newspaper, paper

krantenkiosk (*krahn*-ter-kee-^yosk) *c* (pl ~en) newsstand

krantenverkoper (*krahn*-ter-verr-koa-perr) *m* (pl ~s) newsagent

krap (krahp) *adj* tight

kras (krahss) *c* (pl ~sen) scratch

krassen (*krah*-sern) *v* scratch

krat (kraht) *nt* (pl ~ten) crate

krater (*kraa*-terr) *c* (pl ~s) crater

krediet (krer-*deet*) *nt* (pl ~en) credit

kredietbrief (krer-*deet*-breef) *c* (pl -brieven) letter of credit

kreeft (krayft) *c* (pl ~en) lobster

kreek (krayk) *c* (pl kreken) creek

kreet (krayt) *c* (pl kreten) cry

krekel (*kray*-kerl) *c* (pl ~s) cricket

krenken (*krehng*-kern) *v* offend, injure

krent (krehnt) *c* (pl ~en) currant

kreuken (*krūr*-kern) *v* crease

kreunen (*krūr*-nern) *v* moan, groan

kreupel (*krūr*-perl) *adj* lame, crippled

kribbe (*krı*-ber) *c* (pl ~n) manger

kriebel (*kree*-berl) *c* (pl ~s) itch

***krijgen** (*kray*-gern) *v* *get; receive

krijgsgevangene (*kraykhs*-kher-vah-nger-ner) *c* (pl ~n) prisoner of war

krijgsmacht (*kraykhs*-mahkht) *c* (pl ~en) military force

krijt (krayt) *nt* chalk

krik (krık) *c* (pl ~ken) jack

***krimpen** (*krum*-pern) *v* *shrink

krimpvrij (*krımp*-vray) *adj* shrinkproof

kring (krıng) *c* (pl ~en) ring, circle

kringloop (*krıng*-loap) *c* (pl -lopen) cycle

kristal (krıss-*tahl*) *nt* (pl ~len) crystal

kristallen (krıss-*tah*-lern) *adj* crystal

kritiek (kree-*teek*) *adj* critical; *c* criticism

kritisch (*kree*-teess) *adj* critical

kroeg (krookh) *c* (pl ~en) public house; pub

kroes (krooss) *c* (pl kroezen) mug

krokant (krōā-*kahnt*) *adj* crisp

krokodil (krōā-kōā-*dɪl*) *c* (pl ~len) crocodile

krom (krom) *adj* crooked; curved, bent

kromming (*kro*-mɪng) *c* (pl ~en) curve, bend

kronen (*krōā*-nern) *v* crown

kronkelen (*krong*-ker-lern) *v* *wind

kronkelig (*krong*-ker-lerkh) *adj* winding

kroon (krōān) *c* (pl kronen) crown

kruid (krur^{ew}t) *nt* (pl ~en) herb;
  kruiden spices; *v* flavo(u)r

kruidenier (krur^{ew}-der-*neer*) *m* (pl ~s) grocer

kruidenierswaren (krur^{ew}-der-*neers*-vaa-rern) *pl* groceries *pl*

kruidenierswinkel (krur^{ew}-der-*neers*-vɪng-kerl) *c* (pl ~s) grocer's, grocery

kruier (*krur^{ew}*-err) *m* (pl ~s) porter

kruik (krur^{ew}k) *c* (pl ~en) pitcher

kruimel (*krur^{ew}*-merl) *c* (pl ~s) crumb

*kruipen (*krur^{ew}*-pern) *v* *creep, crawl

kruis (krur^{ew}ss) *nt* (pl ~en) cross

kruisbeeld (*krur^{ew}ss*-bāylt) *nt* (pl ~en) crucifix

kruisbes (*krur^{ew}ss*-behss) *c* (pl ~sen) gooseberry

kruisigen (*krur^{ew}*-ser-gern) *v* crucify

kruisiging (*krur^{ew}*-ser-gɪng) *c* (pl ~en) crucifixion

kruising (*krur^{ew}*-sɪng) *c* (pl ~en) crossing, junction

kruispunt (*krur^{ew}ss*-pernt) *nt* (pl ~en) crossroads, intersection

kruissnelheid (*krur^{ew}*-snehl-hayt) *c* cruising speed

kruistocht (*krur^{ew}ss*-tokht) *c* (pl ~en) crusade

kruit (krur^{ew}t) *nt* gunpowder

kruiwagen (*krur^{ew}*-vaa-gern) *c* (pl ~s) wheelbarrow

kruk (krerk) *c* (pl ~ken) crutch

krul (krerl) *c* (pl ~len) curl

krullen (*krer*-lern) *v* curl; **krullend** curly

krulspeld (*krerl*-spehlt) *c* (pl ~en) curler

kubus (*kēw*-berss) *c* (pl ~sen) cube

kudde (*ker*-der) *c* (pl ~n, ~s) herd, flock

kuiken (*kur^{ew}*-kern) *nt* (pl ~s) chicken

kuil (kur^{ew}l) *c* (pl ~en) hole; pit

kuis (kur^{ew}ss) *adj* chaste

kuit[1] (kur^{ew}t) *c* roe

kuit[2] (kur^{ew}t) *c* (pl ~en) calf

kundig (*kern*-derkh) *adj* capable

*kunnen (*ker*-nern) *v* *can, *be able to; *might, *may; **het aan~** cope

kunst (kernst) *c* (pl ~en) art; **schone kunsten** fine arts

kunstacademie (*kernst*-ah-kaa-dāy-mee) *c* (pl ~s) art school

kunstenaar (*kern*-ster-naar) *c* (f -ares, pl ~s) artist

kunstgalerij (*kernst*-khah-ler-ray) *c* (pl ~en) art gallery

kunstgebit (*kernst*-kher-bɪt) *nt* (pl ~ten) denture, false teeth

kunstgeschiedenis (*kernst*-kher-skhee-der-nɪss) *c* art history

kunstijsbaan (*kernst*-ayss-baan) *c* (pl -banen) skating rink

kunstje (*kern*-sher) *nt* (pl ~s) trick

kunstmatig (kernst-*maa*-terkh) *adj* artificial

kunstnijverheid (kernst-*nay*-verr-hayt) *c* arts and crafts

kunsttentoonstelling (*kerns*-tern-tōān-steh-lɪng) *c* (pl ~en) art exhibition

kunstverzameling (*kernst*-ferr-zaa-mer-lɪng) *c* (pl ~en) art collection

kunstwerk (*kernst*-vehrk) *nt* (pl ∼en) work of art

kunstzijde (*kernst*-say-der) *c* rayon

kunstzinnig (kernst-*sı*-nerkh) *adj* artistic

kurk (kerrk) *c* (pl ∼en) cork

kurketrekker (*kerr*-ker-treh-kerr) *c* (pl ∼s) corkscrew

kus (kerss) *c* (pl ∼sen) kiss

kussen¹ (*ker*-sern) *v* kiss

kussen² (*ker*-sern) *nt* (pl ∼s) cushion; pillow; **kussentje** *nt* pad

kussensloop (*ker*-ser-slōap) *c/nt* (pl -slopen) pillowcase

kust (kerst) *c* (pl ∼en) coast, shore; seaside, seashore

kuur (kēwr) *c* (pl kuren) cure

kwaad¹ (kvaat) *adj* angry, cross; mad; ill

kwaad² (kvaat) *nt* (pl kwaden) evil; mischief, harm

kwaadaardig (kvaa-*daar*-derkh) *adj* malignant

kwadraat (kvaa-*draat*) *nt* (pl -draten) square

kwakzalver (*kvahk*-sahl-verr) *m* (pl ∼s) quack

kwal (kvahl) *c* (pl ∼len) jellyfish

kwalijk *nemen (*kvaa*-lerk *nāy*-mern) resent; **neem me niet kwalijk!** sorry!

kwaliteit (kvaa-lee-*tayt*) *c* (pl ∼en) quality

kwart (kvahrt) *nt* (pl ∼en) quarter

kwartaal (kvahr-*taal*) *nt* (pl -talen) quarter

kwartel (*kvahr*-terl) *c* (pl ∼s) quail

kwartier (kvahr-*teer*) *nt* quarter of an hour

kwast (kvahst) *c* (pl ∼en) brush

kweken (*kvāy*-kern) *v* cultivate, *grow

kwellen (*kveh*-lern) *v* torment

kwelling (*kveh*-lıng) *c* (pl ∼en) torment

kwestie (*kvehss*-tee) *c* (pl ∼s) matter, question, issue

kwetsbaar (*kvehts*-baar) *adj* vulnerable

kwetsen (*kveht*-sern) *v* injure; *hurt, wound; **kwetsend** *adj* hurtful

kwijtraken (*kvayt*-raa-kern) *v* *lose; *mislay

kwik (kvık) *nt* mercury

kwis (kvıss) *c* quiz

kwistig (*kvıss*-terkh) *adj* lavish

kwitantie (kvee-*tahn*-see) *c* (pl ∼s) receipt

L

la (laa) *c* (pl ∼den) drawer

laag¹ (laakh) *adj* low; **lager** *adj* inferior

laag² (laakh) *c* (pl lagen) layer

laagland (*laakh*-lahnt) *nt* lowlands *pl*

laan (laan) *c* (pl lanen) avenue

laars (laars) *c* (pl laarzen) boot

laat (laat) *adj* late; **laatst** *adj* last; ultimate, final; *adv* lately; **later** *adv* afterwards; later; **te ∼** late; overdue

labiel (laa-*beel*) *adj* unstable

laboratorium (laa-bōa-raa-*tōa*-ree-ᵞerm) *nt* (pl -ria) laboratory

lach (lahkh) *c* laugh

***lachen** (*lah*-khern) *v* laugh

ladder (*lah*-derr) *c* (pl ∼s) ladder

lade (*laa*-der) *c* (pl ∼n) drawer

***laden** (*laa*-dern) *v* load; charge

ladenkast (*laa*-der-kahst) *c* (pl ∼en) chest of drawers

lading (*laa*-dıng) *c* (pl ∼en) charge,

load; freight, cargo

laf (lahf) *adj* cowardly

lafaard (*lah*-faart) *m* (pl ~s) coward

lagune (laa-*gew*-ner) *c* (pl ~s) lagoon

lak (lahk) *c* (pl ~ken) lacquer, varnish

laken (*laa*-kern) *nt* (pl ~s) sheet

lakken (*lah*-kern) *v* varnish

lam[1] (lahm) *adj* lame

lam[2] (lahm) *nt* (pl ~meren) lamb

lambrizering (lahm-bree-*zay*-rɪng) *c* panelling

lamp (lahmp) *c* (pl ~en) lamp

lampekap (*lahm*-per-kahp) *c* (pl ~pen) lampshade

lampenpeer (*lahm*-per-payr) *c* (pl ~eren) light bulb

lamsvlees (lahms-flayss) *nt* lamb

lanceren (lahn-*say*-rern) *v* launch

land (lahnt) *nt* (pl ~en) country, land; **aan ~** ashore; **aan ~ *gaan** land

landbouw (*lahnt*-bou) *c* agriculture; **landbouw-** agrarian

landen (*lahn*-dern) *v* land

landgenoot (*lahnt*-kher-*nōat*) *m* (pl -noten) fellow-countryman

landgoed (*lahnt*-khōōt) *nt* (pl ~eren) estate

landhuis (*lahnt*-hur^ew^ss) *nt* (pl -huizen) country house

landkaart (*lahnt*-kaart) *c* (pl ~en) map

landloper (*lahnt*-lōa-perr) *m* (pl ~s) tramp

landschap (*lahnt*-skhahp) *nt* (pl ~pen) scenery, landscape

landsgrens (*lahnts*-khrehns) *c* (pl -grenzen) border

landtong (*lahn*-tong) *c* (pl ~en) headland

lang (lahng) *adj* long; tall

langdurig (lahng-*dew*-rerkh) *adj* long

langs (lahngs) *prep* along; past; down

langspeelplaat (*lahng*-spayl-plaat) *c* (pl -platen) long-playing record

langwerpig (lahng-*vehr*-perkh) *adj*

oblong

langzaam (*lahng*-zaam) *adj* slow

langzamerhand (lahng-zaa-merr-*hahnt*) *adv* gradually

lantaarn (lahn-*taa*-rern) *c* (pl ~s) lantern

lantaarnpaal (lahn-*taa*-rerm-paal) *c* (pl -palen) lamppost

las (lahss) *c* (pl ~sen) joint

lassen (*lah*-sern) *v* weld

last (lahst) *c* (pl ~en) charge; load, burden; trouble, nuisance, bother

laster (*lahss*-terr) *c* slander

lastig (*lahss*-terkh) *adj* troublesome, inconvenient; difficult

*laten (*laa*-tern) *v* *let; allow to; *leave; *have

later (*laa*-ter) *adv* afterwards; later

Latijns-Amerika (lah-tayn-zaa-*may*-ree-kaa) Latin America

Latijns-Amerikaans (lah-tayn-zaa-*may*-ree-*kaans*) *adj* Latin-American

lauw (lou) *adj* lukewarm, tepid

lawaai (laa-*vaa*^ee^) *nt* noise

lawaaierig (laa-*vaa*^ee^-er-rerkh) *adj* noisy

lawine (laa-*vee*-ner) *c* (pl ~s, ~n) avalanche

laxeermiddel (lahk-*sayr*-mɪ-derl) *nt* (pl ~en) laxative

ledemaat (*lay*-der-maat) *c* (pl maten) limb

lederen (*lay*-der-rern) *adj* leather

ledigen (*lay*-der-gern) *v* empty

leed (layt) *nt* sorrow

leeftijd (*layf*-tayt) *c* (pl ~en) age

leeg (laykh) *adj* empty

leek (layk) *m* (pl leken) layman

leer[1] (layr) *c* teachings pl

leer[2] (layr) *nt* leather

leerboek (*layr*-bōōk) *nt* (pl ~en) textbook

leerling (*layr*-lɪng) *m* (f ~e, pl ~en) pupil; apprentice; scholar

leerzaam (*lāyr*-zaam) *adj* instructive
leesbaar (*lāyss*-baar) *adj* legible
leeslamp (*lāyss*-lahmp) *c* (pl ~en) reading lamp
leeszaal (*lāy*-saal) *c* (pl -zalen) reading room
leeuw (lāy^oo) *c* (pl ~en) lion
leeuwerik (*lāy^oo*-er-rık) *c* (pl ~en) lark
lef (lehf) *nt* guts
legalisatie (lāy-gaa-lee-*zaa*-tsee) *c* legalization
legatie (ler-*gaa*-tsee) *c* (pl ~s) legation
leger (*lāy*-gerr) *nt* (pl ~s) army
leggen (*leh*-gern) *v* *lay, *put
legpuzzel (*lehkk*-per-zerl) *c* (pl ~s) jigsaw puzzle
lei (lay) *nt* slate
leiden (*lay*-dern) *v* head, direct; guide, *lead, conduct
leider (*lay*-derr) *m* (f -ster, pl ~s) leader
leiderschap (*lay*-derr-skhahp) *nt* leadership
leiding[1] (*lay*-dıng) *c* lead
leiding[2] (*lay*-dıng) *c* (pl ~en) pipe
leidinggevend (lay-dıng-*kher*-vernt) *adj* executive
lek[1] (lehk) *adj* leaky; punctured
lek[2] (lehk) *nt* (pl ~ken) leak
lekken (*leh*-kern) *v* leak
lekker (*leh*-kerr) *adj* good; nice, enjoyable, delicious, tasty
lekkernij (leh-kerr-*nay*) *c* (pl ~en) delicacy
lelie (*lāy*-lee) *c* (pl ~s) lily
lelijk (*lāy*-lerk) *adj* ugly
lemmet (*leh*-mert) *nt* (pl ~en) blade
lenen (*lāy*-nern) *v* *lend; borrow
lengte (*lehng*-ter) *c* (pl ~n, ~s) length; **in de** ~ lengthways
lengtegraad (*lehng*-ter-graat) *c* (pl -graden) longitude
lenig (*lāy*-nerkh) *adj* supple
lening (*lāy*-nıng) *c* (pl ~en) loan
lens (lehns) *c* (pl lenzen) lens

lente (*lehn*-ter) *c* (pl ~s) spring
lepel (*lāy*-perl) *c* (pl ~s) spoon; spoonful
lepra (*lāy*-praa) *c* leprosy
leraar (*lāy*-raar) *m* (f lerares, pl leraren, ~s) teacher; instructor
leren[1] (*lāy*-rern) *v* *teach; *learn
leren[2] (*lāy*-rern) *adj* leather
les (lehss) *c* (pl ~sen) lesson
leslokaal (lehss-lōa-kaal) *nt* (pl -kalen) classroom
lessenaar (*leh*-ser-naar) *c* (pl ~s) desk
letsel (*leht*-serl) *nt* (pl ~s) injury
letten op (*leh*-tern) attend to, *pay attention to; watch, mind
letter (*leh*-terr) *c* (pl ~s) letter
lettergreep (*leh*-terr-grāyp) *c* (pl -grepen) syllable
letterkundig (leh-terr-*kern*-derkh) *adj* literary
leugen (*lūr*-gern) *c* (pl ~s) lie
leugenaar (*lūr*-ger-naar) *m* (f ~ster, pl ~s) liar
leuk (lūrk) *adj* enjoyable; funny, jolly
leunen (*lūr*-nern) *v* *lean
leuning (*lūr*-nıng) *c* (pl ~en) arm; rail
leunstoel (*lūr*n-stōol) *c* (pl ~en) easy chair, armchair
leus (lūrss) *c* (pl leuzen) slogan
leven[1] (*lāy*-vern) *v* live; **levend** alive; live
leven[2] (*lāy*-vern) *nt* (pl ~s) life; lifetime; **in** ~ alive
levendig (*lāy*-vern-derkh) *adj* lively; brisk, vivid
levensmiddelen (*lāy*-verns-mı-der-lern) *pl* foodstuffs *pl*
levensstandaard (*lāy*-vern-stahn-daart) *c* standard of living
levensverzekering (*lāy*-verns-ferr-zāy-ker-rıng) *c* (pl ~en) life insurance
lever (*lāy*-verr) *c* (pl ~s) liver
leveren (*lāy*-ver-rern) *v* furnish, provide, supply
levering (*lāy*-ver-rıng) *c* (pl ~en)

delivery, supply

*lezen (*lay*-zern) v *read

lezing (*lay*-zing) c (pl ~en) lecture

Libanees¹ (lee-baa-*nayss*) adj Lebanese

Libanees² (lee-bah-*nayss*) m (f Libanese, pl -nezen) Lebanese

Libanon (*lee*-baa-non) Lebanon

liberaal (lee-ber-*raal*) adj liberal

Liberia (lee-*bay*-ree-^yaa) Liberia

Liberiaans (lee-bay-ree-^y*aans*) adj Liberian

licentie (lee-*sehn*-see) c (pl ~s) license Am, licence

lichaam (*li*-khaam) nt (pl lichamen) body

licht¹ (likht) adj light; pale; gentle, slight

licht² (likht) nt (pl ~en) light

lichtbruin (*likht*-brur^{ew}n) adj light brown, fawn

lichtgevend (*likht*-kher-vernt) adj luminous

lichting (*likh*-ting) c (pl ~en) collection; batch

lichtpaars (*likht*-paars) adj mauve

lid (lit) nt (pl leden) member; associate

lidmaatschap (*lit*-maat-skhahp) nt membership

lidwoord (*lit*-vōart) nt (pl ~en) article

lied (leet) nt (pl ~eren) song

lief (leef) adj dear; sweet; affectionate, adorable

liefdadigheid (leef-*daa*-derkh-hayt) c charity

liefde (*leef*-der) c (pl ~s) love

liefdesgeschiedenis (*leef*-derss-kher-skhee-der-niss) c (pl ~sen) love story

*liefhebben (*leef*-heh-bern) v love

liefhebberij (leef-heh-ber-*ray*) c (pl ~en) hobby

liefje (*leef*-^yer) nt (pl ~s) sweetheart

*liegen (*lee*-gern) v lie

lies (leess) c (pl liezen) groin

lieveling (*lee*-ver-ling) c (pl ~en) darling, sweetheart; favo(u)rite, pet; **lievelings-** favo(u)rite, pet

liever (*lee*-verr) adv sooner, rather; ~ ***hebben** prefer

lift (lift) c (pl ~en) lift; elevator nAm

liften (*lif*-tern) v hitchhike

lifter (*lif*-terr) m (f -ster, pl ~s) hitchhiker

*liggen (*li*-gern) v *lie; ***gaan ~** *lie down

ligging (*li*-ging) c location; situation, site

ligstoel (*likh*-stōol) c (pl ~en) deck chair

lijden (*lay*-dern) nt suffering

*lijden (*lay*-dern) v suffer

lijf (layf) nt (pl lijven) body

lijfwacht (*layf*-vahkht) c (pl ~en) bodyguard

lijk (layk) nt (pl ~en) corpse; **levend ~** zombie

*lijken (*lay*-kern) v seem, appear; look; **~ op** resemble

lijm (laym) c glue, gum

lijn (layn) c (pl ~en) line; leash

lijnboot (*layn*-bōat) c (pl -boten) liner

lijst (layst) c (pl ~en) list; frame

lijster (*lay*-sterr) c (pl ~s) thrush

lijvig (*lay*-verkh) adj bulky

likdoorn (*lik*-dōa-rern) c (pl ~s) corn

likeur (lee-*kūrr*) c (pl ~en) liqueur

likken (*li*-kern) v lick, lap

limiet (lee-*meet*) c (pl ~en) limit

limoen (lee-*mōon*) c (pl ~en) lime

limonade (lee-mōa-*naa*-der) c (pl ~s) lemonade

limonadesiroop (lee-mōa-*naa*-der-see-rōap) c (pl ~open) cordial

linde (*lin*-der) c (pl ~n) limetree, lime

lingerie (lang-zher-*ree*) c lingerie

liniaal (lee-nee-^y*aal*) c (pl -alen) ruler

links (lingks) adj left; left-hand

linkshandig (lingks-*hahn*-derkh) adj

left-handed

linnen (*lı-nern*) *nt* linen

linnengoed (*lı-ner-gōōt*) *nt* linen

lint (lınt) *nt* (pl ~en) ribbon; tape

lip (lıp) *c* (pl ~pen) lip

lippenstift (*lı-per-stıft*) *c* lipstick

listig (*lıss-terkh*) *adj* sly

liter (*lee-terr*) *c* (pl ~s) liter *Am*, litre

literair (lee-ter-*rair*) *adj* literary

literatuur (lee-ter-raa-*tēwr*) *c* literature

lits-jumeaux (lee-zhēw-*mōā*) *nt* twin beds

litteken (*lı-tāy-kern*) *nt* (pl ~s) scar

locomotief (*lōā-kōā-mōā-teef*) *c* (pl -tieven) engine, locomotive

loeien (*lōō^{ee}-ern*) *v* roar

lof (lof) *c* glory, praise

logé (*lōā-zhāy*) *c* (pl ~'s) guest

logeerkamer (*lōā-zhāyr-kaa-merr*) *c* (pl ~s) spare room, guest room

logeren (*lōā-zhāy-rern*) *v* stay

logica (*lōā-gee-kaa*) *c* logic

logies (*lōā-zheess*) *nt* lodgings *pl*, accommodation; ~ **en ontbijt** bed and breakfast

logisch (*lōā-geess*) *adj* logical

lokaal (*lōā-kaal*) *adj* local

lol (lol) *c* fun

lonen (*lōā-nern*) *v* *pay

long (long) *c* (pl ~en) lung

longontsteking (*long-ont-stāy-kıng*) *c* (pl ~en) pneumonia

lont (lont) *c* (pl ~en) fuse

lood (lōāt) *nt* lead

loodgieter (*lōāt-khee-terr*) *m* (pl ~s) plumber

loodrecht (*lōāt-rehkht*) *adj* perpendicular

loods (lōāts) *c* (pl ~en) pilot

loon (lōān) *nt* (pl lonen) wages *pl*; salary, pay

loonsverhoging (*lōāns-ferr-hōā-gıng*) *c* (pl ~en) raise *nAm*

loop (lōāp) *c* course; walk

loopbaan (*lōā-baan*) *c* (pl -banen) career

loopplank (*lōā-plahngk*) *c* (pl ~en) gangway

***lopen** (*lōā-pern*) *v* walk; *go

loper (*lōā-per*) *m* (f loopster, pl ~s) runner

los (loss) *adj* loose

losgeld (*loass-khehlt*) *nt* (pl ~en) ransom

losknopen (*loss-knōā-pern*) *v* unbutton; untie

losmaken (*loss-maa-kern*) *v* unfasten, *undo, detach; loosen

losschroeven (*lo-skhrōō-vern*) *v* unscrew

lossen (*lo-sern*) *v* unload, discharge

lot¹ (lot) *nt* lot, fortune, destiny, fate

lot² (lot) *nt* (pl ~en) lot

loterij (*lōā-ter-ray*) *c* (pl ~en) lottery

lotion (*lōā-shon*) *c* (pl ~s) lotion

louter (*lou-terr*) *adj* mere

loven (*lōā-vern*) *v* applaud

loyaal (*lōā-^yaal*) *adj* loyal

lucht (lerkht) *c* air; breath; sky

luchtdicht (*lerkh-dıkht*) *adj* airtight

luchtdruk (*lerkh-drerk*) *c* atmospheric pressure

luchten (*lerkh-tern*) *v* air, ventilate

luchtfilter (*lerkht-fıl-terr*) *nt* (pl ~s) air-filter

luchthaven (*lerkht-haa-vern*) *c* (pl ~s) airport

luchtig (*lerkh-terkh*) *adj* airy

luchtpost (*lerkht-post*) *c* airmail

luchtvaartmaatschappij (*lerkht-faart-maat-skhah-pay*) *c* (pl ~en) airline

luchtverversing (*lerkht-ferr-vehr-sıng*) *c* air conditioning, ventilation

luchtziekte (*lerkht-seek-ter*) *c* airsickness

lucifer (*lēw-see-fehr*) *c* (pl ~s) match

lucifersdoosje (*lēw*-see-fehrs-dōa-sher) *nt* (pl ~s) matchbox
lui (lur*ew*) *adj* lazy; idle
luid (lur*ew*t) *adj* loud
luidspreker (*lurew*t-sprāy-kerr) *c* (pl ~s) loudspeaker
luier (*lurew*-err) *c* (pl ~s) nappy; diaper *nAm*
luik (lur*ew*k) *nt* (pl ~en) hatch; shutter
luis (lur*ew*ss) *c* (pl luizen) louse
luisteraar (*lurew*ss-ter-raar) *m* (f ~ster, pl ~s) listener
luisteren (*lurew*ss-ter-rern) *v* listen
luisterrijk (*lurew*ss-ter-rayk) *adj* magnificent
lukken (*ler*-kern) *v* succeed
lunch (lernsh) *c* (pl ~es) lunch
lus (lerss) *c* (pl ~sen) loop
lusten (*lerss*-tern) *v* like; fancy
luxe (*lēw*k-ser) *c* luxury
luxueus (lēwk-sēw-*ūrss*) *adj* luxurious

M

maag (maakh) *c* (pl magen) stomach; **maag-** gastric
maagd (maakht) *f* (pl ~en) virgin
maagpijn (*maakh*-payn) *c* stomach ache
maagzuur (*maakh*-sēwr) *nt* heartburn
maagzweer (*maakh*-svāyr) *c* (pl -zweren) gastric ulcer
maal[1] (maal) *nt* (pl malen) meal
maal[2] (maal) *c* (pl malen) time
maal[3] (maal) *prep* times
maaltijd (*maal*-tayt) *c* (pl ~en) meal; **warme ~** dinner
maan (maan) *c* (pl manen) moon
maand (maant) *c* (pl ~en) month
maandag (*maan*-dahkh) *c* Monday
maandblad (*maant*-blaht) *nt* (pl ~en) monthly magazine
maandelijks (*maan*-der-lerks) *adj* monthly
maandverband (*maant*-ferr-bahnt) *nt* sanitary towel
maanlicht (*maan*-lıkht) *nt* moonlight
maar (maar) *conj* but; yet; *adv* only
maart (maart) March
maas (maass) *c* (pl mazen) mesh
maat (maat) *c* (pl maten) size, measure;

extra grote ~ outsize; **op ~ gemaakt** tailor-made; made to order
maatregel (*maat*-rāy-gerl) *c* (pl ~en, ~s) measure
maatschappelijk (maat-*skhah*-per-lerk) *adj* social
maatschappij (maat-skhah-*pay*) *c* (pl ~en) company; society
maatstaf (*maat*-stahf) *c* (pl -staven) standard
machine (mah-*shee*-ne) *c* (pl ~s) engine, machine
machinerie (mah-shee-ner-*ree*) *c* machinery
macht (mahkht) *c* (pl ~en) power; force, might; authority
machteloos (*mahkh*-ter-lōass) *adj* powerless
machtig (*mahkh*-terkh) *adj* powerful, mighty
machtiging (*mahkh*-ter-gıng) *c* (pl ~en) authorization
magazijn (maa-gaa-*zayn*) *nt* (pl ~en) store house, warehouse
mager (*maa*-gerr) *adj* lean, thin
magie (maa-*gee*) *c* magic
magistraat (maa-gıss-*traat*) *c* (pl

-straten) magistrate

magneet (mahkh-*nāȳt*) c (pl -neten)
magnet

magnetisch (mahkh-*nāȳ*-teess) *adj*
magnetic

magnetron (*mahkh*-ner-tron) c (pl ~s)
microwave oven

maillot (maa-*ʸōa*) c (pl ~s) tights *pl*

maïs (mighss) c maize

maïskolf (mighss-kolf) c (pl -kolven)
corn on the cob

maître d'hôtel (mai-trer-dōa-*tehl*)
head waiter

maîtresse (meh-*tray*-ser) *f* (pl ~s, ~n)
mistress

majoor (maa-*ʸōār*) *m* (pl ~s) major

mak (mahk) *adj* tame

makelaar (*maa*-ker-laar) *m* (pl ~s)
broker, house agent

maken (*maa*-kern) *v* *make; **te ~
*hebben met** *deal with

makreel (maa-*krāȳl*) c (pl -relen)
mackerel

mal (mahl) *adj* foolish, silly

malaria (maa-*laa*-ree-ʸaa) c malaria

Maleis (maa-*layss*) *nt* Malay

Maleisië (maa-*lay*-zee-ʸer) Malaysia

Maleisisch (maa-*lay*-zeess) *adj*
Malaysian

*malen (*maa*-lern) *v* *grind

mals (mahls) *adj* tender

mammoet (*mah*-mōot) c (pl ~en, ~s)
mammoth

man (mahn) *m* (pl ~nen) man; husband

manchet (mahn-*sheht*) c (pl ~ten) cuff

manchetknopen (mahn-*sheht*-knōa-
pern) *pl* cuff links *pl*

mand (mahnt) c (pl ~en) hamper,
basket

mandaat (mahn-*daat*) *nt* (pl -daten)
mandate

mandarijn (mahn-daa-*rayn*) c (pl ~en)
mandarin, tangerine

manege (maa-*nāȳ*-zher) c (pl ~s) riding

school

manicure (maa-nee-*kēw*-rer) c (pl ~s)
manicure

manicuren (maa-nee-*kēw*-rern) *v*
manicure

manier (maa-*neer*) c (pl ~en) manner;
way, fashion; **op de één of andere ~**
somehow

mank (mahngk) *adj* lame

mannelijk (*mah*-ner-lerk) *adj* male;
masculine

mannequin (mah-ner-*kahng*) c (pl ~s)
model, mannequin

mantel (*mahn*-terl) c (pl ~s) coat, cloak

manuscript (maa-nerss-*krıpt*) *nt* (pl
~en) manuscript

marcheren (mahr-*shāȳ*-rern) *v* march

margarine (mahr-gaa-*ree*-ner) c
margarine

marge (*mahr*-zher) c (pl ~s) margin

marine (maa-*ree*-ner) c navy; **marine-**
naval

maritiem (mah-ree-*teem*) *adj* maritime

markt (mahrkt) c (pl ~en) market;
zwarte ~ black market

marktplein (*mahrkt*-playn) *nt* (pl ~en)
marketplace

marmelade (mahr-mer-*laa*-der) c (pl
~s, ~n) marmalade

marmer (*mahr*-merr) *nt* marble

Marokkaan (mah-ro-*kaan*) *m* (f -se, pl
-kanen) Moroccan

Marokkaans (mah-ro-*kaans*) *adj*
Moroccan

Marokko (maa-*ro*-kōa) Morocco

mars (mahrs) c (pl ~en) march

martelaar (*mahr*-ter-laar) *m* (f -ares, pl
~s, -laren) martyr

martelen (*mahr*-ter-lern) *v* torture

marteling (*mahr*-ter-lıng) c (pl ~en)
torture

mascara (mahss-*kaa*-raa) c mascara

masker (*mahss*-kerr) *nt* (pl ~s) mask

massa (*mah*-saa) c (pl ~'s) bulk, mass;

crowd

massage (mah-*saa*-zher) *c* (pl ∾s) massage

massaproductie (mah-saa-prōa-derk-see) *c* mass production

masseren (mah-*say*-rern) *v* massage

masseur (mah-*surr*) *m* (f masseuse, pl ∾s) masseur

massief (mah-*seef*) *adj* solid, massive

mast (mahst) *c* (pl ∾en) mast

mat¹ (maht) *adj* dull, mat, dim

mat² (maht) *c* (pl ∾ten) mat

materiaal (maa-tree-*ʸaal*) *nt* (pl -rialen) material

materie (mah-*tay*-ree) *c* (pl -riën, ∾s) matter

materieel (maa-tree-*ʸayl*) *adj* material

matig (*maa*-terkh) *adj* moderate

matras (maa-*trahss*) *c* (pl ∾sen) mattress

matroos (maa-*trōass*) *m* (pl matrozen) sailor

mausoleum (mou-sōa-*lay*-ʸerm) *nt* (pl ∾s, -lea) mausoleum

mazelen (*maa*-zer-lern) *pl* measles

me (mer) *pron* me; myself

mechanisch (may-*khaa*-neess) *adj* mechanical

mechanisme (may-khaa-*nuss*-mer) *nt* (pl ∾n) mechanism; machinery

medaille (may-*dah*-ʸer) *c* (pl ∾s) medal

mededelen (*may*-der-day-lern) *v* notify, communicate, inform

mededeling (*may*-der-day-lng) *c* (pl ∾en) communication, information

mededelingenbord (*may*-der-day-lng-ern-bort) *nt* (pl ∾en) bulletin board

medegevoel (*may*-der-ger-vōol) *nt* sympathy

medelijden (*may*-der-lay-dern) *nt* pity; ∾ *hebben met pity

medemens (*may*-der-mehns) *m* (pl ∾en) fellow man

medewerking (*may*-der-vehr-kng) *c* cooperation

media (*may*-dee-yaa) *pl* media

medisch (*may*-deess) *adj* medical

mediteren (may-dee-*tay*-rern) *v* meditate

*meebrengen (*may*-breh-ngern) *v* *bring

meedelen (*may*-day-lern) *v* communicate

meel (mayl) *nt* flour

meemaken (*may*-maa-kern) *v* *go through

*meenemen (*may*-nay-mern) *v* *take away

meer¹ (mayr) *adj* more; ∾ dan over; niet ∾ no longer

meer² (mayr) *nt* (pl meren) lake

meerderheid (*mayr*-derr-hayt) *c* majority; bulk

meerderjarig (mayr-derr-*ʸaa*-rerkh) *adj* of age

meervoud (*mayr*-vout) *nt* (pl ∾en) plural

meest (mayst) *adj* most

meestal (may-*stahl*) *adv* mostly

meester (*may*-sterr) *m* (pl ∾s) master; schoolmaster, teacher

meesteres (may-ster-*rehss*) *f* (pl ∾sen) mistress

meesterwerk (*may*-sterr-vehrk) *nt* (pl ∾en) masterpiece

meetellen (*may*-teh-lern) *v* count

meetkunde (*mayt*-kern-der) *c* geometry

meeuw (mayʷ⁰) *c* (pl ∾en) gull; seagull

mei (may) May

meid (mayt) *f* (pl ∾en) girl; housemaid, maid

meineed (*may*-nayt) *c* (pl -eden) perjury

meisje (*may*-sher) *nt* (pl ∾s) girl; girlfriend

meisjesnaam (*may*-sherss-naam) *c* (pl

-namen) maiden name

mejuffrouw (mer-^yer-frou) miss

melden (*mehl*-dern) *v* report

melding (*mehl*-dɪng) *c* (pl ~en) mention

melk (mehlk) *c* milk

melkboer (*mehlk*-bōōr) *m* (pl ~en) milkman

melodie (māy-lōa-*dee*) *c* (pl ~ën) melody; tune

melodieus (māy-lōa-dee-*y*ūrss) *adj* tuneful

melodrama (māy-lōa-*draa*-maa) *nt* (pl ~'s) melodrama

meloen (mer-*lōōn*) *c* (pl ~en) melon

memorandum (māy-mōa-*rahn*-derm) *nt* (pl -randa) memo

men (mehn) *pron* one

meneer (mer-*nāyr*) mister; sir

menen (*māy*-nern) *v* consider; *mean

mengen (*meh*-ngern) *v* mix

mengsel (*mehng*-serl) *nt* (pl ~s) mixture

menigte (*māy*-nerkh-ter) *c* (pl ~n, ~s) crowd

mening (*māy*-nɪng) *c* (pl ~en) opinion; view; **van ~ verschillen** disagree

mens (mehns) *m* (pl ~en) man; **mensen** people *pl*

menselijk (*mehn*-ser-lerk) *adj* human; **~ wezen** human being

mensheid (*mehns*-hayt) *c* humanity, mankind

menstruatie (mehn-strēw-*vaa*-tsee) *c* menstruation

menukaart (mer-*nēw*-kaart) *c* (pl ~en) menu

merel (*māy*-rerl) *c* (pl ~s) blackbird

merg (mehrkh) *nt* marrow

merk (mehrk) *nt* (pl ~en) brand

merkbaar (*mehrk*-baar) *adj* noticeable, perceptible

merken (*mehr*-kern) *v* notice; mark

merkteken (*mehrk*-tāy-kern) *nt* (pl ~s) mark

merrie (*meh*-ree) *f* (pl ~s) mare

mes (mehss) *nt* (pl ~sen) knife

messing (*meh*-sɪng) *nt* brass

mest (mehst) *c* dung, manure

mesthoop (*mehst*-hōap) *c* (pl -hopen) dunghill

met (meht) *prep* with; by

metaal (māy-*taal*) *nt* (pl metalen) metal

metalen (māy-*taa*-lern) *adj* metal

meteen (mer-*tāyn*) *adv* at once, straight away, immediately, instantly; presently

*meten (*māy*-tern) *v* measure

meter (*māy*-terr) *c* (pl ~s) metre; meter; gauge; godmother

metgezel (*meht*-kher-zehl) *m* (f ~lin, pl ~len) companion

methode (māy-*tōa*-der) *c* (pl ~n, ~s) method

methodisch (māy-*tōa*-deess) *adj* methodical

metrisch (*māy*-treess) *adj* metric

metro (*māy*-trōa) *c* (pl ~'s) underground

metselaar (*meht*-ser-laar) *m* (pl ~s) bricklayer

metselen (*meht*-ser-lern) *v* *lay bricks

meubilair (mūr-bee-*lair*) *nt* furniture

meubileren (mūr-bee-*lāy*-rern) *v* furnish

mevrouw (mer-*vrou*) madam

Mexicaan (mehk-see-*kaan*) *m* (f ~se, pl -canen) Mexican

Mexicaans (mehk-see-*kaans*) *adj* Mexican

Mexico (*mehk*-see-kōa) Mexico

microfoon (mee-krōa-*fōan*) *c* (pl ~s) microphone

middag (*mɪ*-dahkh) *c* (pl ~en) afternoon; midday; noon

middageten (*mɪ*-dahkh-āy-tern) *nt* lunch; dinner

middel¹ (*mɪ*-derl) *nt* (pl ~en) means;

remedy; **insektenwerend** ~ insect
repellent; **kalmerend** ~ tranquillizer,
sedative; **pijnstillend** ~ anaesthetic;
stimulerend ~ stimulant; **verdovend**
~ drug
middel² (*mı-derl*) *nt* (pl ~s) waist
middeleeuwen (*mı-derl-āy⁰⁰-ern*) *pl*
Middle Ages
middeleeuws (*mı-derl-āy⁰⁰ss*) *adj*
mediaeval
Middellandse Zee (*mı-der-lahnt-ser-zāy*) Mediterranean
middelmatig (*mı-derl-maa-terkh*) *adj*
moderate; medium
middelpunt (*mı-derl-pernt*) *nt* (pl ~en)
center *Am*, centre
middelst (*mı-derlst*) *adj* middle
midden (*mı-dern*) *nt* midst, middle;
midden- medium; ~ **in** amid; **te ~ van**
amid; among
middenrif (*mı-dern-rıf*) *nt* diaphragm
middernacht (*mı-derr-nahkht*) *c*
midnight
midzomer (*mıt-sōā-merr*) *c*
midsummer
mier (meer) *c* (pl ~en) ant
mierikswortel (*mee-rıks-vor-terl*) *c* (pl
~s) horseradish
migraine (mee-*grai*-ner) *c* migraine
mijl (mayl) *c* (pl ~en) mile
mijlpaal (*mayl*-paal) *c* (pl -palen)
milestone; landmark
mijn¹ (mayn) *pron* my
mijn² (mayn) *c* (pl ~en) mine
mijnbouw (*mayn*-bou) *c* mining
mijnheer (mer-*nāyr*) *c* mister
mijnwerker (*mayn*-vehr-kerr) *m* (pl ~s)
miner
mikken op (*mı*-kern) aim at
mikpunt (*mık*-pernt) *nt* (pl ~en) target
mild (mılt) *adj* liberal
milieu (meel-*ʸūr*) *nt* (pl ~s) milieu;
environment
militair¹ (mee-lee-*tair*) *adj* military

militair² (mee-lee-*tair*) *m* (pl ~en)
soldier
miljard (mıl-*yahrt*) *nt* billion
miljoen (mıl-*ʸōōn*) *nt* million
miljonair (mıl-*ʸōā-nair*) *m* (f ~e, pl ~s)
millionaire
min (mın) *prep* minus
minachting (*mın*-ahkh-tıng) *c*
contempt
minder (*mın*-derr) *adv* less
minderen (*mın*-der-rern) *v* cut down
minderheid (*mın*-derr-hayt) *c* (pl
-heden) minority
minderjarig (mın-derr-*ʸaa*-rerkh) *adj*
under age
minderjarige (mın-derr-*ʸaa*-rer-ger) *c*
(pl ~n) minor
minderwaardig (mın-derr-*vaar*-
derkh) *adj* inferior
mineraal (mee-ner-*raal*) *nt* (pl -ralen)
mineral
mineraalwater (mee-ner-*raal*-vaa-
terr) *nt* mineral water
miniatuur (mee-nee-*ʸaa-tēwr*) *c* (pl
-turen) miniature
minimum (*mee*-nee-merm) *nt* (pl -ma)
minimum
minister (mee-*nıss*-terr) *c* (pl ~s)
minister
ministerie (mee-nıss-*tāy*-ree) *nt* (pl ~s)
ministry
minnaar (*mı*-naar) *m* (f minnares, pl
~s) lover
minst (mınst) *adj* least
minstens (*mın*-sterns) *adv* at least
minuscuul (mee-nerss-*kēwl*) *adj* tiny,
minute
minuut (mee-*nēwt*) *c* (pl minuten) *c*
minute
mis (miss) *c* (pl ~sen) Mass
misbruik (*mıss*-brur^(ew)k) *nt* misuse,
abuse
misdaad (*mıss*-daat) *c* (pl -daden)
crime

misdadig (miss-*daa*-derkh) *adj*
criminal

misdadiger (miss-daa-der-gerr) *m* (f
-ster, pl ~s) criminal

***misdragen** (miss-*draa*-gern): **zich ~**
misbehave

misgunnen (miss-*kher*-nern) *v* grudge

mishagen (miss-*haa*-gern) *v* displease

miskraam (*muss*-kraam) *c* (pl -kramen)
miscarriage

mislukking (miss-*ler*-king) *c* (pl ~en)
failure

mislukt (miss-*lerkt*) *adj* unsuccessful

mismaakt (miss-*maakt*) *adj* deformed

misplaatst (miss-*plaatst*) *adj*
misplaced

misschien (mi-*skheen*) *adv* perhaps;
maybe

misselijk (*mi*-ser-lerk) *adj* sick

misselijkheid (*mi*-ser-lerk-hayt) *c*
nausea, sickness

missen (*mi*-sern) *v* lack; miss; spare

misstap (*mu*-stahp) *c* (pl ~pen) slip

mist (mist) *c* fog, mist

mistig (*miss*-terkh) *adj* foggy, misty

mistlamp (*mist*-lahmp) *c* (pl ~en)
foglamp

***misverstaan** (*miss*-ferr-staan) *v*
*misunderstand

misverstand (*miss*-ferr-stahnt) *nt* (pl
~en) misunderstanding

misvormd (miss-*formt*) *adj* deformed

mits (mits) *conj* provided that

mixer (*mik*-serr) *c* (pl ~s) mixer

mobiel (mōā-*beel*) *adj* mobile

modder (*mo*-derr) *c* mud

modderig (*mo*-der-rerkh) *adj* muddy

mode (*mōā*-der) *c* (pl ~s) fashion

model (mōā-*dehl*) *nt* (pl ~len) model

modelleren (mōā-deh-*lāy*-rern) *v*
model

modem (mōā-*derm*) *c* (pl ~s) modem

modern (mōā-*dehrn*) *adj* modern

modieus (mōā-dee-^{y}*urss*) *adj*

fashionable, trendy

moe (mōō) *adj* tired; weary

moed (mōōt) *c* courage

moeder (*mōō*-derr) *f* (pl ~s) mother

moedertaal (*mōō*-derr-taal) *c* native
language, mother tongue

moedig (*mōō*-derkh) *adj* brave,
courageous

moeilijk (*mōō^{ee}*-lerk) *adj* difficult; hard

moeilijkheid (*mōō^{ee}*-lerk-hayt) *c* (pl
-heden) difficulty

moeite (*mōō^{ee}*-ter) *c* (pl ~n) trouble;
pains, difficulty; **de ~ waard *zijn** *be
worth-while; **~ *doen** bother

moer (mōōr) *c* (pl ~en) nut

moeras (mōō-*rahss*) *nt* (pl ~sen)
swamp; bog, marsh

moestuin (*mōōss*-tur^{ew}n) *c* (pl ~en)
kitchen garden

***moeten** (*mōō*-tern) *v* *must; *have to;
need to, *ought to, *be obliged to, *be
bound to, *should

mogelijk (*mōā*-ger-lerk) *adj* possible

mogelijkheid (*mōā*-ger-lerk-hayt) *c*
(pl -heden) possibility

***mogen** (*mōā*-gern) *v* *be allowed to; *be
allowed to; *may; like

mogendheid (*mōā*-gernt-hayt) *c* (pl
-heden) power

mohair (mōā-*hair*) *nt* mohair

molen (*mōā*-lern) *c* (pl ~s) mill;
windmill

molenaar (*mōā*-ler-naar) *m* (pl ~s)
miller

mollig (*mo*-lerkh) *adj* plump

moment (mōā-*mehnt*) *nt* (pl ~en)
moment

momentopname (mōā-*mehnt*-op-
naa-mer) *c* (pl ~n) snapshot

monarchie (mōā-nahr-*khee*) *c* (pl ~ën)
monarchy

mond (mont) *c* (pl ~en) mouth

mondeling (*mon*-der-ling) *adj* oral,
verbal

monding (*mon*-dıng) *c* (pl ⁓en) mouth

mondspoeling (*mont*-spoō-lıng) *c* mouthwash

monetair (mōa-nāy-*tair*) *adj* monetary

monnik (*mo*-nerk) *m* (pl ⁓en) monk

monoloog (mōa-nōa-*lōakh*) *c* (pl -logen) monologue

monopolie (mōa-nōa-*pōa*-lee) *nt* (pl ⁓s) monopoly

monster (*mon*-sterr) *nt* (pl ⁓s) sample

monteren (mon-*tāy*-rern) *v* assemble

monteur (mon-*tūrr*) *m* (pl ⁓s) mechanic

montuur (mon-*tēwr*) *nt* (pl -turen) frame

monument (mōa-new-*mehnt*) *nt* (pl ⁓en) monument

mooi (mōaᵉᵉ) *adj* beautiful; pretty, fine; nice, lovely, fair

moord (mōart) *c* (pl ⁓en) assassination, murder

moordenaar (*mōar*-der-naar) *m* (f ⁓ares, pl ⁓s) murderer

mop (mop) *c* (pl ⁓pen) joke

mopperen (*mo*-per-rern) *v* grumble

moraal (mōa-*raal*) *c* moral

moraliteit (mōa-raa-lee-*tayt*) *c* morality

moreel (mōa-*rāyl*) *adj* moral

morfine (mor-*fee*-ner) *c* morphine, morphia

morgen¹ (*mor*-gern) *adv* tomorrow

morgen² (*mor*-gern) *c* (pl ⁓s) morning

morsen (*mor*-sern) *v* *spill

mos (moss) *nt* (pl ⁓sen) moss

moskee (moss-*kāy*) *c* (pl ⁓ën) mosque

mossel (*mo*-serl) *c* (pl ⁓s, ⁓en) mussel

mosterd (*moss*-terrt) *c* mustard

mot (mot) *c* (pl ⁓ten) moth

motel (mōa-*tehl*) *nt* (pl ⁓s) motel

motie (*mōa*-tsee) *c* (pl ⁓s) motion

motief (mōa-*teef*) *nt* (pl motieven) motive; pattern

motor (*mōa*-terr) *c* (pl ⁓en, ⁓s) engine, motor; motorbike

motorboot (*mōa*-terr-bōat) *c* (pl -boten) motorboat

motorfiets (*mōa*-terr-feets) *c* (pl ⁓en) motorcycle

motorkap (*mōa*-terr-kahp) *c* (pl ⁓pen) bonnet; hood *nAm*

motorpech (*mōa*-terr-pehkh) *c* breakdown

motregen (*mot*-rāy-gern) *c* drizzle

mousseline (moō-ser-*lee*-ner) *c* muslin

mousserend (moō-*sāy*-rernt) *adj* sparkling

mouw (mou) *c* (pl ⁓en) sleeve

mozaïek (mōa-zaa-*eek*) *nt* (pl ⁓en) mosaic

mug (merkh) *c* (pl ⁓gen) mosquito

muil (murᵉʷl) *c* (pl ⁓en) mouth

muildier (*murᵉʷl*-deer) *nt* (pl ⁓en) mule

muilezel (*murᵉʷl*-āy-zerl) *c* (pl ⁓s) mule

muis (murᵉʷss) *c* (pl muizen) mouse

muiterij (murᵉʷ-ter-*ray*) *c* (pl ⁓en) mutiny

munt (mernt) *c* (pl ⁓en) coin; token; mint

munteenheid (*mernt*-āyn-hayt) *c* (pl -heden) monetary unit, currency

muntstuk (*mernt*-sterk) *nt* (pl ⁓ken) coin

mus (merss) *c* (pl ⁓sen) sparrow

museum (mēw-*zāy*-ʸerm) *nt* (pl ⁓s, -sea) museum

musical (*mʸoō*-zı-kerl) *c* (pl ⁓s) musical comedy, musical

musicus (*mēw*-zee-kerss) *m* (f musicienne, pl -ci) musician

musket (merss-*keet*) *c* (pl ⁓en) mosquito

muskietennet (merss-*kee*-ter-neht) *nt* (pl ⁓ten) mosquito net

muts (merts) *c* (pl ⁓en) cap

muur (mēwr) *c* (pl muren) wall

muziek (mēw-*zeek*) *c* music
muziekinstrument (mēw-*zeek*-ɪn-strēw-mehnt) *nt* (pl ∼en) musical instrument
muzikaal (mēw-zee-*kaal*) *adj* musical

mysterie (mee-*stāy*-ree) *nt* (pl ∼s) mystery
mysterieus (mee-stāy-ree-ᵛ*ūrss*) *adj* mysterious
mythe (*mee*-ter) *c* (pl ∼n) myth

N

na (naa) *prep* after
naad (naat) *c* (pl naden) seam
naadloos (*naat*-lōass) *adj* seamless
naaien (*naa*ᵉᵉ-ern) *v* sew; *vulgar* fuck
naaimachine (*naa*ᵉᵉ-mah-shee-ner) *c* (pl ∼s) sewing machine
naaister (*naa*ᵉᵉ-sterr) *f* (pl ∼s) dressmaker
naakt (naakt) *adj* nude, naked, bare
naaktstrand (*naakt*-strahnt) *nt* (pl∼en) nudist beach
naald (naalt) *c* (pl ∼en) needle
naam (naam) *c* (pl namen) name; reputation; denomination; **in ∼ van** on behalf of
naar¹ (naar) *prep* to, towards; at, for
naar² (naar) *adj* nasty, unpleasant
naast (naast) *prep* next to, beside
nabij (naa-*bay*) *adj* near, close
nabijheid (naa-*bay*-hayt) *c* vicinity
nabijzijnd (naa-*bay*-zaynt) *adj* nearby
nabootsen (*naa*-bōat-sern) *v* imitate
naburig (naa-*bōō*-rerkh) *adj* neighbo(u)ring
nacht (nahkht) *c* (pl ∼en) night; **'s nachts** by night; overnight
nachtclub (*nahkht*-klerp) *c* (pl ∼s) nightclub
nachtcrème (*nahkht*-kraim) *c* (pl ∼s) night cream
nachtegaal (*nahkh*-ter-gaal) *c* (pl -galen) nightingale
nachtelijk (*nahkh*-ter-lerk) *adj* nightly

nachtjapon (*nahkht*-ᵛaa-pon) *c* (pl ∼nen) nightdress
nachttarief (*nahkh*-taa-reef) *nt* (pl -rieven) night rate
nachttrein (*nahkh*-trayn) *c* (pl ∼en) night train
nachtvlucht (*nahkht*-flerkht) *c* (pl ∼en) night flight
nadat (naa-*daht*) *conj* after
nadeel (naa-*dāyl*) *nt* (pl -delen) disadvantage; handicap
nadelig (naa-*dāy*-lerkh) *adj* harmful
*****nadenken** (*naa*-dehng-kern) *v* *think; **nadenkend** thoughtful
nader (*naa*-derr) *adj* further
naderen (*naa*-der-rern) *v* approach; **naderend** oncoming
naderhand (naa-derr-*hahnt*) *adv* afterwards
nadien (naa-*deen*) *adv* afterwards
nadruk (*naa*-drerk) *c* stress; accent
nagedachtenis (*naa*-ger-dahkh-ter-nɪss) *c* memory
nagel (*naa*-gerl) *c* (pl ∼s) nail
nagelborstel (*naa*-gerl-bors-terl) *c* (pl ∼s) nailbrush
nagellak (*naa*-ger-lahk) *c* nail polish
nagelschaar (*naa*-gerl-skhaar) *c* (pl -scharen) nail scissors *pl*
nagelvijl (*naa*-gerl-vayl) *c* (pl ∼en) nail file
naïef (naa-*eef*) *adj* naïve
najaar (*naa*-ᵛaar) *nt* autumn

*najagen (*naa-ᵞaa*-gern) *v* chase
*nakijken (*naa*-kay-kern) *v* check
*nalaten (*naa*-laa-tern) *v* fail
nalatig (naa-*laa*-terkh) *adj* neglectful
namaak (*naa*-maak) *c* imitation
namaken (*naa*-maa-kern) *v* copy
namelijk (*naa*-mer-lerk) *adv* namely
namens (*naa*-merns) *adv* on behalf of, in the name of
namiddag (naa-*mɪ*-dahkh) *c* (pl ⁓en) afternoon
narcis (nahr-*sɪss*) *c* (pl ⁓sen) daffodil
narcose (nahr-*kōa*-zer) *c* narcosis
narcoticum (nahr-*kōa*-tee-kerm) *nt* (pl -ca) narcotic
narigheid (naa-*rerkh*-hayt) *c* (pl -heden) misery
naseizoen (*naa*-say-zōōn) *nt* low season
nastreven (*naa*-strāy-vern) *v* aim at, pursue
nat (naht) *adj* wet; damp, moist
natie (*naa*-tsee) *c* (pl ⁓s) nation
nationaal (naa-tshōa-*naal*) *adj* national; **nationale klederdracht** national dress
nationaliseren (naa-tshōa-naa-lee-*zāy*-rern) *v* nationalize
nationaliteit (naa-tshōa-naa-lee-*tayt*) *c* (pl ⁓en) nationality
natuur (naa-*tēwr*) *c* nature
natuurkunde (naa-*tēwr*-kern-der) *c* physics
natuurkundige (naa-tēwr-*kern*-der-ger) *c* (pl ⁓n) physicist
natuurlijk (naa-*tēwr*-lerk) *adj* natural; *adv* of course, naturally
natuurreservaat (naa-*tēw*-rāy-zerr-vaat) *nt* (pl -vaten) national park
nauw (nou) *adj* narrow; tight
nauwelijks (*nou*-er-lerks) *adv* hardly; scarcely, barely
nauwkeurig (nou-*kūr*-rerkh) *adj* accurate; precise, careful, exact

navel (*naa*-verl) *c* (pl ⁓s) navel
navigatie (naa-vee-*gaa*-tsee) *c* navigation
navraag (*naa*-vraakh) *c* inquiry; demand
*navragen (*naa*-vraa-gern) *v* query, inquire
*nazenden (*naa*-zehn-dern) *v* forward
nederig (*nāy*-der-rerkh) *adj* humble
nederlaag (*nāy*-derr-laakh) *c* (pl -lagen) defeat
Nederland (*nāy*-derr-lahnt) the Netherlands
Nederlander (*nāy*-derr-lahn-derr) *m* (f -landse, pl ⁓s) Dutchman
Nederlands (*nāy*-derr-lahnts) *adj* Dutch
nee (nāy) no
neef (nāyf) *c* (pl neven) cousin; nephew
neen (nāyn) no
neer (nāyr) *adv* down; downwards
*neerlaten (*nāyr*-laa-tern) *v* lower
*neerslaan (*nāyr*-slaan) *v* knock down
neerslachtig (nāyr-*slahkh*-terkh) *adj* down, low, blue, depressed
neerslachtigheid (nāyr-*slahkh*-terkh-hayt) *c* depression
neerslag (*nāyr*-slahkh) *c* precipitation
neerstorten (*nāyr*-stor-tern) *v* crash
negatief (*nāy*-gaa-teef) *adj* negative
negen (*nāy*-gern) *num* nine
negende (*nāy*-gern-der) *num* ninth
negentien (*nāy*-gern-teen) *num* nineteen
negentiende (*nāy*-gern-teen-der) *num* nineteenth
negentig (*nāy*-gern-terkh) *num* ninety
negeren (ner-*gāy*-rern) *v* ignore
negligé (nāy-glee-*zhāy*) *nt* (pl ⁓s) negligee
neigen (*nay*-gern) *v* *be inclined to; ⁓ **tot** *v* tend to
neiging (*nay*-gɪng) *c* (pl ⁓en) inclination, tendency; **de ⁓ *hebben**

tend

nek (nehk) c (pl ~ken) nape of the neck

*nemen (n$\overline{ay}$-mern) v *take;
gevangen ~ capture; **op zich ~** *take charge of

neon (n$\overline{ay}$-^{y}on) nt neon

nergens (nehr-gerns) adv nowhere

nerts (nehrts) nt (pl ~en) mink

nerveus (nehr-v$\overline{u}$rss) adj nervous

nest (nehst) nt (pl ~en) nest; litter

net¹ (neht) adj tidy, neat

net² (neht) nt (pl ~ten) net

netnummer (neht-ner-merr) nt (pl ~s) area code

netto (neh-t$\overline{oa}$) adj net

netvlies (neht-fleess) nt (pl -vliezen) retina

netwerk (neht-vehrk) nt (pl ~en) network

neuken (n$\overline{u}$-kern) v vulgar fuck

neuriën (n$\overline{u}$r-ree-^{y}ern) v hum

neurose (n$\overline{u}$r-r$\overline{oa}$-zer) c (pl ~n, ~s) neurosis

neus (n$\overline{u}$rss) c (pl neuzen) nose

neusbloeding (n$\overline{u}$rss-bl$\overline{oo}$-d$ı$ng) c (pl ~en) nosebleed

neusgat (n$\overline{u}$rss-khaht) nt (pl ~en) nostril

neushoorn (n$\overline{u}$rss-h$\overline{oa}$rn) c (pl ~s) rhinoceros

neutraal (n$\overline{u}$-traal) adj neutral

nevel (n$\overline{ay}$-verl) c (pl ~s, ~en) haze, mist

nicht (n$ı$kht) f (pl ~en) cousin; niece

nicotine (nee-k$\overline{oa}$-tee-ner) c nicotine

niemand (nee-mahnt) pron nobody, no one

nier (neer) c (pl ~en) kidney

niet (neet) adv not

nietig (nee-terkh) adj petty, insignificant; void

nietje (nee-t^{y}er) nt (pl ~s) staple

niet-roker (neet-r$\overline{oa}$-kerr) m (f -rookster, pl ~s) non-smoker

niets (neets) pron nothing; nil

nietsbetekenend (neets-ber-t$\overline{ay}$-ker-nernt) adj insignificant

nietszeggend (neet-seh-gernt) adj meaningless

niettemin (nee-ter-m$ı$n) adv nevertheless

nieuw (nee^{oo}) adj new

nieuwjaar (nee^{oo}-^{y}aar) New Year

nieuws (nee^{oo}ss) nt news

nieuwsberichten (nee^{oo}ss-ber-r$ı$kh-tern) pl news

nieuwsgierig (nee^{oo}-skhee-rerkh) adj curious, inquisitive, colloquial nosy

nieuwsgierigheid (nee^{oo}-skhee-rerkh-hayt) c curiosity

Nieuw-Zeeland (nee^{oo}-z$\overline{ay}$-lahnt) New Zealand

niezen (nee-zern) v sneeze

Nigeria (nee-g$\overline{ay}$-ree-^{y}aa) Nigeria

Nigeriaan (nee-g$\overline{ay}$-ree-^{y}aan) m (f ~se, pl -rianen) Nigerian

Nigeriaans (nee-g$\overline{ay}$-ree-^{y}aans) adj Nigerian

nijptang (nayp-tahng) c (pl ~en) pincers pl

nikkel (n$ı$-kerl) nt nickel

niks (n$ı$ks) pron nothing

nimmer (n$ı$-merr) adv never

niveau (nee-v$\overline{oa}$) nt (pl ~s) level

nivelleren (nee-ver-l$\overline{ay}$-rern) v level

noch ... noch (nokh) neither ... nor

nodig (n$\overline{oa}$-derkh) adj necessary; ~ *hebben need

noemen (n$\overline{oo}$-mern) v call; name, mention

nog (nokh) adv still, yet; ~ een another; ~ eens once more; ~ wat some more

noga (n$\overline{oa}$-gaa) c nougat

nogal (no-gahl) adv pretty, fairly, rather, quite

nogmaals (nokh-maals) adv once more

nominaal (n$\overline{oa}$-mee-naal) adj nominal

nominatie (n$\overline{oa}$-mee-naa-tsee) c (pl

~s) nomination

non (non) *f* (pl ~nen) nun

nonnenklooster (*no*-ner-klōass-terr) *nt* (pl ~s) nunnery

nonsens (*non*-sehns) *c* nonsense, rubbish

nood (nōat) *c* (pl noden) distress; misery; need

noodgedwongen (nōat-kher-*dvo*-ngern) *adv* by force

noodgeval (*nōat*-kher-vahl) *nt* (pl ~len) emergency

noodlot (nōat-lot) *nt* destiny, fate

noodlottig (nōat-*lo*-terkh) *adj* fatal

noodsein (*nōat*-sayn) *nt* (pl ~en) distress signal

noodtoestand (nōa-tōō-stahnt) *c* emergency

nooduitgang (nōat-ur^(ew)t-khahng) *c* (pl ~en) emergency exit

noodzaak (nōat-saak) *c* need, necessity

noodzakelijk (nōat-*saa*-ker-lerk) *adj* necessary

noodzaken (nōat-saa-kern) *v* force

nooit (nōa^(ee)t) *adv* never

Noor (nōar) *m* (f ~se, pl Noren) Norwegian

noord (nōart) *c* north

noordelijk (*nōar*-der-lerk) *adj* northern, northerly, north

noorden (*nōar*-dern) *nt* north

noordoosten (nōart-*ōass*-tern) *nt* north-east

noordpool (*nōart*-pōal) *c* North Pole

noordwesten (nōart-*vehss*-tern) *nt* north-west

Noors (nōars) *adj* Norwegian

Noorwegen (*nōar*-vāy-gern) Norway

noot (nōat) *c* (pl noten) nut; note

nootmuskaat (nōat-merss-*kaat*) *c* nutmeg

norm (norm) *c* (pl ~en) standard

normaal (nor-*maal*) *adj* normal, regular

nota (*nōa*-taa) *c* (pl ~'s) bill

notaris (nōa-*taa*-rerss) *m* (pl ~sen) notary

notendop (*nōa*-ter-dop) *c* (pl ~pen) nutshell

notenkraker (*nōa*-ter-kraa-kerr) *c* (pl ~s) nutcrackers *pl*

noteren (nōa-*tāy*-rern) *v* note; list

notie (*nōa*-tsee) *c* notion

notitie (nōa-*tee*-tsee) *c* (pl ~s) note

notitieboek (nōa-*tee*-tsee-bōōk) *nt* (pl ~en) notebook

notulen (nōa-*tēw*-lern) *pl* minutes

nou (nou) *adv* now

november (nōa-*vehm*-berr) November

nu (nēw) *adv* now; ~ **en dan** now and then; **tot ~ toe** so far

nuance (nēw-*ahng*-ser) *c* (pl ~s, ~n) nuance

nuchter (*nerkh*-terr) *adj* sober; down-to-earth, matter-of-fact

nucleair (nēw-klāy-^(y)*air*) *adj* nuclear

nul (nerl) *c* (pl ~len) nought, zero

nummer (*ner*-merr) *nt* (pl ~s) number; act

nummerbord (*ner*-merr-bort) *nt* (pl ~en) registration plate; licence plate *Am*

nut (nert) *nt* utility, use

nutteloos (*ner*-ter-lōass) *adj* useless

nuttig (*ner*-terkh) *adj* useful

nuttigen (*ner*-ter-khern) *v* consume

nylon® (*nay*-lon) *nt* nylon®

O

oase (ōa-*vaa*-zer) c (pl ~n, ~s) oasis

ober (ōa-berr) m (pl ~s) waiter

object (op-*ʸehkt*) nt (pl ~en) object

objectief (op-ʸehk-*teef*) adj objective

obligatie (ōa-blee-*gaa*-tsee) c (pl ~s) bond

obsceen (op-*sāyn*) adj obscene

obscuur (op-*skēwr*) adj obscure

observatie (op-sehr-*vaa*-tsee) c (pl ~s) observation

observatorium (op-sehr-vaa-*tōa*-ree-ʸerm) nt (pl -ria) observatory

observeren (op-sehr-*vāy*-rern) v observe

obsessie (op-*seh*-see) c (pl ~s) obsession

obstipatie (op-stee-*paa*-tsee) c constipation

oceaan (ōa-*sāy*-ʸaan) c (pl oceanen) ocean

ochtend (*okh*-ternt) c (pl ~en) morning

ochtendblad (*okh*-ternt-blaht) nt (pl ~en) morning paper

ochtendeditie (*okh*-ternt-*āy*-dee-tsee) c (pl ~s) morning edition

ochtendschemering (*okh*-ternt-skhāy-mer-rıng) c dawn

octopus (*ok*-tōa-perss) c (pl ~sen) octopus

octrooi (ok-*trōa*ᵉᵉ) nt (pl ~en) patent

oefenen (ōō-fer-nern) v practise, exercise

oefening (ōō-fer-nıng) c (pl ~en) exercise

oeroud (ōōr-out) adj ancient

oerwoud (ōōr-vout) nt (pl ~en) jungle

oester (ōōss-terr) c (pl ~s) oyster

oever (ōō-verr) c (pl ~s) river bank; bank, shore

of (of) conj or; whether; ~...of either... or; whether ... or

offensief¹ (o-fehn-*seef*) adj offensive

offensief² (o-fehn-*seef*) nt (pl -sieven) offensive

offer (*o*-ferr) nt (pl ~s) sacrifice

officieel (o-fee-*shāyl*) adj official

officier (o-fee-*seer*) m (pl ~en, ~s) officer

officieus (o-fee-*shērss*) adj unofficial

ofschoon (of-*skhōan*) conj although, though

ogenblik (ōa-germ-blık) nt (pl ~ken) moment, instant

ogenblikkelijk (ōa-germ-*blı*-ker-lerk) adv instantly

oktober (ok-*tōa*-berr) October

olie (ōa-lee) c oil

olieachtig (ōa-lee-ahkh-terkh) adj oily

oliebron (ōa-lee-bron) c (pl ~nen) oil well

oliedruk (ōa-lee-drerk) c oil pressure

oliefilter (ōa-lee-fıl-terr) nt (pl ~s) oil filter

oliën (ōa-lee-ʸern) v lubricate

olieraffinaderij (ōa-lee-rah-fee-naa-der-ray) c (pl ~en) oil refinery

olieverfschilderij (ōa-lee-vehrf-skhıl-der-ray) nt (pl ~en) oil painting

olifant (ōa-lee-fahnt) c (pl ~en) elephant

olijf (ōa-*layf*) c (pl olijven) olive

olijfolie (ōa-*layf*-ōa-lee) c olive oil

om (om) prep round, about, around; ~te to, in order to

oma (ōa-maa) f (pl ~'s) grandmother

***ombrengen** (*om*-breh-ngern) v kill

omcirkelen (om-*sır*-ker-lern) v encircle

omdat (om-*daht*) conj because; as

omdraaien (*om*-draaᵉᵉ-ern) v turn; invert; zich ~ turn round

omelet (ōa-mer-*leht*) nt (pl ~ten) omelette

*omgaan met (*om*-gaan) associate with, mix with

omgang (*om*-gahng) *c* intercourse; contact

omgekeerd (*om*-ger-kāyrt) *adj* reverse

*omgeven (om-gāy-vern) *v* surround, circle

omgeving (om-gāy-vɪng) *c* environment, surroundings *pl*; setting

omheen (om-*hāyn*) *adv* about

omheining (om-*hay*-nɪng) *c* (pl ~en) fence

omhelzen (om-*hehl*-zern) *v* hug, embrace

omhelzing (om-*hehl*-zɪng) *c* (pl ~en) hug, embrace

omhoog (om-*hōāk*h) *adv* up; ~ *gaan ascend

omhullen (om-*her*-lern) *v* envelop

omkeer (om-*kāyr*) *c* reverse

omkeren (om-*kāy*-rern) *v* turn over, turn, turn round; reverse

*omkomen (om-kōā-mern) *v* perish

*omkopen (om-kōā-pern) *v* bribe, corrupt

omkoping (om-kōā-pɪng) *c* (pl ~en) bribery, corruption

omlaag (om-*laakh*) *adv* down

omleiding (om-*lay*-dɪng) *c* (pl ~en) detour

omliggend (om-lɪ-gernt) *adj* surrounding

omloop (om-*lōāp*) *c* circulation; orbit

omrekenen (om-*rāy*-ker-nern) *v* convert

omrekentabel (om-*rāy*-ker-taa-behl) *c* (pl ~len) conversion chart

omringen (om-rɪng-ern) *v* encircle, surround, circle

*omschrijven (oam-*skhray*-vern) *v* define

omslag (om-slahkh) *c/nt* (pl ~en) cover, jacket

omslagdoek (om-slahkh-dōōk) *c* (pl ~en) shawl

omstandigheid (om-*stahn*-derkh-hayt) *c* (pl -heden) circumstance; condition

omstreden (om-*strāy*-dern) *adj* controversial

omstreeks (om-*strāyks*) *adv* about

omtrek (om-*trehk*) *c* (pl ~ken) contour, outline

omtrent (om-*trehnt*) *prep* about, concerning

omvang (*om*-vahng) *c* bulk, size; extent

omvangrijk (om-*vahng*-rayk) *adj* bulky, big; extensive

omvatten (om-*vah*-tern) *v* comprise

omver (om-*vehr*) *adv* down, over

omweg (*om*-vehkh) *c* (pl ~en) detour

omwenteling (*om*-vehn-ter-lɪng) *c* (pl ~en) revolution

omwisselen (*om*-vɪ-ser-lern) *v* switch

omzet (*om*-zeht) *c* (pl ~ten) turnover

omzetbelasting (*om*-zeht-ber-lahss-tɪng) *c* turnover tax; sales tax

onaangenaam (on-*aan*-ger-naam) *adj* unpleasant, disagreeable

onaanvaardbaar (on-aan-*vaart*-baar) *adj* unacceptable

onaardig (on-*aar*-derkh) *adj* unkind

onafgebroken (on-*ahf*-kher-brōā-kern) *adj* continuous

onafhankelijk (on-ahf-*hahng*-ker-lerk) *adj* independent

onafhankelijkheid (on-ahf-*hahng*-ker-lerk-hayt) *c* independence

onbeantwoord (om-ber-*ahnt*-vōārt) *adj* unanswered

onbebouwd (om-ber-*bout*) *adj* uncultivated

onbeduidend (om-ber-*dur*ew-dernt) *adj* petty, insignificant

onbegaanbaar (om-ber-*gaam*-baar) *adj* impassable

onbegrijpelijk (om-ber-*gray*-per-lerk) *adj* puzzling; incomprehensible

onbehaaglijk (om-ber-*haakh*-lerk) *adj* uneasy

onbekend (om-ber-*kehnt*) *adj* unfamiliar, unknown

onbekwaam (om-ber-*kvaam*) *adj* unable, incompetent, incapable

onbelangrijk (om-ber-*lahng*-rayk) *adj* unimportant; insignificant

onbeleefd (om-ber-*lāyft*) *adj* impolite, *colloquial* cheeky

onbemind (om-ber-*mınt*) *adj* unpopular

onbepaald (om-ber-*paalt*) *adj* indefinite; **onbepaalde wijs** infinitive

onbeperkt (om-ber-*pehrkt*) *adj* unlimited

onbeschaamd (om-ber-*skhaamt*) *adj* impudent, impertinent, insolent

onbeschaamdheid (om-ber-*skhaamt*-hayt) *c* impertinence, insolence

onbescheiden (om-ber-*skhay*-dern) *adj* immodest

onbeschermd (om-ber-*skhehrmt*) *adj* unprotected

onbeschoft (oam-ber-*skhoft*) *adj* impertinent

onbetrouwbaar (om-ber-*trou*-baar) *adj* untrustworthy, unreliable

onbevoegd (om-ber-*vōōkht*) *adj* unqualified; unauthorized

onbevredigend (om-ber-*vrāy*-der-gernt) *adj* unsatisfactory

onbewoonbaar (om-ber-*vōām*-baar) *adj* uninhabitable

onbewoond (om-ber-*vōānt*) *adj* uninhabited

onbewust (om-ber-*verst*) *adj* unaware

onbezet (om-ber-*zeht*) *adj* unoccupied

onbezonnen (om-ber-*zo*-nern) *adj* rash

onbezorgd (om-ber-*zorkht*) *adj* carefree

onbillijk (om-*bı*-lerk) *adj* unfair

onbreekbaar (om-ber-*brāyk*-baar) *adj* unbreakable

ondankbaar (on-*dahngk*-baar) *adj* ungrateful

ondanks (*on*-dahngks) *prep* despite, in spite of

ondenkbaar (on-*dehngk*-baar) *adj* inconceivable

onder (*on*-derr) *prep* under; beneath, below; among, amid

onderaan (on-der-*raan*) *adv* below

***onderbreken** (on-derr-*brāy*-kern) *v* interrupt

onderbreking (on-derr-*brāy*-kıng) *c* (pl ~en) interruption

***onderbrengen** (*on*-derr-breh-ngern) *v* accommodate

onderbroek (*on*-derr-brōōk) *c* (pl ~en) briefs *pl*, (*women's*) knickers *pl*, panties *pl*, drawers *pl*; (*men's*) pants *pl*, shorts *plAm*, underpants *plAm*

onderdaan (*on*-derr-daan) *c* (pl -danen) subject

onderdak (*on*-derr-dahk) *nt* accommodation

onderdeel (*on*-derr-dāyl) *nt* (pl -delen) part

onderdrukken (on-derr-*drer*-kern) *v* suppress

***ondergaan** (on-derr-*gaan*) *v* suffer

ondergang (*on*-derr-gahng) *c* destruction; ruin

ondergeschikt (on-derr-ger-*skhıkt*) *adj* subordinate; secondary, minor

ondergoed (*on*-derr-gōōt) *nt* underwear

ondergronds (on-derr-*gronts*) *adj* underground

ondergrondse (on-derr-*gron*-tser) *c* underground, subway *nAm*

onderhandelen (on-derr-*hahn*-der-lern) *v* negotiate

onderhandeling (on-derr-*hahn*-der-lıng) *c* (pl ~en) negotiation

onderhevig aan (on-derr-*hay*-verkh-aan) subject to; liable to; **aan bederf onderhevig** perishable

onderhoud (*on*-derr-hout) nt upkeep; maintenance

***onderhouden** (on-derr-*hou*-dern) v entertain

onderling (*on*-derr-lng) adj mutual

***ondernemen** (on-derr-*nay*-mern) v *undertake

onderneming (on-derr-*nay*-mng) c (pl ~en) enterprise, undertaking; concern, company

onderrichten (on-der-*rkh*-tern) v instruct

onderrok (*on*-derr-rok) c (pl ~ken) slip

onderschatten (on-derr-*skhah*-tern) v underestimate

onderscheid (*on*-derr-skhayt) nt distinction; difference; ~ **maken** distinguish

***onderscheiden** (on-derr-*skhay*-dern) v distinguish

onderst (*on*-derrst) adj bottom

ondersteboven (on-derr-ster-*boa*-vern) adv upside down

ondersteunen (on-derr-*stur*-nern) v *hold up, support

onderstrepen (on-derr-*stray*-pern) v underline

onderstroom (*on*-derr-stroam) c (pl -stromen) undercurrent

ondertekenen (on-derr-*tay*-ker-nern) v sign

ondertitel (*on*-derr-tee-terl) c (pl ~s) subtitle

ondertussen (on-derr-*ter*-sern) adv in the meantime, meanwhile

***ondervinden** (on-derr-*vn*-dern) v experience

ondervoeding (on-derr-*voo*-dng) c malnutrition

***ondervragen** (on-derr-*vraa*-gern) v interrogate, question

onderwerp (*on*-derr-vehrp) nt (pl ~en) subject; topic, theme

***onderwerpen** (on-derr-*vehr*-pern) v subject; **zich ~** submit

onderwijs (*on*-derr-vayss) nt tuition; education, instruction

***onderwijzen** (on-derr-*vay*-zern) v *teach

onderwijzer (on-derr-*vay*-zerr) m (f ~es, pl ~s) schoolteacher, schoolmaster, master, teacher

onderzoek (*on*-derr-zook) nt (pl ~en) enquiry, investigation, inquiry; checkup, examination; research

***onderzoeken** (on-derr-*zoo*-kern) v enquire, investigate, examine; explore

ondeugend (on-*dur*-gernt) adj naughty, mischievous

ondiep (on-*deep*) adj shallow

ondoeltreffend (on-dool-*treh*-fehnt) adj inefficient

ondraaglijk (on-*draakh*-lerk) adj unbearable

onduidelijk (on-*dur*ᵉʷ-der-lerk) adj ambiguous

onecht (on-*ehkht*) adj false

oneens: het ~ *zijn (ert on-*ayns* zayn) disagree

oneerlijk (on-*ayr*-lerk) adj crooked, dishonest; unfair

oneetbaar (on-*ayt*-baar) adj inedible

oneffen (on-*eh*-fern) adj uneven

oneindig (on-*ayn*-derkh) adj infinite, endless; immense

onenigheid (on-*ay*-nerkh-hayt) c (pl -heden) dispute

onervaren (on-ehr-*vaa*-rern) adj inexperienced

oneven (on-*ay*-vern) adj odd

onevenwichtig (on-*ay*-ver-*vkh*-terkh) adj unsteady

onfatsoenlijk (om-faht-*soon*-lerk) adj indecent

ongeacht (ong-*ger-ahkht*) prep in spite

of

ongebruikelijk (ong-ger-*brur^{ew}*-ker-lerk) *adj* unusual

ongeduldig (ong-ger-*derl*-derkh) *adj* impatient; eager

ongedurig (ong-ger-*d$\overline{ew}$*-rerkh) *adj* restless

ongedwongen (ong-ger-*dvo*-ngern) *adj* casual

ongedwongenheid (ong-ger-*dvo*-nger-hayt) *c* ease

ongeldig (ong-*gehl*-derkh) *adj* invalid

ongelegen (ong-ger-*l$\overline{ay}$*-gern) *adj* inconvenient

ongelijk (ong-ger-*layk*) *adj* unequal; uneven; ~ ***hebben** *be wrong

ongelofelijk (ong-ger-*l$\overline{oa}$*-fer-lerk) *adj* incredible

ongeluk (*ong*-ger-lerk) *nt* (pl ~ken) accident; misfortune; ~**je** mishap

ongelukkig (ong-ger-*ler*-kerkh) *adj* unhappy; unlucky, unfortunate

ongelukkigerwijs (ong-ger-ler-ker-gerr-*vayss*) *adv* unfortunately

ongemak (*ong*-ger-mahk) *nt* (pl ~ken) inconvenience

ongemakkelijk (ong-ger-*mah*-ker-lerk) *adj* uncomfortable

ongeneeslijk (ong-ger-*n$\overline{ay}$ss*-lerk) *adj* incurable

ongepast (ong-ger-*pahst*) *adj* unsuitable; improper

ongerief (*ong*-ger-reef) *nt* inconvenience

ongerijmd (ong-ger-*raymt*) *adj* absurd

ongerust (ong-ger-*rerst*) *adj* worried; **zich ~ maken** worry

ongeschikt (ong-ger-*skhikt*) *adj* unfit

ongeschoold (ong-ger-*skh$\overline{oa}$lt*) *adj* uneducated; unskilled

ongetrouwd (ong-ger-*trout*) *adj* single

ongetwijfeld (ong-ger-*tvay*-ferlt) *adv* undoubtedly

ongeval (*ong*-ger-vahl) *nt* (pl ~len) accident

ongeveer (ong-ger-*v$\overline{ay}$r*) *adv* about, approximately

ongevoelig (ong-ger-*v$\overline{oo}$*-lerkh) *adj* insensitive

ongewenst (ong-ger-*vehnst*) *adj* undesirable

ongewoon (ong-ger-*v$\overline{oa}$n*) *adj* uncommon, unusual

ongezond (ong-ger-*z*ont) *adj* unhealthy, unsound

ongunstig (ong-*gerns*-terkh) *adj* unfavo(u)rable

onhandig (on-*hahn*-derkh) *adj* clumsy, awkward

onheil (*on*-hayl) *nt* calamity, disaster; mischief

onheilspellend (on-hayl-*speh*-lernt) *adj* sinister; ominous

onherroepelijk (on-heh-*r$\overline{oo}$*-per-lerk) *adj* irrevocable

onherstelbaar (on-hehr-*stehl*-baar) *adj* irreparable

onjuist (oñ-*ur^{ew}st*) *adj* incorrect

onkosten (*ong*-koss-tern) *pl* expenses *pl*

onkruid (*ong*-krur^{ew}t) *nt* weed

onlangs (*on*-lahngs) *adv* recently; lately

onleesbaar (on-*l$\overline{ay}$ss*-baar) *adj* illegible

onmetelijk (o-*m$\overline{ay}$*-ter-lerk) *adj* vast, immense

onmiddellijk (o-*mı*-der-lerk) *adj* immediate, prompt; *adv* immediately, instantly

onmogelijk (o-*m$\overline{oa}$*-ger-lerk) *adj* impossible

onnauwkeurig (o-nou-*k$\overline{ur}$*-rerkh) *adj* inaccurate; incorrect

onnodig (o-*n$\overline{oa}$*-derkh) *adj* unnecessary

onontbeerlijk (on-ont-*b$\overline{ay}$r*-lerk) *adj* essential

onopvallend (on-op-*fah*-lernt) *adj*
inconspicuous

onopzettelijk (on-op-*seh*-ter-lerk) *adj*
unintentional

onoverkomelijk (on-ōa-verr-*kōa*-mer-lerk) *adj* prohibitive

onovertroffen (on-ōa-verr-*tro*-fern) *adj* unsurpassed

onpartijdig (om-pahr-*tay*-derkh) *adj*
impartial

onpersoonlijk (om-pehr-*sōan*-lerk) *adj* impersonal

onplezierig (om-pler-*zee*-rerkh) *adj*
unpleasant

onrecht (*on*-rehkht) *nt* injustice; wrong; ~ **aandoen* wrong

onrechtvaardig (on-rehkht-*faar*-derkh) *adj* unjust

onredelijk (on-*rāy*-der-lerk) *adj*
unreasonable

onregelmatig (on-rāy-gerl-*maa*-terkh) *adj* irregular

onrein (on-*rayn*) *adj* unclean

onrust (*on*-rerst) *c* unrest

onrustig (on-*rerss*-terkh) *adj* restless

ons (ons) *pron* our; us; ourselves

onschadelijk (on-*skhaa*-der-lerk) *adj*
harmless

onschatbaar (on-*skhaht*-baar) *adj*
priceless

onschuld (*on*-skherlt) *c* innocence

onschuldig (on-*skherl*-derkh) *adj*
innocent

ontbijt (ont-*bayt*) *nt* breakfast

*ontbinden (ont-*bin*-dern) *v* dissolve

*ontbreken (ont-*brāy*-kern) *v* fail; **ontbrekend** missing

ontdekken (on-*deh*-kern) *v* detect, discover

ontdekking (on-*deh*-king) *c* (pl ~en) discovery

ontdooien (on-*dōaᵉᵉ*-ern) *v* thaw

ontevreden (on-ter-*vrāy*-dern) *adj*
dissatisfied; discontented

*ontgaan (ont-*khaan*) *v* escape

ontglippen (ont-*khli*-pern) *v* slip

onthaal (ont-*haal*) *nt* reception

*ontheffen (ont-*heh*-fern) *v* exempt; ~ **van** discharge of

*onthouden (ont-*hou*-dern) *v*
remember; deny; **zich ~ van** abstain from

onthullen (ont-*her*-lern) *v* reveal

onthulling (ont-*her*-ling) *c* (pl ~en) revelation

onthutsen (ont-*hert*-sern) *v*
overwhelm

ontkennen (ont-*keh*-nern) *v* deny; **ontkennend** negative

ontkoppelen (ont-*ko*-per-lern) *v*
disconnect

ontkurken (ont-*kerr*-kern) *v* uncork

ontleden (ont-*lāy*-dern) *v* analyse; **break down*

ontlenen (ont-*lāy*-nern) *v* borrow

ontmoedigen (ont-*mōō*-der-gern) *v*
discourage

ontmoeten (ont-*mōō*-tern) *v*
encounter; **meet*

ontmoeting (ont-*mōō*-ting) *c* (pl ~en) encounter, meeting

*ontnemen (ont-*nāy*-mern) *v* deprive of

ontoegankelijk (on-tōō-*gahng*-ker-lerk) *adj* inaccessible

ontploffen (ont-*plo*-fern) *v* explode

ontplooien (ont-*plōaᵉᵉ*-ern) *v* expand

ontroeren (oant-*rōō*-rern) *v* move

ontroering (oant-*rōō*-ring) *c* emotion

ontrouw (*on*-trou) *adj* unfaithful

ontruimen (ont-*rurᵉʷ*-mern) *v* vacate

ontschepen (ont-*skhāy*-pern) *v*
disembark

*ontslaan (ont-*slaan*) *v* dismiss, fire

ontslag *nemen (ont-*slahkh nāy*-mern) resign

ontslagneming (ont-*slahkh-nāy*-ming) *c* resignation

ontsmetten (ont-*smeh*-tern) *v*
disinfect

ontsmettingsmiddel (ont-*smeh*-tungs-mı-derl) *nt* (pl ~en) disinfectant

ontsnappen (ont-*snah*-pern) *v* escape

ontsnapping (ont-*snah*-pıng) *c* (pl ~en) escape

ontspannen (ont-*spah*-nern) *adj* easy-going

ontspannen (ont-*spah*-nern): **zich ~** relax

ontspanning (ont-*spah*-ning) *c* relaxation; recreation

***ontstaan** (ont-*staan*) *v* *arise

***ontsteken** (ont-*stay*-kern) *v* *become septic

ontsteking (ont-*stay*-kıng) *c* (pl ~en) ignition; ignition coil; inflammation

ontstemmen (ont-*steh*-mern) *v* displease

***ontvangen** (ont-*fah*-ngern) *v* receive; entertain

ontvangst (ont-*fahngst*) *c* (pl ~en) receipt; reception

ontvlambaar (ont-*flahm*-baar) *adj* inflammable

ontvluchten (ont-*flerkh*-tern) *v* escape

ontvouwen (ont-*fou*-ern) *v* unfold

ontwaken (ont-*vaa*-kern) *v* wake up

ontwerp (ont-*vehrp*) *nt* (pl ~en) design

***ontwerpen** (ont-*vehr*-pern) *v* design

***ontwijken** (ont-*vay*-kern) *v* avoid

ontwikkelen (ont-*vı*-ker-lern) *v* develop

ontwikkeling (ont-*vı*-ker-lıng) *c* (pl ~en) development

ontwricht (ont-*frıkht*) *adj* dislocated

ontzag (ont-*sahkh*) *nt* respect

***ontzeggen** (ont-*seh*-gern) *v* deny

ontzettend (ont-*seh*-ternt) *adj* dreadful, terrible

onuitstaanbaar (on-ur^cwt-*staam*-baar) *adj* intolerable

onvast (*on*-vahst) *adj* unsteady

onveilig (on-*vay*-lerkh) *adj* unsafe

onverdiend (*on*-verr-deent) *adj* unearned

onverklaarbaar (on-verr-*klaar*-baar) *adj* unaccountable

onvermijdelijk (on-verr-*may*-der-lerk) *adj* unavoidable, inevitable

onverschillig (on-verr-*skhı*-lerkh) *adj* indifferent

onverstandig (on-verr-*stahn*-derkh) *adj* unwise

onverwacht (*on*-verr-vahkht) *adj* unexpected

onvoldoende (on-vol-*doon*-der) *adj* insufficient; inadequate

onvolledig (on-vo-*lay*-derkh) *adj* incomplete

onvolmaakt (on-vol-*maakt*) *adj* imperfect

onvoorstelbaar (on-voar-*stehl*-baar) *adj* inconceivable

onvoorwaardelijk (on-voar-*vaar*-der-lerk) *adj* unconditional

onvoorzien (on-voar-*zeen*) *adj* unexpected

onvriendelijk (on-*vreen*-der-lerk) *adj* unkind, unfriendly

onwaar (*on*-vaar) *adj* untrue, false

onwaarschijnlijk (on-vaar-*skhayn*-lerk) *adj* unlikely, improbable

onweer (*on*-vayr) *nt* thunderstorm

onweerachtig (*on*-vayr-ahkh-terkh) *adj* thundery

onwel (on-*vehl*) *adj* unwell

onwerkelijk (on-*vehr*-ker-lerk) *adj* unreal

onwetend (on-*vay*-ternt) *adj* ignorant

onwettig (on-*veh*-terkh) *adj* unlawful, illegal

onwillig (on-*vı*-lerkh) *adj* unwilling

onyx (*oa*-nıks) *nt* onyx

onzeker (on-*zay*-kerr) *adj* doubtful, uncertain

onzelfzuchtig (on-zehlf-*serkh*-terkh)

adj unselfish

onzichtbaar (on-*zıkht*-baar) *adj* invisible

onzijdig (on-*zay*-derkh) *adj* neuter

onzin (*on*-zın) *c* nonsense, rubbish

oog (ōakh) *nt* (pl ogen) eye

oogarts (ōakh-ahrts) *c* (pl ~en) oculist

ooggetuige (ōa-kher-tur^(ew)-ger) *c* (pl ~n) eyewitness

ooglid (ōakh-lıt) *nt* (pl -leden) eyelid

oogschaduw (ōa-g-skhaa-dēw^(oo)) *c* eye shadow

oogst (ōakhst) *c* (pl ~en) harvest; crop

oogsten (ōakh-stern) *v* harvest, crop, reap, gather

ooievaar (ōa^(ee)-er-vaar) *c* (pl ~s) stork

ooit (ōa^(ee)t) *adv* ever

ook (ōak) *adv* also, too; as well

oom (ōam) *m* (pl ~s) uncle

oor (ōar) *nt* (pl oren) ear

oorbel (ōar-behl) *c* (pl ~len) earring

oordeel (ōar-dāyl) *nt* (pl -delen) judgment

oordelen (ōar-dāy-lern) *v* judge

oorlog (ōar-lokh) *c* (pl ~en) war

oorlogsschip (ōar-lokh-skhıp) *nt* (pl -schepen) man-of-war

oorpijn (ōar-payn) *c* earache

oorsprong (ōar-sprong) *c* (pl ~en) origin

oorspronkelijk (ōar-*sprong*-ker-lerk) *adj* original

oorzaak (ōar-zaak) *c* (pl -zaken) cause; reason

oost (ōast) *c* east; **oost-** eastern

oostelijk (o-ster-lerk) *adj* eastern, easterly

oosten (ōa-stern) *nt* east

Oostenrijk (ōa-stern-rayk) Austria

Oostenrijker (ōa-stern-ray-kerr) *m* (f -rijkse, pl ~s) Austrian

Oostenrijks (ōa-stern-rayks) *adj* Austrian

oosters (ōa-sterrs) *adj* oriental

op (op) *prep* on, upon; at, in; *adv* up; finished

opa (ōa-paa) *c* (pl ~'s) grandfather, granddad

opaal (ōa-*paal*) *c* (pl opalen) opal

opbellen (o-beh-lern) *v* call, ring up, phone; call up *Am*

***opbergen** (o-behr-gern) *v* *put away

opblaasbaar (o-*blaass*-baar) *adj* inflatable

***opblazen** (o-blaa-zern) *v* inflate; blow up

opbouw (o-bou) *c* construction

opbouwen (o-bou-ern) *v* erect; construct

opbrengst (o-brehngst) *c* (pl ~en) produce

opdat (ob-*daht*) *conj* so that

opdracht (*op*-drahkht) *c* (pl ~en) order; assignment

***opdragen aan** (*oap*-draa-gern) assign to

opeens (op-*ayns*) *adv* suddenly

opeisen (*op*-ay-sern) *v* claim

open (ōa-pern) *adj* open

openbaar (ōa-perm-*baar*) *adj* public

openbaren (ōa-perm-*baa*-rern) *v* reveal

opendraaien (ōa-per-draa^(ee)ern) *v* turn on

openen (ōa-per-nern) *v* unlock; open

opener (ōa-per-ner) *c* (pl ~s) opener

openhartig (ōa-per-*hahr*-terkh) *adj* open

opening (ōa-per-nıng) *c* (pl ~en) opening, gap

openingstijden (ōa-per-nıngs-tay-dern) *pl* business hours

opera (ōa-per-raa) *c* (pl ~'s) opera; opera house

operatie (ōa-per-*raa*-tsee) *c* (pl ~s) operation, surgery

opereren (ōa-per-*rāy*-rern) *v* operate

operette (ōa-per-*reh*-ter) *c* (pl ~s)

operetta

*opgaan (*op*-khaan) *v* *rise

opgeruimd (*op*-kher-rur^(ew)mt) *adj* good-humo(u)red

opgetogen (*oap*-kher-tōā-gern) *adj* delighted

*opgeven (*oap*-khāy-vern) *v* declare; *give up

opgewekt (*op*-kher-vehkt) *adj* cheerful

opgewonden (*op*-kher-von-dern) *adj* ecxited

opgraving (*op*-khraa-vɪng) *c* (pl ~en) excavation

ophaalbrug (*op*-haal-brerkh) *c* (pl ~gen) drawbridge

ophalen (*op*-haa-lern) *v* collect, pick up

*ophangen (*op*-hah-ngern) *v* *hang

ophanging (*op*-hah-ngɪng) *c* suspension

ophef (*op*-hehf) *c* fuss

*opheffen (*op*-heh-fern) *v* discontinue

ophelderen (*op*-hehl-der-rern) *v* clarify

*ophouden (*op*-hou-dern) *v* cease; ~ met stop; quit

opinie (ōā-*pee*-nee) *c* (pl ~s) opinion

opklaren (*op*-klaa-rern) *v* brighten; doen ~ brighten

opkomst (*op*-komst) *c* rise; attendance

oplage (*op*-laa-ger) *c* (pl ~n) issue

opleiden (*op*-lay-dern) *v* educate

opletten (*op*-leh-tern) *v* *pay attention; **oplettend** attentive

oplichten (*op*-lɪkh-tern) *v* cheat, swindle

oplichter (*op*-lɪkh-terr) *m* (f-ster, pl ~s) swindler

*oplopen (*op*-lōā-pern) *v* increase; contract

oplosbaar (*op*-*loss*-baar) *adj* soluble

oplossen (*op*-lo-sern) *v* dissolve; solve

oplossing (*op*-lo-sɪng) *c* (pl ~en) solution

opmerkelijk (op-*mehr*-ker-lerk) *adj* remarkable; noticeable, striking

opmerken (*op*-mehr-kern) *v* notice, note; remark

opmerking (*op*-mehr-kɪng) *c* (pl ~en) remark

opname (*op*-naa-mer) *c* (pl ~n) recording; shot

*opnemen (*op*-nāy-mern) *v* *draw

opnieuw (op-*nee*^(ōō)) *adv* again

opofferen (*op*-o-fer-rern) *v* sacrifice

oponthoud (*op*-ont-hout) *nt* delay

oppassen (*o*-pah-sern) *v* look out, beware

oppasser (*o*-pah-serr) *c* (pl ~s) attendant

opperhoofd (*o*-perr-hōāft) *nt* (pl ~en) chieftain

oppervlakkig (o-perr-*vlah*-kerkh) *adj* superficial

oppervlakte (*o*-perr-vlahk-ter) *c* (pl ~n, ~s) surface; area

oppositie (o-pōā-*see*-tsee) *c* (pl ~s) opposition

oprapen (*op*-raa-pern) *v* pick up

oprecht (op-*rehkht*) *adj* honest, sincere, earnest

oprichten (*op*-rɪkh-tern) *v* found; erect

*oprijzen (*op*-ray-zern) *v* *arise

oproer (*op*-rōōr) *nt* revolt, rebellion

opruimen (*op*-rur^(ew)-mern) *v* tidy up, clear

opruiming (*op*-rur^(ew)-mɪng) *c* clearance sale

opscheppen (*op*-skheh-pern) *v* boast

*opschieten (*op*-skhee-tern) *v* hurry

opschorten (*op*-skhor-tern) *v* *put off

*opschrijven (*op*-skhray-vern) *v* *write down

*opslaan (*op*-slaan) *v* store

opslag^1 (*op*-slahkh) *c* storage

opslag^2 (*op*-slahkh) *c* rise; raise *nAm*

opslagplaats (*op*-slahkh-plaats) *c* (pl

~en) depot

*opsluiten (*op*-slur^(ew)-tern) *v* lock up

opsporen (*op*-spōa-rern) *v* trace

*opstaan (*op*-staan) *v* *get up, *rise

opstand (*op*-stahnt) *c* (pl ~en) rising, revolt, rebellion; **in ~ *komen** revolt

opstapelen (*op*-staa-per-lern) *v* pile

opstel (*op*-stehl) *nt* (pl ~len) essay

opstellen (*op*-steh-lern) *v* *draw up, *make up

*opstijgen (*op*-stay-gern) *v* ascend

optellen (*op*-teh-lern) *v* add; count

optelling (*op*-teh-lɪng) *c* (pl ~en) addition

opticien (op-tee-*shanḡ*) *m* (pl ~s) optician

optillen (*op*-tɪ-lern) *v* lift; raise

optimisme (op-tee-*mɪss*-mer) *nt* optimism

optimist (op-tee-*mɪst*) *m* (f ~e, pl ~en) optimist

optimistisch (op-tee-*mɪss*-teess) *adj* optimistic

optocht (*op*-tokht) *c* (pl ~en) parade

optreden (*op*-trāy-dern) *nt* (pl ~s) appearance

*optreden (*op*-trāy-dern) *v* act; appear

*opvallen (*op*-fah-lern) *v* attract attention; **opvallend** striking

opvatten (*op*-fah-tern) *v* conceive

opvatting (*op*-fah-tɪng) *c* (pl ~en) view

opvoeden (*op*-fōō-dern) *v* *bring up, educate

opvoeding (*op*-fōō-dɪng) *c* education

opvolgen (*op*-fol-gern) *v* succeed

*opvouwen (*op*-fou-ern) *v* fold

opvrolijken (*op*-frōa-ler-kern) *v* cheer up

opvullen (*op*-fer-lern) *v* fill up

*opwinden (*op*-vɪn-dern) *v* *wind; excite

opwinding (*op*-vɪn-dɪng) *c* excitement

opzettelijk (op-*seh*-ter-lerk) *adj* deliberate, intentional; on purpose

opzicht (*op*-sɪkht) *nt* (pl ~en) respect

opzichter (*op*-sɪkh-terr) *m* (pl ~s) supervisor; warden

opzienbarend (op-seen-*baa*-rernt) *adj* sensational

opzij (op-*say*) *adv* aside; sideways

*opzoeken (*op*-sōō-kern) *v* look up

oranje (ōa-*rah*-ñer) *adj* orange

orde[1] (*or*-der) *c* order; method; **in ~** in order; **in orde!** okay!, all right!

orde[2] (*or*-der) *c* (pl ~n, ~s) congregation

ordenen (*or*-der-nern) *v* arrange

ordinair (or-dee-*nair*) *adj* common, vulgar

orgaan (or-*gaan*) *nt* (pl organen) organ

organisatie (or-gaa-nee-*zaa*-tsee) *c* (pl ~s) organization

organisch (or-*gaa*-neess) *adj* organic

organiseren (or-gaa-nee-*zāy*-rern) *v* organize

orgel (*or*-gerl) *nt* (pl ~s) organ

oriënteren (ōa-ree-^(y)ehn-*tāy*-rern): **zich ~** orientate

origine (ōa-ree-*zhee*-ner) *c* origin

origineel (ōa-ree-zhee-*nāyl*) *adj* original

orkaan (or-*kaan*) *c* (pl orkanen) hurricane

orkest (or-*kehst*) *nt* (pl ~en) orchestra; band

orlon (*or*-lon) *nt* orlon

ornamenteel (or-naa-mehn-*tāyl*) *adj* ornamental

orthodox (or-tōa-*doks*) *adj* orthodox

os (oss) *c* (pl ~sen) ox

oud (out) *adj* old; ancient; aged

oudbakken (out-*bah*-kern) *adj* stale

ouder (*ou*-derr) *adj* elder; *c* parent *n*; **ouders** *pl* parents *pl*

ouderdom (*ou*-derr-dom) *c* age; old age

ouderwets (ou-derr-*vehts*) *adj* old-fashioned, ancient; out of date; quaint

oudheden (*out*-hāy-dern) *pl*

antiquities *pl*

Oudheid (*out*-hayt) *c* antiquity

oudheidkunde (*out*-hayt-kern-der) *c* archaeology

oudst (outst) *adj*, **oudste** eldest, elder

ouverture (ōō-verr-*few*-rer) *c* (pl ~s, ~n) overture

ouvreuse (ōō-*vrūr*-zer) *f* (pl ~s) usherette

ovaal (ōā-*vaal*) *adj* oval

oven (*ōā*-vern) *c* (pl ~s) oven; furnace;

over (*ōā*-verr) *prep* about; over; across; in; *adv* over

overal (*ōā*-verr-ahl) *adv* everywhere; anywhere, throughout

overall (*ōā*-ver-*rahl*) *c* (pl ~s) overalls *pl*

*overblijfsel (*ōā*-verr-blayf-serl) *nt* (pl ~s, ~en) remnant

*overblijven (*ōā*-verr-blay-vern) *v* remain

overbodig (*ōā*-verr-*bōā*-derkh) *adj* superfluous; redundant

*overbrengen (*ōā*-verr-breh-ngern) *v* transfer

overdag (*ōā*-verr-*dahkh*) *adv* by day

*overdenken (*ōā*-verr-*dehng*-kern) *v* *think over

*overdrijven (*ōā*-verr-*dray*-vern) *v* exaggerate, magnify, overdo; **overdreven** extravagant, overdone

*overeenkomen (*ōā*-ver-*rāyng*-kōā-mern) *v* agree; correspond

overeenkomst (*ōā*-ver-*rāyng*-komst) *c* (pl ~en) agreement, settlement

overeenkomstig (*ōā*-ver-*rāyng*-*kom*-sterkh) *adj* similar; *prep* according to

overeenstemming (*ōā*-ver-*rāyn*-steh-ming) *c* agreement

overeind (*ōā*-ver-*raynt*) *adv* upright; erect

overgang (*ōā*-ver-gahng) *c* (pl ~en) transition

overgave (*ōā*-verr-gaa-ver) *c* surrender

*overgeven (*ōā*-verr-*gāy*-vern) *v* vomit; **zich *overgeven** surrender

*overgewicht (*ōā*-verr-ger-vikht) *nt* overweight

overhaast (*ōā*-verr-*haast*) *adj* rash

overhalen (*ōā*-verr-haa-lern) *v* persuade

*overhebben (*ōā*-verr-heh-bern) *v* spare

overheersing (*ōā*-verr-*hāyr*-sing) *c* domination

overheid (*ōā*-verr-hayt) *c* (pl -heden) authorities *pl*

overhemd (*ōā*-verr-hehmt) *nt* (pl ~en) shirt

overig (*ōā*-ver-rerkh) *adj* remaining

overigens (*ōā*-ver-rer-gerns) *adv* though

overjas (*ōā*-verr-ʸahss) *c* (pl ~sen) overcoat

overkant (aan der *ōā*-verr-kahnt): **aan de ~** across

overleg (*ōā*-verr-*lehkh*) *nt* deliberation

overleggen (*ōā*-verr-*leh*-gern) *v* deliberate

overleven (*ōā*-verr-*lāy*-vern) *v* survive

overleving (*ōā*-verr-*lāy*ving) *c* survival

*overlijden (*ōā*-verr-*lay*-dern) *v* depart, die

overmaken (*ōā*-verr-maa-kern) *v* remit

overmoedig (*ōā*-verr-*mōō*-derkh) *adj* presumptuous

*overnemen (*ōā*-verr-*nāy*-mern) *v* *take over

overreden (*ōā*-ver-*rāy*-dern) *v* persuade

overschot (*ōā*-verr-skhot) *nt* (pl ~ten) surplus

*overschrijden (*ōā*-verr-*skhray*-dern) *v* exceed

overschrijving (*ōā*-verr-skhray-ving) *c* (pl ~en) money order

*overslaan (*ōā*-verr-slaan) *v* skip

overspannen (ōā-verr-*spah*-nern) *adj*
overstrung; overworked
overstappen (ōā-verr-stah-pern) *v*
change
oversteekplaats (ōā-verr-stāyk-
plaats) *c* (pl ~en) crossing
***oversteken** (ōā-verr-stāy-kern) *v*
cross
overstroming (ōā-verr-*strōā*-mɪng) *c*
(pl ~en) flood
overstuur (ōā-verr-*stewr*) *adj* upset
overtocht (ōā-verr-tokht) *c* (pl ~en)
crossing, passage
***overtreden** (ōā-verr-*trāy*-dern) *v*
offend
overtreding (ōā-verr-*trāy*-dɪng) *c* (pl
~en) offense *Am*, offence
***overtreffen** (ōā-verr-*treh*-fern) *v*
*outdo, exceed
overtuigen (ōā-verr-*tur*ᵉʷ-gern) *v*
convince; persuade
overtuiging (ōā-verr-*tur*ᵉʷ-gɪng) *c* (pl
~en) conviction; persuasion
overval (ōā-verr-vahl) *c* (pl ~len) hold-
up
oververmoeid (ōā-verr-verr-*mōō*ᵉᵉt)

adj over-tired
overvloed (ōā-verr-vlōōt) *c*
abundance; plenty
overvloedig (ōā-verr-*vlōō*-derkh) *adj*
abundant, plentiful
overvol (ōā-verr-vol) *adj* crowded
overweg (ōā-verr-vehkh) *c* (pl ~en)
level crossing, crossing
***overwegen** (ōā-verr-*vāy*-gern) *v*
consider
overweging (ōā-verr-*vāy*-gɪng) *c* (pl
~en) consideration
overweldigen (ōā-verr-*vehl*-der-gern)
v overwhelm
overwerken (ōā-verr-*vehr*-kern): **zich**
~ overwork
overwerkt (ōā-verr-*vehr*-kt)
overworked
***overwinnen** (ōā-verr-*vɪ*-nern) *v*
conquer; *overcome
overwinning (ōā-verr-*vɪ*-nɪng) *c* (pl
~en) victory
overzees (ōā-verr-*zāy*ss) *adj* overseas
overzicht (ōā-verr-zɪkht) *nt* (pl ~en)
survey
ozon (ōā-zon) *c* ozone

P

paal (paal) *c* (pl palen) post, pole
paar (paar) *nt* (pl paren) pair; couple
paard (paart) *nt* (pl ~en) horse
paardebloem (*paar*-der-blōōm) *c* (pl
~en) dandelion
paardekracht (*paar*-der-krahkht) *c*
horsepower
paardesport (*paar*-der-sport) *c* riding
***paardrijden** (*paart*-ray-dern) *v* *ride
paars (paars) *adj* purple
pacht (pahkht) *c* (pl ~en) lease
pacifisme (pah-see-*fɪss*-mer) *nt*

pacifism
pacifist (pah-see-*fɪst*) *m* (f ~e, pl ~en)
pacifist
pacifistisch (pah-see-*fɪss*-teess) *adj*
pacifist
pact (pahkt) *nt* (pl ~en) pact
pad¹ (paht) *nt* (pl ~en) path; lane, trail
pad² (paht) *c* (pl ~den) toad
paddestoel (*pah*-der-stōōl) *c* (pl ~en)
toadstool; mushroom
padvinder (*paht*-fɪn-derr) *m* (pl ~s)
scout, boy scout

padvindster (*paht*-fint-sterr) *f* (pl ~s) girl scout, girl guide

pagina (*paa*-gee-naa) *c* (pl ~'s) page

pak (pahk) *nt* (pl ~ken) package; ~ **slaag** spanking

pakhuis (*pahk*-hur^ew ss) *nt* (pl -huizen) warehouse

Pakistaan (paa-kee-*staan*) *c* (f ~se, pl -stanen) Pakistani

Pakistaans (paa-kee-*staans*) *adj* Pakistani

Pakistan (*paa*-kiss-tahn) Pakistan

pakje (*pahk*-Yer) *nt* (pl ~s) parcel, packet

pakken (*pah*-kern) *v* *take

pakket (pah-*keht*) *nt* (pl ~ten) parcel

pakpapier (*pahk*-paa-peer) *nt* wrapping paper

paleis (paa-*layss*) *nt* (pl paleizen) palace

paling (*paa*-ling) *c* (pl ~en) eel

palm (pahlm) *c* (pl ~en) palm

pan (pahn) *c* (pl ~nen) pan

pand (pahnt) *nt* (pl ~en) security; house, premises *pl*

pandjesbaas (*pahn*-t^Yerss-baass) *m* (pl -bazen) pawnbroker

paneel (paa-*nayl*) *nt* (pl panelen) panel

paniek (paa-*neek*) *c* panic

panne (*pah*-ner) *c* breakdown

pantoffel (pahn-*to*-ferl) *c* (pl ~s) slipper

panty (*pehn*-tee) *c* (pl panties) pantyhose

papa (*pah*-paa) *m* (pl ~'s) daddy

papaver (paa-*paa*-verr) *c* (pl ~s) poppy

papegaai (pah-per-*gaa^ee*) *c* (pl ~en) parrot

papier (paa-*peer*) *nt* (pl ~en) paper

papieren (paa-*pee*-rern) *adj* paper; ~ **servet** paper napkin; ~ **zak** paper bag; ~ **zakdoek** tissue

parade (paa-*raa*-der) *c* (pl ~s) parade

paradijs (paa-*raa*-dayss) *nt* (pl ~zen) paradise

paraferen (paa-raa-*fay*-rern) *v* initial

paragraaf (paa-raa-*graaf*) *c* (pl -grafen) paragraph

parallel (paa-raa-*lehl*) *adj* parallel

paraplu (paa-raa-*plew*) *c* (pl ~'s) umbrella

parasol (paa-raa-*sol*) *c* (pl ~s) sunshade

pardon! (pahr-*don*) sorry!

parel (*paa*-rerl) *c* (pl ~s, ~en) pearl

parelmoer (paar-ler-*moor*) *nt* mother of pearl

parfum (pahr-*ferm*) *nt* (pl ~s) perfume

park (pahrk) *nt* (pl ~en) park

parkeermeter (pahr-*kayr*-may-terr) *c* (pl ~s) parking meter

parkeerplaats (pahr-*kayr*-plaats) *c* (pl ~en) car park; parking lot *Am*

parkeertarief (pahr-*kayr*-taa-reef) *nt* (pl -tarieven) parking fee

parkeerzone (pahr-*kayr*-zaw-ner) *c* (pl ~s) parking zone

parkeren (pahr-*kay*-rern) *v* park

parkiet (pahr-*keet*) *c* (pl ~en) parakeet

parlement (pahr-ler-*mehnt*) *nt* (pl ~en) parliament

parlementair (pahr-ler-mehn-*tair*) *adj* parliamentary

parochie (pah-*ro*-khee) *c* (pl ~s) parish

particulier (pahr-tee-*kew*-leer) *adj* private

partij (pahr-*tay*) *c* (pl ~en) party; side; batch

partijdig (pahr-*tay*-derkh) *adj* partial

partner (*pahrt*-nerr) *c* (pl ~s) partner; associate

pas[1] (pahss) *c* (pl ~sen) step

pas[2] (pahss) *adv* just

Pasen (*paa*-sern) Easter

pasfoto (*pahss*-foa-toa) *c* (pl ~'s) passport photograph

paskamer (*pahss*-kaa-merr) *c* (pl ~s) fitting room

paspoort (*pahss*-poart) *nt* (pl ~en)

passport

paspoortcontrole (*pahss-pōart-kon-traw-ler*) *c* passport control

passage (pah-*saa-*zher) *c* (pl ~s) excerpt; passage

passagier (pah-saa-*zheer*) *m* (f ~e, pl ~s) passenger

passen (*pah-*sern) *v* try on; fit; ~ **bij** match; **passend** appropriate; convenient, adequate, proper; ~ **op** look after; attend to

passeren (pah-*sāy*-rern) *v* pass; by-pass, pass by

passie (*pah-*see) *c* passion

passief (pah-*seef*) *adj* passive

pasta (*pahss-*taa) *c* (pl ~'s) paste

pasteitje (pahss-*tay-*t^yer) *nt* (pl ~s) pasty

pastorie (pahss-tōa-*ree*) *c* (pl ~ën) parsonage, vicarage

patat (paa-*taht*) *pl* chips; French fries

patent (paa-*tehnt*) *nt* (pl ~en) patent; great

pater (*paa-*terr) *m* (pl ~s) father

patiënt (paa-*shehnt*) *m* (f ~e, pl ~en) patient

patrijs (paa-*trayss*) *c* (pl patrijzen) partridge

patrijspoort (paa-*trayss*-pōart) *c* (pl ~en) porthole

patriot (paa-tree-^y*ot*) *m* (pl ~ten) patriot

patroon (paa-*trōan*) *nt* (pl patronen) pattern; *c* cartridge

patrouille (paa-*trōō-*^yer) *c* (pl ~s) patrol

patrouilleren (paa-trōō-^y*āy*-rern) *v* patrol

paus (pouss) *m* (pl ~en) pope

pauw (pou) *c* (pl ~en) peacock

pauze (*pou-*zer) *c* (pl ~s) pause; break; interval, intermission

pauzeren (pou-*zāy*-rern) *v* pause

paviljoen (paa-vıl-*^yōōn*) *nt* (pl ~en, ~s)

pavilion

pech (pehkh) *c* bad luck

pedaal (per-*daal*) *nt/c* (pl pedalen) pedal

peddel (*peh-*derl) *c* (pl ~s) paddle

peen (pāyn) *c* (pl penen) carrot

peer (pāyr) *c* (pl peren) pear; light bulb

pees (pāyss) *c* (pl pezen) sinew, tendon

peettante (*pāyt-*tahn-ter) *f* (pl ~s) godmother

peetoom (*pāyt-* ōam) *m* (pl ~s) godfather

peil (payl) *nt* (pl ~en) level

pelgrim (*pehl-*grım) *c* (pl ~s) pilgrim

pelikaan (pāy-lee-*kaan*) *c* (pl -kanen) pelican

pels (pehls) *c* (pl pelzen) fur

pen (pehn) *c* (pl ~nen) pen

penicilline (pāy-nee-see-*lee*-ner) *c* penicillin

penningmeester (*peh*-nıng-māyss-terr) *m* (pl ~s) treasurer

penseel (pehn-*sāyl*) *nt* (pl -selen) paintbrush

pensioen (pehn-*shōōn*) *nt* (pl ~en) pension; **met ~ gaan** retire

pension (pehn-*shon*) *nt* (pl ~s) board; boardinghouse, guesthouse, pension; **vol ~** full board, board and lodging, bed and board

pensionering (pehn-shōa-*nāy*-rıng) *c* (pl ~en) retirement

peper (*pāy-*perr) *c* pepper

pepermunt (*pāy*-perr-*mernt*) *c* peppermint

per (pehr) *prep* by, per

perceel (pehr-*sāyl*) *nt* (pl -celen) plot

percentage (pehr-sehn-*taa*-zher) *nt* (pl ~s) percentage

percolator (pehr-kōa-*laa*-tor) *c* (pl ~s) percolator

perfectie (pehr-*fehk*-see) *c* perfection

periode (pāy-ree-^y*ōa*-der) *c* (pl ~s, ~n) period; term

periodiek (pāȳ-ree-ʸōa-*deek*) *adj* periodical

permanent (pehr-maa-*nehnt*) *adj* permanent; *nt* perm

permissie (pehr-*mɪ*-see) *c* (pl ~s) permission

perron (peh-*ron*) *nt* (pl ~s) platform

perronkaartje (peh-ron-kaar-tʸer) *nt* (pl ~s) platform ticket

Pers (pehrs) *c* (pl Perzen) Persian

pers (pehrs) *c* press

persconferentie (*pehrs*-kon-fer-rehn-tsee) *c* (pl ~s) press conference

persen (*pehr*-sern) *v* press

personeel (pehr-sōa-*nāyl*) *nt* personnel

personentrein (pehr-*sōa*-ner-trayn) *c* (pl ~en) passenger train

persoon (pehr-*sōan*) *c* (pl -sonen) person; **per ~** per person

persoonlijk (pehr-*sōan*-lerk) *adj* personal; private

persoonlijkheid (pehr-*sōan*-lerk-hayt) *c* (pl -heden) personality

perspectief (pehr-spehk-*teef*) *nt* (pl -tieven) perspective

Perzië (*pehr*-zee-ʸer) Persia

perzik (*pehr*-zɪk) *c* (pl ~en) peach

Perzisch (*pehr*-zeess) *adj* Persian

pessarium (peh-*saa*-ree-ʸerm) *nt* diaphragm

pessimisme (peh-see-*mɪss*-mer) *nt* pessimism

pessimist (peh-see-*mɪst*) *m* (f ~e, pl ~en) pessimist

pessimistisch (peh-see-*mɪss*-teess) *adj* pessimistic

pestkop (*pehst*-kop) *c* (pl ~pen) bully

pet (peht) *c* (pl ~ten) cap

peterselie (pāy-terr-*sāy*-lee) *c* parsley

petitie (per-*tee*-tsee) *c* (pl ~s) petition

petroleum (pāy-*trōa*-lāy-ʸerm) *c* petroleum; kerosene, paraffin

peuter (*pūr*-terr) *m* (pl ~s) toddler

pianist (pee-ʸaa-*nɪst*) *m* (f ~e, pl ~en) pianist

piano (pee-ʸaa-nōa) *c* (pl ~'s) piano

piccolo (*pee*-kōa-lōa) *m* (pl ~'s) pageboy, bellboy

picknick (*pɪk*-nɪk) *c* (pl ~s) picnic

picknicken (*pɪk*-nɪ-kern) *v* picnic

pick-up (pɪk-*erp*) *c* (pl ~s) record player

pienter (*peen*-terr) *adj* bright, smart, clever

pier (peer) *c* (pl ~en) pier, jetty

pijl (payl) *c* (pl ~en) arrow

pijn (payn) *c* (pl ~en) ache, pain; **~ *doen** *hurt; ache

pijnlijk (*payn*-lerk) *adj* sore, painful; embarrassing, awkward

pijn (payn) *c* (pl ~s) painkiller

pijnloos (*payn*-lōass) *adj* painless

pijp (payp) *c* (pl ~en) pipe; tube

pijpenstoker (*pay*-per-stōa-kerr) *c* (pl ~s) pipe cleaner

pijptabak (*payp*-taa-bahk) *c* pipe tobacco

pikant (pee-*kahnt*) *adj* spicy; savo(u)ry

pil (pɪl) *c* (pl ~len) pill

pilaar (pee-*laar*) *c* (pl pilaren) column, pillar

piloot (pee-*lōat*) *c* (pl piloten) pilot

pils (pɪls) *nt* beer

pincet (pɪn-*seht*) *c* (pl ~ten) tweezers *pl*

pinda (*pɪn*-daa) *c* (pl ~'s) peanut

pinguïn (*pɪn*-gvɪn) *c* (pl ~s) penguin

pink (pɪngk) *c* (pl ~en) little finger

Pinksteren (*pɪngk*-ster-rern) Whitsun, *nAm* Pentecost

pion (pee-ʸon) *c* (pl ~nen) pawn

pionier (pee-ʸōa-*neer*) *m* (f ~ster, pl ~s) pioneer

piraat (pee-*raat*) *m* (pl piraten) pirate

piste (*peess*-ter) *c* (pl ~s) ring

pistool (peess-*tōal*) *nt* (pl pistolen) pistol

pit (pɪt) *c* (pl ~ten) stone, pip

pittoresk (pee-tōa-*rehsk*) *adj*

picturesque

plaag (plaakh) *c* (pl plagen) plague

plaat (plaat) *c* (pl platen) plate, sheet; picture

plaats (plaats) *c* (pl ~en) place; spot, locality, site; seat; room; station; **in ~ van** instead of; **open ~** clearing

plaatselijk (*plaat*-ser-lerk) *adj* local; regional

plaatsen (*plaat*-sern) *v* *lay, *put, place; locate

*plaatshebben (*plaats*-heh-bern) *v* *take place

plaatskaartenbureau (*plaats*-kaar-ter-bēw-rōā) *nt* (pl ~s) box office

plaatsvervanger (*plaats*-ferr-vah-ngerr) *m* (pl ~s) deputy, substitute

plafond (plaa-*font*) *nt* (pl ~s) ceiling

plagen (*plaa*-gern) *v* tease

plakband (*plahk*-bahnt) *nt* scotch tape®, adhesive tape

plakboek (*plahk*-bōōk) *nt* (pl ~en) scrapbook

plakken (*plah*-kern) *v* *stick; paste

plan (plahn) *nt* (pl ~nen) plan; project, scheme; **van ~ *zijn** intend

planeet (plaa-*nāyt*) *c* (pl -neten) planet

planetarium (plaa-ner-*taa*-ree-^yerm) *nt* (pl ~s, -ria) planetarium

plank (plahngk) *c* (pl ~en) board, plank; shelf

plannen (*pleh*-nern) *v* plan

plant (plahnt) *c* (pl ~en) plant

plantage (plahn-*taa*-zher) *c* (pl ~s) plantation

planten (*plahn*-tern) *v* plant

plantengroei (*plahn*-ter-grōō^{ee}) *c* vegetation

plantkunde (*plahnt*-kern-der) *c* botany

plantsoen (plahnt-*sōōn*) *nt* (pl ~en) public garden

plas (plahss) *c* (pl ~sen) puddle

plastic (*pleh*-stik) *adj* plastic

plat (plaht) *adj* flat; even, level

platenspeler (*plaa*-ter-spāy-lerr) *c* (pl ~s) record player

platina (*plaa*-tee-naa) *nt* platinum

plattegrond (plah-ter-*gront*) *c* (pl ~en) map, plan

platteland (plah-ter-*lahnt*) *nt* countryside, country; **plattelands-** rural

platzak (*plaht*-sahk) broke

plaveien (plaa-*vay*-ern) *v* pave

plaveisel (plaa-*vay*-serl) *nt* pavement

plechtig (*plehkh*-terkh) *adj* solemn

pleegouders (*plāykh*-ou-derrs) *pl* foster parents *pl*

plegen (*plāy*-gern) *v* commit

pleidooi (play-*dōā^{ee}*) *nt* (pl ~en) plea

plein (playn) *nt* (pl ~en) square

pleister[1] (*play*-sterr) *c* (pl ~s) plaster

pleister[2] (*play*-sterr) *nt* plaster

pleiten (*play*-tern) *v* plead

plek (plehk) *c* (pl ~ken) spot; **blauwe ~** bruise; **zere ~** sore

plezier (pler-*zeer*) *nt* pleasure; fun

plicht (plikht) *c* (pl ~en) duty

ploeg[1] (plōōkh) *c* (pl ~en) plough

ploeg[2] (plōōkh) *c* (pl ~en) team; shift; gang

ploegen (*plōō*-gern) *v* plough

plooi (plōā^{ee}) *c* (pl ~en) crease

plooihoudend (plōā^{ee}-*hou*-dernt) *adj* permanent press

plotseling (*plot*-ser-lɪng) *adj* sudden

plukken (*pler*-kern) *v* pick

plus (plerss) *prep* plus

pneumatisch (pnūr-*maa*-teess) *adj* pneumatic

pocketboek (*po*-kert-bōōk) *nt* (pl ~en) paperback

poeder (*pōō*-derr) *nt/c* (pl ~s) powder

poederdoos (*pōō*-derr-dōāss) *c* (pl -dozen) powder compact

poelier (pōō-*leer*) *m* (pl ~s) poulterer

poes (pōōss) *c* (pl poezen) pussy-cat

poetsen (*pōō*-tsern) *v* brush; polish

pogen (*pōa*-gern) *v* try, attempt

poging (*pōa*-gıng) *c* (pl ⁓en) try, attempt; effort

pokken (*po*-kern) *pl* smallpox

Polen (*pōa*-lern) Poland

polio (*pōa*-lee-ʸōa) *c* polio

polis (*pōa*-lerss) *c* (pl ⁓sen) policy

politicus (pōa-*lee*-tee-kerss) *c* (pl -ci) politician

politie (pōa-*lee*-tsee) *c* police *pl*

politieagent (pōa-*lee*-tsi-aa-gehnt) *m* (pl ⁓en) policeman

politiebureau (pōa-*lee*-tsee-bēw-rōa) *nt* (pl ⁓s) police station

politiek (pōa-lee-*teek*) *adj* political; *c* policy; politics

pols (pols) *c* (pl ⁓en) wrist; pulse

polshorloge (*pols*-hor-lōa-zher) *nt* (pl ⁓s) wristwatch

polsslag (*pol*-slahkh) *c* pulse

pomp (pomp) *c* (pl ⁓en) pump

pompelmoes (*pom*-perl-mōōss) *c* (pl -moezen) grapefruit

pompen (*pom*-pern) *v* pump

pond (pont) *nt* pound

pony (*po*-nee) *c* (pl ⁓'s) pony; fringe

Pool (pōal) *m* (f ⁓se, pl Polen) Pole

Pools (pōals) *adj* Polish

poort (pōart) *c* (pl ⁓en) gate

poosje (*pōa*-sher) *nt* while

poot (pōat) *c* (pl poten) leg; paw

pop (pop) *c* (pl ⁓pen) doll

popmuziek (*pop*-mēw-zeek) *c* pop music

poppenkast (*po*-per-kahst) *c* puppetshow

populair (pōa-pēw-*lair*) *adj* popular

porselein (por-seh-*layn*) *nt* porcelain, china

portefeuille (por-ter-*furᵉʷ-ʸ*er) *c* (pl ⁓s) pocketbook, wallet

portemonnee (por-ter-mo-*nay*) *c* (pl ⁓s) purse

portie (*por*-see) *c* (pl ⁓s) portion; helping

portier (por-*teer*) *m* (pl ⁓s) doorman, doorkeeper, porter

portret (por-*treht*) *nt* (pl ⁓ten) portrait

Portugal (*por*-tēw-gahl) Portugal

Portugees (por-tēw-*gayss*) *adj* Portuguese

positie (pōa-*zee*-tsee) *c* (pl ⁓s) position

positief (*pōa*-zee-*teef*) *adj* positive

post[1] (post) *c* mail, post

post[2] (post) *c* (pl ⁓en) entry

postbode (*post*-bōa-der) *m* (pl ⁓s, ⁓n) postman

postcode (*post*-kōa-der) *c* (pl ⁓s) zip code *Am*

poster (*pōa*-sterr) *c* (pl ⁓s) poster

posten (*poss*-tern) *v* mail, post

poste restante (post-rehss-*tahn*-ter) poste restante

posterijen (poss-ter-*ray*-ern) *pl* postal service

postkantoor (*post*-kahn-tōar) *nt* (pl -toren) post-office

postwissel (*post*-vi-serl) *c* (pl ⁓s) postal order; mail order *Am*

postzegel (*post*-say̆-gerl) *c* (pl ⁓s) postage stamp, stamp

postzegelautomaat (*post*-say̆-gerl-ōa-tōa-maat) *c* (pl -maten) stamp machine

pot (pot) *c* (pl ⁓ten) pot; jar

potlood (*pot*-lōat) *nt* (pl -loden) pencil

praatje (*praa*-tᵉʸer) *nt* (pl ⁓s) chat

pracht (prahkht) *c* splendo(u)r

prachtig (*prahkh*-terkh) *adj* lovely, wonderful, marvel(l)ous; splendid, gorgeous, glorious, enchanting, fine, superb, swell

praktijk (prahk-*tayk*) *c* (pl ⁓en) practice

praktisch (*prahk*-teess) *adj* practical

praten (*praa*-tern) *v* talk

precies (prer-*seess*) *adj* precise, very, exact; *adv* exactly; just

predikant (pray-dee-*kahnt*) m (pl ~en) clergyman, minister, vicar, rector

preek (prayk) c (pl preken) sermon

preekstoel (*prayk*-stool) c (pl ~en) pulpit

preken (*pray*-kern) v preach

premie (*pray*-mee) c (pl ~s) premium

premier (prer-*m^yay*) c (pl ~s) premier, Prime Minister

prent (prehnt) c (pl ~en) picture; print, engraving

prentbriefkaart (*prehnt*-breef-kaart) c (pl ~en) picture postcard

president (*pray*-zee-*dehnt*) m (f ~e, pl ~en) president

prestatie (prehss-*taa*-tsee) c (pl ~s) achievement; feat

presteren (prehss-*tay*-rern) v achieve

prestige (prehss-*tee*-zher) nt prestige

pret (preht) c fun; pleasure

prettig (*preh*-terkh) adj enjoyable, pleasant; nice

preventief (*pray*-vehn-*teef*) adj preventive

priester (*pree*-sterr) m (pl ~s) priest

prijs (prayss) c (pl prijzen) price; charge, cost, rate; prize, award; **op ~ stellen** appreciate

prijsdaling (*prayss*-daa-ling) c (pl ~en) slump

prijslijst (*prayss*-layst) c (pl ~en) price list

prijzen (*pray*-zern) v price

***prijzen** (*pray*-zern) v praise

prijzig (*pray*-zerkh) adj expensive

prik¹ (prik) c (pl ~ken) sting

prik² (prik) c fizz

prikkel (*pri*-kerl) c (pl ~s) impulse

prikkelbaar (*pri*-kerl-baar) adj irritable

prikkelen (*pri*-ker-lern) v irritate

prikken (*pri*-kern) v prick

prima (*pree*-maa) adj first-rate; all right

primair (*pree*-mair) adj primary

principe (prin-*see*-per) nt (pl ~s) principle

prins (prins) m (pl ~en) prince

prinses (prin-*sehss*) f (pl ~sen) princess

prioriteit (pree-^yoa-ree-*tayt*) c (pl ~en) priority

privé (pree-*vay*) adj private

privé-docent (pree-*vay*-*doa*-*sehnt*) m tutor

privéleven (pree-*vay*-*lay*-vern) nt privacy

proberen (proa-*bay*-rern) v try; attempt; test

probleem (proa-*blaym*) nt (pl-blemen) problem

procédé (proa-ser-*day*) nt (pl ~s) process

procedure (proa-ser-*dew*-rer) c (pl ~s) procedure

procent (proa-*sehnt*) nt (pl ~en) per cent

proces (proa-*sehss*) nt (pl ~sen) process; lawsuit

processie (proa-*seh*-see) c (pl ~s) procession

producent (proa-dew-*sehnt*) m (pl ~en) producer

produceren (proa-dew-*say*-rern) v produce

product (proa-*derkt*) nt (pl ~en) product; produce

productie (proa-*derk*-see) c (pl ~s) production; output

proef (proof) c (pl proeven) experiment; trial, test

proeven (*proo*-vern) v taste

profeet (proa-*fayt*) m (pl -feten) prophet

professor (proa-*feh*-sor) c (pl ~en, ~s) professor

profiteren (proa-fee-*tay*-rern) v profit, benefit

programma (proa-*grah*-maa) nt (pl ~'s) programme

progressief (prōa-greh-*seef*) *adj*
progressive

project (prōa-*^yehkt*) *nt* (pl ~en) project

promenade (pro-mer-*naa*-der) *c* (pl ~s) esplanade, promenade

promotie (prōa-*mōa*-tsee) *c* (pl ~s) promotion

prompt (prompt) *adj* prompt

propaganda (prōa-paa-*gahn*-daa) *c* propaganda

propeller (prōa-*peh*-lerr) *c* (pl ~s) propeller

proportie (prōa-*por*-see) *c* (pl ~s) proportion

prospectus (pro-*spehk*-terss) *c* (pl ~sen) prospectus

prostituée (pro-stee-tēw-*vāy*) *f* (pl ~s) prostitute

protest (prōa-*tehst*) *nt* (pl ~en) protest

protestants (prōa-terss-*tahnts*) *adj* Protestant

protesteren (prōa-tehss-*tāy*-rern) *v* protest

provinciaal (prōa-vɪn-*shaal*) *adj* provincial

provincie (prōa-*vɪn*-see) *c* (pl ~s) province

provisie (prōa-*vee*-zee) *c* (pl ~s) commission

provisiekast (prōa-*vee*-zee-kahst) *c* (pl ~en) larder

pruik (prur^{ew}k) *c* (pl ~en) wig

pruim (prur^{ew}m) *c* (pl ~en) plum; prune

prullenmand (*prer*-ler-mahnt) *c* (pl ~en) wastepaper basket

psychiater (psee-khee-*^yaa*-terr) *m* (pl ~s) psychiatrist

psychisch (*psee*-kheess) *adj* psychic

psychologie (psee-khōa-lōa-*gee*) *c* psychology

psychologisch (psee-khōa-*lōa*-geess) *adj* psychological

psycholoog (psee-khōa-*lōakh*) *c* (pl -logen) psychologist

publiceren (pēw-blee-*sāy*-rern) *v* publish

publiciteit (pēw-blee-see-*tayt*) *c* publicity

publiek (pēw-*bleek*) *adj* public; *nt* audience, public

publikatie (pēw-blee-*kaa*-tsee) *c* (pl ~s) publication

puimsteen (*pur^{ew}m*-stāyn) *nt* pumice stone

puistje (*pur^{ew}*-sher) *nt* (pl ~s) pimple

punaise (pēw-*nai*-zer) *c* (pl ~s) drawing pin; thumbtack *nAm*

punctueel (perngk-tēw-*vāyl*) *adj* punctual

punt (pernt) *nt* (pl ~en) point; item, issue; *c* full stop, period, dot; tip

puntesliiper (*pern*-ter-slay-perr) *c* (pl ~s) pencil sharpener

puntkomma (pernt-*ko*-maa) *c* semicolon

put (pert) *c* (pl ~ten) well

puur (pēwr) *adj* neat; sheer

puzzel (*per*-zerl) *c* (pl ~s) puzzle

pyjama (pee-*^yaa*-maa) *c* (pl ~'s) pyjamas *pl*

Q

quarantaine (kaa-rahn-*tai*-ner) *c* quarantine

quota (*kvōa*-taa) *c* (pl ~'s) quota

R

raad¹ (raat) *c* advice, counsel

raad² (raat) *c* (pl raden) council

raadplegen (*raat*-plāy-gern) *v* consult

raadpleging (*raat*-plāy-gɪng) *c* (pl ∼en) consultation

raadsel (*raat*-serl) *nt* (pl ∼s, ∼en) riddle, puzzle; mystery, enigma

raadslid (*raats*-lɪt) *nt* (pl -leden) councillor

raadsman (*raats*-mahn) *m* (pl -lieden) counsellor; solicitor

raaf (raaf) *c* (pl raven) raven

raam (raam) *nt* (pl ramen) window

raar (raar) *adj* curious, odd, strange, queer, quaint

rabarber (raa-*bahr*-berr) *c* rhubarb

*raden (*raa*-dern) *v* guess

radiator (raa-dee-*ÿaa*-tor) *c* (pl ∼s, ∼en) radiator

radicaal (raa-dee-*kaal*) *adj* radical

radijs (raa-*dayss*) *c* (pl radijzen) radish

radio (*raa*-dee-ÿōa) *c* (pl ∼'s) radio

rafelen (*raa*-fer-lern) *v* fray

raffinaderij (rah-fee-naa-der-*ray*) *c* (pl ∼en) refinery

rage (*raa*-zher) *c* (pl ∼s) craze

raken (*raa*-kern) *v* *hit

raket (raa-*keht*) *c* (pl ∼ten) rocket

ramp (rahmp) *c* (pl ∼en) calamity, disaster

rampzalig (rahm-*psaa*-lerkh) *adj* disastrous

rand (rahnt) *c* (pl ∼en) edge, border; brim, rim, verge

rang (rahng) *c* (pl ∼en) rank; class

rangschikken (*rahng*-skhɪ-kern) *v* arrange; sort, grade

rantsoen (rahnt-*sōōn*) *nt* (pl ∼en) ration

ranzig (*rahn*-zerkh) *adj* rancid

rapport (rah-*port*) *nt* (pl ∼en) report

rapporteren (rah-por-*tāy*-rern) *v* report

ras (rahss) *nt* (pl ∼sen) race; breed; **rassen-** racial

rasp (rahsp) *c* (pl ∼en) grater

raspen (*rahss*-pern) *v* grate

rat (raht) *c* (pl ∼ten) rat

rauw (rou) *adj* raw

ravijn (raa-*vayn*) *nt* (pl ∼en) gorge

razen (*raa*-zern) *v* rage

razend (*raa*-zernt) *adj* furious

razernij (raa-zerr-*nay*) *c* rage

reactie (rāy-*ÿahk*-see) *c* (pl ∼s) reaction

reageren (rāy-ÿah-*gāy*-rern) *v* react, respond

recent (rer-*sehnt*) *adj* recent

recept (rer-*sehpt*) *nt* (pl ∼en) recipe; prescription

receptie (rer-*sehp*-see) *c* (pl ∼s) reception office

receptioniste (rer-sehp-shōa-*nɪss*-ter) *f* (pl ∼s) receptionist

recht¹ (rehkht) *nt* (pl ∼en) right; law, justice

recht² (rehkht) *adj* straight

rechtbank (*rehkht*-bahngk) *c* (pl ∼en) court

rechtdoor (rehkh-*dōar*) *adv* straight on, straight ahead

rechter¹ (*rehkh*-terr) *adj* right-hand

rechter² (*rehkh*-terr) *c* (pl ∼s) judge

rechthoek (*rehkht*-hōōk) *c* (pl ∼en) oblong, rectangle

rechthoekig (*rehkht*-hōō-kerkh) *adj* rectangular

rechtopstaand (rehkh-*top*-staant) *adj* erect, upright

rechts (rehkhts) *adj* right-hand, right

rechtschapen (rehkht-*skhaa*-pern) *adj* honourable

rechtstreeks (*rehkht*-strāyks) *adj* direct

rechtszaak (*rehkht*-saak) *c* (pl -zaken)

trial

rechtuit (rehkh-*tur^{ew}t*) *adv* straight ahead

rechtvaardig (raykht-*faar*-derkh) *adj* just, righteous, right

rechtvaardigen (raykht-*faar*-der-khern) *v* justify

rechtvaardigheid (rehkht-*faar*-derkh-hayt) *c* justice

reclame (rer-*klaa*-mer) *c* advertising; advertisement; publicity

reclamespot (rer-*klaa*-mer-spot) *c* (pl ~s) commercial

record (rer-*kawr*) *nt* (pl ~s) record

recreatie (rāy-krāy-ʸ*aa*-tsee) *c* recreation

recreatiecentrum (rāy-krāy-ʸ*aa*-tsee-sehn-trerm) *nt* (pl -tra) recreation center *Am*, recreation centre

rector (*rehk*-tor) *m* (pl ~en, ~s) headmaster, principal

reçu (rer-*sēw*) *nt* (pl ~'s) receipt

recycleerbar (ree-sie-*kleer*-bar) *adj* recyclable

recycleren (ree-sie-*klee*-rern) *v* recycle

redakteur (rāy-dahk-*tūrr*) *c* (pl ~en, ~s) editor

redden (*reh*-dern) *v* save, rescue

redder (*reh*-derr) *m* (pl ~s) saviour

redding (*reh*-dıng) *c* (pl ~en) rescue

reddingsgordel (*reh*-dıngs-khor-derl) *c* (pl ~s) lifebelt

rede[1] (*rāy*-der) *c* sense; reason

rede[2] (*rāy*-der) *c* (pl ~s) speech

redelijk (*rāy*-der-lerk) *adj* reasonable

reden (*rāy*-dern) *c* (pl ~en) reason

redeneren (rāy-der-*nāy*-rern) *v* reason

reder (*rāy*-derr) *c* (pl ~s) shipowner

redetwisten (*rāy*-der-tvıss-tern) *v* argue

redigeren (rāy-dee-*gāy*-rern) *v* edit

reduceren (rāy-dēw-*sāy*-rern) *v* reduce

reductie (rer-*derk*-see) *c* (pl ~s) discount, reduction, rebate

reeds (rāyts) *adv* already

reekalf (*rāy*-kahlf) *nt* (pl -kalveren) fawn

reeks (rāyks) *c* (pl ~en) series; sequence

referentie (rer-fer-*rehn*-tsee) *c* (pl ~s) reference

reflector (rer-*flehk*-tor) *c* (pl ~s, ~en) reflector

reformatie (rāy-for-*maa*-tsee) *c* reformation

regel (*rāy*-gerl) *c* (pl ~s) line; rule; **in de ~** as a rule

regelen (*rāy*-ger-lern) *v* arrange; settle; regulate

regeling (*rāy*-ger-lıng) *c* (pl ~en) arrangement; settlement; regulation

regelmatig (rāy-gerl-*maa*-terkh) *adj* regular

regen (*rāy*-gern) *c* rain

regenachtig (*rāy*-gern-ahkh-terkh) *adj* rainy

regenboog (*rāy*-ger-bōakh) *c* (pl -bogen) rainbow

regenbui (*rāy*-ger-bur^{ew}) *c* (pl ~en) shower

regenen (*rāy*-ger-nern) *v* rain

regenjas (*rāy*-ger-ʸahss) *c* (pl ~sen) mackintosh, raincoat

regeren (rer-*gāy*-rern) *v* rule, govern, reign

regering (rer-*gāy*-rıng) *c* (pl ~en) government; reign

regie (rer-*gee*) *c* (pl ~s) direction

regime (rer-*zheem*) *nt* (pl ~s) régime

regisseren (rāy-gee-*sāy*-rern) *v* direct

regisseur (rāy-gee-*sūrr*) *m* (f regisseuse, pl ~s) director

register (rer-*gıss*-terr) *nt* (pl ~s) record; index

registratie (rāy-gıss-*traa*-tsee) *c* registration

reglement (rāy-gler-*mehnt*) *nt* (pl ~en)

regulation

reiger (*ray*-gerr) c (pl ~s) heron

rein (rayn) adj pure

reinigen (*ray*-ner-gern) v clean;
chemisch ~ dry-clean

reiniging (*ray*-ner-gɪng) c cleaning

reinigingsmiddel (*ray*-ner-gɪngs-mɪ-
derl) nt (pl ~en) cleaning fluid

reis (rayss) c (pl reizen) journey; trip,
voyage

reisagent (*rayss*-aa-gehnt) m (f ~e, pl
~en) travel agent

reisbureau (*rayss*-bēw-rōa) nt (pl ~s)
travel agency

reischeque (*ray*-shehk) c (pl ~s)
traveller's cheque, traveler's check
Am

reisgegevens (*rayss*-ger-gāy-verns) pl
itinerary

reiskosten (*rayss*-koss-tern) pl fare;
travelling expenses

reisplan (*rayss*-plahn) nt (pl ~nen)
itinerary

reisroute (*rayss*-rōō-ter) c (pl ~s, ~n)
itinerary

reisverzekering (*rayss*-ferr-zāy-ker-
rɪng) c travel insurance

reiswieg (*rayss*-veekh) c (pl ~en)
carrycot

reizen (*ray*-zern) v travel

reiziger (*ray*-zer-gerr) m (f reizigster,
pl ~s) travel(l)er

rek (rehk) c elasticity

rekbaar (*rehk*-baar) adj elastic

rekenen (*rāy*-ker-nern) v reckon

rekening (*rāy*-ker-nɪng) c (pl ~en)
account; bill; check nAm

rekenkunde (*rāy*-kerng-kern-der) c
arithmetic

rekenmachine (*ree*-kern-ma-sjiner) c
calculator

rekken (*reh*-kern) v stretch

rekruut (rer-*krēwt*) m (pl rekruten)
recruit

rel (rehl) c (pl ~len) riot

relatie (rer-*laa*-tsee) c (pl ~s) relation;
connection

relatief (rer-laa-*teef*) adj relative;
comparative

reliëf (rerl-ʸ*ehf*) nt (pl ~s) relief

relikwie (rer-ler-*kvee*) c (pl ~ën) relic

reling (*rāy*-lɪng) c (pl ~en) rail

rem (rehm) c (pl ~men) brake

remlichten (*rehm*-lɪkh-tern) pl brake
lights

remtrommel (*rehm*-tro-mehl) c (pl ~s)
brake drum

renbaan (*rehn*-baan) c (pl -banen)
racecourse; track; racetrack

rendabel (rehn-*daa*-berl) adj paying

rendier (*rehn*-deer) nt (pl ~en) reindeer

rennen (*reh*-nern) v *run

renpaard (*rehn*-paart) nt (pl ~en)
racehorse

rente (*rehn*-ter) c (pl ~n, ~s) interest

reparatie (rāy-paa-*raa*-tsee) c (pl ~s)
reparation

repareren (rāy-paa-*rāy*-rern) v repair,
fix; mend

repertoire (rer-pehr-*tvaar*) nt (pl ~s)
repertory

repeteren (rer-per-*tāy*-rern) v rehearse

repetitie (rer-per-*tee*-tsee) c (pl ~s)
rehearsal

representatief (rer-prāy-zehn-taa-
teef) adj representative

reproduceren (rāy-prōa-dēw-*sāy*-
rern) v reproduce

reproductie (rāy-prōa-*derk*-see) c (pl
~s) reproduction

reptiel (rehp-*teel*) nt (pl ~en) reptile

republiek (rāy-pēw-*bleek*) c (pl ~en)
republic

republikeins (rāy-pēw-blee-*kayns*)
adj republican

reputatie (rāy-pēw-*taa*-tsee) c
reputation; fame

reserve (rer-*zehr*-ver) c (pl ~s) reserve;

reserve- spare

reserveband (rer-*zehr*-ver-bahnt) *c* (pl ~en) spare tyre

reserveren (rer-zehr-*vāy*-rern) *v* reserve; book

reservering (rer-zehr-*vāy*-rɪng) *c* (pl ~en) reservation; booking

reservewiel (rer-*zehr*-ver-veel) *nt* (pl ~en) spare wheel

reservoir (rer-zerr-*vvaar*) *nt* (pl ~s) reservoir; container

resoluut (rāy-zōa-*lōōt*) *adj* resolute

respect (reh-*spehkt*) *nt* respect; esteem, regard

respectabel (reh-spehk-*taa*-berl) *adj* respectable

respecteren (reh-spehk-*tāy*-rern) *v* respect

respectievelijk (reh-spehk-*tee*-ver-lerk) *adj* respective

rest (rehst) *c* (pl ~en) rest; remainder; remnant

restant (rehss-*tahnt*) *nt* (pl ~en) remainder; remnant

restaurant (reh-stōa-*rahnt*) *nt* (pl ~s) restaurant

restauratiewagen (rehss-tōa-*raa*-tsee-vaa-gern) *c* (pl ~s) dining car

restriktie (rer-*strɪk*-see) *c* (pl ~s) qualification

resultaat (rāy-zerl-*taat*) *nt* (pl -taten) result; outcome, issue

resulteren (rāy-zerl-*tāy*-rern) *v* result

resumé (rāy-zēw-*māy*) *nt* (pl ~s) summary

retour (rer-*tōōr*) round trip *Am*

retourvlucht (rer-*tōōr*-vlerkht) *c* (pl ~en) return flight

reumatiek (rūr-maa-*teek*) *c* rheumatism

reus (rūrss) *m* (pl reuzen) giant

reusachtig (rūr-*zahkh*-terkh) *adj* huge; gigantic, enormous, immense

revalidatie (rāy-vaa-lee-*daa*-tsee) *c* rehabilitation

revers (rer-*vair*) *c* (pl ~) lapel

reviseren (rāy-vee-*zāy*-rern) *v* overhaul

revolutie (rāy-vōa-*lēw*-tsee) *c* (pl ~s) revolution

revolutionair (rāy-vōa-lēw-tshōa-*nair*) *adj* revolutionary

revolver (rer-*vol*-verr) *c* (pl ~s) gun, revolver

revue (rer-*vēw*) *c* (pl ~s) revue

rib (rɪp) *c* (pl ~ben) rib

ribfluweel (rɪp-flēw-*vāyl*) *nt* corduroy

richten (*rɪkh*-tern) *v* direct; ~ **op** aim at

richting (*rɪkh*-tɪng) *c* (pl ~en) direction; way

richtingaanwijzer (*rɪkh*-tɪng-aan-vay-zerr) *c* (pl ~s) trafficator, indicator; directional signal *Am*

richtlijn (*rɪkht*-layn) *c* (pl ~en) directive; guideline

ridder (*rɪ*-derr) *m* (pl ~s) knight

riem (reem) *c* (pl ~en) belt; strap; lead

riet (reet) *nt* reed; cane

rif (rɪf) *nt* (pl ~fen) reef

rij (ray) *c* (pl ~en) row, rank; line; file, queue; **in de ~** *staan queue; stand in line *Am*

rijbaan (*ray*-baan) *c* (pl -banen) carriageway; roadway *nAm*

rijbewijs (*ray*-ber-vayss) *nt* driving licence, driver's license *Am*

*rijden (*ray*-dern) *v* *drive; *ride; **(te) hard ~** *speed

*rijgen (*ray*-gern) *v* thread

rijk[1] (rayk) *adj* rich; wealthy

rijk[2] (rayk) *nt* (pl ~en) kingdom, empire; **rijks-** imperial

rijkdom (*rayk*-dom) *c* (pl ~men) wealth, riches *pl*

rijm (raym) *nt* (pl ~en) rhyme

rijp (rayp) *adj* ripe, mature

rijpheid (*rayp*-hayt) *c* maturity

rijst (rayst) *c* rice

rijstrook (*ray*-strōāk) *c* (pl -stroken)
lane

rijtuig (*ray*-tur^{ew}g) *nt* (pl ~en) carriage;
coach

rijweg (*ray*-vehkh) *c* drive

rijwiel (*ray*-veel) *nt* (pl ~en) cycle;
bicycle

rillen (*rı*-lern) *v* shiver; tremble

rilling (*rı*-lıng) *c* (pl ~en) chill; shiver,
shudder

rimpel (*rım*-perl) *c* (pl ~s) wrinkle

ring (rıng) *c* (pl ~en) ring

ringweg (*rıng*-vehkh) *c* (pl ~en) by-
pass

riool (ree-^yōāl) *nt* (pl riolen) sewer

risico (*ree*-zee-kōā) *nt* (pl ~'s) risk;
chance, hazard

riskant (rıss-*kahnt*) *adj* risky

rit (rıt) *c* (pl ~ten) ride

ritme (*rıt*-mer) *nt* (pl ~n) rhythm

ritssluiting (*rıt*-slur^{ew}-tıng) *c* (pl ~en)
zipper, zip

rivaal (ree-*vaal*) *m* (f rivale, pl rivalen)
rival

rivaliseren (ree-vaa-lee-*zay*-rern) *v*
rival

rivaliteit (ree-vaa-lee-*tayt*) *c* rivalry

rivier (ree-*veer*) *c* (pl ~en) river

riviermonding (ree-*veer*-mon-dıng) *c*
(pl ~en) estuary

rivieroever (ree-*veer*-ōō-verr) *c* (pl ~s)
riverside

rob (rop) *c* (pl ~ben) seal

robijn (rōā-*bayn*) *c* (pl ~en) ruby

roddelen (*ro*-der-lern) *v* gossip

roede (*rōō*-der) *c* (pl ~n) rod

roeiboot (*rōō^{ee}*-bōāt) *c* (pl -boten)
rowing boat

roeien (*rōō^{ee}*-ern) *v* row

roeiriem (*rōō^{ee}*-reem) *c* (pl ~en) oar

roem (rōōm) *c* glory; celebrity, fame

Roemeen (rōō-*māyn*) *m* (f ~se, pl
-menen) Rumanian

Roemeens (rōō-*māyns*) *adj* Rumanian

Roemenië (rōō-*māy*-nee-^yer)
Rumania

roep (rōōp) *c* call, cry

***roepen** (*rōō*-pern) *v* call; cry, shout

roer (rōōr) *nt* rudder, helm

roeren (*rōō*-rern) *v* stir

roerend (*rōō*-rernt) *adj* movable

roest (rōōst) *nt* rust

roestig (*rōōss*-terkh) *adj* rusty

rok (rok) *c* (pl ~ken) skirt

roken (*rōā*-kern) *v* smoke

roker (*rōā*-kerr) *m* (f rookster, pl ~s)
smoker

rol (rol) *c* (pl ~len) roll

rolgordijn (*rol*-gor-dayn) *nt* (pl ~en)
blind

rollen (*ro*-lern) *v* roll

rolstoel (*rol*-stōōl) *c* (pl ~en)
wheelchair

roltrap (*rol*-trahp) *c* (pl ~pen) escalator

roman (rōā-*mahn*) *c* (pl ~s) novel

romance (rōā-*mahng*-ser) *c* (pl ~s, ~n)
romance

romanschrijver (rōā-*mahn*-skhray-
verr) *m* (f -schrijfster, pl ~s) novelist

romantisch (rōā-*mahn*-teess) *adj*
romantic

romig (*rōā*-merkh) *adj* creamy

rommel (*ro*-merl) *c* mess; litter; trash,
junk

rond (ront) *adj* round; *prep* around

ronde (*ron*-der) *c* (pl ~n, ~s) round

rondom (ront-*om*) *adv* around; *prep*
round

rondreis (*ront*-rayss) *c* (pl -reizen) tour

***rondtrekken** (*ron*-treh-kern) *v* tramp,
tour; migrate

***rondzwerven** (*ront*-svehr-vern) *v*
wander

röntgenfoto (*rernt*-gern-fōā-tōā) *c* (pl
~'s) X-ray

rood (rōāt) *adj* red; **~ staan** *v* *be
overdrawn

roodborstje (*rōāt*-bor-sher) *nt* (pl ~s)

robin

roodkoper (*rōat*-kōa-perr) *nt* copper

roof (rōaf) *c* robbery

roofdier (*rōaf*-deer) *nt* (pl ~en) beast of prey

rook (rōak) *c* smoke

rookcoupé (*rōa*-kōo-pāy) *c* (pl ~s) smoker

room (rōam) *c* cream

roomkleurig (rōam-*klūr*-rerkh) *adj* cream

rooms-katholiek (rōams-kah-tōa-*leek*) *adj* Roman Catholic

roos¹ (rōass) *c* (pl rozen) rose

roos² (rōass) *c* dandruff

rooster (*rōa*-sterr) *nt* (pl ~s) grate; schedule

roosteren (*rōa*-ster-rern) *v* grill, roast

rot (rot) *adj* rotten

rotan (*rōa*-tahn) *nt* cane

rotonde (rōa-*ton*-der) *c* (pl ~s) roundabout

rots (rots) *c* (pl ~en) rock; cliff

rotsachtig (*rot*-sahkh-terkh) *adj* rocky

rotsblok (*rots*-blok) *nt* (pl ~ken) boulder

rouge (*rōo*-zher) *c*/*nt* rouge

roulette (rōo-*leh*-ter) *c* roulette

route (*rōo*-ter) *c* (pl ~s) route

routine (rōo-*tee*-ner) *c* routine

rouw (rou) *c* mourning

royaal (rōa-*ᵞaal*) *adj* generous; liberal

roze (*raw*-zer) *adj* rose, pink

rozenkrans (*rōa*-zer-krahns) *c* (pl ~en) rosary, beads *pl*

rozijn (rōa-*zayn*) *c* (pl ~en) raisin

rubber (*rer*-berr) *nt* rubber

rubriek (rēw-*breek*) *c* (pl ~en) column

rug (rerkh) *c* (pl ~gen) back

ruggegraat (*rer*-ger-graat) *c* spine, backbone

rugpijn (*rerkh*-payn) *c* backache

rugzak (*rerkh*-sahk) *c* (pl ~ken) rucksack

ruien (*rurᵉʷ*y-ern) *v* *shed

***ruiken** (*rurᵉʷ*-kern) *v* *smell

ruil (rurᵉʷl) *c* exchange

ruilen (*rurᵉʷ*-lern) *v* exchange; swap

ruim¹ (rurᵉʷm) *adj* broad, large; roomy, spacious

ruim² (rurᵉʷm) *nt* (pl ~en) hold

ruimte (*rurᵉʷm*-ter) *c* (pl ~s) room, space

ruimtevaarder (*rurᵉʷm*-ter-vaar-derr) *m* (pl ~s) astronaut

ruimteveer (*rurᵉʷm*-ter- *vāyr*) *nt* (pl ~eren) space-shuttle

ruïne (rēw-*vee*-ner) *c* (pl ~s) ruins

ruïneren (rēw-vee-*nāy*-rern) *v* ruin

ruit (rurᵉʷt) *c* (pl ~en) check; pane

ruitenwisser (*rurᵉʷ*-ter-vi-serr) *c* (pl ~s) windscreen wiper; windshield wiper *Am*

ruiter (*rurᵉʷ*-terr) *c* (pl ~s) horseman; rider

ruk (rerk) *c* (pl ~ken) tug, wrench

rumoer (rēw-*mōor*) *nt* noise

rundvlees (*rernt*-flāyss) *nt* beef

Rus (rerss) *m* (f ~sin, pl ~sen) Russian

Rusland (*rerss*-lahnt) Russia

Russisch (*rer*-seess) *adj* Russian

rust (rerst) *c* rest; quiet; half time

rusteloosheid (rerss-ter-*lōass*-hayt) *c* unrest

rusten (*rerss*-tern) *v* rest

rusthuis (*rerst*-hurᵉʷss) *nt* (pl -huizen) rest home

rustiek (rerss-*teek*) *adj* rustic

rustig (*rerss*-terkh) *adj* calm, quiet; restful, tranquil

ruw (rēwᵒᵒ) *adj* rough, harsh

ruzie (*rēw*-zee) *c* (pl ~s) row, quarrel, dispute; ~ **maken** quarrel

S

saai (saa^ee) *adj* dull, boring, square

saamhorig (saam-*hōā*-rerkh) *adj* united

saffier (sah-*feer*) *nt* sapphire

salaris (saa-*laa*-rıss) *nt* (pl ~sen) salary; pay

saldo (*sahl*-dōā) *nt* (pl ~'s, saldi) balance

salon (saa-*lon*) *c* (pl ~s) drawing room, lounge; salon

samen (*saa*-mern) *adv* together

*****samenbinden** (*saa*-mer-bın-dern) *v* bundle

*****samenbrengen** (*saa*-mer-breh-ngern) *v* combine

samenhang (*saa*-mer-hahng) *c* coherence

samenleving (*saa*-mer-lāȳ-vıng) *c* (pl ~en) community

samenloop (*saa*-mer-lōāp) *c* concurrence

samenstellen (*saa*-mer-steh-lern) *v* compose, compile

samenstelling (*saa*-mer-steh-lıng) *c* (pl ~en) composition

*****samenvallen** (*saa*-mer-vah-lern) *v* coincide

samenvatting (*saa*-mer-vah-tıng) *c* (pl ~en) résumé, summary

samenvoegen (*saa*-mer-vōō-gern) *v* join; merge

samenwerken (*saa*-mer-vehr-kern) *v* cooperate, collaborate

samenwerking (*saa*-mer-vehr-kıng) *c* cooperation

*****samenzweren** (*saa*-mer-zvāȳ-rern) *v* conspire

samenzwering (*saa*-mer-zvāȳ-rıng) *c* (pl ~en) plot

sanatorium (saa-naa-*tōā*-ree-ʸerm) *nt* (pl ~s, -ria) sanatorium

sandaal (sahn-*daal*) *c* (pl -dalen) sandal

sanitair (saa-nee-*tair*) *adj* sanitary

Saoedi-Arabië (saa-ōō-dee-aa-*raa*-bee-ʸer) Saudi Arabia

Saoedi-Arabisch (saa-ōō-dee-aa-*raa*-beess) *adj* Saudi Arabian

sap (sahp) *nt* (pl ~pen) juice

sappig (*sah*-perkh) *adj* juicy

sardine (sahr-*dee*-ner) *c* (pl ~s) sardine

satelliet (saa-ter-*leet*) *c* (pl ~en) satellite

satijn (saa-*tayn*) *nt* satin

sauna (*sou*-naa) *c* (pl ~'s) sauna

saus (souss) *c* (pl sauzen) sauce

Scandinavië (skahn-dee-*naa*-vee-ʸer) Scandinavia

Scandinaviër (skahn-dee-*naa*-vee-ʸerr) *m* (f Scandinavische, pl ~s) Scandinavian

Scandinavisch (skahn-dee-*naa*-veess) *adj* Scandinavian

scène (*sai*-ner) *c* (pl ~s) scene

schaafwond (*skhaaf*-vont) *c* (pl ~en) graze

schaak! (skhaak) check!

schaakbord (*skhaak*-bort) *nt* (pl ~en) chessboard

schaakspel (*skhaak*-spehl) *nt* chess

schaal (skhaal) *c* (pl schalen) dish; bowl; scale

schaaldier (*skhaal*-deer) *nt* (pl ~en) shellfish

schaamte (*skhaam*-ter) *c* shame

schaap (skhaap) *nt* (pl schapen) sheep

schaar (skhaar) *c* (pl scharen) scissors *pl*

schaars (skhaars) *adj* scarce

schaarste (*skhaar*-ster) *c* scarcity

schaats (skhaats) *c* (pl ~en) skate

schaatsen (*skhaat*-sern) *v* skate

schade (*skhaa*-der) *c* damage; harm, mischief

schadelijk (*schaa-der-lerk*) *adj*
harmful; hurtful

schadeloosstelling (*schaa-der-lōa-steh-lıng*) *c* (pl ~en) indemnity

schaden (*schaa-dern*) *v* harm

schadevergoeding (*schaa-der-verr-gōō-dıng*) *c* (pl ~en) compensation, indemnity

schaduw (*schaa-dēw⁰⁰*) *c* (pl ~en) shade; shadow

schaduwrijk (*schaa-dēw⁰⁰-rayk*) *adj* shady

schakel (*schaa-kerl*) *c* (pl ~s) link

schakelaar (*schaa-ker-laar*) *c* (pl ~s) switch

schakelbord (*schaa-kerl-bort*) *nt* switchboard

schakelen (*schaa-ker-lern*) *v* change gear

schamen (*schaa-mern*): **zich ~** *be ashamed

schandaal (schahn-*daal*) *nt* (pl -dalen) scandal

schande (*schahn-deh*) *c* disgrace, shame

schapevlees (*schaa-per-vlāyss*) *nt* mutton

scharnier (skhahr-*neer*) *nt* (pl ~en) hinge

schat (skhaht) *c* (pl ~ten) treasure; darling

schatkist (*skhaht-kıst*) *c* treasury

schatten (*skhah-tern*) *v* evaluate, estimate, value; appreciate

schatting (*skhah-tıng*) *c* (pl ~en) estimate; appreciation

schedel (*skhāy-derl*) *c* (pl ~s) skull

scheef (skhāyf) *adj* slanting

scheel (skhāyl) *adj* cross-eyed

scheepswerf (*skhāyps-vehrf*) *c* (pl -werven) shipyard

scheepvaart (*skhāyp-faart*) *c* navigation

scheepvaartlijn (*skhāyp-faart-layn*) *c* (pl ~en) shipping line

scheerapparaat (*skhāyr-ah-paa-raat*) *nt* (pl -raten) safety razor, electric razor, shaver

scheercrème (*skhāyr-kraim*) *c* (pl ~s) shaving cream

scheerkwast (*skhāyr-kvahst*) *c* (pl ~en) shaving brush

scheermesje (*skhāyr-meh-sher*) *nt* (pl ~s) razor blade

scheerzeep (*skhāyr-zāyp*) *c* shavingsoap

***scheiden** (*skhay-dern*) *v* separate; divide, part; divorce

scheiding (*skhay-dıng*) *c* (pl ~en) division; parting

scheidsrechter (*skhayts-rehkh-terr*) *m* (pl ~s) umpire, referee

scheikunde (*skhay-kern-der*) *c* chemistry

scheikundig (skhay-*kern*-derkh) *adj* chemical

***schelden** (*skhehl-dern*) *v* scold

schelm (skhehlm) *m* (pl ~en) rascal

schelp (skhehlp) *c* (pl ~en) shell

schelvis (*skhehl-vıss*) *c* haddock

schema (*skhāy-maa*) *nt* (pl ~'s, ~ta) diagram; scheme

schemering (*skhāy-mer-rıng*) *c* twilight

schenden (*skhehn-dern*) *v* violate; invade

schending (*skhehn-dıng*) *c* (pl ~en) violation

***schenken** (*skhehng-kern*) *v* pour; donate

schenking (*skhehng-kıng*) *c* (pl ~en) donation

***scheppen** (*skheh-pern*) *v* create

schepsel (*skhehp-serl*) *nt* (pl ~s) creature

***scheren** (*skhāy-rern*): **zich ~** shave

scherm (skhehrm) *nt* (pl ~en) screen

schermen (*skhehr-mern*) *v* fence

scherp (skhehrp) *adj* sharp; keen

schets (skhehts) *c* (pl ~en) sketch

schetsen (*skheht*-sern) *v* sketch

scheur (skhūrr) *c* (pl ~en) tear

scheuren (*skhū̄r*-rern) *v* rip, *tear

schiereiland (*skheer*-ay-lahnt) *nt* peninsula

***schieten** (*skhee*-tern) *v* *shoot, fire

schietschijf (*skheet*-skhayf) *c* (pl -schijven) mark

schijf (skhayf) *c* (pl schijven) disc; **harde ~** hard disk

schijn (skhayn) *c* semblance

schijnbaar (*skhaym*-baar) *adj* apparent

***schijnen** (*skhay*-nern) *v* appear, seem; *shine

schijnheilig (skhayn-*hay*-lerkh) *adj* hypocritical

schijnwerper (*skhayn*-vehr-perr) *c* (pl ~s) spotlight, searchlight

schikken (*skhı*-kern) *v* suit

schikking (*skhı*-kıng) *c* (pl ~en) settlement

schil (skhıl) *c* (pl ~len) skin; peel

schilder (*skhıl*-derr) *m* (f ~es, pl ~s) painter

schilderachtig (*skhıl*-derr-ahkh-terkh) *adj* scenic, picturesque

schilderen (*skhıl*-der-rern) *v* paint

schilderij (skhıl-der-*ray*) *nt* (pl ~en) painting, picture

schildpad (*skhıl*-paht) *c* (pl ~den) turtle

schilfer (*skhıl*-ferr) *c* (pl ~s) chip

schillen (*skhı*-lern) *c* peel

schimmel (*skhı*-merl) *c* (pl ~s) mildew

schip (skhıp) *nt* (pl schepen) ship; vessel

schitterend (*skhı*-ter-rernt) *adj* brilliant, splendid

schittering (*skhı*-ter-rıng) *c* (pl ~en) glare

schoeisel (*skhoo*ᵉᵉ-serl) *nt* footwear

schoen (skhōōn) *c* (pl ~en) shoe

schoenmaker (*skhōōn*-maa-kerr) *m* (pl ~s) shoemaker

schoensmeer (*skhōōn*-smāyr) *c* shoe polish

schoenveter (*skhōōn*-fāy-terr) *c* (pl ~s) shoelace

schoenwinkel (*skhōōn*-vıng-kerl) *c* (pl ~s) shoe shop

schoft (skhoft) *c* (pl ~en) bastard

schok (skhok) *c* (pl ~ken) shock

schokbreker (*skhok*-brāy-kerr) *c* (pl ~s) shock absorber

schokken (*skho*-kern) *v* shock

schol (skhol) *c* (pl ~len) plaice

schommel (*skho*-merl) *c* (pl ~s) swing

schommelen (*skho*-mer-lern) *v* rock, *swing

school (skhōāl) *c* (pl scholen) school; college; **middelbare ~** secondary school

schoolbank (*skhōāl*-bahngk) *c* (pl ~en) desk

schoolbord (*skhōāl*-bort) *nt* (pl ~en) blackboard

schoolhoofd (*skhōāl*-hōāft) *nt* (pl ~en) headmaster, headmistress, head, principal

schooljongen (*skhōāl*-ʸo-ngern) *m* (pl ~s) schoolboy

schoolmeester (*skhōāl*-māyss-terr) *m* (pl ~s) teacher

schoolmeisje (*skhōāl*-may-sher) *nt* (pl ~s) schoolgirl

schoolslag (*skhōāl*-slahkh) *c* breaststroke

schooltas (*skhōāl*-tahss) *c* (pl ~sen) satchel

schoon (skhōān) *adj* clean

schoondochter (skhōān-*dokh*-terr) *f* (pl ~s) daughter-in-law

schoonheid (*skhōān*-hayt) *c* (pl -heden) beauty

schoonheidsbehandeling (*skhōān*-

hayts-ber-hahn-der-ling) *c* (pl ~en)
beauty treatment

schoonheidsmasker (*skhōan*-hayts-mahss-kerr) *nt* (pl ~s) face pack

schoonheidsmiddelen (*skhōan*-hayts-mɪ-der-lern) *pl* cosmetics *pl*

schoonheidssalon (*skhōan*-hayts-saa-lon) *c* (pl ~s) beauty salon, beauty parlo(u)r

schoonmaak (*skhōa*-maak) *c* cleaning

schoonmaken (*skhōa*-maa-kern) *v* clean

schoonmoeder (*skhōa*-mōō-derr) *f* (pl ~s) mother-in-law

schoonouders (*skhōan*-ou-derrs) *pl* parents-in-law *pl*

schoonvader (*skhōan*-vaa-derr) *m* (pl ~s) father-in-law

schoonzoon (*skhōan*-zōan) *m* (pl -zonen) son-in-law

schoonzuster (*skhōan*-zerss-terr) *f* (pl ~s) sister-in-law

schoorsteen (*skhōar*-stāyn) *c* (pl -stenen) chimney

schoot (*skhōt*) *c* (pl schoten) lap

schop (skhop) *c* (pl ~pen) kick; spade, shovel

schoppen (*skho*-pern) *v* kick

schor (skhor) *adj* hoarse

schorsen (*skhor*-sern) *v* suspend

schort (skhort) *c* (pl ~en) apron

Schot (skhot) *m* (f ~se, pl ~ten) Scot

schot (skhot) *nt* (pl ~en) shot

schotel (*skhōa*-terl) *c* (pl ~s) dish;
schoteltje *nt* saucer

Schotland (*skhot*-lahnt) Scotland

Schots (skhots) *adj* Scottish, Scotch

schouder (*skhou*-derr) *c* (pl ~s) shoulder

schouwburg (*skhou*-berrkh) *c* (pl ~en) theater *Am*, theatre

schouwspel (*skhou*-spehl) *nt* (pl ~en) spectacle

schram (skhrahm) *c* (pl ~men) scratch

schrappen (*skhrah*-pern) *v* scrape

schrede (*skhrāy*-der) *c* (pl ~n) pace

schreeuw (skhrāy⁰⁰) *c* (pl ~en) scream, cry, shout

schreeuwen (*skhrāy⁰⁰*-ern) *v* scream, cry, shout

schriftelijk (*skhrɪf*-ter-lerk) *adj* written; *adv* in writing

schrijfbehoeften (*skhrayf*-ber-hōōf-tern) *pl* stationery

schrijfblok (*skhrayf*-blok) *nt* (pl ~ken) writing pad

schrijfmachine (*skhrayf*-mah-shee-ner) *c* (pl ~s) typewriter

schrijfmachinepapier (*skhrayf*-mah-shee-ner-paa-peer) *nt* typing paper

schrijfpapier (*skhrayf*-paa-peer) *nt* notepaper; writing paper

schrijftafel (*skhrayf*-taa-ferl) *c* (pl ~s) bureau

schrijn (skhrayn) *c* (pl ~en) shrine

*schrijven (*skhray*-vern) *v* *write

schrijver (*skhray*-vehr) *m* (f schrijfster, pl ~s) author, writer

schrik (skhrɪk) *c* fright, scare; ~
*aanjagen terrify

schrikkeljaar (*skhrɪ*-kerl-ʸaar) *nt* leap year

*schrikken (*skhrɪ*-kern) *v* *be frightened; ***doen** ~ frighten, scare

schrobben (*skhro*-bern) *v* scrub

schroef (skhrōōf) *c* (pl schroeven) screw; propeller

schroefsleutel (*skhrōōf*-slūr-terl) *c* (pl ~s) spanner

schroeven (*skhrōō*-vern) *v* screw

schroevendraaier (*skhrōō*-ver-draa-ʸerr) *c* (pl ~s) screwdriver

schub (skherp) *c* (pl ~ben) scale

schudden (*skher*-dern) *v* *shake; shuffle

schuifdeur (*skhurᵉʷf*-dūr) *c* (pl ~en) sliding door

schuilplaats (*skhurᵉʷl*-plaats) *c* (pl

~en) cover; shelter

schuim (skhur^{ew}m) *nt* froth, lather, foam

schuimen (*skhur^{ew}-mern*) *v* foam

schuimrubber (*skhur^{ew}m-rer-berr*) *nt* foam rubber

schuin (skhur^{ew}n) *adj* slanting

*schuiven (*skhur^{ew}-vern*) *v* push

schuld[1] (skherlt) *c* guilt; fault, blame; **de ~ *geven aan** blame

schuld[2] (skherlt) *c* (pl ~en) debt

schuldeiser (*skherlt-ay-serr*) *m* (pl ~s) creditor

schuldig (*skherl-derkh*) *adj* guilty; ~ ***bevinden** convict; ~ ***zijn** owe

schuur (skhewr) *c* (pl schuren) barn; shed

schuurpapier (*skhewr-paa-peer*) *nt* sandpaper

schuw (skhew^{oo}) *adj* shy

scoren (sko$\overline{a}$-rern) *v* score

seconde (ser-*kon*-der) *c* (pl ~n) second

secretaresse (si-krer-taa-*reh*-ser) *f* (pl ~n) secretary

secretaris (si-krer-*taa*-rerss) *m* (pl ~sen) secretary; clerk

sectie (*sehk*-see) *c* (pl ~s) section

secundair (say-kern-*dair*) *adj* secondary

secuur (ser-*kewr*) *adj* precise

sedert (*say*-derrt) *prep* since

sein (sayn) *nt* (pl ~en) signal

seinen (*say*-nern) *v* signal

seizoen (say-z$\overline{oo}$n) *nt* (pl ~en) season; **buiten het ~** off season

seksualiteit (sehk-sew-vaa-lee-*tayt*) *c* sexuality

seksueel (sehk-sew-*vayl*) *adj* sexual

selderij (*sehl*-der-ray) *c* celery

select (ser-*lehkt*) *adj* select

selecteren (say-lehk-*tay*-rern) *v* select

selectie (say-*lehk*-see) *c* selection

senaat (ser-*naat*) *c* senate

senator (ser-*naa*-tor) *m* (pl ~en) senator

seniel (ser-*neel*) *adj* senile

sensatie (sehn-*zaa*-tsee) *c* (pl ~s) sensation

sensationeel (sehn-zaa-tsh$\overline{oa}$-*nayl*) *adj* sensational

sentimenteel (sehn-tee-mehn-*tayl*) *adj* sentimental

september (sehp-*tehm*-berr) September

septisch (*sehp*-teess) *adj* septic

serie (*say*-ree) *c* (pl ~s) series

serieus (say-ree-$^y\overline{u}$rss) *adj* serious

serum (*say*-rerm) *nt* (pl ~s, sera) serum

serveerster (sehr-*vayr*-sterr) *f* (pl ~s) waitress

servet (sehr-*veht*) *nt* (pl ~ten) napkin, serviette

sfeer (sfayr) *c* atmosphere; sphere

shag (shehk) *c* cigarette tobacco

shampoo (*shahm*-po$\overline{a}$) *c* shampoo

Siamees (see-^{y}aa-*mayss*) *adj* Siamese

sigaar (see-*gaar*) *c* (pl sigaren) cigar

sigarenwinkel (see-*gaa*-rer-v$\imath$ng-kerl) *c* (pl ~s) cigar shop, tobacconist's

sigarenwinkelier (see-*gaa*-rer-v$\imath$ng-ker-leer) *m* (pl ~s) tobacconist

sigaret (see-gaa-*reht*) *c* (pl ~ten) cigarette

sigarettenkoker (see-gaa-*reh*-ter-k$\overline{oa}$-ker) *c* (pl ~s) cigarette case

sigarettepijpje (see-gaa-*reh*-ter-payp-^{y}er) *nt* (pl ~s) cigarette holder

signaal (see-*ñaal*) *nt* (pl nalen) signal

signalement (see-ñaa-ler-*mehnt*) *nt* (pl ~en) description

simpel (*s$\imath$m*-perl) *adj* simple

sinaasappel (*see*-naa-sah-perl) *c* (pl ~en, ~s) orange

sinds (s$\imath$ns) *conj* since

sindsdien (s$\imath$ns-*deen*) *adv* since

sirene (see-*ray*-ner) *c* (pl ~s) siren

siroop (see-*r$\overline{oa}$p*) *c* syrup

situatie (see-t$\overline{ew}$-vaa-tsee) *c* (pl ~s)

situation

sjaal (shaal) c (pl ~s) shawl; scarf

skelet (sker-*leht*) nt (pl ~ten) skeleton

ski (skee) c (pl ~'s) ski

skibroek (skee-brōōk) c (pl ~en) ski pants

skiën (skee-*Y*ern) v ski

skiër (skee-*Y*err) m (f skister, pl ~s) skier

skilift (skee-lift) c (pl ~en) ski lift

skischoenen (skee-skhōō-nern) pl ski boots

skistokken (skee-sto-kern) pl ski sticks; ski poles *Am*

sla (slaa) c lettuce; salad

slaaf (slaaf) m (f slavin, pl slaven) slave

***slaan** (slaan) v *beat; *hit; *strike; smack, slap

slaap¹ (slaap) c sleep; **in ~** asleep

slaap² (slaap) c (pl slapen) temple

slaapkamer (slaap-kaa-merr) c (pl ~s) bedroom

slaappil (slaa-pıl) c (pl ~len) sleeping pill

slaapwagen (slaap-vaa-gern) c (pl ~s) sleeping car, couchette

slaapzaal (slaap-saal) c (pl -zalen) dormitory

slaapzak (slaap-sahk) c (pl ~ken) sleeping bag

slachtoffer (slahkht-o-ferr) nt (pl ~s) victim; casualty

slag¹ (slahkh) c (pl ~en) blow; battle

slag² (slahkh) nt sort

slagader (slahkh-aa-derr) c (pl ~s) artery

slagboom (slahkh-bōam) c (pl -bomen) barrier

slagen (slaa-gern) v manage, succeed; pass

slager (slaa-gerr) m (pl ~s) butcher

slagzin (slahkh-sın) c (pl ~nen) slogan

slak (slahk) c (pl ~ken) snail

slang (slahng) c (pl ~en) snake

slank (slahngk) adj slim, slender

slaolie (slaa-ōā-lee) c salad-oil

slap (slahp) adj limp; weak

slapeloos (slaa-per-lōāss) adj sleepless

slapeloosheid (slaa-per-lōāss-hayt) c insomnia

***slapen** (slaa-pern) v *sleep

slaperig (slaa-per-rerkh) adj sleepy

slecht (slehkht) adj bad; poor; ill; wicked, evil; **slechter** worse; **slechtst** worst

slechts (slehkhts) adv only, merely

slede (slāy-der) c (pl ~n) sledge

slee (slāy) c (pl ~ën) sleigh, sledge

sleepboot (slāy-bōat) c (pl -boten) tug

slepen (slāy-pern) v drag, haul; tug, tow

sleutel (slūr-terl) c (pl ~s) key; wrench

sleutelbeen (slūr-terl-bāyn) nt (pl -beenderen, -benen) collarbone

sleutelgat (slūr-terl-gaht) nt (pl ~en) keyhole

***slijpen** (slay-pern) v sharpen

slijterij (slay-ter-*ray*) c (pl ~en) off-licence, *nAm* liquor store

slikken (slı-kern) v swallow

slim (slım) adj clever

slip (slıp) c (pl ~s) briefs pl; panties pl

slippen (slı-pern) v slip; skid

slof (slof) c (pl ~fen) slipper; carton

slokje (slok-*Y*er) nt (pl ~s) sip

sloot (slōat) c (pl sloten) ditch

slopen (slōā-pern) v demolish

slordig (slor-derkh) adj untidy; slovenly, sloppy, careless

slot¹ (slot) nt (pl ~en) lock; castle; **op ~ *doen** lock

slot² (slot) nt end

sluier (slur*ew*-err) c (pl ~s) veil

sluipschutter (slur*ew*p-skher-terr) m (pl ~s) sniper

sluis (slur*ew*ss) c (pl sluizen) lock, sluice

***sluiten** (slur*ew*-tern) v close, *shut; fasten

sluiting (slur*ew*-tıng) c (pl ~en) fastener

sluw (slew⁰⁰) *adj* cunning

smaak (smaak) *c* (pl smaken) taste; flavo(u)r

smakelijk (*smaa*-ker-lerk) *adj* savo(u)ry, tasty; appetizing

smakeloos (*smaa*-ker-lōass) *adj* tasteless

smaken (*smaa*-kern) *v* taste

smal (smahl) *adj* narrow

smaragd (smaa-*rahkht*) *nt* emerald

smart (smahrt) *c* (pl ~en) grief

smartlap (*smahrt*-lahp) *c* (pl ~pen) tearjerker

smeerolie (*smāyr*-ōā-lee) *c* lubrication oil

smeersysteem (*smāyr*-see-stāym) *nt* lubrication system

smeken (*smāy*-kern) *v* beg

*smelten (*smehl*-tern) *v* melt

smeren (*smāy*-rern) *v* lubricate, grease

smerig (*smāy*-rerkh) *adj* dirty; foul, filthy

smering (*smāy*-rıng) *c* lubrication

smet (smeht) *c* (pl ~ten) blot

smid (smıt) *m* (pl smeden) smith, blacksmith

smoking (*smōā*-kıng) *c* (pl ~s) dinner jacket; tuxedo *nAm*

smokkelen (*smo*-ker-lern) *v* smuggle

snaar (snaar) *c* (pl snaren) string

snavel (*snaa*-verl) *c* (pl ~s) beak

snee (snāy) *c* (pl ~ën) cut; slice

sneeuw (snāy⁰⁰) *c* snow

sneeuwen (*snāy*⁰⁰-ern) *v* snow

sneeuwslik (*snāy*⁰⁰-slık) *nt* slush

sneeuwstorm (*snāy*⁰⁰-storm) *c* (pl ~en) snowstorm, blizzard

snel (snehl) *adj* fast, swift, rapid

snelheid (*snehl*-hayt) *c* (pl -heden) speed; **maximum ~** speed limit

snelheidsbeperking (*snehl*-hayts-ber-pehr-kıng) *c* speed limit

snelheidsmeter (*snehl*-hayts-māy-terr) *c* speedometer

snelheidsovertreding (*snehl*-hayts-ōā-verr-trāy-dıng) *c* speeding

snelkookpan (*snehl*-kōāk-pahn) *c* (pl ~nen) pressure cooker

snellen (*sneh*-lern) *v* dash

sneltrein (*snehl*-trayn) *c* (pl ~en) express train

snelweg (*snehl*-vehkh) *c* (pl ~en) motorway

*snijden (*snay*-dern) *v* *cut; carve

snijwond (*snay*-vont) *c* (pl ~en) cut

snipper (*snu*-perr) *c* (pl ~s) scrap

snoek (snōōk) *c* (pl ~en) pike

snoep (snōōp) *nt* sweets; candy *nAm*

snoepgoed (*snōōp*-khōōt) *nt* sweets; candy *nAm*

snoepje (*snōōp*-ᵞer) *nt* (pl ~s) sweet; candy *nAm*

snoepwinkel (*snōōp*-vıng-kerl) *c* (pl ~s) sweetshop; candy store *Am*

snoer (snōōr) *nt* (pl ~en) line, cord; flex; electric cord

snor (snor) *c* (pl ~ren) moustache

snorkel (*snor*-kerl) *c* (pl ~s) snorkel

snugger (*sner*-gerr) *adj* bright

snuit (snur^cwt) *c* (pl ~en) snout

snurken (*snerr*-kern) *v* snore

sociaal (sōā-*shaal*) *adj* social

socialisme (sōā-shaa-*liss*-mer) *nt* socialism

socialist (sōā-shaa-*lıst*) *m* (f ~e, pl ~en) socialist

socialistisch (sōā-shaa-*lıss*-teess) *adj* socialist

sociëteit (sōā-see-ᵞer-*tayt*) *c* (pl ~en) club

soep (sōōp) *c* (pl ~en) soup

soepbord (*sōō*-bort) *nt* (pl ~en) soup plate

soepel (*sōō*-perl) *adj* supple, flexible

soeplepel (*sōōp*-lāy-perl) *c* (pl ~s) soup spoon

sofa (*sōā*-faa) *c* (pl ~'s) sofa

sok (sok) *c* (pl ~ken) sock

soldaat (sol-*daat*) *m* (pl -daten) soldier

solide (sōā-*lee*-der) *adj* (pl ~en) solid

solitair (sōā-lee-*tehr*) *adj* solitary

sollicitatie (so-lee-see-*taa*-tsee) *c* (pl ~s) application

sollicitatiegesprek (so-lee-see-*taa*-tsee-ger-sprehk) *nt* (pl ~ken) interview

solliciteren (so-lee-see-*tāy*-rern) *v* apply

som (som) *c* (pl ~men) sum; amount; **ronde ~** lump sum

somber (*som*-berr) *adj* gloomy, somber *Am*, sombre

sommige (*so*-mer-ger) *pron* some

soms (soms) *adv* sometimes

soort (sōārt) *c/nt* (pl ~en) sort, kind; breed, species

sorteren (sor-*tāy*-rern) *v* assort, sort

sortering (sor-*tāy*-rıng) *c* (pl ~en) assortment

souterrain (sōō-ter-ra̅ng̅) *nt* (pl ~s) basement

souvenir (sōō-ver-*neer*) *nt* (pl ~s) souvenir; **souvenirwinkel** souvenir shop

spaak (spaak) *c* (pl spaken) spoke

Spaans (spaans) *adj* Spanish

spaarbank (*spaar*-bahngk) *c* (pl ~en) savings bank

spaargeld (*spaar*-gehlt) *nt* savings *pl*

spaarzaam (*spaar*-zaam) *adj* economical

spaarvarken (*spaar*-vahr-kern) *nt* (pl ~s) piggy bank

spade (*spaa*-der) *c* (pl ~n) spade

spalk (spahlk) *c* (pl ~en) splint

Spanjaard (*spah*-ñaart) *m* (f Spaanse, pl ~en) Spaniard

Spanje (*spah*-ñer) Spain

spannend (*spah*-nernt) *adj* exciting

spanning (*spah*-nıng) *c* (pl ~en) tension; pressure, strain, stress

sparen (*spaa*-rern) *v* save; economize

spat (spaht) *c* (pl ~ten) stain, spot, speck

spatader (*spaht*-aa-derr) *c* (pl ~s, ~en) varicose vein

spatiëren (spaa-*tshāy*-rern) *v* space

spatten (*spah*-tern) *v* splash

specerij (spāy-ser-*ray*) *c* (pl ~en) spice

speciaal (spāy-*shaal*) *adj* special; particular, peculiar

specialiseren (spāy-shaa-lee-*zāy*-rern): **zich ~** specialize

specialist (spāy-shaa-*lıst*) *m* (f ~e, pl ~en) specialist

specialiteit (spāy-shaa-lee-*tayt*) *c* (pl ~en) speciality

specifiek (spāy-see-*feek*) *adj* specific

specimen (*spāy*-see-mehn) *nt* (pl ~s) specimen

speculeren (spāy-kēw-*lāy*-rern) *v* speculate

speeksel (*spāyk*-serl) *nt* spit

speelgoed (*spāyl*-gōōt) *nt* toy

speelgoedwinkel (*spāyl*-gōōt-vıng-kerl) *c* (pl ~s) toyshop

speelkaart (*spāyl*-kaart) *c* (pl ~en) playing card

speelplaats (*spāyl*-plaats) *c* (pl ~en) playground

speelterrein (*spāyl*-teh-rayn) *nt* (pl ~en) recreation ground

speer (spāyr) *c* (pl speren) spear

spek (spehk) *nt* bacon

spel¹ (spehl) *nt* (pl ~en) game

spel² (spehl) *nt* (pl ~len) play

speld (spehlt) *c* (pl ~en) pin

spelen (*spāy*-lern) *v* play

speler (*spāy*-lerr) *m* (f speelster, pl ~s) player

spellen (*speh*-lern) *v* *spell

spelling (*speh*-lıng) *c* spelling

spelonk (spāy-*longk*) *c* (pl ~en) cave

spiegel (*spee*-gerl) *c* (pl ~s) looking-glass, mirror

spiegelbeeld (*spee*-gerl-bāylt) *nt* (pl

~en) reflection

spier (speer) *c* (pl ~en) muscle

spijbelen (*spay*-ber-lern) *v* play truant

spijker (*spay*-kerr) *c* (pl ~s) nail

spijkerbroek (*spay*-kerr-brōōk) *c* (pl ~en) jeans *pl*

spijskaart (*spayss*-kaart) *c* (pl ~en) menu

spijsvertering (*spayss*-ferr-tāy-rīng) *c* digestion

spijt (spayt) *c* regret

spikkel (*spi*-kerl) *c* (pl ~s) spat

spin (spin) *c* (pl ~nen) spider

spinazie (spee-*naa*-zee) *c* spinach

***spinnen** (*spi*-nern) *v* *spin

spinnenweb (*spi*-nern-vehp) *nt* spider's web

spion (spee-*y*on) *m* (f ~ne, pl ~nen) spy

spiritusbrander (*spee*-ree-terss-brahn-derr) *c* (pl ~s) spirit stove

spit[1] (spit) *nt* (pl ~ten) spit

spit[2] (spit) *nt* lumbago

spits[1] (spits) *adj* pointed

spits[2] (spits) *c* (pl ~en) peak; spire

spitsuur (*spits*-ēwr) *nt* (pl -uren) rush hour, peak hour

***splijten** (*splay*-tern) *v* *split

splinter (*splin*-terr) *c* (pl ~s) splinter

splinternieuw (*splin*-terr-nee⁰⁰) *adj* brand-new

splitsen (*split*-sern) split; **zich ~** fork

spoed (spōōt) *c* haste, speed

spoedcursus (*spōōt*-kerr-zerss) *c* (pl ~sen) intensive course

spoedgeval (*spōōt*-kher-vahl) *nt* (pl ~len) emergency

spoedig (*spōō*-derkh) *adv* soon, shortly

spoel (spōōl) *c* (pl ~en) spool

spoelen (*spōō*-lern) *v* rinse

spoeling (*spōō*-līng) *c* (pl ~en) rinse

spons (spons) *c* (pl sponzen) sponge

spook (spōak) *nt* (pl spoken) ghost, phantom; spook

spoor (spōar) *nt* (pl sporen) trace; trail, track

spoorbaan (*spōar*-baan) *c* (pl -banen) railway; railroad *nAm*

spoorweg (*spōar*-vehkh) *c* (pl ~en) railway; railroad *nAm*

sport (sport) *c* sport

sportjasje (*sport-y*ah-sher) *nt* (pl ~s) sports jacket, blazer

sportkleding (*sport*-klāy-dīng) *c* sportswear

sportman (*sport*-mahn) *m* (pl ~en) sportsman

sportvrouw (*sport*-frou) *f* (pl ~en) sportswoman

sportwagen (*sport*-vaa-gern) *c* (pl ~s) sports car

spot (spot) *c* mockery

spraak (spraak) *c* speech; **ter sprake *brengen** *bring up

spraakzaam (*spraak*-saam) *adj* talkative

sprakeloos (*spraa*-ker-lōass) *adj* speechless

spreekkamer (*sprāy*-kaa-merr) *c* (pl ~s) surgery

spreekuur (*sprāyk*-ēwr) *nt* (pl -uren) consultation hours

spreekwoord (*sprāyk*-vōart) *nt* (pl ~en) proverb

spreeuw (sprāy⁰⁰) *c* (pl ~en) starling

sprei (spray) *c* (pl ~en) quilt

spreiden (*spray*-dern) *v* *spread

***spreken** (*sprāy*-kern) *v* *speak, talk

***springen** (*spri*-ngern) *v* jump; *leap

springstof (*spring*-stof) *c* (pl ~fen) explosive

sprinkhaan (*springk*-haan) *c* (pl -hanen) grasshopper

sproeier (*sprōō*ᵉᵉ-err) *c* (pl ~s) atomizer

sprong (sprong) *c* (pl ~en) jump; hop, leap

sprookje (*sprōak-y*er) *nt* (pl ~s)

fairytale

spruitjes (*sprur^{ew}-t^{y}erss*) *pl* sprouts *pl*

spuit (*spur^{ew}t*) *c* (pl ~en) syringe

spuitbus (*spur^{ew}t-berss*) *c* (pl ~sen) atomizer

spuiten (*spur^{ew}-tern*) *v* spray

spuitwater (*spur^{ew}t-vaa-terr*) *nt* soda water

spul (*sperl*) *nt* stuff

spuug (*spēwkh*) *nt* spit

spuwen (*spēw^{oo}-ern*) *v* *spit

staal (*staal*) *nt* steel; **roestvrij ~** stainless steel

***staan** (*staan*) *v* *stand; **goed ~** *become; suit

staart (*staart*) *c* (pl ~en) tail

staat (*staat*) *c* (pl staten) state; **in~** able; **in ~ stellen** enable; **in ~ zijn om** *be able to; **staats-** national

staatsburgerschap (*staats-berr-gerr-skhahp*) *nt* citizenship

staatshoofd (*staats-hōaft*) *nt* (pl ~en) head of state

staatsman (*staats-mahn*) *m* (pl -lieden) statesman

stabiel (*staa-beel*) *adj* stable

stad (*staht*) *c* (pl steden) town; city

stadhuis (*staht-hur^{ew}ss*) *nt* (pl -huizen) town hall

stadion (*staa-dee-^{y}on*) *nt* (pl ~s) stadium

stadium (*staa-dee-^{y}erm*) *nt* (pl stadia) stage

stadscentrum (*staht-sehn-trerm*) *nt* (pl -tra) town center *Am*, town centre

stadslicht (*stahts-lıkht*) *nt* (pl ~en) parking light

stadsmensen (*stahts-mehn-sern*) *pl* townspeople *pl*

staf (*stahf*) *c* staff

stagiair (*staa-zhair*) *m* (f ~e, pl ~s) trainee

staken (*staa-kern*) *v* *strike; stop, discontinue

staking (*staa-kıng*) *c* (pl ~en) strike

stal (*stahl*) *c* (pl ~len) stable

stalknecht (*stahl-knehkht*) *m* (pl ~en) groom

stallen (*stah-lern*) *v* garage

stalles (*stah-lerss*) *pl* stall; orchestra seat *Am*

stam (*stahm*) *c* (pl ~men) trunk; tribe

stamelen (*staa-mer-lern*) *v* falter

stampen (*stahm-pern*) *v* stamp, thump

stampvol (*stahmp-fol*) *adj* packed

stand (*stahnt*) *c* score; **tot ~ *brengen** realize

standaard (*stahn-daart*) *c* (pl ~en) standard; stand

standbeeld (*stahnt-bāylt*) *nt* (pl ~en) statue

standpunt (*stahnt-pernt*) *nt* (pl ~en) point of view

standvastig (*stahnt-fahss-terkh*) *adj* steadfast

stang (*stahng*) *c* (pl ~en) rod, bar

stap (*stahp*) *c* (pl ~pen) step; pace; move

stapel (*staa-perl*) *c* (pl ~s) stack, heap, pile

stappen (*stah-pern*) *v* step

staren (*staa-rern*) *v* gaze, stare

start (*stahrt*) *c* take-off

startbaan (*stahrt-baan*) *c* runway

starten (*stahr-tern*) *v* *take off

statiegeld (*staa-tsee-gehlt*) *nt* deposit

station (*staa-shon*) *nt* (pl ~s) station; depot *nAm*

statistiek (*staa-tiss-teek*) *c* (pl ~en) statistics *pl*

stedelijk (*stāy-der-lerk*) *adj* urban

steeds (*stāyts*) *adv* continually

steeg (*stāykh*) *c* (pl stegen) alley, lane

steek (*stāyk*) *c* (pl steken) stitch; sting, bite

steel (*stāyl*) *c* (pl stelen) stem; handle

steelpan (*stāyl-pahn*) *c* (pl ~nen) saucepan

steen (stayn) *c* (pl stenen) stone; brick
steengroeve (stayn-groo-ver) *c* (pl ~n)
quarry
steenpuist (stayn-pur^ew st) *c* (pl ~en)
boil
steigers (stay-gerrs) *pl* scaffolding
steil (stayl) *adj* steep
stekelvarken (stay-kerl-vahr-kern) *nt*
(pl ~s) porcupine
*****steken** (stay-kern) *v* *sting
stekker (steh-kerr) *c* (pl ~s) plug
stel (stehl) *nt* (pl ~len) set
*****stelen** (stay-lern) *v* *steal
stellen (steh-lern) *v* *put
stelling (steh-lıng) *c* (pl ~en) thesis
stelsel (stehl-serl) *nt* (pl ~s) system;
tientallig ~ decimal system
stem (stehm) *c* (pl ~men) voice; vote
stemmen (steh-mern) *v* vote, *go to the
polls
stemming[1] (steh-mıng) *c* mood;
atmosphere; spirits
stemming[2] (steh-mıng) *c* (pl ~en) vote,
poll
stempel (stehm-perl) *c* (pl ~s) stamp
stemrecht (stehm-rehkht) *nt* suffrage
stenen (stay-nern) *adj* stone
stenografie (stay-noa-graa-fee) *c*
shorthand
ster (stehr) *c* (pl ~ren) star
stereo (stay-ree-yoa) *c* stereo
sterfelijk (stehr-fer-lerk) *adj* mortal
steriel (ster-reel) *adj* sterile
steriliseren (stay-ree-li-zay-rern) *v*
sterilize
sterk (stehrk) *adj* powerful, strong;
sterke drank spirits, liquor
sterkte (stehrk-ter) *c* strength
sterrenkunde (steh-rer-kern-der) *c*
astronomy
*****sterven** (stehr-vern) *v* die
steun (stūrn) *c* assistance, support;
relief
steunen (stūr-nern) *v* support

steunkousen (stūrn-kou-sern) *pl*
support hose
steurgarnaal (stūrr-gahr-naal) *c* (pl
-nalen) prawn
stevig (stay-verkh) *adj* solid, firm
stichten (stıkh-tern) *v* found
stichting (stıkh-tıng) *c* (pl ~en)
foundation
stiefkind (steef-kınt) *nt* (pl ~eren)
stepchild
stiefmoeder (steef-moo-derr) *f* (pl ~s)
stepmother
stiefvader (stee-faa-derr) *m* (pl ~s)
stepfather
stier (steer) *c* (pl ~en) bull
stierengevecht (stee-rer-ger-vehkht)
nt (pl ~en) bullfight
stijf (stayf) *adj* stiff
*****stijgen** (stay-gern) *v* *rise; climb
stijging (stay-gıng) *c* rise; climb, ascent
stijl (stayl) *c* (pl ~en) style
stikken (stı-kern) *v* choke
stikstof (stık-stof) *c* nitrogen
stil (stıl) *adj* silent; quiet; still
Stille Oceaan (stı-ler oa-say-aan)
Pacific Ocean
stilstaand (stıl-staant) *adj* stationary
stilte (stıl-ter) *c* (pl ~s) silence; quiet
stimuleren (stee-mew-lay-rern) *v*
stimulate
stipt (stıpt) *adj* punctual
stoel (stool) *c* (pl ~en) chair; seat
stoep (stoop) *c* (pl ~en) sidewalk *nAm*
stoet (stoot) *c* (pl ~en) procession
stof[1] (stof) *nt* dust
stof[2] (stof) *c* (pl ~fen) fabric, cloth,
material; matter; **stoffen** drapery;
vaste ~ solid
stoffelijk (sto-fer-lerk) *adj* substantial,
material
stoffig (sto-ferkh) *adj* dusty
stofzuigen (stof-sur^ew-gern) *v* hoover;

vacuum *vAm*

stofzuiger (*stof*-sur^(ew)-gerr) *c* (pl ~s) vacuum cleaner

stok (stokl) *c* (pl ~ken) stick; cane

stokpaardje (*stok*-paar-t^(y)er) *nt* (pl ~s) hobbyhorse

stola (*stōa*-laa) *c* (pl ~'s) stole

stom (stom) *adj* mute, dumb

stomerij (stōa-mer-*ray*) *c* (pl ~en) dry cleaner's

stomp (stomp) *adj* blunt

stompen (*stom*-pern) *v* punch

stookolie (*stōak*-ōa-lee) *c* fuel oil

stoom (stōam) *c* steam

stoomboot (*stōam*-bōat) *c* (pl boten) steamer

stoot (stōat) *c* (pl stoten) bump

stop (stop) *c* (pl ~pen) stopper, cork

stopgaren (*stop*-khaa-rern) *nt* darning wool

stoplicht (*stop*-lıkht) *nt* (pl ~en) traffic light

stoppen (*sto*-pern) *v* stop, halt, pull up; *put; darn

stoptrein (*stop*-trayn) *c* (pl ~en) stopping train, local train

storen (*stōa*-rern) *v* disturb; trouble

storing (*stōa*-rıng) *c* (pl ~en) disturbance

storm (storm) *c* (pl ~en) storm; gale, tempest

stormachtig (*storm*-ahkh-terkh) *adj* stormy

stormlamp (*storm*-lahmp) *c* (pl ~en) hurricane lamp

stortbui (*stort*-bur^(ew)) *c* (pl ~en) downpour

storten (*stor*-tern) *v* *shed; deposit

storting (*stor*-tıng) *c* (pl ~en) remittance, deposit

***stoten** (*stōa*-tern) *v* bump

stout (stout) *adj* naughty, bad

stoutmoedig (stout-*mōō*-derkh) *adj* bold

straal (straal) *c* (pl stralen) squirt, spout, jet; ray, beam; radius

straalvliegtuig (*straal*-vleekh-tur^(ew)kh) *nt* (pl ~en) turbojet, jet

straat (straat) *c* (pl straten) street; road

straf (strahf) *c* (pl ~fen) punishment; penalty

straffen (*strah*-fern) *v* punish

strafrecht (*strahf*-rehkht) *nt* criminal law

strafschop (*strahf*-skhop) *c* (pl ~pen) penalty kick

strak (strahk) *adj* tight; **strakker maken** tighten

straks (strahks) *adv* in a moment, later

strand (strahnt) *nt* (pl ~en) beach

streek (strāyk) *c* (pl streken) region; district, country, area; trick

streep (strāyp) *c* (pl strepen) line; stripe

streng (strehng) *adj* strict, harsh; severe

stretcher (*streht*-sherr) *c* (pl ~s) camp bed; cot *nAm*

streven (*strāy*-vern) *v* aspire

strijd (strayt) *c* fight, combat, battle; struggle, contest

***strijden** (*stray*-dern) *v* *fight; struggle

strijdkrachten (*strayt*-krahkh-tern) *pl* armed forces

***strijken** (*stray*-kern) *v* iron; *strike, lower

strijkijzer (*strayk*-ay-zerr) *nt* (pl ~s) iron

strikje (*strık*-Y^(e)er) *nt* (pl ~s) bow tie

strikt (strıkt) *adj* strict

stripverhaal (*strıp*-ferr-haal) *nt* (pl -halen) comics *pl*

stro (strōa) *nt* straw

strodak (*strōa*-dahk) *nt* (pl ~en) thatched roof

stromen (*strōa*-mern) *v* stream, flow

stroming (*strōa*-mıng) *c* (pl ~en) current

stront (stront) *c* *vulgar* crap

strook (strōak) *c* (pl stroken) strip

stroom (strōam) *c* (pl stromen) stream; current

stroomafwaarts (strōam-*ahf*-vaarts) *adv* downstream

stroomopwaarts (strōam-*op*-vaarts) *adv* upstream

stroomverdeler (strōam-verr-dāy-lerr) *c* distributor

stroomversnelling (strōam-verr-sneh-lıng) *c* (pl ~en) rapids *pl*

stroop (strōap) *c* syrup

stropen (strōa-pern) *v* poach

structuur (strerk-*tewr*) *c* (pl -turen) structure; fabric, texture

struik (strur^ewk) *c* (pl ~en) scrub, bush, shrub

struikelen (strur^ew-ker-lern) *v* stumble

struisvogel (strurss-fōa-gerl) *c* (pl ~s) ostrich

studeerkamer (stew-*dāyr*-kaa-merr) *c* study

student (stew-*dehnt*) *c* (pl ~en) student

studeren (stew-*dāy*-rern) *v* study

studie (*stew*-dee) *c* (pl ~s) study, studies

studiebeurs (*stew*-dee-burrs) *c* (pl -beurzen) scholarship

stuitend (stur^ew-ternt) *adj* revolting

stuk[1] (sterk) *adj* broken; ~ *gaan* *break down

stuk[2] (sterk) *nt* (pl ~ken) part, piece; lump, chunk; fragment; stretch; ~ *je* bit

sturen (*stew*-rern) *v* *send; navigate; steer

stuurboord (*stewr*-bōart) *nt* starboard

stuurkolom (*stewr*-kōa-lom) *c* steering column

stuurman (*stewr*-mahn) *m* (pl -lieden, -lui) steersman, helmsman

stuurwiel (*stewr*-veel) *nt* steering wheel

subsidie (serp-*see*-dee) *c* (pl ~s)

subsidy

substantie (serp-*stahn*-see) *c* (pl ~s) substance

subtiel (serp-*teel*) *adj* subtle

succes (serk-*sehss*) *nt* (pl ~sen) success

succesvol (serk-*sehss*-fol) *adj* successful

suède (sew-*vai*-der) *nt/c* suede

suf (serf) *adj* dumb

suiker (sur^ew-kerr) *c* sugar

suikerklontje (sur^ew-kerr-klon-t^yer) *nt* (pl ~s) lump of sugar

suikerzieke (sur^ew-kerr-zee-ker) *c* (pl ~n) diabetic

suikerziekte (sur^ew-kerr-zeek-ter) *c* diabetes

suite (svee-ter) *c* (pl ~s) suite

summier (ser-*meer*) *adj* concise

super (*sew*-perr) *adj* super, fantastic

superieur (sew-per-ree-^yurr) *adj* superior

superlatief (sew-perr-laa-*teef*) *c* (pl -tieven) superlative

supermarkt (*sew*-perr-mahrkt) *c* (pl ~en) supermarket

supplement (ser-pler-*mehnt*) *nt* (pl ~en) supplement

surfplank (serrf-plahngk) *c* (pl ~en) surfboard

surveilleren (serr-vay-^yai-rern) *v* patrol

Swahili (svaa-*hee*-lee) *nt* Swahili

symbool (sım-*bōal*) *nt* (pl -bolen) symbol

symfonie (sım-fōa-*nee*) *c* (pl ~ën) symphony

sympathie (sım-paa-*tee*) *c* (pl ~ën) sympathy

sympathiek (sım-paa-*teek*) *adj* nice

symptoom (sım-*tōam*) *nt* (pl -tomen) symptom

synagoge (see-naa-*gōa*-ger) *c* (pl ~n) synagogue

synoniem (see-nōa-*neem*) *nt* (pl ~en)

synonym
synthetisch (sın-*tay*-teess) *adj*
synthetic
Syrië (*see*-ree-*y*er) Syria
Syriër (*see*-ree-*y*err) *m* (pl ~s) Syrian

Syrisch (*see*-reess) *adj* Syrian
systeem (seess-*taym*) *nt* (pl -temen)
system
systematisch (seess-tay-*maa*-teess)
adj systematic

T

taal (taa^ee) *adj* tough
taak (taak) *c* (pl taken) task; duty
taal (taal) *c* (pl talen) language; speech
taalgids (*taal*-gıts) *c* (pl ~en) phrase
book
taart (taart) *c* (pl ~en) cake; pie
tabak (taa-*bahk*) *c* tobacco
tabakswinkel (taa-*bahks*-vıng-kerl) *c*
(pl ~s) tobacconist's
tabakszak (taa-*bahk*-sahk) *c* (pl ~ken)
tobacco pouch
tabel (taa-*behl*) *c* (pl ~len) chart, table
tablet (taa-*bleht*) *nt* (pl ~ten) tablet
taboe (taa-*boo*) *nt* (pl ~s) taboo
tachtig (*tahkh*-terkh) *num* eighty
tactiek (tahk-*teek*) *c* (pl ~en) tactics *pl*
tafel (*taa*-ferl) *c* (pl ~s) table
tafellaken (*taa*-fer-laa-kern) *nt* (pl ~s)
tablecloth
tafeltennis (*taa*-ferl-teh-nerss) *nt* table
tennis, ping-pong
taille (tah-*y*e) *c* (pl ~s) waist
tak (tahk) *c* (pl ~ken) branch
talenpracticum (*taa*-ler-prahk-tee-
kerm) *nt* (pl-tica) language laboratory
talent (taa-*lehnt*) *nt* (pl ~en) faculty,
talent
talkpoeder (*tahlk*-poo-derr) *nt/c* talc
powder
talrijk (*tahl*-rayk) *adj* numerous
tam (tahm) *adj* tame
tamelijk (*taa*-mer-lerk) *adv* pretty,
fairly, quite, rather

tampon (tahm-*pon*) *c* (pl ~s) tampon
tand (tahnt) *c* (pl ~en) tooth
tandarts (*tahn*-dahrts) *c* (pl ~en)
dentist
tandenborstel (*tahn*-der-bors-terl) *c*
(pl ~s) toothbrush
tandenstoker (*tahn*-der-stoa-kerr) *c*
(pl ~s) toothpick
tandpasta (*tahnt*-pahss-taa) *c/nt* (pl
~'s) toothpaste
tandpijn (*tahnt*-payn) *c* toothache
tandpoeder (*tahnt*-poo-derr) *nt/c*
toothpowder
tandvlees (*tahnt*-flayss) *nt* gum
tang (tahng) *c* (pl ~en) tongs *pl*, pliers *pl*
tank (tehngk) *c* (pl ~s) tank
tankschip (*tehnk*-skhıp) *nt* (pl
-schepen) tanker
tante (*tahn*-ter) *f* (pl ~s) aunt
tapijt (taa-*payt*) *nt* (pl ~en) carpet
tarief (taa-*reef*) *nt* (pl tarieven) rate,
tariff; fare
tarwe (*tahr*-ver) *c* wheat
tas (tahss) *c* (pl ~sen) bag
tastbaar (*tahst*-baar) *adj* palpable;
tangible
tastzin (*tahst*-sın) *c* touch
taxeren (tahk-*say*-rern) *v* estimate
taxi (*tahk*-see) *c* (pl ~'s) cab, taxi
taxichauffeur (*tahk*-see-shoa-furr) *m*
(pl ~s) cab driver, taxi driver
taximeter (*tahk*-see-may-terr) *c*
taximeter

taxistandplaats (*tahk*-see-stahnt-plaats) *c* (pl ~en) taxi rank; taxi stand *Am*

te (ter) *adv* too

technicus (*tehkh*-nee-kerss) *m* (pl -ci) technician

techniek (tehkh-*neek*) *c* (pl ~en) technique

technisch (*tehkh*-neess) *adj* technical

technologie (tehkh-nōā-lōā-*gee*) *c* technology

technologisch (tehkh-nōā-*lōā*-geess) *adj* technological

teder (*tāy*-derr) *adj* delicate, tender

teef (tāyf) *c* (pl teven) bitch

teen (tāyn) *c* (pl tenen) toe

teer (tāyr) *adj* gentle, tender; *c*/*nt* tar

tegel (*tāy*-gerl) *c* (pl ~s) tile

tegelijk (ter-ger-*layk*) *adv* at the same time; at once

tegelijkertijd (ter-ger-lay-kerr-*tayt*) *adv* simultaneously

tegemoetkomend (ter-ger-*mōōt*-kōā-mernt) *adj* oncoming

tegemoetkoming (ter-ger-*mōōt*-kōā-mɪng) *c* (pl ~en) concession

tegen (*tāy*-gern) *prep* against

tegendeel (*tāy*-ger-dāyl) *nt* contrary, reverse

tegengesteld (*tāy*-ger-ger-stehlt) *adj* contrary, opposite

tegenkomen (*tāy*-ger-kōā-mern) *v* *come across, *meet; run into

tegenover (tāy-ger-*nōā*-verr) *prep* opposite, facing

tegenslag (*tāy*-ger-slahkh) *c* (pl ~en) misfortune; reverse

tegenspreken (*tāy*-ger-sprāy-kern) *v* contradict

tegenstander (*tāy*-ger-stahn-derr) *m* (f -standster, pl ~s) opponent

tegenstelling (*tāy*-ger-steh-lɪng) *c* (pl ~en) contrast

tegenstrijdig (tāy-ger-*stray*-derkh) *adj* contradictory

tegenvallen (*tāy*-ger-vah-lern) *v* *be disappointing

tegenwerpen (*tāy*-ger-vehr-pern) *v* object

tegenwerping (*tāy*-ger-vehr-pɪng) *c* (pl ~en) objection

tegenwoordig (tāy-ger-*vōār*-derkh) *adj* present; *adv* nowadays

tegenwoordigheid (tāy-ger-*vōār*-derkh-hayt) *c* presence

tegenzin (*tāy*-ger-zɪn) *c* aversion

tehuis (ter-*hur^(ew)ss*) *nt* (pl tehuizen) home; asylum

teint (taint) *c* complexion

teken (*tāy*-kern) *nt* (pl ~s, ~en) sign; indication, signal; token

tekenen (*tāy*-ker-nern) *v* *draw, sketch; sign

tekenfilm (*tāy*-ker-fɪlm) *c* (pl ~s) cartoon

tekening (*tāy*-ker-nɪng) *c* (pl ~en) drawing, sketch

tekort (ter-*kort*) *nt* (pl ~en) shortage; deficit; ~ *schieten fail

tekst (tehkst) *c* (pl ~en) text

tel (tehl) *c* (pl ~len) second

telefoneren (tāy-ler-fōā-*nāy*-rern) *v* phone, call

telefoon (tāy-ler-*fōān*) *c* (pl ~s) phone, telephone; **mobiele ~** cell phone

telefoonboek (tāy-ler-*fōān*-bōōk) *nt* (pl ~en) telephone directory; telephone book *Am*

telefooncel (tāy-ler-*fōān*-sehl) *c* (pl ~len) telephone booth

telefooncentrale (tāy-ler-*fōān*-sehn-traa-ler) *c* (pl ~s) telephone exchange

telefoongesprek (tāy-ler-*fōān*-ger-sprehk) *nt* (pl ~ken) telephone call

telefoongids (tāy-ler-*fōān*-gɪts) *c* (pl ~en) telephone directory; telephone book *Am*

telefoonhoorn (tāy-ler-*fōān*-hōā-rern) *c* (pl ~s) receiver

telefoonkaart (tāy-ler-*fōan*-kaart) *c* (pl ~en) phone card

telefoontje (tāy-ler-*fōan*-tᵞer) *nt* (pl ~s) call

telegram (tāy-ler-*grahm*) *nt* (pl ~men) cable, telegram

telelens (*tāy*-ler-lehns) *c* (pl -lenzen) telephoto lens

telepathie (tāy-lāy-paa-*tee*) *c* telepathy

teleurstellen (ter-*lūr*-steh-lern) *v* disappoint; *let down

teleurstelling (ter-*lūr*-steh-lıng) *c* (pl ~en) disappointment

televisie (tāy-ler-*vee*-zee) *c* television, TV; **cabel-~** cable TV; **satelliet-~** satellite TV

televisietoestel (tāy-ler-*vee*-zee-tōō-stehl) *nt* (pl ~len) television set

telkens (*tehl*-kerns) *adv* again and again

tellen (*teh*-lern) *v* count

telwoord (*tehl*-vōart) *nt* (pl ~en) numeral

temmen (*teh*-mern) *v* tame

tempel (*tehm*-perl) *c* (pl ~s) temple

temperatuur (tehm-per-raa-*tēwr*) *c* (pl -turen) temperature

tempo (*tehm*-pōa) *nt* pace

tendens (tehn-*dehns*) *c* (pl -denzen) tendency

tenminste (ter-*mın*-ster) *adv* at least

tennis (*teh*-nerss) *nt* tennis

tennisbaan (*teh*-nerss-baan) *c* (pl -banen) tennis court

tennisschoenen (*teh*-ner-skhōō-nern) *pl* tennis shoes

tenslotte (tehn-*slo*-ter) *adv* at last; finally

tent (tehnt) *c* (pl ~en) tent

tentdoek (*tehn*-dōōk) *nt* canvas

tentoonstellen (tehn-*tōan*-steh-lern) *v* exhibit; *show

tentoonstelling (tehn-*tōan*-steh-lıng)

c (pl ~en) exposition, exhibition; display, show

tenzij (tehn-*zay*) *conj* unless

teraardebestelling (tehr-*aar*-der-ber-steh-lıng) *c* (pl ~en) burial

terecht (ter-*rehkht*) *adj* just; *adv* rightly

terechtstelling (ter-*rehkht*-steh-lıng) *c* (pl ~en) execution

terloops (tehr-*lōaps*) *adj* casual

term (tehrm) *c* (pl ~en) term

termijn (tehr-*mayn*) *c* (pl ~en) term

terpentijn (tehr-pern-*tayn*) *c* turpentine

terras (teh-*rahss*) *nt* (pl ~sen) terrace

terrein (teh-*rayn*) *nt* (pl ~en) terrain; grounds, site

terreur (teh-*rūr*) *c* terrorism

terrorisme (teh-ro-*rıss*-mer) *nt* terrorism

terrorist (teh-rōa-*rıst*) *m* (f ~e, pl ~en) terrorist

terug (ter-*rerkh*) *adv* back

terugbetalen (ter-*rerkh*-ber-taa-lern) *v* *repay; reimburse, refund

terugbetaling (terrerkh-ber-taa-lıng) *c* (pl ~en) repayment, refund

***terugbrengen** (ter-*rerkh*-brehng-ern) *v* *bring back

***teruggaan** (ter-*rer*-khaan) *v* *go back, *get back

teruggang (ter-*rer*-khahng) *c* depression, recession

terughoudend (ter-rerkh-*hou*-dehnt) *adj* reserved

terugkeer (ter-*rerkh*-kāyr) *c* return

terugkeren (ter-*rerkh*-kāy-rern) *v* return; turn back

***terugkomen** (ter-rerkh-kōa-mern) *v* return

terugreis (ter-*rerkh*-rayss) *c* return journey

***terugroepen** (ter-*rerkh*-rōō-pern) *v* recall

terugsturen (ter-*rerkh*-stēw-rern) *v*

*send back

*terugtrekken (ter-*rerkh*-treh-kern) *v* *withdraw; **zich ~** retire

*terugvinden (ter-*rerkh*-fɪn-dern) *v* recover

terugweg (ter-*rerkh*-vehkh) *c* way back

*terugzenden (ter-*rerkh*-sehn-dern) *v* *send back

terwijl (terr-*vayl*) *conj* whilst, while

terzijde (tehr-*zay*-der) *adv* aside

test (tehst) *c* (pl ~s) test

testament (tehss-taa-*mehnt*) *nt* (pl ~en) will

testen (*tehss*-tern) *v* test

tevens (*tāy*-verns) *adv* also

tevergeefs (ter-verr-*gāyfs*) *adv* in vain

tevoren (ter-*vōa*-rern) *adv* before; **van ~** in advance, before

tevreden (ter-*vrāy*-dern) *adj* satisfied, content; **tevredenstellend** satisfactory

tewaterlating (ter-*vaa*-terr-laa-tɪng) *c* launching

*teweegbrengen (ter-*vāykh*-breh-ngern) *v* effect

tewerkstellen (ter-*vehrk*-steh-lern) *v* employ

tewerkstelling (ter-*vehrk*-steh-lɪng) *c* (pl ~en) employment

textiel (tehks-*teel*) *c/nt* textile

Thailand (*tigh*-lahnt) Thailand

Thailander (*tigh*-lahn-derr) *m* (pl ~s) Thai

Thailands (*tigh*-lahnts) *adj* Thai

thans (tahns) *adv* now

theater (tāy-*ʸaa*-terr) *nt* (pl ~s) theater *Am*, theatre

thee (tāy) *c* tea

theedoek (*tāy*-dōōk) *c* (pl ~en) tea cloth, kitchen towel

theekopje (*tāy*-kop-ʸay) *nt* (pl ~s) teacup

theelepel (*tāy*-lāy-perl) *c* (pl ~s) teaspoon

theepot (*tāy*-pot) *c* (pl ~ten) teapot

theeservies (*tāy*-sehr-veess) *nt* (pl -viezen) tea set

thema (*tāy*-maa) *nt* (pl ~'s) theme; exercise

theologie (tāy-ʸōa-lōa-*gee*) *c* theology

theoretisch (tāy-ʸōa-*rāy*-teess) *adj* theoretical

theorie (tāy-ʸōa-*ree*) *c* (pl ~ën) theory

therapie (tāy-raa-*pee*) *c* (pl ~ën) therapy

thermometer (tehr-mōa-māy-terr) *c* (pl ~s) thermometer

thermosfles (*tehr*-moss-flehss) *c* (pl ~sen) vacuum flask, thermos flask

thermostaat (tehr-moss-*taat*) *c* (pl -staten) thermostat

thuis (tur^ews) *adv* home, at home

tien (teen) *num* ten

tiende (*teen*-der) *num* tenth

tiener (*tee*-nerr) *c* (pl ~s) teenager

tijd (tayt) *c* (pl ~en) time; **de laatste ~** lately; **op ~** in time; **vrije ~** spare time, leisure

tijdbesparend (tayt-ber-*spaa*-rernt) *adj* time-saving

tijdelijk (*tay*-der-lerk) *adj* temporary

tijdens (*tay*-derns) *prep* during

tijdgenoot (*tayt*-kher-nōat) *m* (pl -noten) contemporary

tijdperk (*tayt*-pehrk) *nt* (pl ~en) period

tijdschrift (*tayt*-skhrɪft) *nt* (pl ~en) review, periodical, journal

tijdverdrijf (*tayt*-verr-drayf) *nt* pastime

tijger (*tay*-gerr) *c* (pl ~s) tiger

tijm (taym) *c* thyme

tikken (*tɪ*-kern) *v* type

timmerhout (*tɪ*-merr-hout) *nt* timber

timmerman (*tɪ*-merr-mahn) *m* (pl -lieden, -lui) carpenter

tin (tɪn) *nt* tin, pewter

tint (tɪnt) *nt* shade

tiran (tee-*rahn*) *m* (pl ~nen) tyrant

titel (*tee*-terl) *c* (pl ~s) title; heading;

degree

toch (tokh) *adv* still; *conj* yet

tocht (tokht) *c* draught

toe (tōō) *adj* closed

toebehoren (tōō-ber-hōā-rern) *v* belong; *pl* accessories *pl*

toebrengen (tōō-breh-ngern) *v* inflict

toedienen (tōō-dee-nern) *v* administer

toegang (tōō-gahng) *c* admittance, admission, access; entry, entrance; approach

toegankelijk (tōō-*gahng*-ker-lerk) *adj* accessible

***toegeven** (tōō-gāȳ-vern) *v* admit, acknowledge; *give in, indulge, yield

toehoorder (tōō-hōār-derr) *f* (f-ster, pl ~s) auditor

toekennen (tōō-keh-nern) *v* award

toekomst (tōō-komst) *c* future

toekomstig (tōō-*kom*-sterkh) *adj* future

toelage (tōō-laa-ger) *c* (pl ~n) allowance, grant

***toelaten** (tōō-laa-tern) *v* admit

toelating (tōō-laa-tıng) *c* (pl ~en) admission

toelichten (tōō-lıkh-tern) *v* elucidate

toelichting (tōō-lıkh-tıng) *c* (pl ~en) explanation

toen (tōōn) *conj* when; *adv* then

toename (tōō-naa-mer) *c* increase

***toenemen** (tōō-nāȳ-mern) *v* increase; **toenemend** progressive

toenmalig (tōōn-maa-lerkh) *adj* contemporary

toepassen (tōō-pah-sern) *v* apply, use

toepassing (tōō-pah-sıng) *c* (pl ~en) application, use

toereikend (tōō-*ray*-kernt) *adj* adequate

toerisme (tōō-*rıss*-mer) *nt* tourism

toerist (tōō-*rıst*) *m* (f ~e, pl ~en) tourist

toeristenklasse (tōō-*rıss*-ter-klah-ser) *c* tourist class

toernooi (tōōr-*nōā*ee) *nt* (pl ~en) tournament

toeschouwer (tōō-skhou-err) *m* (f -schouwster, pl ~s) spectator

***toeschrijven aan** (tōō-skhray-vern) assign to

***toeslaan** (tōō-slaan) *v* *strike

toeslag (tōō-slahkh) *c* (pl ~en) surcharge

toespraak (tōō-spraak) *c* (pl -spraken) speech

***toestaan** (tōō-staan) *v* allow, permit

toestand (tōō-stahnt) *c* (pl ~en) state; condition

toestel (tōō-stehl) *nt* (pl ~len) apparatus, appliance; aircraft; extension

toestemmen (tōō-steh-mern) *v* agree, consent

toestemming (tōō-steh-mıng) *c* authorization, permission; consent

toetje (tōō-tᵛer) *nt* (pl ~s) sweet

toeval (tōō-vahl) *nt* chance; luck

toevallig (tōō-*vah*-lerkh) *adj* accidental, casual, incidental; *adv* by chance

toevertrouwen (tōō-verr-trou-ern) *v* commit; confide

toevoegen (tōō-vōō-gern) *v* add

toevoeging (tōō-vōō-gıng) *c* (pl ~en) addition

toewijden (tōō-vay-dern) *v* dedicate

***toewijzen** (tōō-vay-zern) *v* allot

toezicht (tōō-zıkht) *nt* supervision; ~ *houden op** supervise

toffee (to-*faȳ*) *c* (pl ~s) toffee

toilet (tvah-*leht*) *nt* (pl ~ten) toilet, lavatory, bathroom, rest room; *nAm* washroom

toiletbenodigdheden (tvah-*leht*-ber-nōā-derkht-hāȳ-dern) *pl* toiletry

toiletpapier (tvah-*leht*-paa-peer) *nt* toilet paper

toilettafel (tvah-*leh*-taa-ferl) *c* (pl ~s)

dressing table

toilettas (tvah-*leh*-tahss) *c* (pl ~sen)
toilet case

tol (tol) *c* toll

tolk (tolk) *c* (pl ~en) interpreter

tolken (*tol*-kern) *v* interpret

tolweg (*tol*-verkh) *c* (pl ~en) turnpike
nAm

tomaat (tōā-*maat*) *c* (pl tomaten)
tomato

ton (ton) *c* (pl ~nen) cask, barrel; ton

toneel (tōā-*nāyl*) *nt* drama; stage

toneelkijker (tōā-*nāyl*-kay-kerr) *c* (pl
~s) binoculars *pl*

toneelschrijver (tōā-*nāyl*-skhray-
verr) *m* (f -schrijfster, pl ~s) dramatist,
playwright

toneelspelen (tōā-*nāyl*-spāy-lern) *v*
act

toneelspeler (tōā-*nāyl*-spāy-lerr) *m* (f
-speelster, pl ~s) actor; comedian

toneelstuk (tōā-*nāyl*-sterk) *nt* (pl
~ken) play

tonen (*tōā*-nern) *v* *show; display

tong (tong) *c* (pl ~en) tongue; sole

tonicum (*tōā*-nee-kerm) *nt* (pl -ca, ~s)
tonic

tonijn (tōā-*nayn*) *c* (pl ~en) tuna

toon (tōān) *c* (pl tonen) tone; note

toonbank (*tōām*-bahngk) *c* (pl ~en)
counter

toonladder (*tōān*-lah-derr) *c* (pl ~s)
scale

toonzaal (*tōān*-zaal) *c* (pl -zalen)
showroom

toorn (*tōā*-rern) *c* anger

top (top) *c* (pl ~pen) peak; top, summit

toppunt (*to*-pernt) *nt* (pl ~en) height;
zenith

toren (*tōā*-rern) *c* (pl ~s) tower

tot (tot) *prep* until, to, till; *conj* till; ~ **aan**
till; ~ **zover** so far; ~ **kijk** bye-bye; ~
ziens bye-bye

totaal[1] (tōā-*taal*) *adj* total, overall; utter

totaal[2] (tōā-*taal*) *nt* (pl totalen) total; **in**
~ altogether

totalitair (tōā-taa-lee-*tair*) *adj*
totalitarian

totdat (to-*daht*) *conj* till

touw (tou) *nt* (pl ~en) twine, rope, string

toverkunst (*tōā*-verr-kernst) *c* magic

traag (traakh) *adj* slow; slack

traan (traan) *c* (pl tranen) tear

trachten (*trahkh*-tern) *v* try, attempt

tractor (*trahk*-tor) *c* (pl ~en, ~s) tractor

traditie (traa-*dee*-tsee) *c* (pl ~s)
tradition

traditioneel (traa-dee-shōā-*nāyl*) *adj*
traditional

tragedie (traa-*gāy*-dee) *c* (pl ~s)
tragedy

tragisch (*traa*-geess) *adj* tragic

trainen (*trāy*-nern) *v* drill, train

trainer (*trāy*-ner) *m* trainer, coach

tralie (*traa*-lee) *c* (pl ~s) bar

tram (trehm) *c* (pl ~s) tram; streetcar
nAm

transactie (trahn-*zahk*-see) *c* (pl ~s)
deal, transaction

transatlantisch (trahn-zaht-*lahn*-
teess) *adj* transatlantic

transformator (trahns-for-*maa*-tor) *c*
(pl ~en, ~s) transformer

transpiratie (trahn-spee-*raa*-tsee) *c*
perspiration

transpireren (trahn-spee-*rāy*-rern) *v*
perspire

transport (trahn-*sport*) *nt* (pl ~en)
transport, *nAm* transportation

transporteren (trahn-spor-*tāy*-rern) *v*
transport

trap (trahp) *c* (pl ~pen) stairs *pl*,
staircase; kick

trapleuning (*trahp*-lūr-nng) *c* (pl ~en)
banisters *pl*

trappen (*trah*-pern) *v* kick

trechter (*trehkh*-terr) *c* (pl ~s) funnel

trede (*trāy*-der) *c* (pl ~n) step

*treffen (*treh*-fern) *v* *hit; *strike

trefpunt (*trehf*-pernt) *nt* (pl ~en) meeting place

trefwoord (*trehf*-vōart) *nt* (pl ~en) catchword

trein (trayn) *c* (pl ~en) train; **doorgaande** ~ through train

trek[1] (trehk) *c* (pl ~ken) trait

trek[2] (trehk) *c* appetite

*trekken (*treh*-kern) *v* pull; *draw; extract; hike

trekker (*treh*-kerr) *c* (pl ~s) trigger

trekking (*treh*-kıng) *c* (pl ~en) draw

treuren (*trūr*-rern) *v* grieve

treurig (*trūr*-rerkh) *adj* sad

treurspel (*trūrr*-spehl) *nt* (pl ~en) drama

tribune (tree-*bew*-ner) *c* (pl ~s) stand

triest (treest) *adj* depressing

trillen (*trı*-lern) *v* tremble; vibrate

triomf (tree-ʸomf) *c* (pl ~en) triumph

triomfantelijk (tree-ʸom-*fahn*-ter-lerk) *adj* triumphant

troepen (*trōō*-pern) *pl* troops *pl*

trommel (*tro*-merl) *c* (pl ~s) canister; drum

trommelvlies (*tro*-merl-vleess) *nt* (pl -vliezen) eardrum

trompet (trom-*peht*) *c* (pl ~ten) trumpet

troon (trōan) *c* (pl tronen) throne

troost (trōast) *c* comfort

troosten (*trōāss*-tern) *v* comfort

troostprijs (*trōast*-prayss) *c* (pl -prijzen) consolation prize

tropen (*trōā*-pern) *pl* tropics *pl*

tropisch (*trōā*-peess) *adj* tropical

trots (trots) *adj* proud; *c* pride

trottoir (tro-*tvaar*) *nt* (pl ~s) pavement; sidewalk *nAm*

trottoirband (tro-*tvaar*-bahnt) *c* (pl ~en) curb

trouw (trou) *adj* true, faithful

trouwen (*trou*-ern) *v* marry

trouwens (*trou*-erns) *adv* besides

trouwring (*trou*-rıng) *c* (pl ~en) wedding ring

trui (trurʳᵉʷ) *c* (pl ~en) jersey

Tsjech (tsʸehkh) *c* (pl ~en) Czech

Tsjechisch (tsʸeh-kheess) *adj* Czech

tube (*tew*-ber) *c* (pl ~s) tube

tuberculose (tēw-behr-kēw-*lōā*-zer) *c* tuberculosis

tuchtigen (tukh-*ti*-gern) *v* chastise, punish

tuin (turᵉʷn) *c* (pl ~en) garden

tuinbouw (turᵉʷ*m*-bou) *c* horticulture

tuinman (turᵉʷ*n*-mahn) *m* (pl -lieden, -lui) gardener

tuit (turᵉʷt) *c* (pl ~en) nozzle

tulp (terlp) *c* (pl ~en) tulip

tumor (*tew*-mor) *c* (pl ~s) tumo(u)r

tumult (tēw-*merlt*) *c* racket

Tunesië (tēw-*nāy*-zee-ʸer) Tunisia

Tunesiër (tēw-*nāy*-zee-ʸerr) *m* (f Tunesische, pl ~s) Tunisian

Tunesisch (tēw-*nāy*-zeess) *adj* Tunisian

tuniek (*tew*-neek) *c* (pl ~en) tunic

tunnel (*ter*-nerl) *c* (pl ~s) tunnel

turbine (terr-*bee*-ner) *c* (pl ~s) turbine

Turk (terrk) *m* (f ~e, pl ~en) Turk

Turkije (terr-*kay*-er) Turkey

Turks (terrks) *adj* Turkish; ~ **bad** Turkish bath

tussen (*ter*-sern) *prep* between; among, amid

tussenbeide *komen (ter-serm-*bay*-der *kōā*-mern) interfere

tussenpersoon (*ter*-ser-pehr-sōan) *c* (pl -sonen) intermediary

tussenpoos (*ter*-ser-pōass) *c* (pl -pozen) interval

tussenruimte (*ter*-ser-rurᵉʷm-ter) *c* (pl ~n, ~s) space

tussenschot (*ter*-ser-skhot) *nt* (pl ~ten) partition; diaphragm

tussentijd (*ter*-ser-tayt) *c* interim

tv (tāy-*vāy*) *c* (pl ~'s) TV, *colloquial* telly
twaalf (tvaalf) *num* twelve
twaalfde (tvaalf-der) *num* twelfth
twee (tvāy) *num* two
tweede (tvāy-der) *num* second
tweedehands (tvāy-der-*hahnts*) *adj* second-hand
tweedelig (tvāy-*dāy*-lerkh) *adj* two-piece
tweeling (tvāy-ling) *c* (pl ~en) twins *pl*
tweemaal (tvāy-maal) *adv* twice
tweesprong (tvāy-sprong) *c* (pl ~en) fork, road fork
tweetalig (tvāy-*taa*-lerkh) *adj* bilingual
twijfel (tvay-ferl) *c* (pl ~s) doubt;
zonder ~ without doubt

twijfelachtig (tvay-ferl-ahkh-terkh) *adj* doubtful
twijfelen (tvay-fer-lern) *v* doubt
twijg (tvaykh) *c* (pl ~en) twig
twintig (tvin-terkh) *num* twenty
twintigste (tvin-terkh-ster) *num* twentieth
twist (tvist) *c* (pl ~en) quarrel
twisten (tviss-tern) *v* quarrel, dispute
tyfus (tee-ferss) *c* typhoid
type (tee-per) *nt* (pl ~n, ~s) type
typen (tee-pern) *v* type
typisch (tee-peess) *adj* typical
typist (tee-*pi*-ster) *m* (f ~e, pl ~s, ~n) typist

U

u (ēw) *pron* you
ui (ur^{ew}) *c* (pl ~en) onion
uil (ur^{ew}l) *c* (pl ~en) owl
uit (ur^{ew}t) *prep* from, out of; for; *adv* out
uitademen (ur^{ew}t-aa-der-mern) *v* exhale
uitbarsting (ur^{ew}t-bahr-stern) *c* (pl ~en) outbreak
uitbenen (ur^{ew}t-bāy-nern) *v* bone
***uitblinken** (ur^{ew}t-bling-kern) *v* excel
uitbreiden (ur^{ew}t-bray-dern) *v* extend, enlarge, expand
uitbreiding (ur^{ew}t-bray-ding) *c* (pl ~en) extension, expansion
uitbuiten (ur^{ew}t-bur^{ew}-tern) *v* exploit
uitbundig (ur^{ew}t-*bern*-derkh) *adj* exuberant
uitdagen (ur^{ew}-daa-gern) *v* dare, challenge
uitdaging (ur^{ew}-daa-ging) *c* (pl ~en) challenge
uitdelen (ur^{ew}-dāy-lern) *v* distribute;

*deal
***uitdoen** (ur^{ew}-dōon) *v* *put out
uitdrukkelijk (ur^{ew}-*drer*-ker-lerk) *adj* express, explicit
uitdrukken (ur^{ew}-drer-kern) *v* express
uitdrukking (ur^{ew}-drer-king) *c* (pl ~en) expression; phrase
uiteindelijk (ur^{ew}t-*ayn*-der-lerk) *adj* eventual; finally; *adv* at last
uiten (ur^{ew}-tern) *v* express; utter
uiteraard (ur^{ew}-ter-*raart*) *adv* of course, naturally
uiterlijk (ur^{ew}-terr-lerk) *adj* outward, external, exterior; *nt* outside; look
uiterst (ur^{ew}-terrst) *adj* extreme; utmost, very
uiterste (ur^{ew}-terr-ster) *nt* (pl ~n) extreme
***uitgaan** (ur^{ew}t-khaan) *v* *go out
uitgang (ur^{ew}t-khahng) *c* (pl ~en) way out, exit; issue
uitgangspunt (ur^{ew}t-khahngs-pernt)

nt (pl ~en) starting point

uitgave (*ur^ew t*-khaa-ver) *c* (pl ~n) expense, expenditure; edition, issue

uitgebreid (*ur^ew t*-kher-brayt) *adj* comprehensive, extensive

uitgelezen (*ur^ew t*-kher-lāy-zern) *adj* select

uitgestrekt (*ur^ew t*-kher-strehkt) *adj* vast

*uitgeven (*ur^ew t*-khāy-vern) *v* *spend; publish, issue

uitgever (*ur^ew t*-khāy-verr) *c* (pl ~s) publisher

uitgezonderd (*ur^ew t*-kher-zon-derrt) *prep* except

uitgifte (*ur^ew t*-khif-ter) *c* (pl ~n) issue

*uitglijden (*ur^ew t*-khlay-dern) *v* slip

uiting (*ur^ew*-ting) *c* (pl ~en) expression

uitje (*ur^ew t*-t^y er) *c* (pl ~s) outing

*uitkiezen (*ur^ew t*-kee-zern) *v* select

*uitkijken (*ur^ew t*-kay-kern) *v* watch out, look out; ~ **naar** watch for

uitkleden (*ur^ew t*-klāy-dern): **zich ~** undress

*uitkomen (*ur^ew t*-kōa-mern) *v* *come out; *come true; *be convenient; ~ **op** open on

uitkomst (*ur^ew t*-komst) *c* (pl ~en) issue; outcome

uitlaat (*ur^ew t*-laat) *c* (pl -laten) exhaust

uitlaatgassen (*ur^ew t*-laat-khah-sern) *pl* exhaust gases

uitlaatpijp (*ur^ew t*-laat-payp) *c* (pl ~en) exhaust

*uitladen (*ur^ew t*-laa-dern) *v* unload, discharge

uitleg (*ur^ew t*-lehkh) *c* explanation

uitleggen (*ur^ew t*-leh-gern) *v* explain

uitlenen (*ur^ew t*-lāy-nern) *v* *lend

uitleveren (*ur^ew t*-lāy-ver-rern) *v* extradite

uitloggen (*ur^ew t*-lo-gern) *v* log off

uitmaken (*ur^ew t*-maa-kern) *v* matter; determine; *put out

uitnodigen (*ur^ew t*-nōa-der-gern) *v* invite; ask

uitnodiging (*ur^ew t*-nōa-der-ging) *c* (pl ~en) invitation

uitoefenen (*ur^ew t*-ōō-fer-nern) *v* exercise

uitpakken (*ur^ew t*-pah-kern) *v* unpack; unwrap

uitpersen (*ur^ew t*-pehr-sern) *v* squeeze

uitputten (*ur^ew t*-per-tern) *v* exhaust

uitrekenen (*ur^ew t*-rāy-ker-nern) *v* calculate

uitrit (*ur^ew t*-rit) *c* (pl ~ten) exit

uitroep (*ur^ew t*-rōōp) *c* (pl ~en) exclamation

*uitroepen (*ur^ew t*-rōō-pern) *v* exclaim

uitrusten (*ur^ew t*-rerss-tern) *v* rest; equip

uitrusting (*ur^ew t*-rerss-ting) *c* (pl ~en) equipment; gear, kit, outfit

uitschakelen (*ur^ew t*-skhaa-ker-lern) *v* switch off; disconnect

*uitscheiden (*ur^ew t*-skhay-dern) *v* quit

*uitschelden (*ur^ew t*-skhehl-dern) *v* call names

uitslag (*ur^ew t*-slahkh) *c* (pl ~en) result; rash

*uitsluiten (*ur^ew t*-slur^ew-tern) *v* exclude

uitsluitend (ur^ew t-*slur^ew*-ternt) *adv* solely, exclusively

uitspraak (*ur^ew t*-spraak) *c* (pl -spraken) pronunciation; verdict

uitspreiden (*ur^ew t*-spray-dern) *v* expand

*uitspreken (*ur^ew t*-sprāy-kern) *v* pronounce

uitstapje (*ur^ew t*-stahp-^y er) *nt* (pl ~s) trip, excursion

uitstappen (*ur^ew t*-stah-pern) *v* *get off

uitstekend (ur^ew t-*stāy*-kernt) *adj* fine, excellent

uitstel (*ur^ew t*-stehl) *nt* delay; respite

uitstellen (*ur^ew t*-steh-lern) *v* delay,

postpone; adjourn

*uittrekken (*ur^{ew}t*-treh-kern) *v* extract

uitverkocht (*ur^{ew}t*-ferr-kokht) *adj* sold out

uitverkoop (*ur^{ew}t*-ferr-kōap) *c* sales

*uitvinden (*ur^{ew}t*-fin-dern) *v* invent

uitvinder (*ur^{ew}t*-fin-derr) *m* (pl ~s) inventor

uitvinding (*ur^{ew}t*-fin-ding) *c* (pl ~en) invention

uitvoer (*ur^{ew}t*-fōor) *c* exportation

uitvoerbaar (ur^{ew}t-fōor-baar) *adj* feasible

uitvoeren (*ur^{ew}t*-fōo-rern) *v* carry out; implement, perform, execute; export

uitvoerend (*ur^{ew}t*-fōo-rernt) *adj* executive; **uitvoerende macht** executive

uitvoerig (ur^{ew}t-fōo-rerkh) *adj* detailed

uitwerken (*ur^{ew}t*-vehr-kern) *v* elaborate

*uitwijzen (*ur^{ew}t*-vay-zern) *v* expel

uitwisselen (*ur^{ew}t*-vi-ser-lern) *v* exchange

*uitzenden (*ur^{ew}t*-sehn-dern) *v* *broadcast, transmit

uitzending (*ur^{ew}t*-sehn-ding) *c* (pl ~en) broadcast, transmission

uitzicht (*ur^{ew}t*-sikht) *nt* (pl ~en) view

uitzondering (*ur^{ew}t*-son-der-ring) *c* (pl ~en) exception

uitzonderlijk (ur^{ew}t-*son*-derr-lerk) *adj* exceptional

*uitzuigen (*ur^{ew}t*-sur^{ew}-gern) *v* *bleed

ultraviolet (erl-traa-vee-ȳōa-*leht*) *adj* ultraviolet

unaniem (ēw-naa-*neem*) *adj* unanimous

unie (ēw-nee) *c* (pl ~s) union

uniek (ēw-*neek*) *adj* unique

uniform¹ (ēw-nee-*form*) *adj* uniform

uniform² (ēw-nee-form) *nt/c* (pl ~en) uniform

universeel (ēw-nee-vehr-zāyl) *adj* universal

universiteit (ēw-nee-vehr-zee-*tayt*) *c* (pl ~en) university

urgent (err-*gehnt*) *adj* pressing

urgentie (err-*gehn*-see) *c* urgency

urine (ēw-*ree*-ner) *c* urine

Uruguay (ōō-rōō-gvigh) Uruguay

Uruguayaans (ōō-rōō-gvah-^{y}*aans*) *adj* Uruguayan

uur (ēwr) *nt* (pl uren) hour; **om ... ~ at ...** o'clock; **uur-** hourly

uw (ēw^{oo}) *pron* your

V

vaag (vaakh) *adj* vague; faint; dim

vaak (vaak) *adv* often

vaandel (*vaan*-derl) *nt* (pl ~s) banner

vaardig (*vaar*-derkh) *adj* skilled, skil(l)ful

vaardigheid (*vaar*-derkh-hayt) *c* (pl -heden) skill; art

vaart (vaart) *c* speed

vaartuig (*vaar*-tur^{ew}kh) *nt* (pl ~en) vessel

vaarwater (*vaar*-vaa-terr) *nt* waterway

vaas (vaass) *c* (pl vazen) vase

vaatwasmachine (*vaat*-vahs-mah-shee-ner) *c* dishwasher

vaatwerk (*vaat*-vehrk) *nt* crockery

vacant (vaa-*kahnt*) *adj* vacant

vacature (vah-kah-*tēw*-rer) *c* (pl ~s) vacancy

vacuüm (*vaa*-kēw-erm) *nt* vacuum

vader (*vaa*-derr) *m* (pl ~s) father; dad

vaderland (*vaa*-derr-lahnt) *nt* native country

vagebond (*vaa*-ger-bont) *m* (pl ~en) tramp

vak (vahk) *nt* (pl ~ken) profession, trade; section

vakantie (vaa-*kahn*-see) *c* (pl ~s) holiday, vacation; **met ~** on holiday

vakantiekamp (vaa-*kahn*-see-kahmp) *nt* (pl ~en) holiday camp

vakantieoord (vaa-*kahn*-see-ōart) *nt* (pl ~en) holiday resort

vakbond (*vahk*-bont) *c* (pl ~en) trade union

vakkundig (vah-*kern*-derkh) *adj* skilled

vakman (*vahk*-mahn) *m* (f -vrouw, pl -lieden) expert

val¹ (vahl) *c* fall

val² (vahl) *c* (pl ~len) trap

valk (vahlk) *c* (pl ~en) falcon

vallei (vah-*lay*) *c* (pl ~en) valley

*vallen (*vah*-lern) *v* *fall; ***laten ~** drop

vals (vahls) *adj* false

valuta (vaa-*lēw*-taa) *c* (pl ~'s) currency

van (vahn) *prep* of; from; off; with

vanaf (vah-*nahf*) *prep* from, as from

vanavond (vah-*naa*-vernt) *adv* tonight

vandaag (vahn-*daakh*) *adv* today

*vangen (*vah*-ngern) *v* *catch; capture

vangrail (*vahng*-rāyl) *c* (pl ~s) crash barrier

vangst (vahngst) *c* (pl ~en) capture

vanille (vaa-*nee*-ᵞer) *c* vanilla

vanmiddag (vah-*mɪ*-dahkh) *adv* this afternoon

vanmorgen (vah-*mor*-gern) *adv* this morning

vannacht (vah-*nahkht*) *adv* tonight

vanwege (vahn-*vāy*-ger) *prep* on account of, for, owing to, because of, due to

vanzelfsprekend (vahn-zehlf-*sprāy*-kernt) *adj* self-evident

*varen (*vaa*-rern) *v* sail, navigate

variëren (vaa-ree-ᵞ*āy*-rern) *v* vary

variététheater (vaa-ree-ᵞ*āy*-tāy-tāy-'aa-terr) *nt* (pl ~s) variety theater *Am*, variety theatre; music hall

variétévoorstelling (vaa-ree-ᵞ*āy*-tāy-vōar-steh-lɪng) *c* (pl ~en) variety show

varken (*vahr*-kern) *nt* (pl ~s) pig

varkensleer (*vahr*-kerss-lāyr) *nt* pigskin

varkensvlees (*vahr*-kerss-flāyss) *nt* pork

vaseline (vaa-zer-*lee*-ner) *c* vaseline

vast (vahst) *adj* fixed, firm; steady, permanent; *adv* tight; **~ menu** set menu

vastberaden (vahss-ber-*raa*-dern) *adj* resolute

vastbesloten (vahss-ber-slōa-tern) *adj* determined

vasteland (vahss-ter-*lahnt*) *nt* mainland; continent

*vasthouden (*vahst*-hou-dehn) *v* *hold; **zich ~** *hold on

vastklampen (*vahst*-klahm-pern): **zich ~ aan** *v* cling to

vastleggen (*vahst*-leh-gern): **zich ~** *v* commit

vastmaken (*vahst*-maa-kern) *v* fasten; attach

vastomlijnd (vahss-tom-laynt) *adj* definite

vastspelden (*vahst*-spehl-dern) *v* pin

vaststellen (*vahst*-steh-lern) *v* establish, determine

vat (vaht) *nt* (pl ~en) cask, barrel; vessel

*vechten (*vehkh*-tern) *v* *fight; combat, battle

vee (vāy) *nt* cattle *pl*

veearts (*vāy*-ahrts) *c* (pl ~en) veterinary surgeon, vet

veel (vāyl) *adj* much, many; *adv* much,

far
veelbetekenend (vāyl-ber-tāy-ker-nernt) *adj* significant
veelomvattend (vāyl-om-*vah*-ternt) *adj* extensive
veelvuldig (vāyl-*verl*-derkh) *adj* frequent
veelzijdig (vāyl-*zay*-derkh) *adj* allround, versatile
veen (vāyn) *nt* moor
veer (vāyr) *c* (pl veren) feather; spring
veerboot (*vāyr*-bōat) *c* (pl -boten) ferry-boat
veertien (*vāyr*-teen) *num* fourteen; ~ **dagen** fortnight
veertiende (*vāyr*-teen-der) *num* fourteenth
veertig (*vāyr*-terkh) *num* forty
vegen (*vāy*-gern) *v* *sweep; wipe
vegetariër (vāy-ger-*taa*-ree-ʸerr) *m* (pl ~s) vegetarian
veilig (*vay*-lerkh) *adj* safe; secure
veiligheid (*vay*-lerkh-hayt) *c* safety; security
veiligheidsgordel (*vay*-lerkh-hayts-khor-derl) *c* (pl ~s) safety belt; seat belt
veiligheidsspeld (*vay*-lerkh-hayt-spehlt) *c* (pl ~en) safety pin
veiling (*vay*-lıng) *c* (pl ~en) auction
vel (vehl) *nt* (pl ~len) skin
veld (vehlt) *nt* (pl ~en) field
veldbed (*vehlt*-beht) *nt* (pl ~den) camp bed
veldkijker (*vehlt*-kay-kerr) *c* (pl ~s) field glasses
velg (vehlkh) *c* (pl ~en) rim
Venezolaans (vāy-nāy-zōā-*laans*) *adj* Venezuelan
Venezuela (vāy-nāy-zēw-*vāy*-laa) Venezuela
vennoot (ver-*nōāt*) *c* (pl -noten) associate
vensterbank (*vehn*-sterr-bahngk) *c* (pl

~en) windowsill
vent (vehnt) *m* chap, guy
ventiel (vehn-*teel*) *nt* (pl ~en) valve
ventilatie (vehn-tee-*laa*-tsee) *c* (pl ~s) ventilation
ventilator (vehn-ti-*laa*-tor) *c* (pl ~s, ~en) ventilator, fan
ventilatorriem (vehn-tee-*laa*-to-reem) *c* (pl ~en) fan belt
ventileren (vehn-tee-*lāy*-rern) *v* ventilate
ver (vehr) *adj* far; remote, far-away, distant
verachten (verr-*ahkh*-tern) *v* scorn, despise
verachting (verr-*ahkh*-tıng) *c* scorn, contempt
verademing (verr-aa-der-mıng) *c* relief
verafschuwen (verr-*ahf*-skhēwᵒᵒ-ern) *v* detest
veranda (ver-*rahn*-daa) *c* (pl ~'s) veranda
veranderen (verr-*ahn*-der-rern) *v* change; alter, transform; vary; ~ **in** turn into
verandering (verr-*ahn*-der-rıng) *c* (pl ~en) change; alteration; variation; **voor de** ~ for a change
veranderlijk (verr-*ahn*-derr-lerk) *adj* variable
verantwoordelijk (verr-ahnt-*vōār*-der-lerk) *adj* responsible; accountable
verantwoordelijkheid (verr-ahnt-*vōār*-der-lerk-hayt) *c* (pl -heden) responsibility
verantwoorden (verr-*ahnt*-vōār-dern) *v* account for
verband (verr-*bahnt*) *nt* (pl ~en) connection, relation; bandage
verbandkist (verr-*bahnt*-kıst) *c* (pl ~en) first aid kit
verbazen (verr-*baa*-zern) *v* astonish, amaze, surprise; **zich** ~ marvel; **verbazend** *adj* astonishing, amazing

verbazing (verr-*baa*-zing) *c*
astonishment, amazement, surprise;
~**wekkend** astonishing, amazing

verbeelden (verr-*bayl*-dern): **zich ~**
fancy, imagine

verbeelding (verr-*bayl*-ding) *c*
imagination

*verbergen (verr-*behr*-gern) *v* *hide;
conceal

verbeteren (verr-*bay*-ter-rern) *v*
improve; correct

verbetering (verr-*bay*-ter-ring) *c* (pl
~en) improvement; correction

*verbieden (verr-*bee*-dern) *v* prohibit,
*forbid; inhibit

*verbinden (verr-*bin*-dern) *v* link,
connect, join; dress; **zich ~** engage

verbinding (verr-*bin*-ding) *c* (pl ~en)
link; connection; **zich in ~ stellen met**
contact

verbindingsstuk (verr-*bin*-ding-
sturk) *nt* adaptor

verblijf (verr-*blayf*) *nt* (pl -blijven) stay

verblijfsvergunning (verr-*blayfs*-ferr-
ger-ning) *c* (pl ~en) residence permit

*verblijven (verr-*blay*-vern) *v* stay

verblinden (verr-*blin*-dern) *v* blind;
verblindend glaring; dazzling

verbod (verr-*bot*) *nt* (pl ~en)
prohibition

verboden (verr-*boa*-dern) *adj*
prohibited; **~ te parkeren** no parking;
~ te roken no smoking; **~ toegang** no
entry, no admittance; **~ voor
voetgangers** no pedestrians

verbond (verr-*bont*) *nt* (pl ~en) union

verbouwen (verr-*bou*-ern) *v* raise,
cultivate, grow; renovate

verbranden (verr-*brahn*-dern) *v* *burn

verbruiken (verr-*brur*^{ew}-kern) *v* use up

verbruiker (verr-*brur*^{ew}-kerr) *c* (pl ~s)
consumer

verdacht (verr-*dahkht*) *adj* suspicious

verdachte (verr-*dahkh*-teh) *c* (pl ~n)
suspect; accused

verdampen (verr-*dahm*-pern) *v*
evaporate

verdedigen (verr-*day*-der-gern) *v*
defend

verdediging (verr-*day*-der-ging) *c*
defense *Am*, defence

verdelen (verr-*day*-lern) *v* divide

*verdenken (verr-*dehng*-kern) *v*
suspect

verdenking (verr-*dehng*-king) *c* (pl
~en) suspicion

verder (*vehr*-derr) *adj* further, farther;
adv beyond; **~ dan** beyond

verdienen (verr-*dee*-nern) *v* earn;
*make; deserve, merit

verdienste (verr-*deens*-ter) *c* (pl ~n)
merit; **verdiensten** *pl* earnings *pl*

verdieping (verr-*dee*-ping) *c* (pl ~en)
stor(e)y, floor

verdikken (verr-*di*-kern) *v* thicken

verdomd (verr-*domt*) *adj* vulgar
bloody, damn

verdomme (verr-*do*-mer) *adv* vulgar
damn

verdommen (verr-*do*-mern) *v* vulgar
damn

verdoving (verr-*doa*-ving) *c* (pl ~en)
anaesthesia

verdraaien (verr-*draa*^{ee}-ern) *v* wrench

verdrag (verr-*drahkh*) *nt* (pl ~en)
treaty, pact

*verdragen (verr-*draa*-gern) *v* endure,
*bear; sustain

verdriet (verr-*dreet*) *nt* grief, sorrow

verdrietig (verr-*dree*-terkh) *adj* sad

*verdrijven (verr-*dray*-vern) *v* chase

*verdrinken (verr-*dring*-kern) *v*
drown; *be drowned

verdrukken (verr-*drer*-kern) *v* oppress

verduidelijken (verr-*dur*^{ew}-der-ler-
kern) *v* clarify

verduistering (verr-*dur*^{ew}ss-ter-rehn)
c (pl ~en) eclipse

verdunnen (verr-*der*-nern) *v* dilute
verdwaald (verr-*dvaalt*) *adj* lost
***verdwijnen** (verr-*dvay*-nern) *v* vanish, disappear
vereisen (verr-*ay*-sern) *v* demand, require; **vereist** requisite
vereiste (verr-*ayss*-ter) *c* (pl ~n) requirement
verenigd (verr-$\overline{ay}$-nerkhd) united
Verenigde Staten (verr-$\overline{ay}$-nerkh-der-*staa*-tern) United States, the States
verenigen (verr-*$\overline{ay}$*-ner-gern) *v* join; unite; **verenigd** joint
vereniging (verr-$\overline{ay}$-ner-ging) *c* (pl ~en) association; union, society, club
verf (vehrf) *c* (pl verven) paint; dye
verfdoos (*vehrf*-d$\overline{oa}$ss) *c* (pl -dozen) paintbox
verfrissen (verr-*fri*-sern) *v* refresh
verfrissing (verr-*fri*-sing) *c* (pl ~en) refreshment
vergadering (verr-*gaa*-der-ring) *c* (pl ~en) meeting; assembly
vergeefs (verr-*g$\overline{ay}$fs*) *adj* vain; *adv* in vain
vergeetachtig (verr-*g$\overline{ay}$t*-ahkh-terkh) *adj* forgetful
***vergelijken** (vehr-ger-*lay*-kern) *v* compare
vergelijking (vehr-ger-*lay*-king) *c* (pl ~en) comparison
***vergeten** (verr-*g$\overline{ay}$*-tern) *v* *forget
***vergeven** (verr-*g$\overline{ay}$*-vern) *v* *forgive
vergewissen (verr-ger-*vi*-sern): **zich ~ van** ascertain
vergezellen (verr-ger-*zeh*-lern) *v* accompany
vergiet (verr-*geet*) *nt* (pl ~en) strainer
vergif (verr-*gif*) *nt* poison
vergiffenis (verr-*gi*-fer-niss) *c* pardon
vergiftig (verr-*gif*-terkh) *adj* toxic
vergiftigen (verr-*gif*-teh-gern) *v* poison
vergissen (verr-*gi*-sern): **zich ~** *be

mistaken; err
vergissing (verr-*gi*-sing) *c* (pl ~en) oversight; error, mistake
vergoeden (verr-*g$\overline{oo}$*-dern) *v* *make good, reimburse; remunerate
vergoeding (verr-*g$\overline{oo}$*-ding) *c* (pl ~en) remuneration
vergrootglas (verr-*gr$\overline{oa}$t*-khlahss) *nt* (pl -glazen) magnifying glass
vergroten (verr-*gr$\overline{oa}$*-tern) *v* enlarge, magnify
vergroting (verr-*gr$\overline{oa}$*-ting) *c* (pl ~en) enlargement
verguld (verr-*gerlt*) *adj* gilt
vergunning (verr-*ger*-ning) *c* (pl ~en) license *Am*, licence, permit, permission; **een ~ verlenen** license
verhaal (verr-*haal*) *nt* (pl -halen) story; tale
verhandeling (verr-*hahn*-der-ling) *c* (pl ~en) essay
verheugd (verr-*h$\overline{u}$rkht*) *adj* glad
verhinderen (verr-*hin*-der-rern) *v* prevent
verhogen (verr-*h$\overline{oa}$*-gern) *v* raise
verhoging (verr-*h$\overline{oa}$*-ging) *c* (pl ~en) rise, increase
verhoor (verr-*h$\overline{oa}$r*) *nt* (pl -horen) interrogation
verhouding (verr-*hou*-ding) *c* (pl ~en) affair
verhuizen (verr-*hur^{ew}*-zern) *v* move
verhuizing (verr-*hur^{ew}*-zing) *c* (pl ~en) move
verhuren (verr-*h$\overline{ew}$*-rern) *v* *let; lease
verifiëren (v$\overline{ay}$-ree-fee-*$^y\overline{ay}$*-rern) *v* verify
vering (*v$\overline{ay}$*-ring) *c* suspension
verjaardag (verr-*^{y}aar*-dahkh) *c* (pl ~en) birthday; anniversary
***verjagen** (verr-*^{y}aa*-gern) *v* chase
verkeer (verr-*k$\overline{ay}$r*) *nt* traffic
verkeerd (verr-*k$\overline{ay}$rt*) *adj* false, wrong
verkeersbureau (verr-*k$\overline{ay}$rs*-b$\overline{ew}$-r$\overline{oa}$)

nt (pl ~s) tourist office

verkeersopstopping (verr-*kāȳrz*-op-sto-pɪng) *c* (pl ~en) traffic jam

verkennen (verr-*keh*-nern) *v* explore

***verkiezen** (verr-*kee*-zern) *v* elect

verkiezing (verr-*kee*-zɪng) *c* (pl ~en) election

verklaarbaar (verr-*klaar*-baar) *adj* accountable

verklappen (verr-*klah*-pern) *v* give away, tell

verklaren (verr-*klaa*-rern) *v* state, declare; explain, elucidate

verklaring (verr-*klaa*-rɪng) *c* (pl ~en) statement, declaration; explanation

verkleden (verr-*klāȳ*-dern): **zich ~** change

verkleuren (verr-*klūr*-rern) *v* fade; discolo(u)r

verknoeien (verr-*knōōᵉᵉ*-ern) *v* muddle

verkoop (*vehr*-kōap) *c* sale

verkoopbaar (verr-*kōa*-baar) *adj* saleable

verkoopster (verr-*kōap*-sterr) *f* (pl ~s) salesgirl

***verkopen** (verr-*kōa*-pern) *v* *sell; **in het klein ~** retail

verkoper (verr-*kōa*-perr) *m* (pl ~s) salesman; shop assistant

verkorten (verr-*kor*-tern) *v* shorten

verkoudheid (verr-*kout*-hayt) *c* cold

verkrachten (verr-*krahkh*-tern) *v* rape

verkrijgbaar (verr-*kraykh*-baar) *adj* obtainable, available

***verkrijgen** (verr-*kray*-gern) *v* obtain

verkwisten (verr-*kvɪss*-tern) *v* waste; **verkwistend** wasteful

verlagen (verr-*laa*-gern) *v* lower, reduce; *cut

verlammen (verr-*lah*-mern) *v* paralyse

verlangen¹ (verr-*lah*-ngern) *v* wish, desire; **~ naar** long for

verlangen² (verr-*lah*-ngern) *nt* (pl ~s) wish; longing; **verlangend** *adj* anxious

verlaten (verr-*laa*-tern) *adj* desert

***verlaten** (verr-*laa*-tern) *v* *leave; desert

verleden (verr-*lāȳ*-dern) *adj* previous; *nt* past

verlegen (verr-*lāȳ*-gern) *adj* shy; embarrassed

verlegenheid (verr-*lāȳ*-gern-hayt) *c* shyness, timidity; embarrassment; **in ~ *brengen** embarrass

verleiden (verr-*lay*-dern) *v* seduce; tempt

verleiding (verr-*lay*-dɪng) *c* (pl ~en) temptation

verlenen (verr-*lāȳ*-nern) *v* grant; extend

verlengen (verr-*leh*-ngern) *v* lengthen; extend; renew

verlenging (verr-*leh*-ngɪng) *c* (pl ~en) extension

verlengsnoer (verr-*lehng*-snōōr) *nt* (pl ~en) extension cord

verlichten (verr-*lɪkh*-tern) *v* illuminate; relieve

verlichting (verr-*lɪkh*-tɪng) *c* lighting, illumination; relief

verliefd (verr-*leeft*) *adj* in love **~ zijn op** *v* fancy, *have a crush on; *be in love

verlies (verr-*leess*) *nt* (pl -liezen) loss

***verliezen** (verr-*lee*-zern) *v* *lose

verliezer (verr-*lee*-zer) *m* (pl ~s) loser

verlof (verr-*lof*) *nt* (pl -loven) leave; permission

verloofd (verr-*lōaft*) *adj* engaged

verloofde (verr-*lōaf*-der) *c* (pl ~n) fiancé; fiancée

verlossen (verr-*lo*-sern) *v* deliver; redeem

verlossing (verr-*lo*-sɪng) *c* (pl ~en) delivery

verloving (verr-*lōa*-vɪng) *c* (pl ~en) engagement

verlovingsring (verr-*lōā*-vings-ring) *c*
(pl ～en) engagement ring
vermaak (verr-*maak*) *nt*
entertainment, amusement
vermageren (verr-*maa*-ger-rern) *v*
slim
vermakelijk (verr-*maa*-ker-lerk) *adj*
entertaining
vermaken (verr-*maa*-kern) *v* entertain,
amuse
vermeerderen (verr-*māȳr*-der-rern) *v*
increase
vermelden (verr-*mehl*-dern) *v*
mention
vermelding (verr-*mehl*-ding) *c* (pl ～en)
mention
vermengen (verr-*meh*-ngern) *v* mingle
vermenigvuldigen (verr-*māȳ*-nerkh-
ferl-der-dern) *v* multiply
vermenigvuldiging (verr-*māȳ*-nerkh-
ferl-der-ging) *c* (pl ～en) multiplication
***vermijden** (verr-*may*-dern) *v* avoid
verminderen (verr-*min*-der-rern) *v*
decrease, lessen, reduce
vermindering (verr-*min*-der-ring) *c* (pl
～en) decrease
vermiste (verr-*miss*-ter) *c* (pl ～n)
missing person
vermoedelijk (verr-*mōō*-der-lerk) *adj*
presumable, probable
vermoeden (verr-*mōō*-dern) *v* suspect
vermoeid (verr-*mōō^ee*d) *adj* weary,
tired
vermoeien (verr-*mōō^ee*-ern) *v* tire;
vermoeiend tiring
vermogen (verr-*mōā*-gern) *nt* (pl ～s)
ability, faculty; capacity
vermommen (verr-*mo*-mern): **zich ～**
disguise
vermomming (verr-*mo*-ming) *c* (pl
～en) disguise
vermoorden (verr-*mōār*-dern) *v*
murder
vernielen (verr-*nee*-lern) *v* wreck,

destroy, smash
vernietigen (verr-*nee*-ter-gern) *v*
destroy
vernietiging (verr-*nee*-ter-ging) *c*
destruction
vernieuwen (verr-*nee^oo*-ern) *v* renew
vernis (verr-*niss*) *nt/c* varnish
veronderstellen (verr-on-derr-*steh*-
lern) *v* assume, suppose
verontreinigen (verr-ont-*ray*-ner-
gern) *c* pollute
verontreiniging (verr-ont-*ray*-ner-
ging) *c* (pl ～en) pollution
verontschuldigen (verr-ont-*skherl*-
der-gern) *v* excuse; **zich ～** apologize
verontschuldiging (verr-ont-*skherl*-
der-ging) *c* (pl ～en) apology
verontwaardiging (verr-ont-*vaar*-der-
ging) *c* indignation
veroordeelde (verr-*ōār*-dāȳl-der) *c* (pl
～n) convict
veroordelen (verr-*ōār*-dāȳ-lern) *v*
sentence
veroordeling (verr-*ōār*-dāȳ-ling) *c* (pl
～en) conviction
veroorloven (verr-*ōār*-*lōā*-vern) *v*
allow, permit; **zich ～** afford
veroorzaken (verr-*ōār*-zaa-kern) *v*
cause
verouderd (verr-*ou*-derrt) *adj* ancient,
dated
veroveraar (verr-*ōā*-ver-raar) *m* (pl ～s)
conqueror
veroveren (verr-*ōā*-ver-rern) *v*
conquer
verovering (verr-*ōā*-ver-ring) *c* (pl ～en)
conquest
verpachten (verr-*pahkh*-tern) *v* lease
verpakking (verr-*pah*-king) *c* (pl ～en)
packing
verpanden (verr-*pahn*-dern) *v* pawn
verplaatsen (verr-*plaat*-sern) *v* move
verplegen (verr-*plāȳ*-gern) *v* nurse
verpleger (verr-*plāȳ*-gerr) *m* (f

verpleegster, pl ~s nurse
verplicht (verr-*plikht*) *adj* obligatory, compulsory; **~ *zijn om** *be obliged to
verplichten (verr-*plikh*-tern) *v* oblige
verplichting (verr-*plikh*-ting) *c* (pl ~en) engagement
verraad (ver-*raat*) *nt* treason
*verraden (ver-*raa*-dern) *v* betray
verrader (ver-*raa*-derr) *c* (pl ~s) traitor
verrassen (ver-*rah*-sern) *v* surprise
verrassing (ver-*rah*-sing) *c* (pl ~en) surprise
verrekijker (*veh*-rer-kay-kerr) *c* (pl ~s) binoculars *pl*
verreweg (*veh*-rer-vehkh) *adv* by far
verrichten (ver-*rikh*-tern) *v* perform
verrukkelijk (ver-*rer*-ker-lerk) *adj* delightful, wonderful
verrukking (ver-*rer*-king) *c* (pl ~en) delight; **in ~ *brengen** delight
vers¹ (vehrs) *adj* fresh
vers² (vehrs) *nt* (pl verzen) verse
verschaffen (verr-*skhah*-fern) *v* furnish, provide
verscheidene (verr-*skhay*-der-ner) *num* various; several
verscheidenheid (verr-*skhay*-dern-hayt) *c* (pl -heden) variety
verschepen (verr-*skhay*-pern) *v* ship
*verschieten (verr-*skhee*-tern) *v* fade
*verschijnen (verr-*skhay*-nern) *v* appear
verschijnsel (verr-*skhayn*-serl) *nt* (pl ~en, ~s) phenomenon
verschil (verr-*skhil*) *nt* (pl ~len) difference; distinction, contrast
verschillen (verr-*skhi*-lern) *v* differ; vary
verschillend (verr-*skhi*-lernt) *adj* unlike, different; distinct
verschrikkelijk (verr-*skhri*-ker-lerk) *adj* terrible; horrible, frightful, awful
verschuldigd (verr-*skherl*-derkht) *adj* due; **~ *zijn** owe

versie (*vehr*-zee) *c* (pl ~s) version
versieren (verr-*see*-rern) *v* decorate
versiering (verr-*see*-ring) *c* (pl ~en) decoration
versiersel (verr-*seer*-serl) *nt* (pl ~s, ~en) ornament
*verslaan (verr-*slaan*) *v* defeat, *beat
verslag (verr-*slahkh*) *nt* (pl ~en) report, account
verslaggever (verr-*slah*-khāy-verr) *c* (pl ~s) reporter
*verslapen (verr-*slaa*-pern): **zich ~** *oversleep
versleten (verr-*slāy*-tern) *adj* worn-out, worn; threadbare
*verslijten (verr-*slay*-tern) *v* wear out
versnellen (verr-*sneh*-lern) *v* accelerate
versnelling (verr-*sneh*-ling) *c* (pl ~en) gear
versnellingsbak (verr-*sneh*-lings-bahk) *c* (pl ~ken) gearbox
versnellingspook (verr-*sneh*-lings-pōa) *c* gear lever
versperren (verr-*speh*-rern) *v* block
verspillen (verr-*spi*-lern) *v* waste
verspilling (verr-*spi*-ling) *c* waste
verspreiden (verr-*spray*-dern) *v* scatter, *shed; spread
*verstaan (verr-*staan*) *v* *understand
verstand (verr-*stahnt*) *nt* brain; wit, wits *pl*, reason; **gezond ~** sense
verstandig (verr-*stahn*-derkh) *adj* sensible
verstellen (verr-*steh*-lern) *v* patch
verstijfd (verr-*stayft*) *adj* numb
verstoppen (verr-*sto*-pern) *v* *hide
verstoren (verr-*stōa*-rern) *v* disturb; upset
*verstrijken (verr-*stray*-kern) *v* expire
verstuiken (verr-*stur*ᵉʷ-kern) *v* sprain
verstuiking (verr-*stur*ᵉʷ-king) *c* (pl ~en) sprain
verstuiver (verr-*stur*ᵉʷ-verr) *c* (pl ~s)

atomizer, spray

versturen (verr-*stew*-rern) *v* *send off, dispatch

vertalen (verr-*taa*-lern) *v* translate

vertaler (verr-*taa*-lerr) *m* (f vertaalster, pl ⁓s) translator

vertaling (verr-*taa*-lɪng) *c* (pl ⁓en) translation; version

verteerbaar (verr-*tāȳr*-baar) *adj* digestible

vertegenwoordigen (verr-*tāȳ*-ger-*vōar*-der-gern) *v* represent

vertegenwoordiger (verr-*tāȳ*-ger-*vōar*-der-gerr) *m* (f -ster, pl ⁓s) agent

vertegenwoordiging (verr-*tāȳ*-ger-*vōar*-der-gɪng) *c* (pl ⁓en) representation; agency

vertellen (verr-*ter*-lern) *v* *tell; relate

vertelling (verr-*teh*-lɪng) *c* (pl ⁓en) tale

verteren (verr-*tāȳ*-rern) *v* digest

verticaal (vehr-tee-*kaal*) *adj* vertical

vertolken (verr-*tol*-kern) *v* interpret

vertonen (verr-*tōa*-nern) *v* exhibit; display

vertragen (verr-*traa*-gern) *v* delay, slow down

vertraging (verr-*traa*-gɪng) *c* (pl ⁓en) delay

vertrek[1] (verr-*trehk*) *nt* departure

vertrek[2] (verr-*trehk*) *nt* (pl ⁓ken) room

*vertrekken (verr-*treh*-kern) *v* *leave; depart, *set out, pull out

vertrektijd (verr-*trehk*-tayt) *c* (pl ⁓en) time of departure

vertrouwd (verr-*trout*) *adj* familiar

vertrouwelijk (verr-*trou*-er-lerk) *adj* confidential

vertrouwen (verr-*trou*-ern) *nt* confidence, trust, faith; *v* trust; ⁓ **op** rely on

vervaardigen (verr-*vaar*-der-gern) *v* manufacture

vervallen (verr-*vah*-lern) *adj* expired; due

*vervallen (verr-*vah*-lern) *v* expire

vervalsen (verr-*vahl*-sern) *v* forge, counterfeit

vervalsing (verr-*vahl*-sɪng) *c* (pl ⁓en) fake

*vervangen (verr-*vah*-ngern) *v* replace, substitute

vervanging (verr-*vah*-ngɪng) *c* substitute

vervelen (verr-*vāȳ*-lern) *v* bore; bother

vervelend (verr-*vāȳ*-lernt) *adj* dull, boring, annoying; unpleasant

verven (*vehr*-vern) *v* paint; dye

vervloeken (verr-*vlōo*-kern) *v* curse

vervoer (verr-*vōor*) *nt* transport

vervolg (verr-*volkh*) *nt* (pl ⁓en) sequel

vervolgen (verr-*vol*-gern) *v* continue; pursue

vervolgens (verr-*vol*-gerss) *adv* then

vervuilen (verr-*vur^ew*-lern) *c* pollute

vervuiling (verr-*vur^ew*-lɪng) *c* pollution

verwaand (verr-*vaant*) *adj* conceited, snooty

verwaarlozen (verr-*vaar*-lōa-zern) *v* neglect

verwaarlozing (verr-*vaar*-lōa-zɪng) *c* neglect

verwachten (verr-*vahkh*-tern) *v* expect; anticipate

verwachting (verr-*vahkh*-tɪng) *c* (pl ⁓en) expectation; outlook; **in ⁓** pregnant

verwant (verr-*vahnt*) *adj* related

verwante (verr-*vahn*-ter) *c* (pl ⁓n) relation

verward (verr-*vahrt*) *adj* confused

verwarmen (verr-*vahr*-mern) *v* heat, warm

verwarming (verr-*vahr*-mɪng) *c* heating

verwarren (verr-*vah*-rern) *v* confuse; *mistake

verwarring (verr-*vah*-rɪng) *c* confusion; disturbance; **in ⁓ brengen**

embarrass

verwekken (verr-*veh*-kern) *v* generate

verwelkomen (verr-*vehl*-kōā-mern) *v* welcome

verwennen (verr-*veh*-nern) *v* *spoil

*verwerpen (verr-*vehr*-pern) *v* turn down, reject

*verwerven (verr-*vehr*-vern) *v* acquire

verwezenlijken (verr-*vāy*-zer-ler-kern) *v* realize

verwijden (verr-*vay*-dern) *v* widen

verwijderen (verr-*vay*-der-rern) *v* remove

verwijdering (verr-*vay*-der-rıng) *c* removal

verwijt (verr-*vayt*) *nt* (pl ~en) reproach; blame

*verwijten (verr-*vay*-tern) *v* reproach

*verwijzen naar (verr-*vay*-zern) refer to

verwijzing (verr-*vay*-zıng) *c* (pl ~en) reference

verwonden (verr-*von*-dern) *v* wound, injure

verwonderen (verr-*von*-der-rern) *v* amaze

verwondering (verr-*von*-der-rıng) *c* wonder

verwonding (verr-*von*-dıng) *c* (pl ~en) injury

verzachten (verr-*zahkh*-tern) *v* soften

verzamelaar (verr-*zaa*-mer-laar) *m* (f ~ster, pl ~s) collector

verzamelen (verr-*zaa*-mer-lern) *v* gather; collect

verzameling (verr-*zaa*-mer-lıng) *c* (pl ~en) collection

verzekeren (verr-*zāy*-ker-rern) *v* assure; insure

verzekering (verr-*zāy*-ker-rıng) *c* (pl ~en) insurance

verzekeringspolis (verr-*zāy*-ker-rıngs-pōā-lerss) *c* (pl ~sen) insurance policy

*verzenden (verr-*zehn*-dern) *v* despatch, dispatch

verzending (verr-*zehn*-dıng) *c* expedition

verzet (verr-*zeht*) *nt* resistance

verzetten (verr-*zeh*-tern): **zich ~** oppose, resist

verzilveren (verr-*zıl*-ver-rern) *v* cash

*verzinnen (verr-*zı*-nern) *v* invent

verzinsel (verr-*zın*-serl) *nt* (pl ~s) fiction

verzoek (verr-*zōōk*) *nt* (pl ~en) request; appeal

*verzoeken (verr-*zōō*-kern) *v* request, ask; appeal

verzoening (verr-*zōō*-nıng) *c* (pl ~en) reconciliation

verzorgen (verr-*zor*-gern) *v* look after, *take care of; tend; groom

verzorging (verr-*zor*-gıng) *c* care

verzwikken (verr-*zvı*-kern) *v* sprain

vest (vehst) *nt* (pl ~en) cardigan; waistcoat, jacket; vest *nAm*

vestigen (vehss-ter-gern) *v* establish; **zich ~** settle down

vesting (vehss-tıng) *c* (pl ~en) fortress

vet[1] (veht) *adj* fat; greasy

vet[2] (veht) *nt* (pl ~ten) fat; grease

veter (*vāy*-terr) *c* (pl ~s) lace, shoelace

vettig (*veh*-terkh) *adj* greasy, fatty

vezel (*vāy*-zerl) *c* (pl ~s) fibre

via (vee-*ʸ*aa) *prep* per, via, through

vibratie (vee-*braa*-tsee) *c* (pl ~s) vibration

video camera (*vie*-dee-oo *kaa*-mee-raa) *c* video camera

video cassette (*vie*-dee-oo ka-*seter*) *c* (pl ~s) video cassette

video recorder (vie-dee-oo rie-*kor*-derr) *c* (pl ~s) video recorder

vier (veer) *num* four

vierde (*veer*-der) *num* fourth

vieren (*vee*-rern) *v* celebrate

viering (*vee*-rıng) *c* (pl ~en) celebration

vierkant (*veer*-kahnt) *adj* square; *nt* square

vies (veess) *adj* dirty

vijand (*vay*-ahnt) *m* (f ~in, pl ~en) enemy

vijandig (vay-*ahn*-derkh) *adj* hostile

vijf (vayf) *num* five

vijfde (*vayf*-der) *num* fifth

vijftien (*vayf*-teen) *num* fifteen

vijftiende (*vayf*-teen-der) *num* fifteenth

vijftig (*vayf*-terkh) *num* fifty

vijg (vaykh) *c* (pl ~en) fig

vijl (vayl) *c* (pl ~en) file

vijver (*vay*-verr) *c* (pl ~s) pond

villa (*vee*-laa) *c* (pl ~'s) villa

vilt (vilt) *nt* felt

***vinden** (*vin*-dern) *v* *find; *come across; consider

vindingrijk (*vin*-ding-rayk) *adj* inventive

vinger (*vi*-ngerr) *c* (pl ~s) finger, digit

vingerafdruk (*vi*-ngerr-ahf-drerk) *c* (pl ~ken) fingerprint

vingerhoed (*vi*-ngerr-hōot) *c* (pl ~en) thimble

vink (vink) *c* (pl ~en) *c* finch; ~je tick

violet (vee-ʸōa-*leht*) *adj* violet

viool (vee-ʸōal) *c* (pl violen) violin

viooltje (vee-ʸōal-tʸer) *nt* (pl ~s) violet

vis (viss) *c* (pl ~sen) fish

visakte (*viss*-ahk-ter) *c* (pl ~n, ~s) fishing license *Am*, fishing licence

visgraat (*viss*-khraat) *c* (pl -graten) fishbone

vishaak (*viss*-haak) *c* (pl -haken) fishing hook

visie (vee-zee) *c* vision

visite (vee-*zee*-ter) *c* (pl ~s) visit; call

visitekaartje (vi-*zee*-ter-kaar-tʸer) *nt* (pl ~s) visiting-card; business card

viskuit (*viss*-kur^{ew}t) *c* roe

vislijn (*viss*-layn) *c* (pl ~en) fishing line

visnet (*viss*-neht) *nt* (pl ~ten) fishing net

vissen (*vi*-sern) *v* fish

visser (*vi*-serr) *m* (pl ~s) fisherman

visserij (vi-ser-*ray*) *c* fishing industry

vistuig (*viss*-tur^{ew}kh) *nt* fishing tackle, fishing gear

visum (*vee*-zerm) *nt* (pl visa) visa

viswinkel (*viss*-ving-kerl) *c* (pl ~s) fish shop

vitamine (vee-taa-*mee*-ner) *c* (pl ~n, ~s) vitamin

vitrine (vee-*tree*-ner) *c* (pl ~s) showcase

vlag (vlahkh) *c* (pl ~gen) flag

vlak (vlahk) *adj* flat; smooth; level, plane

vlakgom (*vlahk*-khom) *c/nt* (pl ~men) rubber

vlakte (*vlahk*-ter) *c* (pl ~n, ~s) plain

Vlaams (vlaams) *adj* flamish

Vlaanderen (*vlahn*-der-rern) *nt* Flanders

vlam (vlahm) *c* (pl ~men) flame

Vlaming (*vlaa*-ming) *m* (f Vlaamse, pl ~en) Flaming

vlees (vlāyss) *nt* meat; flesh

vlek (vlehk) *c* (pl ~ken) stain, spot, blot

vlekkeloos (*vleh*-ker-lōass) *adj* stainless, spotless

vlekken (*vleh*-kern) *v* stain

vlekkenwater (*vleh*-ker-vaa-terr) *nt* stain remover

vleugel (*vlur*-gerl) *c* (pl ~s) wing; grand piano

vlieg (vleekh) *c* (pl ~en) fly

***vliegen** (*vlee*-gern) *v* *fly

vliegramp (*vleekh*-rahmp) *c* (pl ~en) plane crash

vliegtuig (*vleekh*-tur^{ew}kh) *nt* (pl ~en) aircraft, aeroplane, plane; airplane *nAm*

vliegveld (*vleekh*-fehlt) *nt* (pl ~en) airfield

vlijt (vlayt) *c* diligence

vlijtig (*vlay*-terkh) *adj* industrious;

diligent

vlinder (*vlin*-derr) *c* (pl ~s) butterfly

vlinderdasje (*vlin*-derr-dah-sher) *nt* (pl ~s) bow tie

vlinderslag (*vlin*-derr-slahkh) *c* butterfly stroke

vloed (vloot) *c* flood

vloeibaar (*vlooee*-baar) *adj* liquid, fluid

vloeien (*vlooee*-ern) *v* flow; **vloeiend** fluent

vloeipapier (*vlooee*-paa-peer) *nt* blotting paper

vloeistof (*vlooee*-stof) *c* (pl ~fen) fluid, liquid

vloek (vlook) *c* (pl ~en) curse

vloeken (*vloo*-kern) *v* curse, *swear

vloer (vloor) *c* (pl ~en) floor

vloerkleed (*vloor*-klayt) *nt* (pl -kleden) carpet

vloot (vloat) *c* (pl vloten) fleet

vlot (vlot) *nt* (pl ~ten) raft

vlotter (*vlo*-terr) *c* (pl ~s) float

vlucht (vlerkht) *c* (pl ~en) flight

vluchteling (*vlerkh*-ter-ling) *m* (f ~e, pl ~en) refugee

vluchten (*vlerkh*-tern) *v* escape; flee

vlug (vlerkh) *adj* fast, quick, rapid; *adv* soon

vocaal (võa-*kaal*) *adj* vocal

vocabulaire (võa-kaa-bew-*lair*) *nt* vocabulary

vocht (vokht) *nt* damp

vochtig (*vokh*-terkh) *adj* humid, moist, damp, wet

vochtigheid (*vokh*-terkh-hayt) *c* humidity, moisture

vod (vot) *nt* (pl ~den) rag

voeden (*võo*-dern) *v* *feed

voedsel (*võot*-serl) *nt* food; fare

voedselvergiftiging (*võot*-serl-verr-gif-ter-ging) *c* food poisoning

voedzaam (*võot*-saam) *adj* nutritious, nourishing

voegen (*võo*-gern): **zich ~ bij** join

voelen (*võo*-lern) *v* *feel; sense

voeren (*võo*-rern) *v* carry

voering (*võo*-ring) *c* (pl ~en) lining

voertuig (*võor*-tur^ewkh) *nt* (pl ~en) vehicle

voet (võot) *c* (pl ~en) foot; **te ~** on foot, walking

voetbal (*võot*-bahl) *nt* soccer; football

voetbalwedstrijd (*võot*-bahl-veht-strayt) *c* (pl ~en) football match

voetganger (*võot*-khah-ngerr) *m* (f -gangster, pl ~s) pedestrian

voetpad (*võot*-paht) *nt* (pl ~en) footpath

voetpoeder (*võot*-põo-derr) *nt*/*c* foot powder

voetrem (*võot*-rehm) *c* foot brake

vogel (*võa*-gerl) *c* (pl ~s) bird

vol (vol) *adj* full; full up

***volbrengen** (vol-*breh*-ngern) *v* accomplish

voldaan (vol-*daan*) *adj* satisfied

voldoende (vol-*dõon*-der) *adj* sufficient, enough; **~ *zijn** *do, suffice

voldoening (vol-*dõo*-ning) *c* satisfaction

volgen (*vol*-gern) *v* follow; **volgend** subsequent, next, following

volgens (*vol*-gerns) *prep* according to

volgorde (*vol*-gor-der) *c* order, sequence

***volhouden** (*vol*-hou-dern) *v* *keep up; insist

volk (volk) *nt* (pl ~en, ~eren) people; nation; folk; **volks-** national; popular; vulgar

volkomen (voal-*kõa*-mern) *adj* perfect; *adv* completely

volkorenbrood (vol-*kõa*-rerm-brõat) *nt* wholemeal bread

volksdans (*volks*-dahns) *c* (pl ~en) folk dance

volkslied (*volks*-leet) *nt* (pl ~eren) folk

song; national anthem

volledig (vo-*lay*-derkh) *adj* complete

volmaakt (vol-*maakt*) *adj* perfect

volmaaktheid (vol-*maakt*-hayt) *c* perfection

volslagen (vol-*slaa*-gern) *adj* total, utter

volt (volt) *c* volt

voltage (vol-*taa*-zher) *c/nt* (pl ~s) voltage

voltooien (vol-*tōa^ee*-ern) *v* complete

volume (vōa-*lew*-mer) *nt* (pl ~n, ~s) volume

volwassen (vol-*vah*-sern) *adj* adult; grown-up

volwassene (vol-*vah*-ser-ner) *c* (pl ~n) adult; grown-up

vonk (vongk) *c* (pl ~en) spark

vonnis (*vo*-nerss) *nt* (pl ~sen) verdict, sentence

voogd (vōakht) *m* (pl ~en) tutor, guardian

voogdij (vōakh-*day*) *c* custody

voor (vōar) *prep* before; ahead of, in front of; for; to

vooraanstaand (vōar-*aan*-staant) *adj* leading, outstanding

*****voorafgaan** (vōar-*ahf*-khaan) *v* precede

vooral (vōa-*rahl*) *adv* essentially, especially, most of all

voorbarig (vōar-*baa*-rerkh) *adj* premature

voorbeeld (*vōar*-bāylt) *nt* (pl ~en) example, instance

voorbehoedmiddel (*vōar*-ber-hōot-mɪ-derl) *nt* (pl ~en) contraceptive

voorbehoud (*vōar*-ber-hout) *nt* qualification

voorbereiden (*vōar*-ber-ray-dern) *v* prepare

voorbereiding (*vōar*-ber-ray-dɪng) *c* (pl ~en) preparation

voorbij (vōar-*bay*) *adj* past, over; *prep* past, beyond

*****voorbijgaan** (vōar-*bay*-gaan) *v* pass

voorbijganger (vōar-*bay*-gah-ngerr) *m* (f -gangster, pl ~s) passer-by

voordat (*vōar*-daht) *conj* before

voordeel (*vōar*-dāyl) *nt* (pl -delen) advantage; profit, benefit

voordelig (vōar-*day*-lerkh) *adj* advantageous; cheap

*****voordoen** (*vōar*-dōōn): **zich ~** occur

voorgaand (*vōar*-khaant) *adj* previous, preceding

voorganger (*vōar*-gah-ngerr) *m* (f -gangster, pl ~s) predecessor

voorgerecht (*vōar*-ger-rehkht) *nt* (pl ~en) hors d'œuvre

voorgrond (*vōar*-gront) *c* foreground

voorhanden (vōar-*hahn*-dern) *adj* available

voorheen (vōar-*hāyn*) *adv* formerly

voorhoofd (*vōar*-hōaft) *nt* (pl ~en) forehead

voorjaar (*vōar*-ʸaar) *nt* springtime, spring

voorkant (*vōar*-kahnt) *c* front

voorkeur (*vōar*-kūrr) *c* preference; **de ~ *geven aan** prefer

voorkomen¹ (*vōar*-kōa-mern) *nt* look, appearance

*****voorkomen²** (*vōar*-kōa-mern) *v* occur, happen

*****voorkomen³** (vōar-*kōa*-mern) *v* prevent; anticipate

voorkomend (vōar-*kōa*-mernt) *adj* obliging

voorletter (*vōar*-leh-terr) *c* (pl ~s) initial

voorlopig (vōar-*lōa*-perkh) *adj* provisional, temporary; preliminary

voormalig (vōar-*maa*-lerkh) *adj* former

voorman (*vōar*-mahn) *m* (pl ~nen) foreman

voornaam¹ (vōar-*naam*) *adj*

distinguished; **voornaamst** *adj*
principal, main, leading, chief

voornaam² (*vōar*-naam) *c* (pl -namen)
first name, Christian name

voornaamwoord (*vōar*-naam-vōart)
nt (pl ~en) pronoun

voornamelijk (vōar-*naa*-mer-lerk) *adv*
especially

vooroordeel (*vōar*-ōar-dāyl) *nt* (pl
-delen) prejudice

vooroorlogs (vōar-*ōar*-lokhs) *adj*
prewar

voorraad (*vōa*-raat) *c* (pl -raden) stock,
store, supply; provisions *pl*; **in ~
*hebben** stock

voorrang (*vōa*-rahng) *c* priority; right
of way

voorrecht (*vōa*-rehkht) *nt* (pl ~en)
privilege

voorruit (*vōa*-rur^ew^t) *c* (pl ~en)
windscreen; windshield *nAm*

*voorschieten (*vōar*-skhee-tern) *v*
advance

voorschot (*vōar*-skhot) *nt* (pl ~ten)
advance

voorschrift (*vōar*-skhrıft) *nt* (pl ~en)
regulation

*voorschrijven (*vōar*-skhray-vern) *v*
prescribe

voorspellen (vōar-*speh*-lern) *v* predict,
forecast

voorspelling (vōar-*speh*-lıng) *c* (pl
~en) forecast

voorspoed (*vōar*-spōot) *c* prosperity

voorsprong (*vōar*-sprong) *c* lead

voorstad (*vōar*-staht) *c* (pl -steden)
suburb

voorstander (*vōar*-stahn-derr) *m* (f
-standster, pl ~s) advocate

voorstel (*vōar*-stehl) *nt* (pl ~len)
proposition, proposal; suggestion

voorstellen (*vōar*-steh-lern) *v* propose,
suggest; present, introduce; represent;
zich ~ conceive of, fancy, imagine

voorstelling (*vōar*-steh-lıng) *c* (pl ~en)
show, performance

voortaan (*vōar*-taan) *adv* from now on

voortduren (*vōar*-dēw-rern) *v*
continue; **voortdurend** continuous,
continual

*voortgaan (*vōart*-khaan) *v* continue;
proceed

voortreffelijk (vōar-*treh*-fer-lerk) *adj*
excellent; exquisite

voorts (vōarts) *adv* moreover

voortzetten (*vōart*-seh-tern) *v* carry
on, continue

vooruit (vōa-*rur*^ew^t) *adv* ahead,
forward; in advance

vooruitbetaald (vōa-*rur*^ew^t-ber-taalt)
adj prepaid

*vooruitgaan (vōa-*rur*^ew^t-khaan) *v*
advance

vooruitgang (vōa-*rur*^ew^t-khahng) *c*
progress, advance

vooruitstrevend (vōa-rur^ew^t-*strāy*-
vernt) *adj* progressive

vooruitzicht (vōa-*rur*^ew^t-sıkht) *nt* (pl
~en) prospect

voorvader (*vōar*-vaa-derr) *m* (pl ~s,
~en) ancestor

voorvechter (*vōar*-vehkh-terr) *m* (f
-vechtster, pl ~s) champion; advocate

voorvertoning (*vōar*-vehr tōa-nıng) *c*
(pl ~en) preview

voorvoegsel (*vōar*-vōokh-serl) *nt* (pl
~s) prefix

voorwaarde (*vōar*-vaar-der) *c* (pl ~n)
condition; term

voorwaardelijk (vōar-*vaar*-der-lerk)
adj conditional

voorwaarts (*vōar*-vaarts) *adv* onwards,
forward

voorwenden (*vōar*-vehn-dern) *v*
pretend

voorwendsel (*vōar*-vehnt-serl) *nt* (pl
~s, ~en) pretext, pretence

voorwerp (*vōar*-vehrp) *nt* (pl ~en)

object; **gevonden voorwerpen** lost and found

voorzetsel (*vōar*-zeht-serl) *nt* (pl ~s) preposition

voorzichtig (vōar-*zıkh*-terkh) *adj* careful, cautious; gentle

voorzichtigheid (vōar-*zıkh*-terkh-hayt) *c* caution

voorzien (vōar-*zeen*) *v* anticipate; ~ **van** furnish with

voorziening (vōar-*zee*-nıng) *c* (pl ~en) facilities

voorzitster (*vōar*-zıt-sterr) *f* (pl ~s) chairwoman, president

voorzitter (*vōar*-zı-terr) *m* (pl ~s) chairman, president

voorzorg (*vōar*-zorkh) *c* (pl ~en) precaution

voorzorgsmaatregel (*vōar*-zorkhs-maat-rāy-gerl) *c* (pl ~en) precaution

vorderen (vor-*der*-rern) *v* *get on, progress; confiscate; claim

vorig (*vōa*-rerkh) *adj* last; past

vork (vork) *c* (pl ~en) fork

vorm (vorm) *c* (pl ~en) shape; form

vormen (*vor*-mern) *v* shape; form

vorming (*vor*-mıng) *c* background

vorst¹ (vorst) *m* (f ~in, pl ~en) ruler, monarch, sovereign

vorst² (vorst) *c* frost

vos (voss) *c* (pl ~sen) fox

vouw (vou) *c* (pl ~en) fold; crease

vouwen (*vou*-ern) *v* fold

vraag (vraakh) *c* (pl vragen) question; inquiry, query

vraaggesprek (*vraa*-ger-sprehk) *nt* (pl ~ken) interview

vraagstuk (*vraakh*-sterk) *nt* (pl ~ken) problem, question

vraagteken (*vraakh*-tāy-kern) *nt* (pl ~s) question mark

vracht (vrahkht) *c* (pl ~en) freight, cargo

vrachtwagen (*vrahkht*-vaa-gern) *c* (pl ~s) lorry; truck *nAm*

vragen (*vraa*-gern) *v* ask; beg; question; **vragend** interrogative

vrede (*vrāy*-der) *c* peace

vreedzaam (*vrāyt*-saam) *adj* peaceful

vreemd (vrāymt) *adj* strange; odd, queer; foreign

vreemde (*vrāym*-der) *c* (pl ~n) stranger

vreemdeling (*vrāym*-der-lıng) *m* (f ~e, pl ~en) foreigner; stranger, alien

vrees (vrāyss) *c* dread, fear

vreselijk (*vrāy*-ser-lerk) *adj* terrible; horrible, dreadful, frightful

vreugde (*vrūrkh*-der) *c* (pl ~n) gladness, joy

vrezen (*vrāy*-zern) *v* dread, fear

vriend (vreent) *m* (pl ~en) friend, *colloquial* buddy; boyfriend

vriendelijk (*vreen*-der-lerk) *adj* friendly; kind

vriendin (vreen-*dın*) *f* (pl ~nen) friend; girlfriend

vriendschap (*vreent*-skhahp) *c* (pl ~pen) friendship

vriendschappelijk (vreent-*skhah*-per-lerk) *adj* friendly

vriespunt (*vreess*-pernt) *nt* freezing point

vriezen (*vree*-zern) *v* *freeze

vrij (vray) *adj* free; *adv* pretty, fairly, quite, rather

vrijdag (*vray*-dahkh) *c* Friday

vrijgevig (vray-*gāy*-verkh) *adj* liberal; generous

vrijgezel (vray-ger-*zehl*) *c* (pl ~len) bachelor

vrijheid (*vray*-hayt) *c* (pl -heden) freedom, liberty

vrijkaart (*vray*-kaart) *c* (pl ~en) free ticket

vrijpostig (vray-*poss*-terkh) *adj* bold

vrijspraak (*vray*-spraak) *c* acquittal

vrijstellen (*vray*-steh-lern) *v* exempt; **vrijgesteld** exempt

vrijstelling (*vray*-steh-lıng) *c* (pl ~en) exemption

vrijwel (*vray*-vehl) *adv* practically

vrijwillig (vray-vı-lerkh) *adj* voluntary

vrijwilliger (vray-vı-ler-gerr) *m* (f -ster, pl ~s) volunteer

vroedvrouw (*vrōōt*-frou) *f* (pl ~en) midwife

vroeg (vrōōkh) *adj* early

vroeger (*vrōō*-gerr) *adj* prior, previous, former; *adv* formerly

vrolijk (*vrōā*-lerk) *adj* gay, cheerful, merry, joyful

vroom (vrōām) *adj* pious

vrouw (vrou) *f* (pl ~en) woman; wife; ~ **des huizes** mistress

vrouwelijk (*vrou*-er-lerk) *adj* female; feminine

vrouwenarts (*vrou*-ern-ahrts) *c* (pl ~en) gynaecologist

vrucht (vrerkht) *c* (pl ~en) fruit

vruchtbaar (*vrerkht*-baar) *adj* fertile

vruchtensap (*vrerkh*-ter-sahp) *nt* (pl ~pen) squash

vuil (vur^ewl) *adj* filthy, dirty; *nt* dirt

vuilnis (*vur*^ewl-nıss) *nt* garbage

vuilnisbak (*vur*^ewl-nıss-bahk) *c* (pl ~ken) rubbish bin, dustbin; trash can *Am*

vuist (vur^ewst) *c* (pl ~en) fist

vuistslag (*vur*^ewst-slahkh) *c* (pl ~en) punch

vulgair (verl-*gair*) *adj* vulgar

vulkaan (verl-*kaan*) *c* (pl -kanen) volcano

vullen (*ver*-lern) *v* fill

vulling (*ver*-lıng) *c* (pl ~en) stuffing, filling; refill

vulpen (*verl*-pehn) *c* (pl ~nen) fountain pen

vuur (vewr) *nt* (pl vuren) fire

vuurrood (*vēw*-rōāt) *adj* scarlet, crimson

vuursteen (*vēwr*-stayn) *c* (pl -stenen) flint

vuurtoren (*vēwr*-tōā-rern) *c* (pl ~s) lighthouse

vuurvast (*vēwr*-vahst) *adj* fireproof

W

*waaien (*vaa*^ee-ern) *v* *blow

waaier (*vaa*^ee-err) *c* (pl ~s) fan

waakzaam (*vaak*-saam) *adj* vigilant

waanzin (*vaan*-zın) *c* madness

waanzinnig (vaan-zı-nerkh) *adj* mad

waar[1] (vaar) *adj* true; very

waar[2] (vaar) *adv* where; *conj* where; ~ **dan ook** anywhere; ~ **ook** wherever

waarborg (*vaar*-borkh) *c* (pl ~en) guarantee

waard (vaart) *adj* worthy of; ~ ***zijn** *be worth

waarde (*vaar*-der) *c* (pl ~n) worth, value

waardeloos (vaar-der-*lōāss*) *adj* worthless

waarderen (vaar-*dāy*-rern) *v* appreciate

waardering (vaar-*dāy*-rıng) *c* appreciation

waardevol (*vaar*-der-vol) *adj* valuable

waardig (*vaar*-derkh) *adj* dignified

waardigheid (*vaar*-derkh-hayt) *c* dignity

waarheid (*vaar*-hayt) *c* (pl -heden) truth

waarheidsgetrouw (*vaar*-hayts-kher-trou) *adj* truthful

*waarnemen (*vaar*-nāy-mern) *v* observe

waarneming (*vaar*-nāy-mɪng) *c* (pl ~en) observation

waarom (vaa-*rom*) *adv* why; what for

waarschijnlijk (vaar-*skhayn*-lerk) *adj* probable, likely; *adv* probably

waarschuwen (*vaar*-skhēw^{oo}-ern) *v* warn; caution; notify

waarschuwing (*vaar*-skhēw^{oo}-ɪng) *c* (pl ~en) warning

waas (vaass) *nt* haze

wachten (*vahkh*-tern) *v* wait; ~ **op** await

wachtkamer (*vahkht*-kaa-merr) *c* (pl ~s) waiting room

wachtlijst (*vahkht*-layst) *c* (pl ~en) waiting list

wachtwoord (*vahkht*-vōart) *nt* (pl ~en) password

waden (*vaa*-dern) *v* wade

wafel (*vaa*-ferl) *c* (pl ~s) waffle, wafer

wagen¹ (*vaa*-gern) *c* (pl ~s) cart

wagen² (*vaa*-gerñ) *v* dare, venture, risk

wagon (vaa-*gon*) *c* (pl ~s) carriage, wag(g)on; passenger car *Am*

wakker (*vah*-kerr) *adj* awake; ~ ***worden** wake up

walgelijk (*vahl*-ger-lerk) *adj* revolting, disgusting

walnoot (*vahl*-nōat) *c* (pl -noten) walnut

wals (vahls) *c* (pl ~en) waltz

walvis (*vahl*-vɪss) *c* (pl ~sen) whale

wand (vahnt) *c* (pl ~en) wall

wandelaar (*vahn*-der-laar) *m* (f-ster, pl ~s) walker

wandelen (*vahn*-der-lern) *v* stroll, walk

wandeling (*vahn*-der-lɪng) *c* (pl ~en) stroll, walk

wandelstok (*vahn*-derl-stok) *c* (pl ~ken) walking stick

wang (vahng) *c* (pl ~en) cheek

wanhoop (*vahn*-hōap) *c* despair

wanhopen (vahn-*hōa*-pern) *v* despair

wanhopig (vahn-*hōa*-perkh) *adj* desperate

wankel (*vahn*-kerl) *adj* unsteady

wankelen (*vahn*-ker-lern) *v* falter

wanneer (vah-*nāyr*) *adv* when; *conj* when; ~ **ook** whenever

wanorde (*vahn*-or-der) *c* disorder

want (vahnt) *conj* for

wanten (*vahn*-tern) *pl* mittens *pl*

wapen (*vaa*-pern) *nt* (pl ~s, ~en) weapon, arm

wapenstilstand (*vaa*-pern-stɪl-stant) *c* ceasefire

warboel (*vahr*-bōol) *c* muddle, mess

waren (*vaa*-rern) *pl* goods *pl*, wares *pl*

warenhuis (*vaa*-rer-hur^{ew}ss) *nt* (pl -huizen) department store

warm (vahrm) *adj* warm; hot; ~ ***eten** dine

warmte (*vahrm*-ter) *c* warmth; heat

warmwaterkruik (vahrm-*vaa*-terr-krur^{ew}k) *c* (pl ~en) hot-water bottle

was¹ (vahss) *c* laundry, washing

was² (vahss) *c* wax

wasbaar (*vahss*-baar) *adj* washable

wasbak (*vahss*-bahk) *c* (pl ~ken) washbasin

wasbekken (*vahss*-beh-kern) *nt* (pl ~s) washbasin

wasecht (vahss-*ehkht*) *adj* fast-dyed; washable

wasgoed (*vahss*-khōot) *nt* washing

wasmachine (*vahss*-mah-shee-ner) *c* (pl ~s) washing machine

wasmiddel (*vahss*-mɪ-derl) *nt* (pl ~en) detergent

waspoeder (*vahss*-pōo-derr) *nt* (pl ~s) washing powder

*wassen (*vah*-sern) *v* wash

wassenbeeldenmuseum (vah-ser-bāyl-der-mēw-zāy-^yerm) *nt* (pl ~s,

-musea) waxworks *pl*

wasserette (vah-ser-*reh*-ter) *c* (pl ~s)
launderette

wasserij (vah-ser-*ray*) *c* (pl ~en)
laundry

wasverzachter (*vahss*-ferr-zahkh-
terr) *c* (pl ~s) water softener

wat (vaht) *pron* what; *adv* how; ~ **dan
ook** whatever; anything

water (*vaa*-terr) *nt* water; **hoog** ~ high
tide; **laag** ~ low tide; **stromend** ~
running water; **zoet** ~ fresh water

waterdicht (*vaa*-terr-dıkht) *adj*
rainproof, waterproof

waterkers (*vaa*-terr-kehrs) *c*
watercress

waterketel (*vaa*-terr-kāy-terl) *c* (pl ~s)
kettle

waterkoker (*vaa*-terr-kōā-kerr) *c* (pl
~s) kettle

watermeloen (*vaa*-terr-mer-lōōn) *c* (pl
~en) watermelon

waterpas (*vaa*-terr-pahss) *c* (pl ~sen)
level

waterpokken (*vaa*-terr-po-kern) *pl*
chicken pox

waterpomp (*vaa*-terr-pomp) *c* (pl ~en)
water pump

waterski (*vaa*-terr-skee) *c* (pl ~'s) water
ski

waterstof (*vaa*-terr-stof) *c* hydrogen

waterstofperoxyde (*vaa*-terr-stof-
pehr-ok-see-der) *nt* peroxide

waterval (*vaa*-terr-vahl) *c* (pl ~len)
waterfall

waterverf (*vaa*-terr-vehrf) *c*
watercolo(u)r

watten (*vah*-tern) *pl* cotton wool

wazig (*vaa*-zerkh) *adj* hazy

we (ver) *pron* we

wedden (*veh*-dern) *v* *bet

weddenschap (*veh*-der-skhahp) *c* (pl
~pen) bet

wederverkoper (*vāy*-derr-verr-kōā-

perr) *m* (pl ~s) retailer

wederzijds (vāy-derr-*zayts*) *adj* mutual

wedijveren (*veht*-ay-ver-rern) *v*
compete

wedloop (*veht*-lōāp) *c* (pl -lopen) race

wedstrijd (*veht*-strayt) *c* (pl ~en)
competition, contest; match

weduwe (*vāy*-dēw⁰⁰-er) *f* (pl ~n) widow

weduwnaar (*vāy*-dēw⁰⁰-naar) *m* (pl
~s) widower

weeën (*vāy*-ern) *pl* labo(u)r

weefsel (*vāyf*-serl) *nt* (pl ~s) tissue

weegschaal (*vāykh*-skhaal) *c* (pl
-schalen) weighing machine, scales *pl*

week (vāyk) *c* (pl weken) week

weekblad (*vāyk*-blaht) *c* (pl ~en)
weekly

weekdag (*vāyk*-dahkh) *c* (pl ~en)
weekday

weekend (*vee*-kehnt) *nt* (pl ~s)
weekend

weemoed (*vāy*-mōōt) *c* melancholy

weer¹ (vāyr) *nt* weather

weer² (vāyr) *adv* again

weerbericht (*vāyr*-ber-rıkht) *nt* (pl
~en) weather forecast

*weerhouden (vāyr-*hou*-dern) *v*
restrain

weerkaatsen (vāyr-*kaat*-sern) *v* reflect

weerkaatsing (vāyr-*kaat*-sıng) *c*
reflection

weerklank (*vāyr*-klahngk) *c* echo

weerzinwekkend (vāyr-zın-*veh*-kernt)
adj repulsive, repellent, revolting,
disgusting

wees (vāyss) *c* (pl wezen) orphan

weg¹ (vehkh) *adv* gone, away; lost; off

weg² (vehkh) *c* (pl ~en) way; road;
doodlopende ~ cul-de-sac; **op** ~ **naar**
bound for

*wegen (*vāy*-gern) *v* weigh

wegenkaart (*vāy*-ger-kaart) *c* (pl ~en)
road map

wegnet (*vāy*-ger-neht) *nt* (pl ~ten)

road system

wegens (*vāy*-gerns) *prep* because of, for

*****weggaan** (*veh*-khaan) *v* *go away

*****weggeven** (*veh*-gāy-vern) *v* *give away

wegkant (*vehkh*-kahnt) *c* (pl ~en) roadside, wayside

*****weglaten** (*vehkh*-laa-tern) *v* omit, *leave out

*****wegnemen** (*vehkh*-nāy-mern) *v* *take out, *take away

wegomlegging (*vaykh*-om-leh-gıng) *c* (pl ~en) diversion

wegrestaurant (*vehkh*-rehss-tōā-rahnt) *nt* (pl ~s) roadhouse; roadside restaurant

wegwerp- (*vehkh*-vehrp) disposable

wegwijzer (*vehkh*-vay-zerr) *c* (pl ~s) milepost, signpost

*****wegzenden** (*vehkh*-sehn-dern) *v* dismiss

wei (vay) *c* (pl ~den) meadow

weigeren (*vay*-ger-rern) *v* refuse; deny

weigering (*vay*-ger-rıng) *c* (pl ~en) refusal

weiland (*vay*-lahnt) *nt* (pl ~en) pasture

weinig (*vay*-nerkh) *adj* little; few

wekelijks (*vāy*-ker-lerks) *adj* weekly

weken (*vāy*-kern) *v* soak

wekken (*veh*-kern) *v* *awake, *wake

wekker (*veh*-kerr) *c* (pl ~s) alarm-clock

weldra (*vehl*-draa) *adv* soon, shortly

welk (vehlk) *pron* which; ~ **ook** whichever

welkom (*vehl*-kom) *adj* welcome; *nt* welcome

wellicht (*veh*-lıkht) *adv* perhaps

wellust (*veh*-lerst) *c* (pl ~en) lust

welnu! (vehl-*nēw*) well!

welvaart (*vehl*-vaart) *c* prosperity

welvarend (vehl-*vaa*-rernt) *adj* prosperous

welwillendheid (vehl-*vı*-lernt-hayt) *c* goodwill

welzijn (*vehl*-zayn) *nt* welfare

wending (*vehn*-dıng) *c* (pl ~en) turn

wenk (vehngk) *c* (pl ~en) sign

wenkbrauw (*vehngk*-brou) *c* (pl ~en) eyebrow

wenkbrauwstift (*vehngk*-brou-stıft) *c* (pl ~en) eyebrow pencil

wennen (*veh*-nern) *v* accustom

wens (vehns) *c* (pl ~en) wish, desire

wenselijk (*vehn*-ser-lerk) *adj* desirable

wensen (*vehn*-sern) *v* wish, desire; want

wereld (*vāy*-rerlt) *c* (pl ~en) world

wereldberoemd (*vāy*-rerlt-ber-rōōmt) *adj* world-famous

wereldbol (*vāy*-rerlt-bol) *c* globe

werelddeel (*vāy*-rerl-dāyl) *nt* (pl -delen) continent

wereldomvattend (*vāy*-rerlt-om-vah-ternt) *adj* global, world-wide

wereldoorlog (*vāy*-rerlt-ōar-lokh) *c* (pl ~en) world war

werk (vehrk) *nt* work; labo(u)r; occupation, employment; business; **te** ~ *****gaan** proceed; ~ **in uitvoering** road up

werkdag (*vehrk*-dahkh) *c* (pl ~en) working day

werkelijk (*vehr*-ker-lerk) *adj* actual, true; substantial, very; *adv* really

werkelijkheid (*vehr*-ker-lerk-hayt) *c* reality

werkeloos (*vehr*-ker-lōāss) *adj* unemployed; idle

werkeloosheid (vehr-ker-*lōāss*-hayt) *c* unemployment

werken (*vehr*-kern) *v* work; operate

werkgever (*vehrk*-khāy-verr) *m* (pl ~s) employer

werking (*vehr*-kıng) *c* operation, working; **buiten** ~ out of order

werknemer (*vehrk*-nāy-merr) *m* (f -neemster, pl ~s) employee

werkplaats (*vehrk*-plaats) *c* (pl ~en)
workshop

werktuig (*vehrk*-tur^(cw)kh) *nt* (pl ~en)
tool; utensil, implement

werkvergunning (*vehrk*-ferr-ger-nɪng)
c (pl ~en) work permit; labor permit
Am

werkwoord (*vehrk*-vōārt) *nt* (pl ~en)
verb

***werpen** (*vehr*-pern) *v* *cast, *throw

wesp (vehsp) *c* (pl ~en) wasp

west (vehst) *c* west

westelijk (*vehss*-ter-lerk) *adj* westerly

westen (*vehss*-tern) *nt* west

westers (*vehss*-terrs) *adj* western

wet (veht) *c* (pl ~ten) law

***weten** (*vāy*-tern) *v* *know

wetenschap (*vāy*-ter-skhahp) *c* (pl
~pen) science

wetenschappelijk (vāy-ter-*skhah*-per-
lerk) *adj* scientific

wettelijk (*veh*-ter-lerk) *adj* legal

wettig (*veh*-terkh) *adj* legal, lawful;
legitimate

***weven** (*vāy*-vern) *v* *weave

wever (*vāy*-verr) *m* (f weefster, pl ~s)
weaver

wezen¹ (*vāy*-zern) *nt* (pl ~s) creature,
being

wezen² (*vāy*-zern) *nt* essence

wezenlijk (*vāy*-zer-lerk) *adj* essential

wie (vee) *pron* who; whom; ~ **dan ook**
anybody; ~ **ook** whoever; **van** ~ whose

wieg (veekh) *c* (pl ~en) cradle

wiel (veel) *nt* (pl ~en) wheel

wielrijder (*veel*-ray-derr) *m* (f -ster, pl
~s) cyclist

wierook (*vee*-rōāk) *c* incense

wig (vɪkh) *c* (pl ~gen) wedge

wijd (vayt) *adj* broad, wide

wijden (*vay*-dern) *v* devote

wijk (vayk) *c* (pl ~en) quarter, district

wijn (vayn) *c* (pl ~en) wine

wijngaard (*vayn*-gaart) *c* (pl ~en)
vineyard

wijnkaart (*vayng*-kaart) *c* (pl ~en) wine
list

wijnkelder (*vayng*-kehl-derr) *c* (pl ~s)
wine cellar

wijnkoper (*vayng*-kōā-perr) *m* (pl ~s)
wine merchant

wijnoogst (*vayn*-ōākhst) *c* (pl ~en)
vintage

wijnstok (*vayn*-stok) *c* (pl ~ken) vine

wijs¹ (vayss) *adj* wise

wijs² (vayss) *c* (pl wijzen) tune

wijsbegeerte (*vayss*-ber-gāyr-ter) *c*
philosophy

wijsgeer (*vayss*-khāyr) *m* (pl -geren)
philosopher

wijsheid (*vayss*-hayt) *c* (pl -heden)
wisdom

wijsvinger (*vayss*-fɪ-ngerr) *c* (pl ~s)
index finger

wijting (*vay*-tɪng) *c* (pl ~en) whiting

wijze (*vay*-zer) *c* (pl ~n) manner, way

***wijzen** (*vay*-zern) *v* point; direct

wijzerplaat (*vay*-zerr-plaat) *c* (pl
~aten) dial

wijzigen (*vay*-zer-gern) *v* change, alter,
modify

wijziging (*vay*-zer-gɪng) *c* (pl ~en)
change, alteration

wil (vɪl) *c* will

wild (vɪlt) *adj* wild; savage, fierce; *nt*
game

wildpark (*vɪlt*-pahrk) *nt* (pl ~en) game
reserve

willekeurig (vɪ-ler-*kūr*-rerkh) *adj*
arbitrary

***willen** (*vɪ*-lern) *v* want; *will

wilskracht (*vɪls*-krahkht) *c* willpower

wimper (*vɪm*-perr) *c* (pl ~s) eyelash

wind (vɪnt) *c* (pl ~en) wind

***winden** (*vɪn*-dern) *v* *wind; twist

winderig (*vɪn*-der-rerkh) *adj* windy

windmolen (*vɪnt*-mōā-lern) *c* (pl ~s)
windmill

windstoot (vɪnt-stōat) c (pl -stoten) gust

windvlaag (vɪnt-flaakh) c (pl -vlagen) blow

winkel (vɪng-kerl) c (pl ~s) store, shop

winkelcentrum (vɪng-kerl-sehn-trerm) nt (pl -tra) shopping centre; nAm mall

winkelen (vɪng-ker-lern) v shop

winkelier (vɪng-ker-leer) m (f ~ster, pl ~s) shopkeeper

winnaar (vɪ-naar) m (f winnares, pl ~s) winner

***winnen** (vɪ-nern) v *win; gain

winst (vɪnst) c (pl ~en) profit; gain, winnings pl, benefit

winstgevend (vɪnst-khāy-vernt) adj profitable

winter (vɪn-terr) c (pl ~s) winter

wintersport (vɪn-terr-sport) c winter sports

wip (vɪp) c (pl ~pen) seesaw

wippen (vɪp-pern) v vulgar fuck

wirwar (vɪr-vahr) c muddle

wiskunde (vɪss-kern-der) c mathematics; **wiskundig** adj mathematical

wissel (vɪ-serl) c (pl ~s) draft

wisselen (vɪ-ser-lern) v change; exchange

wisselgeld (vɪ-serl-gehlt) nt change

wisselkantoor (vɪ-serl-kahn-tōar) nt (pl -toren) money exchange, exchange office

wisselkoers (vɪ-serl-kōors) c (pl ~en) exchange rate

wisselstroom (vɪ-serl-strōam) c alternating current

wit (vɪt) adj white

wittebroodsweken (vɪ-ter-brōats-vāy-kern) pl honeymoon

woede (vōō-der) c anger, rage

woeden (vōō-dern) v rage

woedend (vōō-dernt) adj furious

woensdag (vōōns-dahkh) c Wednesday

woest (vōōst) adj wild, fierce; desert

woestijn (vōōss-tayn) c (pl ~en) desert

wol (vol) c wool

wolf (volf) c (pl wolven) wolf

wolk (volk) c (pl ~en) cloud

wolkenkrabber (vol-ker-krah-berr) c (pl ~s) skyscraper

wollen (vo-lern) adj wool(l)en

wond (vont) c (pl ~en) wound

wonder (von-derr) nt (pl ~en) wonder, miracle; marvel

wonderbaarlijk (von-derr-baar-lerk) adj miraculous

wonen (vōa-nern) v live; reside

woning (vōa-nɪng) c (pl ~en) house

woonachtig (vōan-ahkh-terkh) adj resident

woonboot (vōan-bōat) c (pl -boten) houseboat

woonkamer (vōang-kaa-merr) c (pl ~s) living room

woonplaats (vōam-plaats) c (pl ~en) domicile, residence

woonwagen (vōan-vaa-gern) c (pl ~s) caravan

woord (vōart) nt (pl ~en) word

woordenboek (vōar-der-bōok) nt (pl ~en) dictionary

woordenlijst (vōar-der-layst) c (pl ~en) vocabulary

woordenschat (vōar-der-skhaht) c vocabulary

woordenwisseling (vōar-der-vɪ-ser-lɪng) c (pl ~en) argument

woordspeling (vōart-spāy-lɪng) c (pl ~en) pun

***worden** (vor-dern) v *become; *go, *get, *grow

worm (vorm) c (pl ~en) worm

worp (vorp) c (pl ~en) cast; shot

worst (vorst) c (pl ~en) sausage

worstelen (vor-ster-lern) v struggle

worsteling (*voar*-ster-lıng) *c* (pl ~en) struggle

wortel (*vor*-terl) *c* (pl ~s, ~en) root; carrot

woud (vout) *nt* (pl ~en) forest

wraak (vraak) *c* revenge

wrak (vrahk) *nt* (pl ~ken) wreck

wreed (vrāyt) *adj* harsh, cruel

*wrijven (*vray*-vern) *v* rub

wrijving (*vray*-vıng) *c* (pl ~en) friction

wrok (*vrohk*) *c* spite

wurgen (*verr*-gern) *v* strangle, choke

Z

zaad (zaat) *nt* (pl zaden) seed

zaag (zaakh) *c* (pl zagen) saw

zaagsel (*zaakh*-serl) *nt* sawdust

zaaien (*zaa^{ee}*-ern) *v* *sow

zaak (zaak) *c* (pl zaken) cause; case, matter; business

zaal (zaal) *c* (pl zalen) hall

zacht (zahkht) *adj* soft; gentle, smooth, mild, mellow

zadel (*zaa*-derl) *nt* (pl ~s) saddle

zak (zahk) *c* (pl ~ken) pocket; sack, bag

zakdoek (*zahk*-dōōk) *c* (pl ~en) handkerchief; **papieren** ~ tissue

zakelijk (*zaa*-ker-lerk) *adj* business-like

zaken (*zaa*-kern) *pl* business; **voor** ~ on business; ~ ***doen met** *deal with

zakenman (*zaa*-ker-mahn) *m* (pl -lieden, -lui) businessman

zakenreis (*zaa*-ker-rayss) *c* (pl -reizen) business trip

zakenvrouw (*zaa*-ker-vrou) *f* (pl -en) businesswoman, tradeswoman

zakken (*zahk*-kern) *v* fail

zaklantaarn (*zahk*-lahn-taa-rern) *c* (pl ~s) torch, flashlight

zakmes (*zahk*-mehss) *nt* (pl ~sen) pocketknife, penknife

zalf (zahlf) *c* (pl zalven) ointment, salve

zalm (zahlm) *c* (pl ~en) salmon

zand (zahnt) *nt* sand

zanderig (*zahn*-der-rerkh) *adj* sandy

zanger (*zah*-ngerr) *m* (f ~es, pl ~s) vocalist, singer

zappen (*zah*-pern) *v* zap

zaterdag (*zaa*-terr-dahkh) *c* Saturday

ze (zer) *pron* she; they

zebra (*zāy*-braa) *c* (pl ~'s) zebra

zebrapad (*zāy*-braa-paht) *nt* (pl ~en) pedestrian crossing; crosswalk *nAm*

zedelijk (*zāy*-der-lerk) *adj* moral

zeden (*zāy*-dern) *pl* morals

zee (zāy) *c* (pl ~ën) sea

zeeëgel (*zāy*-āy-gerl) *c* (pl ~s) sea urchin

zeef (zāyf) *c* (pl zeven) sieve

zeegezicht (*zāy*-ger-zıkht) *nt* (pl ~en) seascape

zeehaven (*zāy*-haa-vern) *c* (pl ~s) seaport

zeehond (*zāy*-hont) *c* (pl ~en) seal

zeekaart (*zāy*-kaart) *c* (pl ~en) chart

zeekust (*zāy*-kerst) *c* (pl ~en) seashore

zeeman (*zāy*-mahn) *c* (pl -lieden, -lui) seaman

zeemeeuw (*zāy*-māy^{ōō}) *c* (pl ~en) seagull

zeep (zāyp) *c* soap

zeeppoeder (*zāy*-pōō-derr) *nt* soap powder

zeer (zāyr) *adj* sore; *adv* very, quite

zeeschelp (*zāy*-skhehlp) *c* (pl ~en) seashell

zeevogel (*zāy*-vōa-gerl) *c* (pl ~s)

seabird

zeewater (*z$\overline{ay}$*-vaa-terr) *nt* sea water

zeeziek (*z$\overline{ay}$*-zeek) *adj* seasick

zeeziekte (*z$\overline{ay}$*-zeek-ter) *c* seasickness

zegel (*z$\overline{ay}$*-gerl) *nt* (pl ~s) seal

zegen (*z$\overline{ay}$*-gern) *c* blessing

zegenen (*z$\overline{ay}$*-ger-nern) *v* bless

zegevieren (*z$\overline{ay}$*-ger-vee-rern) *v* triumph

*zeggen (*zeh*-gern) *v* *say; *tell

zeil (zayl) *nt* (pl ~en) sail

zeilboot (*zayl*-b$\overline{oa}$t) *c* (pl -boten) sailing boat

zeilclub (*zayl*-klerp) *c* (pl ~s) yacht club

zeilsport (*zayl*-sport) *c* yachting

zeker (*z$\overline{ay}$*-kerr) *adv* surely, certainly; *adj* certain, sure; ~ **niet** by no means

zekering (*z$\overline{ay}$*-ker-rıng) *c* (pl ~en) fuse

zelden (*zehl*-dern) *adv* seldom, rarely

zeldzaam (*zehlt*-saam) *adj* rare; uncommon, infrequent

zelf (zehlf) *pron* myself; yourself; himself; herself; oneself; ourselves; yourselves; themselves; self

zelfbediening (*zehlf*-ber-dee-nıng) *c* self-service

zelfbedieningsrestaurant (*zehlf*-ber-dee-nıngs-rehss-t$\overline{oa}$a-rahnt) *nt* (pl ~s) self-service restaurant

zelfbestuur (*zehlf*-ber-st$\overline{ew}$r) *nt* self-government

zelfde (*zehlf*-der) *adj* same

zelfmoord (*zehlf*-m$\overline{oa}$rt) *c* (pl ~en) suicide

zelfs (zehlfs) *adv* even

zelfstandig (zehlf-*stahn*-derkh) *adj* independent; self-employed; ~ **naamwoord** noun

zelfstrijkend (zehlf-*stray*-kernt) *adj* drip-dry, wash and wear

zelfzuchtig (zehlf-*serkh*-terkh) *adj* egoistic

*zenden (*zehn*-dern) *v* *send

zender (*zehn*-derr) *c* (pl ~s) transmitter

zending (*zehn*-dıng) *c* (pl ~en) consignment, shipment

zenit (*z$\overline{ay}$*-nıt) *nt* zenith

zenuw (*zay*-n$\overline{ew}^{oo}$) *c* (pl ~en) nerve

zenuwachtig (*z$\overline{ay}$*-n$\overline{ew}^{oo}$-ahkh-terkh) *adj* nervous

zenuwpijn (*z$\overline{ay}$*-n$\overline{ew}^{oo}$-payn) *c* (pl ~en) neuralgia

zes (zehss) *num* six

zesde (*zehss*-der) *num* sixth

zestien (*zehss*-teen) *num* sixteen

zestiende (*zehss*-teen-der) *num* sixteenth

zestig (*zehss*-terkh) *num* sixty

zet (zeht) *c* (pl ~ten) move; push

zetel (*z$\overline{ay}$*-terl) *c* (pl ~s) chair; seat

zetpil (*zeht*-pıl) *c* (pl ~len) suppository

zetten (zeh-tern) *v* place; *lay, *set, *put; **in elkaar** ~ assemble

zeurpiet (*z$\overline{ur}$r*-peet) *c* (pl ~en) bore

zeven[1] (*z$\overline{ay}$*-vern) *num* seven

zeven[2] (*z$\overline{ay}$*-vern) *v* strain, sift, sieve

zevende (*z$\overline{ay}$*-vern-der) *num* seventh

zeventien (*z$\overline{ay}$*-vern-teen) *num* seventeen

zeventiende (*z$\overline{ay}$*-vern-teen-der) *num* seventeenth

zeventig (*z$\overline{ay}$*-vern-terkh) *num* seventy

zich (zıkh) *pron* himself; herself; themselves

zicht (zıkht) *nt* sight; visibility; **op** ~ on approval

zichtbaar (*zıkht*-baar) *adj* visible

zichzelf (zıkh-*zehlf*) *nt* self

ziek (zeek) *adj* ill, sick

ziekenauto (*zee*-kern-$\overline{oa}$-t$\overline{oa}$) *c* (pl ~'s) ambulance

ziekenhuis (*zee*-ker-hur^{ew}ss) *nt* (pl -huizen) hospital

ziekte (*zeek*-ter) *c* (pl ~n, ~s) disease; illness, sickness

ziel (zeel) *c* (pl ~en) soul

*zien (zeen) *v* *see; notice; **er uit** ~ look;

*laten ~ *show

zienswijze (*zeens*-vay-zer) *c* (pl ~n) outlook

zijbeuk (*zay*-bürk) *c* (pl ~en) aisle

zijde[1] (*zay*-der) *c* silk

zijde[2] (*zay*-der) *c* (pl ~n) side

zijlicht (*zay*-lıkht) *nt* sidelight

zijn (zayn) *pron* his, its

*zijn (zayn) *v* *be

zijrivier (*zay*-ree-veer) *c* (pl ~en) tributary

zijstraat (*zay*-straat) *c* (pl -straten) side street

zilver (*zıl*-verr) *nt* silver

zilveren (*zıl*-ver-rern) *adj* silver

zilverpapier (*zıl*-verr-paa-peer) *nt* tinfoil

zilversmid (*zıl*-verr-smıt) *m* (pl -smeden) silversmith

zilverwerk (*zıl*-verr-vehrk) *nt* silverware

zin[1] (zın) *c* sense; desire; **~ *hebben in** *feel like, fancy

zin[2] (zın) *c* (pl ~nen) sentence

*zingen (*zı*-ngern) *v* *sing

zink (zıngk) *nt* zinc

*zinken (*zıng*-kern) *v* *sink

zinloos (*zın*-lōass) *adj* senseless

zintuig (*zın*-tur[ew]kh) *nt* (pl ~en) sense

zitkamer (*zıt*-kaa-merr) *c* (pl ~s) sitting room

zitplaats (*zıt*-plaats) *c* (pl ~en) seat

*zitten (*zı*-tern) *v* *sit; ***gaan ~** *sit down, *be seated

zitting (*zı*-tıng) *c* (pl ~en) session

zitvlak (*zıt*-flahk) *nt* bottom

zo (zōā) *adv* so, thus; such; **zo'n** such a

zoals (zōā-*ahls*) *conj* like, as; such as

zodat (zōā-*daht*) *conj* so that

zodra (zōā-*draa*) *conj* as soon as

*zoeken (*zōō*-kern) *v* look for; *seek, search; hunt for

zoeker (*zōō*-kerr) *c* (pl ~s) viewfinder

zoemen (*zōō*-mern) *v* buzz

zoen (zōōn) *c* (pl ~en) kiss

zoet (zōōt) *adj* sweet; good; **~ maken** sweeten

zoetzuur (*zōōt*-sēwr) *nt* pickles pl

zogen (*zōā*-gern) *v* nurse

zogenaamd (zōā-ger-*naamt*) *adj* socalled

zolder (*zol*-derr) *c* (pl ~s) attic

zomer (*zōā*-merr) *c* (pl ~s) summer

zomertijd (*zōā*-merr-tayt) *c* summer time

zon (zon) *c* (pl ~nen) sun

zondag (*zon*-dahkh) *c* Sunday

zonde (*zon*-der) *c* (pl ~n) sin

zondebok (*zon*-der-bok) *c* (pl ~ken) scapegoat

zonder (*zon*-derr) *prep* without

zonderling (*zon*-derr-lıng) *adj* funny, queer

zone (*zaw*-ner) *c* (pl ~s) zone

zonlicht (*zon*-lıkht) *nt* sunlight

zonnebaden (zo-ner-baa-dern) *v* sunbathe

zonnebrand (zo-ner-brahnt) *c* sunburn

zonnebrandolie (zo-ner-brahnt-ōā-lee) *c* suntan oil

zonnebril (zo-ner-brıl) *c* (pl ~len) sunglasses pl

zonnescherm (zo-ner-skhehrm) *nt* (pl ~en) awning

zonneschijn (zo-ner-skhayn) *c* sunshine

zonnesteek (zo-ner-stāyk) *c* sunstroke

zonnestelsel (zo-ner-stehl-serl) *nt* solar system

zonnig (zo-nerkh) *adj* sunny

zonsondergang (zons-*on*-derr-gahng) *c* (pl ~en) sunset

zonsopgang (zons-*op*-khahng) *c* (pl ~en) sunrise

zoogdier (*zōākh*-deer) *nt* (pl ~en) mammal

zool (z$\overline{oo}$al) *c* (pl zolen) sole

zoölogie (z$\overline{oo}$-$\overline{oo}$-l$\overline{oo}$-*gee*) *c* zoology

zoom (z$\overline{oo}$m) *c* (pl zomen) hem

zoon (z$\overline{oo}$n) *m* (pl zonen) son

zorg (zorkh) *c* (pl ~en) concern, worry, care; trouble

zorgen voor (*zor*-gern) look after, *take care of; see to

zorgvuldig (zorkh-*ferl*-derkh) *adj* careful

zorgwekkend (zorkh-*veh*-kernt) *adj* critical

zorgzaam (*zorkh*-saam) *adj* thoughtful

zout (zout) *nt* salt; *adj* salty

zoutvaatje (*zout*-faa-t^{y}er) *nt* (pl ~s) salt cellar, *nAm* salt shaker

zoveel (z$\overline{oo}$-v$\overline{ay}$l) *adv* so much, so many

zowel ... als (z$\overline{oo}$-*veh* ... ahls) both ... and

zuid (zur^{ew}t) *c* south

Zuid-Afrika (zur^{ew}t-*aa*-free-kaa) South Africa

zuidelijk (*zur^{ew}*-der-lerk) *adj* southern, southerly

zuiden (*zur^{ew}*-dern) *nt* south

zuidoosten (zur^{ew}t-$\overline{oo}$ss-tern) *nt* southeast

zuidpool (*zur^{ew}t*-p$\overline{oo}$al) *c* South Pole

zuidwesten (zur^{ew}t-*vehss*-tern) *nt* southwest

zuigeling (*zur^{ew}*-ger-lıng) *m* (pl ~en) infant

***zuigen** (*zur^{ew}*-gern) *v* suck

zuiger (*zur^{ew}*-gerr) *c* (pl ~s) piston

zuigerring (*zur^{ew}*-ger-rıng) *c* (pl ~en) piston ring

zuil (zur^{ew}l) *c* (pl ~en) column, pillar

zuilengang (*zur^{ew}*-ler-gahng) *c* (pl ~en) arcade

zuinig (*zur^{ew}*-nerkh) *adj* economical, thrifty

zuipen (*zur^{ew}*-pern) *v adj colloquial* booze

zuivelwinkel (*zur^{ew}*-verl-vıng-kerl) *c* (pl ~s) dairy

zuiver (*zur^{ew}*-verr) *adj* pure, clean

zulk (zerlk) *adj* such

***zullen** (*zer*-lern) *v* *will, *shall

zus (zerss) *f* (pl ~sen) sister

zuster (*zerss*-terr) *f* (pl ~s) sister; nurse

zuur[1] (z$\overline{ew}$r) *adj* sour

zuur[2] (z$\overline{ew}$r) *nt* (pl zuren) acid

zuurstof (z$\overline{ew}$r-stof) *c* oxygen

zwaaien (zvaa^{ee}-ern) *v* *swing; wave

zwaan (zvaan) *c* (pl zwanen) swan

zwaar (zvaar) *adj* heavy; **te~** too heavy; overweight

zwaard (zvaart) *nt* (pl ~en) sword

zwaartekracht (*zvaar*-ter-krahkht) *c* gravity

zwager (*zvaa*-gerr) *m* (pl ~s) brother-in-law

zwak (zvahk) *adj* feeble, weak; faint; dim

zwakheid (*zvahk*-hayt) *c* (pl -heden) weakness

zwaluw (*zvaa*-l$\overline{ew}^{oo}$) *c* (pl ~en) swallow

zwanger (*zvah*-ngerr) *adj* pregnant

zwart (zvahrt) *adj* black

Zweden (*zv$\overline{ay}$*-dern) Sweden

Zweed (zv$\overline{ay}$t) *m* (f ~se, pl Zweden) Swede

Zweeds (zv$\overline{ay}$ts) *adj* Swedish

zweefvliegtuig (*zv$\overline{ay}$*-fleekh-tur^{ew}kh) *nt* (pl ~en) glider

zweep (zv$\overline{ay}$p) *c* (pl zwepen) whip

zweer (zv$\overline{ay}$r) *c* (pl zweren) ulcer, sore

zweet (zv$\overline{ay}$t) *nt* sweat, perspiration

***zwellen** (*zveh*-lern) *v* *swell

zwelling (*zveh*-lıng) *c* (pl ~en) swelling

zwembad (*zvehm*-baht) *nt* (pl ~en) swimming pool, pool

zwembroek (*zvehm*-br$\overline{oo}$k) *c* (pl ~en) swimming trunks, bathing suit

***zwemmen** (*zveh*-mern) *v* *swim

zwemmer (*zveh*-merr) *m* (f zwemster, pl ~s) swimmer

zwempak (*zvehm*-pahk) *nt* (pl ~ken)
swimsuit, swimming suit

zwemsport (*zvehm*-sport) *c*
swimming

zwemvest (*zvehm*-vehst) *c* (pl ~en) life
jacket

zwendelarij (zvehn-der-laa-*ray*) *c* (pl
~en) swindle

*zweren (*zvāy*-rern) *v* *swear, vow

*zwerven (*zvehr*-vern) *v* roam, wander

zweten (*zvāy*-tern) *v* sweat, perspire

*zwijgen (*zvay*-gern) *v* *be silent,
*keep quiet; **tot ~ *brengen** silence;
zwijgend silent

zwijn (zvayn) *nt* (pl ~en) pig

Zwitser (*zvɪt*-serr) *m* (f ~se, pl ~s) Swiss

Zwitserland (*zvɪt*-serr-lahnt)
Switzerland

Zwitsers (*zvɪt*-serrs) *adj* Swiss

zwoegen (*zvoo*-gern) *v* labo(u)r

Menu Reader

Food

aalbes redcurrant
aardappel potato
  ~ puree mashed potatoes
aardbei strawberry
abrikoos apricot
amandel almond
  ~ broodje a sweet roll with almond-paste filling
ananas pineapple
andijvie endive (US chicory)
  ~ stamppot mashed potato and endive casserole
anijs aniseed
ansjovis anchovy
appel apple
  ~ beignet fritter
  ~ bol dumpling
  ~ flap puff-pastry containing apple
  ~ gebak cake
  ~ moes sauce
Ardense pastei rich pork mixture cooked in a pastry crust, served cold in slices
artisjok artichoke
asperge asparagus
  ~ punt tip
aubergine aubergine (US eggplant)
augurk gherkin (US pickle)
avondeten dinner, supper
azijn vinegar
baars perch, bass
babi pangang slices of roast suckling pig, served with a sweet-and-sour sauce
bami goreng a casserole of noodles, vegetables, diced pork and shrimps
banaan banana
banketletter pastry with an almond-paste filling
basilicum basil

bediening service
belegd broodje roll with a variety of garnishes
belegen kaas pungent-flavoured cheese
biefstuk fillet of beef
  ~ van de haas small round fillet of beef
bieslook chive
bitterbal small, round breaded meatball served as an appetizer
blinde vink veal bird; thin slice of veal rolled around stuffing
bloedworst black pudding (US blood sausage)
  ~ met appelen with cooked apples
bloemkool cauliflower
boerenkool met worst kale mixed with mashed potatoes and served with smoked sausage
boerenomelet omelet with diced vegetables and bacon
bokking bloater
boon bean
borrelhapje appetizer
borststuk breast, brisket
bosbes bilberry (US blueberry)
bot 1) flounder 2) bone
boter butter
boterham slice of buttered bread
bouillon broth
braadhaantje spring chicken
braadworst frying sausage
braam blackberry
brasem bream
brood bread
  ~ maaltijd bread served with cold meat, eggs, cheese, jam or other garnishes
  ~ pudding kind of bread pudding with

eggs, cinnamon and rum flavouring

broodje roll

~ **halfom** buttered roll with liver and salted beef

~ **kaas** buttered roll with cheese

bruine bonen met spek red kidney beans served with bacon

Brussels lof chicory (US endive)

caramelpudding caramel mould

caramelvla caramel custard

champignon mushroom

chocola(de) chocolate

citroen lemon

cordon bleu veal scallop stuffed with ham and cheese

dadel date

dagschotel day's special

dame blanche vanilla ice-cream with hot chocolate sauce

dille dill

doperwt green pea

dragon tarragon

drie-in-de-pan small, fluffy pancake filled with currants

druif grape

duif pigeon

Duitse biefstuk hamburger steak

Edam, Edammer kaas firm, mildflavoured yellow cheese, coated with red wax

eend duck

ei egg

eierpannekoek egg pancake

erwt pea

erwtensoep met kluif pea soup with diced, smoked sausages, pork fat, pig's trotter (US feet), parsley, leeks and celery

exclusief not included

fazant pheasant

filet fillet

~ **américain** steak tartare

flensje small, thin pancake

foe yong hai omelet with leeks, onions, and shrimps served in a sweet-and-sour sauce

forel trout

framboos raspberry

Friese nagelkaas cheese made from skimmed milk, flavoured with cloves

frikadel meatball

frites, frieten chips (US french fries)

gaar well-done

gans goose

garnaal shrimp, prawn

gebak pastry, cake

gebakken fried

gebonden soep cream soup

gebraden roasted

gedroogde pruim prune

gehakt 1) minced 2) minced meat

~ **bal** meatball

gekookt boiled

gekruid seasoned

gemarineerd marinated

gember ginger

~ **koek** gingerbread

gemengd assorted, mixed

gepaneerd breaded

gepocheerd ei poached egg

geraspt grated

gerecht course, dish

gerookt smoked

geroosterd brood toast

gerst barley

gestoofd braised

gevogelte fowl

gevuld stuffed

gezouten salted

Goudakaas, Goudse kaas a renowned Dutch cheese, similar to *Edam*, large, flat and round; it gains in flavour with maturity

graskaas spring cheese

griesmeel semolina

~ **pudding** semolina pudding

griet brill

groente vegetable

Haagse bluf dessert of whipped egg-whites, served with redcurrant sauce
haantje cockerel
haas hare
hachee hash of minced meat, onions and spices
half, halve half
hardgekookt ei hard-boiled egg
haring herring
hart heart
havermoutpap (oatmeal) porridge
hazelnoot hazelnut
heilbot halibut
heldere soep consommé, clear soup
hersenen brains
hete bliksem potatoes, bacon and apples, seasoned with butter, salt and sugar
Hollandse biefstuk loin section of a porterhouse or T-bone steak
Hollandse nieuwe freshly caught, filleted herring
honing honey
houtsnip 1) woodcock 2) cheese sandwich on rye bread
hutspot met klapstuk hotch-potch of mashed potatoes, carrots and onions served with boiled beef
huzarensalade salad of potatoes, hard-boiled eggs, cold meat, gherkins, beetroot and mayonnaise
ijs ice, ice-cream
inclusief included
Italiaanse salade mixed salad with tomatoes, olives and tunny fish
jachtschotel a casserole of meat, onions and potatoes, often served with apple sauce
jonge kaas fresh cheese
jus gravy
kaas cheese
  ~ balletje baked cheese ball
kabeljauw cod
kalfslapje, kalfsoester veal cutlet

kalfsrollade roast veal
kalfsvlees veal
kalkoen turkey
kapucijnrs met spek peas served with fried bacon, boiled potatoes, onions and green salad
karbonade chop, cutlet
karper carp
kastanje chestnut
kaviaar caviar
kerrie curry
kers cherry
kievitsei plover's egg
kip chicken
kippeborst breast of chicken
kippebout leg of chicken
knakworst small frankfurter sausage
knoflook garlic
koek 1) cake 2) gingerbread
koekje biscuit (US cookie)
koffietafel light lunch consisting of bread and butter with a variety of garnishes, served with coffee
kokosnoot coconut
komijnekaas cheese flavoured with cumin seeds
komkommer cucumber
konijn rabbit
koninginnensoep cream of chicken
kool cabbage
  ~ schotel met gehakt casserole of meatballs and cabbage
kotelet chop, cutlet
koud cold
  ~ vlees cold meat (US cold cuts)
krab crab
krabbetje spare rib
krent currant
kroepoek large, deep-fried shrimp wafer
kroket croquette
kruidnagel clove
kruisbes gooseberry
kwark fresh white cheese

kwartel quail
kweepeer quince
lamsbout leg of lamb
lamsvlees lamb
langoest spiny lobster
Leidse kaas cheese flavoured with cumin seeds
lekkerbekje deep-fried, breaded, filleted haddock or plaice
lendestuk sirloin
lever liver
linze lentil
loempia spring roll (US egg roll)
maïskolf corn on the cob
makreel mackerel
mandarijntje tangerine
marsepein marzipan
meikaas a creamy cheese with high fat content
meloen melon
menu van de dag set menu
mossel mussel
mosterd mustard
nagerecht dessert
nasi goreng a casserole of rice, fried onions, meat, chicken, shrimps, vegetables and seasoning, usually topped with a fried egg
nier kidney
  ~ **broodje** roll filled with kidneys and chopped onions
noot nut
oester oyster
olie oil
  ~ **bol** fritter, often with raisins
olijf olive
omelet fines herbes herb omelet
omelet met kippelevertjes chicken liver omelet
omelet nature plain omelet
ongaar underdone (US rare)
ontbijt breakfast
  ~ **koek** honey cake
  ~ **spek** bacon, rasher

ossehaas fillet of beef
ossestaart oxtail
oude kaas any mature and strong cheese
paddestoel mushroom
paling eel
  ~ **in 't groen** braised in white sauce garnished with chopped parsley and other greens
pannenkoek pancake
  ~ **met stroop** pancake served with treacle (US syrup)
pap porridge
paprika green or red (sweet) pepper
patates frites chips (US french fries)
pastei pie, pasty
patrijs partridge
peer pear
pekeltong salt(ed) tongue
pekelvlees slices of salted meat
peper pepper
  ~ **koek** gingerbread
perzik peach
peterselie parsley
piccalilly pickle
pinda peanut
  ~ **kaas** peanut butter
pisang goreng fried banana
poffertje tiny pancake with sugar and butter
pompelmoes grapefruit
portie portion
postelein purslane (edible plant)
prei leek
prinsessenboon French bean (US green bean)
pruim plum
rabarber rhubarb
radijs radish
rauw raw
reebout, reerug venison
reine-claude greengage
rekening bill
ribstuk rib of beef

rijst rice
  ~ tafel an Indonesian preparation composed of some 30 dishes including stewed vegetables, spit-roasted meat and fowl, served with rice, various sauces, fruit, nuts and spices
rivierkreeft crayfish
rode biet beetroot
rode kool red cabbage
roerei scrambled egg
roggebrood rye bread
rolmops Bismarck herring
rolpens fried slices of spiced and pickled minced beef and tripe, topped with an apple slice
rookspek smoked bacon
rookworst smoked sausage
roomboter butter
roomijs ice-cream
rosbief roast beef
rozemarijn rosemary
runderlap beefsteak
rundvlees beef
Russische eieren Russian eggs; hard-boiled egg-halves garnished with mayonnaise, herring, shrimps, capers, anchovies and sometimes caviar; served on lettuce
salade salad
sambal very hot paste consisting mainly of ground pimentos, usually served with *rijsttafel*, *bami* or *nasi goreng*
sardien sardine
saté, sateh skewered pieces of meat covered with a spicy peanut sauce
saucijzebroodje sausage roll
saus sauce, gravy
schaaldier shellfish
schapevlees mutton
scharretong lemon sole
schelvis haddock
schildpadsoep turtle soup
schnitzel cutlet

schol plaice
schuimomelet fluffy dessert omelet
selderij celery
sinaasappel orange
sjaslik skewered chunks of meat, grilled, then braised in a spicy sauce of tomatoes, onions and bacon
sla salad, lettuce
slaboon French bean (US green bean)
slagroom whipped cream
slak snail
sneeuwbal kind of cream puff, sometimes filled with currants and raisins
snijboon sliced French bean
soep soup
  ~ van de dag soup of the day
sorbet water ice (US sherbet)
specerij herb, seasoning
speculaas spiced almond biscuit
spek bacon
sperzieboon French bean (US green bean)
spiegelei fried egg
spijskaart menu, bill of fare
spinazie spinach
sprits a kind of shortbread
spruitje Brussels sprout
stamppot a stew of vegetables and mashed potatoes
steur sturgeon
stokvis stockfish (dried cod)
stroop treacle (US syrup)
suiker sugar
taart cake
tarbot turbot
tartaar steak tartare
  ~ speciaal extra-large portion, of prime quality
tijm thyme
tjap tjoy chop suey; a dish of fried meat and vegetables served with rice
toeristenmenu tourist menu
tomaat tomato

tong 1) tongue 2) sole
tonijn tunny (US tuna)
toost toast
tosti grilled cheese-and-ham sandwich
tournedos thick round fillet cut of prime beef (US rib or rib-eye steak)
truffel truffle
tuinboon broad bean
ui onion
uitsmijter two slices of bread garnished with ham or roast beef and topped with two fried eggs
vanille vanilla
varkenshaas pork tenderloin
varkenslapje pork fillet
varkensvlees pork
venkel fennel
vermicellisoep consommé with thin noodles
vers fresh
vijg fig
vis fish
vla custard
vlaai fruit tart
Vlaamse karbonade small slices of beef and onions braised in broth, with beer sometimes added
vlees meat
voorgerecht starter or first course
vrucht fruit

vruchtensalade fruit salad
wafel wafer
walnoot walnut
warm hot
waterkers watercress
waterzooi chicken poached in white wine and shredded vegetables, cream and egg-yolk
wentelteefje French toast; slice of white bread dipped in egg batter and fried, then sprinkled with cinnamon and sugar
wijnkaart wine list
wijting whiting
wild game
~ zwijn wild boar
wilde eend wild duck
witlof chicory (US endive)
~ op zijn Brussels chicory rolled in a slice of ham and oven-browned with cheese sauce
worst sausage
wortel carrot
zachtgekookt ei soft-boiled egg
zalm salmon
zeekreeft lobster
zeevis saltwater fish
zout salt
zuurkool sauerkraut
zwezerik sweetbread

Drinks

advocaat egg liqueur
ananassap pineapple juice
aperitief aperitif
bessenjenever blackcurrant gin
bier beer
bisschopswijn mulled wine
bittertje bitter-tasting aperitif
boerenjongens Dutch brandy with

raisins
boerenmeisjes Dutch brandy with apricots
borrel shot
brandewijn brandy
cassis blackcurrant liqueur
chocolademelk, chocomel(k) chocolate drink

warme ~ hot cocoa

warme ~ **met slagroom** hot cocoa with whipped cream

citroenbrandewijn lemon brandy

citroenjenever lemon-flavoured gin

citroentje met suiker brandy flavoured with lemon peel, with sugar added

cognac brandy, cognac

donker bier porter; dark sweet-tasting beer

druivensap grape juice

frisdrank soft drink

gekoeld iced

genever see *jenever*

Geuzelambiek a strong Flemish bitter beer brewed from wheat and barley

jenever Dutch gin

jonge jenever/klare young Dutch gin

karnemelk buttermilk

kersenbrandewijn kirsch; spirit distilled from cherries

koffie coffee

~ **met melk** with milk

~ **met room** with cream

~ **met slagroom** with whipped cream

~ **verkeerd** white coffee; equal quantity of coffee and hot milk

zwarte ~ black

Kriekenlambiek a strong Brussels bitter beer flavoured with morello cherries

kwast hot or cold lemon squash

licht bier lager; light beer

likeur liqueur

limonade lemonade

melk milk

mineraalwater mineral water

oude jenever/klare Dutch gin aged in wood casks, yellowish in colour and more mature than *jonge jenever*

oranjebitter orange-flavoured bitter

pils general name for lager, served cold

sap juice

sinas orangeade

spuitwater soda water

sterkedrank liquor, spirit

tafelwater mineral water

thee tea

~ **met citroen** with lemon

~ **met suiker en melk** with sugar and milk

trappistenbier malt beer brewed (originally) by Trappist monks

vieux brandy bottled in Holland

vruchtesap fruit juice

warme chocola hot chocolate

wijn wine

droge ~ dry

rode ~ red

witte ~ white

zoete ~ sweet

wodka vodka

Mini Dutch Grammar

Nouns

Dutch nouns are either masculine, feminine, or neuter.

As masculine and feminine nouns usually have the same article (**de**, see page 179), we have chosen to use the denotation *c* ("common gender") to indicate the so-called "**de**-words".

In the case of living beings *m* and *f* indicate masculine and feminine forms of the nouns, respectively:

Dutch ... Nederlander *m*, Nederlandse *f*

Plural

The most common sign of the plural in Dutch is an **-en** ending:

krant	newspaper	**woord**	word	**dag**	day
kranten	newspapers	**woorden**	words	**dagen**	days

a) In nouns with a double vowel, one vowel is dropped when **-en** is added:

uur	hour	**boot**	boat	**jaar**	year
uren	hours	**boten**	boats	**jaren**	years

b) most nouns ending in **-s** or **-f** change this letter into **-z** and **-v** respectively, when **-en** is added:

prijs	the price	**brief**	letter
prijzen	prices	**brieven**	letters

Another common plural ending in Dutch is **-s**. Nouns ending in an unstressed **-el**, **-em**, **-en**, **-aar** as well as **-je** (diminutives) take an **-s** in the plural:

tafel/tafels	table(s)	**winnaar/winnaars**	winner(s)
deken/dekens	blanket(s)	**dubbeltje/dubbeltjes**	ten-cent piece(s)

Some exceptions:

stad/steden	town(s)	**auto/auto's**	car(s)
ship/schepen	ship(s)	**paraplu/paraplu's**	umbrella(s)
kind/kinderen	child(ren)	**foto/foto's**	photo(s)
ei/eieren	egg(s)	**musicus/musici**	musician(s)

Articles

1) Definite article (the)

The definite article in Dutch is either **de** or **het**. **De** is used with roughly two thirds of all common-gender singular nouns as well as with all plural nouns, while **het** is mainly used with neuter singular nouns and all diminutives:

de straat the street   **het huis** the house   **het katje** the kitten

2) Indefinite article (a; an)

The indefinite article is **een** for all genders, always unstressed and pronounced like *an* in the English word "another". As in English there is no plural. When it bears accent marks (**één**) it means "one" and is pronounced rather like a in "late", but a pure vowel, not a diphthong.

een man	a man	**een vrouw**	a woman	**een kind**	a child
mannen	men	**vrouwen**	women	**kinderen**	children

Adjectives

When the adjective stands immediately before the noun, it usually takes the ending **–e**:

de jonge vrouw	the young woman
een prettige reis	a pleasant trip
aardige mensen	nice people

However, no ending is added to the adjective in the following cases:
1) When the adjective follows the noun:

De stad is groot.	The city is big.
De zon is heet.	The sun is hot.

2) When the noun is neuter singular and preceded by **een** (a/an), or when the words **elk/ieder** (each), **veel** (much), **zulk** (such) and **geen** (no) precede the adjective:

een wit huis	a white house
elk goed boek	each good book
veel vers fruit	much fresh fruit
zulk mooi weer	such good weather
geen warm water	no hot water

Demonstrative adjectives (this/that)

this	**deze**	(with nouns of common gender)
	dit	(with nouns of neuter gender)
that	**die (daar)**	(with nouns of common gender)
	dat	(with nouns of neuter gender)
these	**deze**	(with all plural nouns)

those	**die (daar)**	(with all plural nouns)
Deze stad is groot.		This city is big.
Dat huis is wit.		That house is white.

Possessive adjectives

my	**mijn**
your	**jouw** (fam.)
your	**uw** (pol.)
his	**zijn**
her	**haar**
its	**zijn**
our	**ons** (with singular neuter nouns)
	onze (with singular nouns of common gender and all plurals)
you	**jullie** (fam.)
their	**hun**

Personal pronouns

Subject		Object	
I	**ik**	me	**mij** or **me**
you	**jij** or **je** (fam.)	you	**jou** or **je** (fam.)
you	**u** (polite)	you	**u** (polite)
he	**hij**	him	**hem**
she	**zij** or **ze**	her	**haar**
it	**het**	it	**het**
we	**wij** or **we**	us	**ons**
you	**jullie** (familiar)	you	**jullie** (familiar)
they	**zij** or **ze**	them	**hen**

Verbs

First a few handy irregular verbs. If you learn only these, or even only the "I" and polite "you" forms of them, you'll have made a useful start.

1) The indispensible verbs **hebben** (to have) and **zijn** (to be) in the present:

I have	**ik heb**	I am	**ik ben**
you have	**jij hebt**	you are	**jij bent**
you have	**u hebt**	you are	**u bent**
he/she/it has	**hij/zij/het heeft**	he/she/it is	**hij/zij/het is**
we have	**wij hebben**	we are	**wij zijn**
you have	**jullie hebben**	you are	**jullie zijn**
they have	**zij hebben**	they are	**zij zijn**

2) Some more useful irregular verbs (in the present):

Infinitive		willen (to want)	kunnen (can)	gaan (to go)	doen (to do)	weten(to know)
I	ik	wil	kan	ga	doe	weet
you	jij	wilt	kunt	gaat	doet	weet
you	u	wilt	kunt	gaat	doet	weet
he	hij	wil	kan	gaat	doet	weet
she	zij	wil	kan	gaat	doet	weet
It	het	wil	kan	gaat	doet	weet
we	wij	willen	kunnen	gaan	doen	weten
you	jullie	willen	kunnen	gaan	doen	weten
they	zij	willen	kunnen	gaan	doen	weten

3) Infinitive and verb stem:
In Dutch verbs, the infinitive generally ends in **-en: noemen** (to name).
As the verb stem is usually the base for forming tenses, you need to know how to obtain it. The general rule is: the infinitive less **-en**:

infinitive: **noemen**   stem: **noem**

4) Present and past tenses:
First find the stem of the verb (see under 3 above).
Then add the appropriate endings, where applicable, according to the models given below for present and past tenses.

Note: in forming the past tense, the **-de/-den** endings shown in our example are added after most verb stems. However, if the stem ends in **p, t, k, f, s**, or **ch**, add **te/-ten** instead.

Present tense		Past tense	
ik noem	I name	**ik noemde**	I named
jij noemt	you name	**jij noemde**	you named
u noemt	you name	**u noemde**	you named
hij/zij/het noemt	he/she/it names	**hij/zij/het noemde**	he/she/it named
wij noemen	we name	**wij noemden**	we named
jullie noemen	you name	**jullie noemden**	you named
zij noemen	they name	**zij noemden**	they named

5) Past perfect (e.g.: "I have built"):
This tense is generally formed, as in English, by the verb "to have" (**hebben**) (see page 180) + the past participle.
To form the past participle, start with the verb stem, and add **ge-** to the front of it and **-d** or **-t** to the end:

infinitive:	**bouwen** (to build)
verb stem:	**bouw**
past participle:	**gebouwd**

The past participle must be placed *after* the object of the sentence:

Ik heb een huis gebouwd.   I have built a house.

Note: Verbs prefixed by **be-, er-, her-, ont-** and **ver-** do not take **ge-** in the past participle.

Instead of **hebben**, the verb **zijn** (to be) is used with verbs expressing motion (if the destination is specified or implied) or a change of state:

Wij zijn naar Parijs gevlogen.   We have flown to Paris.
Hij is rijk geworden.   He has become rich.

Negatives

To put a verb into the negative, place **niet** (not) after the verb, or after the direct object if there is one:

Ik rook.	I smoke.	**Ik heb de kaartjes.**	I have the tickets.
Ik rook niet.	I don't smoke.	**Ik heb de kaartjes niet.**	I don't have the tickets.

Questions

In Dutch, questions are formed by placing the subject after the verb:

Hij reist.	He travels.	**Ik betaal.**	I pay.
Reist hij?	Does he travel?	**Betaal ik?**	Do I pay?

Questions are also introduced by the following **interrogative pronouns:**

Wie (who)	Who says so?	**Wie zegt dat?**
	Whose house is that?	**Van wie is dat huis?**
Wat (what)	What does he do?	**Wat doet hij?**
Waar (where)	Where is the hotel?	**Waar is het hotel?**
Hoe (how)	How are you?	**Hoe gaat het met u?**

Irregular verbs

The following list contains the most common strong and irregular verbs (*infinitive, past, and past participle forms*). If a compound verb or a verb with a prefix (*be-, con-, dis-, im-, in-, mis-, om-, on-, ont-, ver-*, etc.) is not listed, its forms may be found by looking up the basic verb, e.g. *verbinden* is conjugated as *binden*.

bakken	bakte	gebakken	*bake*
barsten	barstte	gebarsten	*burst, crack*
bederven	bedierf	bedorven	*spoil*
bedriegen	bedroog	bedrogen	*deceive*
beginnen	begon	begonnen	*begin*
bergen	borg	geborgen	*put*
bevelen	beval	bevolen	*order*
bewegen	bewoog	bewogen	*move*
bezwijken	bezweek	bezweken	*succumb*
bidden	bad	gebeden	*pray*
bieden	bood	geboden	*offer*
bijten	beet	gebeten	*bite*
binden	bond	gebonden	*tie*
blazen	blies	geblazen	*blow*
blijken	bleek	gebleken	*prove to be*
blijven	bleef	gebleven	*remain*
blinken	blonk	geblonken	*shine*
braden	braadde	gebraden	*fry*
breken	brak	gebroken	*break*
brengen	bracht	gebracht	*bring*
buigen	boog	gebogen	*bow*
delven	delfde/dolf	gedolven	*dig up*
denken	dacht	gedacht	*think*
dingen	dong	gedongen	*compete (for)*
doen	deed	gedaan	*do*
dragen	droeg	gedragen	*wear*
drijven	dreef	gedreven	*float*
dringen	drong	gedrongen	*push*
drinken	dronk	gedronken	*drink*
druipen	droop	gedropen	*drip*
duiken	dook	gedoken	*dive*
dwingen	dwong	gedwongen	*force*
eten	at	gegeten	*eat*
fluiten	floot	gefloten	*whistle*
gaan	ging	gegaan	*go*
gelden	gold	gegolden	*be valid*
genezen	genas	genezen	*heal*
genieten	genoot	genoten	*enjoy*

geven	gaf	gegeven	*give*
gieten	goot	gegoten	*pour*
glijden	gleed	gegleden	*slide*
glimmen	glom	geglommen	*shine*
graven	groef	gegraven	*dig*
grijpen	greep	gegrepen	*catch*
hangen	hing	gehangen	*hang*
hebben	had	gehad	*have*
heffen	hief	geheven	*raise*
helpen	hielp	geholpen	*help*
heten	heette	geheten	*be called*
hijsen	hees	gehesen	*hoist*
houden	hield	gehouden	*keep*
jagen	jaagde/joeg	gejaagd	*chase*
kiezen	koos	gekozen	*choose*
kijken	keek	gekeken	*look*
klimmen	klom	geklommen	*climb*
klinken	klonk	geklonken	*sound*
knijpen	kneep	geknepen	*pinch*
komen	kwam	gekomen	*come*
kopen	kocht	gekocht	*buy*
krijgen	kreeg	gekregen	*get*
krimpen	kromp	gekrompen	*shrink*
kruipen	kroop	gekropen	*creep*
kunnen	kon	gekund	*can*
lachen	lachte	gelachen	*laugh*
laden	laadde	geladen	*load*
laten	liet	gelaten	*let*
lezen	las	gelezen	*read*
liegen	loog	gelogen	*tell lies*
liggen	lag	gelegen	*lie*
lijden	leed	geleden	*suffer*
lijken	leek	geleken	*seem*
lopen	liep	gelopen	*walk*
malen	maalde	gemalen	*grind*
meten	mat	gemeten	*measure*
moeten	moest	gemoeten	*must*
mogen	mocht	gemogen/gemoogd	*may*
nemen	nam	genomen	*take*
prijzen	prees	geprezen	*praise*
raden	raadde/ried	geraden	*guess*
rijden	reed	gereden	*ride*
rijgen	reeg	geregen	*thread*
rijzen	rees	gerezen	*rise*

roepen	riep	geroepen	*call*
ruiken	rook	geroken	*smell*
scheiden	scheidde	gescheiden	*separate*
schelden	schold	gescholden	*call names*
schenken	schonk	geschonken	*pour*
scheppen	schiep	geschapen	*create*
scheren	schoor	geschoren	*shave*
schieten	schoot	geschoten	*shoot*
schijnen	scheen	geschenen	*shine, seem to be*
schrijden	schreed	geschreden	*stride*
schrijven	schreef	geschreven	*write*
schrikken	schrok	geschrokken	*be frightened*
chuiven	schoof	geschoven	*shove*
slaan	sloeg	geslagen	*hit*
slapen	sliep	geslapen	*sleep*
slijpen	sleep	geslepen	*sharpen*
slijten	sleet	gesleten	*wear down*
sluipen	sloop	geslopen	*sneak*
sluiten	sloot	gesloten	*close*
smelten	smolt	gesmolten	*melt*
snijden	sneed	gesneden	*cut*
spinnen	spon	gesponnen	*spin*
splijten	spleet	gespleten	*split*
spreken	sprak	gesproken	*speak*
springen	sprong	gesprongen	*jump*
spuiten	spoot	gespoten	*squirt*
staan	stond	gestaan	*stand*
steken	stak	gestoken	*sting*
stelen	stal	gestolen	*steal*
sterven	stierf	gestorven	*die*
stijgen	steeg	gestegen	*rise*
stijven	steef	gesteven	*starch*
stinken	stonk	gestonken	*stink*
stoten	stootte/stiet	gestoten	*push*
strijden	streed	gestreden	*fight*
strijken	streek	gestreken	*iron*
treden	trad	getreden	*tread*
treffen	trof	getroffen	*hit*
trekken	trok	getrokken	*pull*
vallen	viel	gevallen	*fall*
vangen	ving	gevangen	*catch*
varen	voer	gevaren	*sail*
vechten	vocht	gevochten	*fight*
verbergen	verborg	verborgen	*hide*

verdwijnen	verdween	verdwenen	*disappear*
vergeten	vergat	vergeten	*forget*
verliezen	verloor	verloren	*lose*
vermijden	vermeed	vermeden	*avoid*
verslinden	verslond	verslonden	*devour*
vinden	vond	gevonden	*find*
vliegen	vloog	gevlogen	*fly*
voortspruiten	sproot voort	voortgesproten	*result*
vouwen	vouwde	gevouwen	*fold*
vragen	vroeg	gevraagd	*ask*
vriezen	vroor	gevroren	*freeze*
waaien	waaide/woei	gewaaid	*blow*
wassen	waste	gewassen	*wash*
wegen	woog	gewogen	*weigh*
werpen	wierp	geworpen	*throw*
werven	wierf	geworven	*recruit*
weten	wist	geweten	*know*
weven	weefde	geweven	*weave*
wijken	week	geweken	*yield*
wijten	weet	geweten	*impute*
wijzen	wees	gewezen	*show*
willen	wilde/wou	gewild	*want*
winden	wond	gewonden	*wind*
winnen	won	gewonnen	*win*
worden	werd	geworden	*become*
wreken	wreekte	gewroken	*revenge*
wrijven	wreef	gewreven	*rub*
zeggen	zei	gezegd	*say*
zenden	zond	gezonden	*send*
zien	zag	gezien	*see*
zijn	was	geweest	*be*
zingen	zong	gezongen	*sing*
zinken	zonk	gezonken	*sink*
zinnen	zon	gezonnen	*brood*
zitten	zat	gezeten	*sit*
zoeken	zocht	gezocht	*seek*
zuigen	zoog	gezogen	*suck*
zullen	zou	–	*shall, will*
zwellen	zwol	gezwollen	*swell*
zwemmen	zwom	gezwommen	*swim*
1) zweren	zwoer	gezworen	*swear*
2) zweren	zweerde/zwoor	gezworen	*ulcerate*
zwerven	zwierf	gezworven	*wander*
zwijgen	zweeg	gezwegen	*be silent*

Dutch Abbreviations

A°	*anno*	(built) in the year
afd.	*afdeling*	department
alg.	*algemeen*	general
A.N.W.B.	*Algemene Nederlandse Wielrijdersbond*	Dutch Touring Association
a.s.	*aanstaande*	next
a.u.b.	*alstublieft*	please
Bfr.	*Belgische frank*	former Belgian monetary unit
b.g.	*begane grond*	ground floor
b.g.g.	*bij geen gehoor*	if no answer
blz.	*bladzijde*	page
B.R.T.	*Belgische Radio en Televisie*	Belgian Broadcasting Company
B.T.W.	*Belasting Toegevoegde Waarde*	VAT, value added tax
b.v.	*bijvoorbeeld*	e.g.
B.V.	*besloten vennootschap*	limited liability company
C.S.	*Centraal Station*	main railway station
ct.	*cent*	1/100 of the guilder
dhr.	*de heer*	Mr.
drs.	*doctorandus*	Master of Arts
d.w.z.	*dat wil zeggen*	i.e.
EU	*Europese Unie*	EU, European Union
E.H.B.O.	*Eerste Hulp bij Ongelukken*	first aid
enz.	*enzovoort*	etc.
excl.	*exclusief*	exclusive, not included
fl/f	*gulden*	former Dutch monetary unit
geb.	*geboren*	born
H.K.H.	*Hare Koninklijke Hoogheid*	Her Royal Highness
H.M.	*Hare Majesteit*	His/Her Majesty
hs	*huis*	ground floor
incl.	*inclusief*	inclusive, included
ing.	*ingenieur (HBO)*	engineer (higher vocational training)
i.p(l).v.	*in plaats van*	in the place of
ir.	*ingenieur (universiteit)*	engineer (university)
jl.	*jongstleden*	last
K.A.C.B.	*Koninklijke Automobielclub van België*	Royal Automobile Association of Belgium
km/u	*kilometer per uur*	kilometres per hour
K.N.A.C.	*Koninklijke Nederlandse Automobielclub*	Royal Dutch Automobile Association
K.N.M.I.	*Koninklijk Nederlands Meteorologisch Instituut*	Royal Dutch Meteorological Institute

m.a.w.	*met andere woorden*	in other words
Mej.	*mejuffrouw*	Miss
Mevr.	*mevrouw*	Mrs.
Mij.	*maatschappij*	company
Mr.	*meester in de rechten*; *mijnheer*	barrister, lawyer; Mr.
Mw	*mevrouw/mejuffrouw*	Ms.
N.A.V.O.	*Noordatlantische Verdrags-organisatie*	NATO
N.B.T.	*Nederlands Bureau voor Toerisme*	Dutch National Tourist Office
n.Chr.	*na Christus*	A.D.
nl.	*namelijk*	namely
n.m.	*namiddag*	afternoon
N.M.B.S.	*Nationale Maatschappij der Belgische Spoorwegen*	Belgian National Railways
N.P.	*niet parkeren*	no parking
N.S.	*Nederlandse Spoorwegen*	Dutch National Railways
N.V.	*naamloze vennootschap*	Ltd. or Inc.
p.a.	*per adres*	in care of
pk	*paardekracht*	horsepower
r.-k./R.-K.	*rooms-katholiek*	Roman Catholic
t./m.	*tot en met*	up to and including
t.o.v.	*ten opzichte van*	with regard to
v.a.	*volgens anderen, vanaf*	from
V.A.B.	*Vlaamse Automobilistenbond*	Flemish Automobile Association
v.Chr.	*voor Christus*	B.C.
v.m.	*voormiddag*	morning
V.N.	*Verenigde Naties*	UN
V.S.	*Verenigde Staten*	USA
V.T.B.	*Vlaamse Toeristenbond*	Flemish Tourist Association
V.V.V.	*Vereniging voor Vreemdelingenverkeer*	tourist-information office
zgn.	*zogenaamd*	so-called
Z.K.H.	*Zijne Koninklijke Hoogheid*	His Royal Highness
z.o.z.	*zie ommezijde*	pto, please turn over

Numerals

Cardinal numbers

0	nul
1	een
2	twee
3	drie
4	vier
5	vijf
6	zes
7	zeven
8	acht
9	negen
10	tien
11	elf
12	twaalf
13	dertien
14	veertien
15	vijftien
16	zestien
17	zeventien
18	achttien
19	negentien
20	twintig
21	eenentwintig
22	tweeëntwintig
23	drieëntwintig
24	vierentwintig
30	dertig
40	veertig
50	vijftig
60	zestig
70	zeventig
80	tachtig
90	negentig
100	honderd
101	honderdeen
230	tweehonderddertig
1.000	duizend
1.001	duizendeen
1.100	elfhonderd
2.000	tweeduizend
1.000.000	een miljoen

Ordinal numbers

1e	eerste
2e	tweede
3e	derde
4e	vierde
5e	vijfde
6e	zesde
7e	zevende
8e	achtste
9e	negende
10e	tiende
11e	elfde
12e	twaalfde
13e	dertiende
14e	veertiende
15e	vijftiende
16e	zestiende
17e	zeventiende
18e	achttiende
19e	negentiende
20e	twintigste
21e	eenentwintigste
22e	tweeëntwintigste
23e	drieëntwintigste
24e	vierentwintigste
25e	vijfentwintigste
26e	zesentwintigste
30e	dertigste
40e	veertigste
50e	vijftigste
60e	zestigste
70e	zeventigste
80e	tachtigste
90e	negentigste
100e	honderdste
101e	honderdeerste
230e	tweehonderddertigste
1000e	duizendste
1001e	duizendeerste
1100e	elfhonderdste
2000e	tweeduizendste

Time

Although official time in Holland and Belgium is based on the 24-hour clock, the 12-hour system is used in conversation.

To avoid confusion, you can make use of the terms *'s morgens* (morning), and *'s middags* (afternoon) or *'s avonds* (evening).

Ik kom om vier uur 's morgens.	I'll come at 4 a.m.
Ik kom om vier uur 's middags.	I'll come at 4 p.m.
Ik kom om acht uur 's avonds.	I'll come at 8 p.m.

Days of the Week

zondag	Sunday	*donderdag*	Thursday
maandag	Monday	*vrijdag*	Friday
dinsdag	Tuesday	*zaterdag*	Saturday
woensdag	Wednesday		

Some Basic Phrases

Please.
Thank you very much.
Don't mention it.
Good morning.
Good afternoon.
Good evening.
Good night.
Good-bye.
See you later.
Where is/Where are...?
What do you call this?
What does that mean?
Do you speak English?
Do you speak German?
Do you speak French?
Do you speak Spanish?
Do you speak Italian?
Could you speak more slowly, please?
I don't understand.
Can I have...?
Can you show me...?
Can you tell me...?
Can you help me, please?
I'd like...
We'd like...
Please give me...
Please bring me...
I'm hungry.
I'm thirsty.
I'm lost.
Hurry up!
There is/There are...
There isn't/There aren't...

Arrival

Your passport, please.
Have you anything to declare?
No, nothing at all.
Can you help me with my luggage, please?

Enkele nuttige zinnen

Alstublieft.
Hartelijk dank.
Niets te danken.
Goedemorgen.
Goedemiddag.
Goedenavond.
Goedenacht.
Tot ziens.
Tot straks.
Waar is/Waar zijn...?
Hoe noemt u dit?
Wat betekent dat?
Spreekt u Engels?
Spreekt u Duits?
Spreekt u Frans?
Spreekt u Spaans?
Spreekt u Italiaans?
Kunt u wat langzamer spreken, alstublieft?
Ik begrijp het niet.
Mag ik...hebben?
Kunt u mij...tonen?
Kunt u mij zeggen...?
Kunt u me helpen?
Ik wil graag...
Wij willen graag...
Geeft u me..., alstublieft.
Brengt u me..., alstublieft.
Ik heb honger.
Ik heb dorst.
Ik ben verdwaald.
Vlug!
Er is/Er zijn...
Er is geen/Er zijn geen...

Aankomst

Uw paspoort, alstublieft.
Hebt u iets aan te geven?
Nee, helemaal niets.
Kunt u me met mijn bagage helpen, alstublieft?

Where's the bus to the centre of town, please?

Waar is de bus naar het centrum?

This way, please.

Hierlangs, alstublieft.

Where can I get a taxi?

Waar kan ik een taxi krijgen?

What's the fare to…?

Wat kost het naar…?

Take me to this address, please.

Breng me naar dit adres, alstublieft.

I'm in a hurry.

Ik heb haast.

Hotel

Hotel

My name is…

Mijn naam is…

Have you a reservation?

Hebt u gereserveerd?

I'd like a room with a bath.

Ik wil graag een kamer met bad.

What's the price per night?

Hoeveel kost het per nacht?

May I see the room?

Mag ik de kamer zien?

What's my room number, please?

Wat is mijn kamernummer?

There's no hot water.

Er is geen warm water.

May I see the manager, please?

Mag ik de directeur spreken, alstublieft?

Did anyone telephone me?

Heeft er iemand voor mij opgebeld?

Is there any mail for me?

Is er post voor mij?

May I have my bill (check), please?

Mag ik de rekening, alstublieft?

Eating out

Uit eten

Do you have a fixed-price menu?

Hebt u een menu à prix fixe?

May I see the menu?

Mag ik de menukaart zien?

May we have an ashtray, please?

Kunt u ons een asbak brengen, alstublieft?

Where's the toilet, please?

Waar is het toilet?

I'd like an hors d'uvre (starter).

Ik wil graag een voorgerecht.

Have you any soup?

Hebt u soep?

I'd like some fish.

Ik wil graag vis.

What kind of fish do you have?

Wat voor vis hebt u?

I'd like a steak.

Ik wil graag een biefstuk.

What vegetables have you got?

Wat voor groenten hebt u?

Nothing more, thanks.

Niets meer, dank u.

What would you like to drink?

Wat wilt u drinken?

I'll have a lager, please.

Een pils, alstublieft.

I'd like a bottle of wine.

Ik wil graag een fles wijn.

May I have the bill (check), please?

Mag ik de rekening, alstublieft?

Is service included?

Is de bediening inbegrepen?

Thank you, that was a very good meal.

Dank u, het was een uitstekende maaltijd.

Travelling

Where's the railway station, please?
Where's the ticket office, please?
I'd like a ticket to...
First or second class?
First class, please.
Single or return (one way or round-trip)?
Do I have to change trains?
What platform does the train for... leave from?
Where's the nearest underground (subway) station?
Where's the bus station, please?
When's the first bus to...?
Please let me off at the next stop.

Reizen

Waar is het station?
Waar is het loket?
Ik wil graag een kaartje naar...
Eerste of tweede klas?
Eerste klas, alstublieft.
Enkele reis of retour?

Moet ik overstappen?
Van welk perron vertrekt de trein naar...?
Waar is het dichtstbijzijnde metrostation?
Waar is het busstation?
Hoe laat vertrekt de eerste bus naar...?
Wilt u me bij de volgende halte laten uitstappen?

Relaxing

What's on at the cinema (movies)?
What time does the film begin?
Are there any tickets for tonight?
Where can we go dancing?

Ontspanning

Wat wordt er in de bioscoop gegeven?
Hoe laat begint de film?
Zijn er nog plaatsen vrij voor vanavond?
Waar kunnen we gaan dansen?

Meeting people

How do you do.
How are you?
Very well, thank you. And you?
May I introduce...?
My name is...
I'm very pleased to meet you.
How long have you been here?
It was nice meeting you.
Do you mind if I smoke?
Do you have a light, please?
May I get you a drink?
May I invite you for dinner tonight?
Where shall we meet?

Ontmoetingen

Dag mevrouw/juffrouw/ mijnheer.
Hoe maakt u het?
Uitstekend, dank u. En u?
Mag ik u... voorstellen?
Mijn naam is...
Prettig kennis met u te maken.
Hoelang bent u al hier?
Het was mij een genoegen.
Hindert het u als ik rook?
Hebt u een vuurtje, alstublieft?
Mag ik u iets te drinken aanbieden?
Mag ik u vanavond ten eten uitnodigen?
Waar spreken we af?

Shops, stores and services

Where's the nearest bank, please?
Where can I cash some travellers' cheques?

Winkels en diensten

Waar is de dichtstbijzijnde bank?
Waar kan ik reischeques inwisselen?

Can you give me some small change, please? — Kunt u me wat kleingeld geven, alstublieft?

Where's the nearest chemist's (pharmacy)? — Waar is de dichtstbijzijnde apotheek?

How do I get there? — Hoe kom ik daar?

Is it within walking distance? — Is het te lopen?

Can you help me, please? — Kunt u mij helpen, alstublieft?

How much is this? And that? — Hoeveel kost dit? En dat?

It's not quite what I want. — Het is niet precies wat ik zoek.

I like it. — Het bevalt me.

Can you recommend something for sunburn? — Kunt u mij iets tegen zonnebrand aanbevelen?

I'd like a haircut, please. — Knippen, alstublieft.

I'd like a manicure, please. — Ik wil een manicure, alstublieft.

Street directions — **De weg vragen**

Can you show me on the map where I am? — Kunt u mij op de kaart aanwijzen waar ik ben?

You are on the wrong road. — U bent op de verkeerde weg.

Go/Walk straight ahead. — Rij/Ga rechtuit.

It's on the left/on the right. — Het is aan de linkerkant/aan de rechterkant.

Emergencies — **Spoedgevallen**

Call a doctor quickly. — Roep vlug een dokter.

Call an ambulance. — Roep een ambulance.

Please call the police. — Roep de politie, alstublieft.

Engels-Nederlands

English-Dutch

Inleiding

Dit woordenboek is zodanig opgezet, dat het zoveel mogelijk beantwoordt aan de eisen van de praktijk. Onnodige taalkundige aanduidingen zijn achterwege gelaten. De volgorde van de woorden is strikt alfabetisch, ook als het samengestelde woorden of woorden met een koppelteken betreft. Wanneer bij een grondwoord nog daarvan afgeleide samenstellingen of uitdrukkingen zijn gegeven, staan ook deze weer in alfabetische volgorde.

Achter elk grondwoord vindt u een fonetische transcriptie (zie de Gids voor de uitspraak) en vervolgens, wanneer van toepassing, de woordsoort. Wanneer bij hetzelfde grondwoord meerdere woordsoorten behoren, zijn de vertalingen telkens naar woordsoort gegroepeerd. Onregelmatige meervouden van zelfstandige naamwoorden zijn altijd opgenomen; tevens is het meervoud gegeven van bepaalde woorden waarover twijfel zou kunnen bestaan.

Wanneer in onregelmatige meervoudsvormen of in afgeleide samenstellingen en uitdrukkingen het teken ~ wordt gebruikt, duidt dit op een herhaling aan van het grondwoord als geheel.

In onregelmatige meervoudsvormen van samengestelde woorden wordt alleen het gedeelte dat verandert voluit geschreven. Het onveranderde deel wordt aangegeven door een liggend streepje (-).

Een sterretje (*) voor een werkwoord geeft aan dat dit werkwoord onregelmatig is. Voor nadere bijzonderheden kunt u de lijst van onregelmatige werkwoorden raadplegen.

Dit woordenboek is gebaseerd op de Britse spelling. Alle woorden en woordbetekenissen die overwegend Amerikaans zijn, zijn als zodanig aangegeven (zie lijst van gebezigde afkortingen).

Afkortingen

adj	bijvoeglijk naamwoord	*num*	telwoord
adv	bijwoord	*p*	verleden tijd
Am	Amerikaans	*pl*	meervoud
art	lidwoord	*plAm*	meervoud (Amerikaans)
c	gemeenslachtig	*pp*	voltooid deelwoord
conj	voegwoord	*pr*	tegenwoordige tijd
f	vrouwelijk	*pref*	voorvoegsel
m	mannelijk	*prep*	voorzetsel
n	zelfstandig naamwoord	*pron*	voornaamwoord
nAm	zelfstandig naamwoord (Amerikaans)	*v*	werkwoord
nt	onzijdig	*vAm*	werkwoord (Amerikaans)

Uitspraak

Elk trefwoord in dit deel van het woordenboek wordt gevolgd door een transcriptie in het internationale fonetische alfabet (IPA). In dit alfabet vertegenwoordigt elk teken altijd dezelfde klank. Letters die hieronder niet beschreven zijn worden min of meer op dezelfde wijze uitgesproken als in het Nederlands.

Medeklinkers

b	nooit scherp zoals in he**b**
d	nooit scherp zoals in raa**d**
ð	als de **z** in **z**ee, maar lispend uitgesproken
g	als een zachte **k**, zoals in het Franse **g**arçon
ŋ	als de **ng** in ba**ng**
r	plaats de tong eerst als voor de ʒ (zie beneden), open dan de mond enigszins en beweeg de tong daarbij naar beneden
ʃ	als de **sj** in **sj**ofel
θ	als de **s** in **s**amen, maar lispend uitgesproken
v	als de **w** in **w**aar
w	een korte, zwakke **oe**-klank
ʒ	als de **g** in eta**g**e

N.B. De lettergroep **sj** moet worden uitgesproken als een **s** gevolgd door een **j**-klank, maar *niet* als in **sj**ofel.

Klinkers

ɑː	als de **aa** in m**aa**t
æ	een klank tussen de **a** in **a**ls en de **e** in b**e**st
ʌ	min of meer als de **a** in **a**ls
e	als in b**e**st
ɛ	als de **e** in b**e**st, maar met de tong wat lager
ə	als de **e** in acht**e**r
ɔ	min of meer als de **o** in p**o**t
u	als de **oe** in g**oe**d, maar korter

1) Een dubbele punt (ː) geeft aan dat de voorafgaande klinker lang is.
2) Enkele aan het Frans ontleende Engelse woorden bevatten neusklanken, die aangegeven worden d.m.v. een tilde boven de klinker (b. v. ã). Deze worden door de neus en de mond tegelijkertijd uitgesproken.

Tweeklanken

Een tweeklank bestaat uit twee klinkers, waarvan er één sterk is (beklemtoond) en de andere zwak (niet beklemtoond) en die samen als één klinker worden uitgesproken, zoals **ei** in het Nederlands. In het Engels is de tweede klinker altijd zwak. Een tweeklank kan soms gevolgd worden door een [ə]. In dergelijke gevallen heeft de tweede klinker van de tweeklank de neiging zeer zwak te worden.

Klemtoon

Het teken (') geeft aan dat de klemtoon op de volgende lettergreep valt. Als in een woord meer dan één lettergreep wordt beklemtoond, wordt het teken (‚) geplaatst vóór de lettergreep, waarop de bijklemtoon valt.

Amerikaanse uitspraak

Onze transcriptie geeft de gebruikelijke Engelse uitspraak aan. De Amerikaanse uitspraak verschilt in enkele opzichten van het Britse Engels en kent daarbij nog belangrijke regionale verschillen. Hier volgen enkele van de meest opvallende afwijkingen:
1) In tegenstelling tot in het Britse Engels wordt de **r** ook uitgesproken voor een medeklinker en aan het einde van een woord.
2) In vele woorden (b. v. *ask*, *castle*, *laugh* enz.) wordt [ɑː] uitgesproken als [æː].
3) De [ɔ]-klank wordt in het Amerikaans uitgesproken als [ɑ], vaak ook als [ɔː].
4) In woorden als *duty*, *tune*, *new* enz. valt in het Amerikaans de [j]-klank voor de [uː] vaak weg.
5) Bovendien wordt bij een aantal woorden in het Amerikaans de klemtoon anders gelegd.

A

a [ei, ə] *art* (an) een *art*

abbey ['æbi] *n* abdij *c*

abbreviation [ə,briːvi'eiʃən] *n* afkorting *c*

ability [ə'biləti] *n* bekwaamheid *c*; vermogen *nt*

able ['eibəl] *adj* in staat; capabel, bekwaam; ***be ~ to** in staat *zijn om; *kunnen

aboard [ə'bɔːd] *adv* aan boord

abolish [ə'bɔliʃ] *v* afschaffen

abortion [ə'bɔːʃən] *n* abortus *c*

about [ə'baut] *prep* over; betreffende, omtrent; om; *adv* omstreeks, ongeveer; omheen

above [ə'bʌv] *prep* boven; *adv* boven

abroad [ə'brɔːd] *adv* naar het buitenland, in het buitenland

abscess ['æbses] *n* abces *nt*

absence ['æbsəns] *n* afwezigheid *c*

absent ['æbsənt] *adj* afwezig

absolutely ['æbsəluːtli] *adv* absoluut

abstain from [əb'stein] zich *onthouden van

abstract ['æbstrækt] *adj* abstract

absurd [əb'səːd] *adj* absurd, ongerijmd

abundance [ə'bʌndəns] *n* overvloed *c*

abundant [ə'bʌndənt] *adj* overvloedig

abuse [ə'bjuːs] *n* misbruik *nt*

abyss [ə'bis] *n* afgrond *c*

academy [ə'kædəmi] *n* academie *c*

accelerate [æk'seləreit] *v* versnellen

accelerator [æk'seləreitə] *n* gaspedaal *nt*

accent ['æksənt] *n* accent *nt*; nadruk *c*

accept [ək'sept] *v* aanvaarden, *aannemen; accepteren

access ['ækses] *n* toegang *c*

accessible [ək'sesəbəl] *adj* toegankelijk

accessories [ək'sesəriz] *pl* toebehoren *pl*, accessoires *pl*

accident ['æksidənt] *n* ongeluk *nt*, ongeval *nt*

accidental [,æksi'dentəl] *adj* toevallig

accommodate [ə'kɔmədeit] *v* *onderbrengen

accommodation [ə,kɔmə'deiʃən] *n* accommodatie *c*, logies *nt*, onderdak *nt*

accompany [ə'kʌmpəni] *v* vergezellen; begeleiden

accomplish [ə'kʌmpliʃ] *v* *volbrengen; bereiken

accordance: in ~ with [in ə'kɔːdəns wið] ingevolge

according to [ə'kɔːdiŋ tuː] volgens; overeenkomstig

account [ə'kaunt] *n* rekening *c*; verslag *nt*; **~ for** verantwoorden; **on ~ of** vanwege

accountable [ə'kauntəbəl] *adj* verklaarbaar; verantwoordelijk

accurate ['ækjurət] *adj* nauwkeurig

accuse [ə'kjuːz] *v* beschuldigen; aanklagen

accused [ə'kjuːzd] *n* verdachte *c*

accustom [ə'kʌstəm] *v* wennen; **accustomed** gewoon, gewend

ache [eik] *v* pijn *doen; *n* pijn *c*

achieve [ə'tʃiːv] *v* bereiken; presteren

achievement [ə'tʃiːvmənt] *n* prestatie *c*

acid ['æsid] *n* zuur *nt*

acknowledge [ək'nɔlidʒ] *v* erkennen; *toegeven; bevestigen

acne ['ækni] *n* acne *c*

acorn ['eikɔːn] *n* eikel *c*

acquaintance [ə'kweintəns] *n* bekende *c*, kennis *c*

acquire [ə'kwaiə] *v* *verwerven

acquisition [,ækwi'ziʃən] *n* acquisitie *c*

acquittal [ə'kwitəl] n vrijspraak c

across [ə'krɔs] prep over; aan de andere kant van; adv aan de overkant

act [ækt] n daad c; bedrijf nt, akte c; nummer nt; v *optreden, handelen; zich *gedragen; toneelspelen

action ['ækʃən] n actie c, handeling c

active ['æktiv] adj actief; bedrijvig

activity [æk'tivəti] n activiteit c

actor ['æktə] n acteur m, toneelspeler m

actress ['æktris] n actrice f, toneelspeelster f

actual ['æktʃuəl] adj eigenlijk, werkelijk

actually ['æktʃuəli] adv feitelijk

acute [ə'kjuːt] adj acuut

adapt [ə'dæpt] v aanpassen

adaptor [ə'dæptə] n verbindingsstuk nt

add [æd] v optellen; toevoegen

addition [ə'diʃən] n optelling c; toevoeging c

additional [ə'diʃənəl] adj extra; bijkomend; bijkomstig

address [ə'dres] n adres nt; v adresseren; *aanspreken

addressee [,ædre'siː] n geadresseerde c

adequate ['ædikwət] adj toereikend; adequaat, passend

adjective ['ædʒiktiv] n bijvoeglijk naamwoord nt

adjoin [ə'dʒ] v grenzen aan

adjourn [ə'dʒəːn] v uitstellen

adjust [ə'dʒʌst] v afstellen; aanpassen

administer [əd'ministə] v toedienen

administration [əd,mini'streiʃən] n administratie c; beheer nt

administrative [əd'ministrətiv] adj administratief; bestuurlijk; ~ law bestuursrecht nt

admiration [,ædmə'reiʃən] n bewondering c

admire [əd'maiə] v bewonderen

admission [əd'miʃən] n toegang c; toelating c

admit [əd'mit] v *toelaten; *toegeven, bekennen

admittance [əd'mitəns] n toegang c; **no ~** verboden toegang

adopt [ə'dɔpt] v adopteren; *aannemen

adorable [ə'dɔrəbl] adj lief

adult ['ædʌlt] n volwassene c; adj volwassen

advance [əd'vaːns] n vooruitgang c; voorschot nt; v *vooruitgaan; *voorschieten; **in ~** vooruit, van tevoren

advanced [əd'vaːnst] adj gevorderd

advantage [əd'vaːntidʒ] n voordeel nt

advantageous [,ædvən'teidʒəs] adj voordelig

adventure [əd'ventʃə] n avontuur nt

adverb ['ædvəːb] n bijwoord nt

advertisement [əd'vəːtismənt] n advertentie c; reclame c

advertising ['ædvətaiziŋ] n reclame c

advice [əd'vais] n advies nt, raad c

advise [əd'vaiz] v adviseren, *aanraden

advocate ['ædvəkət] n voorstander c, voorvechter c

aerial ['ɛəriəl] n antenne c

aeroplane ['ɛərəplein] n vliegtuig nt

affair [ə'fɛə] n aangelegenheid c; verhouding c, affaire c

affect [ə'fekt] v beïnvloeden; *betreffen

affected [ə'fektid] adj geaffecteerd

affection [ə'fekʃən] n genegenheid c; aandoening c

affectionate [ə'fekʃənit] adj lief, aanhankelijk

affiliated [ə'filieitid] adj aangesloten

affirm [ə'fəːm] v bevestigen, beamen

affirmative [ətiv] adj bevestigend

afford [əˈfɔːd] v zich veroorloven

afraid [əˈfreid] adj angstig, bang; ***be ~** bang *zijn

Africa [ˈæfrikə] Afrika

African [ˈæfrikən] adj Afrikaans; n Afrikaan m, -se f

after [ˈɑːftə] prep na; achter; conj nadat

afternoon [ˌɑːftəˈnuːn] n middag c, namiddag c; **this ~** vanmiddag

afterwards [ˈɑːftəwədz] adv later; nadien, naderhand

again [əˈgen] adv weer; opnieuw; **~and again** telkens

against [əˈgenst] prep tegen

age [eidʒ] n leeftijd c; ouderdom c; **of ~** meerderjarig; **under ~** minderjarig

aged [ˈeidʒid] adj bejaard; oud

agency [ˈeidʒənsi] n agentschap nt; bureau nt; vertegenwoordiging c

agenda [əˈdʒendə] n agenda c

agent [ˈeidʒənt] n vertegenwoordiger m, vertegenwoordigster f, agent m, -e f

aggressive [əˈgresiv] adj agressief

ago [əˈgou] adv geleden

agree [əˈɡriː] v het eens *zijn; toestemmen; *overeenkomen

agreeable [əˈgriːəbəl] adj aangenaam

agreement [əˈgriːmənt] n contract nt; akkoord nt, overeenkomst c, overeenstemming c

agriculture [ˈægrikʌltʃə] n landbouw c

ahead [əˈhed] adv vooruit; **~ of** voor; ***go ~** *doorgaan; **straight ~** rechtuit

aid [eid] n hulp c; v *bijstaan, *helpen

AIDS [eidz] n AIDS

aim [eim] n doel nt; **~ at** richten op, mikken op; beogen, nastreven

air [ɛə] n lucht c; v luchten

air bag [ˈɛəbæg] n airbag c

air conditioning [ˈɛəkən,diʃəniŋ] n airconditioning c, luchtverversing c; **air-conditioned** adj air conditioned

aircraft [ˈɛəkrɑːft] n (pl ~) vliegtuig nt; toestel nt

airfield [ˈɛəfiːld] n vliegveld nt

air-filter [ˈɛə,filtə] n luchtfilter nt

airline [ˈɛəlain] n luchtvaartmaatschappij c

airmail [ˈɛəmeil] n luchtpost c

airplane [ˈɛəplein] nAm vliegtuig nt

airport [ˈɛəpɔːt] n luchthaven c

airsickness [ˈɛə,siknəs] n luchtziekte c

airtight [ˈɛətait] adj luchtdicht

airy [ˈɛəri] adj luchtig

aisle [ail] n zijbeuk c; gangpad nt

alarm [əˈlɑːm] n alarm nt; v alarmeren; **~-clock** wekker c

album [ˈælbəm] n album nt

alcohol [ˈælkəhɔl] n alcohol c

alcoholic [ˌælkəˈhɔlik] adj alcoholisch, n alcoholist c

ale [eil] n bier nt

algebra [ˈældʒibrə] n algebra c

Algeria [ælˈdʒiəriə] Algerije

Algerian [ælˈdʒiəriən] adj Algerijns; n Algerijn m, -se f

alien [ˈeiliən] n buitenlander c; vreemdeling c; adj buitenlands

alike [əˈlaik] adj eender, gelijk

alive [əˈlaiv] adj in leven, levend

all [ɔːl] adj al, allemaal; **~ in** alles inbegrepen; **~ right!** goed!; **at ~** helemaal

allergic [əˈlɔdʒik] adj allergisch

allergy [ˈælədʒi] n allergie c

alley [ˈæli] n steeg c

alliance [əˈlaiəns] n bondgenootschap nt

allow [əˈlau] v veroorloven, *toestaan; **~ to** *laten; ***be allowed** *mogen; ***be allowed to** *mogen

allowance [əˈlauəns] n toelage c

all-round [ˌɔːlˈraund] adj veelzijdig

almond [ˈɑːmənd] n amandel c

almost [ˈɔːlmoust] adv bijna; haast

alone [əˈloun] adv alleen

along [ə'lɔŋ] *prep* langs

aloud [ə'laud] *adv* hardop

alphabet ['ælfəbet] *n* alfabet *nt*

already [ɔːl'redi] *adv* reeds, al

also ['ɔːlsou] *adv* ook; tevens, eveneens

altar ['ɔːltə] *n* altaar *nt*

alter ['ɔːltə] *v* wijzigen, veranderen

alteration [,ɔːltə'reiʃən] *n* wijziging *c*, verandering *c*

alternate [ɔːl'təːnət] *adj* afwisselend

alternative [ɔːl'təːnətiv] *n* alternatief *nt*

although [ɔːl'ðou] *conj* ofschoon, hoewel

altitude ['æltitjuːd] *n* hoogte *c*

alto ['æltou] *n* (pl ∼s) alt *c*

altogether [,ɔːltə'geðə] *adv* helemaal; in totaal

always ['ɔːlweiz] *adv* altijd

am [æm] *v* (pr be)

amaze [ə'meiz] *v* verwonderen, verbazen

amazement [ə'meizmənt] *n* verbazing *c*

amazing [ə'meiziŋ] *adj* verbazingwekkend, verbazend

ambassador [æm'bæsədə] *n* ambassadeur *m*, ambassadrice *f*

amber ['æmbə] *n* barnsteen *nt*; *adj* oranje

ambiguous [æm'bigjuəs] *adj* dubbelzinnig; onduidelijk

ambition [æm'biʃən] *n* ambitie *c*

ambitious [æm'biʃəs] *adj* ambitieus

ambulance ['æmbjuləns] *n* ziekenauto *c*, ambulance *c*

ambush ['æmbuʃ] *n* hinderlaag *c*

America [ə'merikə] Amerika

American [ə'merikən] *adj* Amerikaans; *n* Amerikaan *m*, -se *f*

amethyst ['æmiθist] *n* amethist *c*

amid [ə'mid] *prep* onder; tussen, midden in, te midden van

ammonia [ə'mouniə] *n* ammonia *c*

amnesty ['æmnisti] *n* amnestie *c*

among [ə'mʌŋ] *prep* te midden van; tussen, onder; ∼ **other things** onder andere

amount [ə'maunt] *n* hoeveelheid *c*; som *c*, bedrag *nt*; ∼ **to** *bedragen

amuse [ə'mjuːz] *v* amuseren, vermaken

amusement [ə'mjuːzmənt] *n* amusement *nt*, vermaak *nt*

amusing [ə'mjuːziŋ] *adj* amusant

anaemia [ə'niːmiə] *n* bloedarmoede *c*

anaesthesia [,ænis'θiːziə] *n* verdoving *c*

anaesthetic [,ænis'θetik] *n* pijnstillend middel *nt*

analyse ['ænəlaiz] *v* ontleden, analyseren

analysis [ə'næləsis] *n* (pl -ses) analyse *c*

analyst ['ænəlist] *n* analist *c*; analyticus *c*

anarchy ['ænəki] *n* anarchie *c*

anatomy [ə'nætəmi] *n* anatomie *c*

ancestor ['ænsestə] *n* voorvader *c*

anchor ['æŋkə] *n* anker *c*

anchovy ['æntʃəvi] *n* ansjovis *c*

ancient ['einʃənt] *adj* oud; ouderwets, verouderd; oeroud

and [ænd, ənd] *conj* en

angel ['eindʒəl] *n* engel *c*

anger ['æŋgə] *n* toorn *c*, boosheid *c*; woede *c*

angle ['æŋgəl] *v* hengelen; *n* hoek *c*

angry ['æŋgri] *adj* kwaad

animal ['æniməl] *n* dier *nt*

ankle ['æŋkəl] *n* enkel *c*

annex[1] ['æneks] *n* bijgebouw *nt*; bijlage *c*

annex[2] [ə'neks] *v* annexeren

anniversary [,æni'vəːsəri] *n* verjaardag *c*

announce [ə'nauns] *v* bekendmaken,

aankondigen
announcement [ə'naunsmənt] *n*
aankondiging *c*, bekendmaking *c*
annoy [ə'nɔi] *v* irriteren, ergeren
annoyance [ə'nɔiəns] *n* ergernis *c*
annoying [ə'nɔiiŋ] *adj* vervelend,
hinderlijk
annual ['ænjuəl] *adj* jaarlijks; *n*
jaarboek *nt*
annum: per ~ [pər 'ænəm] jaarlijks
anonymous [ə'nɔniməs] *adj* anoniem
another [ə'nʌðə] *adj* nog een; een
ander
answer ['ɑːnsə] *v* antwoorden;
beantwoorden; *n* antwoord *nt*
ant [ænt] *n* mier *c*
antibiotic [,æntibai'ɔtik] *n*
antibioticum *nt*
anticipate [æn'tisipeit] *v* verwachten,
*voorzien; *voorkomen
antifreeze ['æntifriːz] *n* antivries *c*
antipathy [æn'tipəθi] *n* afkeer *c*
antique [æn'tiːk] *adj* antiek; *n*
antiquiteit *c*; ~ **dealer** antiquair *c*
antiquity [æn'tikwəti] *n* Oudheid *c*;
antiquities *pl* oudheden *pl*
anxiety [æŋ'zaiəti] *n* bezorgdheid *c*
anxious ['æŋkʃəs] *adj* verlangend;
bezorgd
any ['eni] *adj* enig
anybody ['enibɔdi] *pron* wie dan ook
anyhow ['enihau] *adv* hoe dan ook
anyone ['eniwʌn] *pron* iedereen
anything ['eniθiŋ] *pron* wat dan ook
anyway ['eniwei] *adv* in elk geval
anywhere ['eniwɛə] *adv* waar dan ook;
overal
apart [ə'pɑːt] *adv* apart, afzonderlijk; ~
from afgezien van
apartment [ə'pɑːtmənt] *nAm*
appartement *nt*, flat *c*; etage *c*; ~
house *Am* flatgebouw *nt*
aperitif [ə'perətiv] *n* aperitief *nt*/*c*
apologize [ə'pɔlədʒaiz] *v* zich

verontschuldigen
apology [ə'pɔlədʒi] *n* excuus *nt*,
verontschuldiging *c*
apparatus [,æpə'reitəs] *n* apparaat *nt*,
toestel *nt*
apparent [ə'pærənt] *adj* schijnbaar;
duidelijk
apparently [ə'pærəntli] *adv* blijkbaar;
klaarblijkelijk
appeal [ə'piːl] *n* beroep *nt*;
aantrekkingskracht *c*; verzoek *nt*; *v* in
beroep gaan; *aanspreken;
*verzoeken
appear [ə'piə] *v* lijken, *schijnen;
*blijken; *verschijnen; *optreden
appearance [ə'piərəns] *n* voorkomen
nt; aanblik *c*; optreden *nt*
appendicitis [ə,pendi'saitis] *n*
blindedarmontsteking *c*
appendix [ə'pendiks] *n* (pl -dices,
-dixes) blindedarm *c*; bijlage *c*
appetite ['æpətait] *n* trek *c*, eetlust *c*
appetizer ['æpətaizə] *n* borrelhapje *nt*
appetizing ['æpətaiziŋ] *adj* smakelijk
applaud [ə'plɔːd] *v* applaudisseren *nt*,
klappen; loven
applause [ə'plɔːz] *n* applaus *nt*
apple ['æpəl] *n* appel *c*
appliance [ə'plaiəns] *n* toestel *nt*,
apparaat *nt*
application [,æpli'keiʃən] *n*
toepassing *c*; aanvraag *c*; sollicitatie *c*
apply [ə'plai] *v* toepassen; gebruiken;
solliciteren; *gelden
appoint [ə'pɔint] *v* aanstellen,
benoemen
appointment [ə'pɔintmənt] *n*
afspraak *c*; benoeming *c*
appreciate [ə'priːʃieit] *v* schatten;
waarderen, op prijs stellen
appreciation [ə,priːʃi'eiʃən] *n*
schatting *c*; waardering *c*
apprentice [ə'prentis] *n* leerling *c*
approach [ə'proutʃ] *v* naderen; *n*

aanpak c; toegang c

appropriate [ə'proupriət] adj juist, geschikt, passend

approval [ə'pru:vəl] n goedkeuring c; instemming c; **on ~** op zicht

approve [ə'pru:v] v goedkeuren; **~ of** instemmen met

approximate [ə'prɔksimət] adj bij benadering

approximately [ə'prɔksimətli] adv circa, ongeveer

apricot ['eiprikɔt] n abrikoos c

April ['eiprəl] april

apron ['eiprən] n schort c

Arab ['ærəb] adj Arabisch; n Arabier m, Arabische f

arbitrary ['ɑːbitrəri] adj willekeurig

arcade [ɑː'keid] n zuilengang c, galerij c

arch [ɑːtʃ] n boog c; gewelf nt

archaeologist [,ɑːki'ɔlədʒist] n archeoloog m

archaeology [,ɑːki'ɔlədʒi] n oudheidkunde c, archeologie c

archbishop [,ɑːtʃ'biʃəp] n aartsbisschop m

arched [ɑːtʃt] adj boogvormig

architect ['ɑːkitekt] n architect c

architecture ['ɑːkitektʃə] n bouwkunde c, architectuur c

archives ['ɑːkaivz] pl archief nt

are [ɑː] v (pr be)

area ['ɛəriə] n streek c; gebied nt; oppervlakte c; **~ code** netnummer nt

Argentina [,ɑːdʒən'tiːnə] Argentinië

Argentinian [,ɑːdʒən'tiniən] adj Argentijns; n Argentijn m, -se f

argue ['ɑːgjuː] v argumenteren, debatteren, discussiëren; redetwisten

argument ['ɑːgjumənt] n argument nt; discussie c; woordenwisseling c

*arise [ə'raiz] v *oprijzen, *ontstaan

arithmetic [ə'riθmətik] n rekenkunde c

arm [ɑːm] n arm c; wapen nt; leuning c; v bewapenen

armchair ['ɑːmtʃɛə] n fauteuil c, leunstoel c

armed [ɑːmd] adj gewapend; **~ forces** strijdkrachten pl

armour ['ɑːmə] n harnas nt

army ['ɑːmi] n leger nt

aroma [ə'roumə] n aroma nt

around [ə'raund] prep om, rond; adv rondom

arrange [ə'reindʒ] v rangschikken, ordenen; regelen

arrangement [ə'reindʒmənt] n regeling c

arrest [ə'rest] v arresteren; n aanhouding c, arrestatie c

arrival [ə'raivəl] n aankomst c; komst c

arrive [ə'raiv] v *aankomen

arrow ['ærou] n pijl c

art [ɑːt] n kunst c; vaardigheid c; **~ collection** kunstverzameling c; **~ exhibition** kunsttentoonstelling c; **~ gallery** kunstgalerij c; **~ history** kunstgeschiedenis c; **arts and crafts** kunstnijverheid c; **~ school** kunstacademie c

artery ['ɑːtəri] n slagader c

artichoke ['ɑːtitʃouk] n artisjok c

article ['ɑːtikəl] n artikel nt; lidwoord nt

artificial [,ɑːti'fiʃəl] adj kunstmatig

artist ['ɑːtist] n kunstenaar m, kunstenares f

artistic [ɑː'tistik] adj artistiek, kunstzinnig

as [æz] conj als, zoals; even; aangezien, omdat; **~ from** vanaf; met ingang van; **~ if** alsof

asbestos [æz'bestɔs] n asbest nt

ascend [ə'send] v omhoog *gaan; *opstijgen; *beklimmen

ascent [ə'sent] n stijging c; beklimming c

ascertain [,æsə'tein] *v* constateren; zich vergewissen van

ash [æʃ] *n* as *c*

ashamed [ə'ʃeimd] *adj* beschaamd; ***be ~** zich schamen

ashore [ə'ʃɔː] *adv* aan land

ashtray ['æʃtrei] *n* asbak *c*

Asia ['eiʃə] Azië

Asian ['eiʃən] *adj* Aziatisch; *n* Aziaat *m*, Aziatische *f*

aside [ə'said] *adv* opzij, terzijde

ask [ɑːsk] *v* *vragen; *verzoeken; uitnodigen

asleep [ə'sliːp] *adj* in slaap

asparagus [ə'spærəgəs] *n* asperge *c*

aspect ['æspekt] *n* aspect *nt*; aanzien *nt*

asphalt ['æsfælt] *n* asfalt *nt*

aspire [ə'spaiə] *v* streven

aspirin ['æspərin] *n* aspirine *c*

assassination [ə,sæsi'neiʃən] *n* moord *c*

assault [ə'sɔːlt] *v* *aanvallen; aanranden

assemble [ə'sembəl] *v* *bijeenbrengen; in elkaar zetten, monteren

assembly [ə'sembli] *n* vergadering *c*, bijeenkomst *c*

assignment [ə'sainmənt] *n* opdracht *c*

assign to [ə'sain] *opdragen aan; *toeschrijven aan

assist [ə'sist] *v* *bijstaan, *helpen; **~ at** bijwonen

assistance [ə'sistəns] *n* hulp *c*; steun *c*, bijstand *c*

assistant [ə'sistənt] *n* assistent *c*

associate [ə'souʃiət] *n* partner *c*, vennoot *c*; bondgenoot *c*; lid *nt*; *v* associëren; **~ with** *omgaan met

association [ə,sousi'eiʃən] *n* genootschap *nt*, vereniging *c*

assort [ə'sɔːt] *v* sorteren

assortment [ə'sɔːtmənt] *n* assortiment *nt*, sortering *c*

assume [ə'sjuːm] *v* *aannemen, veronderstellen

assure [ə'ʃuə] *v* verzekeren

asthma ['æsmə] *n* astma *nt*

astonish [ə'stɔniʃ] *v* verbazen

astonishing [ə'stɔniʃiŋ] *adj* verbazend, verbazingwekkend

astonishment [ə'stɔniʃmənt] *n* verbazing *c*

astronaut ['æstrənɔːt] *n* astronaut *m*, -e *f*, ruimtevaarder *m*

astronomy [ə'strɔnəmi] *n* sterrenkunde *c*

asylum [ə'sailəm] *n* asiel *nt*; gesticht *nt*, tehuis *nt*

at [æt] *prep* in, bij, op; naar

ate [et] *v* (p eat)

atheist ['eiθiist] *n* atheïst *m*, -e *f*

athlete ['æθliːt] *n* atleet *c*

athletics [æθ'letiks] *pl* atletiek *c*

Atlantic [ət'læntik] Atlantische Oceaan

ATM *n* geldautomaat *c*

atmosphere ['ætməsfiə] *n* atmosfeer *c*; sfeer *c*, stemming *c*

atom ['ætəm] *n* atoom *nt*

atomic [ə'tɔmik] *adj* atomisch; atoom-

atomizer ['ætəmaizə] *n* sproeier *c*; spuitbus *c*, verstuiver *c*

attach [ə'tætʃ] *v* hechten, vastmaken; aanhechten; bijvoegen; **attached to** gehecht aan

attack [ə'tæk] *v* *aanvallen; *n* aanval *c*

attain [ə'tein] *v* bereiken

attainable [ə'teinəbəl] *adj* haalbaar; bereikbaar

attempt [ə'tempt] *v* pogen, proberen, trachten; *n* poging *c*

attend [ə'tend] *v* bijwonen; **~ on** bedienen; **~ to** *passen op, zich *bezighouden met; letten op, aandacht besteden aan

attendance [ə'tendəns] *n* opkomst *c*

attendant [ə'tendənt] *n* oppasser *c*

attention [ə'tenʃən] n aandacht c; ***pay ~** opletten; **attract ~** opvallen

attentive [ə'tentiv] adj oplettend

attest [ə'test] v getuigen; officieel bevestigen

attic ['ætik] n zolder c

attitude ['ætitjuːd] n houding c

attorney [ə'təːni] n advocaat c

attract [ə'trækt] v *aantrekken

attraction [ə'trækʃən] n attractie c; aantrekking c, bekoring c

attractive [ə'træktiv] adj aantrekkelijk

auction ['ɔːkʃən] n veiling c

audible ['ɔːdibəl] adj hoorbaar

audience ['ɔːdiəns] n publiek nt

auditor ['ɔːditə] n toehoorder m, toehoorster f

auditorium [,ɔːdi'tɔːriəm] n aula c

August ['ɔːgəst] augustus

aunt [ɑːnt] n tante f

Australia [ɔ'streiliə] Australië

Australian [ɔ'streiliən] adj Australisch; n Australiër m, Australische f

Austria ['ɔstriə] Oostenrijk

Austrian ['ɔstriən] adj Oostenrijks; n Oostenrijker m, Oostenrijkse f

authentic [ɔː'θentik] adj authentiek; echt

author ['ɔːθə] n auteur c, schrijver m, schrijfster f

authoritarian [ɔː,θori'teəriən] adj autoritair

authority [ɔː'θorəti] n gezag nt; macht c; **authorities** pl autoriteiten pl, overheid c

authorization [,ɔːθərai'zeiʃən] n machtiging c; toestemming c

automatic [,ɔːtə'mætik] adj automatisch

automation [,ɔːtə'meiʃən] n automatisering c

automobile ['ɔːtəməbiːl] n auto c; **~ club** automobielclub c

autonomous [ɔː'tonəməs] adj autonoom

autopsy ['ɔːtopsi] n autopsie c

autumn ['ɔːtəm] n najaar nt, herfst c

available [ə'veiləbəl] adj verkrijgbaar, voorhanden, beschikbaar

avalanche ['ævəlɑːnʃ] n lawine c

avenue ['ævənjuː] n laan c

average ['ævəridʒ] adj gemiddeld; n gemiddelde nt; **on the ~** gemiddeld

averse [ə'vəːs] adj afkerig

aversion [ə'vəːʃən] n tegenzin c

avert [ə'vəːt] v afwenden

avoid [ə'void] v *vermijden; *ontwijken

await [ə'weit] v wachten op, afwachten

awake [ə'weik] adj wakker

*awake [ə'weik] v wekken

award [ə'wɔːd] n prijs c; v toekennen

aware [ə'weə] adj bewust

away [ə'wei] adv weg; ***go ~** v *weggaan

awful ['ɔːfəl] adj afschuwelijk, verschrikkelijk

awkward ['ɔːkwəd] adj pijnlijk; onhandig

awning ['ɔːniŋ] n zonnescherm nt

axe [æks] n bijl c

axle ['æksəl] n as c

B

baby ['beibi] n baby c; ~ **carriage** Am kinderwagen c

babysitter ['beibi,sitə] n babysitter c

bachelor ['bætʃələ] n vrijgezel c

back [bæk] n rug c; adv terug; *go ~ *teruggaan

backache ['bækeik] n rugpijn c

backbone ['bækboun] n ruggegraat c

background ['bækgraund] n achtergrond c; vorming c

backwards ['bækwədz] adv achteruit

bacon ['beikən] n spek nt

bacterium [bæk'ti:riəm] n (pl -ria) bacterie c

bad [bæd] adj slecht; ernstig, erg; stout

bag [bæg] n zak c; tas c, handtas c; koffer c

baggage ['bægidʒ] n bagage c; ~ **deposit office** Am bagagedepot nt; **hand ~** Am handbagage c

bail [beil] n borgsom c

bait [beit] n aas nt

bake [beik] v *bakken

baker ['beikə] n bakker m

bakery ['beikəri] n bakkerij c

balance ['bæləns] n evenwicht nt; balans c; saldo nt

balcony ['bælkəni] n balkon nt

bald [bɔːld] adj kaal

ball [bɔːl] n bal c; bal nt

ballet ['bælei] n ballet nt

balloon [bə'luːn] n ballon c

ballpoint pen ['bɔːlpɔintpen] n ballpoint c

ballroom ['bɔːlruːm] n danszaal c

bamboo [bæm'buː] n (pl ~s) bamboe nt

banana [bə'nɑːnə] n banaan c

band [bænd] n orkest nt; band c

bandage ['bændidʒ] n verband nt

bandit ['bændit] n bandiet m

bangle ['bæŋgəl] n armband c

bank [bæŋk] n oever c; bank c; v deponeren; ~ **account** bankrekening c

banknote ['bæŋknout] n bankbiljet nt

bank rate ['bæŋkreit] n disconto nt

bankrupt ['bæŋkrʌpt] adj failliet, bankroet

banner ['bænə] n vaandel nt

banquet ['bæŋkwit] n banket nt

baptism ['bæptizəm] n doopsel nt, doop c

baptize [bæp'taiz] v dopen

bar [bɑː] n bar c; stang c; tralie c

barbecue ['bɑːbikjuː] n barbecue c; v barbecue

barbed wire ['bɑːbd waiə] n prikkeldraad c

barber ['bɑːbə] n kapper m

bare [bɛə] adj naakt, bloot; kaal

barely ['bɛəli] adv nauwelijks

bargain ['bɑːgin] n koopje nt; v *afdingen

baritone ['bæritoun] n bariton m

bark [bɑːk] n bast c; v blaffen

barley ['bɑːli] n gerst c

barmaid ['bɑːmeid] n barjuffrouw f

barman ['bɑːmən] n (pl -men) barman m

barn [bɑːn] n schuur c

barometer [bə'rɔmitə] n barometer c

baroque [bə'rɔk] adj barok

barracks ['bærəks] pl kazerne c

barrel ['bærəl] n ton c, vat nt

barrier ['bæriə] n barrière c; slagboom c

barrister ['bæristə] n advocaat c

bartender ['bɑː,tendə] n barman m

base [beis] n basis c; grondslag c; v baseren

baseball ['beisbɔːl] n honkbal c

basement ['beismənt] n souterrain nt, kelder

basic ['beisik] adj fundamenteel; ~s n

grondbeginselen *pl*; basiskennis *c*
basilica [bə'zilikə] *n* basiliek *c*
basin ['beisən] *n* kom *c*, bekken *nt*
basis ['beisis] *n* (pl bases) grondslag *c*, basis *c*
basket ['bɑːskit] *n* mand *c*
bass¹ [beis] *n* bas *c*
bass² [bæs] *n* (pl ~) baars *c*
bastard ['bɑːstəd] *n* bastaard *c*; schoft *c*
batch [bætʃ] *n* partij *c*; lichting *c*
bath [bɑːθ] *n* bad *nt*; ~ **salts** badzout *nt*; ~ **towel** badhanddoek *c*
bathe [beið] *v* baden, een bad *nemen
bathing cap ['beiðiŋkæp] *n* badmuts *c*
bathing suit ['beiðiŋsuːt] *n* badpak *nt*; zwembroek *c*
bathing trunks ['beiðiŋtrʌŋks] *n* zwembroek *c*
bathrobe ['bɑːθroub] *n* badjas *c*
bathroom ['bɑːθruːm] *n* badkamer *c*; toilet *nt*
batter ['bætə] *n* beslag *nt*
battery ['bætəri] *n* batterij *c*; accu *c*
battle ['bætəl] *n* slag *c*; strijd *c*, gevecht *nt*; *v* *vechten
bay [bei] *n* baai *c*; *v* blaffen
***be** [biː] *v* *zijn; zich *bevinden
beach [biːtʃ] *n* strand *nt*; **nudist ~** naaktstrand *nt*
bead [biːd] *n* kraal *c*; **beads** *pl* kralensnoer *nt*; rozenkrans *c*
beak [biːk] *n* snavel *c*; bek *c*
beam [biːm] *n* straal *c*; balk *c*
bean [biːn] *n* boon *c*
bear [bɛə] *n* beer *c*
***bear** [bɛə] *v* *dragen; dulden; *verdragen
beard [biəd] *n* baard *c*
bearer ['bɛərə] *n* drager *m*, draagster *f*
beast [biːst] *n* beest *nt*; ~ **of prey** roofdier *nt*
***beat** [biːt] *v* *slaan; *verslaan
beautiful ['bjuːtifəl] *adj* mooi

beauty ['bjuːti] *n* schoonheid *c*; ~ **parlo(u)r** schoonheidssalon *c*; ~ **salon** schoonheidssalon *c*; ~ **treatment** schoonheidsbehandeling *c*
beaver ['biːvə] *n* bever *c*
because [bi'kɔz] *conj* omdat; aangezien; doordat; ~ **of** vanwege, wegens
***become** [bi'kʌm] *v* *worden; goed *staan
bed [bed] *n* bed *nt*; ~ **and board** vol pension, kost en inwoning; ~ **and breakfast** logies en ontbijt
bedding ['bediŋ] *n* beddegoed *nt*
bedroom ['bedruːm] *n* slaapkamer *c*
bee [biː] *n* bij *c*
beech [biːtʃ] *n* beuk *c*
beef [biːf] *n* rundvlees *nt*
beefburger ['biːfbəːgə] *n* hamburger *c*
beehive ['biːhaiv] *n* bijenkorf *c*
been [biːn] *v* (pp be)
beer [biə] *n* bier *nt*; pils *c/nt*
beet [biːt] *n* biet *c*
beetle ['biːtəl] *n* kever *c*
before [bi'fɔː] *prep* voor; *conj* voordat; *adv* van tevoren; eerder, tevoren
beg [beg] *v* bedelen; smeken; *vragen
beggar ['begə] *n* bedelaar *m*, bedelaarster *f*
***begin** [bi'gin] *v* *beginnen; *aanvangen
beginner [bi'ginə] *n* beginneling *c*
beginning [bi'giniŋ] *n* begin *nt*; aanvang *c*
behalf: on ~ of [ɔn bi'hɑːf ɔv] namens, in naam van; ten behoeve van
behave [bi'heiv] *v* zich *gedragen
behavio(u)r [bi'heivjə] *n* gedrag *nt*
behind [bi'haind] *prep* achter; *adv* achteraan; *n* achterwerk *nt*
beige [beiʒ] *adj* beige
being ['biːiŋ] *n* wezen *nt*
Belgian ['beldʒən] *adj* Belgisch; *n* Belg *m*, Belgische *f*

Belgium ['beldʒəm] België

belief [bi'li:f] n geloof nt

believe [bi'li:v] v geloven

bell [bel] n klok c; bel c

bellboy ['belbɔi] n piccolo m

belly ['beli] n buik c

belong [bi'lɔŋ] v toebehoren

belongings [bi'lɔŋiŋz] pl bezittingen pl

beloved [bi'lʌvd] adj bemind

below [bi'lou] prep onder; beneden; adv onderaan, beneden

belt [belt] n riem c; **garter ~** Am jarretelgordel c

bench [bentʃ] n bank c

bend [bend] n bocht c; kromming c

***bend** [bend] v *buigen; **~ down** zich bukken

beneath [bi'ni:θ] prep onder; adv beneden

benefit ['benifit] n winst c, baat c; voordeel nt; v profiteren

bent [bent] adj (pp bend) krom

beret ['berei] n baret c

berry ['beri] n bes c

beside [bi'said] prep naast

besides [bi'saidz] adv bovendien; trouwens; prep behalve

best [best] adj best

bet [bet] n weddenschap c; inzet c

***bet** [bet] v wedden

betray [bi'trei] v *verraden

better ['betə] adj beter

between [bi'twi:n] prep tussen

beverage ['bevəridʒ] n drank c

beware [bi'wɛə] v zich hoeden, oppassen

bewitch [bi'witʃ] v beheksen, betoveren

beyond [bi'jɔnd] prep verder dan; voorbij; behalve; adv verder

bible ['baibəl] n bijbel c

bicycle ['baisikəl] n fiets c; rijwiel nt

bid [bid] n bod nt, nAm aanbod nt; v *bieden; *bevelen

big [big] adj groot; omvangrijk; dik; gewichtig

bike [baik] n fiets c; rijwiel nt; motorfiets c; v fietsen

bile [bail] n gal c

bilingual [bai'liŋgwəl] adj tweetalig

bill [bil] n rekening c; nota c; v factureren

billion ['biljən] n miljard c

billiards ['biljədz] pl biljart nt

***bind** [baind] v *binden

binoculars [bi'nɔkjələz] pl verrekijker c; toneelkijker c

biology [bai'ɔlədʒi] n biologie c

birch [bə:tʃ] n berk c

bird [bə:d] n vogel c; vulgar griet c

biro® ['bairou] n ballpoint c

birth [bə:θ] n geboorte c

birthday ['bə:θdei] n verjaardag c

biscuit ['biskit] n koekje nt

bishop ['biʃəp] n bisschop m

bit [bit] n stukje nt; beetje nt

bitch [bitʃ] n teef c

bite [bait] n hap c; beet c; steek c

***bite** [bait] v *bijten

bitter ['bitə] adj bitter

black [blæk] adj zwart;**~market** zwarte markt

blackberry ['blækbəri] n braam c

blackbird ['blækbə:d] n merel c

blackboard ['blækbɔ:d] n schoolbord nt

blackcurrant [,blæk'kʌrənt] n zwarte bes c

blackmail ['blækmeil] n chantage c; v chanteren

blacksmith ['blæksmiθ] n smid m

bladder ['blædə] n blaas c

blade [bleid] n lemmet nt; **~ of grass** grasspriet c

blame [bleim] n schuld c; verwijt nt; v de schuld *geven aan, beschuldigen

blank [blæŋk] adj blanco

blanket ['blæŋkit] *n* deken *c*

blast [blɑːst] *n* explosie *c*

blazer ['bleizə] *n* sportjasje *nt*, blazer *c*

bleach [bliːtʃ] *v* bleken

bleak [bliːk] *adj* guur

*** bleed** [bliːd] *v* bloeden; *uitzuigen

bless [bles] *v* zegenen

blessing ['blesiŋ] *n* zegen *c*

blind [blaind] *n* rolgordijn *nt*, jaloezie *c*; *adj* blind; *v* verblinden

blister ['blistə] *n* blaar *c*, blaas *c*

blizzard ['blizəd] *n* sneeuwstorm *c*

block [blɔk] *v* versperren, blokkeren; *n* blok *nt*; ~ **of flats** flatgebouw *nt*

blond [blɔnd] *adj* blond; **blonde** *n* blondine *f*

blood [blʌd] *n* bloed *nt*; ~ **poisoning** bloedvergiftiging *c*; ~ **pressure** bloeddruk *c*; ~ **vessel** bloedvat *nt*; ~**y** *adj* bloed-, bebloed, bloederig; *colloquial* verdomd

blossom ['blɔsəm] *n* bloesem *c*

blot [blɔt] *n* vlek *c*; smet *c*; **blotting paper** vloeipapier *nt*

blouse [blauz] *n* blouse *c*

blow [blou] *n* klap *c*, slag *c*; windvlaag *c*

*** blow** [blou] *v* *blazen; *waaien; ~ **up** *opblazen; exploderen, ontploffen

blowout ['blouaut] *n* bandenpech *c*

blue [bluː] *adj* blauw; neerslachtig

blunt [blʌnt] *adj* bot; stomp

blush [blʌʃ] *v* blozen

board [bɔːd] *n* plank *c*; bord *nt*; pension *nt*; bestuur *nt*; ~ **and lodging** vol pension, kost en inwoning

boarder ['bɔːdə] *n* kostganger *m*

boardinghouse ['bɔːdiŋhaus] *n* pension *nt*

boarding school ['bɔːdiŋskuːl] *n* internaat *nt*

boast [boust] *v* opscheppen

boat [bout] *n* schip *nt*, boot *c*

body ['bɔdi] *n* lichaam *nt*; lijf *nt*

bodyguard ['bɔdigɑːd] *n* lijfwacht *c*

bog [bɔg] *n* moeras *nt*

boil [bɔil] *v* koken; *n* steenpuist *c*

bold [bould] *adj* stoutmoedig; vrijpostig, brutaal

Bolivia [bə'liviə] Bolivië

Bolivian [bə'liviən] *adj* Boliviaans; *n* Boliviaan *m*, -se *f*

bolt [boult] *n* grendel *c*; bout *c*

bomb [bɔm] *n* bom *c*; *v* bombarderen

bond [bɔnd] *n* obligatie *c*

bone [boun] *n* been *nt*, bot *nt*; graat *c*; *v* uitbenen

bonnet ['bɔnit] *n* motorkap *c*

book [buk] *n* boek *nt*; *v* reserveren, boeken; *inschrijven

booking ['bukiŋ] *n* reservering *c*, bespreking *c*

bookseller ['buk,selə] *n* boekhandelaar *m*, -ster *f*

bookstand ['bukstænd] *n* boekenstalletje *nt*

bookstore ['bukstɔː] *n* boekwinkel *c*, boekhandel *c*

boot [buːt] *n* laars *c*; bagageruimte *c*

booth [buːð] *n* kraam *c*; hokje *nt*

booze [buːz] *n* alcohol *c*; *v colloquial* *zuipen

border ['bɔːdə] *n* grens *c*; rand *c*; *v* grenzen

bore¹ [bɔː] *v* vervelen; boren; *n* zeurpiet *c*

bore² [bɔː] *v* (p bear)

boring ['bɔːriŋ] *adj* vervelend, saai

born [bɔːn] *adj* geboren

borrow ['bɔrou] *v* lenen; ontlenen

bosom ['buzəm] *n* borst *c*

boss [bɔs] *n* chef *m*, baas *m*, bazin *f*

botany ['bɔtəni] *n* plantkunde *c*

both [bouθ] *adj* beide; **both ... and** zowel ... als

bother ['bɔðə] *v* vervelen, hinderen; moeite *doen; *n* last *c*

bottle ['bɔtəl] *n* fles *c*; ~ **opener** flesopener *c*; **hot-water** ~

warmwaterkruik c

bottleneck ['bɔtəlnek] n flessehals c

bottom ['bɔtəm] n bodem c;
achterwerk nt, zitvlak nt; adj onderst

bought [bɔːt] v (p, pp buy)

boulder ['bouldə] n rotsblok nt

bound [baund] n grens c; ***be ~ to**
*moeten; **~ for** op weg naar

boundary ['baundəri] n grens c

bouquet [bu'kei] n boeket nt

bourgeois ['buəʒwaː] adj burgerlijk

boutique [bu'tiːk] n boutique c, n
boetiek c

bow¹ [bau] v *buigen

bow² [bou] n boog c; **~ tie** vlinderdasje
nt, strikje nt

bowels [bauəlz] pl darmen pl,
ingewanden pl

bowl [boul] n schaal c

bowling ['boulin] n bowling c,
kegelspel nt; **~ alley** kegelbaan c

box¹ [bɔks] v boksen; **boxing match**
bokswedstrijd c

box² [bɔks] n doos c

box office ['bɔks,ɔfis] n
plaatskaartenbureau nt, kassa c

boy [bɔi] n jongen m; joch nt, knaap c;
bediende c; **~friend** vriend m, vrijer m;
~scout padvinder m

bra [braː] n beha c, bustehouder c

bracelet ['breislit] n armband c

braces ['breisiz] pl bretels pl

brain [brein] n hersenen pl; verstand nt;
~ wave inval c

brake [breik] n rem c; **~ drum**
remtrommel c; **~ lights** remlichten pl

branch [braːntʃ] n tak c; filiaal nt

brand [brænd] n merk nt; brandmerk nt

brand-new [ˌbrænd'njuː] adj
splinternieuw

brass [braːs] n messing nt; koper nt,
geelkoper nt; **~ band** n fanfarekorps nt

brave [breiv] adj moedig, dapper; flink

Brazil [brə'zil] Brazilië

Brazilian [brə'ziljən] adj Braziliaans; n
Braziliaan m, -se f

breach [briːtʃ] n bres c

bread [bred] n brood nt; **wholemeal ~**
volkorenbrood nt

breadth [bredθ] n breedte c

break [breik] n breuk c; pauze c

*break [breik] v *breken; **~ down** stuk
*gaan; ontleden

breakdown ['breikdaun] n panne c,
motorpech c

breakfast ['brekfəst] n ontbijt nt

breast [brest] n borst c

breaststroke ['breststrouk] n
schoolslag c

breath [breθ] n adem c; lucht c

breathe [briːð] v ademen

breathing ['briːðiŋ] n ademhaling c

breed [briːd] n ras nt; soort c/nt

*breed [briːd] v fokken

breeze [briːz] n bries c

brew [bruː] v brouwen

brewery ['bruːəri] n brouwerij c

bribe [braib] v *omkopen

bribery ['braibəri] n omkoping c

brick [brik] n steen c, baksteen c

bricklayer ['brikleiə] n metselaar m

bride [braid] n bruid f

bridegroom ['braidgruːm] n
bruidegom m

bridge [bridʒ] n brug c; bridge nt

brief [briːf] adj kort; beknopt

briefcase ['briːfkeis] n aktentas c

briefs [briːfs] pl slip c, onderbroek c

bright [brait] adj helder; blinkend;
snugger, pienter

brighten ['braitən] v opklaren; doen
opklaren

brill [bril] n griet c

brilliant ['briljənt] adj schitterend;
briljant

brim [brim] n rand c

*bring [briŋ] v *brengen;
*meebrengen; **~ back** *terugbrengen;

~ **up** opvoeden, *grootbrengen; ter sprake *brengen

brisk [brisk] *adj* levendig

Britain ['britən] Engeland

British ['britiʃ] *adj* Brits; Engels

Briton ['britən] *n* Brit *c*; Engelsman *m*

broad [brɔ:d] *adj* breed; ruim, wijd; globaal

broadcast ['brɔ:dkɑ:st] *n* uitzending *c*

*broadcast ['brɔ:dkɑ:st] *v* *uitzenden

brochure ['brouʃuə] *n* brochure *c*

broke¹ [brouk] *v* (p break)

broke² [brouk] *adj* platzak

broken ['broukən] *adj* (pp break) stuk, kapot

broker ['broukə] *n* makelaar *m*

bronchitis [brɔŋ'kaitis] *n* bronchitis *c*

bronze [brɔnz] *n* brons *nt*; *adj* bronzen

brooch [broutʃ] *n* broche *c*

brook [bruk] *n* beek *c*

broom [bru:m] *n* bezem *c*

brothel ['brɔθəl] *n* bordeel *nt*

brother ['brʌðə] *n* broer *m*; broeder *m*

brother-in-law ['brʌðərinlɔ:] *n* (pl brothers-) zwager *m*

brought [brɔ:t] *v* (p, pp bring)

brown [braun] *adj* bruin

bruise [bru:z] *n* blauwe plek, kneuzing *c*; *v* kneuzen

brunette [bru:'net] *n* brunette *c*

brush [brʌʃ] *n* borstel *c*; kwast *c*; *v* poetsen, borstelen

brutal ['bru:təl] *adj* beestachtig

bubble ['bʌbəl] *n* bel *c*

buck [bʌk] *n* bok *c*; *colloquial* dollar *c*

bucket ['bʌkit] *n* emmer *c*

buckle ['bʌkəl] *n* gesp *c*

bud [bʌd] *n* knop *c*

buddy ['bʌdi] *n* vriend *c* **budget** ['bʌdʒit] *n* begroting *c*, budget *nt*

buffet [bufei] *n* buffet *nt*

bug [bʌg] *n* wandluis *c*; kever *c*; *nAm* insekt *nt*

*build [bild] *v* bouwen

building ['bildiŋ] *n* gebouw *nt*

bulb [bʌlb] *n* bol *c*; bloembol *c*; **light** ~ gloeilamp *c*, lampenpeer *c*

Bulgaria [bʌl'gɛəriə] Bulgarije

Bulgarian [bʌl'gɛəriən] *adj* Bulgaars; *n* Bulgaar *m*, -se *f*

bulk [bʌlk] *n* omvang *c*; massa *c*; meerderheid *c*

bulky ['bʌlki] *adj* lijvig, omvangrijk

bull [bul] *n* stier *c*

bullet ['bulit] *n* kogel *c*

bulletin ['bulitin] *n* bulletin *nt*; ~ **board** *n* mededelingenbord *nt*

bullfight ['bulfait] *n* stierengevecht *nt*

bullring ['bulriŋ] *n* arena *c*

bully [buli] *n* pestkop *c*, klier *c*

bump [bʌmp] *v* *stoten; botsen; bonzen; *n* stoot *c*, bons *c*

bumper ['bʌmpə] *n* bumper *c*

bumpy ['bʌmpi] *adj* hobbelig

bun [bʌn] *n* broodje *nt*

bunch [bʌntʃ] *n* bos *c*; groep *c*

bundle ['bʌndəl] *n* bundel *c*; *v* *samenbinden, bundelen

bunk [bʌŋk] *n* kooi *c*; slaapbank *c*

buoy ['bɔi] *n* boei *c*

burden ['bə:dən] *n* last *c*

bureau ['bjuərou] *n* (pl ~s) bureau *nt*, schrijftafel *c*; *nAm* commode *c*

bureaucracy [bjuə'rɔkrəsi] *n* bureaucratie *c*

burglar ['bə:glə] *n* inbreker *m*

burgle ['bə:gəl] *v* *inbreken

burial ['beriəl] *n* teraardebestelling *c*, begrafenis *c*

burn [bə:n] *n* brandwond *c*

*burn [bə:n] *v* branden; verbranden; aanbranden

*burst [bə:st] *v* *barsten; *breken

bury ['beri] *v* *begraven; *bedelven

bus [bʌs] *n* bus *c*

bush [buʃ] *n* struik *c*

business ['biznəs] *n* zaken *pl*, handel *c*; bedrijf *nt*, zaak *c*; werk *nt*;

aangelegenheid c; ~ **card**
visitekaartje; ~ **hours** openingstijden
pl, kantooruren pl; ~ **trip** zakenreis c;
on ~ voor zaken
business-like ['biznislaik] adj
zakelijk
businessman ['biznəsmən] n (pl
-men) zakenman c
businesswoman ['biznəswumən] n
(pl -women) zakenvrouw c
bust [bʌst] n buste c
bustle ['bʌsəl] n drukte c
busy ['bizi] adj bezig; druk
but [bʌt] conj maar; doch; prep behalve
butcher ['butʃə] n slager m

butter ['bʌtə] n boter c
butterfly ['bʌtəflai] n vlinder c; ~
stroke vlinderslag c
buttock ['bʌtək] n bil c
button ['bʌtən] n knoop c; v knopen
buttonhole ['bʌtənhoul] n knoopsgat
nt
***buy** [bai] v *kopen; aanschaffen
buyer ['baiə] n koper c
buzz [bʌz] n zoemen, brommen
by [bai] prep door; met, per; bij
bye-bye [bai'bai] colloquial doei!, tot
kijk, tot ziens
by-pass ['baipɑːs] n ringweg c; v
passeren

C

cab [kæb] n taxi c
cabaret ['kæbərei] n cabaret nt
cabbage ['kæbidʒ] n kool c
cab driver ['kæb,draivə] n
taxichauffeur c
cabin ['kæbin] n cabine c; hut c;
kleedhokje nt; kajuit c
cabinet ['kæbinət] n kabinet nt
cable ['keibəl] n kabel c; telegram nt; v
telegraferen
cadre ['kɑːdə] n kader nt
café ['kæfei] n café nt
cafeteria [,kæfə'tiəriə] n cafetaria c
caffeine ['kæfiːn] n coffeïne c
cage [keidʒ] n kooi c
cake [keik] n cake c; gebak nt; taart c,
koek c
calamity [kə'læməti] n onheil nt, ramp
c
calcium ['kælsiəm] n calcium nt
calculate ['kælkjuleit] v uitrekenen,
berekenen
calculation [,kælkju'leiʃən] n

berekening c
calculator ['kælkju'leitə] n
rekenmachine c
calendar ['kæləndə] n kalender c
calf [kɑːf] n (pl calves) kalf nt; kuit c; ~
skin kalfsleer nt
call [kɔːl] v *roepen; noemen;
opbellen, telefoneren; n roep c; visite
c, bezoek nt; telefoontje nt; ***be called**
*heten; ~ **names** *uitschelden; ~ **on**
*bezoeken; ~ **up** Am opbellen
calm [kɑːm] adj rustig, kalm; ~ **down**
kalmeren; bedaren
calorie ['kæləri] n calorie c
came [keim] v (p come)
camel ['kæməl] n kameel m
cameo ['kæmiou] n (pl ~s) camee c
camera ['kæmərə] n fototoestel nt;
filmcamera c; ~ **shop** fotowinkel c
camp [kæmp] n kamp nt; v kamperen; ~
bed veldbed nt, stretcher c
campaign [kæm'pein] n campagne c
camper ['kæmpə] n kampeerder m,

kampeerster f

camping ['kæmpiŋ] n camping c; ~ **site** camping c, kampeerterrein nt

can [kæn] n blik nt; ~ **opener** blikopener c

*can [kæn] v *kunnen

Canada ['kænədə] Canada

Canadian [kə'neidiən] adj Canadees; n Canadees m, Canadese f

canal [kə'næl] n kanaal nt; gracht c

canary [kə'neəri] n kanarie c

cancel ['kænsəl] v annuleren; *afzeggen

cancellation [ˌkænsə'leiʃən] n annulering c

cancer ['kænsə] n kanker c

candidate ['kændidət] n kandidaat m, kandidate f, gegadigde c

candle ['kændəl] n kaars c

candy ['kændi] nAm snoepje nt; snoep nt, snoepgoed nt; ~ **store** Am snoepwinkel c

cane [kein] n riet nt, rotan c/nt; stok c

canister ['kænistə] n trommel c, bus c

canoe [kə'nu:] n kano c

canteen [kæn'ti:n] n kantine c

canvas ['kænvəs] n tentdoek nt

cap [kæp] n pet c, muts c

capable ['keipəbəl] adj kundig, bekwaam

capacity [kə'pæsəti] n capaciteit c; vermogen nt; bekwaamheid c

cape [keip] n cape c; kaap c

capital ['kæpitəl] n hoofdstad c; kapitaal nt; adj belangrijk, hoofd-; ~ **letter** hoofdletter c

capitalism ['kæpitəlizəm] n kapitalisme nt

capitulation [kəˌpitju'leiʃən] n capitulatie c

capsule ['kæpsju:l] n capsule c

captain ['kæptin] n kapitein m; gezagvoerder m

capture ['kæptʃə] v gevangen *nemen, *vangen; *innemen; n vangst c; inneming c

car [ka:] n auto c; ~ **hire** autoverhuur c; ~ **park** parkeerplaats c; ~ **rental** Am autoverhuur c

caramel ['kærəməl] n karamel c

carat ['kærət] n karaat nt

caravan ['kærəvæn] n caravan c; woonwagen c

carburettor [ˌka:bju'retə] n carburateur c

card [ka:d] n kaart c; briefkaart c

cardboard ['ka:dbɔ:d] n karton nt; adj kartonnen

cardigan ['ka:digən] n vest nt

cardinal ['ka:dinəl] n kardinaal m; adj kardinaal, hoofd-

care [kɛə] n verzorging c; zorg c; ~ **about** zich bekommeren om; ~ **for** *houden van; ***take ~ of** zorgen voor, verzorgen

career [kə'riə] n loopbaan c, carrière c

carefree ['kɛəfri:] adj onbezorgd

careful ['kɛəfəl] adj voorzichtig; zorgvuldig, nauwkeurig

careless ['kɛələs] adj achteloos, slordig

caretaker ['kɛəˌteikə] n conciërge c

cargo ['ka:gou] n (pl ~es) lading c, vracht c

carnival ['ka:nivəl] n carnaval nt

carp [ka:p] n (pl ~) karper c

carpenter ['ka:pintə] n timmerman m

carpet ['ka:pit] n vloerkleed nt, tapijt nt

carriage ['kæridʒ] n wagon c; koets c, rijtuig nt

carriageway ['kæridʒwei] n rijbaan c

carrot ['kærət] n peen c, wortel c

carry ['kæri] v *dragen; voeren; ~ **on** voortzetten; *doorgaan; ~ **out** uitvoeren

carrycot ['kærikɔt] n reiswieg c

cart [ka:t] n kar c, wagen c

cartilage ['ka:tilidʒ] n kraakbeen nt

carton ['kɑːtən] n kartonnen doos; slof c

cartoon [kɑː'tuːn] n tekenfilm c

cartridge ['kɑːtridʒ] n patroon c

carve [kɑːv] v *snijden; kerven, *houtsnijden

carving ['kɑːviŋ] n houtsnijwerk nt

case [keis] n geval nt; zaak c; koffer c; etui nt; **attaché ~** aktentas c; **in ~** indien; **in ~ of** in geval van

cash [kæʃ] n contanten pl, contant geld nt; v verzilveren, incasseren, innen; **~ dispenser** geldautomaat c; **~ point** geldautomaat c

cashier [kæ'ʃiə] n kassier m, caissière f

cashmere ['kæʃmiə] n kasjmier nt

casino [kə'siːnou] n (pl ~s) casino nt

cask [kɑːsk] n ton c, vat nt

cassette [kə'set] n cassette c

cast [kɑːst] n worp c

***cast** [kɑːst] v gooien, *werpen; **cast iron** gietijzer nt

castle ['kɑːsəl] n slot nt, kasteel nt

casual ['kæʒuəl] adj ongedwongen; terloops, toevallig

casualty ['kæʒuəlti] n slachtoffer nt

cat [kæt] n kat c

catacomb ['kætəkoum] n catacombe c

catalogue ['kætələg] n catalogus c

catarrh [kə'tɑː] n catarre c

catastrophe [kə'tæstrəfi] n catastrofe c

***catch** [kætʃ] v *vangen; *grijpen; betrappen; *nemen, halen

catchword ['kætʃwəːd] n trefwoord nt

category ['kætigəri] n categorie c

cathedral [kə'θiːdrəl] n dom c, kathedraal c

catholic ['kæθəlik] adj katholiek

cattle ['kætəl] pl vee nt

caught [kɔːt] v (p, pp catch)

cauliflower ['kɔliflauə] n bloemkool c

cause [kɔːz] v veroorzaken; aanrichten; n oorzaak c; beweegreden c, aanleiding c; zaak c; **~ to** *doen

caution ['kɔːʃən] n voorzichtigheid c; v waarschuwen

cautious ['kɔːʃəs] adj bedachtzaam; voorzichtig

cave [keiv] n grot c; spelonk c

cavern ['kævən] n hol nt

caviar ['kæviɑː] n kaviaar c

cavity ['kævəti] n holte c

CD [siː'diː] n CD; **~ player** CD-speler c; **CD-ROM** CD-ROM c

cease [siːs] v *ophouden

ceasefire ['siːsfaiə] n wapenstilstand c

ceiling ['siːliŋ] n plafond nt

celebrate ['selibreit] v vieren

celebration [,seli'breiʃən] n viering c

celebrity [si'lebrəti] n roem c

celery ['seləri] n selderij c

celibacy ['selibəsi] n celibaat nt

cell [sel] n cel c

cellar ['selə] n kelder c

cellophane ['seləfein] n cellofaan nt

cell phone ['selfoun] n mobiele telefoon c

cement [si'ment] n cement nt

cemetery ['semitri] n begraafplaats c, kerkhof nt

censorship ['sensəʃip] n censuur c

center ['sentə] nAm centrum nt; middelpunt nt; adj midden

centigrade ['sentigreid] adj celsius

centimeter Am, **centimetre** ['sentimiːtə] n centimeter c

central ['sentrəl] adj centraal; **~ heating** centrale verwarming; **~ station** centraal station

centralize ['sentrəlaiz] v centraliseren

centre ['sentə] n centrum nt; middelpunt nt

century ['sentʃəri] n eeuw c

ceramics [si'ræmiks] pl aardewerk nt, keramiek c

ceremony ['serəməni] n ceremonie c

certain ['səːtən] adj zeker; bepaald

certainly ['sɜːtənli] *adv* zeker, beslist

certificate [sə'tifikət] *n* certificaat *nt*; attest *nt*, akte *c*, diploma *nt*, getuigschrift *nt*

chain [tʃein] *n* keten *c*, ketting *c*

chair [tʃɛə] *n* stoel *c*; zetel *c*

chairman ['tʃɛəmən] *n* (pl -men) voorzitter *m*

chairwoman ['tʃɛəwumən] *n* (pl -women) voorzitster *f*

chalet ['ʃælei] *n* chalet *nt*

chalk [tʃɔːk] *n* krijt *nt*

challenge ['tʃæləndʒ] *v* uitdagen; *n* uitdaging *c*

chamber ['tʃeimbə] *n* kamer *c*

champagne [ʃæm'pein] *n* champagne *c*

champion ['tʃæmpjən] *n* kampioen *m*, -e *f*; voorvechter *c*

chance [tʃɑːns] *n* toeval *nt*; kans *c*, gelegenheid *c*; risico *nt*; gok *c*; **by ~** toevallig

change [tʃeindʒ] *v* wijzigen, veranderen; wisselen; zich verkleden; overstappen; *n* wijziging *c*, verandering *c*; wisselgeld *nt*, kleingeld *nt*; **for a ~** voor de verandering, voor de afwisseling

channel ['tʃænəl] *n* kanaal *nt*; **English Channel** het Kanaal

chaos ['keiɔs] *n* chaos *c*

chaotic [kei'ɔtik] *adj* chaotisch

chap [tʃæp] *n* vent *c*

chapel ['tʃæpəl] *n* kerk *c*, kapel *c*

chaplain ['tʃæplin] *n* kapelaan *m*

character ['kærəktə] *n* karakter *nt*

characteristic [ˌkærəktə'ristik] *adj* kenmerkend, karakteristiek; *n* kenmerk *nt*; karaktertrek *c*

characterize ['kærəktəraiz] *v* kenmerken

charcoal ['tʃɑːkoul] *n* houtskool *c*

charge [tʃɑːdʒ] *v* berekenen; belasten; aanklagen; *laden; *n* prijs *c*; belasting *c*, lading *c*; last *c*; aanklacht *c*; **~ plate** *Am* credit card; **free of ~** kosteloos; **in ~ of** belast met; ***take ~ of** op zich *nemen

charity ['tʃærəti] *n* liefdadigheid *c*

charm [tʃɑːm] *n* bekoring *c*, charme *c*; amulet *c*

charming ['tʃɑːmin] *adj* charmant

chart [tʃɑːt] *n* tabel *c*; grafiek *c*; zeekaart *c*; **conversion ~** omrekentabel *c*

chase [tʃeis] *v* *najagen; *verdrijven, *verjagen; *n* jacht *c*

chasm ['kæzəm] *n* kloof *c*

chassis ['ʃæsi] *n* (pl ~) chassis *nt*

chaste [tʃeist] *adj* kuis

chastise [tʃæs'taiz] *v* tuchtigen

chat [tʃæt] *v* kletsen, babbelen; *n* babbeltje *nt*, praatje *nt*, geklets *nt*

chatterbox ['tʃætəbɔks] *n* babbelkous *c*

chauffeur ['ʃoufə] *n* chauffeur *c*

cheap [tʃiːp] *adj* goedkoop; voordelig

cheat [tʃiːt] *v* *bedriegen; oplichten

check [tʃek] *v* controleren, *nakijken; *n* ruit *c*; *nAm* rekening *c*; cheque *c*; **check!** schaak!; **~ in** zich *inschrijven

checkbook ['tʃekbuk] *nAm* chequeboekje *nt*

checkerboard ['tʃekəbɔːd] *nAm* dambord *nt*

checkers ['tʃekəz] *plAm* damspel *nt*

checkroom ['tʃekruːm] *nAm* garderobe *c*

checkup ['tʃekʌp] *n* onderzoek *nt*

cheek [tʃiːk] *n* wang *c*

cheekbone ['tʃiːkboun] *n* jukbeen *nt*

cheeky ['tʃiːki] *adj colloquial* brutaal, onbeleefd

cheer [tʃiə] *v* juichen; **~ up** opvrolijken

cheerful ['tʃiəfəl] *adj* opgewekt, vrolijk

cheese [tʃiːz] *n* kaas *c*

chef [ʃef] *n* chef-kok *c*

chemical ['kemikəl] *adj* scheikundig, chemisch

chemist ['kemist] *n* apotheker *c*; chemist's apotheek *c*; drogisterij *c*

chemistry ['kemistri] *n* scheikunde *c*, chemie *c*

cheque [tʃek] *n* cheque *c*

chequebook ['tʃekbuk] *n* chequeboekje *c*

chequered ['tʃekəd] *adj* geruit, geblokt

cherry ['tʃeri] *n* kers *c*

chess [tʃes] *n* schaakspel *nt*

chest [tʃest] *n* borst *c*; borstkas *c*; kist *c*; ~ of drawers ladenkast *c*

chestnut ['tʃesnʌt] *n* kastanje *c*

chew [tʃu:] *v* kauwen

chewing gum ['tʃu:iŋɡʌm] *n* kauwgom *c/nt*

chicken ['tʃikin] *n* kip *f*; kuiken *nt*

chicken pox ['tʃikinpɔks] *n* waterpokken *pl*

chief [tʃi:f] *n* chef *c*; *adj* hoofd-, voornaamst

chieftain ['tʃi:ftən] *n* opperhoofd *nt*

child [tʃaild] *n* (pl children) kind *nt*

childbirth ['tʃaildbə:θ] *n* bevalling *c*

childhood ['tʃaildhud] *n* jeugd *c*

Chile ['tʃili] Chili

Chilean ['tʃiliən] *adj* Chileens; *n* Chileen *m*, -se *f*

chill [tʃil] *n* rilling *c*

chilly ['tʃili] *adj* kil

chimes [tʃaimz] *pl* carillon *nt*

chimney ['tʃimni] *n* schoorsteen *c*

chin [tʃin] *n* kin *c*

China ['tʃainə] China

china ['tʃainə] *n* porselein *nt*

Chinese [tʃai'ni:z] *adj* Chinees; *n* Chinees *m*, Chinese *f*

chip [tʃip] *n* schilfer *c*; fiche *c*; *v* *afsnijden, *afbreken; chips frites *pl*

chisel ['tʃizəl] *n* beitel *c*

chives [tʃaivz] *pl* bieslook *nt*

chlorine ['klɔ:ri:n] *n* chloor *nt*

chocolate ['tʃɔklət] *n* chocola *c*; bonbon *c*; chocolademelk *c*

choice [tʃɔis] *n* keuze *c*; keus *c*

choir [kwaiə] *n* koor *nt*

choke [tʃouk] *v* stikken; wurgen; *n* choke *c*

*choose [tʃu:z] *v* *kiezen

chop [tʃɔp] *n* kotelet *c*, karbonade *c*; *v* hakken

Christ [kraist] Christus

christen ['krisən] *v* dopen

christening ['krisəniŋ] *n* doop *c*

Christian ['kristʃən] *adj* christelijk; *n* christen *c*; ~ name voornaam *c*

Christmas ['krisməs] Kerstmis

chromium ['kroumiəm] *n* chroom *nt*

chronic ['krɔnik] *adj* chronisch

chronological [ˌkrɔnə'lɔdʒikəl] *adj* chronologisch

chuckle ['tʃʌkəl] *v* grinniken

chunk [tʃʌŋk] *n* stuk *nt*

church [tʃə:tʃ] *n* kerk *c*

churchyard ['tʃə:tʃjɑ:d] *n* kerkhof *nt*

cigar [si'ɡɑ:] *n* sigaar *c*; ~ shop sigarenwinkel *c*

cigarette [ˌsiɡə'ret] *n* sigaret *c*; ~ tobacco shag *c*; ~ case sigarettenkoker *c*; ~ holder sigarettepijpje *nt*; ~ lighter aansteker *c*

cinema ['sinəmə] *n* bioscoop *c*

cinnamon ['sinəmən] *n* kaneel *c*

circle ['sə:kəl] *n* cirkel *c*; kring *c*; balkon *nt*; *v* omringen, *omgeven

circulation [ˌsə:kju'leiʃən] *n* circulatie *c*; bloedsomloop *c*; omloop *c*

circumstance ['sə:kəmstæns] *n* omstandigheid *c*

circus ['sə:kəs] *n* circus *nt*

citizen ['sitizən] *n* burger *m*

citizenship ['sitizənʃip] *n* staatsburgerschap *nt*

city ['siti] *n* stad *c*

civic ['sivik] *adj* burger-

civil ['sivəl] *adj* civiel; beleefd; **~ law** burgerlijk recht; **~ servant** ambtenaar *m*, ambtenares *f*

civilian [si'viljən] *adj* burger-; *n* burger *m*

civilization [ˌsivəlai'zeiʃən] *n* beschaving *c*

civilized ['sivəlaizd] *adj* beschaafd

claim [kleim] *v* vorderen, opeisen; beweren; *n* eis *c*, aanspraak *c*

clamp [klæmp] *n* klem *c*; klemschroef *c*

clap [klæp] *v* applaudisseren, klappen

clarify ['klærifai] *v* ophelderen, verduidelijken

class [kla:s] *n* rang *c*, klasse *c*; klas *c*

classical ['klæsikəl] *adj* klassiek

classify ['klæsifai] *v* indelen

classmate ['kla:smeit] *n* klasgenoot *m*

classroom ['kla:sru:m] *n* leslokaal *nt*

clause [klɔ:z] *n* clausule *c*

claw [klɔ:] *n* klauw *c*

clay [klei] *n* klei *c*

clean [kli:n] *adj* zuiver, schoon; *v* schoonmaken, reinigen

cleaning ['kli:niŋ] *n* schoonmaak *c*, reiniging *c*; **~ fluid** reinigingsmiddel *nt*

clear [kliə] *adj* helder; duidelijk; *v* opruimen

clearing ['kliəriŋ] *n* open plaats

cleft [kleft] *n* kloof *c*

clergyman ['klə:dʒimən] *n* (pl -men) dominee *m*, predikant *m*; geestelijke *m*

clerk [kla:k] *n* kantoorbediende *c*, beambte *c*; klerk *m*; secretaris *m*, secretaresse *f*

clever ['klevə] *adj* intelligent; slim, pienter, knap

click [klik] *v* klikken; **~ into place** op zijn plaats vallen

client ['klaiənt] *n* klant *c*; cliënt *m*, -e *f*

cliff [klif] *n* rots *c*, klip *c*

climate ['klaimit] *n* klimaat *nt*

climb [klaim] *v* *klimmen; *stijgen; *n* stijging *c*

cling [kliŋ] *v*: **~ to** zich vastklampen; aanhangen

clinic ['klinik] *n* kliniek *c*

cloak [klouk] *n* mantel *c*

cloakroom ['kloukru:m] *n* garderobe *c*

clock [klɔk] *n* klok *c*; **at ... o'clock** om ... uur

clog [klɔg] *n* klomp *c*

close¹ [klouz] *v* *sluiten; **closed** *adj* toe, dicht, gesloten

close² [klous] *adj* nabij

closet ['klɔzit] *n* kast *c*; *nAm* kleerkast *c*

cloth [klɔθ] *n* stof *c*; doek *c*

clothes [klouðz] *pl* kleding *c*, kleren *pl*

clothing ['klouðiŋ] *n* kleding *c*

cloud [klaud] *n* wolk *c*; **clouds** bewolking *c*

cloudy ['klaudi] *adj* betrokken, bewolkt

clover ['klouvə] *n* klaver *c*

clown [klaun] *n* clown *c*

club [klʌb] *n* club *c*; sociëteit *c*, vereniging *c*; knots *c*, knuppel *c*

clumsy ['klʌmzi] *adj* onhandig

clutch [klʌtʃ] *n* koppeling *c*; greep *c*

coach [koutʃ] *n* bus *c*; rijtuig *nt*; koets *c*; trainer *c*

coal [koul] *n* kolen *pl*

coarse [kɔ:s] *adj* grof

coast [koust] *n* kust *c*

coat [kout] *n* mantel *c*, jas *c*; **~ hanger** kleerhanger *c*

cocaine [kou'kein] *n* cocaïne *c*

cock [kɔk] *n* haan *m*

cocktail ['kɔkteil] *n* cocktail *c*

cocoa ['koukə] *n* warme chocolademelk *c*

coconut ['koukənʌt] *n* kokosnoot *c*

cod [kɔd] *n* (pl ~) kabeljauw *c*

code [koud] *n* code *c*

coffee ['kɔfi] *n* koffie *c*

cognac ['kɔnjæk] *n* cognac *c*

coherence [kou'hiərəns] n
samenhang c

coin [kɔin] n munt c; geldstuk nt,
muntstuk nt

coincide [ˌkouin'said] v *samenvallen

cold [kould] adj koud; n kou c;
verkoudheid c; **catch a ~** kou vatten

collaborate [kə'læbərait] v
samenwerken; collaboreren (met de
vijand)

collapse [kə'læps] v *bezwijken,
instorten

collar [kɔlə] n halsband c; boord nt/c,
kraag c; **~ stud** boordenknoopje nt

collarbone ['kɔləboun] n sleutelbeen
nt

colleague ['kɔliːg] n collega c

collect [kə'lekt] v verzamelen;
ophalen, afhalen; collecteren

collection [kə'lekʃən] n collectie c,
verzameling c; lichting c

collective [kə'lektiv] adj collectief

collector [kə'lektə] n verzamelaar m,
-ster f; collectant m, -e f

college ['kɔlidʒ] n instelling voor
hoger onderwijs; school c

collide [kə'laid] v botsen

collision [kə'liʒən] n aanrijding c,
botsing c; aanvaring c

Colombia [kə'lɔmbiə] Colombia

Colombian [kə'lɔmbiən] adj
Colombiaans; n Colombiaan m, -se f

colonel ['kəːnəl] n kolonel m

colony ['kɔləni] n kolonie c

colo(u)r ['kʌlə] n kleur c; v kleuren; ~
film kleurenfilm c

colo(u)r-blind ['kʌləblaind] adj
kleurenblind

colo(u)red ['kʌləd] adj gekleurd

colo(u)rful ['kʌləfəl] adj bont,
kleurrijk

column ['kɔləm] n pilaar c, zuil c;
kolom c; rubriek c; kolonne c

coma ['koumə] n coma nt

comb [koum] v kammen; n kam c

combat ['kɔmbæt] n strijd c, gevecht
nt; v *bestrijden, *vechten

combination [ˌkɔmbi'neiʃən] n
combinatie c

combine [kəm'bain] v combineren;
*samenbrengen

***come** [kʌm] v *komen; ~ **across**
*tegenkomen; *vinden; ~ **true**
*uitkomen

comedian [kə'miːdiən] n toneelspeler
m; komiek m

comedy ['kɔmədi] n blijspel nt,
komedie c; **musical ~** musical c

comfort ['kʌmfət] n gemak nt, komfort
nt, gerief nt; troost c; v troosten

comfortable ['kʌmfətəbəl] adj
gerifelijk, comfortabel

comic ['kɔmik] adj komisch

comics ['kɔmiks] pl stripverhaal nt

coming ['kʌmiŋ] n komst c

comma ['kɔmə] n komma c

command [kə'mɑːnd] v *bevelen; n
bevel nt

commander [kə'mɑːndə] n
bevelhebber m

commemoration [kəˌmemə'reiʃən] n
herdenking c

commence [kə'mens] v *beginnen

comment ['kɔment] n commentaar nt;
v aanmerken

commerce ['kɔmɔːs] n handel c

commercial [kə'mɔːʃəl] adj handels-,
commercieel; n reclamespot c; ~ **law**
handelsrecht nt

commission [kə'miʃən] n commissie
c; provisie c

commit [kə'mit] v toevertrouwen;
plegen, *begaan; zich vastleggen

committee [kə'miti] n commissie c,
comité nt

common ['kɔmən] adj
gemeenschappelijk; gebruikelijk;
gewoon; ordinair

commune ['kɔmju:n] *n* commune *c*

communicate [kə'mju:nikeit] *v* meedelen, mededelen

communication [kə,mju:ni'kei∫ən] *n* communicatie *c*; mededeling *c*

communiqué [kə'mju:nikei] *n* communiqué *nt*

communism ['kɔmjunizəm] *n* communisme *nt*

communist ['kɔmjunist] *n* communist *c*

community [kə'mju:nəti] *n* samenleving *c*, gemeenschap *c*

commuter [kə'mju:tə] *n* forens *c*

compact ['kɔmpækt] *adj* compact

compact disc ['kɔmpækt disk] *n* compact disc *c*; ~ **player** compact disc speler *c*

companion [kəm'pænjən] *n* metgezel *m*, -lin *f*

company ['kʌmpəni] *n* gezelschap *nt*; maatschappij *c*; firma *c*; onderneming *c*

comparative [kəm'pærətiv] *adj* relatief

compare [kəm'pεə] *v* *vergelijken

comparison [kəm'pærisən] *n* vergelijking *c*

compartment [kəm'pɑ:tmənt] *n* coupé *c*

compass ['kʌmpəs] *n* kompas *nt*

compel [kəm'pel] *v* *dwingen

compensate ['kɔmpənseit] *v* compenseren

compensation [,kɔmpən'sei∫ən] *n* compensatie *c*; schadevergoeding *c*

compete [kəm'pi:t] *v* wedijveren

competition [,kɔmpə'ti∫ən] *n* wedstrijd *c*; concurrentie *c*

competitor [kəm'petitər] *n* concurrent *m*, -e *f*

compile [kəm'pail] *v* samenstellen

complain [kəm'plein] *v* klagen

complaint [kəm'pleint] *n* klacht *c*

complete [kəm'pli:t] *adj* compleet, volledig; *v* voltooien

completely [kəm'pli:tli] *adv* helemaal, volkomen, geheel

complex ['kɔmpleks] *adj* ingewikkeld

complexion [kəm'plek∫ən] *n* teint *c*

complicated ['kɔmplikeitid] *adj* gecompliceerd, ingewikkeld

compliment ['kɔmplimənt] *n* compliment *nt*; *v* gelukwensen, feliciteren

compose [kəm'pouz] *v* samenstellen

composer [kəm'pouzə] *n* componist *m*, -e *f*

composition [,kɔmpə'zi∫ən] *n* compositie *c*; samenstelling *c*

comprehensive [,kɔmpri'hensiv] *adj* uitgebreid

comprise [kəm'praiz] *v* omvatten

compromise ['kɔmprəmaiz] *n* compromis *c*

compulsory [kəm'pʌlsəri] *adj* verplicht

computer [kəm'pjutə] *n* computer *c*

comrade ['kɔmreid] *n* kameraad *m*

conceal [kən'si:l] *v* *verbergen

conceited [kən'si:tid] *adj* verwaand

conceive [kən'si:v] *v* opvatten; ~ **of** zich voorstellen

concentrate ['kɔnsəntreit] *v* concentreren

concentration [,kɔnsən'trei∫ən] *n* concentratie *c*

conception [kən'sep∫ən] *n* begrip *nt*; conceptie *c*

concern [kən'sə:n] *v* *aangaan, *betreffen; *n* zorg *c*; aangelegenheid *c*; bedrijf *nt*, onderneming *c*

concerned [kən'sə:nd] *adj* bezorgd; betrokken

concerning [kən'sə:niŋ] *prep* omtrent, betreffende

concert ['kɔnsət] *n* concert *nt*; ~ **hall** concertzaal *c*

concession [kən'seʃən] n concessie c, tegemoetkoming c

concise [kən'sais] adj beknopt, summier

conclusion [kəŋ'kluːʒən] n gevolgtrekking c, conclusie c

concrete ['kɔŋkriːt] adj concreet; n beton nt

concurrence [kəŋ'kʌrəns] n samenloop c

concussion [kəŋ'kʌʃən] n hersenschudding c

condition [kən'diʃən] n voorwaarde c; toestand c; omstandigheid c; conditie c

conditional [kən'diʃənəl] adj voorwaardelijk

conditioner [kən'diʃənə] n conditioner

condom ['kɔndəm] n condoom nt

conduct¹ ['kɔndʌkt] n gedrag nt

conduct² [kən'dʌkt] v leiden; begeleiden; dirigeren

conductor [kən'dʌktə] n conducteur m, -trice f; dirigent m, -e f

confectioner [kən'fekʃənə] n banketbakker m, -bakster f

conference ['kɔnfərəns] n conferentie c

confess [kən'fes] v bekennen; biechten; *belijden

confession [kən'feʃən] n bekentenis c; biecht c

confide [kən'faid] n toevertrouwen

confidence ['kɔnfidəns] n vertrouwen nt

confident ['kɔnfidənt] adj gerust

confidential [ˌkɔnfi'denʃəl] adj vertrouwelijk

confirm [kən'fəːm] v bevestigen

confirmation [ˌkɔnfə'meiʃən] n bevestiging c

confiscate ['kɔnfiskeit] v vorderen, beslag leggen op

conflict ['kɔnflikt] n conflict nt

confuse [kən'fjuːz] v verwarren

confused [kən'fjuːʒd] adj in de war, verward

confusion [kən'fjuːʒən] n verwarring c

congratulate [kəŋ'grætʃuleit] v feliciteren, gelukwensen

congratulation [kəŋˌgrætʃu'leiʃən] n felicitatie c, gelukwens c

congregation [ˌkɔŋgri'geiʃən] n gemeente c; orde c, congregatie c

congress ['kɔŋgres] n congres nt; bijeenkomst c

connect [kə'nekt] v *verbinden; *aansluiten

connection [kə'nekʃən] n relatie c; verband nt; aansluiting c, verbinding c

connoisseur [ˌkɔnə'səː] n kenner m

connotation [ˌkɔnə'teiʃən] n bijbetekenis c

conquer ['kɔŋkə] v veroveren; *overwinnen

conqueror ['kɔŋkərə] n veroveraar m

conquest ['kɔŋkwest] n verovering c

conscience ['kɔnʃəns] n geweten nt

conscious ['kɔnʃəs] adj bewust

consciousness ['kɔnʃəsnəs] n bewustzijn nt

conscript ['kɔnskript] n dienstplichtige c

consent [kən'sent] v toestemmen; instemmen; n instemming c, toestemming c

consequence ['kɔnsikwəns] n consequentie c, gevolg nt

consequently ['kɔnsikwəntli] adv bijgevolg

conservative [kən'səːvətiv] adj behoudend, conservatief

consider [kən'sidə] v beschouwen; *overwegen; menen, *vinden

considerable [kən'sidərəbəl] adj aanzienlijk; flink, aanmerkelijk

considerate [kən'sidərət] *adj* attent

consideration [kən,sidə'reiʃən] *n* overweging *c*; consideratie *c*, aandacht *c*

considering [kən'sidəriŋ] *prep* gezien

consignment [kən'sainmənt] *n* zending *c*

consist of [kən'sist] *bestaan uit

consolation [kɔnsə'leiʃn] *n* (ver)troosting *c*, troost *c*; ~ **prize** troostprijs *c*

conspire [kən'spaiə] *v* *samenzweren

constant ['kɔnstənt] *adj* aanhoudend

constipation [,kɔnsti'peiʃən] *n* obstipatie *c*, constipatie *c*

constituency [kən'stitʃuənsi] *n* kiesdistrict *nt*

constitution [,kɔnsti'tju:ʃən] *n* grondwet *c*

construct [kən'strʌkt] *v* bouwen; opbouwen, construeren

construction [kən'strʌkʃən] *n* constructie *c*; opbouw *c*; gebouw *nt*, bouw *c*

consul ['kɔnsəl] *n* consul *m*

consulate ['kɔnsjulət] *n* consulaat *nt*

consult [kən'sʌlt] *v* raadplegen

consultation [,kɔnsəl'teiʃən] *n* raadpleging *c*; consult *nt*; ~ **hours** *n* spreekuur *nt*

consume [kən'sju:m] *v* consumeren, nuttigen

consumer [kən'sju:mə] *n* verbruiker *c*, consument *m*, -e *f*

contact ['kɔntækt] *n* contact *nt*; omgang *c*; aanraking *c*; *v* zich in verbinding stellen met; ~ **lenses** contactlenzen *pl*

contagious [kən'teidʒəs] *adj* aanstekelijk, besmettelijk

contain [kən'tein] *v* bevatten; *inhouden

container [kən'teinə] *n* reservoir *nt*; container *c*

contemporary [kən'tempərəri] *adj* eigentijds; toenmalig; hedendaags; *n* tijdgenoot *m*

contempt [kən'tempt] *n* verachting *c*, minachting *c*

content [kən'tent] *adj* tevreden

contents ['kɔntents] *pl* inhoud *c*

contest ['kɔntest] *n* strijd *c*; wedstrijd *c*

continent ['kɔntinənt] *n* continent *nt*, werelddeel *nt*; vasteland *nt*

continental [,kɔnti'nentəl] *adj* continentaal

continual [kən'tinjuəl] *adj* voortdurend; **continually** *adv* steeds

continue [kən'tinju:] *v* voortzetten, vervolgen; *voortgaan, *doorgaan, voortduren

continuous [kən'tinjuəs] *adj* voortdurend, doorlopend, onafgebroken

contour ['kɔntuə] *n* omtrek *c*

contraceptive [,kɔntrə'septiv] *n* voorbehoedmiddel *nt*

contract¹ ['kɔntrækt] *n* contract *nt*

contract² [kən'trækt] *v* *oplopen

contractor [kən'træktə] *n* aannemer *c*

contradict [,kɔntrə'dikt] *v* *tegenspreken

contradictory [,kɔntrə'diktəri] *adj* tegenstrijdig

contrary ['kɔntrəri] *n* tegendeel *nt*; *adj* tegengesteld; **on the** ~ integendeel

contrast ['kɔntrɑ:st] *n* contrast *nt*; verschil *nt*, tegenstelling *c*

contribution [,kɔntri'bju:ʃən] *n* bijdrage *c*

control [kən'troul] *n* controle *c*; *v* controleren

controversial [,kɔntrə'və:ʃəl] *adj* controversieel, omstreden

convenience [kən'vi:njəns] *n* gemak *nt*

convenient [kən'vi:njənt] *adj* gerielijk; geschikt, passend, gemakkelijk; **be ~** v uitkomen

convent ['kɔnvənt] n klooster nt

conversation [,kɔnvə'seiʃən] n conversatie c, gesprek nt

convert [kən'vəːt] v bekeren; omrekenen

convict[1] [kən'vikt] v schuldig *bevinden

convict[2] ['kɔnvikt] n veroordeelde c

conviction [kən'vikʃən] n overtuiging c; veroordeling c

convince [kən'vins] v overtuigen

convulsion [kən'vʌlʃən] n kramp c

cook [kuk] n kok m, kokkin f; v koken; bereiden, klaarmaken

cookbook ['kukbuk] nAm kookboek nt

cooker ['kukə] n fornuis nt; **gas ~** gasfornuis nt

cookery book ['kukəribuk] n kookboek nt

cookie ['kuki] nAm biscuit nt; koekje

cool [kuːl] adj koel

cooperation [kou,ɔpə'reiʃən] n samenwerking c; medewerking c

co-operative [kou'ɔpərətiv] adj coöperatief; gewillig, bereidwillig; n coöperatie c

coordinate [kou'ɔːdineit] v coördineren

coordination [kou,ɔːdi'neiʃən] n coördinatie c

cope [koup] v het aankunnen

copper ['kɔpə] n roodkoper nt, koper nt

copy ['kɔpi] n kopie c; afschrift nt; exemplaar nt; v kopiëren; namaken; **carbon ~** doorslag c

coral ['kɔrəl] n koraal c

cord [kɔːd] n koord nt; snoer nt

cordial ['kɔːdiəl] adj hartelijk; n ranja c, limonadesiroop c

corduroy ['kɔːdərɔi] n ribfluweel nt

core [kɔː] n kern c; klokhuis nt

cork [kɔːk] n kurk c; stop c

corkscrew ['kɔːkskruː] n kurketrekker c

corn [kɔːn] n korrel c; graan nt, koren nt; eksteroog nt, likdoorn c; **~ on the cob** maïskolf c

corner ['kɔːnə] n hoek c

cornfield ['kɔːnfiːld] n korenveld nt

corpse [kɔːps] n lijk nt

corpulent ['kɔːpjulənt] adj corpulent; gezet, dik

correct [kə'rekt] adj goed, correct, juist; v corrigeren, verbeteren

correction [kə'rekʃən] n correctie c; verbetering c

correctness [kə'rektnəs] n juistheid c

correspond [,kɔri'spɔnd] v corresponderen; *overeenkomen

correspondence [,kɔri'spɔndəns] n briefwisseling c, correspondentie c

correspondent [,kɔri'spɔndənt] n correspondent m, -e f

corridor ['kɔridɔː] n gang c

corrupt [kə'rʌpt] adj corrupt; v *omkopen

corruption [kə'rʌpʃən] n omkoping c

corset ['kɔːsit] n korset nt

cosmetics [kɔz'metiks] pl kosmetica pl, schoonheidsmiddelen pl

cost [kɔst] n kosten pl; prijs c

***cost** [kɔst] v kosten

cosy ['kouzi] adj knus, gezellig

cot [kɔt] nAm stretcher c

cottage ['kɔtidʒ] n buitenhuis nt

cotton ['kɔtən] n katoen nt/c; katoenen; **~ wool** watten pl

couch [kautʃ] n divan c

couchette [kuː'ʃet] n slaapwagen c

cough [kɔf] n hoest c; v hoesten

could [kud] v (p can)

council ['kaunsəl] n raad c

councillor ['kaunsələ] n raadslid nt

counsel ['kaunsəl] n raad c

counsellor ['kaunsələ] n raadsman m

count [kaunt] v tellen; optellen; meetellen; achten; n graaf m

counter ['kauntə] n toonbank c; balie c

counterfeit ['kauntəfiːt] v vervalsen

counterfoil ['kauntəfɔil] n controlestrook c

countess ['kauntis] n gravin f

country ['kʌntri] n land nt; platteland nt; streek c; ~ **house** landhuis nt

countryman ['kʌntrimən] n (pl -men) landgenoot m

countryside ['kʌntrisaid] n platteland nt

county ['kaunti] n graafschap nt

couple ['kʌpəl] n paar nt

coupon ['kuːpɔn] n coupon c, bon c

courage ['kʌridʒ] n dapperheid c, moed c

courageous [kə'reidʒəs] adj dapper, moedig

course [kɔːs] n koers c; gang c; loop c; cursus c; **intensive** ~ spoedcursus c; **of** ~ uiteraard, natuurlijk

court [kɔːt] n rechtbank c; hof nt

courteous ['kəːtiəs] adj hoffelijk

cousin ['kʌzən] n nicht f, neef m

cover ['kʌvə] v bedekken; n schuilplaats c, beschutting c, deksel nt; omslag c/nt

cow [kau] n koe f

coward ['kauəd] n lafaard m

cowardly ['kauədli] adj laf

crab [kræb] n krab c

crack [kræk] n gekraak nt; barst c; v kraken; *breken, barsten

cradle ['kreidəl] n wieg c; bakermat c

crap [kræp] n vulgar stront c

cramp [kræmp] n kramp c

crane [krein] n hijskraan c

crash [kræʃ] n botsing c; v botsen; neerstorten; ~ **barrier** vangrail c

crate [kreit] n krat nt

crater ['kreitə] n krater c

crawl [krɔːl] v *kruipen

craze [kreiz] n rage c

crazy ['kreizi] adj gek; dwaas, krankzinnig

creak [kriːk] v kraken

cream [kriːm] n crème c; room c; adj roomkleurig

creamy ['kriːmi] adj romig

crease [kriːs] v kreuken; n vouw c; plooi c

create [kri'eit] v *scheppen; creëren

creative [kri'eitiv] adj creatief

creature ['kriːtʃə] n schepsel nt; wezen nt

credible ['kredibəl] adj geloofwaardig

credit ['kredit] n krediet nt; v crediteren; ~ **card** credit card

creditor ['kreditə] n schuldeiser m

credulous ['kredjuləs] adj goedgelovig

creek [kriːk] n inham c, kreek c

***creep** [kriːp] v *kruipen

creepy ['kriːpi] adj eng, griezelig

cremate [kri'meit] v cremeren

cremation [kri'meiʃən] n crematie c

crew [kruː] n bemanning c

cricket ['krikit] n cricket nt; krekel c

crime [kraim] n misdaad c

criminal ['kriminəl] n delinquent c, misdadiger m, misdadigster f; adj crimineel, misdadig; ~ **law** strafrecht nt

criminality [,krimi'næləti] n criminaliteit c

crimson ['krimzən] adj vuurrood

crippled ['kripəld] adj kreupel

crisis ['kraisis] n (pl crises) crisis c

crisp [krisp] adj krokant, knapperig

critic ['kritik] n criticus m

critical ['kritikəl] adj kritisch; kritiek, hachelijk, zorgwekkend

criticism ['kritisizəm] n kritiek c

criticize ['kritisaiz] v bekritiseren

crochet ['krouʃei] v haken

crockery ['krɔkəri] n aardewerk nt,

vaatwerk *nt*

crocodile ['krɔkədail] *n* krokodil *c*

crooked ['krukid] *adj* krom; oneerlijk

crop [krɔp] *n* oogst *c*

cross [krɔs] *v* *oversteken; *adj* kwaad, boos; *n* kruis *nt*

cross-eyed ['krɔsaid] *adj* scheel

crossing ['krɔsiŋ] *n* overtocht *c*; kruising *c*; oversteekplaats *c*; overweg *c*

crossroads ['krɔsroudz] *n* kruispunt *nt*

crosswalk ['krɔswɔːk] *nAm* zebrapad *nt*

crow [krou] *n* kraai *c*

crowbar ['kroubɑː] *n* breekijzer *nt*

crowd [kraud] *n* massa *c*, menigte *c*

crowded ['kraudid] *adj* druk; overvol

crown [kraun] *n* kroon *c*; *v* kronen; bekronen

crucifix ['kruːsifiks] *n* kruisbeeld *nt*

crucifixion [,kruːsi'fikʃən] *n* kruisiging *c*

crucify ['kruːsifai] *v* kruisigen

cruel [kruəl] *adj* wreed

cruise [kruːz] *n* boottocht *c*, cruise *c*

crumb [krʌm] *n* kruimel *c*

crusade [kruː'seid] *n* kruistocht *c*

crust [krʌst] *n* korst *c*

crutch [krʌtʃ] *n* kruk *c*

cry [krai] *v* huilen; schreeuwen; *roepen; *n* kreet *c*, schreeuw *c*; roep *c*

crystal ['kristəl] *n* kristal *nt*; *adj* kristallen

Cuba ['kjuːbə] Cuba

Cuban ['kjuːbən] *adj* Cubaans; *n* Cubaan *m*, -se *f*

cube [kjuːb] *n* kubus *c*; blokje *nt*

cuckoo ['kukuː] *n* koekoek *c*

cucumber ['kjuːkʌmbə] *n* komkommer *c*

cuddle ['kʌdəl] *v* knuffelen

cuff [kʌf] *n* manchet *c*; ~ **links** *pl* manchetknopen *pl*

cul-de-sac ['kʌldəsæk] *n* doodlopende weg

cultivate ['kʌltiveit] *v* bebouwen; verbouwen, kweken

culture ['kʌltʃə] *n* cultuur *c*; beschaving *c*

cultured ['kʌltʃəd] *adj* beschaafd

cunning ['kʌniŋ] *adj* sluw

cup [kʌp] *n* kopje *nt*; beker *c*

cupboard ['kʌbəd] *n* kast *c*

curb [kəːb] *n* trottoirband *c*; *v* beteugelen

cure [kjuə] *v* *genezen; *n* kuur *c*; genezing *c*

curiosity [,kjuəri'ɔsəti] *n* nieuwsgierigheid *c*

curious ['kjuəriəs] *adj* benieuwd, nieuwsgierig; raar

curl [kəːl] *v* krullen; *n* krul *c*

curler ['kəːlə] *n* krulspeld *c*

curly ['kəːli] *adj* krullend

currant ['kʌrənt] *n* krent *c*; bes *c*

currency ['kʌrənsi] *n* valuta *c*, munteenheid *c*; **foreign ~** buitenlands geld

current ['kʌrənt] *n* stroming *c*; stroom *c*; *adj* gangbaar, huidig; **alternating ~** wisselstroom *c*; **direct ~** gelijkstroom *c*

curry ['kʌri] *n* kerrie *c*

curse [kəːs] *v* vloeken; vervloeken; *n* vloek *c*

curtain ['kəːtən] *n* gordijn *nt*; doek *nt*

curve [kəːv] *n* kromming *c*; bocht *c*

curved [kəːvd] *adj* krom, gebogen

cushion ['kuʃən] *n* kussen *nt*

custody ['kʌstədi] *n* hechtenis *c*; hoede *c*; voogdij *c*

custom ['kʌstəm] *n* gewoonte *c*; gebruik *nt*

customary ['kʌstəməri] *adj* gebruikelijk, gewoon, gewoonlijk

customer ['kʌstəmə] *n* klant *c*; cliënt *m*, -e *f*

customs ['kʌstəmz] *pl* douane *c*; ~

duty accijns c; **~ officer**
douanebeambte c
cut [kʌt] n snee c; snijwond c
*cut [kʌt] v *snijden; knippen;
verlagen; **~ down** minderen; **~ off**
*afsnijden; afknippen; *afsluiten
cutlery ['kʌtləri] n bestek nt
cutlet ['kʌtlət] n karbonade c
cycle ['saikəl] n fiets c; rijwiel nt;

kringloop c, cyclus c
cyclist ['saiklist] n fietser m, fietsster f;
wielrijder m, wielrijdster f
cylinder ['silində] n cilinder c; **~ head**
cilinderkop c
cynical ['sinikəl] adj cynisch
cystitis [si'staitis] n blaasontsteking c
Czech [tʃek] adj Tsjechisch; n Tsjech
m, Tsjechische f

D

dad [dæd] n vader m
daddy ['dædi] n papa m
daffodil ['dæfədil] n narcis c
daily ['deili] adj dagelijks; n dagblad nt
dairy ['deəri] n zuivelwinkel c
dam [dæm] n dam c; dijk c
damage ['dæmidʒ] n schade c; v
beschadigen
damn [dæm] v vulgar verdommen; ~!
verdomme!
damp [dæmp] adj vochtig; nat; n vocht
nt; v bevochtigen
dance [dɑːns] v dansen; n dans c
dandelion ['dændilaiən] n
paardebloem c
dandruff ['dændrəf] n roos c
Dane [dein] n Deen m, -se f
danger ['deindʒə] n gevaar nt
dangerous ['deindʒərəs] adj
gevaarlijk
Danish ['deiniʃ] adj Deens
dare [deə] v wagen, durven; uitdagen
daring ['deəriŋ] adj gedurfd
dark [dɑːk] adj duister, donker; n
duisternis c
darling ['dɑːliŋ] n schat c, lieveling c
darn [dɑːn] v stoppen
dash [dæʃ] v snellen; n
gedachtenstreepje nt

dashboard ['dæʃbɔːd] n dashboard nt
data ['deitə] pl gegeven nt
date¹ [deit] n datum c; afspraakje c; v
dateren; **out of ~** ouderwets; **dated**
verouderd
date² [deit] n dadel c
daughter ['dɔːtə] n dochter f
daughter-in-law ['dɔːtərinlɔː] n (pl
daughters-) schoondochter f
dawn [dɔːn] n ochtendschemering c;
dageraad c
day [dei] n dag c; **by ~** overdag; **~ trip**
excursie c; **per ~** per dag; **the ~ before
yesterday** eergisteren
daybreak ['deibreik] n dageraad c
daylight ['deilait] n daglicht nt
dazzling [d] adj verbazend
dead [ded] adj dood; gestorven
deaf [def] adj doof
deal [diːl] n transactie c, affaire c
*deal [diːl] v uitdelen; **~ with** v te maken
*hebben met; zaken *doen met
dealer ['diːlə] n koopman m, handelaar
m, -ster f
dear [diə] adj lief; duur; dierbaar; **~ Sir/
Madam** geachte heer
death [deθ] n dood c; **~ penalty**
doodstraf c
debate [di'beit] n debat nt

debit ['debit] n debet nt
debt [det] n schuld c
decaf(feinated) [di:'kæf(ineitid)] adj cafeïnevrij, coffeïnevrij
deceit [di'si:t] n bedrog nt
deceive [di'si:v] v *bedriegen
December [di'sembə] december
decency ['di:sənsi] n fatsoen nt
decent ['di:sənt] adj fatsoenlijk
decide [di'said] v beslissen, *besluiten
decision [di'siʒən] n beslissing c, besluit nt
deck [dek] n dek nt; ~ **cabin** dekhut c; ~ **chair** ligstoel c
declaration [,deklə'reiʃən] n verklaring c; aangifte c
declare [di'kleə] v verklaren; *opgeven; *aangeven
decorate ['dekəreit] v versieren; inrichten
decoration [,dekə'reiʃən] n versiering c
decrease [di:'kri:s] v verminderen; *afnemen; n vermindering c
dedicate ['dedikeit] v toewijden
deduce [di'dju:s] v afleiden
deduct [di'dʌkt] v *aftrekken
deed [di:d] n handeling c, daad c
deep [di:p] adj diep
deep-freeze [,di:p'fri:z] n diepvrieskast c
deer [diə] n (pl ~) hert nt
defeat [di'fi:t] v *verslaan; n nederlaag c
defective [di'fektiv] adj gebrekkig, defect
defence [di'fens] n verdediging c; defensie c
defend [di'fend] v verdedigen
defense [di'fens] nAm verdediging c; defensie c
deficiency [di'fiʃənsi] n gebrek nt
deficit ['defisit] n tekort nt
define [di'fain] v *omschrijven, bepalen, definiëren
definite ['definit] adj bepaald; vastomlijnd
definition [,defi'niʃən] n bepaling c, definitie c
deformed [di'fɔ:md] adj misvormd, mismaakt
degree [di'gri:] n graad c; titel c
delay [di'lei] v vertragen; uitstellen; n oponthoud nt, vertraging c; uitstel nt
delegate ['deligət] n gedelegeerde c
delegation [,deli'geiʃən] n delegatie c, afvaardiging c
deliberate¹ [di'libəreit] v beraadslagen, overleggen
deliberate² [di'libərət] adj opzettelijk
deliberation [di,libə'reiʃən] n beraad nt, overleg nt
delicacy ['delikəsi] n lekkernij c, delicatesse c
delicate ['delikət] adj fijn; teder; delikaat
delicatessen [,delikə'tesən] n delicatessen pl; delicatessenwinkel c
delicious [di'liʃəs] adj lekker, heerlijk
delight [di'lait] n genot nt, verrukking c; v in verrukking *brengen; **delighted** opgetogen
delightful [di'laitfəl] adj heerlijk, verrukkelijk
deliver [di'livə] v afleveren, bezorgen; verlossen
delivery [di'livəri] n levering c, bezorging c; bevalling c; verlossing c; ~ **van** bestelauto c
demand [di'mɑ:nd] v vereisen, eisen; n eis c; navraag c
democracy [di'mɔkrəsi] n democratie c
democratic [,demə'krætik] adj democratisch
demolish [di'mɔliʃ] v slopen
demolition [,demə'liʃən] n afbraak c
demonstrate ['demənstreit] v

aantonen; demonstreren, betogen

demonstration [,demən'streiʃən] n
demonstratie c; betoging c

den [den] n hol nt

Denmark ['denmɑːk] Denemarken

denomination [di,nɔmi'neiʃən] n
benaming c, naam c

dense [dens] adj dicht

dent [dent] n deuk c

dentist ['dentist] n tandarts c

denture ['dentʃə] n kunstgebit nt

deny [di'nai] v ontkennen;
*onthouden, weigeren, *ontzeggen

deodorant [diː'oudərənt] n deodorant
c

depart [di'pɑːt] v *heengaan,
*vertrekken; *overlijden

department [di'pɑːtmənt] n
departement nt, afdeling c; ~ **store**
warenhuis nt

departure [di'pɑːtʃə] n vertrek nt

dependant [di'pendənt] adj
afhankelijk

depend on [di'pend] *afhangen van
that depends dat hangt ervan af

deposit [di'pɔzit] n storting c;
statiegeld nt; bezinksel nt, afzetting c;
v storten; deponeren

depository [di'pɔzitəri] n bergplaats c

depot ['depou] n opslagplaats c; nAm
station nt

depress [di'pres] v deprimeren

depressed [di'prest] adj neerslachtig

depressing [di'presiŋ] adj triest

depression [di'preʃən] n
neerslachtigheid c; depressie c;
teruggang c

deprive of [di'praiv] *ontnemen

depth [depθ] n diepte c

deputy ['depjuti] n afgevaardigde c;
plaatsvervanger m

descend [di'send] v dalen

descendant [di'sendənt] n
afstammeling m

descent [di'sent] n afdaling c

describe [di'skraib] v *beschrijven

description [di'skripʃən] n
beschrijving c; signalement nt

desert¹ ['dezət] n woestijn c; adj woest,
verlaten

desert² [di'zəːt] v deserteren;
*verlaten

deserve [di'zəːv] v verdienen

design [di'zain] v *ontwerpen; n
ontwerp nt; doel nt

designate ['dezigneit] v *aanwijzen

desirable [di'zaiərəbəl] adj begeerlijk,
wenselijk

desire [di'zaiə] n wens c; zin c, begeerte
c; v begeren, verlangen, wensen

desk [desk] n bureau nt; lessenaar c;
schoolbank c

despair [di'spɛə] n wanhoop c; v
wanhopen

despatch [di'spætʃ] v *verzenden

desperate ['despərət] adj wanhopig

despise [di'spaiz] v verachten

despite [di'spait] prep ondanks

dessert [di'zəːt] n dessert nt

destination [,desti'neiʃən] n
bestemming c

destine ['destin] v bestemmen

destiny ['destini] n noodlot nt, lot nt

destroy [di'strɔi] v vernielen,
vernietigen

destruction [di'strʌkʃən] n
vernietiging c; ondergang c

detach [di'tætʃ] v losmaken

detail ['diːteil] n bijzonderheid c, detail
nt

detailed ['diːteild] adj uitvoerig,
gedetailleerd

detect [di'tekt] v ontdekken

detective [di'tektiv] n detective m; ~
story detectiveroman c

detergent [di'təːdʒənt] n wasmiddel nt

determine [di'təːmin] v vaststellen,
bepalen, uitmaken

determined [di'tə:mind] *adj* vastbesloten

detest [di'test] *v* verafschuwen

detour ['di:tuə] *n* omweg *c*; omleiding *c*

devaluation [,di:vælju'eiʃən] *n* devaluatie *c*

devalue [,di:'vælju:] *v* devalueren

develop [di'veləp] *v* ontwikkelen

development [di'veləpmənt] *n* ontwikkeling *c*

deviate ['di:vieit] *v* *afwijken

deviation [di:vi'eiʃn] *n* afwijking *c*

devil ['devəl] *n* duivel *m*

devise [di'vaiz] *v* beramen

devote [di'vout] *v* wijden

dew [dju:] *n* dauw *c*

diabetes [,daiə'bi:ti:z] *n* diabetes *c*, suikerziekte *c*

diabetic [,daiə'betik] *n* suikerzieke *c*, diabeticus *m*, diabetica *f*

diagnose [,daiəg'nouz] *v* een diagnose stellen; constateren

diagnosis [,daiəg'nousis] *n* (pl -ses) diagnose *c*

diagonal [dai'ægənəl] *n* diagonaal *c*; *adj* diagonaal

diagram ['daiəgræm] *n* schema *nt*, diagram *c*; figuur *c*, grafiek *c*

dial ['daiəl] *n* wijzerplaat *c*; *v* *kiezen

dialect ['daiəlekt] *n* dialect *nt*

diamond ['daiəmənd] *n* diamant *c*

diaper ['daiəpə] *nAm* luier *c*

diaphragm ['daiəfræm] *n* pessarium *nt*; middenrif *nt*; tussenschot *nt*

diarrh(o)ea [daiə'riə] *n* diarree *c*

diary ['daiəri] *n* agenda *c*; dagboek *nt*

dictaphone ['diktəfoun] *n* dictafoon *c*

dictate [dik'teit] *v* dicteren

dictation [dik'teiʃən] *n* dictaat *nt*; dictee *nt*

dictator [dik'teitə] *n* dictator *m*

dictionary ['dikʃənəri] *n* woordenboek *nt*

did [did] *v* (p do)

die [dai] *v* *sterven; *overlijden

diesel ['di:zəl] *n* diesel *c*

diet ['daiət] *n* dieet *nt*

differ ['difə] *v* verschillen

difference ['difərəns] *n* verschil *nt*; onderscheid *nt*

different ['difərənt] *adj* verschillend; ander

difficult ['difikəlt] *adj* moeilijk; lastig

difficulty ['difikəlti] *n* moeilijkheid *c*; moeite *c*

*dig [dig] *v* *graven; *delven

digest [di'dʒest] *v* verteren

digestible [di'dʒestəbəl] *adj* verteerbaar

digestion [di'dʒestʃən] *n* spijsvertering *c*

digit ['didʒit] *n* cijfer *nt*; vinger *c*

digital [didʒitəl] *adj* digitaal

dignified ['dignifaid] *adj* waardig

dignity ['digniti] *n* waardigheid *c*

dike [daik] *n* dijk *c*; dam *c*

dilapidated [di'læpideitid] *adj* bouwvallig

diligence ['dilidʒəns] *n* vlijt *c*, ijver *c*

diligent ['dilidʒənt] *adj* vlijtig, ijverig

dilute [dai'lju:t] *v* aanlengen, verdunnen

dim [dim] *adj* dof, mat; donker, zwak, vaag

dine [dain] *v* warm *eten; dineren

dinghy ['diŋgi] *n* bootje *nt*

dining car ['dainiŋka:] *n* restauratiewagen *c*

dining room ['dainiŋru:m] *n* eetkamer *c*; eetzaal *c*

dinner ['dinə] *n* warme maaltijd; avondeten *nt*, middageten *nt*; ~ **jacket** smoking *c*; ~ **service** eetservies *nt*

diphtheria [dif'θiəriə] *n* difterie *c*

diploma [di'ploumə] *n* diploma *nt*

diplomat ['dipləmæt] *n* diplomaat *m*

direct¹ ['direkt] *adj* rechtstreeks, direct

direct² [di'rekt] *v* richten; *wijzen;

leiden; regisseren

direction [di'rekʃən] n richting c; instructie c; regie c; bestuur nt; **directional signal** Am richtingaanwijzer c; **directions for use** gebruiksaanwijzing c

directive [di'rektiv] n richtlijn c

director [di'rektə] n directeur m, directrice f; regisseur m, regisseuse f

directory [di'rektəri] n telefoonboek nt

dirt [də:t] n vuil nt

dirty ['də:ti] adj smerig, vies, vuil

disabled [di'seibəld] adj gehandicapt, invalide

disadvantage [ˌdisəd'vɑːntidʒ] n nadeel nt

disagree [ˌdisə'gri:] v het oneens *zijn, van mening verschillen

disagreeable [ˌdisə'gri:əbəl] adj onaangenaam

disappear [ˌdisə'piə] v *verdwijnen

disappoint [ˌdisə'pɔint] v teleurstellen; ***be disappointing** *tegenvallen

disappointment [ˌdisə'pɔintmənt] n teleurstelling c

disapprove [ˌdisə'pru:v] v afkeuren

disaster [di'zɑːstə] n ramp c; catastrofe c, onheil nt; fiasco nt

disastrous [di'zɑːstrəs] adj rampzalig

disc [disk] n schijf c; **slipped ~** hernia c

discard [di'skɑːd] v afdanken

discharge [dis'tʃɑːdʒ] v lossen, *uitladen; **~ of** *ontheffen van

discipline ['disiplin] n discipline c

discolo(u)r [di'skʌlə] v verkleuren

disconnect [ˌdiskə'nekt] v ontkoppelen; uitschakelen

discontented [ˌdiskən'tentid] adj ontevreden

discontinue [ˌdiskən'tinju:] v *opheffen, staken

discount ['diskaunt] n korting c, reductie c

discourage [di'skʌridʒ] v ontmoedigen

discover [di'skʌvə] v ontdekken

discovery [di'skʌvəri] n ontdekking c

discuss [di'skʌs] v *bespreken; discussiëren

discussion [di'skʌʃən] n discussie c; gesprek nt, bespreking c, debat nt

disease [di'ziːz] n ziekte c

disembark [ˌdisim'bɑːk] v van boord *gaan, ontschepen

disgrace [dis'greis] n schande c

disguise [dis'gaiz] v zich vermommen; n vermomming c

disgust [dis'gʌst] n afschuw, weerzin; v doen walgen

disgusting [dis'gʌstiŋ] adj walgelijk, afschuwelijk

dish [diʃ] n bord nt; schotel c, schaal c; gerecht nt

dishonest [di'sɔnist] adj oneerlijk

dishwasher ['diʃwɔʃə] n afwasmachine, vaatwasmachine

disinfect [ˌdisin'fekt] v ontsmetten

disinfectant [ˌdisin'fektənt] n ontsmettingsmiddel nt

dislike [di'slaik] v een hekel *hebben aan, niet *houden van; n afkeer c, hekel c, antipathie c

dislocated ['dislə keitid] adj ontwricht

dismiss [dis'mis] v *wegzenden; *ontslaan

disorder [di'sɔːdə] n wanorde c

dispatch [di'spætʃ] v versturen, *verzenden

display [di'splei] v vertonen; tonen; n tentoonstelling c; display

displease [di'spliːz] v ontstemmen, mishagen

disposable [di'spouzəbəl] adj wegwerp-

disposal [di'spouzəl] n beschikking c

dispose of [di'spouz] beschikken over

dispute [di'spju:t] *n* onenigheid *c*; ruzie *c*, geschil *nt*; *v* twisten, betwisten

dissatisfied [di'sætisfaid] *adj* ontevreden

dissolve [di'zɔlv] *v* oplossen; *ontbinden

dissuade from [di'sweid] *afraden

distance ['distəns] *n* afstand *c*; ~ **in kilometers** *Am*, **kilometres** kilometertal *nt*

distant ['distənt] *adj* ver

distinct [di'stiŋkt] *adj* duidelijk; verschillend

distinction [di'stiŋkʃən] *n* onderscheid *nt*, verschil *nt*

distinguish [di'stiŋgwiʃ] *v* onderscheid maken, *onderscheiden

distinguished [di'stiŋgwiʃt] *adj* voornaam

distress [di'stres] *n* nood *c*; ~ **signal** noodsein *nt*

distribute [di'stribju:t] *v* uitdelen

distributor [di'stribjutə] *n* agent *m*, -e *f*; stroomverdeler *c*

district ['distrikt] *n* district *nt*; streek *c*; wijk *c*

disturb [di'stə:b] *v* storen, verstoren

disturbance [di'stə:bəns] *n* storing *c*; verwarring *c*

ditch [ditʃ] *n* greppel *c*, sloot *c*

dive [daiv] *v* *duiken

diversion [dai'və:ʃən] *n* wegomlegging *c*; afleiding *c*

divide [di'vaid] *v* delen; verdelen; *scheiden

divine [di'vain] *adj* goddelijk

division [di'viʒən] *n* deling *c*; scheiding *c*; afdeling *c*

divorce [di'vɔ:s] *n* echtscheiding *c*; *v* *scheiden

dizziness ['dizinəs] *n* duizeligheid *c*

dizzy ['dizi] *adj* duizelig

*do [du:] *v* *doen; voldoende *zijn

dock [dɔk] *n* dok *nt*; kade *c*; *v* aanleggen

docker ['dɔkə] *n* havenarbeider *m*

doctor ['dɔktə] *n* arts *c*, dokter *c*; doctor *c*

document ['dɔkjumənt] *n* document *nt*

dog [dɔg] *n* hond *c*

dogged ['dɔgid] *adj* hardnekkig

doll [dɔl] *n* pop *c*

dollar ['dɔlə] *n* dollar *c*

dome [doum] *n* koepel *c*

domestic [də'mestik] *adj* huiselijk; binnenlands; *n* bediende *c*; ~ **animal** huisdier *nt*

domicile ['dɔmisail] *n* woonplaats *c*

domination [,dɔmi'neiʃən] *n* overheersing *c*

dominion [də'minjən] *n* heerschappij *c*

donate [dou'neit] *v* *schenken

donation [dou'neiʃən] *n* schenking *c*, gift *c*

done [dʌn] *v* (pp do)

donkey ['dɔŋki] *n* ezel *c*

donor ['dounə] *n* donateur *c*; donor *c*

door [dɔ:] *n* deur *c*; **revolving ~** draaideur *c*; **sliding ~** schuifdeur *c*

doorbell ['dɔ:bel] *n* deurbel *c*

doorkeeper ['dɔ:,ki:pə] *n* portier *m*

doorman ['dɔ:mən] *n* (pl -men) portier *m*

dormitory ['dɔ:mitri] *n* slaapzaal *c*

dose [dous] *n* dosis *c*

dot [dɔt] *n* punt *c*

double ['dʌbəl] *adj* dubbel

doubt [daut] *v* betwijfelen, twijfelen; *n* twijfel *c*; **without ~** zonder twijfel

doubtful ['dautfəl] *adj* twijfelachtig; onzeker

dough [dou] *n* deeg *nt*

down¹ [daun] *adv* neer; omlaag, naar beneden, omver; *adj* neerslachtig; *prep* langs, van … af; ~ **payment** aanbetaling *c*

down² [daun] *n* dons *nt*

downpour ['daunpɔ:] n stortbui c

downstairs [,daun'stɛəz] adv naar beneden, beneden

downstream [,daun'stri:m] adv stroomafwaarts

down-to-earth [,dauntu'ə:θ] adj nuchter

downwards ['daunwədz] adv neer, naar beneden

dozen ['dʌzən] n (pl ~, ~s) dozijn nt

draft [drɑ:ft] n wissel c

drag [dræg] v slepen

dragon ['drægən] n draak c

drain [drein] v droogleggen; afwateren; n afvoer c

drama ['drɑ:mə] n drama nt; treurspel nt; toneel nt

dramatic [drə'mætik] adj dramatisch

dramatist ['dræmətist] n toneelschrijver m, toneelschrijfster f

drank [dræŋk] v (p drink)

drapery ['dreipəri] n stoffen

draught [drɑ:ft] n tocht c; **draughts** damspel nt; ~ **beer** bier uit het vat

draw [drɔ:] n trekking c

*****draw** [drɔ:] v tekenen; *trekken; *opnemen; ~ **up** opstellen

drawbridge ['drɔ:bridʒ] n ophaalbrug c

drawer ['drɔ:ə] n la c, lade c; **drawers** onderbroek c

drawing ['drɔ:iŋ] n tekening c; ~ **pin** punaise c; ~ **room** salon c

dread [dred] v vrezen; n vrees c

dreadful ['dredfəl] adj vreselijk, ontzettend

dream [dri:m] n droom c

*****dream** [dri:m] v dromen

dress [dres] v aankleden; zich kleden, zich aankleden; *verbinden; n japon c, jurk c

dressing gown ['dresiŋgaun] n kamerjas c

dressing room ['dresiŋru:m] n kleedkamer c

dressing table ['dresiŋ,teibəl] n toilettafel c

dressmaker ['dres,meikə] n naaister f

drill [dril] v boren; trainen; n boor c

drink [driŋk] n borrel c, drank c

*****drink** [driŋk] v *drinken

drinking water ['driŋkiŋ,wɔ:tə] n drinkwater nt

drip-dry [,drip'drai] adj zelfstrijkend, no-iron

drive [draiv] n rijweg c; autorit c

*****drive** [draiv] v *rijden; besturen

driver ['draivə] n chauffeur c

driver's licence, Brit **driving licence** rijbewijs

drizzle ['drizəl] n motregen c

drop [drɔp] v *laten vallen; n druppel c

drought [draut] n droogte c

drown [draun] v *verdrinken; *be **drowned** *verdrinken

drug [drʌg] n verdovend middel; geneesmiddel nt

drugstore ['drʌgstɔ:] nAm drogisterij c, apotheek c; warenhuis nt

drum [drʌm] n trommel c

drunk [drʌŋk] adj (pp drink) dronken

dry [drai] adj droog; v drogen; afdrogen

dry-clean [,drai'kli:n] v chemisch reinigen

dry cleaner's [,drai'kli:nəz] n stomerij c

dryer ['draiə] n centrifuge c

duchess [dʌt∫is] n hertogin f

duck [dʌk] n eend c

due [dju:] adj verwacht; verschuldigd; vervallen; ~ **to** vanwege

dues [dju:z] pl schulden pl

dug [dʌg] v (p, pp dig)

duke [dju:k] n hertog m

dull [dʌl] adj vervelend, saai; flets, mat; bot

dumb [dʌm] adj stom; suf, dom

dune [dju:n] n duin nt

dung [dʌŋ] *n* mest *c*
dunghill ['dʌŋhil] *n* mesthoop *c*
duration [dju'reiʃən] *n* duur *c*
during ['djuəriŋ] *prep* gedurende, tijdens
dusk [dʌsk] *n* avondschemering *c*
dust [dʌst] *n* stof *nt*
dustbin ['dʌstbin] *n* vuilnisbak *c*, container *c*
dusty ['dʌsti] *adj* stoffig
Dutch [dʌtʃ] *adj* Nederlands,
Hollands; **she's ~** zij is Nederlandse; **the ~** de Nederlanders
Dutchman ['dʌtʃmən] *n* (pl -men) Nederlander *m*, Hollander *m*
duty ['djuːti] *n* plicht *c*; taak *c*; invoerrecht *nt*; **Customs ~** accijns *c*
duty-free [,djuːti'friː] *adj* belastingvrij
dwarf [dwɔːf] *n* dwerg *c*
dye [dai] *v* verven; *n* verf *c*
dynamo ['dainəmou] *n* (pl ~s) dynamo *c*

E

each [iːtʃ] *adj* elk, ieder; **~ other** elkaar
eager ['iːgə] *adj* verlangend, ongeduldig
eagle ['iːgəl] *n* arend *c*
ear [iə] *n* oor *nt*
earache ['iəreik] *n* oorpijn *c*
eardrum ['iədrʌm] *n* trommelvlies *nt*
earl [əːl] *n* graaf *m*
early ['əːli] *adj* vroeg
earn [əːn] *v* verdienen
earnest ['əːnist] *adj* oprecht
earnings ['əːniŋz] *pl* inkomsten *pl*, verdiensten *pl*
earring ['iəriŋ] *n* oorbel *c*
earth [əːθ] *n* aarde *c*; grond *c*
earthquake ['əːθkweik] *n* aardbeving *c*
ease [iːz] *n* ongedwongenheid *c*, gemak *nt*
east [iːst] *n* oost *c*, oosten *nt*
Easter ['iːstə] Pasen
easterly ['iːstəli] *adj* oostelijk
eastern ['iːstən] *adj* oost-, oostelijk
easy ['iːzi] *adj* gemakkelijk; geriefelijk; **~ chair** leunstoel *c*
easy-going ['iːzi,gouiŋ] *adj* ontspannen

*eat [iːt] *v* *eten
eavesdrop ['iːvzdrɔp] *v* afluisteren
ebony ['ebəni] *n* ebbehout *nt*
eccentric [ik'sentrik] *adj* excentriek
echo ['ekou] *n* (pl ~es) weerklank *c*, echo *c*
eclipse [i'klips] *n* verduistering *c*
economic [,iːkə'nɔmik] *adj* economisch
economical [,iːkə'nɔmikəl] *adj* spaarzaam, zuinig
economist [i'kɔnəmist] *n* econoom *m*
economize [i'kɔnəmaiz] *v* sparen
economy [i'kɔnəmi] *n* economie *c*
ecstasy ['ekstəzi] *n* extase *c*
Ecuador ['ekwədɔː] Ecuador
Ecuadorian [,ekwə'dɔːriən] *n* Ecuadoriaan *m*, -se *f*
eczema ['eksimə] *n* eczeem *nt*
edge [edʒ] *n* kant *c*, rand *c*
edible ['edibəl] *adj* eetbaar
edit ['edit] *v* bewerken, redigeren
edition [i'diʃən] *n* editie *c*, uitgave *c*; **morning ~** ochtendeditie *c*
editor ['editə] *n* redakteur *c*
educate ['edʒukeit] *v* opleiden, opvoeden

education [ˌedʒu'keiʃən] *n* onderwijs *nt*; opvoeding *c*

eel [i:l] *n* aal *c*, paling *c*

effect [i'fekt] *n* gevolg *nt*, effect *nt*; *v* *teweegbrengen; **in ~** feitelijk

effective [i'fektiv] *adj* doeltreffend, effectief

efficient [i'fiʃənt] *adj* efficiënt, doelmatig

effort ['efət] *n* inspanning *c*; poging *c*

egg [eg] *n* ei *nt*; **~ yolk** *n* eierdooier *c*

eggcup ['egkʌp] *n* eierdopje *nt*

eggplant ['eglɑ:nt] *n* aubergine *c*

ego(t)istic [ˌegou'tistik] *adj* egoïstisch, zelfzuchtig

Egypt ['i:dʒipt] Egypte

Egyptian [i'dʒipʃən] *adj* Egyptisch; *n* Egyptenaar *m*, Egyptenares *f*

eiderdown ['aidədaun] *n* donzen dekbed

eight [eit] *num* acht

eighteen [ˌei'ti:n] *num* achttien

eighteenth [ˌei'ti:nθ] *num* achttiende

eighth [eitθ] *num* achtste

eighty ['eiti] *num* tachtig

either ['aiðə] *pron* een van beide; **either ... or** hetzij ... hetzij, of ... of

elaborate [i'læbəreit] *v* uitwerken

elastic [i'læstik] *adj* elastisch; rekbaar; elastiek *nt*

elasticity [ˌelæ'stisəti] *n* rek *c*

elbow ['elbou] *n* elleboog *c*

elder ['eldə] *adj* ouder

elderly ['eldəli] *adj* bejaard

eldest ['eldist] *adj* oudst

elect [i'lekt] *v* *kiezen, *verkiezen

election [i'lekʃən] *n* verkiezing *c*

electric [i'lektrik] *adj* elektrisch; **~ razor** scheerapparaat *nt*; **~ cord** snoer *nt*

electrician [ˌilek'triʃən] *n* elektricien *m*

electricity [ˌilek'trisəti] *n* elektriciteit *c*

electronic [ilek'trɔnik] *adj* elektronisch; **~ game** elektronisch spel

elegance ['eligəns] *n* elegantie *c*

elegant ['eligənt] *adj* elegant

element ['elimənt] *n* bestanddeel *nt*, element *nt*

elephant ['elifənt] *n* olifant *c*

elevator ['eliveitə] *nAm* lift *c*

eleven [i'levən] *num* elf

eleventh [i'levənθ] *num* elfde

elf [elf] *n* (pl elves) elf *c*

eliminate [i'limineit] *v* elimineren

elm [elm] *n* iep *c*

else [els] *adv* anders

elsewhere [ˌel'sweə] *adv* elders

elucidate [i'lu:sideit] *v* toelichten, verklaren

e-mail ['i:meil] *n* e-mail *c*; *v* e-mailen, mailen

emancipation [iˌmænsi'peiʃən] *n* emancipatie *c*

embankment [im'bæŋkmənt] *n* kade *c*

embargo [em'bɑ:gou] *n* (pl ~es) embargo *nt*

embark [im'bɑ:k] *v* inschepen; instappen

embarkation [ˌembɑ:'keiʃən] *n* inscheping *c*

embarrass [im'bærəs] *v* in verwarring brengen; in verlegenheid *brengen; **embarrassed** *adj* verlegen, gegeneerd; **embarrassing** *adj* pijnlijk; **~ment** verlegenheid *c*

embassy ['embəsi] *n* ambassade *c*

emblem ['embləm] *n* embleem *nt*

embrace [im'breis] *v* omhelzen; *n* omhelzing *c*

embroider [im'brɔidə] *v* borduren

embroidery [im'brɔidəri] *n* borduurwerk *nt*

emerald ['emərəld] *n* smaragd *c*

emergency [i'mə:dʒənsi] *n* spoedgeval *nt*, noodgeval *nt*;

noodtoestand *c*; ~ **exit** nooduitgang *c*

emigrant ['emigrǝnt] *n* emigrant *m*, -e *f*

emigrate ['emigreit] *v* emigreren

emigration [,emi'greiʃǝn] *n* emigratie *c*

emotion [i'mouʃǝn] *n* ontroering *c*, emotie *c*

emperor ['empǝrǝ] *n* keizer *m*

emphasize ['emfǝsaiz] *v* benadrukken

empire ['empaiǝ] *n* keizerrijk *nt*, rijk *nt*

employ [im'plɔi] *v* tewerkstellen; gebruiken

employee [,emplɔi'i:] *n* werknemer *m*, werkneemster *f*, employé *m*, employee *f*

employer [im'plɔiǝ] *n* werkgever *m*

employment [im'plɔimǝnt] *n* tewerkstelling *c*, werk *nt*

empress ['empris] *n* keizerin *f*

empty ['empti] *adj* leeg; *v* ledigen

enable [i'neibǝl] *v* in staat stellen

enamel [i'næmǝl] *n* email *nt*

enamelled [i'næmǝld] *adj* geëmailleerd

enchanting [in'tʃɑːntiŋ] *adj* prachtig, betoverend

encircle [in'sǝːkǝl] *v* omcirkelen, omringen; *insluiten

enclose [iŋ'klouz] *v* *bijsluiten, *insluiten

enclosure [iŋ'klouʒǝ] *n* bijlage *c*

encounter [iŋ'kauntǝ] *v* ontmoeten; *n* ontmoeting *c*

encourage [iŋ'kʌridʒ] *v* aanmoedigen

encyclop(a)edia [en,saiklǝ'piːdiǝ] *n* encyclopedie *c*

end [end] *n* einde *nt*; slot *nt*; *v* beëindigen; *aflopen

ending ['endiŋ] *n* einde *nt*

endless ['endlǝs] *adj* oneindig

endorse [in'dɔːs] *v* bekrachtigen; aftekenen

endure [in'djuǝ] *v* *verdragen

enemy ['enǝmi] *n* vijand *c*

energetic [,enǝ'dʒetik] *adj* energiek

energy ['enǝdʒi] *n* energie *c*; kracht *c*

engage [iŋ'geidʒ] *v* in dienst *nemen; zich *verbinden; **engaged** verloofd; bezig, bezet

engagement [iŋ'geidʒmǝnt] *n* verloving *c*; verplichting *c*; afspraak *c*; ~ **ring** verlovingsring *c*

engine ['endʒin] *n* machine *c*, motor *c*; locomotief *c*

engineer [,endʒi'niǝ] *n* ingenieur *c*

England ['iŋglǝnd] Engeland

English ['iŋgliʃ] *adj* Engels; **the** ~ de Engelsen

Englishman ['iŋgliʃwmǝn] *n* (pl -men) Engelsman *m*

Englishwoman ['iŋgliʃwumǝn] *n* (pl -women) Engelse *f*

engrave [iŋ'greiv] *v* graveren

engraver [iŋ'greivǝ] *n* graveur *c*

engraving [iŋ'greiviŋ] *n* gravure *c*

enigma [i'nigmǝ] *n* raadsel *nt*

enjoy [in'dʒɔi] *v* *genieten van

enjoyable [in'dʒɔiǝbǝl] *adj* fijn, prettig, leuk; lekker

enjoyment [in'dʒɔimǝnt] *n* genot *nt*

enlarge [in'lɑːdʒ] *v* vergroten; uitbreiden

enlargement [in'lɑːdʒmǝnt] *n* vergroting *c*

enormous [i'nɔːmǝs] *adj* reusachtig, enorm

enough [i'nʌf] *adv* genoeg; *adj* voldoende

enquire [iŋ'kwaiǝ] *v* informeren; *onderzoeken

enquiry [iŋ'kwaiǝri] *n* informatie *c*; onderzoek *nt*; enquête *c*

enter ['entǝ] *v* *betreden, *binnengaan, *binnenkomen; *inschrijven

enterprise ['entǝpraiz] *n*

onderneming c

entertain [ˌentə'tein] v vermaken, *onderhouden; *ontvangen

entertainer [ˌentə'teinə] n conferencier c

entertaining [ˌentə'teiniŋ] adj vermakelijk, amusant

entertainment [ˌentə'teinmənt] n vermaak nt, amusement nt

enthusiasm [in'θjuːziæzəm] n enthousiasme nt

enthusiastic [inˌθjuːzi'æstik] adj enthousiast

entire [in'taiə] adj heel, geheel

entirely [in'taiəli] adv helemaal

entrance ['entrəns] n ingang c; toegang c; binnenkomst c; ~ fee entree c

entry ['entri] n ingang c, entree c; toegang c; post c; no ~ verboden toegang

envelop [in'veləp] v omhullen

envelope ['envəloup] n envelop c

envious ['enviəs] adj afgunstig, jaloers

environment [in'vaiərənmənt] n milieu nt; omgeving c

envoy ['envɔi] n gezant c

envy ['envi] n afgunst c, jaloezie c; v benijden

epic ['epik] n epos nt; adj episch

epidemic [ˌepi'demik] n epidemie c

epilepsy ['epilepsi] n epilepsie c

epilogue ['epilɔg] n epiloog c

episode ['episoud] n episode c

equal ['iːkwəl] adj gelijk; v evenaren

equality [i'kwɔləti] n gelijkheid c

equalize ['iːkwəlaiz] v gelijk maken

equally ['iːkwəli] adv even

equator [i'kweitə] n evenaar c

equip [i'kwip] v uitrusten

equipment [i'kwipmənt] n uitrusting c

equivalent [i'kwivələnt] adj equivalent, gelijkwaardig

eraser [i'reizə] n gom c/nt

erect [i'rekt] v opbouwen, oprichten; adj overeind, rechtstaand

err [əː] v zich vergissen; dwalen

errand ['erənd] n boodschap c

error ['erə] n fout c, vergissing c

escalator ['eskəleitə] n roltrap c

escape [i'skeip] v ontsnappen; vluchten, ontvluchten, *ontgaan; n ontsnapping c

escort[1] ['eskɔːt] n escorte nt

escort[2] [i'skɔːt] v escorteren

especially [i'speʃəli] adv voornamelijk, vooral

esplanade [ˌesplə'neid] n promenade c

essay ['esei] n essay nt; verhandeling c, opstel nt

essence ['esəns] n essentie c; kern c, wezen nt

essential [i'senʃəl] adj onontbeerlijk; wezenlijk, essentieel

essentially [i'senʃəli] adv vooral

establish [i'stæbliʃ] v vestigen; vaststellen

estate [i'steit] n landgoed nt

esteem [i'stiːm] n respect nt, achting, aanzien c; v achten

estimate[1] ['estimeit] v taxeren, schatten

estimate[2] ['estimət] n schatting c

estuary ['estʃuəri] n riviermonding c

etcetera [et'setərə] enzovoort

etching ['etʃiŋ] n ets c

eternal [i'təːnəl] adj eeuwig

eternity [i'təːnəti] n eeuwigheid c

ether ['iːθə] n ether c

Ethiopia [iθi'oupiə] Ethiopië

Ethiopian [iθi'oupiən] adj Ethiopisch; n Ethiopiër m, Ethiopische f

EU ['iː'ju] EU, Europese Unie

euro ['juːrou] n euro

Europe ['juərəp] Europa

European [ˌjuərə'piːən] adj Europees; n Europeaan m, Europese f

European Union [juərə'piːən 'juːnjən] Europese Unie

evacuate [i'vækjueit] v evacueren

evaluate [i'væljueit] v schatten

evaporate [i'væpəreit] v verdampen

even ['iːvən] adj effen, plat, gelijk; constant; even; adv zelfs

evening ['iːvniŋ] n avond c; ~ **dress** avondkleding c

event [i'vent] n gebeurtenis c; geval nt

eventual [i'ventʃuəl] adj eventueel; uiteindelijk

eventually [i'ventʃuəli] adv tenslotte, uiteindelijk

ever ['evə] adv ooit; altijd

every ['evri] adj ieder, elk

everybody ['evri,bɔdi] pron iedereen

everyday ['evridei] adj alledaags

everyone ['evriwʌn] pron ieder, iedereen

everything ['evriθiŋ] pron alles

everywhere ['evriweə] adv overal

evidence ['evidəns] n bewijs nt

evident ['evidənt] adj duidelijk

evil ['iːvəl] n kwaad nt; adj slecht

evolution [,iːvə'luːʃən] n evolutie c

exact [ig'zækt] adj nauwkeurig, precies

exactly [ig'zæktli] adv precies

exaggerate [ig'zædʒəreit] v *overdrijven

exam [ig'zæmi] colloquial, **examination** [ig,zæmi'neiʃən] n examen nt; onderzoek nt;

examine [ig'zæmin] v *onderzoeken

example [ig'zɑːmpəl] n voorbeeld nt; **for** ~ bijvoorbeeld

excavation [ekskə'veiʃn] n opgraving c

exceed [ik'siːd] v *overschrijden; *overtreffen

excel [ik'sel] v *uitblinken

excellent ['eksələnt] adj voortreffelijk, uitstekend

except [ik'sept] prep uitgezonderd, behalve

exception [ik'sepʃən] n uitzondering c

exceptional [ik'sepʃənəl] adj buitengewoon, uitzonderlijk

excerpt ['eksəːpt] n passage c

excess [ik'ses] n exces nt

excessive [ik'sesiv] adj buitensporig

exchange [iks'tʃeindʒ] v uitwisselen, wisselen, ruilen; n ruil c; beurs c; ~ **office** wisselkantoor nt; ~ **rate** koers c

excite [ik'sait] v *opwinden

excited [ik'saitəd] adj opgewonden, geprikkeld

excitement [ik'saitmənt] n drukte c, opwinding c

exciting [ik'saitiŋ] adj spannend

exclaim [ik'skleim] v *uitroepen

exclamation [,eksklə'meiʃən] n uitroep c

exclude [ik'skluːd] v *uitsluiten

exclusive [ik'skluːsiv] adj exclusief

exclusively [ik'skluːsivli] adv uitsluitend

excursion [ik'skəːʃən] n uitstapje nt, excursie c

excuse¹ [ik'skjuːs] n excuus nt

excuse² [ik'skjuːz] v verontschuldigen, excuseren

execute ['eksikjuːt] v uitvoeren

execution [,eksi'kjuːʃən] n terechtstelling c

executioner [,eksi'kjuːʃənə] n beul m

executive [ig'zekjutiv] adj uitvoerend; leidinggevend

exempt [ig'zempt] v *ontheffen, vrijstellen; adj vrijgesteld

exemption [ig'zempʃən] n vrijstelling c

exercise ['eksəsaiz] n oefening c; thema nt; v oefenen; uitoefenen

exhale [eks'heil] v uitademen

exhaust [ig'zɔːst] n uitlaatpijp c, uitlaat c; v uitputten; ~ **gases**

exhibit 240

uitlaatgassen *pl*

exhibit [ig'zibit] *v* tentoonstellen; vertonen

exhibition [,eksi'biʃən] *n* expositie *c*, tentoonstelling *c*

exile ['eksail] *n* ballingschap *c*; balling *c*

exist [ig'zist] *v* *bestaan

existence [ig'zistəns] *n* bestaan *nt*

exit ['eksit] *n* uitgang *c*; uitrit *c*

exotic [ig'zɔtik] *adj* exotisch

expand [ik'spænd] *v* uitbreiden; uitspreiden; ontplooien

expansion [ik'spænʃən] *n* uitbreiding *c*

expect [ik'spekt] *v* verwachten

expectation [,ekspek'teiʃən] *n* verwachting *c*

expedition [,ekspə'diʃən] *n* verzending *c*; expeditie *c*

expel [ik'spel] *v* *uitwijzen

expenditure [ik'spenditʃə] *n* kosten *pl*, uitgave *c*

expense [ik'spens] *n* uitgave *c*; **expenses** *pl* onkosten *pl*

expensive [ik'spensiv] *adj* prijzig, duur; kostbaar

experience [ik'spiəriəns] *n* ervaring *c*; *v* *ervaren, *ondervinden, beleven; **experienced** ervaren

experiment [ik'sperimənt] *n* proef *c*, experiment *nt*; *v* experimenteren

expert ['ekspə:t] *n* deskundige *c*, vakman *m*, vakvrouw *f*, expert *c*; *adj* deskundig

expire [ik'spaiə] *v* *vervallen, *aflopen, *verstrijken; **expired** vervallen

explain [ik'splein] *v* verklaren, uitleggen

explanation [,eksplə'neiʃən] *n* toelichting *c*, uitleg *c*, verklaring *c*

explicit [ik'splisit] *adj* uitdrukkelijk, expliciet

explode [ik'sploud] *v* ontploffen, exploderen

exploit [ik'splɔit] *v* uitbuiten, exploiteren

explore [ik'splɔ:] *v* verkennen, *onderzoeken

explosion [ik'splouʒən] *n* explosie *c*

explosive [ik'splousiv] *adj* explosief; *n* springstof *c*

export[1] [ik'spɔ:t] *v* uitvoeren, exporteren

export[2] ['ekspɔ:t] *n* export *c*

exportation [,ekspɔ:'teiʃən] *n* uitvoer *c*

exports ['ekspɔ:ts] *pl* export *c*

expose [ik'spous] *v* blootstellen

exposition [,ekspə'ziʃən] *n* tentoonstelling *c*

exposure [ik'spouʒə] *n* blootstelling *c*; belichting *c*; ~ **meter** belichtingsmeter *c*

express [ik'spres] *v* uitdrukken; betuigen, uiten; *adj* expresse-; uitdrukkelijk; ~ **train** sneltrein *c*

expression [ik'spreʃən] *n* uitdrukking *c*; uiting *c*

exquisite [ik'skwizit] *adj* voortreffelijk

extend [ik'stend] *v* verlengen; uitbreiden; verlenen

extension [ik'stenʃən] *n* verlenging *c*; uitbreiding *c*; toestel *nt*; ~ **cord** verlengsnoer *nt*

extensive [ik'stensiv] *adj* omvangrijk; veelomvattend, uitgebreid

extent [ik'stent] *n* omvang *c*

exterior [ek'stiəriə] *adj* uiterlijk; *n* buitenkant *c*

external [ek'stə:nəl] *adj* uiterlijk

extinguish [ik'stiŋgwiʃ] *v* blussen, doven

extort [ik'stɔ:t] *v* *afdwingen

extortion [ik'stɔ:ʃən] *n* afpersing *c*

extra ['ekstrə] *adj* extra

extract[1] [ik'strækt] *v* *uittrekken,

*trekken
extract² ['ekstrækt] *n* fragment *nt*
extradite ['ekstrədait] *v* uitleveren
extraordinary [ik'strɔːdənri] *adj*
buitengewoon
extravagant [ik'strævəgənt] *adj*
overdreven, extravagant
extreme [ik'striːm] *adj* extreem;
hoogst, uiterst; *n* uiterste *nt*

exuberant [ig'zjuːbərənt] *adj*
uitbundig
eye [ai] *n* oog *nt*; ~ **shadow**
oogschaduw *c*
eyebrow ['aibrau] *n* wenkbrauw *c*; ~
pencil wenkbrauwpotlood *c*
eyelash ['ailæʃ] *n* wimper *c*
eyelid ['ailid] *n* ooglid *nt*
eyewitness ['ai,witnəs] *n* ooggetuige *c*

F

fable ['feibəl] *n* fabel *c*
fabric ['fæbrik] *n* stof *c*; structuur *c*
façade [fə'sɑːd] *n* gevel *c*
face [feis] *n* gezicht *nt*; *v* het hoofd
*bieden aan; ~ **cream** gezichtscrème
c; ~ **massage** gezichtsmassage *c*; ~
pack schoonheidsmasker *nt*
face-powder ['feis,paudə] *n*
gezichtspoeder *nt/c*
facilities [fə'silətis] *pl* voorziening *c*;
installatie *c*; **cooking** ~
kookgelegenheid *c*
facing tegenover
fact [fækt] *n* feit *nt*; **in** ~ in feite
factor ['fæktə] *n* factor *c*
factory ['fæktəri] *n* fabriek *c*
factual ['fæktʃuəl] *adj* feitelijk
faculty ['fækəlti] *n* vermogen *nt*; gave
c, talent *nt*, bekwaamheid *c*; faculteit *c*
fade [feid] *v* verkleuren, *verschieten
fail [feil] *v* falen; tekort *schieten;
*ontbreken; *nalaten; zakken;
without ~ beslist
failure ['feiljə] *n* mislukking *c*; fiasco *nt*
faint [feint] *v* *flauwvallen; *adj* zwak,
vaag, flauw
fair [fɛə] *n* kermis *c*; beurs *c*; *adj* billijk,
eerlijk; blond; mooi
fairly ['fɛəli] *adv* vrij, nogal, tamelijk

fairy ['fɛəri] *n* fee *f*
fairytale ['fɛəriteil] *n* sprookje *nt*
faith [feiθ] *n* geloof *nt*; vertrouwen *nt*
faithful ['feiθful] *adj* trouw
fake [feik] *n* vervalsing *c*
falcon [f] *n* valk *c*
fall [fɔːl] *n* val *c*; *nAm* herfst *c*
***fall** [fɔːl] *v* *vallen
false [fɔːls] *adj* vals; verkeerd, onwaar,
onecht; ~ **teeth** kunstgebit *nt*
falter ['fɔːltə] *v* wankelen; stamelen
fame [feim] *n* faam *c*, roem *c*; reputatie
c
familiar [fə'miljə] *adj* vertrouwd;
familiair
family ['fæməli] *n* gezin *nt*; familie *c*; ~
name achternaam *c*
famous ['feiməs] *adj* beroemd
fan [fæn] *n* ventilator *c*; waaier *c*; fan *c*; ~
belt ventilatorriem *c*
fanatical [fə'nætikəl] *adj* fanatiek
fancy ['fænsi] *v* lusten, zin *hebben in;
verliefd zijn op; zich verbeelden, zich
voorstellen; *n* gril *c*; fantasie *c*
fantastic [fæn'tæstik] *adj* fantastisch
fantasy ['fæntəzi] *n* fantasie *c*
far [fɑː] *adj* ver; *adv* veel; **by** ~ verreweg;
so ~ tot nu toe; ~ **away** ver, ver weg
fare [fɛə] *n* reiskosten *pl*, tarief *nt*; kost

c, voedsel nt

farm [fɑ:m] n boerderij c

farmer ['fɑ:mə] n boer m; **farmer's wife** boerin f

farmhouse ['fɑ:mhaus] n boerderij c

far-off ['fɑ:rɔf] adj afgelegen

farther ['fɑ:ðə] adj verder

fascinate ['fæsineit] v boeien

fascism ['fæʃizəm] n fascisme nt

fascist ['fæʃist] adj fascistisch; n fascist c

fashion ['fæʃən] n mode c; manier c

fashionable ['fæʃənəbəl] adj modieus

fast [fɑ:st] adj vlug, snel; vast

fasten ['fɑ:sən] v vastmaken, bevestigen; *sluiten

fastener ['fɑ:sənə] n sluiting c

fat [fæt] adj vet, dik; n vet nt

fatal ['feitəl] adj fataal, dodelijk, noodlottig

fate [feit] n lot nt, noodlot nt

father ['fɑ:ðə] n vader m; pater m

father-in-law ['fɑ:ðərinlɔ:] n (pl fathers-) schoonvader m

fatness ['fætnəs] n dikte c

fatty ['fæti] adj vettig

faucet ['fɔ:sit] nAm kraan c

fault [fɔ:lt] n schuld c; fout c, defect nt, gebrek nt

faultless ['fɔ:ltləs] adj foutloos; feilloos

faulty ['fɔ:lti] adj gebrekkig, defect

favo(u)r ['feivə] n gunst c; v begunstigen, bevoorrechten

favo(u)rable ['feivərəbəl] adj gunstig

favo(u)rite ['feivərit] n lieveling c, favoriet c; adj lievelings-

fawn [fɔ:n] adj lichtbruin; n reekalf nt

fax [fæks] n fax c; **send a** ~ en fax versturen

fear [fiə] n vrees c, angst c; v vrezen

feasible ['fi:zəbəl] adj uitvoerbaar; haalbaar

feast [fi:st] n feest nt

feat [fi:t] n prestatie c

feather ['feðə] n veer c

feature ['fi:tʃə] n kenmerk nt; gelaatstrek c

February ['februəri] februari

federal ['fedərəl] adj federaal

federation [,fedə'reiʃən] n federatie c; bond c

fee [fi:] n honorarium nt

feeble ['fi:bəl] adj zwak

***feed** [fi:d] v voeden; **fed up with** beu

***feel** [fi:l] v voelen; betasten; ~ **like** zin *hebben in

feeling ['fi:liŋ] n gevoel nt

feet (pl foot)

fell [fel] v (p fall)

fellow ['felou] n kerel m; ~ **countryman** n landgenoot m; ~ **man** n medemens m

felt¹ [felt] n vilt nt

felt² [felt] v (p, pp feel)

female ['fi:meil] adj vrouwelijk

feminine ['feminin] adj vrouwelijk

fence [fens] n omheining c; hek nt; v schermen

ferment [fə'ment] v gisten

ferry-boat ['feribout] n veerboot c

fertile ['fə:tail] adj vruchtbaar

festival ['festivəl] n festival nt

festive ['festiv] adj feestelijk

fetch [fetʃ] v halen; afhalen

feudal ['fju:dəl] adj feodaal

fever ['fi:və] n koorts c

feverish ['fi:vəriʃ] adj koortsig

few [fju:] adj weinig

fiancé [fi'ɑ:sei] n verloofde c

fiancée [fi'ɑ:sei] n verloofde c

fibre ['faibə] n vezel c

fiction ['fikʃən] n fictie c, verzinsel nt

field [fi:ld] n akker c, veld nt; gebied nt; ~ **glasses** veldkijker c

fierce [fiəs] adj wild; woest, fel

fifteen [,fif'ti:n] num vijftien

fifteenth [,fif'ti:nθ] num vijftiende

fifth [fifθ] *num* vijfde

fifty ['fifti] *num* vijftig

fig [fig] *n* vijg *c*

fight [fait] *n* strijd *c*, gevecht *nt*

*****fight** [fait] *v* *strijden, *vechten

figure ['figə] *n* gestalte *c*, figuur *c*; cijfer *nt*

file [fail] *n* vijl *c*; dossier *nt*; rij *c*

fill [fil] *v* vullen; **~ in** invullen; **filling station** benzinestation *nt*; **~ out** *Am* invullen; **~ up** opvullen

filling ['filiŋ] *n* vulling *c*

film [film] *n* film *c*; *v* filmen

filter ['filtə] *n* filter *nt*

filthy ['filθi] *adj* smerig, vuil

final ['fainəl] *adj* laatst

finally ['fainəli] *adv* tenslotte, uiteindelijk

finance [fai'næns] *v* financieren

finances [fai'nænsiz] *pl* financiën *pl*

financial [fai'nænʃəl] *adj* financieel

finch [fintʃ] *n* vink *c*

*****find** [faind] *v* *vinden

fine [fain] *n* boete *c*; *adj* fijn; mooi; uitstekend, prachtig; **~ arts** schone kunsten

finger ['fiŋgə] *n* vinger *c*; **little ~** pink *c*

fingerprint ['fiŋgəprint] *n* vingerafdruk *c*

finish ['finiʃ] *v* afmaken, beëindigen; eindigen; *n* einde *nt*; eindstreep *c*; **finished** af; op

Finland ['finlənd] Finland

Finn [fin] *n* Fin *m*, -se *f*

Finnish ['finiʃ] *adj* Fins

fire [faiə] *n* vuur *nt*; brand *c*; *v* *schieten; *ontslaan; **~ alarm** brandalarm *nt*; **~ brigade** brandweer *c*; **~ escape** brandtrap *c*; **~ extinguisher** brandblusapparaat *nt*

firefighter ['faiə,faitə] *n* brandweerman *c*

fireplace ['faiəpleis] *n* haard *c*

fireproof ['faiəpruːf] *adj* brandvrij;

vuurvast

firm [fəːm] *adj* vast; stevig; *n* firma *c*

first [fəːst] *num* eerst; **at ~** eerst; aanvankelijk; **~ name** voornaam *c*

first aid [,fəːst'eid] *n* eerste hulp; **~ kit** verbandkist *c*; **~ post** eerste hulppost

first-class [,fəːst'klɑːs] *adj* eersteklas

first-rate [,fəːst'reit] *adj* eersterangs, prima

fir tree ['fəːtriː] *n* dennenboom *c*, den *c*

fish¹ [fiʃ] *n* (pl ~, ~es) vis *c*; **~ shop** viswinkel *c*

fish² [fiʃ] *v* vissen; hengelen; **fishing gear** vistuig *nt*; **fishing hook** vishaak *c*; **fishing industry** visserij *c*; **fishing licence**, *Am* **fishing license** visakte *c*; **fishing line** vislijn *c*; **fishing net** visnet *nt*; **fishing rod** hengel *c*; **fishing tackle** vistuig *nt*

fishbone ['fiʃboun] *n* graat *c*, visgraat *c*

fisherman ['fiʃəmən] *n* (pl -men) visser *m*

fist [fist] *n* vuist *c*

fit [fit] *adj* geschikt; *n* aanval *c*; *v* passen; **fitting room** paskamer *c*

five [faiv] *num* vijf

fix [fiks] *v* repareren

fixed [fikst] *adj* vast

fizz [fiz] *n* prik *c*

flag [flæg] *n* vlag *c*

flame [fleim] *n* vlam *c*

flamingo [flə'miŋgou] *n* (pl ~s, ~es) flamingo *c*

flannel ['flænəl] *n* flanel *nt*

flash [flæʃ] *n* flits *c*; **~ bulb** flitslampje *nt*

flashlight ['flæʃlait] *n* zaklantaarn *c*

flask [flɑːsk] *n* flacon *c*; **thermos ~** thermosfles *c*

flat [flæt] *adj* vlak, plat; *n* flat *c*; **~ tyre** lekke band

flavo(u)r ['fleivə] *n* smaak *c*; *v* kruiden

flee [fliː] *v* vluchten

fleet [fliːt] *n* vloot *c*

flesh [fleʃ] *n* vlees *nt*

flew [flu:] *v* (p fly)

flex [fleks] *n* snoer *nt*

flexible ['fleksibəl] *adj* buigbaar; soepel

flight [flait] *n* vlucht *c*; **charter ~** chartervlucht *c*

flint [flint] *n* vuursteen *c*

float [flout] *v* *drijven; *n* vlotter *c*

flock [flɔk] *n* kudde *c*

flood [flʌd] *n* overstroming *c*; vloed *c*

floor [flɔ:] *n* vloer *c*; etage *c*, verdieping *c*; **~ show** floor-show *c*

florist ['flɔrist] *n* bloemist *m*, -e *f*

flour [flauə] *n* bloem *c*, meel *nt*

flow [flou] *v* vloeien, stromen

flower [flauə] *n* bloem *c*; **~ shop** bloemenwinkel *c*

flowerbed ['flauəbed] *n* bloemperk *nt*

flown [floun] *v* (pp fly)

flu [flu:] *n* griep *c*

fluent ['flu:ənt] *adj* vloeiend

fluid ['flu:id] *adj* vloeibaar; *n* vloeistof *c*

flute [flu:t] *n* fluit *c*

fly [flai] *n* vlieg *c*; gulp *c*

***fly** [flai] *v* *vliegen

foam [foum] *n* schuim *nt*; *v* schuimen; **~ rubber** schuimrubber *nt*

focus ['foukəs] *n* brandpunt *nt*

fog [fɔg] *n* mist *c*

foggy ['fɔgi] *adj* mistig

foglamp ['fɔglæmp] *n* mistlamp *c*

fold [fould] *v* *vouwen; *opvouwen; *n* vouw *c*

folk [fouk] *n* volk *nt*; **~ dance** volksdans *c*; **~ song** volkslied *nt*

folklore ['fouklɔ:] *n* folklore *c*

follow ['fɔlou] *v* volgen; **following** *adj* eerstvolgende, volgend

fond: ***be ~ of** [bi: fɔnd ɔv] *houden van

food [fu:d] *n* voedsel *nt*; eten *nt*, kost *c*; **~ poisoning** voedselvergiftiging *c*

foodstuffs ['fu:dstʌfs] *pl* levensmiddelen *pl*

fool [fu:l] *n* gek *c*, dwaas *c*; *v* foppen

foolish ['fu:liʃ] *adj* mal, dwaas

foot [fut] *n* (pl feet) voet *c*; **~ powder** voetpoeder *nt/c*; **on ~** te voet

football ['futbɔ:l] *n* voetbal *c*; **~ match** voetbalwedstrijd *c*

foot brake ['futbreik] *n* voetrem *c*

footpath ['futpɑ:θ] *n* voetpad *nt*

footwear ['futwɛə] *n* schoeisel *nt*

for [fɔ:, fə] *prep* voor; gedurende; naar; vanwege, wegens, uit; *conj* want

***forbid** [fə'bid] *v* *verbieden

force [fɔ:s] *v* noodzaken, *dwingen; forceren; *n* macht *c*, kracht *c*; geweld *nt*; **by ~** noodgedwongen; **driving ~** drijfkracht *c*

forecast ['fɔ:kɑ:st] *n* voorspelling *c*; *v* voorspellen

foreground ['fɔ:graund] *n* voorgrond *c*

forehead ['fɔred] *n* voorhoofd *nt*

foreign ['fɔrin] *adj* buitenlands; vreemd

foreigner ['fɔrinə] *n* buitenlander *m*, buitenlandse *f*; vreemdeling *m*, -e *f*

foreman ['fɔ:mən] *n* (pl -men) voorman *m*

foremost ['fɔ:moust] *adj* hoogst

forest ['fɔrist] *n* woud *nt*, bos *nt*

forester ['fɔristə] *n* boswachter *m*

forever, for ever [fə'revə] *adv* eeuwig, voor goed; altijd

forge [fɔ:dʒ] *v* vervalsen

***forget** [fə'get] *v* *vergeten

forgetful [fə'getfəl] *adj* vergeetachtig

***forgive** [fə'giv] *v* *vergeven

fork [fɔ:k] *n* vork *c*; tweesprong *c*; *v* zich splitsen

form [fɔ:m] *n* vorm *c*; formulier *nt*; klas *c*; *v* vormen

formal ['fɔ:məl] *adj* formeel

formality [fɔ:'mæləti] *n* formaliteit *c*

former ['fɔ:mə] *adj* voormalig; vroeger; **formerly** voorheen, vroeger

formula ['fɔ:mjulə] n (pl ~e, ~s)
formule c

fortnight ['fɔ:tnait] n veertien dagen

fortress ['fɔ:tris] n vesting c

fortunate ['fɔ:tʃənət] adj gelukkig

fortunately adv gelukkig

fortune ['fɔ:tʃu:n] n fortuin nt; lot nt,
geluk nt

forty ['fɔ:ti] num veertig

forward ['fɔ:wəd] adv vooruit,
voorwaarts; v *nazenden; doorsturen

foster parents ['fɔstə,pɛərənts] pl
pleegouders pl

fought [fɔ:t] v (p, pp fight)

foul [faul] adj smerig; gemeen

found[1] [faund] v (p, pp find)

found[2] [faund] v oprichten, stichten

foundation [faun'deiʃən] n stichting c;
~ **cream** basiscrème c

fountain ['fauntin] n fontein c; bron c

fountain pen ['fauntinpen] n vulpen c

four [fɔ:] num vier

fourteen [,fɔ:'ti:n] num veertien

fourteenth [,fɔ:'ti:nθ] num veertiende

fourth [fɔ:θ] num vierde

fowl [faul] n (pl ~s, ~) gevogelte nt

fox [fɔks] n vos c

foyer ['fɔiei] n foyer c

fraction ['frækʃən] n fractie c

fracture ['fræktʃə] v *breken; n breuk c

fragile ['frædʒail] adj breekbaar; broos

fragment ['frægmənt] n fragment nt;
stuk nt

frame [freim] n lijst c; montuur nt

France [frɑ:ns] Frankrijk

franchise ['fræntʃaiz] n kiesrecht c

fraternity [frə'tə:nəti] n broederschap
c

fraud [frɔ:d] n fraude c, bedrog nt

fray [frei] v rafelen

free [fri:] adj vrij; gratis; ~ **of charge**
gratis; ~ **ticket** vrijkaart c

freedom ['fri:dəm] n vrijheid c

***freeze** [fri:z] v *vriezen; *bevriezen

freezer ['fri:zə] n diepvries c

freezing ['fri:ziŋ] adj ijskoud

freezing point ['fri:ziŋpɔint] n
vriespunt nt

freight [freit] n lading c, vracht c

freight train ['freittrein] nAm
goederentrein c

French [frentʃ] adj Frans; **she's
French** zij is Franse; **the** ~ pl de
Fransen; ~ **fries** pl patat, friet

frequency ['fri:kwənsi] n frequentie
c

frequent ['fri:kwənt] adj veelvuldig,
frequent; **frequently** dikwijls

fresh [freʃ] adj vers; fris; ~ **water** zoet
water

friction ['frikʃən] n wrijving c

Friday ['fraidi] vrijdag c

fridge [fridʒ] n koelkast c, ijskast c

friend [frend] n vriend m; vriendin f

friendly ['frendli] adj vriendelijk;
amicaal, vriendschappelijk

friendship ['frendʃip] n vriendschap c

fright [frait] n angst c, schrik c

frighten ['fraitən] v *doen schrikken

frightened ['fraitənd] adj bang; *be ~
*schrikken

frightful ['fraitfəl] adj verschrikkelijk,
vreselijk

fringe [frindʒ] n franje c

frock [frɔk] n jurk c

frog [frɔg] n kikker c

from [frɔm] prep van; uit; vanaf

front [frʌnt] n voorkant c; **in** ~ **of** voor

frontier ['frʌntiə] n grens c

frost [frɔst] n vorst c

froth [frɔθ] n schuim nt

frozen ['frouzən] adj bevroren; ~ **food**
diepvriesproducten

fruit [fru:t] n fruit nt; vrucht c

fry [frai] v *bakken; *braden

frying pan ['fraiiŋpæn] n koekepan c

fuck [fʌk] v vulgar neuken, naaien,
wippen

fuel ['fju:əl] n brandstof c; benzine c; ~
  pump Am benzinepomp c
full [ful] adj vol; ~ **board** vol pension; ~
  stop punt c; ~ **up** vol
fun [fʌn] n plezier nt, pret c; lol c
function ['fʌŋkʃən] n functie c
fund [fʌnd] n fonds nt
fundamental [,fʌndə'mentəl] adj
  fundamenteel
funeral ['fju:nərəl] n begrafenis c
funnel ['fʌnəl] n trechter c
funny ['fʌni] adj leuk, grappig;
  zonderling
fur [fə:] n pels c; ~ **coat** bontjas c
furious ['fjuəriəs] adj razend,
  woedend

furnace ['fə:nis] n oven c
furnish ['fə:niʃ] v leveren, verschaffen;
  inrichten, meubileren; ~ **with**
  *voorzien van
furniture ['fə:nitʃə] n meubilair nt;
  meubels pl
furrier ['fʌriə] n bontwerker c
further ['fə:ðə] adj verder; nader
furthermore ['fə:ðəmɔ:] adv
  bovendien
furthest ['fə:ðist] adj verst
fuse [fju:z] n zekering c; lont c
fuss [fʌs] n drukte c; ophef c, herrie c
future ['fju:tʃə] n toekomst c; adj
  toekomstig

G

gable ['geibəl] n geveltop c
gadget ['gædʒit] n technisch snufje c
gain [gein] v *winnen; n winst c
gale [geil] n storm c
gall [gɔ:l] n gal c; ~ **bladder** galblaas c
gallery ['gæləri] n galerij c
gallon ['gælən] n gallon (Brit 4.55 l;
  Am 3.79 l) c/nt
gallop ['gæləp] n galop c
gallows ['gælouz] pl galg c
gallstone ['gɔ:lstoun] n galsteen c
game [geim] n spel nt; wild nt; ~
  reserve wildpark nt
gang [gæŋ] n bende c; ploeg c
gangway ['gæŋwei] n loopplank c
gap [gæp] n bres c, opening c, gat nt
garage ['gærɑ:ʒ] n garage c; v stallen
garbage ['gɑ:bidʒ] n vuilnis nt, afval nt
garden ['gɑ:dən] n tuin c; **public ~**
  plantsoen nt; **zoo ~** dierentuin c;
  zoological gardens dierentuin c
gardener ['gɑ:dənə] n tuinman m;

  tuinier m, tuinierster f
gargle ['gɑ:gəl] v gorgelen
garlic ['gɑ:lik] n knoflook nt/c
gas [gæs] n gas nt; nAm benzine c; ~
  cooker gasstel nt; ~ **pump** Am
  benzinepomp c; ~ **station** Am
  benzinestation nt; ~ **stove** gaskachel c
gasoline ['gæsəli:n] nAm benzine c
gastric ['gæstrik] adj maag-; ~ **ulcer**
  maagzweer c
gasworks ['gæswə:ks] n gasfabriek c
gate [geit] n poort c; hek nt
gather ['gæðə] v verzamelen;
  *bijeenkomen; oogsten
gauge [geidʒ] n meter c
gave [geiv] v (p give)
gay [gei] adj vrolijk; homoseksueel
gaze [geiz] v staren
gear [giə] n versnelling c; uitrusting c;
  change ~ schakelen; ~ **lever**
  versnellingspook c
gearbox ['giəbɔks] n versnellingsbak c

geese (pl goose)

gem [dʒem] n juweel nt, edelsteen c; kleinood nt

gender ['dʒendə] n geslacht nt

general ['dʒenərəl] adj algemeen; n generaal c; ~**practitioner** huisarts c; **in** ~ in het algemeen

generate ['dʒenəreit] v verwekken

generation [,dʒenə'reiʃən] n generatie c

generator ['dʒenəreitər] n generator c

generosity [,dʒenə'rɔsəti] n edelmoedigheid c, gulheid c

generous ['dʒenərəs] adj gul, royaal, vrijgevig

genital ['dʒenitəl] adj geslachtelijk

genius ['dʒiːniəs] n genie nt

gentle ['dʒentəl] adj zacht; teer, licht; voorzichtig

gentleman ['dʒentəlmən] n (pl -men) heer m

genuine ['dʒenjuin] adj echt

geography [dʒi'ɔgrəfi] n aardrijkskunde c

geology [dʒi'ɔlədʒi] n geologie c

geometry [dʒi'ɔmətri] n meetkunde c

germ [dʒəːm] n bacil c; kiem c

German ['dʒəːmən] adj Duits; n Duitser m, Duitse f

Germany ['dʒəːməni] Duitsland

gesticulate [dʒi'stikjuleit] v gebaren

*get [get] v *krijgen; halen; *worden; ~ **back** *teruggaan; ~ **dressed** aankleden; ~ **off** uitstappen; ~ **on** instappen; vorderen; ~ **up** *opstaan

ghost [goust] n spook nt; geest c

giant ['dʒaiənt] n reus m

giddiness ['gidinəs] n duizeligheid c

giddy ['gidi] adj duizelig

gift [gift] n geschenk nt, cadeau nt; gave c

gifted ['giftid] adj begaafd

gigantic [dʒai'gæntik] adj reusachtig

giggle ['gigəl] v giechelen

gill [gil] n kieuw c

gilt [gilt] adj verguld

ginger ['dʒindʒə] n gember c

girl [gəːl] n meisje nt; ~ **guide** padvindster f; ~ **scout** padvindster f

girlfriend ['gəːlfrend] n vriendin f, meisje nt

*give [giv] v *geven; *aangeven; ~ **away** verklappen; weggeven; ~ **in** *toegeven; ~ **up** *opgeven

glacier ['glæsiə] n gletsjer c

glad [glæd] adj verheugd, blij; **gladly** graag, gaarne

gladness ['glædnəs] n vreugde c

glamorous ['glæmərəs] adj betoverend, fascinerend

glance [glɑːns] n blik c; v een blik *werpen

gland [glænd] n klier c

glare [glɛə] n scherp licht nt; schittering c; woedende blik c

glaring ['glɛəriŋ] adj verblindend

glass [glɑːs] n glas nt; glazen; **glasses** bril c; **magnifying** ~ vergrootglas nt

glaze [gleiz] v emailleren

glide [glaid] v *glijden

glider ['glaidə] n zweefvliegtuig nt

glimpse [glimps] n blik c; glimp c; v even *zien

global ['gloubəl] adj wereldomvattend

globe [gloub] n wereldbol c, aardbol c

gloom [gluːm] n duister nt

gloomy ['gluːmi] adj somber

glorious ['glɔːriəs] adj prachtig

glory ['glɔːri] n glorie c, roem c; eer c, lof c

gloss [glɔs] n glans c

glossy ['glɔsi] adj glanzend

glove [glʌv] n handschoen c

glow [glou] v gloeien; n gloed c

glue [gluː] n lijm c

*go [gou] v *gaan; *lopen; *worden; ~ **ahead** *doorgaan; ~ **away** *weggaan; ~ **back** *teruggaan; ~ **home** naar huis

*gaan; ~ **in** *binnengaan; ~ **on** *doorgaan; ~ **out** *uitgaan; ~ **through** meemaken, doormaken

goal [goul] *n* doel *nt*; doelpunt *nt*

goalkeeper ['goul,ki:pə] *n* doelman *m*

goat [gout] *n* bok *c*, geit *c*

god [gɔd] *n* god *m*

goddess ['gɔdis] *n* godin *f*

godfather ['gɔd,fɑ:ðə] *n* peetvader *m*

godmother ['gɔd,mʌðə] *n* peettante *f*, meter *f*

goggles ['gɔgəlz] *pl* duikbril *c*

gold [gould] *n* goud *nt*; ~ **leaf** bladgoud *nt*

golden ['gouldən] *adj* gouden

goldmine ['gouldmain] *n* goudmijn *c*

goldsmith ['gouldsmiθ] *n* goudsmid *m*

golf [gɔlf] *n* golf *nt*; ~ **course** golfbaan *c*; ~ **links** golfbaan *c*

golfclub ['gɔlfklʌb] *n* golfclub *c*

gondola ['gɔndələ] *n* gondel *c*

gone [gɔn] *adv* (pp go) weg

good [gud] *adj* goed; lekker; zoet; braaf

goodbye! [,gud'bai] dag!, tot ziens

good-humo(u)red [,gud'hju:məd] *adj* opgeruimd

good-looking [,gud'lukiŋ] *adj* knap

good-natured [,gud'neitʃəd] *adj* goedhartig

goods [gudz] *pl* waren *pl*, goederen *pl*; ~ **train** goederentrein *c*

good-tempered [,gud'tempəd] *adj* goedgestemd, goedgeluimd

goodwill [,gud'wil] *n* welwillendheid *c*

goose [gu:s] *n* (pl geese) gans *c*; ~ **flesh** kippevel *nt*

gooseberry ['guzbəri] *n* kruisbes *c*

gorge [gɔ:dʒ] *n* ravijn *nt*

gorgeous ['gɔ:dʒəs] *adj* prachtig

gospel ['gɔspəl] *n* evangelie *nt*

gossip ['gɔsip] *n* geroddel *nt*; *v* roddelen

got [gɔt] *v* (p, pp get)

gourmet ['guəmei] *n* fijnproever *m*

gout [gaut] *n* jicht *c*

govern ['gʌvən] *v* regeren

governess ['gʌvənis] *n* gouvernante *f*

government ['gʌvənmənt] *n* bewind *nt*, regering *c*

governor ['gʌvənə] *n* gouverneur *m*

gown [gaun] *n* japon *c*

grab [græb] *n* greep *c*; roof *c*

grace [greis] *n* gratie *c*; genade *c*

graceful ['greisfəl] *adj* bevallig

grade [greid] *n* graad *c*; *v* rangschikken

gradient ['greidiənt] *n* helling *c*

gradual ['grædʒuəl] *adj* geleidelijk; **gradually** *adv* langzamerhand

graduate ['grædʒueit] *v* een diploma behalen

grain [grein] *n* korrel *c*, graan *nt*, koren *nt*

gram [græm] *n* gram *nt*

grammar ['græmə] *n* grammatica *c*

grammatical [grə'mætikəl] *adj* grammaticaal

grand [grænd] *adj* groots

grandchild ['græn,tʃaild] *n* kleinkind *nt*

granddad ['grændæd] *n* opa *m*

granddaughter ['græn,dɔ:tə] *n* kleindochter *f*

grandfather ['græn,fɑ:ðə] *n* grootvader *m*; opa *m*

grandmother ['græn,mʌðə] *n* grootmoeder *f*; oma *f*

grandparents ['græn,pɛərənts] *pl* grootouders *pl*

grandson ['grænsʌn] *n* kleinzoon *m*

granite ['grænit] *n* graniet *nt*

grant [grɑ:nt] *v* gunnen, verlenen; inwilligen; *n* toelage *c*, beurs *c*

grape [greip] *n* druif *c*

grapefruit ['greipfru:t] *n* pompelmoes *c*

graph [græf] *n* grafiek *c*

graphic ['græfik] *adj* grafisch

grasp [grɑ:sp] *v* *grijpen; *n* greep *c*

grass [grɑːs] *n* gras *nt*

grasshopper ['grɑːs,hɔpə] *n* sprinkhaan *c*

grate [greit] *n* rooster *nt*; *v* raspen

grateful ['greitfəl] *adj* erkentelijk, dankbaar

grater ['greitə] *n* rasp *c*

gratis ['grætis] *adj* gratis

gratitude ['grætitjuːd] *n* dankbaarheid *c*

gratuity [grə'tjuːəti] *n* fooi *c*

grave [greiv] *n* graf *nt*; *adj* ernstig

gravel ['grævəl] *n* kiezel *c*, grind *nt*

gravestone ['greivstoun] *n* grafsteen *c*

graveyard ['greivjɑːd] *n* kerkhof *nt*

gravity ['grævəti] *n* zwaartekracht *c*; ernst *c*

gravy ['greivi] *n* jus *c*

graze [greiz] *v* grazen; *n* schaafwond *c*

grease [griːs] *n* vet *nt*; *v* smeren

greasy ['griːsi] *adj* vet, vettig

great [greit] *adj* groot; patent; **Great Britain** Groot-Brittannië

Greece [griːs] Griekenland

greed [griːd] *n* hebzucht *c*

greedy ['griːdi] *adj* hebzuchtig; gulzig

Greek [griːk] *adj* Grieks; *n* Griek *m*, -se *f*

green [griːn] *adj* groen; **~ card** groene kaart

greengrocer ['griːn,grousə] *n* groenteboer *m*

greenhouse ['griːnhaus] *n* broeikas *c*, kas *c*

greet [griːt] *v* groeten

greeting ['griːtiŋ] *n* groet *c*

grey [grei] *adj* grijs; grauw

greyhound ['greihaund] *n* hazewind *c*

grief [griːf] *n* verdriet *nt*; bedroefdheid *c*, smart *c*

grieve [griːv] *v* treuren

grill [gril] *n* grill *c*; *v* roosteren

grillroom ['grilruːm] *n* grillroom *c*

grim [grim] *adj* grimmig

grin [grin] *v* grijnzen; *n* grijns *c*

*grind [graind] *v* *malen; fijnmalen

grip [grip] *v* *grijpen; *n* houvast *nt*, greep *c*

grit [grit] *n* gruis *nt*

groan [groun] *v* kreunen

grocer ['grousə] *n* kruidenier *m*; **grocer's**, **grocery** kruidenierswinkel *c*

groceries ['grousəriz] *pl* kruidenierswaren *pl*

groin [grɔin] *n* lies *c*

groom [gruːm] *n* bruidegom *m*, stalknecht *m*; *v* verzorgen

groove [gruːv] *n* groef *c*

gross¹ [grous] *n* (pl ~) gros *nt*

gross² [grous] *adj* grof; bruto

grotto ['grɔtou] *n* (pl ~es, ~s) grot *c*

ground¹ [graund] *n* bodem *c*, grond *c*; **~ floor** begane grond; **grounds** terrein *nt*

ground² [graund] *v* (p, pp grind)

group [gruːp] *n* groep *c*

grouse [graus] *n* (pl ~) korhoen *nt*

grove [grouv] *n* bosje *nt*

*grow [grou] *v* groeien; kweken, verbouwen; *worden

growl [graul] *v* grommen

grown-up ['grounʌp] *adj* volwassen; *n* volwassene *c*

growth [grouθ] *n* groei *c*; gezwel *nt*

grudge [grʌdʒ] *v* misgunnen

grumble ['grʌmbəl] *v* mopperen

guarantee [,gærən'tiː] *n* garantie *c*; waarborg *c*; *v* garanderen

guard [gɑːd] *n* bewaker *m*; *v* bewaken

guardian ['gɑːdiən] *n* voogd *m*

guess [ges] *v* *raden; *denken, gissen; *n* gissing *c*

guest [gest] *n* logé *c*, gast *c*; **~ room** logeerkamer *c*

guesthouse ['gesthaus] *n* pension *nt*

guide [gaid] *n* gids *c*; *v* leiden

guidebook ['gaidbuk] *n* gids *c*

guide dog ['gaiddɔg] n geleidehond c

guideline ['gaidlain] n richtlijn c

guilt [gilt] n schuld c

guilty ['gilti] adj schuldig

guinea pig ['ginipig] n cavia c

guitar [gi'tɑː] n gitaar c

gulf [gʌlf] n golf c

gull [gʌl] n meeuw c

gum [gʌm] n tandvlees nt; gom c

gun [gʌn] n geweer nt, revolver c; kanon nt

gunpowder ['gʌn,paudə] n kruit nt

gust [gʌst] n windstoot c

gut [gʌt] n darm c; **guts** lef nt

gutter ['gʌtə] n goot c

guy [gai] n vent m

gymnasium [dʒim'neiziəm] n (pl ~s, -sia) gymlokaal nt, gymnastiekzaal c

gymnast ['dʒimnæst] n gymnast c

gymnastics [dʒim'næstiks] pl gymnastiek c

gynaecologist [,gainə'kɔlədʒist] n gynaecoloog m, gynaecologe f, vrouwenarts c

H

habit ['hæbit] n gewoonte c

habitable ['hæbitəbəl] adj bewoonbaar

habitual [hə'bitʃuəl] adj gewoon

had [hæd] v (p, pp have)

haddock ['hædək] n (pl ~) schelvis c

h(a)emorrhage ['heməridʒ] n bloeding c

haemorrhoids ['hemərɔidz] pl aambeien pl

hail [heil] n hagel c

hair [heə] n haar nt; ~ **cream** haarcrème c; ~ **gel** haargel; ~ **piece** haarstukje nt; ~ **spray** haarlak c

hairbrush ['heəbrʌʃ] n haarborstel c

hairdo ['heəduː] n kapsel nt, coiffure c

hairdresser ['heə,dresə] n kapper m, kapster f

hairdrier, hairdryer ['heədraiə] n haardroger c

hairgrip ['heəgrip] n haarspeld c

hairpin ['heəpin] n haarspeld c

hairy ['heəri] adj harig

half[1] [hɑːf] adj half

half[2] [hɑːf] n (pl halves) helft c

half time [,hɑːf'taim] n rust c

halfway [,hɑːf'wei] adv halverwege

halibut ['hælibət] n (pl ~) heilbot c

hall [hɔːl] n hal c; zaal c

halt [hɔːlt] v stoppen

halve [hɑːv] v halveren

ham [hæm] n ham c

hamburger ['hæmbə] n hamburger c

hamlet ['hæmlət] n gehucht nt

hammer ['hæmə] n hamer c

hammock ['hæmək] n hangmat c

hamper ['hæmpə] n mand c

hand [hænd] n hand c; v *aangeven; ~ **cream** handcrème c

handbag ['hændbæg] n handtas c

handbook ['hændbuk] n handboek nt

handbrake ['hændbreik] n handrem c

handcuffs ['hændkʌfs] pl handboeien pl

handful ['hændful] n handvol c

handicap ['hændikæp] n handicap c; nadeel nt

handicraft ['hændikrɑːft] n handenarbeid c; handwerk nt

handkerchief ['hæŋkətʃif] n zakdoek c

handle ['hændəl] n steel c, handvat nt; v

hanteren; behandelen
hand-made [ˌhænd'meid] adj met de hand gemaakt
handshake ['hændʃeik] n handdruk c
handsome ['hænsəm] adj knap
handwork ['hændwə:k] n handwerk nt
handwriting ['hænd,raitiŋ] n handschrift nt
handy ['hændi] adj handig
*****hang** [hæŋ] v *ophangen; *hangen
hanger ['hæŋə] n kleerhanger c
hangover ['hæŋ,ouvə] n kater c
happen ['hæpən] v *voorkomen, gebeuren
happening ['hæpəniŋ] n gebeurtenis c
happiness ['hæpinəs] n geluk nt
happy ['hæpi] adj blij, gelukkig
harbour ['hɑ:bə] n haven c
hard [hɑ:d] adj hard; moeilijk; n ~ **disk** harde schijf c
hardly ['hɑ:dli] amper, nauwelijks
hardware ['hɑ:dwɛə] n ijzerwaren pl; ~ **store** handel in ijzerwaren
hare [hɛə] n haas c
harm [hɑ:m] n schade c; kwaad nt; v schaden
harmful ['hɑ:mfəl] adj nadelig, schadelijk
harmless ['hɑ:mləs] adj onschadelijk
harmony ['hɑ:məni] n harmonie c
harp [hɑ:p] n harp c
harpsichord ['hɑ:psikɔ:d] n clavecimbel c
harsh [hɑ:ʃ] adj ruw; streng; wreed
harvest ['hɑ:vist] n oogst c, v oogsten
has [hæz] v (pr have)
haste [heist] n spoed c, haast c
hasten ['heisən] v zich haasten
hasty ['heisti] adj haastig
hat [hæt] n hoed c; ~ **rack** kapstok c
hatch [hætʃ] n luik nt
hate [heit] v een hekel *hebben aan; haten; n haat c
hatred ['heitrid] n haat c

haughty ['hɔ:ti] adj hooghartig
haul [hɔ:l] v slepen
*****have** [hæv] v *hebben; *laten; ~ **to** *moeten
hawk [hɔ:k] n havik c
hay [hei] n hooi nt; ~ **fever** hooikoorts c
hazard ['hæzəd] n risico nt
haze [heiz] n nevel c; waas nt
hazelnut ['heizəlnʌt] n hazelnoot c
hazy ['heizi] adj heiig; wazig
he [hi:] pron hij
head [hed] n hoofd nt; kop c; v leiden; ~ **of state** staatshoofd nt; ~ **waiter** maître d'hotel m
headache ['hedeik] n hoofdpijn c
heading ['hediŋ] n titel c
headlamp ['hedlæmp] n koplamp c
headland ['hedlənd] n landtong c
headlight ['hedlait] n koplamp c
headline ['hedlain] n kop c
headmaster [ˌhed'mɑ:stə] n schoolhoofd nt; rector m, directeur m
headquarters [ˌhed'kwɔ:təz] pl hoofdkwartier nt, hoofdkantoor nt
headstrong ['hedstrɔŋ] adj koppig
heal [hi:l] v *genezen
health [helθ] n gezondheid c; ~ **center** Am, ~ **centre** consultatiebureau nt; ~ **certificate** gezondheidsattest nt
healthy ['helθi] adj gezond
heap [hi:p] n stapel c, hoop c
*****hear** [hiə] v horen
hearing ['hiəriŋ] n gehoor nt, hoorzitting c
heart [hɑ:t] n hart nt; kern c; **by** ~ uit het hoofd; ~ **attack** hartaanval c
heartburn ['hɑ:tbə:n] n maagzuur nt
hearth [hɑ:θ] n haard c
heartless ['hɑ:tləs] adj harteloos
hearty ['hɑ:ti] adj hartelijk
heat [hi:t] n warmte c, hitte c; v verwarmen; **heating pad** elektrisch kussen
heater ['hi:tə] n kachel c; **immersion ~**

dompelaar *c*

heath [hi:θ] *n* heide *c*

heathen ['hi:ðən] *n* heiden *c*; heidens

heather ['heðə] *n* heide *c*

heating ['hi:tiŋ] *n* verwarming *c*

heaven ['hevən] *n* hemel *c*

heavy ['hevi] *adj* zwaar

Hebrew ['hi:bru:] *n* Hebreeuws *nt*

hedge [hedʒ] *n* heg *c*

hedgehog ['hedʒhɔg] *n* egel *c*

heel [hi:l] *n* hiel *c*; hak *c*

height [hait] *n* hoogte *c*; toppunt *nt*, hoogtepunt *nt*

heir [eə] *n* erfgenaam *m*

heiress ['eəres] *n* erfgename *f*

helicopter ['helikʌptə] *n* helicopter *c*

hell [hel] *n* hel *c*

hello! [he'lou] hallo!; dag!; **say hello to** (be)groeten

helm [helm] *n* roer *nt*

helmet ['helmit] *n* helm *c*

helmsman ['helmzmən] *n* stuurman *m*

help [help] *v* *helpen; *n* hulp *c*

helper ['helpə] *n* helper *c*

helpful ['helpfəl] *adj* hulpvaardig

helping ['helpiŋ] *n* portie *c*

hem [hem] *n* zoom *c*

hemp [hemp] *n* hennep *c*

hen [hen] *n* hen *f*; kip *c*

her [hə:] *pron* haar

herb [hə:b] *n* kruid *nt*

herd [hə:d] *n* kudde *c*

here [hiə] *adv* hier; **~ you are** alstublieft

hereditary [hi'reditəri] *adj* erfelijk

hernia ['hə:niə] *n* breuk *c*

hero ['hiərou] *n* (pl ~es) held *m*

heron ['herən] *n* reiger *c*

herring ['heriŋ] *n* (pl ~, ~s) haring *c*

herself [hə:'self] *pron* zich; zelf

hesitate ['heziteit] *v* aarzelen

heterosexual [,hetərə'sekʃuəl] *adj* heteroseksueel

hiccup ['hikʌp] *n* hik *c*

hide [haid] *n* huid *c*

*hide [haid] *v* *verbergen; verstoppen

hideous ['hidiəs] *adj* afschuwelijk

hierarchy ['haiəra:ki] *n* hiërarchie *c*

high [hai] *adj* hoog

highway ['haiwei] *n* hoofdweg *c*; *nAm* autoweg *c*

hijack ['haidʒæk] *v* kapen

hijacker ['haidʒækə] *n* kaper *c*

hike [haik] *v* *trekken

hill [hil] *n* heuvel *c*

hillock ['hilək] *n* lage heuvel *nt*

hillside ['hilsaid] *n* helling *c*

hilltop ['hiltɔp] *n* heuveltop *c*

hilly ['hili] *adj* heuvelachtig

him [him] *pron* hem

himself [him'self] *pron* zich; zelf

hinder ['hində] *v* hinderen

hinge [hindʒ] *n* scharnier *nt*

hint [hint] *n* aanwijzing *c*; hint *c*; *v* aanwijzigingen geven

hip [hip] *n* heup *c*

hire [haiə] *v* huren; **for ~** te huur

hire purchase [,haiə'pə:tʃəs] *n* huurkoop *c*

his [hiz] *adj* zijn

historian [hi'stɔ:riən] *n* geschiedkundige *c*

historic [hi'stɔrik] *adj* historisch

historical [hi'stɔrikəl] *adj* geschiedkundig

history ['histəri] *n* geschiedenis *c*

hit [hit] *n* hit *c*

*hit [hit] *v* *slaan; raken, *treffen

hitchhike ['hitʃhaik] *v* liften

hitchhiker ['hitʃ,haikə] *n* lifter *m*, liftster *f*

hoarse [hɔ:s] *adj* schor, hees

hobby ['hɔbi] *n* liefhebberij *c*, hobby *c*

hobbyhorse ['hɔbihɔ:s] *n* hobbelpaard *nt*; stokpaardje *nt*

hockey ['hɔki] *n* hockey *nt*

hoist [hɔist] *v* *hijsen

hold [hould] *n* ruim *nt*

*hold [hould] *v* *vasthouden, *houden;

bewaren; ~ **on** zich *vasthouden; ~ **up** ondersteunen

hold-up ['houldʌp] *n* overval *c*

hole [houl] *n* kuil *c*, gat *nt*

holiday ['hɔlədi] *n* vakantie *c*; feestdag *c*; ~ **camp** vakantiekamp *nt*; ~ **resort** vakantieoord *nt*; **on** ~ met vakantie

Holland ['hɔlənd] Holland

hollow ['hɔlou] *adj* hol

holy ['houli] *adj* heilig

homage ['hɔmidʒ] *n* hulde *c*

home [houm] *n* thuis *nt*; tehuis *nt*, huis *nt*; *adv* naar huis; **at** ~ thuis

homemade [,houm'meid] *adj* eigengemaakt

homesickness ['houm,siknəs] *n* heimwee *nt*

homosexual [,houmə'sekʃuəl] *adj* homoseksueel

homework ['houm,wə:k] *n* huiswerk *nt*

honest ['ɔnist] *adj* eerlijk; oprecht

honesty ['ɔnisti] *n* eerlijkheid *c*

honey ['hʌni] *n* honing *c*

honeymoon ['hʌnimu:n] *n* huwelijksreis *c*, wittebroodsweken *pl*

honk [hʌŋk] *v Am* claxonneren

honour ['ɔnə] *n* eer *c*; *v* eren, huldigen

honourable ['ɔnərəbəl] *adj* eervol, eerzaam; rechtschapen

hood [hud] *n* kap *c*; *nAm* motorkap *c*

hoof [hu:f] *n* hoef *c*

hook [huk] *n* haak *c*

hoot [hu:t] *v* claxonneren

hooter ['hu:tə] *n* claxon *c*

hoover ['hu:və] *v* stofzuigen

hop[1] [hɔp] *v* huppelen; *n* sprong *c*

hop[2] [hɔp] *n* hop *c*

hope [houp] *n* hoop *c*; *v* hopen

hopeful ['houpfəl] *adj* hoopvol

hopeless ['houpləs] *adj* hopeloos

horizon [hə'raizən] *n* kim *c*, horizon *c*

horizontal [,hɔri'zɔntəl] *adj* horizontaal

horn [hɔ:n] *n* hoorn *c*; claxon *c*

horrible ['hɔribəl] *adj* vreselijk; verschrikkelijk, gruwelijk, afschuwelijk

horror ['hɔrə] *n* afgrijzen *nt*, afschuw *c*

hors d'œuvre [ɔ:'də:vr] *n* hors d'œuvre *c*, voorgerecht *nt*

horse [hɔ:s] *n* paard *nt*

horseman ['hɔ:smən] *n* (pl -men) ruiter *m*

horsepower ['hɔ:s,pauə] *n* paardekracht *c*

horserace ['hɔ:sreis] *n* harddraverij *c*, paardenrace *c*

horseradish ['hɔ:s,rædiʃ] *n* mieriksworteI *c*

horseshoe ['hɔ:sʃu:] *n* hoefijzer *nt*

horticulture ['hɔ:tikʌltʃə] *n* tuinbouw *c*

hospitable ['hɔspitəbəl] *adj* gastvrij

hospital ['hɔspitəl] *n* hospitaal *nt*, ziekenhuis *nt*

hospitality [,hɔspi'tæləti] *n* gastvrijheid *c*

host [houst] *n* gastheer *m*

hostage ['hɔstidʒ] *n* gijzelaar *m*, -ster *f*

hostel ['hɔstəl] *n* herberg *c*

hostess ['houstis] *n* gastvrouw *f*

hostile ['hɔstail] *adj* vijandig

hot [hɔt] *adj* warm, heet

hotel [hou'tel] *n* hotel *nt*

hot-tempered [,hɔt'tempəd] *adj* driftig

hour [auə] *n* uur *nt*

hourly ['auəli] *adj* uur-

house [haus] *n* huis *nt*; woning *c*; pand *nt*; ~ **agent** makelaar *m*; **public** ~ kroeg *c*

houseboat ['hausbout] *n* woonboot *c*

household ['haushould] *n* huishouden *nt*

housekeeper ['haus,ki:pə] *n* huishoudster *f*

housekeeping ['haus,ki:piŋ] *n*

huishouden *nt*
housemaid ['hausmeid] *n* dienstmeid *f*
housewife ['hauswaif] *n* huisvrouw *f*
housework ['hauswə:k] *n* huishouden *nt*
how [hau] *adv* hoe; wat; ~ **many** hoeveel; ~ **much** hoeveel
however [hau'evə] *conj* evenwel, echter
hug [hʌg] *v* omhelzen; *n* omhelzing *c*
huge [hju:dʒ] *adj* geweldig, enorm, reusachtig
hum [hʌm] *v* neuriën
human ['hju:mən] *adj* menselijk; ~ **being** menselijk wezen
humanity [hju'mænəti] *n* mensheid *c*
humble ['hʌmbəl] *adj* nederig
humid ['hju:mid] *adj* vochtig
humidity [hju'midəti] *n* vochtigheid *c*
humorous ['hju:mərəs] *adj* grappig, geestig, humoristisch
humo(u)r ['hju:mə] *n* humor *c*
hundred ['hʌndrəd] *n* honderd *c*
Hungarian [hʌŋ'geəriən] *adj* Hongaars; *n* Hongaar *m*, -se *f*
Hungary ['hʌŋgəri] Hongarije

hunger ['hʌŋgə] *n* honger *c*
hungry ['hʌŋgri] *adj* hongerig
hunt [hʌnt] *v* jagen; *n* jacht *c*; ~ **for** *zoeken
hunter ['hʌntə] *n* jager *c*
hurricane ['hʌrikən] *n* orkaan *c*; ~ **lamp** stormlamp *c*
hurry ['hʌri] *v* *opschieten, zich haasten; *n* haast *c*; **in a** ~ haastig
hurt [hə:t] *v* pijn *doen, bezeren; kwetsen
hurtful ['hə:tfəl] *adj* schadelijk; kwetsend
husband ['hʌzbənd] *n* echtgenoot *m*, man *m*
hut [hʌt] *n* hut *c*
hydrogen ['haidrədʒən] *n* waterstof *c*
hygiene ['haidʒi:n] *n* hygiëne *c*
hygienic [hai'dʒi:nik] *adj* hygiënisch
hymn [him] *n* gezang *nt*
hyphen ['haifən] *n* koppelteken *nt*
hypocrisy [hi'pɔkrəsi] *n* huichelarij *c*
hypocrite ['hipəkrit] *n* huichelaar *m*, -ster *f*
hypocritical [ˌhipə'kritikəl] *adj* huichelachtig, hypocriet, schijnheilig
hysterical [hi'sterikəl] *adj* hysterisch

I

I [ai] *pron* ik
ice [ais] *n* ijs *nt*; ~ **bag** koeltas *c*; ~ **cream** ijs *nt*, ijsje *nt*
Iceland ['aislənd] IJsland
Icelander ['aisləndə] *n* IJslander *c*
Icelandic [ais'lændik] *adj* IJslands
icon ['aikɔn] *n* ikoon *c*
ID card [ˌai'di:ka:d] *n* identiteitskaart *c*
idea [ai'diə] *n* idee *nt/c*; inval *c*, gedachte *c*; denkbeeld *nt*, begrip *nt*
ideal [ai'diəl] *adj* ideaal; *n* ideaal *nt*

identical [ai'dentikəl] *adj* identiek
identification [ai,dentifi'keiʃən] *n* identificatie *c*
identify [ai'dentifai] *v* identificeren
identity [ai'dentəti] *n* identiteit *c*; ~ **card** identiteitskaart *c*
idiom ['idiəm] *n* idioom *nt*
idiomatic [ˌidiə'mætik] *adj* idiomatisch
idiot ['idiət] *n* idioot *c*
idiotic [ˌidi'ɔtik] *adj* idioot

idle ['aidəl] *adj* werkeloos; lui; ijdel

idol ['aidəl] *n* afgod *c*; idool *nt*

if [if] *conj* als; indien

ignition [ig'niʃən] *n* ontsteking *c*; **~coil** ontsteking *c*

ignorant ['ignərənt] *adj* onwetend

ignore [ig'nɔ:] *v* negeren

ill [il] *adj* ziek; slecht; kwaad

illegal [i'li:gəl] *adj* illegaal, onwettig

illegible [i'ledʒəbəl] *adj* onleesbaar

illiterate [i'litərət] *n* analfabeet *m*, analfabete *f*

illness ['ilnəs] *n* ziekte *c*

illuminate [i'lu:mineit] *v* verlichten

illumination [i,lu:mi'neiʃən] *n* verlichting *c*

illusion [i'lu:ʒən] *n* illusie *c*; droombeeld *nt*

illustrate ['iləstreit] *v* illustreren

illustration [,ilə'streiʃən] *n* illustratie *c*

image ['imidʒ] *n* beeld *nt*

imaginary [i'mædʒinəri] *adj* denkbeeldig

imagination [i,mædʒi'neiʃən] *n* verbeelding *c*

imagine [i'mædʒin] *v* zich voorstellen; zich verbeelden; zich *indenken

imitate ['imiteit] *v* nabootsen, imiteren

imitation [,imi'teiʃən] *n* namaak *c*, imitatie *c*

immediate [i'mi:djət] *adj* onmiddellijk

immediately [i'mi:djətli] *adv* meteen, dadelijk, onmiddellijk

immense [i'mens] *adj* oneindig, reusachtig, onmetelijk

immigrant ['imigrənt] *n* immigrant *m*, -e *f*

immigrate ['imigreit] *v* immigreren

immigration [,imi'greiʃən] *n* immigratie *c*

immodest [i'mɔdist] *adj* onbescheiden

immunity [i'mju:nəti] *n* immuniteit *c*

immunize ['imjunaiz] *v* immuun maken

impartial [im'pɑ:ʃəl] *adj* onpartijdig

impassable [im'pɑ:səbəl] *adj* onbegaanbaar

impatient [im'peiʃənt] *adj* ongeduldig

impede [im'pi:d] *v* belemmeren

impediment [im'pedimənt] *n* beletsel *nt*, belemmering *c*

imperfect [im'pə:fikt] *adj* onvolmaakt

imperial [im'piəriəl] *adj* keizerlijk; rijks-

impersonal [im'pə:sənəl] *adj* onpersoonlijk

impertinence [im'pə:tinəns] *n* onbeschaamdheid *c*

impertinent [im'pə:tinənt] *adj* brutaal, onbeschoft, onbeschaamd

implement[1] ['implimənt] *n* werktuig *nt*, gereedschap *nt*

implement[2] ['impliment] *v* uitvoeren

implicate ['implikeit] *v* *betrekken

imply [im'plai] *v* impliceren; *inhouden

impolite [,impə'lait] *adj* onbeleefd

import[1] [im'pɔ:t] *v* invoeren, importeren

import[2] ['impɔ:t] *n* import *c*, invoer *c*; **~ duty** invoerrecht *nt*

importance [im'pɔ:təns] *n* belang *nt*

important [im'pɔ:tənt] *adj* gewichtig, belangrijk

importer [im'pɔ:tə] *n* importeur *c*

imposing [im'pouziŋ] *adj* indrukwekkend

impossible [im'pɔsəbəl] *adj* onmogelijk

impotence ['impətəns] *n* impotentie *c*

impotent ['impətənt] *adj* impotent

impress [im'pres] *v* imponeren, indruk maken op

impression [im'preʃən] *n* indruk *c*

impressive [im'presiv] *adj* indrukwekkend

imprison [im'prizən] v gevangen zetten

imprisonment [im'prizənmənt] n gevangenschap c

improbable [im'prɔbəbəl] adj onwaarschijnlijk

improper [im'prɔpə] adj ongepast

improve [im'pru:v] v verbeteren

improvement [im'pru:vmənt] n verbetering c

improvise ['imprəvaiz] v improviseren

impudent ['impjudənt] adj onbeschaamd

impulse ['impʌls] n impuls c; prikkel c

impulsive [im'pʌlsiv] adj impulsief

in [in] prep in; over, op; binnen

inaccessible [i,næk'sesəbəl] adj ontoegankelijk

inaccurate [i'nækjurət] adj onnauwkeurig

inadequate [i'nædikwət] adj onvoldoende

incapable [iŋ'keipəbəl] adj onbekwaam

incense ['insens] n wierook c

inch ['intʃ] n duim (2.54 cm) c

incident ['insidənt] n incident nt

incidental [,insi'dentəl] adj toevallig

incite [in'sait] v aansporen

inclination [,iŋkli'neiʃən] n neiging c

incline [iŋ'klain] n helling c

inclined [iŋ'klaind] adj genegen, geneigd; *be ~ to v neigen

include [iŋ'klu:d] v bevatten, *insluiten; **included** inbegrepen

inclusive [iŋ'klu:siv] adj inclusief

income ['iŋkəm] n inkomen nt; ~ tax inkomstenbelasting c

incompetent [iŋ'kɔmpətənt] adj onbekwaam

incomplete [,iŋkəm'pli:t] adj onvolledig, incompleet

incomprehensible [,iŋkəmpri'hensibəl] adj onbegrijpelijk

inconceivable [,iŋkən'si:vəbəl] adj ondenkbaar, onvoorstelbaar

inconspicuous [,iŋkən'spikjuəs] adj onopvallend

inconvenience [,iŋkən'vi:njəns] n ongemak nt, ongerief nt

inconvenient [,iŋkən'vi:njənt] adj ongelegen; lastig

incorrect [,iŋkə'rekt] adj onnauwkeurig, onjuist

increase[1] [iŋ'kri:s] v vermeerderen; *oplopen, *toenemen

increase[2] ['iŋkri:s] n toename c; verhoging c

incredible [iŋ'kredəbəl] adj ongelofelijk

incurable [iŋ'kjuərəbəl] adj ongeneeslijk

indecent [in'di:sənt] adj onfatsoenlijk

indeed [in'di:d] adv inderdaad

indefinite [in'definit] adj onbepaald

indemnity [in'demnəti] n schadeloosstelling c, schadevergoeding c

independence [,indi'pendəns] n onafhankelijkheid c

independent [,indi'pendənt] adj onafhankelijk; zelfstandig

index ['indeks] n register nt, index c; ~ finger wijsvinger c

India ['indiə] India

Indian ['indiən] adj Indisch; Indiaans; n Indiër m, Indische f; Indiaan m, -se f

indicate ['indikeit] v *aangeven, aanduiden

indication [,indi'keiʃən] n teken nt, aanwijzing c

indicator ['indikeitə] n richtingaanwijzer c

indifferent [in'difərənt] adj onverschillig

indigestion [,indi'dʒestʃən] n

indigestie *c*

indignation [,indig'neiʃən] *n* verontwaardiging *c*

indirect [,indi'rekt] *adj* indirect

individual [,indi'vidʒuəl] *adj* afzonderlijk, individueel; *n* enkeling *c*, individu *nt*

Indonesia [,ində'ni:ziə] Indonesië

Indonesian [,ində'ni:ziən] *adj* Indonesisch; *n* Indonesiër *m*, Indonesische *f*

indoor ['indɔ:] *adj* binnen

indoors [,in'dɔ:z] *adv* binnen

indulge [in'dʌldʒ] *v* *toegeven

industrial [in'dʌstriəl] *adj* industrieel; ~ **area** industriegebied *nt*

industrious [in'dʌstriəs] *adj* vlijtig, bedrijvig

industry ['indəstri] *n* industrie *c*

inedible [i'nedibəl] *adj* oneetbaar

inefficient [,ini'fiʃənt] *adj* ondoeltreffend

inevitable [i'nevitəbəl] *adj* onvermijdelijk

inexpensive [,inik'spensiv] *adj* goedkoop

inexperienced [,inik'spiəriənst] *adj* onervaren

infallible [in'fæləbl] *adj* feilloos

infant ['infənt] *n* zuigeling *c*

infantry ['infəntri] *n* infanterie *c*

infect [in'fekt] *v* besmetten, *aansteken

infection [in'fekʃən] *n* infectie *c*

infectious [in'fekʃəs] *adj* besmettelijk

infer [in'fə:] *v* afleiden

inferior [in'fiəriə] *adj* inferieur, minderwaardig; lager

infinite ['infinət] *adj* oneindig

infinitive [in'finitiv] *n* onbepaalde wijs

inflammable [in'flæməbəl] *adj* ontvlambaar

inflammation [,inflə'meiʃən] *n* ontsteking *c*

inflatable [in'fleitəbəl] *adj* opblaasbaar

inflate [in'fleit] *v* *opblazen

inflation [in'fleiʃən] *n* inflatie *c*

inflict [in'flikt] *v* toebrengen

influence ['influəns] *n* invloed *c*; *v* beïnvloeden

influential [,influ'enʃəl] *adj* invloedrijk

influenza [,influ'enzə] *n* griep *c*

inform [in'fɔ:m] *v* informeren; inlichten, mededelen

informal [in'fɔ:məl] *adj* informeel

information [,infə'meiʃən] *n* informatie *c*; inlichting *c*, mededeling *c*; ~ **bureau** inlichtingenkantoor *nt*

infra-red [,infrə'red] *adj* infrarood

infrequent [in'fri:kwənt] *adj* zeldzaam

ingredient [in'gri:diənt] *n* ingrediënt *nt*, bestanddeel *nt*

inhabit [in'hæbit] *v* bewonen

inhabitable [in'hæbitəbəl] *adj* bewoonbaar

inhabitant [in'hæbitənt] *n* inwoner *m*, inwoonster *f*; bewoner *m*, bewoonster *f*

inhale [in'heil] *v* inademen

inherit [in'herit] *v* erven

inheritance [in'heritəns] *n* erfenis *c*

inhibit [in'hibit] *v* verbieden; hinderen

initial [i'niʃəl] *adj* begin-, eerst; *n* voorletter *c*; *v* paraferen

initiate [i'niʃieit] *v* beginnen; inwijden

initiative [i'niʃətiv] *n* initiatief *nt*

inject [in'dʒekt] *v* *inspuiten

injection [in'dʒekʃən] *n* injectie *c*

injure ['indʒə] *v* verwonden, kwetsen; krenken

injured ['indʒəd] *adj* gewond

injury ['indʒəri] *n* verwonding *c*; letsel *nt*, blessure *c*

injustice [in'dʒʌstis] *n* onrecht *nt*

ink [iŋk] *n* inkt *c*

inlet ['inlet] *n* inham *c*
inn [in] *n* herberg *c*
inner ['inə] *adj* inwendig; ~ **tube** binnenband *c*
innocence ['inəsəns] *n* onschuld *c*
innocent ['inəsənt] *adj* onschuldig
inoculate [i'nɔkjuleit] *v* inenten
inoculation [i,nɔkju'leiʃən] *n* inenting *c*
inquire [iŋ'kwaiə] *v* *navragen, informatie *inwinnen
inquiry [iŋ'kwaiəri] *n* vraag *c*, navraag *c*; onderzoek *nt*; ~ **office** informatiebureau *nt*
inquisitive [iŋ'kwizətiv] *adj* nieuwsgierig
insane [in'sein] *adj* krankzinnig
inscription [in'skripʃən] *n* inscriptie *c*
insect ['insekt] *n* insekt *nt*; ~ **repellent** insektenwerend middel
insecticide [in'sektisaid] *n* insekticide *c*
insensitive [in'sensətiv] *adj* ongevoelig
insert [in'sə:t] *v* invoegen
inside [,in'said] *n* binnenkant *c*; *adj* binnenst; *adv* binnen; van binnen; *prep* in, binnen; ~ **out** binnenste buiten; **insides** ingewanden *pl*
insight ['insait] *n* inzicht *nt*
insignificant [,insig'nifikənt] *adj* onbelangrijk; onbeduidend, nietsbetekenend; nietig
insist [in'sist] *v* *aandringen; *aanhouden, *volhouden
insolence ['insələns] *n* onbeschaamdheid *c*
insolent ['insələnt] *adj* brutaal, onbeschaamd
insomnia [in'sɔmniə] *n* slapeloosheid *c*
inspect [in'spekt] *v* inspecteren
inspection [in'spekʃən] *n* inspectie *c*; controle *c*

inspector [in'spektə] *n* inspecteur *m*, inspectrice *f*
inspire [in'spaiə] *v* bezielen
install [in'stɔ:l] *v* installeren
installation [,instə'leiʃən] *n* installatie *c*
instal(l)ment [in'stɔ:lmənt] *n* afbetaling *c*; ~ **plan** *nAm* huurkoop *c*
instance ['instəns] *n* voorbeeld *nt*; geval *nt*; **for** ~ bijvoorbeeld
instant ['instənt] *n* ogenblik *nt*
instantly ['instəntli] *adv* ogenblikkelijk, onmiddellijk, meteen
instead of [in'sted ɔv] in plaats van
instinct ['instiŋkt] *n* instinct *nt*
institute ['institju:t] *n* instituut *nt*; instelling *c*; *v* instellen
institution [,insti'tju:ʃən] *n* inrichting *c*, instelling *c*
instruct [in'strʌkt] *v* onderrichten
instruction [in'strʌkʃən] *n* onderwijs *nt*
instructive [in'strʌktiv] *adj* leerzaam
instructor [in'strʌktə] *n* leraar *m*, lerares *f*
instrument ['instrumənt] *n* instrument *nt*; **musical** ~ muziekinstrument *nt*
insufficient ['insə'fiʃənt] *adj* onvoldoende
insulate ['insjuleit] *v* isoleren
insulation [,insju'leiʃən] *n* isolatie *c*
insulator ['insjuleitə] *n* isolator *c*
insult[1] [in'sʌlt] *v* beledigen
insult[2] ['insʌlt] *n* belediging *c*
insurance [in'ʃuərəns] *n* assurantie *c*, verzekering *c*; ~ **policy** verzekeringspolis *c*
insure [in'ʃuə] *v* verzekeren
intact [in'tækt] *adj* intact
integrate ['intəgreit] *v* integreren
intellect ['intəlekt] *n* intellect *nt*
intellectual [,intə'lektʃuəl] *adj* intellectueel

intelligence [in'telidʒəns] n
intelligentie c

intelligent [in'telidʒənt] adj
intelligent

intend [in'tend] v van plan *zijn,
bedoelen

intense [in'tens] adj intens; hevig

intention [in'tenʃən] n bedoeling c

intentional [in'tenʃənəl] adj
opzettelijk

intercourse ['intəkɔ:s] n omgang c;
gemeenschap c; (**sexual**) ~
geslachtsgemeenschap c

interest ['intrəst] n interesse c,
belangstelling c; belang nt; rente c; v
interesseren

interested ['intristid] adj
geïnteresseerd, belangstellend;
betrokken

interesting ['intrəstiŋ] adj interessant

interfere [,intə'fiə] v tussenbeide
*komen; ~ **with** zich bemoeien met

interference [,intə'fiərəns] n
inmenging c

interim ['intərim] n tussentijd c

interior [in'tiəriə] n binnenkant c

interlude ['intəlu:d] n intermezzo nt

intermediary [,intə'mi:djəri] n
tussenpersoon c

intermission [,intə'miʃən] n pauze c

internal [in'tə:nəl] adj intern, inwendig

international [,intə'næʃənəl] adj
internationaal

Internet ['intənet] n Internet nt

interpret [in'tə:prit] v tolken;
vertolken

interpreter [in'tə:pritə] n tolk c

interrogate [in'terəgeit] v
*ondervragen

interrogation [in,terə'geiʃən] n
verhoor nt

interrogative [,intə'rɔgətiv] adj
vragend

interrupt [,intə'rʌpt] v *onderbreken

interruption [,intə'rʌpʃən] n
onderbreking c

intersection [,intə'sekʃən] n
kruispunt nt

interval ['intəvəl] n pauze c;
tussenpoos c

intervene [,intə'vi:n] v *ingrijpen

interview ['intəvju:] n
sollicitatiegesprek nt; interview nt,
vraaggesprek nt

intestine [in'testin] n darm c;
intestines ingewanden pl

intimate ['intimət] adj intiem

into ['intu] prep in

intolerable [in'tɔlərəbəl] adj
onuitstaanbaar

intoxicated [in'tɔksikeitid] adj
dronken

intrigue [in'tri:g] n komplot nt

introduce [,intrə'dju:s] v
introduceren, voorstellen; inleiden;
invoeren

introduction [,intrə'dʌkʃən] n
inleiding c

invade [in'veid] v *binnenvallen,
*invallen; *schenden

invalid¹ ['invəli:d] n invalide c; adj
invalide

invalid² [in'vælid] adj ongeldig

invasion [in'veiʒən] n inval c, invasie c

invent [in'vent] v *uitvinden;
*verzinnen

invention [in'venʃən] n uitvinding c

inventive [in'ventiv] adj vindingrijk

inventor [in'ventə] n uitvinder m,
uitvindster f

inventory ['invəntri] n inventaris c

invert [in'və:t] v omdraaien

invest [in'vest] v investeren; beleggen

investigate [in'vestigeit] v
*onderzoeken

investigation [in,vesti'geiʃən] n
onderzoek nt

investment [in'vestmənt] n

investering c; belegging c,
geldbelegging c
investor [in'vestə] n investeerder m
invisible [in'vizəbəl] adj onzichtbaar
invitation [,invi'teiʃən] n uitnodiging c
invite [in'vait] v inviteren, uitnodigen
invoice ['invɔis] n factuur c
involve [in'vɔlv] v impliceren;
involved betrokken
inwards ['inwədz] adv naar binnen
iodine ['aiədi:n] n jodium nt
Iran [i'rɑ:n] Iran
Iranian [i'reiniən] adj Iraans; n Iraniër m
Iraq [i'rɑ:k] Irak
Iraqi [i'rɑ:ki] adj Iraaks; n Irakees m
Ireland ['aiələnd] Ierland
Irish ['aiəriʃ] adj Iers; **I'm ~** ik ben
Ier(se); **the ~** de Ieren
Irishman ['aiəriʃmən] n (pl -men) Ier m
Irishman ['aiəriʃwumən] n (pl
-women) Ierse f
iron ['aiən] n ijzer nt; strijkijzer nt;
ijzeren; v *strijken
ironical [ai'rɔnikəl] adj ironisch
irony ['aiərəni] n ironie c
irregular [i'regjulə] adj onregelmatig
irreparable [i'repərəbəl] adj
onherstelbaar

irrevocable [i'revəkəbəl] adj
onherroepelijk
irritable ['iritəbəl] adj prikkelbaar
irritate ['iriteit] v prikkelen, irriteren
is [iz] v (pr be)
island ['ailənd] n eiland nt
isolate ['aisəleit] v isoleren
isolation [,aisə'leiʃən] n isolement nt;
isolatie c
Israel ['izreil] Israël
Israeli [iz'reili] adj Israëlisch; n
Israëliër m
issue ['iʃu:] v *uitgeven; n uitgifte c,
oplage c, uitgave c; kwestie c, punt nt;
uitkomst c, resultaat nt, gevolg nt, slot
nt, einde nt; uitgang c
it [it] pron het
Italian [i'tæljən] adj Italiaans; n
Italiaan m, -se f
Italy ['itəli] Italië
itch [itʃ] n jeuk c; kriebel c; v jeuken
item ['aitəm] n artikel nt; punt nt
itinerary [ai'tinərəri] n reisplan nt,
reisgegevens, reisroute c
its zijn, haar
itself [it'self] zich, zichzelf; **by ~** alleen
ivory ['aivəri] n ivoor nt
ivy ['aivi] n klimop c

J

jack [dʒæk] n krik c
jacket ['dʒækit] n jasje nt, colbert c,
vest nt; omslag c/nt
jade [dʒeid] n jade nt/c
jail [dʒeil] n gevangenis c
jam [dʒæm] n jam c;
verkeersopstopping c
janitor ['dʒænitə] n conciërge c
January ['dʒænjuəri] januari
Japan [dʒə'pæn] Japan

Japanese [,dʒæpə'ni:z] adj Japans; n
Japanner m, Japanse f
jar [dʒɑ:] n pot c
jaundice ['dʒɔ:ndis] n geelzucht c
jaw [dʒɔ:] n kaak c
jealous ['dʒeləs] adj jaloers
jealousy ['dʒeləsi] n jaloezie c
jeans [dʒi:nz] pl spijkerbroek c
jelly ['dʒeli] n gelei c; jam
jellyfish ['dʒelifiʃ] n kwal c

jersey ['dʒəːzi] n jersey c; trui c

jet [dʒet] n straal c; straalvliegtuig nt

jetty ['dʒeti] n pier c

Jew [dʒuː] n jood m, jodin f

jewel ['dʒuːəl] n juweel nt

jeweller ['dʒuːələ] n juwelier c

jewellery ['dʒuːəlri] n juwelen; bijouterie c

jewelry ['dʒuːəlri] nAm juwelen; bijouterie c

Jewish ['dʒuːiʃ] adj joods

job [dʒɔb] n karwei nt; betrekking c, baan c; ~ center Am, ~ centre arbeidsbureau nt

jobless ['dʒɔbləs] adj zonder werk

jockey ['dʒɔki] n jockey m

join [dʒɔin] v *verbinden; zich voegen bij; zich *aansluiten bij; samenvoegen, verenigen

joint [dʒɔint] n gewricht nt; las c; adj verenigd, gezamenlijk

jointly ['dʒɔintli] adv gezamenlijk

joke [dʒouk] n mop c, grap c

jolly ['dʒɔli] adj leuk

Jordan ['dʒɔːdən] Jordanië

Jordanian [dʒɔː'deiniən] adj Jordaans; n Jordaniër m

journal ['dʒəːnəl] n tijdschrift nt

journalism ['dʒəːnəlizəm] n journalistiek c

journalist ['dʒəːnəlist] n journalist m,
-e f

journey ['dʒəːni] n reis c

joy [dʒɔi] n genot nt, vreugde c

joyful ['dʒɔifəl] adj blij, vrolijk

jubilee ['dʒuːbiliː] n jubileum nt

judge [dʒʌdʒ] n rechter c; v oordelen; beoordelen

judgment ['dʒʌdʒmənt] n oordeel nt; beoordeling c

jug [dʒʌg] n kan c

juggle ['dʒʌgəl] v jongleren, goochelen

juice [dʒuːs] n sap nt

juicy ['dʒuːsi] adj sappig

July [dʒu'lai] juli

jump [dʒʌmp] v *springen; n sprong c

jumper ['dʒʌmpə] n jumper c

junction ['dʒʌŋkʃən] n kruising c; knooppunt nt

June [dʒuːn] juni

jungle ['dʒʌŋgəl] n oerwoud nt, jungle c

junior ['dʒuːnjə] adj jonger

junk [dʒʌŋk] n rommel c

jury ['dʒuəri] n jury c

just [dʒʌst] adj terecht, rechtvaardig; juist; adv pas; precies; alleen, slechts

justice ['dʒʌstis] n recht nt; gerechtigheid c, rechtvaardigheid c

justify ['dʒʌstifai] v rechtvaardigen

juvenile ['dʒuːvənail] adj jeugdig

K

kangaroo [ˌkæŋgə'ruː] n kangoeroe c

keel [kiːl] n kiel c

keen [kiːn] adj enthousiast; scherp

*keep [kiːp] v *houden; bewaren; *blijven; ~ away from niet *betreden; ~ off *afblijven; ~ on *doorgaan met; ~ quiet *zwijgen; ~ up *volhouden; ~ up

with *bijhouden

keep [kiːp] n aandenken

kennel ['kenəl] n hondehok nt; kennel c

Kenya ['kenjə] Kenya

kerosene ['kerəsiːn] n petroleum c

kettle ['ketəl] n ketel c, fluitketel c,

waterketel *c*; waterkoker *c*
key [kiː] *n* sleutel *c*
keyhole ['kiːhoul] *n* sleutelgat *nt*
khaki ['kɑːki] *n* kaki *nt*
kick [kik] *v* trappen, schoppen; *n* trap *c*, schop *c*
kickoff [ˌki'kɔf] *n* aftrap *c*
kid [kid] *n* kind *nt*; geiteleer *nt*; *v* *beetnemen
kidney ['kidni] *n* nier *c*
kill [kil] *v* *ombrengen, doden
kilogram ['kiləgræm] *n* kilo *nt*
kilometer *nAm*, **kilometre** ['kiləˌmiːtə] *n* kilometer *c*
kind [kaind] *adj* aardig, vriendelijk; goed; *n* soort *c/nt*
kindergarten ['kindəˌgɑːtən] *n* kleuterschool *c*
king [kiŋ] *n* koning *m*
kingdom ['kiŋdəm] *n* koninkrijk *nt*; rijk *nt*
kiosk ['kiːɔsk] *n* kiosk *c*

kiss [kis] *n* zoen *c*, kus *c*; *v* kussen
kit [kit] *n* uitrusting *c*
kitchen ['kitʃin] *n* keuken *c*; **~ garden** moestuin *c*; **~ towel** theedoek
knapsack ['næpsæk] *n* knapzak *c*
knave [neiv] *n* boer *m*
knee [niː] *n* knie *c*
kneecap ['niːkæp] *n* knieschijf *c*
*kneel [niːl] *v* knielen
knew [njuː] *v* (p know)
knife [naif] *n* (pl knives) mes *nt*
knight [nait] *n* ridder *m*
*knit [nit] *v* breien
knob [nɔb] *n* knop *c*
knock [nɔk] *v* kloppen; *n* klop *c*; **~ against** *stoten tegen; **~ down** *neerslaan
knot [nɔt] *n* knoop *c*; *v* knopen
*know [nou] *v* *weten, kennen
knowledge ['nɔlidʒ] *n* kennis *c*
knuckle ['nʌkəl] *n* knokkel *c*

L

label ['leibəl] *n* etiket *nt*; *v* etiketteren
laboratory [lə'bɔrətəri] *n* laboratorium *nt*
labo(u)r ['leibə] *n* werk *nt*, arbeid *c*; weeën *pl*; *v* zwoegen; **labor permit** *Am* werkvergunning *c*
labo(u)rer ['leibərə] *n* arbeider *m*
labo(u)r-saving ['leibəˌseiviŋ] *adj* arbeidbesparend
labyrinth ['læbərinθ] *n* doolhof *nt*
lace [leis] *n* kant *nt*; veter *c*
lack [læk] *n* gemis *nt*, gebrek *nt*; *v* missen
lacquer ['lækə] *n* lak *c*
lad [læd] *n* jongen *m*, joch *nt*
ladder ['lædə] *n* ladder *c*

lady ['leidi] *n* dame *f*; **ladies' room** damestoilet *nt*
lagoon [lə'guːn] *n* lagune *c*
lake [leik] *n* meer *nt*
lamb [læm] *n* lam *nt*; lamsvlees *nt*
lame [leim] *adj* lam, mank, kreupel
lamentable ['læməntəbəl] *adj* erbarmelijk
lamp [læmp] *n* lamp *c*
lamppost ['læmppoust] *n* lantaarnpaal *c*
lampshade ['læmpʃeid] *n* lampekap *c*
land [lænd] *n* land *nt*; *v* landen; aan land *gaan
landlady ['lændˌleidi] *n* hospita *f*
landlord ['lændlɔːd] *n* huisbaas *m*;

hospes *m*

landmark ['lændmɑ:k] *n* baken *nt*; mijlpaal *c*

landscape ['lændskeip] *n* landschap *nt*

lane [lein] *n* steeg *c*, pad *nt*; rijstrook *c*

language ['læŋgwidʒ] *n* taal *c*; ~ **laboratory** talenpracticum *nt*

lantern ['læntən] *n* lantaarn *c*

lap ['læp] *n* schoot *c*; etappe *c*; *v* likken

lapel [lə'pel] *n* revers *c*

larder ['lɑ:də] *n* provisiekast *c*

large [lɑ:dʒ] *adj* groot; ruim

lark [lɑ:k] *n* leeuwerik *c*

laryngitis [,lærin'dʒaitis] *n* keelontsteking *c*

last [lɑ:st] *adj* laatst; vorig; *v* duren; **at ~** eindelijk; tenslotte, uiteindelijk

lasting ['lɑ:stiŋ] *adj* blijvend, duurzaam

latchkey ['lætʃki:] *n* huissleutel *c*

late [leit] *adj* laat; te laat

lately ['leitli] *adv* de laatste tijd, onlangs, laatst

later ['l] *adv* later; in a moment

lather ['lɑ:ðə] *n* schuim *nt*

Latin America ['lætin ə'merikə] Latijns-Amerika

Latin-American [,lætinə'merikən] *adj* Latijns-Amerikaans

latitude ['lætitju:d] *n* breedtegraad *c*

laugh [lɑ:f] *v* *lachen; *n* lach *c*

laughter ['lɑ:ftə] *n* gelach *nt*

launch [lɔ:ntʃ] *v* inzetten; lanceren

launching ['lɔ:ntʃiŋ] *n* tewaterlating *c*

launderette [,lɔ:ndə'ret] *n* wasserette *c*

laundry ['lɔ:ndri] *n* wasserij *c*; was *c*

lavatory ['lævətəri] *n* toilet *nt*

lavish ['læviʃ] *adj* kwistig

law [lɔ:] *n* wet *c*; recht *nt*; ~ **court** gerecht *nt*

lawful ['lɔ:fəl] *adj* wettig

lawn [lɔ:n] *n* grasveld *nt*, gazon *nt*

lawsuit ['lɔ:su:t] *n* proces *nt*, geding *nt*

lawyer ['lɔ:jə] *n* advocaat *m*, advocate *f*; jurist *m*, -e *f*

laxative ['læksətiv] *n* laxeermiddel *nt*

***lay** [lei] *v* plaatsen, zetten, leggen; ~ **bricks** metselen

layer [leiə] *n* laag *c*

layman ['leimən] *n* leek *m*

lazy ['leizi] *adj* lui

lead¹ [li:d] *n* voorsprong *c*; leiding *c*; riem *c*

lead² [led] *n* lood *nt*

***lead** [li:d] *v* leiden

leader ['li:də] *n* aanvoerder *m*, aanvoerster *f*, leider *m*, leidster *f*

leadership ['li:dəʃip] *n* leiderschap *nt*

leading ['li:diŋ] *adj* vooraanstaand, voornaamst

leaf [li:f] *n* (pl leaves) blad *nt*

league [li:g] *n* bond *c*

leak [li:k] *v* lekken; *n* lek *nt*

leaky ['li:ki] *adj* lek

lean [li:n] *adj* mager

***lean** [li:n] *v* leunen

leap [li:p] *n* sprong *c*

***leap** [li:p] *v* *springen

leap year ['li:pjiə] *n* schrikkeljaar *nt*

***learn** [lə:n] *v* leren

learner ['lə:nə] *n* beginneling *m*, -e *f*, beginner *c*

lease [li:s] *n* huurcontract *nt*; pacht *c*; *v* verpachten, verhuren; huren

leash [li:ʃ] *n* lijn *c*

least [li:st] *adj* geringst, minst; kleinst; **at ~** minstens; tenminste

leather ['leðə] *n* leer *nt*; lederen, leren

leave [li:v] *n* verlof *nt*

***leave** [li:v] *v* *vertrekken, *verlaten; *laten; ~ **behind** *achterlaten; ~ **out** *weglaten

Lebanese [,lebə'ni:z] *adj* Libanees; *n* Libanees *m*, Libanese *f*

Lebanon ['lebənən] Libanon

lecture ['lektʃə] *n* college *nt*, lezing *c*

left¹ [left] *adj* links

left² [left] *v* (p, pp leave)
left-hand ['lefthænd] *adj* links
left-handed [,left'hændid] *adj* linkshandig
leg [leg] *n* poot *c*, been *nt*
legacy ['legəsi] *n* erfenis *c*
legal ['li:gəl] *adj* wettig, wettelijk; juridisch
legalization [,li:gəlai'zeiʃən] *n* legalisatie *c*
legation [li'geiʃən] *n* legatie *c*
legible ['ledʒibəl] *adj* leesbaar
legitimate [li'dʒitimət] *adj* wettig
leisure ['leʒə] *n* vrije tijd; gemak *nt*
lemon ['lemən] *n* citroen *c*
lemonade [,lemə'neid] *n* limonade *c*
*lend [lend] *v* lenen, uitlenen
length [leŋθ] *n* lengte *c*
lengthen ['leŋθən] *v* verlengen
lengthways ['leŋθweiz] *adv* in de lengte
lens [lenz] *n* lens *c*; **telephoto ~** telelens *c*; **zoom ~** zoomlens *c*
leprechaun [lepre'kɔ:n] *n* kabouter *m*
leprosy ['leprəsi] *n* lepra *c*
less [les] *adv* minder
lessen ['lesən] *v* verminderen
lesson ['lesən] *n* les *c*
*let [let] *v* *laten; verhuren; **~ down** teleurstellen
letter ['letə] *n* brief *c*; letter *c*; **~ of credit** kredietbrief *c*; **~ of recommendation** aanbevelingsbrief *c*
letterbox ['letəbɔks] *n* brievenbus *c*
lettuce ['letis] *n* sla *c*
level ['levəl] *adj* egaal; plat, vlak, effen, gelijk; *n* peil *nt*, niveau *nt*; waterpas *c*; *v* egaliseren, nivelleren; **~ crossing** overweg *c*
lever ['li:və] *n* hefboom *c*, hendel *c*
liability [,laiə'biləti] *n* aansprakelijkheid *c*
liable ['laiəbəl] *adj* aansprakelijk; **~ to** onderhevig aan

liar ['laiə] *n* leugenaar *m*, -ster *f*
liberal ['libərəl] *adj* liberaal; mild, royaal, vrijgevig
liberation [,libə'reiʃən] *n* bevrijding *c*
Liberia [lai'biəriə] Liberia
Liberian [lai'biəriən] *adj* Liberiaans; *n* Liberiaan *m*
liberty ['libəti] *n* vrijheid *c*
library ['laibrəri] *n* bibliotheek *c*
licence ['laisəns] *n* licentie *c*; vergunning *c*; **driving ~** rijbewijs *nt*; **~ number** *Am* kenteken *nt*; **~ plate** *Am* nummerbord *nt*
license ['laisəns] *v* een vergunning verlenen; *nAm* vergunning *c*; **~ plate** *Am* nummerbord *nt*
lick [lik] *v* likken
lid [lid] *n* deksel *nt*
lie [lai] *v* *liegen; *n* leugen *c*
*lie [lai] *v* *liggen; **~ down** *gaan liggen
life [laif] *n* (pl lives) leven *nt*; **~ insurance** levensverzekering *c*; **~ jacket** zwemvest *nt*
lifebelt ['laifbelt] *n* reddingsgordel *c*
lifetime ['laiftaim] *n* leven *nt*
lift [lift] *v* optillen; *n* lift *c*
light [lait] *n* licht *nt*; *adj* licht; **~ bulb** peer *c*
*light [lait] *v* *aansteken
lighter ['laitə] *n* aansteker *c*
lighthouse ['laithaus] *n* vuurtoren *c*
lighting ['laitiŋ] *n* verlichting *c*
lightning ['laitniŋ] *n* bliksem *c*
like [laik] *v* *houden van; *mogen, lusten; *adj* gelijk; *conj* zoals; *prep* als
likely ['laikli] *adj* waarschijnlijk
like-minded [,laik'maindid] *adj* gelijkgezind
likewise ['laikwaiz] *adv* evenzo, eveneens
lily ['lili] *n* lelie *c*
limb [lim] *n* ledemaat *c*
lime [laim] *n* kalk *c*; linde *c*; limoen *c*
limetree ['laimtri:] *n* linde *c*

limit ['limit] n limiet c; v beperken

limp [limp] v hinken; adj slap

line [lain] n regel c; streep c; snoer nt; lijn c; rij c; **stand in ~** Am in de rij *staan

linen ['linin] n linnen nt; linnengoed c

liner ['lainə] n lijnboot c

lingerie ['lõʒəri:] n lingerie c

lining ['lainiŋ] n voering c

link [liŋk] v *verbinden; n verbinding c; schakel c

lion ['laiən] n leeuw c

lip [lip] n lip c

lipstick ['lipstik] n lippenstift c

liqueur [li'kjuə] n likeur c

liquid ['likwid] adj vloeibaar; n vloeistof c

liquor ['likə] n sterke drank; **~ store** nAm slijterij c

liquorice ['likəris] n drop c

list [list] n lijst c; v noteren

listen ['lisən] v aanhoren, luisteren

listener ['lisnə] n luisteraar m, -ster f

litre ['li:tə] nAm liter c

literary ['litrəri] adj letterkundig, literair

literature ['litrətʃə] n literatuur c

litre ['li:tə] n liter c

litter ['litə] n afval nt; rommel c; nest nt

little ['litəl] adj klein; weinig

live¹ [liv] v leven; wonen

live² [laiv] adj levend

livelihood ['laivlihud] n kost c

lively ['laivli] adj levendig

liver ['livə] n lever c

living ['liviŋ] n inkomen nt; adj levend; **~ creatures** pl levende wezens pl; **~ room** woonkamer c, huiskamer c

lizard ['lizəd] n hagedis c

load [loud] n lading c; last c; v *laden

loaf [louf] n (pl loaves) brood nt

loan [loun] n lening c

lobby ['lɔbi] n hal c; foyer c

lobster ['lɔbstə] n kreeft c

local ['loukəl] adj lokaal, plaatselijk; ~

call lokaal gesprek; **~ train** stoptrein c

locality [lou'kæləti] n plaats c

locate [lou'keit] v plaatsen

location [lou'keiʃən] n ligging c

lock [lɔk] v op slot *doen; n slot nt; sluis c; **~ up** *opsluiten

locker ['lɔkə] n kluisje nt

locomotive [,loukə'moutiv] n locomotief c

lodge [lɔdʒ] v herbergen; n jachthuis nt

lodger ['lɔdʒə] n kamerbewoner m

lodgings ['lɔdʒiŋz] pl logies nt

log [lɔg] n houtblok n; **~ in** v inloggen; **~ off** v uitloggen

logic ['lɔdʒik] n logica c

logical ['lɔdʒikəl] adj logisch

lonely ['lounli] adj eenzaam

long¹ [lɔŋ] adj lang; langdurig; **no longer** niet meer

long² [lɔŋ] v: **~ for** verlangen naar

long-distance call [lɔŋ'distəns,kɔ:l] n interlokaal gesprek

longing ['lɔŋiŋ] n verlangen nt

longitude ['lɔndʒitju:d] n lengtegraad c

look [luk] v *kijken; *lijken, er uit *zien; n kijkje nt, blik c; uiterlijk nt, voorkomen nt; **~ after** verzorgen, zorgen voor, passen op; **~ at** *aankijken, *kijken naar; **~ for** *zoeken; **~ out** *uitkijken, oppassen; **~ up** *opzoeken

looking-glass ['lukiŋglɑ:s] n spiegel c

loop [lu:p] n lus c

loose [lu:s] adj los

loosen ['lu:sən] v losmaken

lord [lɔ:d] n lord m, heer m

lorry ['lɔri] n vrachtwagen c

***lose** [lu:z] v kwijtraken, *verliezen

loser ['lu:sə] n verliezer c

loss [lɔs] n verlies nt

lost [lɔst] adj verdwaald; weg; **~ and found** gevonden voorwerpen; **~ property office** bureau voor

gevonden voorwerpen
lot [lɔt] *n* lot *nt*; hoop *c*, boel *c*
lotion ['louʃən] *n* lotion *c*; **aftershave**
~ after shave
lottery ['lɔtəri] *n* loterij *c*
loud [laud] *adj* hard, luid
loudspeaker [,laud'spi:kə] *n*
luidspreker *c*
lounge [laundʒ] *n* salon *c*
louse [laus] *n* (pl lice) luis *c*
love [lʌv] *v* *houden van, *liefhebben;
n liefde *c*; **in** ~ verliefd
lovely ['lʌvli] *adj* heerlijk, prachtig,
mooi
lover ['lʌvə] *n* minnaar *m*, minnares *f*
love story ['lʌv,stɔ:ri] *n*
liefdesgeschiedenis *c*
low [lou] *adj* laag; diep; neerslachtig; ~
tide eb *c*
lower ['louə] *v* *neerlaten; verlagen;
*strijken; *adj* onderst, lager
lowlands ['louləndz] *pl* laagland *nt*
loyal ['lɔiəl] *adj* loyaal
lubricate ['lu:brikeit] *v* oliën, smeren
lubrication [,lu:bri'keiʃən] *n* smering
c; ~ **oil** smeerolie *c*; ~ **system**

smeersysteem *nt*
luck [lʌk] *n* geluk *nt*; toeval *nt*; **bad** ~
pech *c*; **good** ~! succes!
lucky charm amulet *c*
ludicrous ['lu:dikrəs] *adj* belachelijk,
bespottelijk
luggage ['lʌgidʒ] *n* bagage *c*; **hand** ~
handbagage *c*; **left** ~ **office**
bagagedepot *nt*; ~ **rack** bagagerek *nt*,
bagagenet *nt*; ~ **van** bagagewagen *c*
lukewarm ['lu:kwɔ:m] *adj* lauw
lumbago [lʌm'beigou] *n* spit *nt*
luminous ['lu:minəs] *adj* lichtgevend
lump [lʌmp] *n* brok *nt*, klont *c*, stuk *nt*;
bult *c*; ~ **of sugar** suikerklontje *nt*; ~
sum ronde som
lumpy ['lʌmpi] *adj* klonterig
lunacy ['lu:nəsi] *n* krankzinnigheid *c*
lunatic ['lu:nətik] *adj* krankzinnig; *n*
krankzinnige *c*
lunch [lʌntʃ] *n* lunch *c*, middageten *nt*
lung [lʌŋ] *n* long *c*
lust [lʌst] *n* wellust *c*
luxurious [lʌg'ʒuəriəs] *adj* luxueus
luxury ['lʌkʃəri] *n* luxe *c*

M

machine [mə'ʃi:n] *n* apparaat *nt*,
machine *c*
machinery [mə'ʃi:nəri] *n* machinerie
c; mechanisme *nt*
mackerel ['mækrəl] *n* (pl ~) makreel *c*
mackintosh ['mækintɔʃ] *n* regenjas *c*
mad [mæd] *adj* krankzinnig,
waanzinnig, gek; kwaad
madam ['mædəm] *n* mevrouw
madness ['mædnəs] *n* waanzin *c*
magazine [,mægə'zi:n] *n* blad *nt*
magic ['mædʒik] *n* toverkunst *c*, magie

c; *adj* tover-
magician [mə'dʒiʃən] *n* goochelaar *m*,
-ster *f*
magistrate ['mædʒistreit] *n*
magistraat *c*
magnet ['mæg'ni:tou] *n* (pl ~s)
magneet *c*
magnetic [mæg'netik] *adj* magnetisch
magnificent [mæg'nifisənt] *adj*
prachtig; groots; luisterrijk
magnify ['mægnifai] *v* vergroten;
overdrijven

magpie ['mægpai] *n* ekster *c*

maid [meid] *n* meid *f*

maiden name ['meidən neim] meisjesnaam *c*

mail [meil] *n* post *c*; *v* posten; **~ order** *Am* postwissel *c*

mailbox ['meilbɔks] *nAm* brievenbus *c*

main [mein] *adj* hoofd-, voornaamst; grootst; **~ deck** bovendek *nt*; **~ line** hoofdlijn *c*; **~ road** hoofdweg *c*; **~ street** hoofdstraat *c*

mainland ['meinlənd] *n* vasteland *nt*

mainly ['meinli] *adv* hoofdzakelijk

mains [meinz] *pl* hoofdleiding *c*

maintain [mein'tein] *v* handhaven

maintenance ['meintənəns] *n* onderhoud *nt*

maize [meiz] *n* maïs *c*

major ['meidʒə] *adj* groot; groter; grootst; *n* majoor *m*

majority [mə'dʒɔrəti] *n* meerderheid *c*

*make [meik] *v* maken; verdienen; halen; **~ do with** zich *behelpen met; **~ good** vergoeden; **~ up** opstellen

make-up ['meikʌp] *n* make-up *c*

malaria [mə'lɛəriə] *n* malaria *c*

Malay [mə'lei] *n* Maleis *nt*

Malaysia [mə'leiziə] Maleisië

Malaysian [mə'leiziən] *adj* Maleisisch

male [meil] *adj* mannelijk

malicious [mə'liʃəs] *adj* boosaardig

malignant [mə'lignənt] *adj* kwaadaardig

mall [mɔːl] *nAm* (overdekt) winkelcentrum *nt*

mallet ['mælit] *n* houten hamer

malnutrition [,mælnju'triʃən] *n* ondervoeding *c*

mammal ['mæməl] *n* zoogdier *nt*

mammoth ['mæməθ] *n* mammoet *c*

man [mæn] *n* (pl men) man *m*; mens *m*; **men's room** herentoilet *nt*

manage ['mænidʒ] *v* beheren; slagen

manageable ['mænidʒəbəl] *adj* hanteerbaar

management ['mænidʒmənt] *n* directie *c*; beheer *nt*

manager ['mænidʒə] *n* chef *m*, -in *f*, directeur *m*, directrice *f*

mandarin ['mændərin] *n* mandarijn *c*

mandate ['mændeit] *n* mandaat *nt*

manger ['meindʒə] *n* kribbe *c*

manicure ['mænikjuə] *n* manicure *c*; *v* manicuren

mankind [mæn'kaind] *n* mensheid *c*

mannequin ['mænəkin] *n* mannequin *c*

manner ['mænə] *n* wijze *c*, manier *c*; **manners** *pl* manieren

man-of-war [,mænəv'wɔː] *n* oorlogsschip *nt*

manor house ['mænəhaus] *n* herenhuis *nt*

mansion ['mænʃən] *n* herenhuis *nt*

manual ['mænjuəl] *adj* hand-; handboek *nt*

manufacture [,mænju'fæktʃə] *v* vervaardigen, fabriceren

manufacturer [,mænju'fæktʃərə] *n* fabrikant *m*, -e *f*

manure [mə'njuə] *n* mest *c*

manuscript ['mænjuskript] *n* manuscript *nt*

many ['meni] *adj* veel

map [mæp] *n* kaart *c*; landkaart *c*; plattegrond *c*

maple ['meipəl] *n* esdoorn *c*

marble ['mɑːbəl] *n* marmer *nt*; knikker *c*

March [mɑːtʃ] maart

march [mɑːtʃ] *v* marcheren; *n* mars *c*

mare [mɛə] *n* merrie *f*

margarine [,mɑːdʒə'riːn] *n* margarine *c*

margin ['mɑːdʒin] *n* kantlijn *c*, marge *c*

maritime ['mæritaim] *adj* maritiem

mark [mɑːk] *v* aankruisen; merken;

kenmerken; *n* merkteken *nt*; cijfer *nt*;
schietschijf *c*

market ['mɑ:kit] *n* markt *c*

marketplace ['mɑ:kitpleis] *n*
marktplein *nt*

marmalade ['mɑ:məleid] *n*
marmelade *c*

marriage ['mæridʒ] *n* huwelijk *nt*

marrow ['mærou] *n* merg *nt*

marry ['mæri] *v* huwen, trouwen;
married couple echtpaar *nt*

marsh [mɑ:ʃ] *n* moeras *nt*

martyr ['mɑ:tə] *n* martelaar *m*,
martelares *f*

marvel ['mɑ:vəl] *n* wonder *nt*; *v* zich
verbazen

marvel(l)ous ['mɑ:vələs] *adj* prachtig

mascara [mæˈskɑ:rə] *n* mascara *c*

masculine ['mæskjulin] *adj* mannelijk

mash [mæʃ] *v* fijnstampen; **mashed
potatoes** *pl* aardappelpuree

mask [mɑ:sk] *n* masker *nt*

Mass [mæs] *n* mis *c*

mass [mæs] *n* massa *c*; **~ production**
massaproductie *c*

massage ['mæsɑ:ʒ] *n* massage *c*; *v*
masseren

masseur [mæˈsə:] *n* masseur *m*,
masseuse *f*

massive ['mæsiv] *adj* massief

mast [mɑ:st] *n* mast *c*

master ['mɑ:stə] *n* meester *m*; baas *m*;
leraar *m*, onderwijzer *m*; *v* beheersen

masterpiece ['mɑ:stəpi:s] *n*
meesterwerk *nt*

mat [mæt] *n* mat *c*; *adj* mat, dof

match [mætʃ] *n* lucifer *c*; wedstrijd *c*; *v*
passen bij

matchbox ['mætʃbɔks] *n*
lucifersdoosje *nt*

material [məˈtiəriəl] *n* materiaal *nt*;
stof *c*; *adj* stoffelijk, materieel

mathematical [ˌmæθəˈmætikəl] *adj*
wiskundig

mathematics [ˌmæθəˈmætiks] *n*
wiskunde *c*

matrimony ['mætriməni] *n* echt *c*

matter ['mætə] *n* stof *c*, materie *c*;
aangelegenheid *c*, kwestie *c*, zaak *c*; *v*
van belang *zijn; **as a ~ of fact**
feitelijk, eigenlijk

matter-of-fact [ˌmætərəvˈfækt] *adj*
nuchter

mattress ['mætrəs] *n* matras *c*

mature [məˈtjuə] *adj* rijp

maturity [məˈtjuərəti] *n* rijpheid *c*

mausoleum [ˌmɔ:səˈli:əm] *n*
mausoleum *nt*

mauve [mouv] *adj* lichtpaars

May [mei] mei

***may** [mei] *v* *kunnen; *mogen

maybe ['meibi:] *adv* misschien

mayor [mɛə] *n* burgemeester *m*

maze [meiz] *n* doolhof *nt*

me [mi:] *pron* me

meadow ['medou] *n* wei *c*

meal [mi:l] *n* maaltijd *c*, maal *nt*

mean [mi:n] *adj* gemeen; *n* gemiddelde
nt

***mean** [mi:n] *v* betekenen; bedoelen;
menen

meaning ['mi:niŋ] *n* betekenis *c*

meaningless ['mi:niŋləs] *adj*
nietszeggend

means [mi:nz] *n* middel *nt*; **by no ~**
zeker niet, geenszins

meantime: in the ~ [in ðə ˈmi:ntaim]
inmiddels, ondertussen

meanwhile ['mi:nwail] *adv* intussen,
ondertussen

measles ['mi:zəlz] *n* mazelen *pl*

measure ['meʒə] *v* *meten; *n* maat *c*;
maatregel *c*

meat [mi:t] *n* vlees *nt*

mechanic [miˈkænik] *n* monteur *m*

mechanical [miˈkænikəl] *adj*
mechanisch

mechanism ['mekənizəm] *n*

mechanisme *nt*

medal ['medəl] *n* medaille *c*

media ['mi:diə] *pl* media *pl*

mediaeval [,medi'i:vəl] *adj* middeleeuws

mediate ['mi:dieit] *v* bemiddelen

mediator ['mi:dieitə] *n* bemiddelaar *c*

medical ['medikəl] *adj* geneeskundig, medisch

medicine ['medsin] *n* geneesmiddel *nt*; geneeskunde *c*

meditate ['mediteit] *v* mediteren

Mediterranean [,meditə'reiniən] Middellandse Zee

medium ['mi:diəm] *adj* middelmatig, gemiddeld, midden-

*meet [mi:t] *v* ontmoeten; *tegenkomen

meeting ['mi:tiŋ] *n* vergadering *c*, bijeenkomst *c*; ontmoeting *c*

meeting place ['mi:tiŋpleis] *n* trefpunt *nt*

melancholy ['melənkəli] *n* weemoed *c*

mellow ['melou] *adj* zacht

melodrama ['melə,drɑ:mə] *n* melodrama *nt*

melody ['melədi] *n* melodie *c*

melon ['melən] *n* meloen *c*

melt [melt] *v* *smelten

member ['membə] *n* lid *nt*; **Member of Parliament** kamerlid *nt*

membership ['membəʃip] *n* lidmaatschap *nt*

memo ['memou] *n* (pl ∼s) memorandum *nt*

memorable ['memərəbəl] *adj* gedenkwaardig

memorial [mə'mɔ:riəl] *n* gedenkteken *nt*

memorize ['meməraiz] *v* uit het hoofd leren

memory ['meməri] *n* geheugen *nt*; herinnering *c*; nagedachtenis *c*

mend [mend] *v* herstellen, repareren

menstruation [,menstru'eiʃən] *n* menstruatie *c*

mental ['mentəl] *adj* geestelijk

mention ['menʃən] *v* noemen, vermelden; *n* melding *c*, vermelding *c*

menu ['menju:] *n* spijskaart *c*, menukaart *c*

merchandise ['mə:tʃəndaiz] *n* handelswaar *c*, koopwaar *c*

merchant ['mə:tʃənt] *n* handelaar *m*, -ster *f*, koopman *m*

merciful ['mə:sifəl] *adj* barmhartig

mercury ['mə:kjuri] *n* kwik *nt*

mercy ['mə:si] *n* genade *c*, clementie *c*

mere [miə] *adj* louter

merely ['miəli] *adv* slechts

merge [mə:dʒ] *v* fuseren; samenvoegen

merger ['mə:dʒə] *n* fusie *c*

merit ['merit] *v* verdienen; *n* verdienste *c*

merry ['meri] *adj* vrolijk

merry-go-round ['merigou,raund] *n* draaimolen *c*

mesh [meʃ] *n* maas *c*

mess [mes] *n* rommel *c*, warboel *c*; ∼ **up** *bederven

message ['mesidʒ] *n* boodschap *c*, bericht *nt*

messenger ['mesindʒə] *n* bode *m*

metal ['metəl] *n* metaal *nt*; metalen

meter ['mi:tə] *n* meter *c*

method ['meθəd] *n* aanpak *c*, methode *c*; orde *c*

methodical [mə'θɔdikəl] *adj* methodisch

metre ['mi:tə] *n* meter *c*

metric ['metrik] *adj* metrisch

Mexican ['meksikən] *adj* Mexicaans; *n* Mexicaan *m*, -se *f*

Mexico ['meksikou] Mexico

mice (pl mouse)

microphone ['maikrəfoun] *n* microfoon *c*

midday ['middei] n middag c
middle ['midəl] n midden nt; adj
 middelst; **Middle Ages**
 middeleeuwen pl; **middle-class** adj
 burgerlijk
midnight ['midnait] n middernacht c
midst [midst] n midden nt
midsummer ['mid,sʌmə] n midzomer
 c
midwife ['midwaif] n (pl -wives)
 vroedvrouw f
might [mait] n macht c
***might** [mait] v *kunnen
mighty ['maiti] adj machtig
migraine ['migrein] n migraine c
migrate ['migreit] v rondtrekken
mild [maild] adj zacht
mildew ['mildju] n schimmel c
mile [mail] n mijl c
mileage ['mailidʒ] n afstand in mijlen
milepost ['mailpoust] n wegwijzer c
milestone ['mailstoun] n mijlpaal c
milieu ['miːljəː] n milieu nt
military ['militəri] adj militair; ~ **force**
 krijgsmacht c
milk [milk] n melk c
milkman ['milkmən] n (pl -men)
 melkboer m
milkshake ['milkʃeik] n milk shake
mill [mil] n molen c; fabriek c
miller ['milə] n molenaar m
million ['miljən] n miljoen nt
millionaire [,miljə'nɛə] n miljonair m,
 -e f
mince [mins] v fijnhakken
mind [maind] n geest c; v bezwaar
 *hebben tegen; letten op; *geven om
mine [main] n mijn c
miner ['mainə] n mijnwerker m
mineral ['minərəl] n delfstof c,
 mineraal nt; ~ **water** mineraalwater nt
mingle ['mingl] v zich begeven onder;
 vermengen
miniature ['minjətʃə] n miniatuur c

minimum ['miniməm] n minimum nt
mining ['mainiŋ] n mijnbouw c
minister ['ministə] n minister c;
 predikant m; **Prime Minister** premier
 c
ministry ['ministri] n ministerie nt
mink [miŋk] n nerts nt
minor ['mainə] adj klein, gering,
 kleiner; ondergeschikt; n
 minderjarige c
minority [mai'nɔrəti] n minderheid c
mint [mint] n munt c
minus ['mainəs] prep min
minute[1] ['minit] n minuut c; **minutes**
 notulen pl
minute[2] [mai'njuːt] adj minuscuul
miracle ['mirəkəl] n wonder nt
miraculous [mi'rækjuləs] adj
 wonderbaarlijk
mirror ['mirə] n spiegel c
misbehave [,misbi'heiv] v zich
 *misdragen
miscarriage [mis'kæridʒ] n miskraam
 c
miscellaneous [,misə'leiniəs] adj
 gemengd
mischief ['mistʃif] n kattekwaad nt;
 onheil nt, schade c, kwaad nt
mischievous ['mistʃivəs] adj
 ondeugend
miserable ['mizərəbəl] adj beroerd,
 ellendig
misery ['mizəri] n narigheid c, ellende
 c; nood c
misfortune [mis'fɔːtʃen] n tegenslag
 c, ongeluk nt
mishap ['mishæp] n ongelukje nt
***mislay** [mis'lei] v kwijtraken
misplaced [mis'pleist] adj misplaatst
mispronounce [,misprə'nauns] v
 verkeerd *uitspreken
miss[1] [mis] mejuffrouw, juffrouw f
miss[2] [mis] v missen
missing ['misiŋ] adj ontbrekend; ~

person vermiste c
mist [mist] n nevel c, mist c
mistake [mi'steik] n abuis nt, vergissing c, fout c
***mistake** [mi'steik] v verwarren
mistaken [mi'steikən] adj fout; ***be ~** zich vergissen
mister ['mistə] meneer, mijnheer
mistress ['mistrəs] n lerares f, onderwijzeres f; meesteres f; maîtresse f
mistrust [mis'trʌst] v wantrouwen
misty ['misti] adj mistig
***misunderstand** [,misʌndə'stænd] v *misverstaan
misunderstanding [,misʌndə'stændiŋ] n misverstand nt
misuse [mis'ju:s] n misbruik nt
mittens ['mitənz] pl wanten pl
mix [miks] v mengen; **~ with** *omgaan met
mixed [mikst] adj gemêleerd, gemengd
mixer ['miksə] n mixer c
mixture ['mikstʃə] n mengsel nt
moan [moun] v kreunen
moat [mout] n gracht c
mobile ['moubail] adj beweeglijk, mobiel; **~ phone** mobiele telefoon c, GSM c
mock [mɔk] v bespotten
mockery ['mɔkəri] n spot c
model ['mɔdəl] n model nt; mannequin c; v modelleren, boetseren
modem ['moudem] n modem c
moderate ['mɔdərət] adj gematigd, matig; middelmatig
modern ['mɔdən] adj modern
modest ['mɔdist] adj discreet, bescheiden
modesty ['mɔdisti] n bescheidenheid c
modify ['mɔdifai] v wijzigen
mohair ['mouhɛə] n mohair nt

moist [mɔist] adj nat, vochtig
moisten ['mɔisən] v bevochtigen
moisture ['mɔistʃə] n vochtigheid c; **moisturizing cream** vochtinbrengende crème
molar ['moulə] n kies c
moment ['moumənt] n moment nt, ogenblik nt; **in a ~** straks
momentary ['moumən təri] adj kortstondig
monarch ['mɔnək] n vorst m, -in f
monarchy ['mɔnəki] n monarchie c
monastery ['mɔnəstri] n klooster nt
Monday ['mʌndi] maandag c
monetary ['mʌnitəri] adj monetair; **~ unit** munteenheid c
money ['mʌni] n geld nt; **~ exchange** wisselkantoor nt; **~ order** overschrijving c
monk [mʌŋk] n monnik m
monkey ['mʌŋki] n aap c
monologue ['mɔnələg] n monoloog c
monopoly [mə'nɔpəli] n monopolie nt
monotonous [mə'nɔtənəs] adj eentonig
month [mʌnθ] n maand c
monthly ['mʌnθli] adj maandelijks; **~ magazine** maandblad nt
monument ['mɔnjumənt] n gedenkteken nt, monument nt
mood [mu:d] n humeur nt, stemming c
moon [mu:n] n maan c
moonlight ['mu:nlait] n maanlicht nt
moor [muə] n heide c, veen nt
moose [mu:s] n (pl ~, ~s) eland c
moped ['mouped] n bromfiets c
moral ['mɔrəl] n moraal c; adj zedelijk, moreel; **morals** zeden pl
morality [mə'ræləti] n moraliteit c
more [mɔ:] adj meer; **once ~** nogmaals
moreover [mɔ:'rouvə] adv voorts, bovendien
morning ['mɔ:niŋ] n ochtend c, morgen c; **~ paper** ochtendblad nt;

this ~ vanmorgen
Moroccan [məˈrɔkən] *adj*
Marokkaans; *n* Marokkaan *m*, -se *f*
Morocco [məˈrɔkou] Marokko
morphia [ˈmɔːfiə] *n* morfine *c*
morphine [ˈmɔːfiːn] *n* morfine *c*
morsel [ˈmɔːsəl] *n* brok *nt*
mortal [ˈmɔːtəl] *adj* dodelijk, sterfelijk
mortgage [ˈmɔːgidʒ] *n* hypotheek *c*
mosaic [məˈzeiik] *n* mozaïek *nt*
mosque [mɔsk] *n* moskee *c*
mosquito [məˈskiːtou] *n* (pl ~es) mug
c; muskiet *c*; ~ **net** muskietennet *nt*
moss [mɔs] *n* mos *nt*
most [moust] *adj* meest; **at** ~
hoogstens, hooguit; ~ **of all** vooral
mostly [ˈmoustli] *adv* meestal
motel [mouˈtel] *n* motel *nt*
moth [mɔθ] *n* mot *c*
mother [ˈmʌðə] *n* moeder *f*; ~ **of pearl**
parelmoer *nt*; ~ **tongue** moedertaal *c*
mother-in-law [ˈmʌðərinlɔ:] *n* (pl
mothers-) schoonmoeder *f*
motion [ˈmouʃən] *n* beweging *c*; motie
c
motivate [ˈmoutiveit] *v* aanzetten tot
motive [ˈmoutiv] *n* motief *nt*
motor [ˈmoutə] *n* motor *c*; *v*
*autorijden; ~ **body** *Am* carrosserie *c*;
starter ~ startmotor *c*
motorbike [ˈmoutəbaik] motor *c*; *nAm*
brommer *c*
motorboat [ˈmoutəbout] *n* motorboot
c
motorcar [ˈmoutəkɑ:] *n* auto *c*
motorcycle [ˈmoutə,saikəl] *n*
motorfiets *c*
motoring [ˈmoutəriŋ] *n*
automobilisme *nt*
motorist [ˈmoutərist] *n* automobilist *c*
motorway [ˈmoutəwei] *n* snelweg *c*
motto [ˈmɔtou] *n* (pl ~es, ~s) devies *nt*
mouldy [ˈmouldi] *adj* beschimmeld
mound [maund] *n* heuvel *c*

mount [maunt] *v* *bestijgen; *n* berg *c*
mountain [ˈmauntin] *n* berg *c*; ~ **pass**
bergpas *c*; ~ **range** bergketen *c*
mountaineering [,maunti'niəriŋ] *n*
bergsport *c*
mountainous [ˈmauntinəs] *adj*
bergachtig
mourning [ˈmɔːniŋ] *n* rouw *c*
mouse [maus] *n* (pl mice) muis *c*
moustache [məˈstɑːʃ] *n* snor *c*
mouth [mauθ] *n* mond *c*; muil *c*, bek *c*;
monding *c*
mouthwash [ˈmauθwɔʃ] *n*
mondspoeling *c*
movable [ˈmuːvəbəl] *adj* roerend
move [muːv] *v* *bewegen; verplaatsen;
verhuizen; ontroeren; *n* zet *c*, stap *c*;
verhuizing *c*
movement [ˈmuːvmənt] *n* beweging *c*
movie [ˈmuːvi] *n* film *c*; ~ **theater** *Am*
bioscoop *c*; **movies** *Am* bioscoop *c*
much [mʌtʃ] *adj* veel; **as** ~ evenveel;
evenzeer
muck [mʌk] *n* drek *c*
mud [mʌd] *n* modder *c*
muddle [ˈmʌdəl] *n* warboel *c*; *v*
verknoeien
muddy [ˈmʌdi] *adj* modderig
muffler [ˈmʌflə] *nAm* knalpot *c*;
geluiddemper *c*
mug [mʌg] *n* beker *c*, kroes *c*
mule [mjuːl] *n* muildier *nt*, muilezel *c*
multiplication [,mʌltipli'keiʃən] *n*
vermenigvuldiging *c*
multiply [ˈmʌltiplai] *v*
vermenigvuldigen
mumps [mʌmps] *n* bof *c*
municipal [mjuːˈnisipəl] *adj*
gemeentelijk
municipality [mjuː,nisi'pæləti] *n*
gemeentebestuur *nt*
murder [ˈmɔːdə] *n* moord *c*; *v*
vermoorden
murderer [ˈmɔːdərə] *n* moordenaar *m*,

mordenares *f*
muscle ['mʌsəl] *n* spier *c*
muscular ['mʌskjulə] *adj* gespierd
museum [mjuː'ziːəm] *n* museum *nt*
mushroom ['mʌʃruːm] *n* champignon *c*; paddestoel *c*
music ['mjuːzik] *n* muziek *c*; ~ **hall** variététheater *nt*; ~ **academy** conservatorium *nt*
musical ['mjuːzikəl] *adj* muzikaal; *n* musical *c*
musician [mjuː'ziʃən] *n* musicus *m*, musicienne *f*
muslin ['mʌzlin] *n* mousseline *c*
mussel ['mʌsəl] *n* mossel *c*

*must [mʌst] *v* *moeten
mustard ['mʌstəd] *n* mosterd *c*
mute [mjuːt] *adj* stom
mutiny ['mjuːtini] *n* muiterij *c*
mutton ['mʌtən] *n* schapevlees *nt*
mutual ['mjuːtʃuəl] *adj* onderling, wederzijds
my [mai] *adj* mijn
myself [mai'self] *pron* me; zelf
mysterious [mi'stiəriəs] *adj* mysterieus, geheimzinnig
mystery ['mistəri] *n* raadsel *nt*, mysterie *nt*
myth [miθ] *n* mythe *c*

N

nail [neil] *n* nagel *c*; spijker *c*; ~ **file** nagelvijl *c*; ~ **polish** nagellak *c*; ~ **scissors** *pl* nagelschaar *c*
nailbrush ['neilbrʌʃ] *n* nagelborstel *c*
naïve [naː'iːv] *adj* naïef
naked ['neikid] *adj* bloot, naakt; kaal
name [neim] *n* naam *c*; *v* noemen; **in the ~ of** namens
namely ['neimli] *adv* namelijk
nap [næp] *n* dutje *nt*
napkin ['næpkin] *n* servet *nt*
nappy ['næpi] *n* luier *c*
narcosis [naː'kousis] *n* (pl -ses) narcose *c*
narcotic [naː'kɔtik] *n* narcoticum *nt*
narrow ['nærou] *adj* eng, smal, nauw
narrow-minded [,nærou'maindid] *adj* bekrompen
nasty ['naːsti] *adj* naar, akelig
nation ['neiʃən] *n* natie *c*; volk *nt*
national ['næʃənəl] *adj* nationaal; volks-; staats-; ~ **anthem** volkslied *nt*; ~ **dress** nationale klederdracht; ~ **park** natuurreservaat *nt*
nationality [,næʃə'næləti] *n* nationaliteit *c*
nationalize ['næʃənəlaiz] *v* nationaliseren
native ['neitiv] *n* inboorling *m*, -e *f*; *adj* inheems; ~ **country** vaderland *nt*, geboorteland *nt*; ~ **language** moedertaal *c*
natural ['nætʃərəl] *adj* natuurlijk; aangeboren
naturally ['nætʃərəli] *adv* natuurlijk, uiteraard
nature ['neitʃə] *n* natuur *c*; aard *c*
naughty ['nɔːti] *adj* ondeugend, stout
nausea ['nɔːsiə] *n* misselijkheid *c*
naval ['neivəl] *adj* marine-
navel ['neivəl] *n* navel *c*
navigable ['nævigəbəl] *adj* bevaarbaar
navigate ['nævigeit] *v* *varen; sturen
navigation [,nævi'geiʃən] *n* navigatie *c*; scheepvaart *c*

navy ['neivi] *n* marine *c*

near [niə] *prep* bij; *adj* nabij, dichtbij

nearby ['niəbai] *adj* nabijzijnd

nearly ['niəli] *adv* haast, bijna

neat [ni:t] *adj* keurig, net; puur

necessary ['nesəsəri] *adj* nodig, noodzakelijk

necessity [nə'sesəti] *n* noodzaak *c*

neck [nek] *n* hals *c*; **nape of the ~** nek *c*

necklace ['nekləs] *n* halsketting *c*

necktie ['nektai] *n* das *c*

need [ni:d] *v* hoeven, behoeven, nodig *hebben; *n* nood *c*, behoefte *c*; **~ to** *moeten

needle ['ni:dəl] *n* naald *c*

needlework ['ni:dəlwə:k] *n* handwerk *nt*

negative ['negətiv] *adj* ontkennend, negatief; *n* negatief *nt*

neglect [ni'glekt] *v* verwaarlozen; *n* verwaarlozing *c*

neglectful [ni'glektfəl] *adj* nalatig

negligee ['negliʒei] *n* negligé *nt*

negotiate [ni'gouʃieit] *v* onderhandelen

negotiation [ni,gouʃi'eiʃən] *n* onderhandeling *c*

neighbo(u)r ['neibə] *n* buur *m*, buurman *m*, buurvrouw *f*

neighbo(u)rhood ['neibəhud] *n* buurt *c*

neighbo(u)ring ['neibəriŋ] *adj* aangrenzend, naburig

neither ['naiðə] *pron* geen van beide; **neither ... nor** noch ... noch

neon ['ni:ɔn] *n* neon *nt*

nephew ['nefju:] *n* neef *m*

nerve [nə:v] *n* zenuw *c*; durf *c*

nervous ['nə:vəs] *adj* nerveus, zenuwachtig

nest [nest] *n* nest *nt*

net [net] *n* net *nt*; *adj* netto

Netherlands: the ~ ['neðələndz] Nederland

network ['netwə:k] *n* netwerk *nt*

neuralgia [njuə'rældʒə] *n* zenuwpijn *c*

neurosis [njuə'rousis] *n* neurose *c*

neuter ['nju:tə] *adj* onzijdig

neutral ['nju:trəl] *adj* neutraal

never ['nevə] *adv* nimmer, nooit

nevertheless [,nevəðə'les] *adv* niettemin

new [nju:] *adj* nieuw; **New Year** nieuwjaar

news [nju:z] *n* nieuwsberichten *pl*, nieuws *nt*; journaal *nt*

newsagent ['nju:,zeidʒənt] *n* krantenverkoper *m*

newspaper ['nju:z,peipə] *n* krant *c*

newsreel ['nju:zri:l] *n* filmjournaal *nt*

newsstand ['nju:zstænd] *n* krantenkiosk *c*

New Zealand [nju: 'zi:lənd] Nieuw-Zeeland

next [nekst] *adj* volgend; **~ to** naast

nice [nais] *adj* aardig, mooi, prettig; lekker; sympathiek

nickel ['nikəl] *n* nikkel *nt*

nickname ['nikneim] *n* bijnaam *c*

nicotine ['nikəti:n] *n* nicotine *c*

niece [ni:s] *n* nicht *f*

Nigeria [nai'dʒiəriə] Nigeria

Nigerian [nai'dʒiəriən] *adj* Nigeriaans; *n* Nigeriaan *m*, -se *f*

night [nait] *n* nacht *c*; avond *c*; **by ~** 's nachts; **~ flight** nachtvlucht *c*; **~ rate** nachttarief *nt*; **~ train** nachttrein *c*

nightclub ['naitklʌb] *n* nachtclub *c*

night cream ['naitkri:m] *n* nachtcrème *c*

nightdress ['naitdres] *n* nachtjapon *c*

nightingale ['naitiŋgeil] *n* nachtegaal *c*

nightly ['naitli] *adj* nachtelijk

nil [nil] niets

nine [nain] *num* negen

nineteen [,nain'ti:n] *num* negentien

nineteenth [,nain'ti:nθ] *num* negentiende

ninety ['nainti] *num* negentig

ninth [nainθ] *num* negende

nitrogen ['naitrədʒən] *n* stikstof *c*

no [nou] neen, nee; *adj* geen; **~ one** niemand

nobility [nou'biləti] *n* adel *c*

noble ['noubəl] *adj* adellijk; edel

nobody ['noubɔdi] *pron* niemand

nod [nɔd] *n* knik *c*; *v* knikken

noise [nɔiz] *n* geluid *nt*; herrie *c*, rumoer *c*, lawaai *nt*

noisy ['nɔizi] *adj* lawaaierig; gehorig

nominal ['nɔminəl] *adj* nominaal

nominate ['nɔmineit] *v* benoemen

nomination [,nɔmi'neiʃən] *n* nominatie *c*; benoeming *c*

none [nʌn] *pron* geen

nonsense ['nɔnsəns] *n* onzin *c*, nonsens *c*

non-smoker [,nɔn'smoukə] *n* niet-roker *m*, niet-rookster *f*

noon [nu:n] *n* middag *c*

nor ['nɔ:] ook niet; **neither ... nor** noch ... noch

normal ['nɔ:məl] *adj* gewoon, normaal

north [nɔ:θ] *n* noorden *nt*; noord *c*; *adj* noordelijk; **North Pole** noordpool *c*

north-east [,nɔ:θ'i:st] *n* noordoosten *nt*

northerly ['nɔ:ðəli] *adj* noordelijk

northern ['nɔ:ðən] *adj* noordelijk

north-west [,nɔ:θ'west] *n* noordwesten *nt*

Norway ['nɔ:wei] Noorwegen

Norwegian [nɔ:'wi:dʒən] *adj* Noors; *n* Noor *m*, -se *f*

nose [nouz] *n* neus *c*

nosebleed ['nouzbli:d] *n* neusbloeding *c*

nostril ['nɔstril] *n* neusgat *nt*

nosy ['nouzi] *adj colloquial* nieuwsgierig

not [nɔt] *adv* niet

notary ['noutəri] *n* notaris *m*

note [nout] *n* aantekening *c*, notitie *c*; noot *c*; toon *c*; *v* noteren; opmerken, constateren

notebook ['noutbuk] *n* notitieboek *nt*; notebook *c*

noted ['noutid] *adj* befaamd

notepaper ['nout,peipə] *n* schrijfpapier *nt*, briefpapier *nt*

nothing ['nʌθiŋ] *n* niks, niets

notice ['noutis] *v* bemerken, merken, opmerken; *zien; *n* aankondiging *c*, bericht *nt*; notitie *c*, aandacht *c*

noticeable ['noutisəbəl] *adj* merkbaar; opmerkelijk

notify ['noutifai] *v* mededelen; waarschuwen

notion ['nouʃən] *n* begrip *nt*, notie *c*

notorious [nou'tɔ:riəs] *adj* berucht

nougat ['nu:ga:] *n* noga *c*

nought [nɔ:t] *n* nul *c*

noun [naun] *n* zelfstandig naamwoord *c*

nourishing ['nʌriʃiŋ] *adj* voedzaam

novel ['nɔvəl] *n* roman *c*

novelist ['nɔvəlist] *n* romanschrijver *m*, -schrijfster *f*

November [nou'vembə] november

now [nau] *adv* nu, nou; thans; **~ and then** nu en dan

nowadays ['nauədeiz] *adv* tegenwoordig

nowhere ['nouwɛə] *adv* nergens

nozzle ['nɔzəl] *n* tuit *c*

nuance [nju:'ɑ̃:s] *n* nuance *c*

nuclear ['nju:kliə] *adj* kern-, nucleair; **~ energy** kernenergie *c*

nucleus ['nju:kliəs] *n* kern *c*

nude [nju:d] *adj* naakt; *n* naakt *nt*

nuisance ['nju:səns] *n* last *c*

numb [nʌm] *adj* gevoelloos; verstijfd

number ['nʌmbə] *n* nummer *nt*; cijfer *nt*, getal *nt*; aantal *nt*

numeral ['nju:mərəl] *n* telwoord *nt*

numerous ['nju:mərəs] *adj* talrijk

nun [nʌn] *n* non *f*

nunnery ['nʌnəri] *n* nonnenklooster *nt*

nurse [nɔːs] *n* zuster *f*, verpleger *m*, verpleegster *f*; kinderjuffrouw *f*; *v* verplegen; zogen

nursery ['nəːsəri] *n* kinderkamer *c*; crèche *c*; boomkwekerij *c*

nut [nʌt] *n* noot *c*; moer *c*

nutcrackers ['nʌt,krækəz] *pl* notenkraker *c*

nutmeg ['nʌtmeg] *n* nootmuskaat *c*

nutritious [nju:'triʃəs] *adj* voedzaam

nutshell ['nʌtʃel] *n* notendop *c*

nylon® ['nailɔn] *n* nylon® *nt*

O

oak [ouk] *n* eik *c*

oar [ɔː] *n* roeiriem *c*

oasis [ou'eisis] *n* (pl oases) oase *c*

oath [ouθ] *n* eed *c*

oats [outs] *pl* haver *c*

obedience [ə'bi:diəns] *n* gehoorzaamheid *c*

obedient [ə'bi:diənt] *adj* gehoorzaam

obey [ə'bei] *v* gehoorzamen

object¹ ['ɔbdʒikt] *n* object *nt*; voorwerp *nt*; doel *nt*

object² [əb'dʒekt] *v* *tegenwerpen; ~ **to** bezwaar *hebben tegen

objection [əb'dʒekʃən] *n* bezwaar *nt*, tegenwerping *c*

objective [əb'dʒektiv] *adj* objectief; *n* doel *nt*

obligatory [ə'bligətəri] *adj* verplicht

oblige [ə'blaidʒ] *v* verplichten; ***be obliged to** verplicht *zijn om; *moeten

obliging [ə'blaidʒiŋ] *adj* voorkomend

oblong ['ɔblɔŋ] *adj* langwerpig; *n* rechthoek *c*

obscene [əb'si:n] *adj* obsceen

obscure [əb'skjuə] *adj* obscuur, duister

observation [,ɔbzə'veiʃən] *n* observatie *c*, waarneming *c*

observatory [əb'zə:vətri] *n* observatorium *nt*

observe [əb'zəːv] *v* observeren, *waarnemen

obsession [əb'seʃən] *n* obsessie *c*

obstacle ['ɔbstəkəl] *n* hindernis *c*

obstinate ['ɔbstinət] *adj* koppig; hardnekkig

obtain [əb'tein] *v* behalen, *verkrijgen, *betrekken

obtainable [əb'teinəbəl] *adj* verkrijgbaar

obvious ['ɔbviəs] *adj* duidelijk

occasion [ə'keiʒən] *n* gelegenheid *c*; aanleiding *c*

occasionally [ə'keiʒənəli] *adv* af en toe, nu en dan

occupant ['ɔkjupənt] *n* bewoner *c*

occupation [,ɔkju'peiʃən] *n* werk *nt*; bezetting *c*

occupy ['ɔkjupai] *v* *innemen, bezetten; **occupied** *adj* bezet

occur [ə'kəː] *v* gebeuren, *voorkomen, zich *voordoen

occurrence [ə'kʌrəns] *n* gebeurtenis *c*

ocean ['ouʃən] *n* oceaan *c*

October [ɔk'toubə] oktober

octopus ['ɔktəpəs] *n* octopus *c*

oculist ['ɔkjulist] *n* oogarts *c*

odd [ɔd] *adj* raar, vreemd; oneven

odo(u)r ['oudə] *n* geur *c*

277 **order**

of [ɔv, əv] *prep* van

off [ɔf] *adv* af; weg; *prep* van

offence [ə'fens] *n* overtreding *c*;
beleediging *c*, aanstoot *c*

offend [ə'fend] *v* krenken, beledigen;
*overtreden

offense [ə'fens] *nAm* overtreding *c*;
beleediging *c*, aanstoot *c*

offensive [ə'fensiv] *adj* offensief;
beleedigend, aanstootgevend; *n*
offensief *nt*

offer ['ɔfə] *v* *aanbieden; *bieden; *n*
aanbieding *c*, aanbod *nt*

office ['ɔfis] *n* bureau *nt*, kantoor *nt*;
ambt *nt*; **~ hours** kantooruren *pl*

officer ['ɔfisə] *n* officier *m*; ambtenaar
m, ambtenares *f*

official [ə'fiʃəl] *adj* officieel

off-licence ['ɔf,laisəns] *n* slijterij *c*

often ['ɔfən] *adv* vaak, dikwijls

oil [ɔil] *n* olie *c*; **fuel~** stookolie *c*; **~ filter**
oliefilter *nt*; **~ painting**
olieverfschilderij *nt*; **~ pressure**
oliedruk *c*; **~ refinery** olieraffinaderij
c; **~ well** oliebron *c*

oily ['ɔili] *adj* olieachtig

ointment ['ɔintmənt] *n* zalf *c*

okay! [,ou'kei] in orde!

old [ould] *adj* oud; **~ age** ouderdom *c*

old-fashioned [,ould'fæʃənd] *adj*
ouderwets

olive ['ɔliv] *n* olijf *c*; **~ oil** olijfolie *c*

omelette ['ɔmlət] *n* omelet *nt*

ominous ['ɔminəs] *adj* onheilspellend

omit [ə'mit] *v* *weglaten

omnipotent [ɔm'nipətənt] *adj*
almachtig

on [ɔn] *prep* op; aan

once [wʌns] *adv* eenmaal, eens; **at ~**
meteen, dadelijk; ineens; tegelijk; **for
~** voor deze keer, eenmalig; **~ more**
nog eens, nogmaals

oncoming ['ɔn,kʌmiŋ] *adj*
tegemoetkomend, naderend

one [wʌn] *num* een; *pron* men

oneself [wʌn'self] *pron* zelf

onion ['ʌnjən] *n* ui *c*

only ['ounli] *adj* enig; *adv* slechts,
alleen, maar; *conj* maar

onwards ['ɔnwədz] *adv* voorwaarts

onyx ['ɔniks] *n* onyx *nt*

opal ['oupəl] *n* opaal *c*

open ['oupən] *v* openen; *adj* open;
openhartig; **opener** opener

opening ['oupəniŋ] *n* opening *c*

opera ['ɔpərə] *n* opera *c*; **~ house** opera
c

operate ['ɔpəreit] *v* opereren, werken

operation [,ɔpə'reiʃən] *n* werking *c*;
operatie *c*

operator ['ɔpəreitə] *n* telefonist *m*, -e *f*

operetta [,ɔpə'retə] *n* operette *c*

opinion [ə'pinjən] *n* opinie *c*, mening *c*

opponent [ə'pounənt] *n* tegenstander
m

opportunity [,ɔpə'tju:nəti] *n*
gelegenheid *c*, kans *c*

oppose [ə'pouz] *v* zich verzetten

opposite ['ɔpəzit] *prep* tegenover; *adj*
tegengesteld

opposition [,ɔpə'ziʃən] *n* oppositie *c*

oppress [ə'pres] *v* beklemmen,
verdrukken

optician [ɔp'tiʃən] *n* opticien *m*

optimism ['ɔptimizəm] *n* optimisme *nt*

optimist ['ɔptimist] *n* optimist *m*, -e *f*

optimistic [,ɔpti'mistik] *adj*
optimistisch

optional ['ɔpʃənəl] *adj* facultatief

or [ɔː] *conj* of

oral ['ɔːrəl] *adj* mondeling

orange ['ɔrindʒ] *n* sinaasappel *c*; *adj*
oranje

orbit ['ɔːbit] *n* omloop *c*; baan *c*

orchard ['ɔːtʃəd] *n* boomgaard *c*

orchestra ['ɔːkistrə] *n* orkest *nt*; **~ seat**
Am stalles *pl*

order ['ɔːdə] *v* *bevelen; bestellen; *n*

volgorde c; orde c; opdracht c, bevel nt;
bestelling c; **in ~** in orde; **in ~ to** om te;
made to ~ op maat gemaakt; **out of ~**
buiten werking; **postal ~** postwissel c

order form ['ɔːdəfɔːm] n
bestelformulier nt

ordinary ['ɔːdənri] adj alledaags,
gewoon

ore [ɔː] n erts nt

organ ['ɔːgən] n orgaan nt; orgel nt

organic [ɔː'gænik] adj organisch

organization [ˌɔːgənai'zeiʃən] n
organisatie c

organize ['ɔːgənaiz] v organiseren

Orient ['ɔːriənt] n Oosten nt

oriental [ˌɔːri'entəl] adj oosters

orientate ['ɔːriənteit] v zich oriënteren

origin ['ɔridʒin] n origine c, oorsprong
c; afstamming c, herkomst c

original [ə'ridʒinəl] adj
oorspronkelijk, origineel

originally [ə'ridʒinəli] adv
aanvankelijk

ornament ['ɔːnəmənt] n versiersel nt

ornamental [ˌɔːnə'mentəl] adj
ornamenteel

orphan ['ɔːfən] n wees c

orthodox ['ɔːθədɔks] adj orthodox

ostrich ['ɔstritʃ] n struisvogel c

other ['ʌðə] adj ander

otherwise ['ʌðəwaiz] conj anders

*ought to [ɔːt] *moeten, zou *moeten

ounce [auns] n ons (28.35 gr) nt; beetje
nt

our [auə] adj ons

ours ['auəz] pron van ons

ourselves [auə'selvz] pron ons; zelf

out [aut] adv buiten, uit; **~ of** buiten, uit

outbreak ['autbreik] n uitbarsting c

outcome ['autkʌm] n resultaat nt;
uitkomst

*outdo [ˌaut'duː] v *overtreffen

outdoors [ˌaut'dɔːz] adv buiten

outfit ['autfit] n uitrusting c

outing ['autiŋ] n uitje nt

outline ['autlain] n omtrek c; v schetsen

outlook ['autluk] n verwachting c;
zienswijze c

output ['autput] n productie c

outrage ['autreidʒ] n gewelddaad c

outside [ˌaut'said] adv buiten; prep
buiten; n uiterlijk nt, buitenkant c

outsize ['autsaiz] n extra grote maat

outskirts ['autskəːts] pl buitenwijk c

outstanding [ˌaut'stændiŋ] adj
eminent, vooraanstaand

outward ['autwəd] adj uiterlijk

outwards ['autwədz] adv naar buiten

oval ['ouvəl] adj ovaal

oven ['ʌvən] n oven c; **microwave ~**
magnetron c

over ['ouvə] prep boven, over; meer
dan; adv over; omver; adj voorbij; **~
there** ginds

overall ['ouvərɔːl] adj totaal

overalls ['ouvərɔːlz] pl overall c

overcast ['ouvəkɑːst] adj betrokken

overcoat ['ouvəkout] n overjas c

*overcome [ˌouvə'kʌm] v
*overwinnen

overdo [ˌouvə'duː] v overdrijven; fig te
ver gaan

overdraft ['ouvədrɑːft] n tekort nt,
debet nt, roodstand c

overdraw [ˌouvə'drɔː] v debet staan,
rood (gaan) staan

overdue [ˌouvə'djuː] adj te laat;
achterstallig

overgrown [ˌouvə'groun] adj
begroeid

overhaul [ˌouvə'hɔːl] v reviseren

overlook [ˌouvə'luk] v over het hoofd
*zien

overnight [ˌouvə'nait] adv 's nachts

overseas [ˌouvə'siːz] adj overzees

oversight ['ouvəsait] n vergissing c

*oversleep [ˌouvə'sliːp] v zich
*verslapen

overstrung [ˌouvə'strʌŋ] *adj*
overspannen

***overtake** [ˌouvə'teik] *v* inhalen; **no overtaking** inhalen verboden

over-tired [ˌouvə'taiəd] *adj*
oververmoeid

overture ['ouvətʃə] *n* ouverture *c*

overweight ['ouvəweit] *n*
bagageoverschot *nt*; overgewicht *nt*;
adj te zwaar

overwhelm [ˌouvə'welm] *v* onthutsen,
overweldigen

overwork [ˌouvə'wə:k] *v* zich
overwerken

owe [ou] *v* verschuldigd *zijn, schuldig
*zijn; te danken *hebben aan; **owing
to** vanwege, ten gevolge van

owl [aul] *n* uil *c*

own [oun] *v* *bezitten; *adj* eigen

owner ['ounə] *n* bezitter *m*, bezitster *f*,
eigenaar *c*, eigenares *f*

ox [ɔks] *n* (pl oxen) os *c*

oxygen ['ɔksidʒən] *n* zuurstof *c*

oyster ['ɔistə] *n* oester *c*

ozone ['ouzoun] *n* ozon *nt*

P

pace [peis] *n* gang *c*; schrede *c*, stap *c*;
tempo *nt*

Pacific Ocean [pə'sifik 'ouʃən] Stille
Oceaan

pacifism ['pæsifizəm] *n* pacifisme *nt*

pacifist ['pæsifist] *n* pacifist *m*, -e *f*;
pacifistisch

pack [pæk] *v* inpakken; ~ **up** inpakken

package ['pækidʒ] *n* pak *nt*

packet ['pækit] *n* pakje *nt*

packing ['pækiŋ] *n* verpakking *c*

pact ['pækt] *n* pact *nt*, verdrag *nt*

pad [pæd] *n* kussentje *nt*; blocnote *c*

paddle ['pædəl] *n* peddel *c*

padlock ['pædlɔk] *n* hangslot *nt*

pagan ['peigən] *adj* heidens; *n* heiden *c*

page [peidʒ] *n* pagina *c*, bladzijde *c*

pageboy ['peidʒbɔi] *n* piccolo *m*

pail [peil] *n* emmer *c*

pain [pein] *n* pijn *c*; **pains** moeite *c*

painful ['peinfəl] *adj* pijnlijk

painkiller ['peinkilə] *n* pijnstiller *c*

painless ['peinləs] *adj* pijnloos

paint [peint] *n* verf *c*; *v* schilderen;
verven

paintbox ['peintbɔks] *n* verfdoos *c*

paintbrush ['peintbrʌʃ] *n* penseel *nt*

painter ['peintə] *n* schilder *m*, -es *f*

painting ['peintiŋ] *n* schilderij *nt*

pair [pɛə] *n* paar *nt*

Pakistan [ˌpɑːki'stɑːn] Pakistan

Pakistani [ˌpɑːki'stɑːni] *adj*
Pakistaans; *n* Pakistaan *m*, -se *f*

palace ['pæləs] *n* paleis *nt*

pale [peil] *adj* bleek; licht

palm [pɑːm] *n* palm *c*; handpalm *c*

palpable ['pælpəbəl] *adj* tastbaar

palpitation [ˌpælpi'teiʃən] *n*
hartklopping *c*

pan [pæn] *n* pan *c*

pane [pein] *n* ruit *c*

panel ['pænəl] *n* paneel *nt*

panelling ['pænəliŋ] *n* lambrizering *c*

panic ['pænik] *n* paniek *c*

pant [pænt] *v* hijgen

panties ['pæntiz] *pl* onderbroek *c*, slip
c

pants [pænts] *pl* onderbroek *c*; *plAm*
broek *c*

pant suit ['pæntsuːt] *n* broekpak *nt*

panty hose ['pæntihouz] *n* panty *c*

paper ['peipə] *n* papier *nt*; krant *c*; papieren; **carbon ~** carbonpapier *nt*; **~ bag** papieren zak; **~ napkin** papieren servet; **typing ~** schrijfmachinepapier *nt*; **wrapping ~** pakpapier *nt*

paperback ['peipəbæk] *n* pocketboek *nt*

paper knife ['peipənaif] *n* briefopener *c*

parade [pə'reid] *n* parade *c*, optocht *c*

paradise ['pærədais] *n* paradijs *nt*

paraffin ['pærəfin] *n* petroleum *c*

paragraph ['pærəgra:f] *n* alinea *c*, paragraaf *c*

parakeet ['pærəki:t] *n* parkiet *c*

paralyse, *Am* **paralyze** ['pærəlaiz] *v* verlammen

parallel ['pærəlel] *adj* evenwijdig, parallel; *n* parallel *c*

parcel ['pɑ:səl] *n* pakket *nt*, pakje *nt*

pardon ['pɑ:dən] *n* vergiffenis *c*; gratie *c*

parent ['pɛərənts] *n* ouder

parents-in-law ['pɛərəntsinlɔ:] *pl* schoonouders *pl*

parish ['pæriʃ] *n* parochie *c*

park [pɑ:k] *n* park *nt*; *v* parkeren; **no parking** verboden te parkeren; **parking fee** parkeertarief *nt*; **parking light** stadslicht *nt*; **parking lot** *Am* parkeerplaats *c*; **parking meter** parkeermeter *c*; **parking zone** parkeerzone *c*

parliament ['pɑ:ləmənt] *n* parlement *nt*

parliamentary [,pɑ:lə'mentəri] *adj* parlementair

parrot ['pærət] *n* papegaai *c*

parsley ['pɑ:sli] *n* peterselie *c*

parson ['pɑ:sən] *n* dominee *m*

parsonage ['pɑ:sənidʒ] *n* pastorie *c*

part [pɑ:t] *n* gedeelte *nt*, deel *nt*; stuk *nt*; *v* *scheiden; **spare ~** onderdeel *nt*

partial ['pɑ:ʃəl] *adj* gedeeltelijk; partijdig

participant [pɑ:'tisipənt] *n* deelnemer *m*, deelneemster *f*

participate [pɑ:'tisipeit] *v* *deelnemen

particular [pə'tikjulə] *adj* bijzonder, speciaal; kieskeurig; **in ~** in het bijzonder

parting ['pɑ:tiŋ] *n* afscheid *nt*; scheiding *c*

partition [pɑ:'tiʃən] *n* tussenschot *nt*

partly ['pɑ:tli] *adv* deels, gedeeltelijk

partner ['pɑ:tnə] *n* partner *c*; compagnon *c*

partridge ['pɑ:tridʒ] *n* patrijs *c*

party ['pɑ:ti] *n* partij *c*; fuif *c*, feestje *nt*; groep *c*

pass [pɑ:s] *v* *voorbijgaan, passeren; *aangeven; slagen; *v Am* inhalen; **no passing** *Am* inhalen verboden; **~ by** passeren; **~ through** *gaan door

passage ['pæsidʒ] *n* doorgang *c*; overtocht *c*; passage *c*; doorreis *c*

passenger ['pæsəndʒə] *n* passagier *m*; **~ car** *Am* wagon *c*; **~ train** personentrein *c*

passer-by [,pɑ:sə'bai] *n* voorbijganger *m*

passion ['pæʃən] *n* hartstocht *c*, passie *c*; drift *c*

passionate ['pæʃənət] *adj* hartstochtelijk

passive ['pæsiv] *adj* passief

passport ['pɑ:spɔ:t] *n* paspoort *nt*; **~ control** paspoortcontrole *c*; **~ photograph** pasfoto *c*

password ['pɑ:swə:d] *n* wachtwoord *nt*

past [pɑ:st] *n* verleden *nt*; *adj* vorig, afgelopen, voorbij; *prep* langs, voorbij

paste [peist] *n* pasta *c*; *v* plakken

pastime ['pɑ:staim] *n* tijdverdrijf *nt*

pastry ['peistri] *n* gebak *nt*; **~ shop**

banketbakkerij c

pasture ['pɑːstʃə] n weiland nt

pasty ['peisti] n pasteitje nt

patch [pætʃ] v verstellen

patent ['peitənt] n patent nt, octrooi nt

path [pɑːθ] n pad nt

patience ['peiʃəns] n geduld nt

patient ['peiʃənt] adj geduldig; n patiënt m, -e f

patriot ['peitriət] n patriot m

patrol [pə'troul] n patrouille c; v patrouilleren; surveilleren

pattern ['pætən] n motief nt, patroon nt

pause [pɔːz] n pauze c; v pauzeren

pave [peiv] v plaveien, bestraten

pavement ['peivmənt] n trottoir nt; plaveisel nt

pavilion [pə'viljən] n paviljoen nt

paw [pɔː] n poot c

pawn [pɔːn] v verpanden; n pion c

pawnbroker ['pɔːn,broukə] n pandjesbaas m

pay [pei] n salaris nt, loon nt

***pay** [pei] v betalen; lonen; ~ **attention to** letten op; ~ **off** aflossen; ~ **on account** afbetalen; **paying** rendabel

pay desk ['peidesk] n kassa c

payee [pei'iː] n begunstigde c

payment ['peimənt] n betaling c

pea [piː] n erwt c

peace [piːs] n vrede c

peaceful ['piːsfəl] adj vreedzaam

peach [piːtʃ] n perzik c

peacock ['piːkɔk] n pauw c

peak [piːk] n top c; spits c; ~ **hour** spitsuur nt; ~ **season** hoogseizoen nt

peanut ['piːnʌt] n pinda c

pear [pɛə] n peer c

pearl [pəːl] n parel c

peasant ['pezənt] n boer m

pebble ['pebəl] n kiezel c

peculiar [pi'kjuːljə] adj eigenaardig; speciaal, bijzonder

peculiarity [pi,kjuːli'ærəti] n

eigenaardigheid c

pedal ['pedəl] n pedaal nt/c

pedestrian [pi'destriən] n voetganger m, voetgangster f; ~ **crossing** zebrapad nt; **no pedestrians** verboden voor voetgangers

peel [piːl] v schillen c; n schil c

peep [piːp] v gluren

peg [peg] n klerenhaak c

pelican ['pelikən] n pelikaan c

pelvis ['pelvis] n bekken nt

pen [pen] n pen c

penalty ['penəlti] n boete c; straf c; ~ **kick** strafschop c

pencil ['pensəl] n potlood nt; ~ **sharpener** n punteslijper c

penetrate ['penitreit] v *doordringen

penguin ['peŋgwin] n pinguin c

penicillin [,peni'silin] n penicilline c

peninsula [pə'ninsjulə] n schiereiland nt

penknife ['pennaif] n (pl -knives) zakmes nt

penny ['peni] n; (pl pennies, pence) penny c

pension¹ ['pɑːsiɔ̃ː] n pension nt

pension² ['penʃən] n pensioen nt

Pentecost ['pentikɔst] n Pinksteren

people ['piːpəl] pl mensen; n volk nt

pepper ['pepə] n peper c

peppermint ['pepəmint] n pepermunt c

per [pəː] prep per, via; ~ **cent** procent

perceive [pə'siːv] v bemerken

percent [pə'sent] n procent nt

percentage [pə'sentidʒ] n percentage nt

perceptible [pə'septibəl] adj merkbaar

perception [pə'sepʃən] n gewaarwording c

perch [pəːtʃ] (pl ~) baars c

percolator ['pəːkəleitə] n percolator c

perfect ['pəːfikt] adj volkomen,

volmaakt

perfection [pə'fekʃən] *n* perfectie *c*,
volmaaktheid *c*

perform [pə'fɔːm] *v* uitvoeren,
verrichten

performance [pə'fɔːməns] *n*
voorstelling *c*

perfume ['pəːfjuːm] *n* parfum *nt*

perhaps [pə'hæps] *adv* misschien;
wellicht

peril ['peril] *n* gevaar *nt*

perilous ['periləs] *adj* gevaarlijk

period ['piəriəd] *n* tijdperk *nt*, periode
c; punt *c*

periodical [,piəri'ɔdikəl] *n* tijdschrift
nt; *adj* periodiek

perish ['periʃ] *v* *omkomen

perishable ['periʃəbəl] *adj* aan bederf
onderhevig

perjury ['pəːdʒəri] *n* meineed *c*

perm ['pəːm] *n* permanent *c*

permanent ['pəːmənənt] *adj* blijvend,
permanent, duurzaam; bestendig,
vast; **~ press** plooihoudend

permission [pə'miʃən] *n* toestemming
c, permissie *c*; verlof *nt*, vergunning *c*

permit[1] [pə'mit] *v* *toestaan,
veroorloven

permit[2] ['pəːmit] *n* vergunning *c*

peroxide [pə'rɔksaid] *n*
waterstofperoxyde *nt*

perpendicular [,pəːpən'dikjulə] *adj*
loodrecht

Persia ['pəːʃə] Perzië

Persian ['pəːʃən] *adj* Perzisch; *n* Pers *c*

person ['pəːsən] *n* persoon *c*; **per ~** per
persoon

personal ['pəːsənəl] *adj* persoonlijk

personality [,pəːsə'næləti] *n*
persoonlijkheid *c*

personnel [,pəːsə'nel] *n* personeel *nt*

perspective [pə'spektiv] *n* perspectief
nt

perspiration [,pəːspə'reiʃən] *n*

transpiratie *c*, zweet *nt*

perspire [pə'spaiə] *v* transpireren,
zweten

persuade [pə'sweid] *v* overreden,
overhalen; overtuigen

persuasion [pə'sweiʒən] *n*
overtuiging *c*

pessimism ['pesimizəm] *n*
pessimisme *c*

pessimist ['pesimist] *n* pessimist *m*, -e
f

pessimistic [,pesi'mistik] *adj*
pessimistisch

pet [pet] *n* huisdier *nt*; lieveling *c*

petal ['petəl] *n* bloemblad *nt*

petition [pi'tiʃən] *n* petitie *c*

petrol ['petrəl] *n* benzine *c*; **unleaded~**
loodvrije benzine *c*; **~ pump**
benzinepomp *c*; **~ station**
benzinestation *nt*; **~ tank** benzinetank
c

petroleum [pi'trouliəm] *n* petroleum *c*

petty ['peti] *adj* klein, nietig,
onbeduidend; **~ cash** kleingeld *nt*

pewit ['pjuːt] *n* kievit *c*

pewter ['pjuːtə] *n* tin *nt*

phantom ['fæntəm] *n* spook *nt*

pharmacist ['faːməsist] *n* apotheker
m, apotheekeres *f*

pharmacology [,faːmə'kɔlədʒi] *n*
farmacologie *c*

pharmacy ['faːməsi] *n* apotheek *c*;
drogisterij *c*

phase [feiz] *n* fase *c*

pheasant ['fezənt] *n* fazant *c*

phenomenon [fe'nɔmənon] *n*
verschijnsel *nt*

Philippine ['filipain] *adj* Filippijns

Philippines ['filipiːnz] *pl* Filippijnen
pl

philosopher [fi'lɔsəfə] *n* wijsgeer *c*,
filosoof *m*, filosofe *f*

philosophy [fi'lɔsəfi] *n* wijsbegeerte *c*,
filosofie *c*

phone [foun] *n* telefoon *c*; *v* opbellen, telefoneren; **~ card** *n* telefoonkaart *c*

phonetic [fə'netik] *adj* fonetisch

photo ['foutou] *n* (pl ~s) foto *c*

photocopy ['foutəkopi] *n* fotocopie *c*

photograph ['foutəgra:f] *n* foto *c*; *v* fotograferen

photographer [fə'tɔgrəfə] *n* fotograaf *m*, fotografe *f*

photography [fə'tɔgrəfi] *n* fotografie *c*

phrase [freiz] *n* uitdrukking *c*

phrase book ['freizbuk] *n* taalgids *c*

physical ['fizikəl] *adj* fysiek

physician [fi'ziʃən] *n* dokter *c*

physicist ['fizisist] *n* natuurkundige *c*

physics ['fiziks] *n* fysica *c*, natuurkunde *c*

physiology [,fizi'ɔlədʒi] *n* fysiologie *c*

pianist ['pi:ənist] *n* pianist *m*, -e *f*

piano [pi'ænou] *n* piano *c*; **grand ~** vleugel *c*

pick [pik] *v* plukken; *kiezen; *n* keus *c*; **~ up** oprapen; ophalen; **pick-up van** bestelauto *c*

pickles ['pikəlz] *pl* zoetzuur *nt*

picnic ['piknik] *n* picknick *c*; *v* picknicken

picture ['piktʃə] *n* schilderij *nt*; plaat *c*, prent *c*; beeld *nt*, afbeelding *c*; **~ postcard** ansichtkaart *c*, prentbriefkaart *c*; **pictures** bioscoop *c*

picturesque [,piktʃə'resk] *adj* pittoresk, schilderachtig

pie [pai] *n* taart *c*; pastei *c*

piece [pi:s] *n* stuk *nt*

pier [piə] *n* pier *c*

pierce [piəs] *v* doorboren

pig [pig] *n* varken *nt*; zwijn *nt*

pigeon ['pidʒən] *n* duif *c*

piggy bank ['pigibæŋk] *n* spaarvarken *nt*

pig-headed [,pig'hedid] *adj* eigenwijs

piglet ['piglət] *n* big *c*

pigskin ['pigskin] *n* varkensleer *nt*

pike [paik] (pl ~) snoek *c*

pile [pail] *n* stapel *c*; *v* opstapelen; **piles** *pl* aambeien *pl*

pilgrim ['pilgrim] *n* pelgrim *m*

pilgrimage ['pilgrimidʒ] *n* bedevaart *c*

pill [pil] *n* pil *c*

pillar ['pilə] *n* zuil *c*, pilaar *c*

pillarbox ['piləbɔks] *n* brievenbus *c*

pillow ['pilou] *n* kussen *nt*, hoofdkussen *nt*

pillowcase ['piloukeis] *n* kussensloop *c/nt*

pilot ['pailət] *n* piloot *c*; loods *c*

pimple ['pimpəl] *n* puistje *nt*

pin [pin] *n* speld *c*; *v* vastspelden; **bobby ~** *Am* haarspeld *c*

pincers ['pinsəz] *pl* nijptang *c*

pinch [pintʃ] *v* *knijpen

pineapple ['pai,næpəl] *n* ananas *c*

ping-pong ['piŋpɔŋ] *n* tafeltennis *nt*

pink [piŋk] *adj* roze

pioneer [,paiə'niə] *n* pionier *m*, -ster *f*

pious ['paiəs] *adj* vroom

pip [pip] *n* pit *c*

pipe [paip] *n* pijp *c*; leiding *c*; **~ cleaner** pijpenstoker *c*; **~ tobacco** pijptabak *c*

pirate ['paiərət] *n* piraat *m*

pistol ['pistəl] *n* pistool *nt*

piston ['pistən] *n* zuiger *c*; **~ ring** zuigerring *c*

pit [pit] *n* kuil *c*; groeve *c*

pitcher ['pitʃə] *n* kruik *c*

pity ['piti] *n* medelijden *nt*; *v* medelijden *hebben met, beklagen; **what a pity!** jammer!

placard ['plæka:d] *n* aanplakbiljet *nt*

place [pleis] *n* plaats *c*; *v* zetten, plaatsen; **~ of birth** geboorteplaats *c*; *take ~ *plaatshebben

plague [pleig] *n* plaag *c*

plaice [pleis] (pl ~) schol *c*

plain [plein] *adj* duidelijk; gewoon,

eenvoudig; *n* vlakte *c*

plan [plæn] *n* plan *nt*; plattegrond *c*; *v* plannen

plane [plein] *adj* vlak; *n* vliegtuig *nt*; ~ **crash** vliegramp *c*

planet ['plænit] *n* planeet *c*

planetarium [,plæni'tɛəriəm] *n* planetarium *c*

plank [plæŋk] *n* plank *c*

plant [plɑːnt] *n* plant *c*; bedrijf *nt*; *v* planten

plantation [plæn'teiʃən] *n* plantage *c*

plaster ['plɑːstə] *n* pleister *nt*, gips *nt*; pleister *c*

plastic ['plæstik] *adj* plastic; *n* plastic *nt*

plate [pleit] *n* bord *nt*; plaat *c*

plateau ['plætou] *n* (pl ~x, ~s) hoogvlakte *c*

platform ['plætfɔːm] *n* perron *nt*; ~ **ticket** perronkaartje *nt*

platinum ['plætinəm] *n* platina *nt*

play [plei] *v* spelen; bespelen; *n* spel *nt*; toneelstuk *nt*; **one-act** ~ eenakter *c*; ~ **truant** spijbelen

player [pleiə] *n* speler *m*, speelster *f*

playground ['pleigraund] *n* speelplaats *c*

playing card ['pleiiŋkɑːd] *n* speelkaart *c*

playwright ['pleirait] *n* toneelschrijver *m*, toneelschrijfster *f*

plea [pliː] *n* pleidooi *nt*

plead [pliːd] *v* pleiten

pleasant ['plezənt] *adj* prettig, aardig, aangenaam

please [pliːz] alstublieft; *v* *bevallen; **pleased** ingenomen; **pleasing** aangenaam

pleasure ['pleʒə] *n* genoegen *nt*, pret *c*, plezier *nt*

plentiful ['plentifəl] *adj* overvloedig

plenty ['plenti] *n* overvloed *c*; heleboel *c*

pliers [plaiəz] *pl* tang *c*

plimsolls ['plimsəlz] *pl* gymschoenen *pl*

plot [plɔt] *n* samenzwering *c*, komplot *nt*; handeling *c*; perceel *nt*

plough [plau] *n* ploeg *c*; *v* ploegen

plucky ['plʌki] *adj* flink

plug [plʌg] *n* stekker *c*; ~ **in** inschakelen

plum [plʌm] *n* pruim *c*

plumber ['plʌmə] *n* loodgieter *m*

plump [plʌmp] *adj* mollig

plural ['pluərəl] *n* meervoud *nt*

plus [plʌs] *prep* plus

pneumatic [njuː'mætik] *adj* pneumatisch

pneumonia [njuː'mouniə] *n* longontsteking *c*

poach [poutʃ] *v* stropen

pocket ['pɔkit] *n* zak *c*

pocketbook ['pɔkitbuk] *n* portefeuille *c*

pocketknife ['pɔkitnaif] *n* (pl -knives) zakmes *nt*

poem ['pouim] *n* gedicht *nt*

poet ['pouit] *n* dichter *m*, -es *f*

poetry ['pouitri] *n* dichtkunst *c*

point [pɔint] *n* punt *nt*; punt *c*; *v* *wijzen; ~ **of view** standpunt *nt*; ~ **out** *aanwijzen

pointed ['pɔintid] *adj* spits

poison ['pɔizən] *n* vergif *nt*; *v* vergiftigen

poisonous ['pɔizənəs] *adj* giftig

Poland ['poulənd] Polen

Pole [poul] *n* Pool *m*, Poolse *f*

pole [poul] *n* paal *c*

police [pə'liːs] *pl* politie *c*; ~ **station** politiebureau *nt*

policeman [pə'liːsmən] *n* (pl -men) agent *m*, politieagent *m*

policewoman [pə'liːswumən] *n* (pl -women) agente *f*, politieagente *f*

policy ['pɔlisi] *n* beleid *nt*, politiek *c*; polis *c*

polio ['pouliou] *n* polio *c*,

kinderverlamming c
Polish ['pouliʃ] adj Pools
polish ['pɔliʃ] v poetsen
polite [pə'lait] adj beleefd
political [pə'litikəl] adj politiek
politician [ˌpɔli'tiʃən] n politicus c
politics ['pɔlitiks] n politiek c
poll [poul] n stemming c; **go to the polls** stemmen
pollute [pə'luːt] v vervuilen, verontreinigen
pollution [pə'luːʃən] n vervuiling c, verontreiniging c
pond [pɔnd] n vijver c
pony ['pouni] n pony c
pool [puːl] n zwembad nt; poel c; biljart nt; ~ **attendant** badmeester m
poor [puə] adj arm; armoedig; slecht
pope [poup] n paus m
pop music [pɔp 'mjuːzik] popmuziek c
poppy ['pɔpi] n klaproos c; papaver c
popular ['pɔpjulə] adj populair; volks-
population [ˌpɔpju'leiʃən] n bevolking c
populous ['pɔpjuləs] adj dichtbevolkt
porcelain ['pɔːsəlin] n porselein nt
porcupine ['pɔːkjupain] n stekelvarken nt
pork [pɔːk] n varkensvlees nt
port [pɔːt] n haven c; bakboord nt
portable ['pɔːtəbəl] adj draagbaar
porter ['pɔːtə] n kruier m; portier m
porthole ['pɔːthoul] n patrijspoort c
portion ['pɔːʃən] n portie c
portrait ['pɔːtrit] n portret nt
Portugal ['pɔːtjugəl] Portugal
Portuguese [ˌpɔːtju'giːz] adj Portugees; n Portugees m, Portugese f
posh [pɔʃ] adj colloquial chic, kak
position [pə'ziʃən] n positie c; houding c; betrekking c, functie c
positive ['pɔzətiv] adj positief; n positief nt

possess [pə'zes] v *bezitten; **possessed** adj bezeten
possession [pə'zeʃən] n bezit nt; **possessions** eigendom nt
possibility [ˌpɔsə'biləti] n mogelijkheid c
possible ['pɔsəbəl] adj mogelijk; eventueel
post [poust] n paal c; betrekking c; post c; v posten; **post-office** postkantoor nt
postage ['poustidʒ] n frankering c; ~ **paid** franko; ~ **stamp** postzegel c
postcard ['poustkɑːd] n briefkaart c; ansichtkaart c
poster ['poustə] n affiche nt, poster c
poste restante [poust re'stɑːt] poste restante
postman ['poustmən] n (pl -men) postbode m
post-paid [ˌpoust'peid] adj franko
postpone [pə'spoun] v uitstellen
pot [pɔt] n pot c
potato [pə'teitou] n (pl ~es) aardappel c
pottery ['pɔtəri] n aardewerk nt
pouch [pautʃ] n buidel c
poulterer ['poultərə] n poelier m
poultry ['poultri] n gevogelte nt
pound [paund] n pond nt
pour [pɔː] v *inschenken, *schenken, *gieten
poverty ['pɔvəti] n armoede c
powder ['paudə] n poeder nt/c; ~ **compact** poederdoos c; **talc** ~ talkpoeder nt/c; ~ **room** damestoilet nt
power [pauə] n kracht c; energie c; macht c; mogendheid c; ~ **station** elektriciteitscentrale c
powerful ['pauəfəl] adj machtig; sterk
powerless ['pauələs] adj machteloos
practical ['præktikəl] adj praktisch
practically ['præktikli] adv vrijwel
practice ['præktis] n praktijk c

practise ['præktis] v beoefenen;
oefenen

praise [preiz] v *prijzen; n lof c

pram [præm] n kinderwagen c

prawn [prɔ:n] n garnaal c, steurgarnaal
c

pray [prei] v *bidden

prayer [prɛə] n gebed nt

preach [pri:tʃ] v preken

precarious [pri'kɛəriəs] adj hachelijk

precaution [pri'kɔ:ʃən] n voorzorg c;
voorzorgsmaatregel c

precede [pri'si:d] v *voorafgaan

preceding [pri'si:diŋ] adj voorgaand

precious ['preʃəs] adj kostbaar;
dierbaar

precipice ['presipis] n afgrond c

precipitation [pri,sipi'teiʃən] n
neerslag c

precise [pri'sais] adj precies, exact,
nauwkeurig; secuur

predecessor ['pri:disesə] n
voorganger m, voorgangster f

predict [pri'dikt] v voorspellen

prefer [pri'fə:] v de voorkeur *geven
aan, liever *hebben

preferable ['prefərəbəl] adj te
verkiezen, verkieselijker, de voorkeur
verdienend

preference ['prefərəns] n voorkeur c

prefix ['pri:fiks] n voorvoegsel nt

pregnant ['pregnənt] adj in
verwachting, zwanger

prejudice ['predʒədis] n vooroordeel
nt

preliminary [pri'liminəri] adj
inleidend; voorlopig

premature ['premətʃuə] adj voorbarig

premier ['premiə] n premier c

premises ['premisiz] pl pand nt

premium ['pri:miəm] n premie c

prepaid [,pri:'peid] adj vooruitbetaald

preparation [,prepə'reiʃən] n
voorbereiding c

prepare [pri'pɛə] v voorbereiden;
klaarmaken

prepared [pri'pɛəd] adj bereid

preposition [,prepə'ziʃən] n
voorzetsel nt

prescribe [pri'skraib] v
*voorschrijven

prescription [pri'skripʃən] n recept nt

presence ['prezəns] n aanwezigheid c;
tegenwoordigheid c

present[1] ['prezənt] n geschenk nt,
cadeau nt; heden nt; adj tegenwoordig;
aanwezig

present[2] [pri'zent] v voorstellen;
*aanbieden

presently ['prezəntli] adv meteen,
dadelijk

preservation [,prezə'veiʃən] n
bewaring c

preserve [pri'zə:v] v bewaren;
inmaken

president ['prezidənt] n president m,
-e f; voorzitter m, voorzitster f

press [pres] n pers c; v indrukken,
drukken; persen; ~ **conference**
persconferentie c

pressing ['presiŋ] adj urgent,
dringend

pressure ['preʃə] n druk c; spanning c;
atmospheric ~ luchtdruk c; ~ **cooker**
snelkookpan c

prestige [pre'sti:ʒ] n prestige nt

presumable [pri'zju:məbəl] adj
vermoedelijk

presumptuous [pri'zʌmpʃəs] adj
overmoedig; arrogant

pretence [pri'tens] n voorwendsel nt

pretend [pri'tend] v *doen alsof,
voorwenden

pretext ['pri:tekst] n voorwendsel nt

pretty ['priti] adj mooi, knap; adv vrij,
tamelijk, nogal

prevent [pri'vent] v beletten,
verhinderen; *voorkomen

preventive [pri'ventiv] *adj* preventief

preview ['pri:vju:] *n* voorvertoning *c*

previous ['pri:viəs] *adj* verleden, vroeger, voorgaand

pre-war [,pri:'wɔ:] *adj* vooroorlogs

price [prais] *n* prijs; *v* prijzen; **~ list** prijslijst *c*

priceless ['praisləs] *adj* onschatbaar

prick [prik] *v* prikken

pride [praid] *n* trots *c*

priest [pri:st] *n* priester *m*

primary ['praiməri] *adj* primair; eerst, hoofd-; elementair

prince [prins] *n* prins *m*

princess [prin'ses] *n* prinses *c*

principal ['prinsəpəl] *adj* voornaamst; *n* rector *c*, schoolhoofd *nt*, directeur *c*

principle ['prinsəpəl] *n* beginsel *nt*, principe *nt*

print [print] *v* drukken; *n* afdruk *c*; prent *c*; **printed matter** drukwerk *nt*

prior [praiə] *adj* vroeger

priority [prai'ɔrəti] *n* prioriteit *c*, voorrang *c*

prison ['prizən] *n* gevangenis *c*

prisoner ['prizənə] *n* gedetineerde *c*, gevangene *c*;**~of war** krijgsgevangene *c*

privacy ['praivəsi] *n* privacy *c*, privéleven *nt*

private ['praivit] *adj* particulier, privé; persoonlijk

privilege ['privilidʒ] *n* voorrecht *nt*

prize [praiz] *n* prijs *c*; beloning *c*

probable ['prɔbəbəl] *adj* vermoedelijk, waarschijnlijk

probably ['prɔbəbli] *adv* waarschijnlijk

problem ['prɔbləm] *n* probleem *nt*; vraagstuk *nt*

procedure [prə'si:dʒə] *n* procedure *c*

proceed [prə'si:d] *v* *voortgaan; te werk *gaan

process ['prouses] *n* proces *nt*, procédé *nt*

procession [prə'seʃən] *n* processie *c*, stoet *c*

proclaim [prə'kleim] *v* afkondigen

produce[1] [prə'dju:s] *v* produceren

produce[2] ['prɔdju:s] *n* opbrengst *c*, product *nt*

producer [prə'dju:sə] *n* producent *m*

product ['prɔdʌkt] *n* product *nt*

production [prə'dʌkʃən] *n* productie *c*

profession [prə'feʃən] *n* vak *nt*, beroep *nt*

professional [prə'feʃənəl] *adj* beroeps-

professor [prə'fesə] *n* hoogleraar *m*, professor *c*

profit ['prɔfit] *n* voordeel *nt*, winst *c*; baat *c*; *v* profiteren

profitable ['prɔfitəbəl] *adj* winstgevend

profound [prə'faund] *adj* diepzinnig

programme ['prougræm] *n* programma *nt*

progress[1] ['prougres] *n* vooruitgang *c*

progress[2] [prə'gres] *v* vorderen

progressive [prə'gresiv] *adj* vooruitstrevend, progressief; toenemend

prohibit [prə'hibit] *v* *verbieden

prohibition [,proui'biʃən] *n* verbod *nt*

prohibitive [prə'hibitiv] *adj* onoverkomelijk

project ['prɔdʒekt] *n* plan *nt*, project *nt*

promenade [,prɔmə'na:d] *n* promenade *c*

promise ['prɔmis] *n* belofte *c*; *v* beloven

promote [prə'mout] *v* bevorderen

promotion [prə'mouʃən] *n* promotie *c*

prompt [prɔmpt] *adj* onmiddellijk, prompt

pronoun ['prounaun] *n* voornaamwoord *nt*

pronounce [prə'nauns] *v* *uitspreken

pronunciation [ˌprənʌnsiˈeiʃən] *n*
uitspraak *c*

proof [pru:f] *n* bewijs *nt*

propaganda [ˌprɔpəˈgændə] *n*
propaganda *c*

propel [prəˈpel] *v* *aandrijven

propeller [prəˈpelə] *n* schroef *c*,
propeller *c*

proper [ˈprɔpə] *adj* juist; behoorlijk,
passend, geschikt, gepast

property [ˈprɔpəti] *n* bezit *nt*,
eigendom *nt*; eigenschap *c*

prophet [ˈprɔfit] *n* profeet *m*

proportion [prəˈpɔːʃən] *n* proportie *c*

proportional [prəˈpɔːʃənəl] *adj*
evenredig

proposal [prəˈpouzəl] *n* voorstel *nt*

propose [prəˈpouz] *v* voorstellen

proposition [ˌprɔpəˈziʃən] *n* voorstel
nt

proprietor [prəˈpraiətə] *n* eigenaar *m*,
eigenares *f*

prospect [ˈprɔspekt] *n* vooruitzicht *nt*

prospectus [prəˈspektəs] *n*
prospectus *c*

prosperity [prɔˈsperəti] *n* voorspoed *c*,
welvaart *c*

prosperous [ˈprɔspərəs] *adj*
welvarend

prostitute [ˈprɔstitjuːt] *n* prostituée *f*

protect [prəˈtekt] *v* beschermen

protection [prəˈtekʃən] *n*
bescherming *c*

protein [ˈproutiːn] *n* eiwit *nt*

protest[1] [ˈproutest] *n* protest *nt*

protest[2] [prəˈtest] *v* protesteren

Protestant [ˈprɔtistənt] *adj*
protestants

proud [praud] *adj* trots; hoogmoedig

prove [pruːv] *v* aantonen, *bewijzen;
*blijken

proverb [ˈprɔvəːb] *n* spreekwoord *nt*

provide [prəˈvaid] *v* leveren,
verschaffen; **provided that** mits

province [ˈprɔvins] *n* provincie *c*;
gewest *nt*

provincial [prəˈvinʃəl] *adj* provinciaal

provisional [prəˈviʒənəl] *adj*
voorlopig

provisions [prəˈviʒənz] *pl* voorraad *c*

prune [pruːn] *n* pruim *c*

psychiatrist [saiˈkaiətrist] *n*
psychiater *m*

psychic [ˈsaikik] *adj* helderziend;
psychisch

psychoanalyst [ˌsaikouˈænəlist] *n*
analyticus *c*

psychological [ˌsaikəˈlɔdʒikəl] *adj*
psychologisch

psychologist [saiˈkɔlədʒist] *n*
psycholoog *m*

psychology [saiˈkɔlədʒi] *n*
psychologie *c*

pub [pʌb] *n* café *nt*; kroeg *c*

public [ˈpʌblik] *adj* publiek, openbaar;
algemeen; *n* publiek *nt*; ~ **garden**
plantsoen *nt*; ~ **house** café *nt*

publication [ˌpʌbliˈkeiʃən] *n*
publikatie *c*

publicity [pʌˈblisəti] *n* reclame *c*;
publiciteit *c*

publish [ˈpʌbliʃ] *v* publiceren,
*uitgeven

publisher [ˈpʌbliʃə] *n* uitgever *m*

puddle [ˈpʌdəl] *n* plas *c*

pull [pul] *v* *trekken; ~ **out**
*vertrekken; ~ **up** stoppen

pulley [ˈpuli] *n* (pl ~s) katrol *c*

Pullman [ˈpulmən] *n* slaaprijtuig *nt*

pullover [ˈpuˌlouvə] *n* pullover *c*

pulpit [ˈpulpit] *n* kansel *c*, preekstoel *c*

pulse [pʌls] *n* polsslag *c*, pols *c*

pump [pʌmp] *n* pomp *c*; *v* pompen

pun [pʌn] *n* woordspeling *c*

punch [pʌntʃ] *v* stompen; *n* vuistslag *c*

punctual [ˈpʌŋktʃuəl] *adj* stipt,
punctueel

puncture [ˈpʌŋktʃə] *n* lekke band,

bandepech *c*

punctured ['pʌŋktʃəd] *adj* lek

punish ['pʌniʃ] *v* straffen

punishment ['pʌniʃmənt] *n* straf *c*

pupil ['pju:pəl] *n* leerling *m*, -e *f*

puppet show ['pʌpitʃou] *n* poppenkast *c*

purchase ['pə:tʃəs] *v* *kopen; *n* aankoop *c*, koop *c*; ~ **price** koopprijs *c*; ~ **tax** omzetbelasting *c*

purchaser ['pə:tʃəsə] *n* koper *m*, koopster *f*

pure [pjuə] *adj* rein, zuiver

purple ['pə:pəl] *adj* paars

purpose ['pə:pəs] *n* bedoeling *c*, doel *nt*; **on** ~ opzettelijk

purse [pə:s] *n* beurs *c*, portemonnee *c*

pursue [pə'sju:] *v* vervolgen; nastreven

pus [pʌs] *n* etter *c*

push [puʃ] *n* zet *c*, duw *c*; *v* duwen; *schuiven; *dringen

push button ['puʃ,bʌtən] *n* drukknop *c*

***put** [put] *v* plaatsen, leggen, zetten; stoppen; stellen; ~ **away** *opbergen; ~ **off** opschorten; ~ **on** *aantrekken; ~ **out** *uitdoen

puzzle ['pʌzəl] *n* puzzel *c*; raadsel *nt*; *v* in verwarring *brengen; **jigsaw** ~ legpuzzel *c*

puzzling ['pʌzliŋ] *adj* onbegrijpelijk

pyjamas [pə'dʒɑ:məz] *pl* pyjama *c*

Q

quack [kwæk] *n* kwakzalver *m*, charlatan *m*

quail [kweil] *n* (pl ~, ~s) kwartel *c*

quaint [kweint] *adj* raar; ouderwets

qualification [,kwɔlifi'keiʃən] *n* bevoegdheid *c*; voorbehoud *nt*, restriktie *c*

qualified ['kwɔlifaid] *adj* gediplomeerd; bevoegd

qualify ['kwɔlifai] *v* geschikt *zijn

quality ['kwɔləti] *n* kwaliteit *c*; eigenschap *c*

quantity ['kwɔntəti] *n* hoeveelheid *c*; aantal *nt*

quarantine ['kwɔrəntiːn] *n* quarantaine *c*

quarrel ['kwɔrəl] *v* twisten, ruzie maken; *n* twist *c*, ruzie *c*

quarry ['kwɔri] *n* steengroeve *c*

quarter ['kwɔ:tə] *n* kwart *nt*; kwartaal *nt*; wijk *c*; ~ **of an hour** kwartier *nt*

quarterly ['kwɔ:təli] *adj* driemaandelijks

quay [ki:] *n* kade *c*

queen [kwi:n] *n* koningin *f*

queer [kwiə] *adj* zonderling, raar; vreemd

query ['kwiəri] *n* vraag *c*; *v* *navragen; betwijfelen

question ['kwestʃən] *n* vraag *c*; kwestie *c*, vraagstuk *nt*; *v* *vragen, *ondervragen; in twijfel *trekken; ~ **mark** vraagteken *nt*

queue [kju:] *n* rij *c*; *v* in de rij *staan

quick [kwik] *adj* vlug

quick-tempered [,kwik'tempəd] *adj* driftig

quiet ['kwaiət] *adj* stil, kalm, bedaard, rustig; *n* stilte *c*, rust *c*

quilt [kwilt] *n* sprei *c*

quit [kwit] *v* *ophouden met, *uitscheiden

quite [kwait] *adv* helemaal; tamelijk, vrij, nogal; zeer, heel
quiz [kwiz] *n* (pl ~zes) quiz *c*, kwis *c*
quota ['kwoutə] *n* quota *c*

quotation [kwou'teiʃən] *n* citaat *nt*; ~ **marks** aanhalingstekens *pl*
quote [kwout] *v* citeren, aanhalen

R

rabbit ['ræbit] *n* konijn *nt*
rabies ['reibiz] *n* hondsdolheid *c*
race [reis] *n* wedloop *c*, race *c*; ras *nt*
racecourse ['reiskɔːs] *n* renbaan *c*
racehorse ['reishɔːs] *n* renpaard *nt*
racetrack ['reistræk] *n* renbaan *c*
racial ['reiʃəl] *adj* rassen-
racket ['rækit] *n* kabaal *nt*, tumult *nt*; racket *nt*
radiator ['reidieitə] *n* radiator *c*
radical ['rædikəl] *adj* radicaal
radio ['reidiou] *n* radio *c*
radish ['rædiʃ] *n* radijs *c*
radius ['reidiəs] *n* (pl radii) straal *c*
raft [rɑːft] *n* vlot *nt*
rag [ræg] *n* vod *nt*
rage [reidʒ] *n* razernij *c*, woede *c*; *v* razen, woeden
raid [reid] *n* inval *c*
rail [reil] *n* leuning *c*, reling *c*
railing ['reiliŋ] *n* hek *nt*
railroad ['reilroud] *nAm* spoorbaan *c*, spoorweg *c*
railway ['reilwei] *n* spoorweg *c*, spoorbaan *c*
rain [rein] *n* regen *c*; *v* regenen
rainbow ['reinbou] *n* regenboog *c*
raincoat ['reinkout] *n* regenjas *c*
rainproof ['reinpruːf] *adj* waterdicht
rainy ['reini] *adj* regenachtig
raise [reiz] *v* optillen; verhogen; *grootbrengen, verbouwen, fokken; *heffen; *nAm* loonsverhoging *c*, opslag *c*

raisin ['reizən] *n* rozijn *c*
rake [reik] *n* hark *c*
rally ['ræli] *n* bijeenkomst *c*
ramp [ræmp] *n* glooiing *c*
ramshackle ['ræm,ʃækəl] *adj* gammel
rancid ['rænsid] *adj* ranzig
rang [ræŋ] *v* (p ring)
range [reindʒ] *n* bereik *nt*; ~ **finder** afstandsmeter *c*
rank [ræŋk] *n* rang *c*; rij *c*
ransom ['rænsəm] *n* losgeld *nt*
rape [reip] *v* verkrachten
rapid ['ræpid] *adj* vlug, snel
rapids ['ræpidz] *pl* stroomversnelling *c*
rare [rɛə] *adj* zeldzaam
rarely ['rɛəli] *adv* zelden
rascal ['rɑːskəl] *n* schelm *m*, deugniet *m*
rash [ræʃ] *n* uitslag *c*, huiduitslag *c*; *adj* overhaast, onbezonnen
raspberry ['rɑːzbəri] *n* framboos *c*
rat [ræt] *n* rat *c*
rate [reit] *n* prijs *c*, tarief *nt*; snelheid *c*; **at any ~** hoe dan ook, in elk geval; ~ **of exchange** wisselkoers *c*
rather ['rɑːðə] *adv* vrij, tamelijk, nogal; liever, eerder
ration ['ræʃən] *n* rantsoen *nt*
raven ['reivən] *n* raaf *c*
raw [rɔː] *adj* rauw; ~ **material** grondstof *c*
ray [rei] *n* straal *c*
rayon ['reiɔn] *n* kunstzijde *c*
razor ['reizə] *n* scheerapparaat *nt*; ~

blade scheermesje nt

reach [riːtʃ] v bereiken; n bereik nt

react [riˈækt] v reageren

reaction [riˈækʃən] n reactie c

*read [riːd] v *lezen

reading lamp [ˈriːdiŋlæmp] n leeslamp c

reading room [ˈriːdiruːm] n leeszaal c

ready [ˈredi] adj gereed, klaar

ready-made [ˌrediˈmeid] adj confectie-

real [riəl] adj echt

reality [riˈæləti] n werkelijkheid c

realizable [ˈriəlaizəbəl] adj haalbaar

realize [ˈriəlaiz] v beseffen; tot stand *brengen, verwezenlijken

really [ˈriəli] adv echt, werkelijk; eigenlijk

reap [riːp] v oogsten

rear [riə] n achterkant c; v *grootbrengen; ~ **light** achterlicht nt

reason [ˈriːzən] n oorzaak c, reden c; verstand nt, rede c; v redeneren

reasonable [ˈriːzənəbəl] adj redelijk; billijk

reassure [ˌriːəˈʃuə] v geruststellen

rebate [ˈriːbeit] n korting c, reductie c

rebellion [riˈbeljən] n opstand c, oproer nt

recall [riˈkɔːl] v zich herinneren; *terugroepen; *herroepen

receipt [riˈsiːt] n kwitantie c, reçu nt; ontvangst c

receive [riˈsiːv] v *krijgen, *ontvangen

receiver [riˈsiːvə] n telefoonhoorn c

recent [ˈriːsənt] adj recent

recently [ˈriːsəntli] adv kort geleden, onlangs

reception [riˈsepʃən] n ontvangst c; onthaal nt; ~ **office** receptie c

receptionist [riˈsepʃənist] n receptioniste f

recession [riˈseʃən] n teruggang c

recipe [ˈresipi] n recept nt

recital [riˈsaitəl] n recital nt

reckon [ˈrekən] v rekenen; beschouwen; *denken

recognition [ˌrekəgˈniʃən] n erkenning c

recognize [ˈrekəgnaiz] v herkennen; erkennen

recollect [ˌrekəˈlekt] v zich herinneren

recommence [ˌriːkəˈmens] v hervatten

recommend [ˌrekəˈmend] v *aanprijzen, *aanbevelen; *aanraden

recommendation [ˌrekəmenˈdeiʃən] n aanbeveling c

reconciliation [ˌrekənsiliˈeiʃən] n verzoening c

record¹ [ˈrekɔːd] n grammofoonplaat c; record nt; register nt; ~ **player** platenspeler c, pick-up c

record² [riˈkɔːd] v aantekenen

recorder [riˈkɔːdə] n bandrecorder c

recording [riˈkɔːdiŋ] n opname c

recover [riˈkʌvə] v *terugvinden; zich herstellen, *genezen

recovery [riˈkʌvəri] n genezing c, herstel nt

recreation [ˌrekriˈeiʃən] n recreatie c, ontspanning c; ~ **center** Am, ~ **centre** recreatiecentrum nt; ~ **ground** speelterrein nt

recruit [riˈkruːt] n rekruut m

rectangle [ˈrektæŋgəl] n rechthoek c

rectangular [rekˈtæŋgjulə] adj rechthoekig

rectum [ˈrektəm] n endeldarm c

recyclable [ˌriˈsaikləbəl] adj recycleerbar

recycle [ˌriˈsaikəl] v recycleren

red [red] adj rood

redeem [riˈdiːm] v verlossen

reduce [riˈdjuːs] v reduceren, verminderen, verlagen

reduction [riˈdʌkʃən] n korting c, reductie c

redundant [ri'dʌndənt] *adj* overbodig
reed [ri:d] *n* riet *nt*
reef [ri:f] *n* rif *nt*
referee [ˌrefə'ri:] *n* scheidsrechter *m*
reference ['refrəns] *n* referentie *c*,
verwijzing *c*; betrekking *c*; **with ~ to**
met betrekking tot
refer to [ri'fə:] *verwijzen naar
refill ['ri:fil] *n* vulling *c*
refinery [ri'fainəri] *n* raffinaderij *c*
reflect [ri'flekt] *v* weerkaatsen
reflection [ri'flekʃən] *n* weerkaatsing
c; spiegelbeeld *nt*
reflector [ri'flektə] *n* reflector *c*
reformation [ˌrefə'meiʃən] *n*
reformatie *c*
refresh [ri'freʃ] *v* verfrissen
refreshment [ri'freʃmənt] *n*
verfrissing *c*
refrigerator [ri'fridʒəreitə] *n* koelkast
c, ijskast *c*
refugee [ˌrefju'dʒi:] *n* vluchteling *m*,
-e *f*
refund¹ [ri'fʌnd] *v* terugbetalen
refund² ['ri:fʌnd] *n* terugbetaling *c*
refusal [ri'fju:zəl] *n* weigering *c*
refuse¹ [ri'fju:z] *v* weigeren
refuse² ['refju:s] *n* afval *nt*
regard [ri'ɡɑ:d] *v* beschouwen;
*bekijken; *n* respect *nt*; **as regards**
betreffende, aangaande, wat betreft;
kind regards met vriendelijke groet
regarding [ri'ɡɑ:diŋ] *prep* met
betrekking tot, betreffende; ten
aanzien van
regatta [ri'ɡætə] *n* regatta *c*
regime [rei'ʒi:m] *n* regime *c*
region ['ri:dʒən] *n* streek *c*; gebied *nt*
regional ['ri:dʒənəl] *adj* plaatselijk
register ['redʒistə] *v* zich *inschrijven;
aantekenen; **registered letter**
aangetekende brief
registration [ˌredʒi'streiʃən] *n*
registratie *c*; **~ form**

inschrijvingsformulier *nt*; **~ number**
kenteken *nt*; **~ plate** nummerbord *nt*
regret [ri'ɡret] *v* betreuren; *n* spijt *c*
regular ['reɡjulə] *adj* geregeld,
regelmatig; gewoon, normaal
regulate ['reɡjuleit] *v* regelen
regulation [ˌreɡju'leiʃən] *n* reglement
nt, voorschrift *nt*; regeling *c*
rehabilitation [ˌri:hə,bili'teiʃən] *n*
revalidatie *c*
rehearsal [ri'hə:səl] *n* repetitie *c*
rehearse [ri'hə:s] *v* repeteren
reign [rein] *n* regering *c*; *v* regeren
reimburse [ˌri:im'bə:s] *v*
terugbetalen, vergoeden
reindeer ['reindiə] *n* (pl ~) rendier *nt*
reject [ri'dʒekt] *v* *afwijzen,
*verwerpen; afkeuren
relate [ri'leit] *v* vertellen
related [ri'leitid] *adj* verwant
relation [ri'leiʃən] *n* relatie *c*, verband
nt; verwante *c*
relative ['relətiv] *n* familielid *nt*; *adj*
betrekkelijk, relatief
relax [ri'læks] *v* zich ontspannen
relaxation [ˌrilæk'seiʃən] *n*
ontspanning *c*
reliable [ri'laiəbəl] *adj* betrouwbaar
relic ['relik] *n* relikwie *c*
relief [ri'li:f] *n* verademing *c*,
verlichting *c*; steun *c*; reliëf *nt*
relieve [ri'li:v] *v* verlichten; aflossen
religion [ri'lidʒən] *n* godsdienst *c*
religious [ri'lidʒəs] *adj* godsdienstig
rely on [ri'lai] vertrouwen op
remain [ri'mein] *v* *blijven;
*overblijven
remainder [ri'meində] *n* restant *nt*, rest
c
remaining [ri'meiniŋ] *adj* overig,
overblijvend
remark [ri'mɑ:k] *n* opmerking *c*; *v*
opmerken
remarkable [ri'mɑ:kəbəl] *adj*

opmerkelijk

remedy ['remədi] n geneesmiddel nt; middel nt

remember [ri'membə] v zich herinneren; *onthouden

remembrance [ri'membrəns] n aandenken nt, herinnering c

remind [ri'maind] v herinneren

remit [ri'mit] v overmaken

remittance [ri'mitəns] n storting c

remnant ['remnənt] n overblijfsel nt, restant nt, rest c

remote [ri'mout] adj afgelegen, ver

removal [ri'mu:vəl] n verwijdering c

remove [ri'mu:v] v verwijderen

remunerate [ri'mju:nəreit] v vergoeden

remuneration [ri,mju:nə'reiʃən] n vergoeding c

renew [ri'nju:] v vernieuwen; verlengen

renovate ['renoveit] v verbouwen

rent [rent] v huren; n huur c

repair [ri'pɛə] v herstellen, repareren; n herstel nt

reparation [,repə'reiʃən] n reparatie c

***repay** [ri'pei] v terugbetalen

repayment [ri'peimənt] n terugbetaling c

repeat [ri'pi:t] v herhalen

repellent [ri'pelənt] adj weerzinwekkend, afstotelijk

repentance [ri'pentəns] n berouw nt

repertory ['repətəri] n repertoire nt

repetition [,repə'tiʃən] n herhaling c

replace [ri'pleis] v *vervangen

reply [ri'plai] v antwoorden; n antwoord nt; **in ~** als antwoord

report [ri'pɔ:t] v rapporteren; melden; zich aanmelden; n verslag nt, rapport nt

reporter [ri'pɔ:tə] n verslaggever m, reporter c

represent [,repri'zent] v vertegenwoordigen; voorstellen

representation [,reprizen'teiʃən] n vertegenwoordiging c

representative [,repri'zentətiv] adj representatief

reprimand ['reprimɑ:nd] v berispen

reproach [ri'proutʃ] n verwijt nt; v *verwijten

reproduce [,ri:prə'dju:s] v reproduceren

reproduction [,ri:prə'dʌkʃən] n reproductie c

reptile ['reptail] n reptiel nt

republic [ri'pʌblik] n republiek c

republican [ri'pʌblikən] adj republikeins

repulsive [ri'pʌlsiv] adj weerzinwekkend

reputation [,repju'teiʃən] n reputatie c; naam c

request [ri'kwest] n verzoek nt; v *verzoeken

require [ri'kwaiə] v vereisen

requirement [ri'kwaiəmənt] n vereiste c

requisite ['rekwizit] adj vereist

rescue ['reskju:] v redden; n redding c

research [ri'sə:tʃ] n onderzoek nt

resemblance [ri'zembləns] n gelijkenis c

resemble [ri'zembəl] v *lijken op

resent [ri'zent] v kwalijk *nemen

reservation [,rezə'veiʃən] n reservering c

reserve [ri'zə:v] v reserveren; *bespreken; n reserve c

reserved [ri'zə:vd] adj terughoudend; gereserveerd

reservoir ['rezəvwɑ:] n reservoir nt

reside [ri'zaid] v wonen

residence ['rezidəns] n woonplaats c; **~ permit** verblijfsvergunning c

resident ['rezidənt] n inwoner m, inwoonster f; adj woonachtig; intern

resign [ri'zain] v ontslag *nemen

resignation [,rezig'neiʃən] n ontslagneming c

resin ['rezin] n hars nt/c

resist [ri'zist] v zich verzetten

resistance [ri'zistəns] n verzet nt

resolute ['rezəluːt] adj resoluut, vastberaden

respect [ri'spekt] n respect nt; ontzag nt, achting c, eerbied c; opzicht nt; v respecteren

respectable [ri'spektəbəl] adj eerzaam, respectabel

respectful [ri'spektfəl] adj eerbiedig

respective [ri'spektiv] adj respectievelijk

respiration [,respə'reiʃən] n ademhaling c

respite ['respait] n uitstel nt

respond [ri,spɔnd] v reageren

responsibility [ri,spɔnsə'biləti] n verantwoordelijkheid c; aansprakelijkheid c

responsible [ri'spɔnsəbəl] adj verantwoordelijk; aansprakelijk

rest [rest] n rust c; rest c; v uitrusten, rusten

restaurant ['restərɔː] n restaurant nt

restful ['restfəl] adj rustig

rest home ['resthoum] n rusthuis nt

restless ['restləs] adj onrustig; ongedurig

restrain [ri'strein] v *inhouden, *weerhouden

restriction [ri'strikʃən] n beperking c

rest room ['restruːm] nAm toilet nt

result [ri'zʌlt] n resultaat nt; gevolg nt; uitslag c; v resulteren

resume [ri'zjuːm] v hervatten

résumé ['rezjumei] n samenvatting c

retail ['riːteil] v in het klein *verkopen; ~ trade kleinhandel c, detailhandel c

retailer ['riːteilə] n detaillist m, kleinhandelaar m; wederverkoper m

retina ['retinə] n netvlies nt

retire [ri'taiə] v met pensioen gaan; zich terugtrekken

retired [ri'taiəd] adj gepensioneerd

retirement [ri'taiəmənt] n pensionering c

rid [rid] v: ~ of bevrijden van; get ~ of kwijtraken

return [ri'təːn] v *terugkomen, terugkeren; n terugkeer c; ~ flight retourvlucht c; ~ journey terugreis c

reunite [,riːjuː'nait] v herenigen

reveal [ri'viːl] v openbaren, onthullen

revelation [,revə'leiʃən] n onthulling c

revenge [ri'vendʒ] n wraak c

revenue ['revənjuː] n inkomen nt

reverse [ri'vəːs] n tegendeel nt; keerzijde c; omkeer c; tegenslag c; adj omgekeerd; v *achteruitrijden

review [ri'vjuː] n bespreking c; tijdschrift nt

revise [ri'vaiz] v *herzien

revision [ri'viʒən] n herziening c

revival [ri'vaivəl] n herstel nt

revolt [ri'voult] v in opstand *komen; n opstand c, oproer nt

revolting [ri'voultiŋ] adj walgelijk, stuitend, weerzinwekkend

revolution [,revə'luːʃən] n revolutie c; omwenteling c

revolutionary [,revə'luːʃənəri] adj revolutionair

revolver [ri'vɔlvə] n revolver c

revue [ri'vjuː] n revue c

reward [ri'wɔːd] n beloning c; v belonen

rheumatism ['ruːmətizəm] n reumatiek c

rhinoceros [rai'nɔsərəs] n (pl ~, ~es) neushoorn c

rhubarb ['ruːbɑːb] n rabarber c

rhyme [raim] n rijm nt

rhythm ['riðəm] n ritme nt

rib [rib] n rib c

ribbon ['ribən] n lint nt

rice [rais] n rijst c

rich [ritʃ] adj rijk

riches ['ritʃiz] pl rijkdom c

riddle ['ridəl] n raadsel nt

ride [raid] n rit c

*ride [raid] v *rijden; *paardrijden

rider ['raidə] n ruiter m

ridge [ridʒ] n bergrug c

ridicule ['ridikju:l] v bespotten

ridiculous [ri'dikjuləs] adj bespottelijk, belachelijk

riding ['raidiŋ] n paardesport c; ~ **school** manege c

rifle ['raifəl] v geweer nt

right [rait] n recht nt; adj goed, juist; recht; rechts; billijk, rechtvaardig; *be ~ gelijk *hebben; ~ **of way** voorrang c; **all right!** in orde!

righteous ['raitʃəs] adj rechtvaardig

right-hand ['raithænd] adj rechter, rechts

rightly ['raitli] adv terecht

rim [rim] n velg c; rand c

ring [riŋ] n ring c; kring c; piste c

*ring [riŋ] v bellen; ~ **up** opbellen

rinse [rins] v spoelen; n spoeling c

riot ['raiət] n rel c

rip [rip] v scheuren

ripe [raip] adj rijp

rise [raiz] n opslag c, verhoging c; stijging c; opkomst c

*rise [raiz] v *opstaan; *opgaan; *stijgen

rising ['raiziŋ] n opstand c

risk [risk] n risico nt; gevaar nt; v wagen

risky ['riski] adj gewaagd, riskant

rival ['raivəl] n rivaal m, rivale f; concurrent m, -e f; v rivaliseren

rivalry ['raivəlri] n rivaliteit c; concurrentie c

river ['rivə] n rivier c; ~ **bank** oever c

riverside ['rivəsaid] n rivieroever c

roach [routʃ] n (pl ~) blankvoorn c

road [roud] n straat c, weg c; ~ **fork** n tweesprong c; ~ **map** wegenkaart c; ~ **system** wegennet nt; ~ **up** werk in uitvoering

roadhouse ['roudhaus] n wegrestaurant nt

roadside ['roudsaid] n wegkant c; ~ **restaurant** wegrestaurant nt

roadway ['roudwei] nAm rijbaan c

roam [roum] v *zwerven

roar [rɔ:] v loeien, brullen; n gebrul nt, geraas nt

roast [roust] v *braden, roosteren

rob [rɔb] v beroven

robber ['rɔbə] n dief m

robbery ['rɔbəri] n roof c, diefstal c, beroving c

robe [roub] n jurk c; gewaad c

robin ['rɔbin] n roodborstje nt

robust [rou'bʌst] adj fors

rock [rɔk] n rots c; v schommelen

rocket ['rɔkit] n raket c

rock-'n-roll [,rɔkən'roul] n rock en roll c

rocky ['rɔki] adj rotsachtig

rod [rɔd] n stang c, roede c

roe [rou] n kuit c, viskuit c

roll [roul] v rollen; n rol c; broodje nt

Roman Catholic ['roumən 'kæθəlik] rooms-katholiek

romance [rə'mæns] n romance c

romantic [rə'mæntik] adj romantisch

roof [ru:f] n dak nt; **thatched** ~ strodak nt

room [ru:m] n vertrek nt, kamer c; ruimte c, plaats c; ~ **and board** kost en inwoning; ~ **service** bediening op de kamer; ~ **temperature** kamertemperatuur c

roomy ['ru:mi] adj ruim

root [ru:t] n wortel c

rope [roup] n touw nt

rosary ['rouzəri] n rozenkrans c

rose [rouz] n roos c; adj roze

rotten ['rɔtən] *adj* rot
rouge [ru:ʒ] *n* rouge *c/nt*
rough [rʌf] *adj* ruw
roulette [ru:'let] *n* roulette *c*
round [raund] *adj* rond; *prep* rondom, om; *n* ronde *c*; ~ **trip** *Am* retour
roundabout ['raundəbaut] *n* rotonde *c*
rounded ['raundid] *adj* afgerond
route [ru:t] *n* route *c*
routine [ru:'ti:n] *n* routine *c*
row[1] [rou] *n* rij *c*; *v* roeien
row[2] [rau] *n* ruzie *c*
rowdy ['raudi] *adj* baldadig
rowing boat ['rouiŋbout] *n* roeiboot *c*
royal ['rɔiəl] *adj* koninklijk
rub [rʌb] *v* *wrijven
rubber ['rʌbə] *n* rubber *nt*; vlakgom *c/nt*; ~ **band** elastiek *nt*
rubbish ['rʌbiʃ] *n* afval *nt*; geklets *nt*, onzin *c*; **talk** ~ uit je nek kletsen; ~ **bin** vuilnisbak *c*
ruby ['ru:bi] *n* robijn *c*
rucksack ['rʌksæk] *n* rugzak *c*
rudder ['rʌdə] *n* roer *nt*
rude [ru:d] *adj* grof
rug [rʌg] *n* kleedje *nt*
ruin ['ru:in] *v* ruïneren; *n* ondergang *c*;

ruins *pl* ruïne *c*
rule [ru:l] *n* regel *c*; bewind *nt*, bestuur *nt*, heerschappij *c*; *v* heersen, regeren; **as a** ~ gewoonlijk, in de regel
ruler ['ru:lə] *n* vorst *m*, -in *f*, heerser *m*, -es *f*; liniaal *c*
Rumania [ru:'meiniə] Roemenië
Rumanian [ru:'meiniən] *adj* Roemeens; *n* Roemeen *m*, -se *f*
rumour ['ru:mə] *n* gerucht *nt*
***run** [rʌn] *v* rennen; ~ **into** *tegenkomen
runaway ['rʌnəwei] *n* ontsnapte gevangene
rung [rʌn] *v* (pp ring)
runner ['rʌnə] *n* loper *m*, loopster *f*
runway ['rʌnwei] *n* startbaan *c*
rural ['ruərəl] *adj* plattelands-
rush [rʌʃ] *v* zich haasten; *n* bies *c*
rush hour ['rʌʃauə] *n* spitsuur *nt*
Russia ['rʌʃə] Rusland
Russian ['rʌʃən] *adj* Russisch; *n* Rus *m*, Russin *f*
rust [rʌst] *n* roest *nt*
rustic ['rʌstik] *adj* rustiek
rusty ['rʌsti] *adj* roestig

S

sack [sæk] *n* zak *c*
sacred ['seikrid] *adj* heilig
sacrifice ['sækrifais] *n* offer *nt*; *v* opofferen
sacrilege ['sækrilidʒ] *n* heiligschennis *c*
sad [sæd] *adj* bedroefd; verdrietig, droevig, treurig
saddle ['sædəl] *n* zadel *nt*
sadness ['sædnəs] *n* bedroefdheid *c*
safe [seif] *adj* veilig; *n* brandkast *c*,

kluis *c*
safety ['seifti] *n* veiligheid *c*; ~ **belt** veiligheidsgordel *c*; ~ **pin** veiligheidsspeld *c*; ~ **razor** scheerapparaat *nt*
sail [seil] *v* *bevaren, *varen; *n* zeil *nt*
sailing boat ['seiliŋbout] *n* zeilboot *c*
sailor ['seilə] *n* matroos *m*
saint [seint] *n* heilige *c*
salad ['sæləd] *n* sla *c*
salad oil ['sælədɔil] *n* slaolie *c*

salary ['sæləri] n loon nt, salaris nt

sale [seil] n verkoop c; **clearance ~** opruiming c; **for ~** te koop; **sales** pl uitverkoop c; **sales tax** omzetbelasting c

saleable ['seiləbəl] adj verkoopbaar

salesgirl ['seilzgə:l] n verkoopster f

salesman ['seilzmən] n (pl -men) verkoper m

salmon ['sæmən] n (pl ~) zalm c

salon ['sælõ:] n salon c

saloon [sə'lu:n] n bar c

salt [sɔ:lt] n zout nt; **~ cellar**, nAm **~ shaker** n zoutvaatje nt

salty ['sɔ:lti] adj zout

salute [sə'lu:t] v groeten

salve [sɑ:v] n zalf c

same [seim] adj zelfde

sample ['sɑ:mpəl] n monster nt

sanatorium [,sænə'tɔ:riəm] n (pl ~s, -ria) sanatorium nt

sand [sænd] n zand nt

sandal ['sændəl] n sandaal c

sandpaper ['sænd,peipə] n schuurpapier nt

sandwich ['sænwidʒ] n boterham c

sandy ['sændi] adj zanderig

sanitary ['sænitəri] adj sanitair; **~ towel** maandverband nt

sapphire ['sæfaiə] n saffier nt

sardine [sɑ:'di:n] n sardine c

satchel ['sætʃəl] n schooltas c

satellite ['sætəlait] n satelliet c

satin ['sætin] n satijn nt

satisfaction [,sætis'fækʃən] n bevrediging c, voldoening c

satisfactory [,sætis'fæktəri] adj bevredigend, tevredenstellend

satisfy ['sætisfai] v bevredigen; **satisfied** voldaan, tevreden

Saturday ['sætədi] zaterdag c

sauce [sɔ:s] n saus c

saucepan ['sɔ:spən] n steelpan c

saucer ['sɔ:sə] n schoteltje nt

Saudi Arabia [,saudiə'reibiə] Saoedi-Arabië

Saudi Arabian [,saudiə'reibiən] adj Saoedi-Arabisch

sauna ['sɔ:nə] n sauna c

sausage ['sɔsidʒ] n worst c

savage ['sævidʒ] adj wild

save [seiv] v redden; sparen

savings ['seiviŋz] pl spaargeld nt; **~ bank** spaarbank c

saviour ['seivjə] n redder m

savo(u)ry ['seivəri] adj smakelijk; pikant

saw¹ [sɔ:] v (p see)

saw² [sɔ:] n zaag c

sawdust ['sɔ:dʌst] n zaagsel nt

sawmill ['sɔ:mil] n houtzagerij c

***say** [sei] v *zeggen

scaffolding ['skæfəldiŋ] n steigers pl

scale [skeil] n schaal c; toonladder c; schub c; **scales** pl weegschaal c

scandal ['skændəl] n schandaal nt

Scandinavia [,skændi'neiviə] Scandinavië

Scandinavian [,skændi'neiviən] adj Scandinavisch; n Scandinaviër m, Scandinavische f

scapegoat ['skeipgout] n zondebok c

scar [skɑ:] n litteken nt

scarce [skeəs] adj schaars

scarcely ['skeəsli] adv nauwelijks

scarcity ['skeəsəti] n schaarste c

scare [skeə] v *doen schrikken; n schrik c

scarf [skɑ:f] n (pl ~s, scarves) das c, sjaal c

scarlet ['skɑ:lət] adj vuurrood

scary ['skeəri] adj griezelig

scatter ['skætə] v verspreiden

scene [si:n] n scène c

scenery ['si:nəri] n landschap nt

scenic ['si:nik] adj schilderachtig

scent [sent] n geur c

schedule ['ʃedju:l] n dienstregeling c,

scheme 298

rooster *nt*

scheme [ski:m] *n* schema *nt*; plan *nt*

scholar ['skɔlə] *n* geleerde *c*; leerling *m*, -e *f*

scholarship ['skɔləʃip] *n* studiebeurs *c*

school [sku:l] *n* school *c*

schoolboy ['sku:lbɔi] *n* schooljongen *m*

schoolgirl ['sku:lgə:l] *n* schoolmeisje *nt*

schoolmaster ['sku:l,mɑ:stə] *n* onderwijzer *m*, meester *m*

schoolteacher ['sku:l,ti:tʃə] *n* onderwijzer *m*, -es *f*

science ['saiəns] *n* wetenschap *c*

scientific [,saiən'tifik] *adj* wetenschappelijk

scientist ['saiəntist] *n* geleerde *c*

scissors ['sizəz] *pl* schaar *c*

scold [skould] *v* berispen; *schelden

scooter ['sku:tə] *n* scooter *c*; autoped *c*

score [skɔ:] *n* stand *c*; *v* scoren

scorn [skɔ:n] *n* hoon *c*, verachting *c*; *v* verachten

Scot [skɔt] *n* Schot *m*, -se *f*

Scotch [skɔtʃ] *adj* Schots; **scotch tape®** plakband *nt*

Scotland ['skɔtlənd] Schotland

Scottish ['skɔtiʃ] *adj* Schots

scout [skaut] *n* padvinder *m*, padvindster *f*

scrap [skræp] *n* snipper *c*

scrapbook ['skræpbuk] *n* plakboek *nt*

scrape [skreip] *v* schrappen

scratch [skrætʃ] *v* krassen, krabben; *n* kras *c*, schram *c*

scream [skri:m] *v* gillen, schreeuwen; *n* gil *c*, schreeuw *c*

screen [skri:n] *n* scherm *nt*; beeldscherm *nt*

screw [skru:] *n* schroef *c*; *v* schroeven

screwdriver ['skru:,draivə] *n* schroevendraaier

scrub [skrʌb] *v* schrobben; *n* struik *c*

sculptor ['skʌlptə] *n* beeldhouwer *c*

sculpture ['skʌlptʃə] *n* beeldhouwwerk *nt*

sea [si:] *n* zee *c*; ~ **urchin** zeeëgel *c*; ~ **water** zeewater *nt*

seabird ['si:bə:d] *n* zeevogel *c*

seacoast ['si:koust] *n* zeekust *c*

seagull ['si:gʌl] *n* meeuw *c*, zeemeeuw *c*

seal [si:l] *n* zegel *nt*; rob *c*, zeehond *c*

seam [si:m] *n* naad *c*

seaman ['si:mən] *n* (pl -men) zeeman *m*

seamless ['si:mləs] *adj* naadloos

seaport ['si:pɔ:t] *n* zeehaven *c*

search [sə:tʃ] *v* *zoeken; fouilleren, *doorzoeken

searchlight ['sə:tʃlait] *n* schijnwerper *c*

seascape ['si:skeip] *n* zeegezicht *nt*

seashell ['si:ʃel] *n* zeeschelp *c*

seashore ['si:ʃɔ:] *n* kust *c*

seasick ['si:sik] *adj* zeeziek

seasickness ['si:,siknəs] *n* zeeziekte *c*

seaside ['si:said] *n* kust *c*; ~ **resort** badplaats *c*

season ['si:zən] *n* jaargetijde *nt*, seizoen *nt*; **high** ~ hoogseizoen *nt*; **low** ~ naseizoen *nt*; **off** ~ buiten het seizoen; ~ **ticket** abonnementskaart *c*

seat [si:t] *n* stoel *c*; plaats *c*, zitplaats *c*; zetel *c*; ~ **belt** veiligheidsgordel *c*

second ['sekənd] *num* tweede; *n* seconde *c*; tel *c*

secondary ['sekəndəri] *adj* secundair, ondergeschikt; ~ **school** middelbare school

second-hand [,sekənd'hænd] *adj* tweedehands

secret ['si:krət] *n* geheim *nt*; *adj* geheim

secretary ['sekrətri] secretaris *m*, secretaresse *f*

section ['sekʃən] n sectie c; afdeling c,
vak nt
secure [si'kjuə] adj veilig; v
bemachtigen
security [si'kjuərəti] n veiligheid c;
pand nt
sedative ['sedətiv] n kalmerend
middel
seduce [si'dju:s] v verleiden
***see** [si:] v *zien; *begrijpen, *inzien; ~
to zorgen voor
seed [si:d] n zaad nt
***seek** [si:k] v *zoeken
seem [si:m] v *lijken, *schijnen
seen [si:n] v (pp see)
seesaw ['si:sɔ:] n wip c
seize [si:z] v *grijpen
seldom ['seldəm] adv zelden
select [si'lekt] v selecteren,
*uitkiezen; adj select, uitgelezen
selection [si'lekʃən] n keuze c, selectie
c
self [self] zelf; zichzelf; ik
self-centered Am, **self-centred**
[,self'sentəd] adj egocentrisch
self-employed [,selfim'plɔid] adj
zelfstandig
self-evident [,sel'fevidənt] adj
vanzelfsprekend
self-government [,self'gʌvəmənt] n
zelfbestuur c
selfish ['selfiʃ] adj egoïstisch
selfishness ['selfiʃnəs] n egoïsme nt
self-service [,self'sə:vis] n
zelfbediening c; ~ **restaurant**
zelfbedieningsrestaurant nt
***sell** [sel] v *verkopen
semblance ['sembləns] n schijn c
semi- ['semi] half
semicircle ['semi,sə:kəl] n halve
cirkel
semicolon [,semi'koulən] n
puntkomma c
senate ['senət] n senaat c

senator ['senətə] n senator m
***send** [send] v sturen, *zenden; ~ **back**
terugsturen, *terugzenden; ~ **for**
*laten halen; ~ **off** versturen
sender ['sendə] n afzender m,
afzendster f
senile ['si:nail] adj seniel
sensation [sen'seiʃən] n sensatie c;
gewaarwording c, gevoel nt
sensational [sen'seiʃənəl] adj
sensationeel, opzienbarend
sense [sens] n zintuig nt; gezond
verstand, rede c; zin c, betekenis c; v
voelen; ~ **of honour** eergevoel nt
senseless ['sensləs] adj zinloos
sensible ['sensəbəl] adj verstandig
sensitive ['sensitiv] adj gevoelig
sentence ['sentəns] n zin c; vonnis nt; v
veroordelen
sentimental [,senti'mentəl] adj
sentimenteel
separate¹ ['sepəreit] v *scheiden
separate² ['sepərət] adj afzonderlijk,
gescheiden
separately ['sepərətli] adv apart
September [sep'tembə] september
septic ['septik] adj septisch; *become
~ *ontsteken
sequel ['si:kwəl] n vervolg nt
sequence ['si:kwəns] n volgorde c;
reeks c
serene [sə'ri:n] adj kalm; helder
serial ['siəriəl] n feuilleton nt
series ['siəri:z] n (pl ~) reeks c, serie c
serious ['siəriəs] adj serieus, ernstig
seriousness ['siəriəsnəs] n ernst c
sermon ['sə:mən] n preek c
serum ['siərəm] n serum nt
servant ['sə:vənt] n bediende c
serve [sə:v] v bedienen
service ['sə:vis] n dienst c; bediening c;
~ **charge** bedieningsgeld nt; ~ **station**
benzinestation nt
serviette [,sə:vi'et] n servet nt

session ['seʃən] n zitting c

set [set] n stel nt, groep c

*set [set] v zetten; ~ **menu** vast menu; ~ **out** *vertrekken

setting ['setiŋ] n omgeving c; ~ **lotion** haarversteviger c

settle ['setəl] v afhandelen, regelen; ~ **down** zich vestigen

settlement ['setəlmənt] n regeling c, schikking c, overeenkomst c

seven ['sevən] num zeven

seventeen [,sevən'ti:n] num zeventien

seventeenth [,sevən'ti:nθ] num zeventiende

seventh ['sevənθ] num zevende

seventy ['sevənti] num zeventig

several ['sevərəl] adj ettelijk, verscheidene

severe [si'viə] adj hevig, streng, ernstig

sew [sou] v naaien; ~ **up** hechten

sewer ['su:ə] n riool nt

sewing machine ['souiŋmə,ʃi:n] n naaimachine c

sex [seks] n geslacht nt; sex c

sexual ['sekʃuəl] adj seksueel

sexuality [,sekʃu'æləti] n seksualiteit c

shade [ʃeid] n schaduw c; tint c

shadow ['ʃædou] n schaduw c

shady ['ʃeidi] adj schaduwrijk

*shake [ʃeik] v schudden

shaky ['ʃeiki] adj gammel

*shall [ʃæl] v *zullen; *moeten

shallow ['ʃælou] adj ondiep

shambles ['ʃæmbəls] n janboel c

shame [ʃeim] n schaamte c; schande c; **shame!** foei!

shampoo [ʃæm'pu:] n shampoo c

shamrock ['ʃæmrɔk] n klaver c

shape [ʃeip] n vorm c; v vormen

share [ʃɛə] v delen; n deel nt; aandeel nt

shark [ʃɑ:k] n haai c

sharp [ʃɑ:p] adj scherp

sharpen ['ʃɑ:pən] v *slijpen

shave [ʃeiv] v zich *scheren

shaver ['ʃeivə] n scheerapparaat nt

shaving brush ['ʃeivinbrʌʃ] n scheerkwast c

shaving cream ['ʃeivinkri:m] n scheercrème c

shaving soap ['ʃeivinsoup] n scheerzeep c

shawl [ʃɔ:l] n omslagdoek c, sjaal c

she [ʃi:] pron ze

shed [ʃed] n schuur c

*shed [ʃed] v storten; verspreiden; ruien

sheep [ʃi:p] n (pl ~) schaap nt

sheer [ʃiə] adj absoluut, puur; dun, doorzichtig

sheet [ʃi:t] n laken nt; blad nt; plaat c

shelf [ʃelf] n (pl shelves) plank c

shell [ʃel] n schelp c; dop c

shellfish ['ʃelfiʃ] n schaaldier nt

shelter ['ʃeltə] n beschutting c, schuilplaats c; v beschutten

shepherd ['ʃepəd] n herder m, -in f

shift [ʃift] n ploeg c

*shine [ʃain] v *schijnen; glanzen, *blinken

ship [ʃip] n schip nt; v verschepen; **shipping line** scheepvaartlijn c

shipment ['ʃipmənt] n zending c

shipowner ['ʃi,pounə] n reder m

shipyard ['ʃipjɑ:d] n scheepswerf c

shirt [ʃə:t] n hemd nt, overhemd nt

shiver ['ʃivə] v bibberen, rillen; n rilling c

shock [ʃɔk] n schok c; v schokken; ~ **absorber** schokbreker c

shocking ['ʃɔkiŋ] adj schokkend

shoe [ʃu:] n schoen c; ~ **polish** schoensmeer c; ~ **shop** schoenwinkel c; **gym shoes** gymschoenen pl

shoelace ['ʃu:leis] n schoenveter c

shoemaker ['ʃu:,meikə] n schoenmaker m

shook [ʃuk] v (p shake)

*shoot [ʃuːt] v *schieten

shop [ʃɔp] n winkel c; v winkelen; ~ **assistant** verkoper c; **shopping bag** boodschappentas c; **shopping centre** winkelcentrum nt

shopkeeper ['ʃɔp,kiːpə] n winkelier m, -ster f

shopwindow [,ʃɔp'windou] n etalage c

shore [ʃɔː] n oever c, kust c

short [ʃɔːt] adj kort; klein; ~ **circuit** kortsluiting c

shortage ['ʃɔːtidʒ] n tekort nt, gebrek nt

shorten ['ʃɔːtən] v verkorten

shorthand ['ʃɔːthænd] n stenografie c

shortly ['ʃɔːtli] adv weldra, binnenkort, spoedig

shorts [ʃɔːts] pl korte broek; plAm onderbroek c

short-sighted [,ʃɔːt'saitid] adj bijziend

shot [ʃɔt] n schot nt, worp c; injectie c; opname c

*should [ʃud] v *moeten

shoulder ['ʃouldə] n schouder c

shout [ʃaut] v schreeuwen, *roepen; n schreeuw c

shovel ['ʃʌvəl] n schop c

show [ʃou] n voorstelling c; tentoonstelling c

*show [ʃou] v tonen; *laten zien, tentoonstellen; aantonen

showcase ['ʃoukeis] n vitrine c

shower [ʃauə] n douche c; bui c, regenbui c

showroom ['ʃouruːm] n toonzaal c

shriek [ʃriːk] v gillen; n gil c

shrimp [ʃrimp] n garnaal c

shrine [ʃrain] n heiligdom nt, schrijn c

*shrink [ʃriŋk] v *krimpen

shrinkproof ['ʃriŋkpruːf] adj krimpvrij

shrub [ʃrʌb] n struik c

shudder ['ʃʌdə] n rilling c

shuffle ['ʃʌfəl] v schudden

*shut [ʃʌt] v *sluiten; ~ **in** *insluiten

shut [ʃʌt] adj dicht, gesloten

shutter ['ʃʌtə] n luik nt, blind nt

shy [ʃai] adj schuw, verlegen

shyness ['ʃainəs] n verlegenheid c

Siamese [,saiə'miːz] adj Siamees

sick [sik] adj ziek; misselijk

sickness ['siknəs] n ziekte c; misselijkheid c

side [said] n kant c, zijde c; partij c; **one-sided** adj eenzijdig

sideburns ['saidbəːnz] pl bakkebaarden pl

sidelight ['saidlait] n zijlicht nt

side street ['saidstriːt] n zijstraat c

sidewalk ['saidwɔːk] nAm stoep c, trottoir nt

sideways ['saidweiz] adv opzij

siege [siːdʒ] n belegering c

sieve [siv] n zeef c; v zeven

sift [sift] v zeven

sight [sait] n zicht nt; gezicht nt, aanblik c; bezienswaardigheid c

sign [sain] n teken nt; gebaar nt, wenk c; v ondertekenen, tekenen

signal ['signəl] n signaal nt; sein nt, teken nt; v seinen

signature ['signətʃə] n handtekening c

significant [sig'nifikənt] adj veelbetekenend

signpost ['sainpoust] n wegwijzer c

silence ['sailəns] n stilte c; v tot zwijgen *brengen

silencer ['sailənsə] n knalpot c

silent ['sailənt] adj zwijgend, stil; ***be ~** *zwijgen

silk [silk] n zijde c

silly ['sili] adj mal, dwaas

silver ['silvə] n zilver nt; zilveren

silversmith ['silvəsmiθ] n zilversmid m

silverware ['silvəwɛə] *n* zilverwerk *nt*

similar ['similə] *adj* dergelijk, overeenkomstig

similarity [,simi'lærəti] *n* gelijkenis *c*

simple ['simpəl] *adj* simpel, eenvoudig; gewoon

simply ['simpli] *adv* eenvoudig, gewoonweg

simulate ['simjuleit] *v* huichelen

simultaneous [,siməl'teiniəs] *adj* gelijktijdig; **simultaneously** *adv* tegelijkertijd

sin [sin] *n* zonde *c*

since [sins] *prep* sedert; *adv* sindsdien; *conj* sinds; aangezien

sincere [sin'siə] *adj* oprecht, eerlijk; **yours sincerely** hoogachtend

sinew ['sinju:] *n* pees *c*

***sing** [siŋ] *v* *zingen

singer ['siŋə] *n* zanger *m*, -es *f*

single ['siŋgəl] *adj* enkel; ongetrouwd

singular ['siŋgjulə] *n* enkelvoud *nt*; *adj* eigenaardig

sinister ['sinistə] *adj* onheilspellend

sink [siŋk] *n* gootsteen *c*

***sink** [siŋk] *v* *zinken

sip [sip] *n* slokje *nt*

sir [sə:] meneer

siren ['saiərən] *n* sirene *c*

sister ['sistə] *n* zuster *f*, zus *f*

sister-in-law ['sistərinlɔ:] *n* (pl sisters-in-law) schoonzuster *f*

***sit** [sit] *v* *zitten; **~ down** *gaan zitten

site [sait] *n* plaats *c*; ligging *c*; terrein

sitting room ['sitiŋru:m] *n* zitkamer *c*

situated ['sitʃueitid] *adj* gelegen

situation [,sitʃu'eiʃən] *n* situatie *c*; ligging *c*

six [siks] *num* zes

sixteen [,siks'ti:n] *num* zestien

sixteenth [,siks'ti:nθ] *num* zestiende

sixth [siksθ] *num* zesde

sixty ['siksti] *num* zestig

size [saiz] *n* grootte *c*, maat *c*; afmeting *c*, omvang *c*; formaat *nt*

skate [skeit] *v* schaatsen; *n* schaats *c*

skating rink kunstijsbaan *c*, ijsbaan *c*

skeleton ['skelitən] *n* skelet *nt*, geraamte *nt*

sketch [sketʃ] *n* tekening *c*, schets *c*; *v* tekenen, schetsen

ski¹ [ski:] *v* skiën

ski² [ski:] *n* (pl ~, ~s) ski *c*; **~ boots** skischoenen *pl*; **~ lift** skilift *c*; **~ pants** skibroek *c*; **~ poles** *Am* skistokken *pl*; **~ sticks** skistokken *pl*

skid [skid] *v* slippen

skier ['ski:ə] *n* skiër *m*, skister *f*

skil(l)ful ['skilfəl] *adj* bekwaam, behendig, vaardig

skill [skil] *n* vaardigheid *c*

skilled [skild] *adj* vaardig, vakkundig

skin [skin] *n* vel *nt*, huid *c*; schil *c*; **~ cream** huidcrème *c*

skip [skip] *v* huppelen; *overslaan

skirt [skə:t] *n* rok *c*

skull [skʌl] *n* schedel *c*

sky [skai] *n* hemel *c*; lucht *c*

skyscraper ['skai,skreipə] *n* wolkenkrabber *c*

slack [slæk] *adj* traag

slacks [slæks] *pl* broek *c*

slam [slæm] *v* *dichtslaan

slander ['slɑːndə] *n* laster *c*

slang [slæŋ] *n* slang *c*, jargon *nt*

slant [slɑːnt] *v* hellen

slanting ['slɑːntiŋ] *adj* schuin, hellend, scheef

slap [slæp] *v* *slaan; *n* klap *c*

slate [sleit] *n* lei *nt*

slave [sleiv] *n* slaaf *m*, slavin *f*

sledge [sledʒ] *n* slee *c*, slede *c*

sleep [sli:p] *n* slaap *c*

***sleep** [sli:p] *v* slapen

sleeping bag ['sli:piŋbæg] *n* slaapzak *c*

sleeping car ['sli:piŋkɑː] *n* slaapwagen *c*

sleeping pill ['sli:piŋpil] *n* slaappil *c*

sleepless ['sli:pləs] *adj* slapeloos

sleepy ['sli:pi] *adj* slaperig

sleeve [sli:v] *n* mouw *c*; hoes *c*

sleigh [slei] *n* slee *c*, ar *c*

slender ['slendə] *adj* slank

slice [slais] *n* snee *c*

slide [slaid] *n* glijbaan *c*; dia *c*

***slide** [slaid] *v* *glijden

slight [slait] *adj* licht; gering

slim [slim] *adj* slank; *v* vermageren

slip [slip] *v* slippen, *uitglijden; ontglippen; *n* misstap *c*; onderrok *c*

slipper ['slipə] *n* slof *c*, pantoffel *c*

slippery ['slipəri] *adj* glibberig, glad

slogan ['slougən] *n* leus *c*, slagzin *c*

slope [sloup] *n* helling *c*; *v* glooien

sloping ['sloupiŋ] *adj* afhellend

sloppy ['slopi] *adj* slordig

slot [slot] *n* gleuf *c*; ~ **machine** automaat *c*

slovenly ['slʌvənli] *adj* slordig

slow [slou] *adj* traag, langzaam; ~ **down** vertragen; afremmen

sluice [slu:s] *n* sluis *c*

slum [slʌm] *n* achterbuurt *c*

slump [slʌmp] *n* prijsdaling *c*

slush [slʌʃ] *n* sneeuwslik *nt*

sly [slai] *adj* listig

smack [smæk] *v* *slaan; *n* klap *c*

small [smɔ:l] *adj* klein; gering

smallpox ['smɔ:lpoks] *n* pokken *pl*

smart [smɑ:t] *adj* chic; knap, pienter

smash [smæʃ] *n* dreun *c*; *v* dreunen; vernielen

smell [smel] *n* geur *c*

***smell** [smel] *v* *ruiken; *stinken

smelly ['smeli] *adj* stinkend

smile [smail] *v* glimlachen; *n* glimlach *c*

smith [smiθ] *n* smid *m*

smoke [smouk] *v* roken; *n* rook *c*; **no smoking** verboden te roken

smoker ['smoukə] *n* roker *m*, rookster *f*; rookcoupé *c*

smoking compartment ['smoukiŋkəm,pɑ:tmənt] *n* coupé voor rokers

smooth [smu:ð] *adj* effen, vlak, glad; zacht

smuggle ['smʌgəl] *v* smokkelen

snack [snæk] *n* snack *c*

snack bar ['snækbɑ:] *n* snackbar *c*

snail [sneil] *n* slak *c*

snake [sneik] *n* slang *c*

snapshot ['snæpʃot] *n* kiekje *nt*, momentopname *c*

sneakers ['sni:kəz] *plAm* gymschoenen *pl*

sneeze [sni:z] *v* niezen

sniper ['snaipə] *n* sluipschutter *m*

snooty ['snu:ti] *adj* verwaand

snore [snɔ:] *v* snurken

snorkel ['snɔ:kəl] *n* snorkel *c*

snout [snaut] *n* snuit *c*

snow [snou] *n* sneeuw *c*; *v* sneeuwen

snowstorm ['snoustɔ:m] *n* sneeuwstorm *c*

snowy ['snoui] *adj* besneeuwd

so [sou] *conj* dus; *adv* zo; dermate; **and ~ on** enzovoort; ~ **far** tot zover; ~ **many** zoveel; ~ **much** zoveel; ~ **that** zodat, opdat

soak [souk] *v* weken, doorweken

soap [soup] *n* zeep *c*; ~ **powder** zeeppoeder *nt*

sober ['soubə] *adj* nuchter; bezonnen

so-called [,sou'kɔ:ld] *adj* zogenaamd

soccer ['sokə] *n* voetbal *nt*; ~ **team** elftal *nt*

social ['souʃəl] *adj* maatschappelijk, sociaal; ~ **security** bijstand *c*

socialism ['souʃəlizəm] *n* socialisme *nt*

socialist ['souʃəlist] *adj* socialistisch; *n* socialist *m*, -e *f*

society [sə'saiəti] *n* maatschappij *c*; genootschap *nt*, vereniging *c*; gezelschap *nt*

sock [sɔk] *n* sok *c*

socket ['sɔkit] *n* fitting *c*

soda ['soudə] *nAm* frisdrank *c*; ~ **water** spuitwater *nt*

sofa ['soufə] *n* sofa *c*

soft [sɔft] *adj* zacht; ~ **drink** frisdrank *c*

soften ['sɔfən] *v* verzachten

software ['sɔftweə] *n* software *c*

soil [sɔil] *n* grond *c*; bodem *c*, aarde *c*

soiled [sɔild] *adj* bevuild

solar ['soulə] *adj* zonne-; ~ **system** zonnestelsel *nt*

sold [sould] *v* (p, pp sell); ~ **out** uitverkocht

soldier ['sould3ə] *n* militair *m*, soldaat *m*

sole[1] [soul] *adj* enig

sole[2] [soul] *n* zool *c*; tong *c*

solely ['soulli] *adv* uitsluitend

solemn ['sɔləm] *adj* plechtig

solicitor [sə'lisitə] *n* raadsman *m*, advocaat *m*

solid ['sɔlid] *adj* stevig, solide; massief; *n* vaste stof

solitary ['sɔlitəri] *adj* solitair

soluble ['sɔljubəl] *adj* oplosbaar

solution [sə'lu:ʃən] *n* oplossing *c*

solve [sɔlv] *v* oplossen

somber *Am*, **sombre** ['sɔmbə] *adj* somber

some [sʌm] *adj* enige, enkele; *pron* sommige; iets; ~ **day** eens; ~ **more** nog wat; ~ **time** eens

somebody ['sʌmbədi] *pron* iemand

somehow ['sʌmhau] *adv* op de een of andere manier

someone ['sʌmwʌn] *pron* iemand

something ['sʌmθiŋ] *pron* iets

sometimes ['sʌmtaimz] *adv* soms

somewhat ['sʌmwɔt] *adv* enigszins

somewhere ['sʌmweə] *adv* ergens

son [sʌn] *n* zoon *m*

song [sɔŋ] *n* lied *nt*

son-in-law ['sʌninlɔ:] *n* (pl sons-)

schoonzoon *m*

soon [su:n] *adv* vlug, gauw, weldra, spoedig; **as** ~ **as** zodra

sooner ['su:nə] *adv* liever

sore [sɔ:] *adj* pijnlijk, zeer; *n* zere plek; zweer *c*; ~ **throat** keelpijn *c*

sorrow ['sɔrou] *n* droefheid *c*, leed *nt*, verdriet *nt*

sorry ['sɔri] *adj* bedroefd; **sorry!** neem me niet kwalijk!, sorry!, pardon!

sort [sɔ:t] *v* sorteren, rangschikken; *n* slag *nt*, soort *c/nt*; **all sorts of** allerlei

soul [soul] *n* ziel *c*; geest *c*

sound [saund] *n* klank *c*, geluid *nt*; *v* *klinken; *adj* degelijk

soundproof ['saundpru:f] *adj* geluiddicht

soup [su:p] *n* soep *c*; ~ **plate** soepbord *nt*; ~ **spoon** soeplepel *c*

sour [sauə] *adj* zuur

source [sɔ:s] *n* bron *c*

south [sauθ] *n* zuid *c*, zuiden *nt*; **South Pole** zuidpool *c*

South Africa [sauθ 'æfrikə] Zuid-Afrika

southeast [,sauθ'i:st] *n* zuidoosten *nt*

southerly ['sʌðəli] *adj* zuidelijk

southern ['sʌðən] *adj* zuidelijk

southwest [,sauθ'west] *n* zuidwesten *nt*

souvenir ['su:vəniə] *n* souvenir *nt*; ~ **shop** souvenirwinkel *c*

sovereign ['sɔvrin] *n* vorst *m*

Soviet ['souviət] *adj* Sovjet-

***sow** [sou] *v* zaaien

spa [spɑ:] *n* geneeskrachtige bron

space [speis] *n* ruimte *c*; afstand *c*, tussenruimte *c*; heelal *c*; *v* spatiëren; ~ **shuttle** ruimteveer

spacious ['speiʃəs] *adj* ruim

spade [speid] *n* schop *c*, spade *c*

Spain [spein] Spanje

Spaniard ['spænjəd] *n* Spanjaard *m*, Spaanse *f*

Spanish ['spæniʃ] *adj* Spaans

spanking ['spæŋkiŋ] *n* pak slaag

spanner ['spænə] *n* schroefsleutel *c*; moersleutel *c*

spare [spɛə] *adj* reserve-, extra; *v* missen; ~ **part** reserveonderdeel *nt*; ~ **room** logeerkamer *c*; ~ **time** vrije tijd; ~ **tyre** reserveband *c*; ~ **wheel** reservewiel *nt*

spark [spɑ:k] *n* vonk *c*

sparking plug ['spɑ:kiŋplʌg] *n* bougie *c*

sparkling ['spɑ:kliŋ] *adj* fonkelend; mousserend

sparrow ['spærou] *n* mus *c*

***speak** [spi:k] *v* *spreken

spear [spiə] *n* speer *c*

special ['speʃəl] *adj* bijzonder, speciaal; ~ **delivery** expresse-

specialist ['speʃəlist] *n* specialist *m*, -e *f*

speciality [,speʃi'æləti] *n* specialiteit *c*

specialize ['speʃəlaiz] *v* zich specialiseren

specially ['speʃəli] *adv* in het bijzonder

species ['spi:ʃi:z] *n* (pl ~) soort *c/nt*

specific [spə'sifik] *adj* specifiek

specimen ['spesimən] *n* exemplaar *nt*, specimen *nt*

speck [spek] *n* spat *c*

spectacle ['spektəkəl] *n* schouwspel *nt*; **spectacles** bril *c*

spectator [spek'teitə] *n* kijker *c*, toeschouwer *m*, toeschouwster *f*

speculate ['spekjuleit] *v* speculeren

speech [spi:tʃ] *n* spraak *c*; rede *c*, toespraak *c*; taal *c*

speechless ['spi:tʃləs] *adj* sprakeloos

speed [spi:d] *n* snelheid *c*; vaart *c*, spoed *c*; **cruising** ~ kruissnelheid *c*; ~ **limit** maximum snelheid, snelheidsbeperking *c*

***speed** [spi:d] *v* hard *rijden; te hard

*rijden

speeding ['spi:diŋ] *n* snelheidsovertreding *c*

speedometer [spi:'dɔmitə] *n* snelheidsmeter *c*

spell [spel] *n* betovering *c*

***spell** [spel] *v* spellen

spelling ['speliŋ] *n* spelling *c*

***spend** [spend] *v* *uitgeven, besteden; *doorbrengen

sphere [sfiə] *n* bol *c*; sfeer *c*

spice [spais] *n* specerij *c*; **spices** *pl* kruiden

spiced [spaist] *adj* gekruid

spicy ['spaisi] *adj* pikant

spider ['spaidə] *n* spin *c*; **spider's web** spinnenweb *nt*

***spill** [spil] *v* morsen

***spin** [spin] *v* *spinnen; draaien

spinach ['spinidʒ] *n* spinazie *c*

spine [spain] *n* ruggegraat *c*

spinster ['spinstə] *n* oude vrijster

spire [spaiə] *n* spits *c*

spirit ['spirit] *n* geest *c*; ~ **stove** spiritusbrander *c*; **spirits** *pl* sterke drank; stemming *c*

spiritual ['spiritʃuəl] *adj* geestelijk

spit [spit] *n* spuug *nt*, speeksel *nt*; spit *nt*

***spit** [spit] *v* spuwen

spite [spait] *n* wrok; *v* dwarsbomen; **in** ~ **of** ongeacht, ondanks; **out of** ~ uit kwaadaardigheid

spiteful ['spaitfəl] *adj* hatelijk

splash [splæʃ] *v* spatten

splendid ['splendid] *adj* schitterend, prachtig

splendo(u)r ['splendə] *n* pracht *c*

splint [splint] *n* spalk *c*

splinter ['splintə] *n* splinter *c*

***split** [split] *v* *splijten, splitsen

***spoil** [spɔil] *v* *bederven; verwennen

spoke¹ [spouk] *v* (p speak)

spoke² [spouk] *n* spaak *c*

sponge [spʌndʒ] *n* spons *c*

spook [spuːk] n spook nt

spool [spuːl] n spoel c

spoon [spuːn] n lepel c

spoonful ['spuːnful] n lepel c

sport [spɔːt] n sport c

sports car ['spɔːtskaː] n sportwagen c

sports jacket ['spɔːts,dʒækit] n sportjasje nt

sportsman ['spɔːtsmən] n (pl -men) sportman m

sportswear ['spɔːtswɛə] n sportkleding c

sportswoman ['spɔːtswumən] n (pl -women) sportvrouw v

spot [spɔt] n spat c, vlek c; plek c, plaats c

spotless ['spɔtləs] adj vlekkeloos

spotlight ['spɔtlait] n schijnwerper c

spotted ['spɔtid] adj gespikkeld

spout [spaut] n straal c

sprain [sprein] v verstuiken, verzwikken; n verstuiking c

spray [sprei] n verstuiver c; v spuiten

*spread [spred] v spreiden

spring [sprɪŋ] n voorjaar nt, lente c; veer c; bron c

springtime ['sprɪŋtaim] n voorjaar nt

sprouts [sprauts] pl spruitjes pl

spy [spai] n spion m, spionne f

squadron ['skwɔdrən] n eskader nt

square [skwɛə] adj vierkant; saai; burgerlijk; n kwadraat nt, vierkant nt; plein nt

squash [skwɔʃ] n vruchtensap nt

squeeze [skwiːz] v uitpersen; knijpen

squirrel ['skwirəl] n eekhoorn c

squirt [skwəːt] n straal c

stable ['steibəl] adj stabiel; n stal c

stack [stæk] n stapel c

stadium ['steidiəm] n stadion nt

staff [staːf] n staf c

stage [steidʒ] n toneel nt; fase c, stadium nt; etappe c

stain [stein] v vlekken; n spat c, vlek c; ~

remover vlekkenwater nt; **stained glass** gebrandschilderd glas

stainless ['steinləs] adj vlekkeloos; ~ **steel** roestvrij staal

staircase ['stɛəkeis] n trap c

stairs [stɛəz] pl trap c

stale [steil] adj oudbakken

stall [stɔːl] n kraam c; stalles pl

stamp [stæmp] n postzegel c; stempel c; v frankeren; stampen; ~ **machine** postzegelautomaat c

stand [stænd] n kraam c; tribune c

*stand [stænd] v *staan

standard ['stændəd] n norm c, maatstaf c; standaard-; ~ **of living** levensstandaard c

stanza ['stænzə] n couplet nt

staple ['steipəl] n nietje nt

star [staː] n ster c

starboard ['staːbəd] n stuurboord nt

stare [stɛə] v staren

starling ['staːlɪŋ] n spreeuw c

start [staːt] v *beginnen; n begin nt

starting point ['staːtɪŋpɔint] n uitgangspunt nt

state [steit] n staat c; toestand c; v verklaren; **the States** Verenigde Staten

statement ['steitmənt] n verklaring c

statesman ['steitsmən] n (pl -men) staatsman m

station ['steiʃən] n station nt; plaats c

stationary ['steiʃənəri] adj stilstaand

stationer's ['steiʃənəz] n kantoorboekhandel c

stationery ['steiʃənəri] n schrijfbehoeften pl

statistics [stə'tistiks] pl statistiek c

statue ['stætʃuː] n standbeeld nt

stay [stei] v *blijven; logeren, *verblijven; n verblijf nt

steadfast ['stedfaːst] adj standvastig

steady ['stedi] adj vast

steak [steik] n biefstuk c

*steal [sti:l] *v* *stelen
steam [sti:m] *n* stoom *c*
steamer ['sti:mə] *n* stoomboot *c*
steel [sti:l] *n* staal *nt*
steep [sti:p] *adj* steil
steeple ['sti:pəl] *n* kerktoren *c*
steer [stiə] *v* sturen
steering column ['stiəriŋ,kɔləm] *n* stuurkolom *c*
steering wheel ['stiəriŋwi:l] *n* stuurwiel *nt*
steersman ['stiəzmən] *n* (pl -men) stuurman *m*
stem [stem] *n* steel *c*
step [step] *n* pas *c*, stap *c*; trede *c*; *v* stappen
stepchild ['steptʃaild] *n* (pl -children) stiefkind *nt*
stepfather ['step,fɑ:ðə] *n* stiefvader *m*
stepmother ['step,mʌðə] *n* stiefmoeder *f*
stereo [steriou] *n* stereo *nt*
sterile ['sterail] *adj* steriel
sterilize ['sterilaiz] *v* steriliseren
steward ['stju:əd] *n* steward *m*
stewardess ['stju:ədes] *n* stewardess *f*
stick [stik] *n* stok *c*
*stick [stik] *v* kleven, plakken
sticker ['stikə] *n* sticker
sticky ['stiki] *adj* kleverig
stiff [stif] *adj* stijf
still [stil] *adv* nog; toch; *adj* stil
stimulant ['stimjulənt] *n* stimulerend middel
stimulate ['stimjuleit] *v* stimuleren
sting [stiŋ] *n* prik *c*, steek *c*
*sting [stiŋ] *v* *steken
stingy ['stindʒi] *adj* gierig
*stink [stiŋk] *v* *stinken
stipulate ['stipjuleit] *v* bepalen
stipulation [,stipju'leiʃən] *n* bepaling *c*
stir [stə:] *v* *bewegen; roeren
stitch [stitʃ] *n* steek *c*; hechting *c*

stock [stɔk] *n* voorraad *c*; *v* in voorraad *hebben; ~ **exchange** effectenbeurs *c*, beurs *c*; ~ **market** effectenbeurs *c*; **stocks and shares** effecten
stocking ['stɔkiŋ] *n* kous *c*
stole¹ [stoul] *v* (p steal)
stole² [stoul] *n* stola *c*
stomach ['stʌmək] *n* maag *c*; ~ **ache** buikpijn *c*, maagpijn *c*
stone [stoun] *n* steen *c*; edelsteen *c*; pit *c*; stenen; **pumice** ~ puimsteen *nt*
stood [stud] *v* (p, pp stand)
stop [stɔp] *v* stoppen; *ophouden met, staken; *n* halte *c*; **stop!** halt!
stopper ['stɔpə] *n* stop *c*
storage ['stɔ:ridʒ] *n* opslag *c*
store [stɔ:] *n* voorraad *c*; winkel *c*; *v* *opslaan; ~ **house** magazijn *nt*; **liquor** ~ *nAm* slijterij *c*
storey ['stɔ:ri] *n* etage *c*, verdieping *c*
stork [stɔ:k] *n* ooievaar *c*
storm [stɔ:m] *n* storm *c*
stormy ['stɔ:mi] *adj* stormachtig
story ['stɔ:ri] *n* verhaal *nt*; *nAm* etage *c*, verdieping *c*
stout [staut] *adj* dik, gezet, corpulent
stove [stouv] *n* kachel *c*; fornuis *nt*
straight [streit] *adj* recht; eerlijk; *adv* recht; ~ **ahead** rechtdoor; ~ **away** direct, meteen; ~ **on** rechtdoor
strain [strein] *n* inspanning *c*; spanning *c*; *v* forceren; zeven
strainer ['streinə] *n* vergiet *nt*
strange [streindʒ] *adj* vreemd; raar
stranger ['streindʒə] *n* vreemdeling *m*, -e *f*; vreemde *c*
strangle ['stræŋgəl] *v* wurgen
strap [stræp] *n* riem *c*
straw [strɔ:] *n* stro *nt*
strawberry ['strɔ:bəri] *n* aardbei *c*
stream [stri:m] *n* beek *c*; stroom *c*; *v* stromen
street [stri:t] *n* straat *c*
streetcar ['stri:tkɑ:] *nAm* tram *c*

strength [streŋθ] *n* sterkte *c*, kracht *c*

stress [stres] *n* spanning *c*; nadruk *c*; *v* benadrukken

stretch [stretʃ] *v* rekken; *n* stuk *nt*

strict [strikt] *adj* strikt; streng

strike [straik] *n* staking *c*

*strike [straik] *v* *slaan; *toeslaan; *treffen; staken; *strijken

striking [straikiŋ] *adj* frappant, opmerkelijk, opvallend

string [striŋ] *n* touw *nt*; snaar *c*

strip [strip] *n* strook *c*

stripe [straip] *n* streep *c*

striped [straipt] *adj* gestreept

stroke [strouk] *n* beroerte *c*

stroll [stroul] *v* wandelen; *n* wandeling *c*

strong [strɔŋ] *adj* sterk; krachtig

stronghold ['strɔŋhould] *n* burcht *c*

structure ['strʌktʃə] *n* structuur *c*

struggle ['strʌgəl] *n* strijd *c*, worsteling *c*; *v* worstelen, *strijden

stub [stʌb] *n* controlestrook *c*

stubborn ['stʌbən] *adj* hardnekkig, eigenwijs

student ['stjuːdənt] *n* student *c*

studies ['stʌdiz] *pl* studie

study ['stʌdi] *v* studeren; *n* studie *c*; studeerkamer *c*

stuff [stʌf] *n* stof *c*; spul *nt*

stuffed [stʌft] *adj* gevuld

stuffing ['stʌfiŋ] *n* vulling *c*

stuffy ['stʌfi] *adj* benauwd

stumble ['stʌmbəl] *v* struikelen

stung [stʌŋ] *v* (p, pp sting)

stupid ['stjuːpid] *adj* dom

style [stail] *n* stijl *c*

subject¹ ['sʌbdʒikt] *n* onderwerp *nt*; onderdaan *c*; ~ **to** onderhevig aan

subject² [səb'dʒekt] *v* *onderwerpen

submarine ['sʌbməriːn] *n* duikboot *c*

submit [səb'mit] *v* zich *onderwerpen

subordinate [sə'bɔːdinət] *adj* ondergeschikt; bijkomstig

subscriber [səb'skraibə] *n* abonnee *c*

subscription [səb'skripʃən] *n* abonnement *nt*

subsequent ['sʌbsikwənt] *adj* volgend

subsidy ['sʌbsidi] *n* subsidie *c*

substance ['sʌbstəns] *n* substantie *c*

substantial [səb'stænʃəl] *adj* stoffelijk; werkelijk; aanzienlijk

substitute ['sʌbstitjuːt] *v* *vervangen; *n* vervanging *c*; plaatsvervanger *m*

subtitle ['sʌb,taitəl] *n* ondertitel *c*

subtle ['sʌtəl] *adj* subtiel

subtract [səb'trækt] *v* *aftrekken

suburb ['sʌbəːb] *n* buitenwijk *c*, voorstad *c*

suburban [sə'bəːbən] *adj* van de voorstad, voorstedelijk

subway ['sʌbwei] *nAm* ondergrondse *c*

succeed [sək'siːd] *v* slagen; opvolgen

success [sək'ses] *n* succes *nt*

successful [sək'sesfəl] *adj* succesvol

succumb [sə'kʌm] *v* *bezwijken

such [sʌtʃ] *adj* dergelijk, zulk; *adv* zo; ~ **as** zoals

suck [sʌk] *v* *zuigen

sudden ['sʌdən] *adj* plotseling

suddenly ['sʌdənli] *adv* opeens, ineens

suede [sweid] *n* suède *nt/c*

suffer ['sʌfə] *v* *lijden; *ondergaan

suffering ['sʌfəriŋ] *n* lijden *nt*

suffice [sə'fais] *v* voldoende *zijn

sufficient [sə'fiʃənt] *adj* voldoende, genoeg

suffrage ['sʌfridʒ] *n* stemrecht *nt*, kiesrecht *nt*

sugar ['ʃugə] *n* suiker *c*

suggest [sə'dʒest] *v* voorstellen

suggestion [sə'dʒestʃən] *n* voorstel *nt*

suicide ['suːisaid] *n* zelfmoord *c*

suit [suːt] *v* schikken; aanpassen; goed

*staan; n kostuum nt

suitable ['suːtəbəl] adj gepast, geschikt

suitcase ['suːtkeis] n koffer c

suite [swiːt] n suite c

sum [sʌm] n som c

summary ['sʌməri] n resumé nt, samenvatting c

summer ['sʌmə] n zomer c; ~ **time** zomertijd c

summit ['sʌmit] n top c

sun [sʌn] n zon c

sunbathe ['sʌnbeið] v zonnebaden

sunburn ['sʌnbɔːn] n zonnebrand c

Sunday ['sʌndi] zondag c

sunglasses ['sʌn,glɑːsiz] pl zonnebril c

sunlight ['sʌnlait] n zonlicht nt

sunny ['sʌni] adj zonnig

sunrise ['sʌnraiz] n zonsopgang c

sunset ['sʌnset] n zonsondergang c

sunshade ['sʌnʃeid] n parasol c

sunshine ['sʌnʃain] n zonneschijn c

sunstroke ['sʌnstrouk] n zonnesteek c

suntan oil ['sʌntænɔil] zonnebrandolie c

super ['sjuːpə] adj colloquial super, fantastisch

superb [su'pəːb] adj groots, prachtig

superficial [,suːpə'fiʃəl] adj oppervlakkig

superfluous [su'pəːfluəs] adj overbodig

superior [su'piəriə] adj beter, groter, hoger, superieur

superlative [su'pəːlətiv] adj overtreffend; n superlatief c

supermarket ['suːpə,maːkit] n supermarkt c

superstition [,suːpə'stiʃən] n bijgeloof nt

supervise ['suːpəvaiz] v toezicht *houden op

supervision [,suːpə'viʒən] n controle c, toezicht nt

supervisor ['suːpəvaizə] n opzichter m, -es f

supper ['sʌpə] n avondeten nt

supple ['sʌpəl] adj soepel, lenig, buigzaam

supplement ['sʌplimənt] n supplement nt

supply [sə'plai] n aanvoer c, levering c; voorraad c; aanbod nt; v leveren, bezorgen

support [sə'pɔːt] v ondersteunen, steunen; n steun c; ~ **hose** steunkousen pl

supporter [sə'pɔːtə] n supporter m

suppose [sə'pouz] v *aannemen, veronderstellen; **supposing that** aangenomen dat

suppository [sə'pɔzitəri] n zetpil c

suppress [sə'pres] v onderdrukken

surcharge ['səːtʃɑːdʒ] n toeslag c

sure [ʃuə] adj zeker

surely ['ʃuəli] adv zeker

surface ['səːfis] n oppervlakte c

surfboard ['səːfbɔːd] n surfplank c

surgeon ['səːdʒən] n chirurg m; **veterinary ~** veearts c

surgery ['səːdʒəri] n operatie c; spreekkamer c

surname ['səːneim] n achternaam c

surplus ['səːpləs] n overschot nt

surprise [sə'praiz] n verrassing c; verbazing c; v verrassen; verbazen

surrender [sə'rendə] v zich *overgeven; n overgave c

surround [sə'raund] v omringen, *omgeven

surrounding [sə'raundiŋ] adj omliggend

surroundings [sə'raundiŋz] pl omgeving c

survey ['səːvei] n overzicht nt

survival [sə'vaivəl] n overleving c

survive [sə'vaiv] v overleven

suspect¹ [sə'spekt] v *verdenken; vermoeden

suspect² ['sʌspekt] n verdachte c

suspend [sə'spend] v schorsen

suspenders [sə'spendəz] plAm bretels pl

suspension [sə'spenʃən] n vering c, ophanging c; ~ **bridge** hangbrug c

suspicion [sə'spiʃən] n verdenking c; wantrouwen nt, argwaan c

suspicious [sə'spiʃəs] adj verdacht; argwanend, achterdochtig

sustain [sə'stein] v *verdragen

Swahili [swə'hi:li] n Swahili nt

swallow ['swɔlou] v inslikken, slikken; n zwaluw c

swam [swæm] v (p swim)

swamp [swɔmp] n moeras nt

swan [swɔn] n zwaan c

swap [swɔp] v ruilen

*swear [swɛə] v *zweren; vloeken

sweat [swet] n zweet nt; v zweten

sweater ['swetə] n sweater c

Swede [swi:d] n Zweed m, -se f

Sweden ['swi:dən] Zweden

Swedish ['swi:diʃ] adj Zweeds

*sweep [swi:p] v vegen

sweet [swi:t] adj zoet; lief; n snoepje nt; toetje nt; **sweets** snoep nt, snoepgoed nt

sweeten ['swi:tən] v zoet maken

sweetheart ['swi:thɑ:t] n liefje nt, lieveling c

sweetshop ['swi:tʃɔp] n snoepwinkel c

*swell [swel] v *zwellen

swelling ['sweliŋ] n zwelling c

swift [swift] adj snel

*swim [swim] v *zwemmen

swimmer ['swimə] n zwemmer m, zwemster f

swimming ['swimiŋ] n zwemsport c; ~ **pool** zwembad nt; ~ **suit** n zwempak nt; ~ **trunks** ['swimiŋtrʌŋks] n zwembroek c

swimsuit ['swimsu:t] n zwempak nt

swindle ['swindəl] v oplichten; n zwendelarij c

swindler ['swindlə] n oplichter m

swing [swiŋ] n schommel c

*swing [swiŋ] v zwaaien; schommelen

Swiss [swis] adj Zwitsers; n Zwitser m

switch [switʃ] n schakelaar c; v omwisselen; ~ **off** uitschakelen; ~ **on** inschakelen

switchboard ['switʃbɔ:d] n schakelbord nt

Switzerland ['switsələnd] Zwitserland

sword [sɔ:d] n zwaard nt

swum [swʌm] v (pp swim)

syllable ['siləbəl] n lettergreep c

symbol ['simbəl] n symbool nt

sympathetic [ˌsimpə'θetik] adj hartelijk, begrijpend

sympathy ['simpəθi] n sympathie c; medegevoel nt

symphony ['simfəni] n symfonie c

symptom ['simtəm] n symptoom nt

synagogue ['sinəgɔg] n synagoge c

synonym ['sinənim] n synoniem nt

synthetic [sin'θetik] adj synthetisch

Syria ['siriə] Syrië

Syrian ['siriən] adj Syrisch; n Syriër m

syringe [si'rindʒ] n spuit c

syrup ['sirəp] n stroop c, siroop c

system ['sistəm] n systeem nt; stelsel nt; **decimal** ~ tientallig stelsel

systematic [ˌsistə'mætik] adj systematisch

T

table ['teibəl] *n* tafel *c*; tabel *c*; **~ of contents** inhoudsopgave *c*; **~ tennis** tafeltennis

tablecloth ['teibəlklɔθ] *n* tafellaken *nt*

tablespoon ['teibəlspu:n] *n* eetlepel *c*

tablet ['tæblit] *n* tablet *nt*

taboo [tə'bu:] *n* taboe *nt*

tactics ['tæktiks] *pl* tactiek *c*

tag [tæg] *n* etiket *nt*

tail [teil] *n* staart *c*

taillight ['teillait] *n* achterlicht *nt*

tailor ['teilə] *n* kleermaker *m*

tailor-made ['teiləmeid] *adj* op maat gemaakt

***take** [teik] *v* *nemen; pakken; *brengen; *begrijpen, snappen; **~ away** *meenemen; *afnemen, *wegnemen; **~ effect** ingaan; **~ off** starten; **~ out** *wegnemen; **~ over** *overnemen; **~ place** *plaatshebben; **~ up** *innemen

take-off ['teikɔf] *n* start *c*

tale [teil] *n* verhaal *nt*, vertelling *c*

talent ['tælənt] *n* aanleg *c*, talent *nt*

talented ['tæləntid] *adj* begaafd

talk [tɔ:k] *v* *spreken, praten; *n* gesprek *nt*

talkative ['tɔ:kətiv] *adj* spraakzaam

tall [tɔ:l] *adj* hoog; lang, groot

tame [teim] *adj* mak, tam; *v* temmen

tampon ['tæmpən] *n* tampon *c*

tan [tæn] *n* bruin kleurtje door de (hoogte)zon

tangerine [,tændʒə'ri:n] *n* mandarijn *c*

tangible ['tændʒibəl] *adj* tastbaar

tank [tæŋk] *n* tank *c*

tanker ['tæŋkə] *n* tankschip *nt*

tanned [tænd] *adj* gebruind

tap [tæp] *n* kraan *c*; klop *c*; *v* kloppen

tape [teip] *n* band *c*; lint *nt*; **adhesive ~** plakband *nt*; hechtpleister *c*; **~ measure** centimeter *c*; **~ recorder**

bandrecorder *c*

tar [ta:] *n* teer *c/nt*

target ['ta:git] *n* doel *nt*, mikpunt *nt*

tariff ['tærif] *n* tarief *nt*

task [ta:sk] *n* taak *c*

taste [teist] *n* smaak *c*; *v* smaken; proeven

tasteless ['teistləs] *adj* smakeloos

tasty ['teisti] *adj* lekker, smakelijk

taught [tɔ:t] *v* (p, pp teach)

tavern ['tævən] *n* herberg *c*

tax [tæks] *n* belasting *c*; *v* belasten

taxation [tæk'seiʃən] *n* belasting *c*

tax-free ['tæksfri:] *adj* belastingvrij

taxi ['tæksi] *n* taxi *c*; **~ driver** taxichauffeur *m*; **~ rank** taxistandplaats *c*; **~ stand** *Am* taxistandplaats *c*

taximeter ['tæksi,mi:tə] *n* taximeter *c*

tea [ti:] *n* thee *c*; **~ set** theeservies *nt*

***teach** [ti:tʃ] *v* leren, *onderwijzen

teacher ['ti:tʃə] *n* docent *m*, -e *f*, leraar *m*, lerares *f*; onderwijzer *m*, -es *f*, meester *m*, schoolmeester *m*

teaching ['ti:tʃiŋz] *pl* leer *c*

tea cloth ['ti:klɔθ] *n* theedoek *c*

teacup ['ti:kʌp] *n* theekopje *nt*

team [ti:m] *n* equipe *c*, ploeg *c*

teapot ['ti:pɔt] *n* theepot *c*

tear[1] [tiə] *n* traan *c*

tear[2] [tɛə] *n* scheur *c*; ***tear** *v* scheuren

tease [ti:z] *v* plagen

tea-shop ['ti:ʃɔp] *n* tearoom *c*

teaspoon ['ti:spu:n] *n* theelepel *c*

teaspoonful ['ti:spu:n,ful] *n* theelepel *c*

technical ['teknikəl] *adj* technisch

technician [tek'niʃən] *n* technicus *m*

technique [tek'ni:k] *n* techniek *c*

technological [,teknə'lɔdʒikəl] *adj* technologisch

technology [tek'nɔlədʒi] *n*

technologie *c*

teenager ['ti:ˌneidʒə] *n* tiener *c*

teetotaller [ti:'toutələ] *n* geheelonthouder *c*

telegram ['teligræm] *n* telegram *nt*

telepathy [ti'lepəθi] *n* telepathie *c*

telephone ['telifoun] *n* telefoon *c*; ~ **book** *Am* telefoongids *c*, telefoonboek *nt*; ~ **booth** telefooncel *c*; ~ **call** telefoongesprek *nt*; ~ **directory** telefoonboek *nt*, telefoongids *c*

television ['teliviʒən] *n* televisie *c*; ~ **set** televisietoestel *nt*; **cable** ~ kabel-tv; **satellite** ~ satelliettv

*tell [tel] *v* *zeggen; vertellen; verklappen

telly ['teli] *n colloquial* tv *c*, buis *c*, televisie *c*

temper ['tempə] *n* boosheid *c*

temperature ['temprətʃə] *n* temperatuur *c*

tempest ['tempist] *n* storm *c*

temple ['tempəl] *n* tempel *c*; slaap *c*

temporary ['tempərəri] *adj* voorlopig, tijdelijk

tempt [tempt] *v* *aantrekken

temptation [temp'teiʃən] *n* verleiding *c*

ten [ten] *num* tien

tenant ['tenənt] *n* huurder *m*, huurster *f*

tend [tend] *v* de neiging *hebben; verzorgen; ~ **to** neigen tot

tendency ['tendənsi] *n* neiging *c*, tendens *c*

tender ['tendə] *adj* teder, teer; mals

tendon ['tendən] *n* pees *c*

tennis ['tenis] *n* tennis *nt*; ~ **court** tennisbaan *c*; ~ **shoes** tennisschoenen *pl*

tense [tens] *adj* gespannen

tension ['tenʃən] *n* spanning *c*

tent [tent] *n* tent *c*

tenth [tenθ] *num* tiende

tepid ['tepid] *adj* lauw

term [tə:m] *n* term *c*; periode *c*, termijn *c*; voorwaarde *c*

terminal ['tə:minəl] *n* eindpunt *nt*

terrace ['terəs] *n* terras *nt*

terrain [te'rein] *n* terrein *nt*

terrible ['teribəl] *adj* verschrikkelijk, ontzettend, vreselijk

terrific [tə'rifik] *adj* geweldig

terrify ['terifai] *v* schrik *aanjagen; **terrifying** angstwekkend

territory ['teritəri] *n* gebied *nt*

terror ['terə] *n* angst *c*

terrorism ['terərizəm] *n* terrorisme *nt*, terreur *c*

terrorist ['terərist] *n* terrorist *m*, -e *f*

test [test] *n* proef *c*, test *c*; *v* proberen, testen

testify ['testifai] *v* getuigen

text [tekst] *n* tekst *c*; *v* ~ **someone** een sms-bericht verzenden naar

textbook ['teksbuk] *n* leerboek *nt*

textile ['tekstail] *n* textiel *c/nt*

texture ['tekstʃə] *n* structuur *c*

Thai [tai] *adj* Thailands; *n* Thailander *m*

Thailand ['tailænd] Thailand

than [ðæn] *conj* dan

thank [θæŋk] *v* bedanken, danken; ~ **you** dank u

thankful ['θæŋkfəl] *adj* dankbaar

that [ðæt] *adj* die, dat; *conj* dat

thaw [θɔ:] *v* dooien, ontdooien; *n* dooi *c*

the [ðə, ði] *art* de *art*, het; **the ... the** hoe ... hoe

theater *Am*, **theatre** ['θiətə] *n* schouwburg *c*, theater *nt*

theft [θeft] *n* diefstal *c*

their [ðeə] *adj* hun

them [ðem] *pron* hen; **of** ~ van hen; er

theme [θi:m] *n* thema *nt*, onderwerp *nt*

themselves [ðəm'selvz] *pron* zich; zelf

then [ðen] *adv* toen; vervolgens, dan

theology [θɪ'ɔlədʒi] *n* theologie *c*

theoretical [θɪə'retikəl] *adj* theoretisch

theory ['θɪəri] *n* theorie *c*

therapy ['θerəpi] *n* therapie *c*

there [ðɛə] *adv* daar; daarheen; er

therefore ['ðɛəfɔ:] *conj* daarom

thermometer [θə'mɔmitə] *n* thermometer *c*

thermostat ['θə:məstæt] *n* thermostaat *c*

these [ði:z] *adj* deze

thesis ['θi:sis] *n* (pl theses) stelling *c*

they [ðei] *pron* ze

thick [θik] *adj* dik; dicht

thicken ['θikən] *v* verdikken

thickness ['θiknəs] *n* dikte *c*

thief [θi:f] *n* (pl thieves) dief *m*, dievegge *f*

thigh [θai] *n* dij *c*

thimble ['θimbəl] *n* vingerhoed *c*

thin [θin] *adj* dun; mager

thing [θiŋ] *n* ding *nt*

***think** [θiŋk] *v* *denken; *nadenken; ~ of *denken aan; *bedenken; ~ over *overdenken

thinker ['θiŋkə] *n* denker *m*

third [θə:d] *num* derde

thirst [θə:st] *n* dorst *c*

thirsty ['θə:sti] *adj* dorstig

thirteen [,θə:'ti:n] *num* dertien

thirteenth [,θə:'ti:nθ] *num* dertiende

thirtieth ['θə:tiəθ] *num* dertigste

thirty ['θə:ti] *num* dertig

this [ðis] *adj* dit, deze

thistle ['θisəl] *n* distel *c*

thorn [θɔ:n] *n* doorn *c*

thorough ['θʌrə] *adj* grondig, degelijk

thoroughfare ['θʌrəfɛə] *n* hoofdweg *c*, hoofdstraat *c*

those [ðouz] *adj* die

though [ðou] *conj* hoewel, ofschoon, alhoewel; *adv* overigens

thought¹ [θɔ:t] *v* (p, pp think)

thought² [θɔ:t] *n* gedachte *c*

thoughtful ['θɔ:tfəl] *adj* nadenkend; zorgzaam

thousand ['θauzənd] *num* duizend

thread [θred] *n* draad *c*; garen *nt*; *v* *rijgen

threadbare ['θredbɛə] *adj* versleten

threat [θret] *n* dreigement *nt*, bedreiging *c*

threaten ['θretən] *v* dreigen, bedreigen; **threatening** dreigend

three [θri:] *num* drie

three-quarter [,θri:'kwɔ:tə] *adj* driekwart

threshold ['θreʃould] *n* drempel *c*

threw [θru:] *v* (p throw)

thrifty ['θrifti] *adj* zuinig

throat [θrout] *n* keel *c*; hals *c*

throne [θroun] *n* troon *c*

through [θru:] *prep* door, via

throughout [θru:'aut] *adv* overal

throw [θrou] *n* gooi *c*

***throw** [θrou] *v* *werpen, gooien

thrush [θrʌʃ] *n* lijster *c*

thumb [θʌm] *n* duim *c*

thumbtack ['θʌmtæk] *nAm* punaise *c*

thump [θʌmp] *v* stampen

thunder ['θʌndə] *n* donder *c*; *v* donderen

thunderstorm ['θʌndəstɔ:m] *n* onweer *nt*

thundery ['θʌndəri] *adj* onweerachtig

Thursday ['θə:zdi] donderdag *c*

thus [ðʌs] *adv* zo

thyme [taim] *n* tijm *c*

tick [tik] *n* streepje *nt*, vinkje *nt*; ~ off aanstrepen

ticket ['tikit] *n* kaartje *nt*; bon *c*; ~ collector conducteur *m*, conductrice *f*; ~ machine kaartenautomaat *c*

tickle ['tikəl] *v* kietelen

tide [taid] *n* getij *nt*; high ~ hoog water; low ~ laag water

tidy ['taidi] *adj* net; ~ up opruimen

tie [tai] *v* knopen, *binden; *n* das *c*

tiger ['taigə] *n* tijger *c*

tight [tait] *adj* strak; nauw, krap; *adv* vast

tighten ['taitən] *v* aanhalen, *aantrekken; strakker maken; strakker *worden

tights [taits] *pl* maillot *c*

tile [tail] *n* tegel *c*; dakpan *c*

till [til] *prep* tot aan, tot; *conj* tot, totdat

timber ['timbə] *n* timmerhout *nt*

time [taim] *n* tijd *c*; maal *c*, keer *c*; **all the ~** aldoor; **in ~** op tijd; **~ of arrival** aankomsttijd *c*; **~ of departure** vertrektijd *c*

time-saving ['taim,seiviŋ] *adj* tijdbesparend

timetable ['taim,teibəl] *n* dienstregeling *c*

timid ['timid] *adj* bedeesd

timidity [ti'midəti] *n* verlegenheid *c*

tin [tin] *n* tin *nt*; bus *c*, blik *nt*; **tinned food** conserven *pl*; **~ opener** blikopener *c*

tinfoil ['tinfɔil] *n* zilverpapier *nt*

tiny ['taini] *adj* minuscuul

tip [tip] *n* punt *c*; fooi *c*

tire[1] [taiə] *n* band *c*

tire[2] [taiə] *v* vermoeien

tired [taiəd] *adj* vermoeid, moe; **~ of** beu

tiring ['taiəriŋ] *adj* vermoeiend

tissue ['tiʃu:] *n* weefsel *nt*; papieren zakdoek

title ['taitəl] *n* titel *c*

to [tu:] *prep* tot; aan, voor, bij, naar; om te

toad [toud] *n* pad *c*

toadstool ['toudstu:l] *n* paddestoel *c*

toast [toust] *n* toast *c*

tobacco [tə'bækou] *n* (pl ~s) tabak *c*; **~ pouch** tabakszak *c*

tobacconist [tə'bækənist] *n* sigarenwinkelier *m*; **tobacconist's** tabakswinkel *c*

today [tə'dei] *adv* vandaag

toddler ['tɔdlə] *n* peuter *m*

toe [tou] *n* teen *c*

toffee ['tɔfi] *n* toffee *c*

together [tə'geðə] *adv* bijeen, samen

toilet ['tɔilət] *n* toilet *nt*; **~case** toilettas *c*; **~ paper** closetpapier *nt*, toiletpapier *nt*

toiletry ['tɔilətri] *n* toiletbenodigdheden *pl*

token ['toukən] *n* teken *nt*; bewijs *nt*; munt *c*

told [tould] *v* (p, pp tell)

tolerable ['tɔlərəbəl] *adj* draaglijk

toll [toul] *n* tol *c*

tomato [tə'mɑ:tou] *n* (pl ~es) tomaat *c*

tomb [tu:m] *n* graf *nt*

tombstone ['tu:mstoun] *n* grafsteen *c*

tomorrow [tə'mɔrou] *adv* morgen

ton [tʌn] *n* ton *c*

tone [toun] *n* toon *c*; klank *c*

tongs [tɔŋz] *pl* tang *c*

tongue [tʌŋ] *n* tong *c*

tonic ['tɔnik] *n* tonicum *nt*

tonight [tə'nait] *adv* vannacht, vanavond

tonsilitis [,tɔnsə'laitis] *n* amandelontsteking *c*

tonsils ['tɔnsəlz] *pl* amandelen

too [tu:] *adv* te; ook

took [tuk] *v* (p take)

tool [tu:l] *n* werktuig *nt*, gereedschap *nt*; **~ kit** gereedschapskist *c*

toot [tu:t] *vAm* claxonneren

tooth [tu:θ] *n* (pl teeth) tand *c*

toothache ['tu:θeik] *n* tandpijn *c*

toothbrush ['tu:θbrʌʃ] *n* tandenborstel *c*

toothpaste ['tu:θpeist] *n* tandpasta *c*/*nt*

toothpick ['tu:θpik] *n* tandenstoker *c*

toothpowder ['tu:θ,paudə] *n* tandpoeder *nt*/*c*

top [tɔp] n top c; bovenkant c; deksel nt; bovenst; **on ~ of** bovenop; **~ side** bovenkant c

topic ['tɔpik] n onderwerp nt

topical ['tɔpikəl] adj actueel

torch [tɔːtʃ] n fakkel c; zaklantaarn c

torment[1] [tɔːˈment] v kwellen

torment[2] [ˈtɔːment] n kwelling c

torture [ˈtɔːtʃə] n marteling c; v martelen

toss [tɔs] v gooien

tot [tɔt] n kleuter m

total [ˈtoutəl] adj totaal; geheel, volslagen; n totaal nt

totalitarian [ˌtoutæliˈtɛəriən] adj totalitair

touch [tʌtʃ] v aanraken; *betreffen; n contact nt, aanraking c; tastzin c

touching [ˈtʌtʃiŋ] adj aandoenlijk

tough [tʌf] adj taai

tour [tuə] n rondreis c; v rondtrekken

tourism [ˈtuərizəm] n toerisme nt

tourist [ˈtuərist] n toerist m, -e f; **~ class** toeristenklasse c; **~ office** verkeersbureau nt

tournament [ˈtuənəmənt] n toernooi nt

tow [tou] v slepen

towards [təˈwɔːdz] prep naar; jegens

towel [tauəl] n handdoek c

towel(l)ing [ˈtauəliŋ] n badstof c

tower [tauə] n toren c

town [taun] n stad c; **~ center** Am, **~ centre** stadscentrum nt; **~ hall** stadhuis nt

townspeople [ˈtaunzˌpiːpəl] pl stadsmensen pl

toxic [ˈtɔksik] adj vergiftig

toy [tɔi] n speelgoed nt

toyshop [ˈtɔiʃɔp] n speelgoedwinkel c

trace [treis] n spoor nt; v opsporen

track [træk] n spoor nt; renbaan c

tractor [ˈtræktə] n tractor c

trade [treid] n koophandel c, handel c; ambacht nt, vak nt; v handel *drijven

trademark [ˈtreidmɑːk] n handelsmerk nt

trader [ˈtreidə] n handelaar m

tradesman [ˈtreidzmən] n (pl -men) handelaar m

tradeswoman [ˈtreidzwumən] n (pl -women) zakenvrouw f

trade union [ˌtreidˈjuːnjən] n vakbond c

tradition [trəˈdiʃən] n traditie c

traditional [trəˈdiʃənəl] adj traditioneel

traffic [ˈtræfik] n verkeer nt; **~ jam** verkeersopstopping c; **~ light** stoplicht nt; **one-way ~** eenrichtingsverkeer nt

trafficator [ˈtræfikeitə] n richtingaanwijzer c

tragedy [ˈtrædʒədi] n tragedie c

tragic [ˈtrædʒik] adj tragisch

trail [treil] n spoor nt, pad nt

trailer [ˈtreilə] n aanhangwagen c; nAm kampeerwagen c

train [trein] n trein c; v dresseren, trainen; **stopping ~** stoptrein c; **through ~** doorgaande trein

trainee [treiˈniː] n stagiair m, stagiaire f

trainer [ˈtreinə] n trainer m

training [ˈtreiniŋ] n training c

trait [treit] n trek c

traitor [ˈtreitə] n verrader c

tram [træm] n tram c

tramp [træmp] n landloper m, vagebond m; v *rondtrekken

tranquil [ˈtræŋkwil] adj rustig

tranquillizer [ˈtræŋkwilaizə] n kalmerend middel

transaction [trænˈzækʃən] n transactie c

transatlantic [ˌtrænzətˈlæntik] adj transatlantisch

transfer [trænsˈfəː] v *overbrengen

transform [trænsˈfɔːm] v veranderen

transformer [træns'fɔːmə] n
transformator c

transition [træn'siʃən] n overgang c

translate [træns'leit] v vertalen

translation [træns'leiʃən] n vertaling c

translator [træns'leitə] n vertaler m,
vertaalster f

transmission [trænz'miʃən] n
uitzending c

transmit [trænz'mit] v *uitzenden

transmitter [trænz'mitə] n zender c

transparent [træn'spɛərənt] adj
doorzichtig

transport[1] ['trænspɔːt] n vervoer nt

transport[2] [træn'spɔːt] v
transporteren

transportation [ˌtrænspɔː'teiʃən]
nAm transport nt

trap [træp] n val c

trash [træʃ] n rommel c; ~ **can** Am
vuilnisbak c

travel ['trævəl] v reizen; ~ **agency**
reisbureau nt; ~ **agent** reisagent m, -e
f; ~ **insurance** reisverzekering c;
travelling expenses reiskosten pl

travel(l)er ['trævələ] n reiziger m,
reizigster f; **traveller's cheque**, Am
traveler's check reischeque c

tray [trei] n dienblad nt

treason ['triːzən] n verraad nt

treasure ['treʒə] n schat c

treasurer ['treʒərə] n penningmeester
m

treasury ['treʒəri] n schatkist c

treat [triːt] v behandelen

treatment ['triːtmənt] n behandeling c

treaty ['triːti] n verdrag nt

tree [triː] n boom c

tremble ['trembəl] v rillen, beven;
trillen

tremendous [tri'mendəs] adj enorm

trendy ['trendi] adj colloquial
modieus, in

trespasser ['trespəsə] n indringer m,
indringster f

trial [traiəl] n rechtszaak c; proef c

triangle ['traiæŋgəl] n driehoek c

triangular [trai'æŋgjulə] adj
driehoekig

tribe [traib] n stam c

tributary ['tribjutəri] n zijrivier c

tribute ['tribjuːt] n hulde c

trick [trik] n streek c; foefje nt, kunstje
nt

trigger ['trigə] n trekker c

trim [trim] v bijknippen

trip [trip] n uitstapje nt, reis c

triumph ['traiəmf] n triomf c; v
zegevieren

triumphant [trai'ʌmfənt] adj
triomfantelijk

troops [truːps] pl troepen pl

tropical ['trɔpikəl] adj tropisch

tropics ['trɔpiks] pl tropen pl

trouble ['trʌbəl] n zorg c, moeite c, last
c; v storen

troublesome ['trʌbəlsəm] adj lastig

trousers ['trauzəz] pl broek c

trout [traut] n (pl ~) forel c

truck [trʌk] nAm vrachtwagen c

true [truː] adj waar; werkelijk, echt;
getrouw, trouw

trumpet ['trʌmpit] n trompet c

trunk [trʌŋk] n koffer c; stam c; nAm
kofferruimte c; **trunks** pl
gymnastiekbroek c

trust [trʌst] v vertrouwen; n
vertrouwen nt

trustworthy ['trʌst,wəːði] adj
betrouwbaar

truth [truːθ] n waarheid c

truthful ['truːθfəl] adj
waarheidsgetrouw

try [trai] v proberen; trachten, pogen; n
poging c; ~ **on** passen

tube [tjuːb] n pijp c, buis c; tube c

tuberculosis [tjuːˌbəːkju'lousis] n
tuberculose c

Tuesday ['tju:zdi] dinsdag c

tug [tʌg] v slepen; n sleepboot c; ruk c

tuition [tju:'iʃən] n onderwijs nt

tulip ['tju:lip] n tulp c

tumbler ['tʌmblə] n beker c

tumo(u)r ['tju:mə] n gezwel nt, tumor c

tuna ['tju:nə] n (pl ~, ~s) tonijn c

tune [tju:n] n wijs c, melodie c; ~ **in** afstemmen

tuneful ['tju:nfəl] adj melodieus

tunic ['tju:nik] n tuniek c

Tunisia [tju:'niziə] Tunesië

Tunisian [tju:'niziən] adj Tunesisch; n Tunesiër m

tunnel ['tʌnəl] n tunnel c

turbine ['tə:bain] n turbine c

turbojet [,tə:bou'dʒet] n straalvliegtuig nt

Turk [tə:k] n Turk m, -e f

Turkey ['tə:ki] Turkije

turkey ['tə:ki] n kalkoen c

Turkish ['tə:kiʃ] adj Turks; ~ **bath** Turks bad

turn [tə:n] v draaien, keren; omkeren, omdraaien; n wending c, draai c; bocht c; beurt c; ~ **back** terugkeren; ~ **down** *verwerpen; ~ **into** veranderen in; ~ **off** dichtdraaien; ~ **on** aanzetten; opendraaien; ~ **over** omkeren; ~ **round** omkeren; zich omdraaien

turning ['tə:niŋ] n bocht c

turning point ['tə:niŋpoint] n keerpunt nt

turnover ['tə:,nouvə] n omzet c; ~ **tax** omzetbelasting c

turnpike ['tə:npaik] nAm tolweg c

turpentine ['tə:pəntain] n terpentijn c

turtle ['tə:təl] n schildpad c

tutor ['tju:tə] n prive-docent m; voogd m

tuxedo [tʌk'si:dou] nAm (pl ~s, ~es) smoking c

TV [,ti:'vi:] n tv c, colloquial buis c, televisie c; **on** ~ op tv

tweed [twi:d] n tweed nt

tweezers ['twi:zəz] pl pincet c

twelfth [twelfθ] num twaalfde

twelve [twelv] num twaalf

twentieth ['twentiəθ] num twintigste

twenty ['twenti] num twintig

twice [twais] adv tweemaal

twig [twig] n twijg c

twilight ['twailait] n schemering c

twine [twain] n touw nt

twins [twinz] pl tweeling c; **twin beds** lits-jumeaux c

twist [twist] v *winden; draaien; n draai c

two [tu:] num twee

two-piece [,tu:'pi:s] adj tweedelig

type [taip] v tikken, typen; n type nt

typewriter ['taipraitə] n schrijfmachine c

typhoid ['taifoid] n tyfus c

typical ['tipikəl] adj kenmerkend, typisch

typist ['taipist] n typist m, -e f

tyrant ['taiərənt] n tiran m

tyre [taiə] n band c; ~ **pressure** bandenspanning c

U

ugly ['ʌgli] adj lelijk

ulcer ['ʌlsə] n zweer c

ultimate ['ʌltimət] adj laatst

ultraviolet [,ʌltrə'vaiələt] adj ultraviolet

umbrella [ʌm'brelə] n paraplu c

umpire ['ʌmpaiə] n scheidsrechter m

unable [ʌ'neibəl] adj onbekwaam

unacceptable [ˌʌnək'septəbəl] adj onaanvaardbaar

unaccountable [ˌʌnə'kauntəbəl] adj onverklaarbaar

unaccustomed [ˌʌnə'kʌstəmd] adj niet gewend

unanimous [juː'næniməs] adj unaniem

unanswered [ˌʌ'nɑːnsəd] adj onbeantwoord

unauthorized [ˌʌ'nɔːθəraizd] adj onbevoegd

unavoidable [ˌʌnə'vɔidəbəl] adj onvermijdelijk

unaware [ˌʌnə'weə] adj onbewust

unbearable [ʌn'bɛərəbəl] adj ondraaglijk

unbreakable [ˌʌn'breikəbəl] adj onbreekbaar

unbroken [ˌʌn'broukən] adj heel

unbutton [ˌʌn'bʌtən] v losknopen

uncertain [ʌn'səːtən] adj onzeker

uncle ['ʌŋkəl] n oom m

unclean [ˌʌn'kliːn] adj onrein

uncomfortable [ʌn'kʌmfətəbəl] adj ongemakkelijk

uncommon [ʌn'kɔmən] adj ongewoon, zeldzaam

unconditional [ˌʌnkən'diʃənəl] adj onvoorwaardelijk

unconscious [ʌn'kɔnʃəs] adj bewusteloos

uncork [ˌʌn'kɔːk] v ontkurken

uncover [ʌn'kʌvə] v blootleggen

uncultivated [ˌʌn'kʌltiveitid] adj onbebouwd

under ['ʌndə] prep beneden, onder

undercurrent ['ʌndəˌkʌrənt] n onderstroom c

underestimate [ˌʌndə'restimeit] v onderschatten

underground ['ʌndəgraund] adj ondergronds; n metro c, ondergrondse

underline [ˌʌndə'lain] v onderstrepen

underneath [ˌʌndə'niːθ] adv beneden

underpants ['ʌndəpænts] plAm onderbroek c

undershirt ['ʌndəʃəːt] n hemd nt

*understand [ˌʌndə'stænd] v *begrijpen; verstaan

understanding [ˌʌndə'stændiŋ] n begrip nt

understate [ˌʌndə'steit] v afzwakken

understatement [ˌʌndə'steitmənt] n understatement c

*undertake [ˌʌndə'teik] v *ondernemen

undertaking [ˌʌndə'teikiŋ] n onderneming c

underwater ['ʌndəˌwɔːtə] adj onderwater-

underwear ['ʌndəweə] n ondergoed nt

undesirable [ˌʌndi'zaiərəbəl] adj ongewenst

*undo [ˌʌn'duː] v losmaken

undoubtedly [ʌn'dautidli] adv ongetwijfeld

undress [ʌn'dres] v zich uitkleden

unearned [ˌʌ'nəːnd] adj onverdiend

uneasy [ʌ'niːzi] adj onbehaaglijk

uneducated [ˌʌ'nedjukeitid] adj ongeschoold

unemployed [ˌʌnim'plɔid] adj werkeloos

unemployment [ˌʌnim'plɔimənt] n werkeloosheid c

unequal [ˌʌ'niːkwəl] adj ongelijk

uneven [ˌʌ'niːvən] adj ongelijk, oneffen

unexpected [ˌʌnik'spektid] adj onvoorzien, onverwacht

unfair [ˌʌn'feə] adj oneerlijk, onbillijk

unfaithful [ˌʌn'feiθfəl] adj ontrouw

unfamiliar [ˌʌnfə'miljə] adj onbekend

unfasten [ˌʌn'fɑːsən] v losmaken

unfavo(u)rable [ˌʌn'feivərəbəl] adj

ongunstig

unfit [ˌʌn'fit] *adj* ongeschikt

unfold [ʌn'fould] *v* ontvouwen

unfortunate [ʌn'fɔːtʃənət] *adj* ongelukkig

unfortunately [ʌn'fɔːtʃənətli] *adv* helaas, ongelukkigerwijs

unfriendly [ˌʌn'frendli] *adj* onvriendelijk

ungrateful [ʌn'greitfəl] *adj* ondankbaar

unhappy [ʌn'hæpi] *adj* ongelukkig

unhealthy [ʌn'helθi] *adj* ongezond

unhurt [ˌʌn'həːt] *adj* heelhuids

uniform ['juːnifɔːm] *n* uniform *nt/c*; *adj* uniform

unimportant [ˌʌnim'pɔːtənt] *adj* onbelangrijk

uninhabitable [ˌʌnin'hæbitəbəl] *adj* onbewoonbaar

uninhabited [ˌʌnin'hæbitid] *adj* onbewoond

unintentional [ˌʌnin'tenʃənəl] *adj* onopzettelijk

union ['juːnjən] *n* vereniging *c*; verbond *nt*, unie *c*

unique [juː'niːk] *adj* uniek

unit ['juːnit] *n* eenheid *c*

unite [juː'nait] *v* verenigen

united [juː'naitid] *adj* verenigd; saamhorig; **United States** [juː'naitid steits] Verenigde Staten

unity ['juːnəti] *n* eenheid *c*

universal [ˌjuːni'vəːsəl] *adj* algemeen, universeel

universe ['juːnivəːs] *n* heelal *nt*

university [ˌjuːni'vəːsəti] *n* universiteit *c*

unjust [ˌʌn'dʒʌst] *adj* onrechtvaardig

unkind [ʌn'kaind] *adj* onaardig, onvriendelijk

unknown [ˌʌn'noun] *adj* onbekend

unlawful [ˌʌn'lɔːfəl] *adj* onwettig

unlearn [ˌʌn'ləːn] *v* afleren

unless [ən'les] *conj* tenzij

unlike [ˌʌn'laik] *adj* verschillend

unlikely [ʌn'laikli] *adj* onwaarschijnlijk

unlimited [ʌn'limitid] *adj* grenzeloos, onbeperkt

unload [ˌʌn'loud] *v* lossen, *uitladen

unlock [ˌʌn'lɔk] *v* openen

unlucky [ʌn'lʌki] *adj* ongelukkig

unnecessary [ʌn'nesəsəri] *adj* onnodig

unoccupied [ˌʌ'nɔkjupaid] *adj* onbezet

unofficial [ˌʌnə'fiʃəl] *adj* officieus, onofficieel

unpack [ˌʌn'pæk] *v* uitpakken

unpleasant [ʌn'plezənt] *adj* onaangenaam, onplezierig; naar, vervelend

unpopular [ˌʌn'pɔpjulə] *adj* impopulair, onbemind

unprotected [ˌʌnprə'tektid] *adj* onbeschermd

unqualified [ˌʌn'kwɔlifaid] *adj* onbevoegd

unreal [ˌʌn'riəl] *adj* onwerkelijk

unreasonable [ʌn'riːzənəbəl] *adj* onredelijk

unreliable [ˌʌnri'laiəbəl] *adj* onbetrouwbaar

unrest [ˌʌn'rest] *n* onrust *c*; rusteloosheid *c*

unsafe [ˌʌn'seif] *adj* onveilig

unsatisfactory [ˌʌnsætis'fæktəri] *adj* onbevredigend

unscrew [ˌʌn'skruː] *v* losschroeven

unselfish [ˌʌn'selfiʃ] *adj* onzelfzuchtig

unskilled [ˌʌn'skild] *adj* ongeschoold

unsound [ˌʌn'saund] *adj* ongezond

unstable [ˌʌn'steibəl] *adj* labiel

unsteady [ˌʌn'stedi] *adj* wankel, onvast; onevenwichtig

unsuccessful [ˌʌnsək'sesfəl] *adj*

mislukt

unsuitable [,ʌn'suːtəbəl] *adj* ongepast

unsurpassed [,ʌnsə'pɑːst] *adj* onovertroffen

untidy [ʌn'taidi] *adj* slordig

untie [,ʌn'tai] *v* losknopen

until [ən'til] *prep* tot

untrue [,ʌn'truː] *adj* onwaar

untrustworthy [,ʌn'trʌst,wəːði] *adj* onbetrouwbaar

unusual [ʌn'juːʒuəl] *adj* ongebruikelijk, ongewoon

unwell [,ʌn'wel] *adj* onwel

unwilling [,ʌn'wiliŋ] *adj* onwillig

unwise [,ʌn'waiz] *adj* onverstandig

unwrap [,ʌn'ræp] *v* uitpakken

up [ʌp] *adv* naar boven, omhoog, op

upholster [ʌp'houlstə] *v* bekleden

upkeep ['ʌpkiːp] *n* onderhoud *nt*

uplands ['ʌpləndz] *pl* hoogvlakte *c*

upon [ə'pɔn] *prep* op

upper ['ʌpə] *adj* hoger, bovenst

upright ['ʌprait] *adj* rechtopstaand; *adv* overeind

upset [ʌp'set] *v* verstoren; *adj* overstuur

upside down [,ʌpsaid'daun] *adv* ondersteboven

upstairs [,ʌp'stɛəz] *adv* boven; naar boven

upstream [,ʌp'striːm] *adv* stroomopwaarts

upwards ['ʌpwədz] *adv* naar boven

urban ['əːbən] *adj* stedelijk

urge [əːdʒ] *v* aansporen; *n* drang *c*

urgency ['əːdʒənsi] *n* urgentie *c*

urgent ['əːdʒənt] *adj* dringend

urine ['juərin] *n* urine *c*

Uruguay ['juərəgwai] Uruguay

us [ʌs] *pron* ons

usable ['juːzəbəl] *adj* bruikbaar

usage ['juːzidʒ] *n* gebruik *nt*

use¹ [juːz] *v* gebruiken, toepassen; ~ up verbruiken; *be used to gewoon *zijn

use² [juːs] *n* gebruik *nt*, toepassing *c*; nut *nt*; *be of ~ baten

useful ['juːsfəl] *adj* bruikbaar, nuttig

useless ['juːsləs] *adj* nutteloos

user ['juːzə] *n* gebruiker *m*, gebruikster *f*

usherette [,ʌʃə'ret] *n* ouvreuse *f*

usual ['juːʒuəl] *adj* gebruikelijk

usually ['juːʒuəli] *adv* gewoonlijk

utensil [juː'tensəl] *n* gereedschap *nt*, werktuig *nt*; gebruiksvoorwerp *nt*

utility [juː'tiləti] *n* nut *nt*

utilize ['juːtilaiz] *v* benutten

utmost ['ʌtmoust] *adj* uiterst

utter ['ʌtə] *adj* volslagen, totaal; *v* uiten

V

vacancy ['veikənsi] *n* vacature *c*

vacant ['veikənt] *adj* vacant

vacate [və'keit] *v* ontruimen

vacation [və'keiʃən] *n* vakantie *c*

vaccinate ['væksineit] *v* inenten

vaccination [,væksi'neiʃən] *n* inenting *c*

vacuum ['vækjuəm] *n* vacuüm *nt*; *vAm* stofzuigen; ~ cleaner stofzuiger *c*; ~ flask thermosfles *c*

vague [veig] *adj* vaag

vain [vein] *adj* ijdel; vergeefs; in ~ vergeefs, tevergeefs

valet ['vælit] *n* bediende *c*

valid ['vælid] *adj* geldig

valley ['væli] *n* dal *nt*, vallei *c*

valuable ['væljubəl] *adj* waardevol,
kostbaar; **valuables** *pl*
kostbaarheden *pl*

value ['vælju:] *n* waarde *c*; *v* schatten

valve [vælv] *n* ventiel *nt*

van [væn] *n* bestelauto *c*

vanilla [və'nilə] *n* vanille *c*

vanish ['væniʃ] *v* *verdwijnen

vapo(u)r ['veipə] *n* damp *c*

variable ['vɛəriəbəl] *adj* veranderlijk

variation [,vɛəri'eiʃən] *n* afwisseling *c*;
verandering *c*

varied ['vɛərid] *adj* gevarieerd

variety [və'raiəti] *n* verscheidenheid *c*;
~ **show** variétévoorstelling *c*; ~
theater *Am*, ~ **theatre** variététheater
nt

various ['vɛəriəs] *adj* allerlei,
verscheidene

varnish ['vɑ:niʃ] *n* lak *c*, vernis *nt/c*; *v*
lakken

vary ['vɛəri] *v* variëren, afwisselen;
veranderen; verschillen

vase [vɑ:z] *n* vaas *c*

vaseline ['væsəli:n] *n* vaseline *c*

vast [vɑ:st] *adj* onmetelijk, uitgestrekt

vault [vɔ:lt] *n* gewelf *nt*; kluis *c*

veal [vi:l] *n* kalfsvlees *nt*

vegetable ['vedʒətəbəl] *n* groente *c*; ~
merchant groenteboer *m*

vegetarian [,vedʒi'tɛəriən] *n*
vegetariër *m*

vegetation [,vedʒi'teiʃən] *n*
plantengroei *c*

vehicle ['vi:əkəl] *n* voertuig *nt*

veil [veil] *n* sluier *c*

vein [vein] *n* ader *c*; **varicose** ~
spatader *c*

velvet ['velvit] *n* fluweel *nt*

velveteen [,velvi'ti:n] *n*
katoenfluweel *nt*

venerable ['venərəbəl] *adj*
eerbiedwaardig

venereal disease [vi'niəriəl di'zi:z]

geslachtsziekte *c*

Venezuela [,veni'zweilə] Venezuela

Venezuelan [,veni'zweilən] *adj*
Venezolaans; *n* Venezolaan *c*

ventilate ['ventileit] *v* ventileren;
luchten

ventilation [,venti'leiʃən] *n* ventilatie
c; luchtverversing *c*

ventilator ['ventileitə] *n* ventilator *c*

venture ['ventʃə] *v* wagen

veranda [və'rændə] *n* veranda *c*

verb [və:b] *n* werkwoord *nt*

verbal ['və:bəl] *adj* mondeling

verdict ['və:dikt] *n* vonnis *nt*, uitspraak
c

verge [və:dʒ] *n* rand *c*; *v* grenzen

verify ['verifai] *v* verifiëren

versatile ['və:s] *adj* veelzijdig

verse [və:s] *n* vers *nt*; couplet

version ['və:ʃən] *n* versie *c*; vertaling *c*

versus ['və:səs] *prep* contra

vertical ['və:tikəl] *adj* verticaal

very ['veri] *adv* erg, zeer; *adj* precies,
waar, werkelijk; uiterst

vessel ['vesəl] *n* vaartuig *nt*, schip *nt*;
vat *nt*

vest [vest] *n* hemd *nt*; *nAm* vest *c*

veterinary surgeon
['vetrinəri'sə:dʒən] dierenarts *c*,
veearts *c*

via [vaiə] *prep* via

viaduct ['vaiədʌkt] *n* viaduct *c/nt*

vibrate [vai'breit] *v* trillen

vibration [vai'breiʃən] *n* vibratie *c*

vicar [vi'k] *n* predikant *m*

vicarage [vi'k] *n* pastorie *c*

vicinity [vi'sinəti] *n* nabijheid *c*, buurt *c*

vicious ['viʃəs] *adj* boosaardig

victim ['viktim] *n* slachtoffer *nt*; dupe *c*

victory ['viktəri] *n* overwinning *c*

video ['vidiou] *n* video *c*; ~ **camera**
video camera; ~ **cassette** video
cassette; ~ **game** computerspel *nt*; ~
recorder video recorder

view [vju:] *n* uitzicht *nt*; opvatting *c*, mening *c*; *v* *bekijken
viewfinder ['vju:,faində] *n* zoeker *c*
vigilant ['vidʒilənt] *adj* waakzaam
villa ['vilə] *n* villa *c*
village ['vilidʒ] *n* dorp *nt*
villain ['vilən] *n* boef *m*
vine [vain] *n* wijnstok *c*
vinegar ['vinigə] *n* azijn *c*
vineyard ['vinjəd] *n* wijngaard *c*
vintage ['vintidʒ] *n* wijnoogst *c*
violation [vaiə'leiʃən] *n* schending *c*
violence ['vaiələns] *n* geweld *nt*
violent ['vaiələnt] *adj* gewelddadig; hevig, heftig
violet ['vaiələt] *n* viooltje *nt*; *adj* violet
violin [vaiə'lin] *n* viool *c*
VIP [,vi: ai 'pi:] *n* beroemdheid *c*
virgin ['və:dʒin] *n* maagd *f*
virtue ['və:tʃu:] *n* deugd *c*
visa ['vi:zə] *n* visum *nt*
visibility [,vizə'bilǝti] *n* zicht *nt*
visible ['vizəbəl] *adj* zichtbaar
vision ['viʒən] *n* visie *c*
visit ['vizit] *v* *bezoeken; *n* visite *c*, bezoek *nt*; **visiting hours** bezoekuren *pl*
visiting card ['vizitiŋkɑ:d] *n* visitekaartje *nt*
visitor ['vizitə] *n* bezoeker *m*, -ster *f*
vital ['vaitəl] *adj* essentieel

vitamin ['vitəmin] *n* vitamine *c*
vivid ['vivid] *adj* levendig
vocabulary [və'kæbjuləri] *n* vocabulaire *nt*, woordenschat *c*; woordenlijst *c*
vocal ['voukəl] *adj* vocaal
vocalist ['voukəlist] *n* zanger *m*, -es *f*
voice [vɔis] *n* stem *c*
void [vɔid] *adj* nietig
volcano [vɔl'keinou] *n* (pl ~es, ~s) vulkaan *c*
volt [voult] *n* volt *c*
voltage ['voultidʒ] *n* voltage *c*/*nt*
volume ['vɔljum] *n* volume *nt*; deel *nt*
voluntary ['vɔləntəri] *adj* vrijwillig
volunteer [,vɔlən'tiə] *n* vrijwilliger *m*, vrijwilligster *f*
vomit ['vɔmit] *v* braken, *overgeven
vote [vout] *v* stemmen; *n* stem *c*; stemming *c*
voter ['voutə] *n* kiezer *m*, -es *f*
voucher ['vautʃə] *n* bon *c*, bewijs *nt*
vow [vau] *n* gelofte *c*, eed *c*; *v* *zweren
vowel [vauəl] *n* klinker *c*
voyage ['vɔiidʒ] *n* reis *c*
vulgar ['vʌlgə] *adj* vulgair; volks-, ordinair
vulnerable ['vʌlnərəbəl] *adj* kwetsbaar
vulture ['vʌltʃə] *n* gier *c*

W

wade [weid] *v* waden
wafer ['weifə] *n* wafel *c*
waffle ['wɔfəl] *n* wafel *c*
wages ['weidʒiz] *pl* loon *nt*
wag(g)on ['wægən] *n* wagon *c*
waist [weist] *n* taille *c*, middel *nt*
waistcoat ['weiskout] *n* vest *nt*

wait [weit] *v* wachten; ~ **on** bedienen
waiter ['weitə] *n* ober *m*, kelner *m*
waiting *n* het wachten; ~ **list** wachtlijst *c*; ~ **room** wachtkamer *c*
waitress ['weitris] *n* serveerster *f*
***wake** [weik] *v* wekken; ~ **up** ontwaken, wakker *worden

walk [wɔːk] v *lopen; wandelen; n wandeling c; loop c; **walking** te voet

walker ['wɔːkə] n wandelaar m, -ster f

walking stick ['wɔːkiŋstik] n wandelstok c

wall [wɔːl] n muur c; wand c

wallet ['wɔlit] n portefeuille c

wallpaper ['wɔːl,peipə] n behang nt

walnut ['wɔːlnʌt] n walnoot c

waltz [wɔːls] n wals c

wander ['wɔndə] v *rondzwerven, *zwerven

want [wɔnt] v *willen; wensen; n behoefte c; gebrek nt, gemis nt

war [wɔː] n oorlog c

warden ['wɔːdən] n bewaker m, bewaakster f, opzichter m, -es f

wardrobe ['wɔːdroub] n klerenkast c, garderobe c

warehouse ['wɛəhaus] n magazijn nt, pakhuis nt

wares [wɛəz] pl waren pl

warm [wɔːm] adj heet, warm; v verwarmen

warmth [wɔːmθ] n warmte c

warn [wɔːn] v waarschuwen

warning ['wɔːniŋ] n waarschuwing c

wary ['wɛəri] adj behoedzaam

was [wɔz] v (p be)

wash [wɔʃ] v *wassen; ~ **and wear** zelfstrijkend; ~ **up** afwassen

washable ['wɔʃəbəl] adj wasbaar; wasecht

washbasin ['wɔʃ,beisən] n wasbak c, wasbekken nt

washing ['wɔʃiŋ] n was c; wasgoed nt; ~ **machine** wasmachine c; ~ **powder** waspoeder nt

washroom ['wɔʃruːm] nAm toilet nt

wasp [wɔsp] n wesp c

waste [weist] v verspillen; n verspilling c; adj braak

wasteful ['weistfəl] adj verkwistend

wastepaper basket [weist'peipə,bɑːskit] n prullenmand c

watch [wɔtʃ] v *kijken naar, *gadeslaan; letten op; n horloge nt; ~ **for** *uitkijken naar; ~ **out** *uitkijken

watchmaker ['wɔtʃ,meikə] n horlogemaker m

watchstrap ['wɔtʃstræp] n horlogebandje nt

water ['wɔːtə] n water nt; **iced** ~ ijswater nt; **running** ~ stromend water; ~ **pump** waterpomp c; ~ **ski** waterski c; ~ **softener** wasverzachter c

watercolo(u)r ['wɔːtə,kʌlə] n waterverf c; aquarel c

watercress ['wɔːtəkres] n waterkers c

waterfall ['wɔːtəfɔːl] n waterval c

watermelon ['wɔːtə,melən] n watermeloen c

waterproof ['wɔːtəpruːf] adj waterdicht

waterway ['wɔːtəwei] n vaarwater nt

watt [wɔt] n watt c

wave [weiv] n golf c; v zwaaien

wavelength ['weivleŋθ] n golflengte c

wavy ['weivi] adj golvend

wax [wæks] n was c

waxworks ['wækswɔːks] pl wassenbeeldenmuseum nt

way [wei] n manier c, wijze c; weg c; kant c, richting c; afstand c; **any** ~ hoe dan ook; **by the** ~ tussen twee haakjes; **out of the** ~ afgelegen; **the other** ~ **round** andersom; ~ **back** terugweg c; ~ **in** ingang c; ~ **out** uitgang c

wayside ['weisaid] n wegkant c

we [wiː] pron we

weak [wiːk] adj zwak; slap

weakness ['wiːknəs] n zwakheid c

wealth [welθ] n rijkdom c

wealthy ['welθi] adj rijk

weapon ['wepən] n wapen nt

*wear [wɛə] v *aanhebben, *dragen; ~ **out** *verslijten

weary ['wiəri] adj moe, vermoeid

weather ['weðə] n weer nt; ~ **forecast** weerbericht nt

*__weave__ [wi:v] v *weven

weaver ['wi:və] n wever m

wedding ['wediŋ] n huwelijk nt, bruiloft c; ~ **ring** trouwring c

wedge [wedʒ] n wig c

Wednesday ['wenzdi] woensdag c

weed [wi:d] n onkruid nt

week [wi:k] n week c

weekday ['wi:kdei] n weekdag c

weekly ['wi:kli] adj wekelijks

*__weep__ [wi:p] v huilen

weigh [wei] v *wegen

weighing machine ['weiiŋmə,ʃi:n] n weegschaal c

weight [weit] n gewicht nt

welcome ['welkəm] adj welkom; n welkom nt; v verwelkomen

weld [weld] v lassen

welfare ['welfɛə] n welzijn nt; nAm bijstand c

well[1] [wel] adv goed; adj gezond; **as ~** ook, eveneens; **as ~ as** evenals; **well!** welnu!

well[2] [wel] n bron c, put c

well-founded [,wel'faundid] adj gegrond

well-known ['welnoun] adj bekend

well-to-do [,weltə'du:] adj bemiddeld

went [went] v (p go)

were [wə:] v (p be)

west [west] n west c, westen nt

westerly ['westəli] adj westelijk

western ['westən] adj westers

wet [wet] adj nat; vochtig

whale [weil] n walvis c

wharf [wɔ:f] n (pl ~s, wharves) kade c

what [wɔt] pron wat; ~ **for** waarom

whatever [wɔ'tevə] pron wat dan ook

wheat [wi:t] n tarwe c

wheel [wi:l] n wiel nt

wheelbarrow ['wi:l,bærou] n kruiwagen c

wheelchair ['wi:ltʃɛə] n rolstoel c

when [wen] adv wanneer; conj als, toen, wanneer

whenever [we'nevə] conj wanneer ook

where [wɛə] adv waar; conj waar

wherever [wɛə'revə] conj waar ook

whether [weðə] conj of; **whether ... or** of ... of

which [witʃ] pron welk; dat

whichever [wi'tʃevə] adj welk ook

while [wail] conj terwijl; n poosje nt

whilst [wailst] conj terwijl

whim [wim] n gril c, bevlieging c

whimper [wimp] v janken

whine [wain] v janken

whip [wip] n zweep c; v kloppen

whiskers ['wiskəz] pl bakkebaarden pl

whisper ['wispə] v fluisteren; n gefluister nt

whistle ['wisəl] v *fluiten; n fluitje nt

white [wait] adj wit; blank

whiting ['waitiŋ] n (pl ~) wijting c

Whitsun ['witsən] Pinksteren

who [hu:] pron wie; die

whoever [hu:'evə] pron wie ook

whole [houl] adj geheel, heel; n geheel nt

wholesale ['houlseil] n groothandel c; ~ **dealer** grossier m

wholesome ['houlsəm] adj gezond

wholly ['houlli] adv helemaal

whom [hu:m] pron wie

whore [hɔ:] n hoer c

whose [hu:z] pron wiens; van wie

why [wai] adv waarom

wicked ['wikid] adj slecht

wide [waid] adj wijd, breed

widen ['waidən] v verwijden

widow ['widou] n weduwe f

widower ['widouə] n weduwnaar m

width [widθ] n breedte c

wife [waif] *n* (pl wives) echtgenote *c*, vrouw *f*

wig [wig] *n* pruik *c*

wild [waild] *adj* wild; woest

will [wil] *n* wil *c*; testament *nt*

*****will** [wil] *v* *willen; *zullen

willing ['wiliŋ] *adj* bereid

willingly ['wiliŋli] *adv* graag

willpower ['wilpauə] *n* wilskracht *c*

*****win** [win] *v* *winnen

wind [wind] *n* wind *c*

*****wind** [waind] *v* kronkelen; *opwinden, *winden

winding ['waindiŋ] *adj* kronkelig

windmill ['windmil] *n* molen *c*, windmolen *c*

window ['windou] *n* raam *nt*

windowsill ['windousil] *n* vensterbank *c*

windscreen ['windskri:n] *n* voorruit *c*; ~ **wiper** ruitenwisser *c*

windshield ['windʃi:ld] *n Am* voorruit *c*; ~ **wiper** *Am* ruitenwisser *c*

windy ['windi] *adj* winderig

wine [wain] *n* wijn *c*; ~**cellar** wijnkelder *c*; ~ **list** wijnkaart *c*

wing [wiŋ] *n* vleugel *c*

winkle ['wiŋkəl] *n* alikruik *c*

winner ['winə] *n* winnaar *m*, winnares *f*

winning ['winiŋ] *adj* winnend; **winnings** *pl* winst *c*

winter ['wintə] *n* winter *c*; ~ **sports** wintersport *c*

wipe [waip] *v* vegen, afvegen

wire [waiə] *n* draad *c*; ijzerdraad *nt*

wireless ['waiələs] *adj* draadloos

wisdom ['wizdəm] *n* wijsheid *c*

wise [waiz] *adj* wijs

wish [wiʃ] *v* verlangen, wensen; *n* verlangen *nt*, wens *c*

wit ['wit] *n* gevatheid *c*; verstand *nt*

witch [witʃ] *n* heks *f*

with [wið] *prep* met; bij; van

*****withdraw** [wið'drɔ:] *v* *terugtrekken

within [wi'ðin] *prep* binnen; *adv* van binnen

without [wi'ðaut] *prep* zonder

witness ['witnəs] *n* getuige *c*

wits [wits] *pl* verstand *nt*

witty ['witi] *adj* geestig

wolf [wulf] *n* (pl wolves) wolf *c*

woman ['wumən] *n* (pl women) vrouw *f*

womb [wu:m] *n* baarmoeder *c*

won [wʌn] *v* (p, pp win)

wonder ['wʌndə] *n* wonder *nt*; verwondering *c*; *v* zich *afvragen

wonderful ['wʌndəfəl] *adj* prachtig, verrukkelijk; heerlijk

wood [wud] *n* hout *nt*; bos *nt*; ~ **carving** houtsnijwerk *nt*

wooded ['wudid] *adj* bebost

wooden ['wudən] *adj* houten; ~ **shoe** klomp *c*

woodland ['wudlənd] *n* bebost gebied

wool [wul] *n* wol *c*; **darning** ~ stopgaren *nt*

wool(l)en ['wulən] *adj* wollen

word [wə:d] *n* woord *nt*

wore [wɔ:] *v* (p wear)

work [wə:k] *n* werk *nt*; arbeid *c*; *v* werken; functioneren; **working day** werkdag *c*; ~ **of art** kunstwerk *nt*; ~ **permit** werkvergunning *c*

worker ['wə:kə] *n* arbeider *m*, arbeidster *f*

working ['wə:kiŋ] *n* werking *c*

working day ['wə:kiŋ] *n* werkdag *c*

workman ['wə:kmən] *n* (pl -men) arbeider *m*

works [wə:ks] *pl* fabriek *c*

workshop ['wə:kʃɔp] *n* werkplaats *c*

world [wə:ld] *n* wereld *c*; ~ **war** wereldoorlog *c*

world-famous [,wə:ld'feiməs] *adj* wereldberoemd

world-wide ['wə:ldwaid] *adj* wereldomvattend

worm [wə:m] *n* worm *c*

worn [wɔ:n] *adj* (pp wear) versleten

worn-out [ˌwɔ:n'aut] *adj* versleten

worried ['wʌrid] *adj* ongerust

worry ['wʌri] *v* zich ongerust maken; *n* zorg *c*, bezorgdheid *c*

worse [wə:s] *adj* slechter; *adv* erger

worship ['wə:ʃip] *v* *aanbidden; *n* eredienst *c*

worst [wə:st] *adj* slechtst; *adv* ergst

worth [wə:θ] *n* waarde *c*; ***be ~** waard *zijn; ***be worth-while** de moeite waard *zijn

worthless ['wə:θləs] *adj* waardeloos

worthy of ['wə:ði əv] waard

would [wud] *v* (p will) gewoon *zijn

wound¹ [wu:nd] *n* wond *c*; *v* kwetsen, verwonden

wound² [waund] *v* (p, pp wind)

wrap [ræp] *v* inpakken

wreck [rek] *n* wrak *nt*; *v* vernielen

wrench [rentʃ] *n* sleutel *c*; ruk *c*; *v* verdraaien

wrinkle ['riŋkəl] *n* rimpel *c*

wrist [rist] *n* pols *c*

wristwatch ['ristwɔtʃ] *n* polshorloge *nt*

*write [rait] *v* *schrijven; **in writing** schriftelijk; **~ down** *opschrijven

writer ['raitə] *n* schrijver *m*, schrijfster *f*

writing pad ['raitiŋpæd] *n* blocnote *c*, schrijfblok *nt*

writing paper ['raitiŋˌpeipə] *n* schrijfpapier *nt*

written ['ritən] *adj* (pp write) schriftelijk

wrong [rɔŋ] *adj* verkeerd, fout; *n* onrecht *nt*; *v* onrecht *aandoen; ***be ~** ongelijk *hebben

wrote [rout] *v* (p write)

X

Xmas ['krisməs] Kerstmis

X-ray ['eksrei] *n* röntgenfoto *c*; *v* doorlichten

Y

yacht [jɔt] *n* jacht *nt*; **~ club** zeilclub *c*

yachting ['jɔtiŋ] *n* zeilsport *c*

yard [jɑ:d] *n* erf *nt*

yarn [jɑ:n] *n* garen *nt*

yawn [jɔ:n] *v* gapen, geeuwen

year [jiə] *n* jaar *nt*

yearly ['jiəli] *adj* jaarlijks

yeast [ji:st] *n* gist *c*

yell [jel] *v* gillen; *n* gil *c*

yellow ['jelou] *adj* geel

yelp ['jelp] *v* janken

yes [jes] ja

yesterday ['jestədi] *adv* gisteren

yet [jet] *adv* nog; *conj* toch, echter, maar

yield [ji:ld] *v* *opbrengen; *toegeven

yoke [jouk] *n* juk *nt*

yolk [jouk] *n* dooier *c*

you [ju:] *pron* je, jij; jou; u; jullie

young [jʌŋ] *adj* jong

your [jɔː] *adj* uw; jouw; jullie
yours [jɔːz] *pron* van jou; van jullie
yourself [jɔːˈself] *pron* je; zelf

yourselves [jɔːˈselvz] *pron* je; zelf
youth [juːθ] *n* jeugd *c*; ~ **hostel** jeugdherberg *c*

Z

Zaire [zaːˈiə] Zaïre
zeal [ziːl] *n* ijver *c*
zealous [ˈzeləs] *adj* ijverig
zebra [ˈziːbrə] *n* zebra *c*
zap [zæp] *v* zappen
zebra crossing [ˈziːbrə krɔsiŋ] *n* zebrapad *nt*
zenith [ˈzeniθ] *n* zenit *nt*; toppunt *nt*
zero [ˈziərou] *n* (pl ~s) nul *c*
zest [zest] *n* animo *c*

zinc [ziŋk] *n* zink *nt*
zip [zip] *n* ritssluiting *c*; ~ **code** *Am* postcode *c*
zipper [ˈzipə] *n* ritssluiting *c*
zodiac [ˈzoudiæk] *n* dierenriem *c*
zombie [ˈzɔmbi] *n* zombie, levend lijk
zone [zoun] *n* zone *c*; gebied *nt*
zoo [zuː] *n* (pl ~s) dierentuin *c*
zoology [zouˈɔlədʒi] *n* zoölogie *c*

Culinaire woordenlijst

Spijzen

almond amandel

anchovy ansjovis

angel food cake witte, ronde cake, gemaakt van suiker, eiwit en bloem

angels on horseback geroosterde, met spek omwikkelde oesters

appetizer borrelhapje

apple appel

~ **charlotte** lagen van appels en sneetjes boord met vanille en slagroom

~ **dumpling** appelbol

~ **sauce** appelmoes

apricot abrikoos

Arbroath smoky gerookte schelvis

artichoke artisjok

asparagus asperge

~ **tip** aspergepunt

aspic koude schotel in gelei

assorted gevarieerd, gemengd

bacon spek

~ **and eggs** spiegeleieren met spek

bagel klein kransvormig broodje

baked in de oven gebakken, gebraden

~ **Alaska** omelette sibérienne

~ **beans** witte bonen in tomatensaus

~ **potato** hele, ongeschilde aardappel, in de oven gebakken

Bakewell tart amandeltaart met jam

baloney worstsoort

banana banaan

~ **split** in de lengte gehalveerde banaan met ijs, noten en overgoten met vruchtensiroop of vloeibare chocolade

barbecue 1) gehakt rundvlees in tomatensaus in een broodje geserveerd 2) maaltijd van geroosterd vlees in de open lucht

~ **sauce** zeer scherpe tomatensaus

barbecued geroosterd op houtskool

basil basilicum

bass baars

bean boon

beef rundvlees

~ **olive** blinde vink

beefburger gehakte, geroosterde biefstuk geserveerd in een broodje

beet, beetroot rode biet

bilberry blauwe bosbes

bill rekening

~ **of fare** menu

biscuit 1) koekje (GB) 2) broodje (US)

black pudding bloedworst

blackberry braam

blackcurrant zwarte bes

bloater verse bokking

blood sausage bloedworst

blueberry blauwe bosbes

boiled gekookt

Bologna (sausage) worstsoort

bone bot

boned ontbeend

Boston baked beans witte bonen met stukjes spek en stroop

Boston cream pie taart met vlavulling en chocoladeglazuur

brains hersenen

braised gestoofd

bramble pudding bramenpudding, vaak met schijfjes appel erin

braunschweiger gerookte leverworst

bread brood

breaded gepaneerd

breakfast ontbijt

bream brasem

breast borst (stuk)

brisket borststuk

broad bean tuinboon

broth bouillon

brown Betty afwisselende lagen appel, perzik of kers en paneermeel, met suiker en specerijen, in de oven gebakken

brunch ontbijt en lunch gecombineerd

Brussels sprout spruitje

bubble and squeak soort pannekoek van gebakken aardappelen en kool, soms met vlees

bun 1) krentebroodje (GB) 2) klein, luchtig broodje (US)

butter boter

buttered beboterd

cabbage kool

Caesar salad sla met geroosterde, naar knoflook smakende brooddobbelsteentjes, anjovis en geraspte kaas

cake gebak, koek, cake, taart

cakes koekjes, taartjes

calf kalfsvlees

Canadian bacon gerookt spek in dikke plakken gesneden

canapé belegd sneetje brood

cantaloupe wratmeloen, kanteloep

caper kappertje

capercaillie, capercailzie auerhoen

carp karper

carrot wortel

cashew vrucht van de cajouboom

casserole gestoofd

catfish meerval (vis)

catsup ketchup

cauliflower bloemkool

celery selderie

cereal graansoorten voor bij het ontbijt, zoals maïsvlokken, havermout, met melk en suiker

hot ~ havermoutpap

chateaubriand dubbele biefstuk van de haas

check rekening

Cheddar (cheese) stevige kaas met een milde, zurige smaak

cheese kaas

~ board kaasassortiment

~ cake kwarktaart

cheeseburger gehakte, geroosterde biefstuk met schijfje kaas, opgediend in een broodje

chef's salad salade van ham, kip, eieren, tomaten, sla en kaas

cherry kers

chestnut tamme kastanje

chicken kip

chicory 1) witlof 2) Brussels lof (GB) 3) andijvie (US)

chili con carne gehakt rundvlees gestoofd met bruine bonen, Spaanse pepers en komijn

chili pepper rode Spaanse pepers

chips 1) patates frites (GB) 2) aardappel chips (US)

chitt(er)lings varkenspens

chive bieslook

chocolate chocolade

~ pudding 1) chocoladepudding bereid met verkruimelde koekjes, suiker, eieren en bloem (GB) 2) chocolademousse (US)

choice keus

chop kotelet

~ suey gerecht, bereid uit fijngesneden varkensvlees en kip, groenten en rijst (tjap tjoy)

chopped fijngehakt

chowder dikke soep van vis, schaal- en schelpdieren of kip, met groenten

Christmas pudding speciaal kerstgebak, soms geflambeerd

chutney sterke Indische specerij

cinnamon kaneel

clam steenmossel

club sandwich dubbele sandwich met kip, spek, sla, tomaat en mayonaise

cobbler vruchtenmoes met deeg, soms met ijs

cock-a-leekie soup preisoep met kip

coconut kokosnoot

cod kabeljauw

Colchester oyster beste soort Engelse oester

cold cuts/meat koud vlees

coleslaw koolsla

compote vruchten op sap

condiment specerij

consommé heldere soep

cooked gekookt

cookie koekje

corn 1) koren (GB) 2) maïs (US)
~ **on the cob** maïskolf

cornflakes maïsvlokken

cottage cheese witte, verse kaas

cottage pie gehakt vlees met uien, bedekt met aardappelpuree in de oven gebakken

course gerecht

cover charge couvert

crab krab

cracker droog beschuit van bladerdeeg

cranberry veenbes
~ **sauce** veenbessengelei

crawfish, **crayfish** 1) rivierkreeft 2) langoest (GB) 3) steurgarnaal (US)

cream 1) room 2) vlaai (dessert) 3) gebonden soep
~ **cheese** roomkaas
~ **puff** roomsoes

creamed potatoes aardappelen in witte roomsaus

creole op Creoolse wijze bereid; over het algemeen zeer pikant, met tomaten, paprika's en uien, geserveerd met rijst

cress waterkers

crisps chips

croquette kroket

crumpet rond, licht broodje, geroosterd en beboterd

cucumber komkommer

Cumberland ham zeer fijne, gerookte Engelse ham

Cumberland sauce rode bessengelei, op smaak gemaakt met wijn, sinaasappelsap en specerijen

cupcake klein rond gebakje

cured gezouten, gerookt, gepekeld (vis en vlees)

currant krent

curried met kerrie

curry kerrie

custard custardvla

cutlet vleeslapje, kotelet

dab schar

Danish pastry soort luchtig koffiebrood

date dadel

Derby cheese gele kaas met pikante smaak

devilled sterk gekruid

devil's food cake machtige chocoladetaart

devils on horseback gekookte pruimen, gevuld met amandelen en ansjovis, omwikkeld met spek, geroosterd en geserveerd op toost

Devonshire cream dikke, klonterige room

diced in dobbelsteentjes gesneden

diet food volgens voedselleer bereid

dill dille

dinner diner, avondeten

dish schotel, gerecht

donut, **doughnut** soort oliebol

double cream volle room

Dover sole tong uit Dover, in Engeland zeer gewaardeerd

dressing 1) slasaus 2) vulsel voor kalkoen (US)

Dublin Bay prawn steurgarnaal

duck eend

duckling jonge eend

dumpling knoedel

Dutch apple pie appeltaart bedekt met een mengsel van boter en bruine suiker

éclair langwerpig, met chocolade of caramel geglaceerd roomtaartje
eel paling
egg ei
  boiled ~ gekookt
  fried ~ spiegelei
  hard-boiled ~ hardgekookt
  poached ~ gepocheerd
  scrambled ~ roerei
  soft-boiled ~ zachtgekookt
  eggplant aubergine, eierplant
endive 1) andijvie (GB) 2) Brussels lof (US)
entrecôte tussenrib
entrée 1) voorgerecht (GB) 2) hoofdgerecht (US)
escalope schnitzel
fennel venkel
fig vijg
filet mignon kalfs- of varkenshaasje
fillet filet van vlees of vis
finnan haddock gerookte schelvis
fish vis
  ~ **and chips** gebakken vis met frites
  ~ **cake** viskoekje
flan vla, ronde taart met vruchten
flapjack (appel)flap
flounder bot
forcemeat farce, gehakt
fowl gevogelte
frankfurter knakworst
French bean slaboon
French bread stokbrood
French dressing 1) slasaus in olie, azijn en tuinkruiden (GB) 2) romige slasaus met ketchup (US)
french fries patates frites
French toast wentelteefje
fresh vers
fricassée ragoût, vleeshachee
fried gebakken in een koekepan of in de olie
fritter beignet, poffertje
frogs' legs kikkerbilletjes

frosting suikerglazuur
fruit vrucht
fry bakken
game wild
gammon gerookte ham
garfish geep (snoekachtige zeevis)
garlic knoflook
garnish garnituur
gherkin augurkje
giblets afval van gevogelte
ginger gember
goose gans
  ~ **berry** kruisbes
grape druif
  ~ **fruit** pompelmoes
grated geraspt
gravy vleesjus
grayling vlagzalm
green bean slaboon
green pepper groene paprika
green salad sla
greens groenten
grilled geroosterd
grilse jonge zalm
grouse korhoen
gumbo 1) groente van Afrikaanse afkomst 2) Creools gerecht van vlees, kip of vis, met *okra* zaden, uien, tomaten en kruiden
haddock gerookte schelvis
haggis hart, longen en lever van een schaap fijn gehakt en in de maag gekookt met reuzel, havermeel en uien
hake stokvis
halibut heilbot
ham and eggs spiegeleieren met ham
hamburger gehakt, geroosterd rundvlees opgediend in een broodje
hare haas
haricot bean prinsessenboon, witte boon
hash 1) gehakt of fijngesneden vlees 2) hachee met aardappelen en groenten

hazelnut hazelnoot
heart hart
herb tuinkruid
herring haring
home-made eigengemaakt, van het huis
hominy grits brij van maïsgrutten
honey honing
  ~ **dew melon** zoete meloen met geelgroen vruchtvlees
hors-d'œuvre voorgerecht (Engeland)
horse-radish mierikswortel
hot 1) heet, warm 2) sterk gekruid
  ~ **cross bun** fijn broodje gevuld met rozijnen en kruisvormig bedekt met glazuur, wordt in de vastentijd gegeten (brioche)
  ~ **dog** hot dog, warme worst in een broodje
huckleberry blauwe bosbes
hush puppy beignet van maïsmeel en uien
ice-cream ijs
iced gekoeld
icing suikerglazuur
Idaho baked potato soort bintje, ongeschild in de oven gepoft
Irish stew hutspot van schapevlees, aardappelen en uien
Italian dressing slasaus van olie, azijn en tuinkruiden
jellied in gelei
Jell-O gelatinedessert
jelly jam; gelei
Jerusalem artichoke aardpeer
John Dory zonnevis (zeevis)
jugged hare hazepeper
juice sap
juniper berry jeneverbes
junket gestremde melk (wrongel), gesuikerd
kale boerenkool
kedgeree stukjes vis met rijst, eieren,

boter, wordt vaak als warm gerecht aan het ontbijt geserveerd
kidney nier
kipper bokking
lamb lamsvlees
Lancashire hot pot schotel in de oven van ragoût van lamsvlees en nieren met uien, specerijen en aardappelen
larded gelardeerd
lean mager
leek prei
leg bout
lemon citroen
  ~ **sole** scharretong
lentil linze
lettuce kropsla, veldsla
lima bean tuinboon
lime limoen, kleine groene citroen
liver lever
loaf brood
lobster kreeft
loin lendestuk
Long Island duck eend van Long Island, in de VS zeer goed bekend staande soort
low-calorie laag caloriegehalte
lox gerookte zalm
macaroon bitterkoekje
mackerel makreel
maize maïs
mandarin mandarijntje
maple syrup ahornstroop
marinated gemarineerd
marjoram marjolein
marmalade marmelade van sinaasappelen of andere citrusvruchten
marrow beenmerg
  ~ **bone** mergpijp
marshmallow Amerikaans snoepgoed; *marshmallows* worden vaak aan warme chocola en allerlei soorten desserts toegevoegd
marzipan marsepein

mashed potatoes aardappelpuree

meal maaltijd

meat vlees

~ **ball** gehaktbal

~ **loaf** gehaktbrood

~ **pâté** vleespastei

medium (done) net gaar

melon meloen

melted gesmolten

Melton Mowbray pie pastei bestaande uit gehakt vlees en kruiden

meringue schuimgebak, schuimpje

milk melk

mince fijnhakken

~ **pie** pasteitje met krenten, rozijnen, fijngehakte geconfijte vruchten en appelen (met of zonder vlees)

minced fijngehakt

~ **meat** fijngehakt vlees

mint munt (kruid)

minute steak kort gebakken biefstuk

mixed gemengd

~ **grill** aan een stokje geregen, geroosterde stukjes vlees

molasses melasse, stroop

morel morille, zeer gewaardeerde paddestoelsoort

mousse 1) dessert van geklopte eieren en slagroom 2) luchtig pasteitje

mulberry moerbei

mullet harder (vis gelijkend op een karper)

mulligatawny soup zeer sterk gekruide soep van Indische afkomst met wortels, uien, *chutney* en kip met kerrie

mushroom paddestoel

muskmelon meloen

mussel mossel

mustard mosterd

mutton schapevlees

noodle noedel

nut noot

oatmeal (porridge) havermoutpap

oil olie

okra zaad van de *gumbo*, wordt gebruikt om soepen en ragoûtsausen aan te dikken

olive olijf

onion ui

orange sinaasappel

ox tongue ossetong

oxtail ossestaart

oyster oester

pancake pannenkoek

Parmesan (cheese) Parmezaanse kaas

parsley peterselie

parsnip pastinaak, witte peen

partridge patrijs

pastry banket, gebakje, taartje

pasty pastei

pea doperwt

peach perzik

peanut olienoot, pinda

~ **butter** pindakaas

pear peer

pearl barley parelgerst

pepper peper

~ **mint** pepermunt

perch baars

persimmon dadelpruim

pheasant fazant

pickerel jonge snoek

pickle 1) groente of geconfijte vrucht in pekelzuur 2) in het bijzonder augurkje (US)

pickled in pekel bewaard

pie pastei, vaak met een deksel van bladerdeeg, gevuld met vlees, groenten of vruchten

pig varken

pigeon duif

pike snoek

pineapple ananas

plaice schol

plain natuur, zonder iets erin

plate bord, schaal

plum pruim
  ~ **pudding** speciaal kerstgebak, soms geflambeerd
poached gepocheerd
popcorn gepofte maïskorrels
popover klein, luchtig broodje
pork varkensvlees
porridge havermoutpap
porterhouse steak biefstuk van de haas
pot roast met groenten gesmoord rundvlees
potato aardappel
  ~ **chips** 1) patates frites (GB) 2) aardappel chips (US)
  ~ **in its jacket** aardappel in de schil gekookt en opgediend
potted shrimps garnalen in gesmolten boter, koud opgediend in een vorm
poultry gevogelte, pluimvee
prawn grote garnaal
prune gedroogde pruim
ptarmigan sneeuwhoen
pudding soepel of stevig beslag van meel en eieren, gegarneerd met vlees, vis, groenten of vruchten, in de oven gebakken of gaargestoomd; nagerecht
pumpernickel zwart roggebrood
pumpkin pompoen
quail kwartel
quince kweepeer
rabbit konijn
radish radijs
rainbow trout regenboogforel
raisin rozijn
rare ongaar
raspberry framboos
raw rauw
red mullet soort harder (zeevis)
red (sweet) pepper rode paprika
redcurrant rode bes
relish specerij gemaakt van fijngesneden groente in azijn

rhubarb rabarber
rib (of beef) ribstuk (van het rund)
rib-eye steak entrecôte
rice rijst
rissole vlees- of viskroket
river trout rivierforel
roast braadstuk
roasted gebraden
Rock Cornish hen piepkuiken
roe viskuit
roll broodje
rollmop herring rolmops, gemarineerde haringfilet
round steak runderschijf
Rubens sandwich cornedbeef op een toostje, met zuurkool, kaas en slasaus; warm opgediend
rump steak biefstuk
rusk beschuit
rye bread roggebrood
saddle lendestuk
saffron saffraan
sage salie
salad sla
  ~ **bar** verschillende soorten slaatjes, tomaten, prinsessenbonen
  ~ **cream** slasaus, licht gezoet
  ~ **dressing** slasaus
salmon zalm
  ~ **trout** zalmforel
salt zout
salted gezouten
sardine sardien
sauce saus
sauerkraut zuurkool
sausage worst
sauté(ed) snel in boter, olie of vet gebakken
scallop 1) kamschelp 2) kalfslapje
scampi steurgarnaal
scone zacht broodje, warm geserveerd, met boter en jam
Scotch broth runder- of schapebouillon met groenten

Scotch woodcock toost met roerei en ansjovis

sea bass zeebaars

sea kale zeekool

seafood zeebanket

(in) season (in het) seizoen

seasoning specerij

service bediening

~ **charge** bedieningstarief

~ **included** inclusief bediening

~ **not included** exclusief bediening

set menu menu van de dag

shad elft (zeevis)

shallot sjalot

shellfish schelp- en schaaldieren

sherbet sorbet

shoulder schouderstuk

shredded wheat gesponnen tarwe, wordt bij het ontbijt gegeten

shrimp garnaal

silverside (of beef) onderste deel van runderschenkel

sirloin steak lendestuk (van het rund)

skewer vleespen

slice sneet(je), plak

sliced in plakken gesneden

sloppy Joe gehakt vlees in scherpe tomatensaus, geserveerd in een broodje

smelt spiering

smoked gerookt

snack hapje, snack

sole tong (vis)

soup soep

sour zuur

soused herring gepekelde haring

spare rib krabbetje

spice specerij

spinach spinazie

spiny lobster langoest

(on a) spit (aan het) spit

sponge cake Moscovisch gebak

sprat sprot

squash mergpompoen

starter voorgerecht

steak and kidney pie pastei in bladerdeeg van niertjes en rundvlees

steamed gekookt

stew stoofschotel

Stilton (cheese) een van de beste Engelse kazen, wit of blauw geaderd

strawberry aardbei

string bean slaboon

stuffed gevuld

stuffing vulling

suck(l)ing pig speenvarken

sugar suiker

sugarless zonder suiker

sundae roomijs met vruchten, noten, slagroom en siroop

supper avondmaaltijd

swede knolraap

sweet 1) zoet 2) dessert

~ **corn** zoete maïs

~ **potato** bataat, knol van een oorspronkelijk tropisch gewas, rijk aan zetmeel en suiker

sweetbread zwezerik

Swiss cheese Emmentaler kaas

Swiss roll opgerold gebak met jam ertussen (koninginnenbrood)

Swiss steak met groenten en specerijen gestoofde runderlappen

T-bone steak lendestuk van het rund met een T-vormig bot erin

table d'hôte open tafel in een hotel

tangerine mandarijntje

tarragon dragon

tart (vruchten)taart

tenderloin filet van vlees

Thousand Island dressing slasaus, bestaande uit mayonaise met piment, noten, olijven, selderie, uien, peterselie en eieren

thyme tijm

toad-in-the-hole rundvlees (of worstjes) in beslag gedoopt en in de oven gebakken

toast geroosterd brood
toasted getoost
  ~ cheese toost met gesmolten kaas
tomato tomaat
tongue tong (vlees)
tournedos ossehaas in dikke plakken
treacle melasse, stroop
trifle cake met amandelen en gelei, in sherry (of brandewijn) gedrenkt, opgediend met vla of slagroom
tripe pens
trout forel
truffle truffel (paddestoel)
tuna, tunny tonijn
turbot tarbot
turkey kalkoen
turnip raap, knol
turnover flap
turtle schildpad
underdone ongaar
vanilla vanille
veal kalfsvlees
  ~ bird blinde vink
  ~ escalope kalfsoester
vegetable groente
  ~ marrow mergpompoen, courgette
venison wildbraad
vichyssoise preisoep, koud geserveerd
vinegar azijn

Virginia baked ham ham in de oven geroosterd, in inkepingen in het vel worden stukjes ananas, kersen en kruidnagels gestoken waarna de ham met het vruchtesap geglaceerd wordt
wafer wafeltje
waffle warme wafel met boter, stroop of honing
walnut walnoot
water ice sorbet
watercress waterkers
watermelon watermeloen
well-done gaar
Welsh rabbit/rarebit gesmolten kaas op geroosterd brood
whelk kinkhoorn (wulk)
whipped cream slagroom
whitebait witvis
wine list wijnkaart
woodcock (hout)snip
Worcestershire sauce zoetzure saus bestaande uit soja en vele andere ingrediënten
York ham zeer goed bekend staande ham, opgediend in dunne plakken
Yorkshire pudding knappend gebakken deeg, geserveerd met rosbief
zucchini mergpompoen, courgette
zwieback hard beschuit

Dranken

ale donker, zoetachtig bier, onder hoge temperatuur gegist
  bitter ~ bitter bier, nogal zwaar
  brown~ gebotteld, zoetachtig donker bier
  light ~ gebotteld licht bier
  mild~ donker bier van het vat met een zeer uitgesproken smaak

  pale ~ gebotteld licht bier
applejack Amerikaanse appelbrandewijn
Athol Brose haver vermengd met kokend water, honing en whisky
Bacardi cocktail cocktail van rum en gin met grenadinesiroop en limoensap

barley water frisdrank gemaakt van parelgerst met citroensmaak

barley wine donker bier met hoog alcoholgehalte

beer bier

  bottled ~ gebotteld bier

  draft, draught ~ getapt bier, bier van het vat

bitters kruidenaperitieven, de spijsvertering bevorderende alcoholische dranken

black velvet champagne met toevoeging van *stout* (vaak ter begeleiding van oesters)

bloody Mary cocktail van wodka, tomatensap en specerijen

bourbon Amerikaanse whisky, hoofdzakelijk van mais gestookt

brandy 1) verzamelnaam voor brandewijnsoorten gemaakt van druiven en andere vruchten 2) cognac

  ~ Alexander cocktail van brandewijn, crème de cacao en room

British wines wijnen in Engeland gegist; gemaakt van geïmporteerde druiven (of van geïmporteerd druivensap)

cherry brandy kersenlikeur

chocolate chocolademelk

cider cider

  ~ cup mengsel van cider, specerijen, suiker en ijs

claret rode Bordeauxwijn

cobbler *long drink* gemaakt van vruchten, waaraan men wijn of alcohol toevoegt

coffee koffie

  ~ with cream met room

  black ~ zonder melk

  caffeine-free ~ cafeïnevrij

  white ~ half koffie, half melk; koffie verkeerd

cordial 1) hartversterking 2) limonadesiroop

cream room

cup verfrissende drank gemaakt van gekoelde wijn, sodawater en een likeur of andere sterke drank met een schijfje citroen of sinaasappel

daiquiri cocktail van rum, suiker, limoensap

double dubbele portie

Drambuie likeur gemaakt van whisky en honing

dry martini 1) droge vermouth (GB) 2) cocktail van droge vermouth en gin (US)

egg-nog alcoholische drank op basis van rum of andere sterke drank, vermengd met geklopt eigeel en suiker

gin and it gin met Italiaanse vermouth

gin-fizz gin met citroensap, sodawater en suiker

ginger ale frisdrank met gembersmaak

ginger beer gemberbier

grasshopper cocktail van crème de menthe, crème de cacao en room

Guinness (stout) donker zoetsmakend bier met een hoog mout- en hopgehalte

half pint ongeveer 3 dl

highball alcoholische drank, zoals whisky, vermengd met water, sodawater of *ginger ale*

iced gekoeld, ijskoud

Irish coffee koffie met suiker en slagroom, waaraan men een scheut Ierse whisky toevoegt

Irish Mist Ierse likeur van whisky en honing

Irish whiskey Ierse whisky minder scherp dan Schotse whisky, bevat naast gerst ook rogge, haver en tarwe

juice sap

lager pilsener, koud geserveerd

lemon squash kwast

lemonade limonade

lime juice limoensap
liqueur likeur
liquor sterke drank
long drink sterke drank met tonic, sodawater of gewoon water en ijsblokjes
madeira madera
Manhattan cocktail van Amerikaanse whisky en vermouth met angostura
milk melk
mineral water mineraalwater
mulled wine bisschopswijn; warme, gekruide wijn
neat onvermengd, puur, zonder water of ijs
old-fashioned cocktail van whisky, angostura, sinaasappel schijfje, suiker en maraskijnkersen
on the rocks met ijsblokjes
Ovaltine ovomaltine
Pimm's cup(s) sterke drank met vruchtesap, eventueel aangelengd met sodawater
  ~ No. 1 met gin
  ~ No. 2 met whisky
  ~ No. 3 met rum
  ~ No. 4 met brandewijn
pink champagne roze champagne
pink lady cocktail van eiwit, calvados, citroensap, grenadine en gin
pint ongeveer 6 dl
porter donker, bitter bier
quart 1.14 l (US 0.95 l)
root beer gezoete frisdrank met aroma uit plantenwortels en kruiden
rye (whiskey) whisky uit rogge gestookt; zwaarder en scherper van smaak dan *bourbon*

scotch (whisky) Schotse whisky, een uit gerst en maïs (grain whisky) gestookte sterke drank, vaak vermengd met malt whisky, uitsluitend uit gemoute gerst gestookt
screwdriver wodka met sinaasappelsap
shandy *bitter ale* vermengd met limonade of met *ginger beer*
short drink sterke drank, onverdund gedronken
shot scheut sterke drank
sloe gin-fizz sleepruimlikeur (vrucht van de sleedoorn) met citroensap en sodawater
soda water sodawater, spuitwater
soft drink frisdrank
spirits gedistilleerde dranken
stinger cognac en crème de menthe
stout donker bier met veel hop gebrouwen
straight sterke drank onverdund gedronken, puur
tea thee
toddy grog
Tom Collins *long drink* van gin, citroensap, spuitwater en suiker
tonic (water) tonic, spuitwater met kininesmaak
vodka wodka
whisky sour whisky, citroensap, suiker en sodawater
wine wijn; **dessert ~** zoete
  dry ~ droge
  red ~ rode
  sparkling ~ mousserende
  sweet ~ zoete (dessertwijn)
  white ~ witte

Mini-grammatica

Het lidwoord

Het bepaald lidwoord heeft slechts één vorm: *the*.

the room, the rooms   de kamer, de kamers

Het onbepaald lidwoord heeft twee vormen: *a* voor woorden die met een medeklinker beginnen en *an* voor woorden die met een klinker of stomme h beginnen.

a coat   een jas
an umbrella   een paraplu
an hour   een uur

Het zelfstandig naamwoord

Het meervoud van de meeste zelfstandige naamwoorden wordt gevormd door aan het enkelvoud -(*e*)*s* toe te voegen.

cup – cups (kopje - kopjes)   **dress – dresses** (jurk - jurken)

N.B. Wanneer een zelfstandig naamwoord op -*y* eindigt en de voorlaatste letter een medeklinker is, wordt de meervoudsuitgang -*ies*; als de voorlaatste letter echter een klinker is dan wordt het meervoud op de normale wijze gevormd.

lady – ladies (dame - dames)   **key – keys** (sleutel - sleutels)

Enkele zelfstandige naamwoorden met een onregelmatig meervoud zijn:

man – men (man - mannen)   **child – children** (kind - kinderen)
woman – women (vrouw - vrouwen)
foot – feet (voet - voeten)

Genitief

1. Als de bezitter een mens is en het zelfstandig naamwoord niet met -*s* eindigt, dan wordt '*s* toegevoegd.

the boy's room   de kamer van de jongen
the children's clothes   de kleren van de kinderen

Eindigt het zelfstandig naamwoord met -*s*, dan wordt alleen een apostrophe (') toegevoegd.

the boys' room   de kamer van de jongens

2. Als de bezitter een ding is, gebruikt men het voorzetsel *of*.

the key of the door   de sleutel van de deur

Het bijvoeglijk naamwoord

De bijvoeglijke naamwoorden staan gewoonlijk voor het zelfstandig naamwoord.

a large brown suitcase   een grote bruine koffer

De vergrotende en overtreffende trap van een bijvoeglijk naamwoord kunnen op twee manieren gevormd worden.

1. Alle bijvoeglijke naamwoorden van één lettergreep en vele van twee lettergrepen krijgen -(*e*)*r* en -(*e*)*st*.

small (klein) – **smaller** – **smallest**
pretty (aardig) – **prettier** – **prettiest***

2. Bijvoeglijke naamwoorden van drie of meer lettergrepen en enkele van twee die eindigen op -*ful* en -*less* maken de vergrotende en overtreffende trap met *more* en *most*.

expensive (duur) – **more expensive** – **most expensive**
careful (voorzichtig) – **more careful** – **most careful**

De volgende bijvoeglijke naamwoorden zijn onregelmatig:

good (goed)	**better**	**best**
bad (slecht)	**worse**	**worst**
little (weinig)	**less**	**least**
much/many (veel)	**more**	**most**

Het bijwoord

De meeste bijwoorden worden gemaakt door aan het bijvoeglijk naamwoord -*ly* toe te voegen.

quick/quickly (vlug)   **slow/slowly** (langzaam)

Uitzonderingen:

good/well (goed)   **fast/fast** (snel)

---

* *y* wordt *i* als er een medeklinker aan voorafgaat.

Voornaamwoorden

	persoonlijk		bezittelijk voornaamwoord	
	onderwerp	lijdend en meew. vw.	1	2
ik	I	me	my	mine
jij	you	you	your	yours
hij	he	him	his	his
zij	she	her	her	hers
het	it	it	its	–
wij	we	us	our	ours
u	you	you	your	yours
zij	they	them	their	theirs

De vormen onder 1 worden gebruikt vóór een zelfstandig naamwoord, die onder 2 staan op zichzelf.

Where's my key?   Waar is mijn sleutel?
That's not mine.   Dat is niet de mijne.

N.B. Het Engels kent geen onderscheid tussen "jij" en "u", in beide gevallen zegt men *you*.

He came with you.   Hij kwam met jou/u.

Onregelmatige werkwoorden

De onderstaande lijst geeft de Engelse onregelmatige werkwoorden aan. De samengestelde werkwoorden of werkwoorden met een voorvoegsel worden als de grondwerkwoorden vervoegd, bijvoorbeeld: *withdraw* wordt vervoegd als *draw* en *rebuild* als *build*.

Onbepaalde wijs	Onvoltooid verleden tijd	Verleden deelwoord	
arise	arose	arisen	*opstaan*
awake	awoke	awoken	*ontwaken*
be	was	been	*zijn*
bear	bore	borne	*dragen*
beat	beat	beaten	*slaan*
become	became	become	*worden*
begin	began	begun	*aanvangen*
bend	bent	bent	*buigen*
bet	bet	bet	*wedden*
bid	bade/bid	bidden/bid	*verzoeken*
bind	bound	bound	*binden*
bite	bit	bitten	*bijten*
bleed	bled	bled	*bloeden*
blow	blew	blown	*blazen*
break	broke	broken	*breken*
breed	bred	bred	*fokken*
bring	brought	brought	*brengen*
build	built	built	*bouwen*
burn	burnt/burned	burnt/burned	*branden*
burst	burst	burst	*barsten*
buy	bought	bought	*kopen*
can*	could	–	*kunnen*
cast	cast	cast	*werpen*
catch	caught	caught	*vangen*
choose	chose	chosen	*kiezen*
cling	clung	clung	*vastklemmen*
clothe	clothed/clad	clothed/clad	*kleden*
come	came	come	*komen*
cost	cost	cost	*kosten*
creep	crept	crept	*kruipen*
cut	cut	cut	*snijden*
deal	dealt	dealt	*uitdelen*
dig	dug	dug	*graven*
do (he does)	did	done	*doen*

---

* tegenwoordige tijd

draw	drew	drawn	*trekken*
dream	dreamt/dreamed	dreamt/dreamed	*dromen*
drink	drank	drunk	*drinken*
drive	drove	driven	*rijden*
dwell	dwelt	dwelt	*vertoeven*
eat	ate	eaten	*eten*
fall	fell	fallen	*vallen*
feed	fed	fed	*voeden*
feel	felt	felt	*voelen*
fight	fought	fought	*vechten*
find	found	found	*vinden*
flee	fled	fled	*vluchten*
fling	flung	flung	*werpen*
fly	flew	flown	*vliegen*
forsake	forsook	forsaken	*verzaken*
freeze	froze	frozen	*vriezen*
get	got	got	*krijgen*
give	gave	given	*geven*
go	went	gone	*gaan*
grind	ground	ground	*malen*
grow	grew	grown	*groeien*
hang	hung	hung	*(op)hangen*
have	had	had	*hebben*
hear	heard	heard	*horen*
hew	hewed	hewed/hewn	*hakken*
hide	hid	hidden	*verstoppen*
hit	hit	hit	*slaan*
hold	held	held	*houden*
hurt	hurt	hurt	*pijn doen*
keep	kept	kept	*houden*
kneel	knelt	knelt	*knielen*
knit	knitted/knit	knitted/knit	*breien*
know	knew	known	*weten*
lay	laid	laid	*leggen*
lead	led	led	*leiden*
lean	leant/leaned	leant/leaned	*leunen*
leap	leapt/leaped	leapt/leaped	*springen*
learn	learnt/learned	learnt/learned	*leren*
leave	left	left	*verlaten*
lend	lent	lent	*lenen(aan)*
let	let	let	*laten*
lie	lay	lain	*liggen*
light	lit/lighted	lit/lighted	*aansteken*
lose	lost	lost	*verliezen*

make	made	made	*maken*
may*	might	–	*mogen, kunnen*
mean	meant	meant	*bedoelen*
meet	met	met	*ontmoeten*
mow	mowed	mowed/mown	*maaien*
must*	–	–	*moeten*
ought (to)*	–	–	*moeten*
pay	paid	paid	*betalen*
put	put	put	*zetten*
read	read	read	*lezen*
rid	rid	rid	*zich ontdoen (van)*
ride	rode	ridden	*rijden*
ring	rang	rung	*bellen*
rise	rose	risen	*opstaan*
run	ran	run	*rennen*
saw	sawed	sawn	*zagen*
say	said	said	*zeggen*
see	saw	seen	*zien*
seek	sought	sought	*zoeken*
sell	sold	sold	*verkopen*
send	sent	sent	*verzenden*
set	set	set	*zetten*
sew	sewed	sewed/sewn	*naaien*
shake	shook	shaken	*schudden*
shall*	should	–	*zullen*
shed	shed	shed	*vergieten*
shine	shone	shone	*schijnen*
shoot	shot	shot	*schieten*
show	showed	shown	*tonen*
shrink	shrank	shrunk	*krimpen*
shut	shut	shut	*sluiten*
sing	sang	sung	*zingen*
sink	sank	sunk	*zinken*
sit	sat	sat	*zitten*
sleep	slept	slept	*slapen*
slide	slid	slid	*glijden*
sling	slung	slung	*slingeren*
slink	slunk	slunk	*sluipen*
slit	slit	slit	*opensnijden*
smell	smelled/smelt	smelled/smelt	*ruiken*
sow	sowed	sown/sowed	*zaaien*
speak	spoke	spoken	*spreken*

* tegenwoordige tijd

speed	sped/speeded	sped/speeded	*zich haasten*
spell	spelt/spelled	spelt/spelled	*spellen*
spend	spent	spent	*uitgeven*
spill	spilt/spilled	spilt/spilled	*morsen*
spin	spun	spun	*spinnen*
spit	spat	spat	*spuwen*
split	split	split	*splijten*
spoil	spoilt/spoiled	spoilt/spoiled	*bederven*
spread	spread	spread	*spreiden*
spring	sprang	sprung	*ontspringen*
stand	stood	stood	*staan*
steal	stole	stolen	*stelen*
stick	stuck	stuck	*kleven*
sting	stung	stung	*steken*
stink	stank/stunk	stunk	*stinken*
strew	strewed	strewed/strewn	*strooien*
stride	strode	stridden	*schrijden*
strike	struck	struck/stricken	*slaan*
string	strung	strung	*rijgen*
strive	strove	striven	*streven*
swear	swore	sworn	*zweren*
sweep	swept	swept	*vegen*
swell	swelled	swollen	*zwellen*
swim	swam	swum	*zwemmen*
swing	swung	swung	*slingeren*
take	took	taken	*nemen*
teach	taught	taught	*onderwijzen*
tear	tore	torn	*scheuren*
tell	told	told	*vertellen*
think	thought	thought	*denken*
throw	threw	thrown	*werpen*
thrust	thrust	thrust	*duwen*
tread	trod	trodden	*treden*
wake	woke/waked	woken/waked	*wekken*
wear	wore	worn	*dragen*
weave	wove	woven	*weven*
weep	wept	wept	*huilen*
will*	would	–	*zullen*
win	won	won	*winnen*
wind	wound	wound	*opwinden*
wring	wrung	wrung	*wringen*
write	wrote	written	*schrijven*

* tegenwoordige tijd

Engelse afkortingen

AA	*Automobile Association*	Britse Automobielclub
AAA	*American Automobile Association*	Amerikaanse Automobielclub
ABC	*American Broadcasting Company*	Amerikaanse radio- en televisie-maatschappij
A.D.	*anno Domini*	na Christus
Am.	*America, American*	Amerika; Amerikaans
a.m.	*ante meridiem (before noon)*	de tijd tussen 0 en 12 uur
Amtrak	*American railroad corporation*	Amerikaanse spoorwegmaatschappij
Ave.	*avenue*	avenue
BBC	*British Broadcasting Corporation*	Britse radio- en televisiemaatschappij
B.C.	*before Christ*	voor Christus
bldg.	*building*	gebouw
Blvd.	*boulevard*	boulevard
B.R.	*British Rail*	Britse Spoorwegen
Brit.	*Britain; British*	Groot-Brittannië, Brits
Bros.	*brothers*	gebroeders
¢	*cent*	1/100 van een dollar
Can.	*Canada; Canadian*	Canada; Canadees
CBS	*Columbia Broadcasting System*	Amerikaanse radio- en televisie-maatschappij
CID	*Criminal Investigation Department*	afdeling criminele recherche van Scotland Yard
CNR	*Canadian National Railway*	Canadese Nationale Spoorwegen
c/o	*(in) care of*	per adres
Co.	*company*	maatschappij
Corp.	*corporation*	vennootschap
CPR	*Canadian Pacific Railways*	Canadese spoorwegmaatschappij
D.C.	*District of Columbia*	district in de V.S. waarin de hoofdstad Washington ligt
DDS	*Doctor of Dental Science*	doctor in de tandheelkunde
dept.	*department*	departement, afdeling
EU	*European Union*	EU, Europese Unie
e.g.	*for instance*	bijvoorbeeld
Eng.	*England; English*	Engeland; Engels
excl.	*excluding; exclusive*	exclusief
ft.	*foot/feet*	voet
GB	*Great Britain*	Groot-Brittannië
H.E.	*His/Her Excellency; His Eminence*	Zijne/Hare Excellentie; Zijne Eminentie
H.H.	*His Holiness*	Zijne Heiligheid

H.M.	*His/Her Majesty*	Zijne/Hare Majesteit
H.M.S.	*Her Majesty's ship*	Harer Majesteits schip (Brits oorlogsschip)
hp	*horsepower*	paardekracht
Hwy	*highway*	autoweg
i.e.	*that is to say*	d.w.z., dat wil zeggen
in.	*inch*	duim (2,54 cm)
Inc.	*incorporated*	naamloze vennootschap
incl.	*including, inclusive*	inclusief
£	*pound sterling*	pond sterling
L.A.	*Los Angeles*	Los Angeles
Ltd.	*limited*	naamloze vennootschap
M.D.	*Doctor of Medicine*	arts
M.P.	*Member of Parliament*	lid van het Lagerhuis (Engeland)
mph	*miles per hour*	Engelse mijl per uur
Mr.	*Mister*	meneer
Mrs.	*Missis*	mevrouw
Ms.	*Missis/Miss*	mevrouw/mejuffrouw
nat.	*national*	nationaal
NBC	*National Broadcasting Company*	Amerikaanse radio- en televisiemaatschappij
No.	*number*	nummer
N.Y.C.	*New York City*	New York City
O.B.E.	*Officer (of the Order) of the British Empire*	Officier in de Orde van het Britse Imperium
p.	*page; penny/pence*	bladzijde; 1/100 van een pond
p.a.	*per annum*	per jaar
Ph.D.	*Doctor of Philosophy*	doctor in de wijsbegeerte
p.m.	*post meridiem (after noon)*	de tijd tussen 12 en 24 uur
PO	*Post Office*	postkantoor
POO	*post office order*	postorder
pop.	*population*	bevolking
P.T.O.	*please turn over*	zie ommezijde, a.u.b.
RAC	*Royal Automobile Club*	Koninklijke Britse Automobielclub
RCMP	*Royal Canadian Mounted Police*	Koninklijke Canadese Bereden Politie
Rd.	*road*	weg
ref.	*reference*	verwijzing
Rev.	*reverend*	dominee
RFD	*rural free delivery*	landelijke postbus
RR	*railroad*	spoorweg
RSVP	*please reply*	verzoeke gaarne antwoord
$	*dollar*	dollar
Soc.	*society*	maatschappij, genootschap

St.	*saint; street*	sint; straat
STD	*Subscriber Trunk Dialling*	automatisch telefoonverkeer
UN	*United Nations*	V.N., Verenigde Naties
UPS	*United Parcel Service*	Amerikaanse pakketdienst
US	*United States*	Verenigde Staten
USS	*United States Ship*	Amerikaans oorlogsschip
VAT	*value added tax*	B.T.W.
VIP	*very important person*	zeer belangrijke persoon
Xmas	*Christmas*	Kerstmis
yd.	*yard*	yard (91,44 cm)
YMCA	*Young Men's Christian Association*	Christelijke Jongeren Vereniging
YWCA	*Young Women's Christian Association*	Christelijke Meisjes Vereniging
ZIP	*ZIP code*	postnummer